"The burgeoning field of Petrine studies has recently cast up several important monographs on the apostle Peter. Dr. Bayer's welcome addition appeals to the full range of New Testament materials, and carefully distinguishes between his 'non-transferable' functions as part of the historical 'bedrock' that mediates Jesus to later generations, and his 'transferable' functions, which model the character and virtues of genuine disciples of Christ. Worked out across the field of New Testament sources, that simple distinction proves to be both evocative and seminal."

—D. A. Carson
Research Professor, Trinity Evangelical Divinity School (TEDS),
Deerfield, Illinois, USA

"Usually when one hears the term apostolic, one thinks of the historical and doctrinal roots of the faith, especially when combined with the image of bedrock. Hans Bayer gives us a fresh look at doctrine and history by pointing to these elements in Scripture's presentation of Peter. He shows how the themes Peter raises contribute to and even aim at character, identity, and spiritual development. What a refreshing new take on these themes. When biblical teaching, identity, and ethics come together, it makes for powerful teaching."

—Darrell Bock
Senior Research Professor of New Testament Studies and
Executive Director for Cultural Engagement
The Hendricks Center, Dallas Theological Seminary,
Dallas, Texas, USA

"Hans Bayer has written a wonderful and informative summary of Peter's canonical testimony. He masterfully describes Peter's transformation from rock-headed disciple to becoming the pastor-in-chief of the Christian churches of the west. Utilizing the Petrine perspective the Gospel of Mark, the speeches of Peter in Acts, and the two epistles attributed to Peter, Bayer lays out Peter's witness to Jesus and Peter's contribution to the formation of followers of Jesus. The result is a bountiful feast of Peter's testimony, exhortations, and spirituality that will benefit many."

—Michael F. Bird, PhD University of Queensland
Lecturer in Theology, Ridley College

"Hans Bayer's new book, *Apostolic Bedrock*, serves the church, the scholarly community, and the wider society in manifold ways. It exegetes many New Testament texts related to the apostle Peter in a fresh way, showing how these texts preserved reliable traditions about the saving work of Jesus Christ, the Son of God. The book also contributes to our knowledge about the formation of the canon, especially of the Gospels, Acts, and 1 and 2 Peter. When it summarizes key aspects of how Peter's identity and characteristics were formed by his Master, it points to our only hope in today's turmoil in our personal and communal lives: how we and our fellow human beings can be changed to become Christ-like personalities. The world needs this transformation—we all need it; this book is a great help to achieve it."

—Péter Balla
Chair of New Testament Studies
Rector Károli Gáspár University of the Reformed Church
Budapest, Hungary

(February 16, 2017, review posted on Amazon.com) "In this refreshing monograph, Dr. Hans Bayer makes a strong case for the unity of the Petrine corpus (including the Gospel of Mark, sermons in Acts, and 2 Peter), based on the common themes and patterns of Christology and Christ-like Christian identity. Dr. Bayer has meticulously collected traceable NT clues of the apostle Peter's spirituality, and makes a convincing case that the Petrine writings preserved a homologous pattern when it comes to the identity of Christ and the character formation of the disciples of Christ. This study indirectly supports the common witness behind these writings, but the real focus of the thesis is the authority and content of Peter's personal example.

According to Dr. Bayer, the apostle Peter is a unique authority as a representative eye-witness to Christ, but is also an example of the general patterns of Christian discipleship. On the one hand, Peter preaches the Ebed-Jahve as a specially authorized, trustworthy witness to Him, with the authority and urgency that is comparable to an OT repentance preacher. On the other hand, Peter embodies his unique apostolic witness in his downward movement into humility, and thus is an example to every disciple. Peter, the Rock, has a non-transferable role as a witness, and a transferable role as an example. In this sense, the Church of Jesus Christ is truly built on him.

Dr. Bayer's fresh, creative thesis feeds the mind of the scholar looking for information and new ideas. At the same time it challenges our hearts and does not let us remain neutral about Christ and the state of our character. I whole-heartedly recommend this volume to both lovers of New Testament theology and students of Christian spirituality. Bayer's book is a brilliant combination of the two worlds, which in Peter's mind—as we learn—was still one."

—Ádám Szabados
Ph.D. candidate under Prof. P. Balla, Budapest, Hungary
Pastor, Evangelical Christian Church, Veszprém, Hungary

"Is there a unity between theology and character formation? In his forthcoming book, Dr. Hans Bayer, based on the part of the New Testament associated with Peter, would say there is. If we put all the Peter-related material of the Bible—the Gospel of Mark, Peter's speeches in Acts, and his letters, especially I Peter—we have a distinct Petrine witness. Then, one of the main themes that emerge from this distinct witness is a unity between theology and character formation.

Within this diverse, yet distinct witness, one helpful way of organizing Peter's legacy is to think in terms of things non-transferable, semi-transferable, and wholly transferable. Regarding things non-transferable, for example, Peter serves as an irreplaceable, apostolic witness, a spokesperson for the collective, apostolic witness. As such, as in one of the earliest expressions of the gospel story in Acts 10:34–43, Peter has the non-transferable status of a guarantor of the safe transmission of that story. Also in this category of things non-transferable is Jesus' declaration of Peter as the rock. While we agree with the Catholic Church that Peter with the apostles was the foundation of the church in a non-transferable way (no apostolic succession), we must not confuse the foundation with the cornerstone (Ephesians 2:20).

Some elements of the Petrine witness, though, are more transferable, though still unique. Jesus called Peter as a fisher of men (Mark 1:16) and a shepherd of his sheep (John 21), which, while we may participate in these roles, we do so only derivatively.

Finally, some elements of the Petrine witness are wholly transferable without any condition. This is where Christology and character formation powerfully converge. Rooted in Peter's Christology, we have, what Bayer calls, 'essential, Christ-driven character traits,' consistent throughout the Petrine witness. There are, above all, six in order of priority: faith and trust, courageous witness, pursuing purity of heart, humility and service, overcoming in suffering, and surrender with obedience.

Now, the Petrine witness may lack Pauline sophistication and polish at times, as in places like I Peter 3:18, where surely Paul would have said something more "profound" about what Christ's death did for us. However, while the Pauline witness overshadows the Petrine in a way, the legacy of Jesus, Bayer argues, is more directly carried on in Peter than Paul. Paul himself does not see himself on the same level as the original team of apostles (Acts 13:31) who were direct eyewitnesses of 'his majesty' (2 Peter 1:16). The gospel that Paul proclaimed he himself received (I Corinthians 15:1-11).

It made me proud to watch Dr. Bayer tell us all this. As a young man, Bayer says, he would never have imagined this kind of project. For him, it would have either been a study of high and lofty Christology or character study, but never together. If he had a choice, he said, he probably would never have undertaken a character study, opting for something more polished and sophisticated. While Bayer spoke, it really did occur to me that there is a distinct Petrine witness, a clear Petrine voice with its own strength, vitality and emphasis, a voice I never discerned amidst the symphony of New Testament witness. I hereby resolve, therefore, to listen for it more carefully, and from now on, with Bayer's help, more knowledgeably.

What struck me is that to grasp the character formation that Peter himself experienced through a lifetime of walking with Jesus, Peter's Christology must become our Christology. We must devote ourselves to this Apostle's teaching (Acts 2:42) as a non-transferable guarantor of the Jesus story, so that, in some semi-transferable and some wholly transferable ways, we may become participants in the kind of discipleship to which the Petrine witness invites us. For this apostle, therefore, there was no distinction between theology and practice; neither should there be for us."

—**Pastor Samuel Belz, M.Div.**
Covenant Theological Seminary

PETER AS APOSTOLIC BEDROCK

**CHRISTOLOGY AND DISCIPLESHIP
ACCORDING TO HIS CANONICAL TESTIMONY**

Peter as Apostolic Bedrock

**Christology and Discipleship
According to His Canonical Testimony**

Hans F. Bayer

WIPF & STOCK · Eugene, Oregon

Wipf and Stock Publishers
199 W 8th Ave, Suite 3
Eugene, OR 97401

Peter as Apostolic Bedrock
Christology and Discipleship According to His Canonical Testimony
By Bayer, Hans
Copyright©2016 by Bayer, Hans
ISBN 13: 978-1-5326-7479-2
Publication date 5/21/2019
Previously published by Paternoster, 2016

Dedicated to Christopher, Benjamin, and Katharine

Contents

Preface: The Human Need for Sustained Transformation	xiii
Acknowledgements	xvii
Abbreviations	xix
Introduction	1

PART ONE The Apostolic Foundation: Non-Transferable and Semi-Transferable Aspects of Peter's Work and Witness — 8

Chapter 1 Peter's Development in the Setting of First-Century Palestinian Judaism — 9
- The Names of Peter — 9
- Peter's Shaping Influences Prior to Becoming a Disciple of Jesus — 10
- Peter as a Disciple of Jesus — 35

Chapter 2 Non-Transferable Aspects of Peter's Work and Witness — 50
- Peter and His Confession as the Foundational 'Rock' of Jesus's Nascent Church (Matt 16:18-19) — 50
- Peter's Apostolic Witness in Acts and Old Testament Prophetic Repentance Speeches — 63

Chapter 3 Peter's Non-Transferable Contributions to the Content and Formation of the New Testament Canon — 82
- Peter as Key Guarantor and Transmitter of Oral Jesus-Tradition in the Form of the Earliest Gospel Witness — 82
- Peter as the Source of the Gospel of Mark, the Petrine Sections in Acts, and as the Author of 1 and 2 Peter — 103
- Peter as a Foundation-Laying Contributor to the New Testament Canon — 117

Chapter 4 Semi-Transferable Aspects of Peter's Work and Witness — 125
- Peter as a 'Fisher of Men' (Mark 1:16) — 125
- Peter as Shepherd of God's Jewish and Gentile People (John 21:15-19 and Luke 22:31-32) — 128

PART TWO Transferable Aspects of Peter's Witness Embedded in His Apostolic Functions — 133

Chapter 5 Christology, Identity, and Character Formation in the Gospel of Mark — 135
- Christology — 135
- Identity and Character Formation — 155
- The Dynamic Between Christology, Identity, and Character Formation in Mark's Gospel — 163

Chapter 6 Christology, Identity, and Character Formation in the Petrine Sections of Acts — 165
- Petrine Material in Acts — 165
- Peter's Apostolic Witness to Christ — 167
- Peter's Witness to Christ-Centered Identity and Character Formation — 187
- The Dynamic Between Christology, Identity, and Character Formation in Acts — 195

Chapter 7 Christology, Identity, and Character Formation in 1 and 2 Peter — 197
- Characteristic Christological Themes — 200
- Identity and Character Formation — 202
- The Dynamic Between Christology, Identity, and Character Formation in 1 and 2 Peter — 209

Chapter 8 Characteristic Dynamics Between Christology, Identity, and Character Formation in Peter's Canonical Testimony — 211
- The Thematic Cohesion of Peter's Testimony Despite the Virtual Absence of Literary Indicators — 211
- The Complementary Portraits of Peter — 213
- Characteristic Christological Connections in Peter's Testimony — 214
- Characteristic, Christ-Centered Identity and Character Formation according to Peter's Testimony — 219
- The Dynamic Between Christology, Identity, and Character Formation according to Peter's Testimony — 226

PART THREE Universal Watermarks of Jesus: Contours of Christ-Driven Character Formation according to the Apostle Peter — 228

Chapter 9 Essential Christ-Driven Character Traits Derived from Identity Formation — 229
- The Foundation of Christ-Driven Identity — 229
- Prominent Christ-Driven Character Traits — 230

Conclusions — 268
Author Index — 274
Subject and Place Index — 279
Index of Biblical and Extrabiblical Writings — 292
Bibliography — 322

PREFACE

The Human Need for Sustained Transformation

Regardless of our respective approaches to life, one of the most arresting phenomena in any culture, religion, and philosophy of life is the sustained and authentic transformation of a person for the better. The need for such personal and systemic transformation becomes particularly pressing when we seek to ameliorate political, social, and economic ills such as oppression, the sex trade, drug trafficking, child slavery, exploitation, gangs, and corruption, to mention but a few.[1]

Many of our contemporaries who are most keenly concerned about personal and societal change are cognizant of the fact that even the most researched and optimally implemented programs for societal and systemic change are, at times, rendered ineffective because there is no concurrent transformation of the respective people's attitudes. The reason for this phenomenon lies, e.g., in a fixed cultural mindset, a certain religious persuasion, a traditional practice, or a personal attitude, preference, and need.[2]

The cynical side in us maintains that we will always be the disconcerting selves that we are (including negative genetic predispositions, dysfunctional family systems, and flawed personalities). At times, we merely camouflage our problems with sundry religious disciplines, philanthropic and optimistic altruism, or euphemistic speech.[3] In the end, however, everything stays the same. One reason why we become, at times, cynical is the frustration over hypocritical, idealistic, or utopian political, economic, and/or ecclesiastical changes that merely mask the foul core inside. We must be prepared to face the fact that there is some bitter truth to this. Is history not our best teacher of this disheartening phenomenon? Have communism, fascism, the medieval Crusades, and many other movements not taught us this lesson once and for

---

[1] See D. Brooks, *The Social Animal: The Hidden Source of Love, Character, and Achievement* (New York, NY: Random House, 2011).
[2] From an economic standpoint, see, e.g., the work of the economist and 1988 Nobel laureate A. Sen, *Inequality Reexamined* (Boston, MA: Harvard University Press, 1992).
[3] See D.G. Benner, *The Gift of Loving Yourself: The Sacred Call to Self-Discovery* (Downers Grove, IL: IVP, 2004).

all? Despite the fact that lasting change in human beings is elusive, we are heartened to discover that Jesus takes up this challenge by demonstrating that true, radical change is indeed possible.

The following study explores Jesus's approach to deep transformation of the inner human person and community, not only in terms of transformation (discipleship), but also in terms of mentoring leadership (shepherding) that affects and benefits a given community. Jesus's radical claim is, however, hard to swallow. He calls for a reconciliation with—and dependence upon—the Creator of this universe.[4] Such reconciliation aims at the progressive realization of the purposes and aims of God as Creator and ruler of all of life. Jesus focuses on this root problem, seemingly skirting the pressing issues of societal ills, such as Roman political and economic oppression of Palestine in the first century AD.

Especially for the past two hundred years, we can trace not only an intellectual atheism as a red thread throughout the history of Western society, but also a practical atheism or agnosticism. The following study discusses Jesus's challenge of such atheistic autonomy of the mind and the will, and thus of the inner human being. Jesus implies that rationalistic and self-sufficient life patterns hinder true transformation. He insists that barring a foundational reconciliation with our Maker, we will remain, in one way or another, enslaved to our individual and communal self-centered greed, bound to our addictions and idols, our autonomous reflexes, our self-asphyxiation, and our ideologies at the expense of the dignity and growth that God intended for us and our communities. The perplexing disequilibrium which Jesus triggers in human lives arises from his appeal that healing a broken relationship with God lies at the heart of sustained change. To some, invoking a god to find true and sustained change in human life looks like an extraneous excursion into irrelevant territory.[5] A person with a naturalistic, materialistic worldview, for example, might say that we can and do achieve sustained change without such an unnecessary and unfounded detour. Another default reaction to Jesus's call to true change is the widespread, often unconscious resistance toward a higher being to whom we might be accountable. In the recesses of our autonomous, inner being, we insist on being the masters of our own destiny. We tend to

---

[4] Contrast, e.g., I. Kant's *Critique of Pure Reason* (London: Penguin Classics, 2008 [1781]) with J.G. Hamann's critique of Kant (see, e.g., R.A. Sparling, *Johann Georg Hamann and the Enlightenment Project* [Toronto: University of Toronto Press, 2011]).

[5] To some, this might sound like K. Marx's *dictum* that 'religion . . . is the opium of the people' (K. Marx, 'Zur Kritik der Hegel'schen Rechts-Philosophie: Einleitung', *Deutsch-Französische Jahrbücher*, Paris, 7 and 10 February, 1844, n.p.).

resist any form of outside interference, especially from an unseen and inaudible Supreme Being.[6]

Should the above-mentioned challenges pose no obstacles to the reader, he or she is then faced with the following questions: who is this Jesus and what is his brand of *true* transformation? In the following pages, we seek to give an answer to this crucial question in the context of the overall mission and purpose of God. To accomplish this, we shall trace the astonishing life and transformation of the lower middle-class, Galilean fisherman Peter. We shall learn how radically Jesus changes this average man into a purified, God dependent, non-violent and ethical person who cares deeply about the personal and corporate purity and life of those he is to mentor and lead. He becomes a man who pursues individual and corporate growth in the midst of suffering and injustice, and who seeks lasting change in the midst of an oppressive society. Peter arises as *the* witness to the transforming presence and power of Jesus. As a consequence, the identity and character of those who listen to Peter's testimony are radically changed. As we shall see especially in the book of Acts and in 1 Peter, Peter mobilizes transformed followers to participate in the divine mission that breaks through cultural, philosophical, economic, and religious barriers to expand and deepen such individual and communal transformation.[7]

The pursuit of this kind of far-reaching transformation could sound overwhelming. As we follow, however, along the road of Peter's testimony, transformation, and leadership, we are encouraged to discover simplicity, clarity, and focus.

---

[6] Contrast this with Peter's statement in 1 Pet 1:8.

[7] My colleague, Mark Ryan, made me aware of various current sociological studies on transformation (see, e.g., J.D. Hunter, *To Change the World: The Irony, Tragedy, and Possibility of Christianity in the Late Modern World* [Oxford: Oxford University Press, 2010]). Jesus calls individuals to discipleship which, in turn, issues in community development where maturing occurs and in which such transformation is exemplified and lived out (Hunter speaks of 'faithful presence'; note that our study does not focus on Hunter's main question of meaningful Christian engagement in civil and political society). Concerning a helpful proposal for community engagement cf. T. Keller, *Center Church: Doing Balanced, Gospel-Centered Ministry in Your City* (Grand Rapids, MI: Zondervan, 2012).

Acknowledgements

My sincere gratitude goes to participants of a seminar on Peter, Jan. 14-23, 2015 (including Mark Ryan and Tim Baldwin) at Covenant Theological Seminary, Saint Louis, Missouri, who gave me significant feedback and encouragement on a draft of the present work. I am also very thankful for the board and administration of Covenant Theological Seminary to have afforded me a sabbatical leave in the spring semester of 2012 in order to begin work on this project. My colleagues at Covenant Seminary have been a wonderful source of inspiration in pursuit of this topic. The personal encouragement of Sam Belz, Don Carson, Jon Coody, Amy Felt, Daniel Gleich, Traugott Hopp, May Huang, Werner Neuer, Carey Newman, Dane Ortlund, Jay Sklar, Mark Stirling, Adam Szabados, Tim Vickers, and Robert Yarbrough is deeply appreciated. The careful editorial help of Rick Matt and Alissa Rockney was substantial and invaluable. Additionally, Alissa Rockney competently produced the three indexes. My wife, Susan, did not only give me much insightful feedback on a draft of this book but encouraged me, during a hike in the mountains of Mittersill, Austria, to pursue this topic. Finally, I would like to thank Dr Mike Parsons and the editorial board at Paternoster Press for accepting this work for publication and for Reuben Sneller's kind and helpful assistance in carefully guiding me through the publication process.

Select material on pages 87–93; 106–109; 112; 127–28; 135–37; 141–62; 232–45; 247–49; 257–58; 267–68 was partially taken from H.F. Bayer, *A Theology of Mark*, 2012, ISBN 978-1-59638-119-3, published by P&R Publishing Co., P.O. Box 817, Phillipsburg, N.J., 08865; www.prpbooks.com. Used with permission.

Some content on pages 64–68 and some material on pages 170–75; 180–82, and 184–88 was partially taken from H.F. Bayer, 'Christ-Centered Eschatology in Acts 3:17-26', in *Jesus of Nazareth: Lord and Christ. Essays on the Historical Jesus and New Testament Christology.* Ed. J.B. Green and M. Turner, FS I.H. Marshall, Grand Rapids, MI/Carlisle: Eerdmans/ Paternoster, 1994, 236–50. Used with permission.

Select content on pp. 63–81; 171–73, and 180–82 was partially taken from H.F. Bayer, 'The Preaching of Peter in Acts' in I.H. Marshall and D. Peterson (eds), *Witness to the Gospel: The Theology of Acts*. Grand Rapids, MI: Eerdmans, 1998, 257–74.

Hans F. Bayer, Saint Louis, June 2015

Abbreviations

Primary Sources

1 Clem.	*1 Clement*
1 En.	*1 Enoch (Ethiopic Apocalypse)*
1–2 Macc	1–2 Maccabees
1QapGen	Excavated frags. from cave col. I
1QH	*Hymns of Thanksgiving*
1QIsa[a]	Isaiah[a]
1QM	*Milḥamah* or *War Scroll*
1QpHab	*Pesher Habakkuk*
1QS	*Serek Hayaḥad* or *Rule of the Community*
1QSa	*Rule of the Congregation* (Appendix a to 1QS)
2 Bar.	*2 Baruch (Syriac Apocalypse)*
4 Ezra	*4 Ezra*
4 Macc.	*4 Maccabees*
4QCommGen A	*Commentary on Genesis*
4QDibHam[a]	*Dibre Hameʾorot*[a]
4QFlor	*Florilegium*
4QMessAp	*Messianic Apocalypse*
4QTest	*Testimonia*
11QMel	*Melchizedek*
11QPs[a]	*Psalms Scroll*[a]
11QtgJob	*Targum of Job*
ʾAbot	*Avot*
ʾAbot R. Nat.	*Avot of Rabbi Nathan*
Acts Pet. 12 Apos.	*Acts of Peter and the Twelve Apostles*
Acts Pet. Andr.	*Acts of Peter and Andrew*
Acts Pet. Paul	*Acts of Peter and Paul*
Acts Pet.	*Acts of Peter*
Ag. Ap.	*Against Apion*
Ann.	*Annales/Annals*
Ant.	*Jewish Antiquities*
Ap. John	*Apocryphon of John*

Apoc. Pet.	*Apocalypse of Peter*
Apol.	*Apology (1 and 2)*
As. Mos.	*Assumption of Moses*
Aug.	*Life of Augustus*
b.	Babylonian Talmud
B. Bat.	*Bava Batra*
Bar	Baruch
Ber.	*Berakhot*
CD	*Damascus Document*
Cels.	*Contra Celsum/Against Celsus*
Chron.	*Chronicle*
Claud.	*Life of Claudius*
Comm. Matt.	*Commentarium in evangelium Matthaei*
Cons.	*De Consensu Evangelistarum/Harmony of the Gospels*
Cor.	*De Corona/On the Crown*
Dial.	*Dialogue with Trypho*
Did.	*Didache*
Ep.	*Epistula (ae)*
Ep. Pet. Phil.	*Letter of Peter to Philip*
Gen. Rab.	*Genesis Rabbah*
Geogr.	*Geography*
Gos. Heb.	*Gospel of the Hebrew*
Gos. Pet.	*Gospel of Peter*
H.Ar.	*Historia Arianorum/History of the Arians*
Haer.	*Adversus haereses/Against Heresies*
Ḥag.	*Hagigah*
Her./Heir	*Quis rerum divinarum heres sit/Who is the Heir?*
Hist.	*Historiae/Histories*
Hist. eccl.	*Historia ecclesiastica /Ecclesiastical History*
Ign. *Rom.*	Ignatius, *To the Romans*
Ign. *Smyrn.*	Ignatius, *To Smyrnaeans*
Il.	*Iliad*
Jdt	Judith
J.W.	*Jewish War*
Jub.	*Jubilees*
L.A.B. (Ps.-Philo)	*Liber antiquitatum biblicarum (Pseudo-Philo)*
Legat./Embassy	*Legatio ad Gaium/On the Embassy to Gaius*
Life	*The Life*
m.	Mishnah
Mak.	*Makkot*

Abbreviations

Marc.	*Adversus Marcionem/Against Marcion,* Tertullian
Meg.	*Megillah*
Menaḥ.	*Menahot*
Nero	*Life of Nero*
Oed. col.	*Oedipus coloneus*
Opif./Creation	*De opificio mundi/On the Creation of the World*
POxy	Oxyrhynchus papyri
Pol. *Phil.*	Polycarp, *To the Philippians*
Praescr.	*De praescriptione haereticorum/Prescription against Heretics*
Pre. Pet.	*Preaching of Peter*
Pss. Sol.	*Psalms of Solomon*
Pud.	*De pudicitia/Modesty*
Resp.	*De republica*
Šabb.	*Šabbat*
Sanh.	*Sanhedrin*
Scorp.	*Scorpiace/Antidote for the Scorpion's Sting*
Serm.	*Sermones*
Sib. Or.	*Sibylline Oracles*
Sir	Sirach/Ecclesiasticus
Sukkah	*Sukkah*
t.	Tractates of Tosefta
T. 12 Patr.	*Testaments of the Twelve Patriarchs*
T. Ash.	*Testament of Asher*
T. Benj.	*Testament of Benjamin*
T. Dan	*Testament of Dan*
T. Iss.	*Testament of Issachar*
T. Jud.	*Testament of Judah*
T. Levi	*Testament of Levi*
T. Naph.	*Testament of Naphtali*
T. Sol.	*Testament of Solomon*
T. Zeb.	*Testament of Zebulun*
Tg. Isa.	*Targum Isaiah*
Tob	Tobit
Unit. eccl.	*De catholicae ecclesiae unitate/The Unity of the Catholic Church*
Vesp.	*Life of Vespasian*
Vir. ill.	*De viris illustribus/Lives of illustrious Men*
Wis	Wisdom of Solomon

Secondary Sources

ABRL	Anchor Bible Reference Library
ACCS	Ancient Christian Commentary on Scripture
AJT	*Asia Journal of Theology*
ANF	*Ante-Nicene Fathers*
ANRW	*Aufstieg und Niedergang der römischen Welt: Geschichte und Kultur Roms im Spiegel der neueren Forschung.* Edited by H. Temporini and W. Haase. Berlin, 1972–
BA	*Biblical Archaeologist*
BBR	*Bulletin for Biblical Research*
BDAG	Bauer, W., F.W. Danker, W.F. Arndt, and F.W. Gingrich. *Greek-English Lexicon of the New Testament and Other Early Christian Literature.* 3rd ed., Chicago, IL, 1999
BDB	Brown, F., S. R. Driver, and C.A. Briggs. *A Hebrew and English Lexicon of the Old Testament.* Oxford, 1907
Bib	*Biblica*
BR	*Biblical Research*
BTB	*Biblical Theology Bulletin*
BZ	*Biblische Zeitschrift*
CBQ	*Catholic Biblical Quarterly*
CIJ	*Corpus inscriptionum judaicarum*
DNTB	*Dictionary of New Testament Background.* Edited by C.A. Evans and S.E. Porter. Downers Grove, IL: Inter-Varsity, 2000
EDNT	*Exegetical Dictionary of the New Testament.* Edited by H. Balz and G. Schneider. ET. Grand Rapids, MI, 1990–93
Enc	*Encounter*
ESV	English Standard Version
ExpTim	*Expository Times*
FRLANT	Forschungen zur Religion und Literatur des Alten und Neuen Testaments
ICC	International Critical Commentary
Int	*Interpretation*
ISBE	*International Standard Bible Encyclopedia.* Edited by G.W. Bromiley. 4 vols, Grand Rapids, MI, 1979–88
JBL	*Journal of Biblical Literature*

JETS	*Journal of the Evangelical Theological Society*
JGRChJ	*Journal of Greco-Roman Christianity and Judaism*
JSOT	*Journal for the Study of the Old Testament*
JTS	*Journal of Theological Studies*
LASBF	*Liber annuus Studii biblici franciscani*
L&N	*Greek-English Lexicon of the New Testament: Based on Semantic Domains.* Edited by J.P. Louw and E.A. Nida. 2nd ed. New York, NY, 1989
NICOT	New International Commentary on the Old Testament
NIDNTT	*New International Dictionary of New Testament Theology.* Edited by C. Brown. 4 vols. Grand Rapids, MI, 1975–1985
NIGTC	New International Greek Testament Commentary
NovT	*Novum Testamentum*
NTOA	Novum Testamentum et Orbis Antiquus
NTS	*New Testament Studies*
OTP	*Old Testament Pseudepigrapha.* Edited by J.H. Charlesworth. 2 vols. New York, NY: Doubleday, 1985
PRSt	*Perspectives in Religious Studies*
QD	Quaestiones Disputatae
RGG	*Religion in Geschichte und Gegenwart.* Edited by K. Galling. 7 vols, 3rd ed. Tübingen, 1957–65.
RTR	*Reformed Theological Review*
SBL	Society of Biblical Literature
SBLMS	Society of Biblical Literature Monograph Series
SBLSP	*Society of Biblical Literature Seminar Papers*
Scr	Scripture
SJLA	Studies in Judaism in Late Antiquity
Str-B	Strack, H.L., and P. Billerbeck. *Kommentar zum Neuen Testament aus Talmud und Midrasch.* 2nd ed. 6 vols, Munich: C.H. Beck, 1922–61
TANZ	Texte und Arbeiten zum neutestamentlichen Zeitalter
TBei	*Theologische Beiträge*
TDNT	*Theological Dictionary of the New Testament.* Edited by G. Kittel and G. Friedrich. Trans. G.W. Bromiley. 10 vols, Grand Rapids, MI, 1964–76
TLZ	*Theologische Literaturzeitung*
TNTC	Tyndale New Testament Commentaries

TQ	*Theologische Quartalschrift*
TSK	*Theologische Studien und Kritiken*
TynBul	*Tyndale Bulletin*
TZ	*Theologische Zeitschrift*
WBC	Word Biblical Commentary
WMANT	Wissenschaftliche Monographien zum Alten und Neuen Testament
WUNT	Wissenschaftliche Untersuchungen zum Neuen Testament
ZNW	*Zeitschrift für die neutestamentliche Wissenschaft und die Kunde der älteren Kirche*

Miscellaneous abbreviations

/	Old and New Testament echoes or parallels
CTS	Covenant Theological Seminary, Saint Louis, Missouri, USA
FS	Festschrift
HL	*hapax legomenon*
n.p.	no page
par(r).	synoptic parallel(s)

Italicized references to the Old and New Testaments are given for emphasis

Introduction

In the following study we seek to isolate key issues of Christology and identity and character formation in select New Testament writings which are, in one way or another, historically associated with Peter's Christ-centered witness, transformation, and mentoring. Throughout this study we will repeatedly refer to three bodies of writings: (1) two letters attributed to Peter (1 and 2 Peter), (2) an account of which Peter is said to be the primary source (the Gospel of Mark), and (3) an account in which Peter is prominently featured (Luke's report of Peter's acts and speeches, roughly covering the first half of Acts). As we discuss the historical and historical-critical issues surrounding these texts, we will call these groups of writings *Peter's canonical testimony*. We avoid the nomenclature *corpus Petrinum* since this phrase refers more specifically to a collection of works written by a particular author. Furthermore, we will not so much focus on precise literary connections between the books associated with Peter as we will on various compatible Petrine concepts and emphases of Christology and identity and character formation nestled within the early Christian witness.

A Consistent, Uniquely Petrine Testimony

Our contention is that the historical figure of Peter stands behind the canonical testimony associated with his name. Regarding the various historical questions, we keep in mind what Cullmann remarked in the preface to the second edition of his classic work on Peter: 'Often, unfortunately, with the somewhat primitive prejudice, whose day one would have thought was past, that to pronounce something "spurious" is a mark of scientific method while results of the opposite kind are suspicious signs of an "uncritical" attitude!'[1]

Furthermore, we will isolate not so much a comprehensive 'characteristic Petrine theology' in Peter's canonical testimony as we will seek to identify—and come face-to-face with—Peter's bedrock witness and unique impact upon early Christianity. Cullmann cautions: 'In view of the nature of the sources it would be a rash undertaking to try to present a "theology" of the apostle Peter.

---

[1] O. Cullmann, *Peter: Disciple, Apostle, Martyr* (Waco, TX: Baylor Univ. Press, 2011), 8 n. 1.

Even if one holds that the First Epistle of Peter was written by the apostle himself, the basis for this undertaking is too small'.[2] Bond aptly adds:

> Peter remains an elusive character without a clear voice of his own. The great apostle was clearly one of the most influential people in the early church, but researchers today are left to reconstruct his actions and significance from the writings of others, writings that often tell us as much about the interests of various early Christian groups as they do about the man who inspired them.[3]

Bockmuehl likewise observes: 'Indeed it is remarkably difficult to identify distinctive theological themes associated with Peter'.[4] On the other hand, we offer in the present work much that commends Peter as the key 'rock' of reliable testimony to Jesus's identity and character formation ministry, with a witness spanning the forty years from approximately AD 27 until AD 67. In comparison, Paul is merely a significant supplementary witness to Jesus, building on Peter (Gal 1:18; Acts 13:31).

Generally speaking, then, we seek to trace Petrine emphases and selections from the common early Christian witness and teaching, especially in Mark and the Petrine sections in Acts. We believe it is a false dichotomy to claim that this material stems *either* from Peter or from the early Christian witness. Rather, we see Peter as a *central and driving force amidst* the early Christian witness. We take Acts 15 seriously and do not identify it as an early Christian synthesis devoid of historical fact. We are convinced that James,[5] Peter, Barnabas, and Paul essentially *share* the early Christian conviction that Jesus's claims and life, especially his atoning death and resurrection, are true and real. We thus see Peter as a significant, central, and mediating spokesperson for the early Christian testimony. Even if that accords with the historical facts, it will not be easy to isolate unique and characteristic theological emphases of Peter. What we can expect, however, is to point the reader to selections and emphases in Mark and the Petrine sections in Acts that most likely have Peter as a source, especially when supported by 1 and 2 Peter. While the present work does not,

---

[2] Cullmann, *Peter*, 66.

[3] H.K. Bond, 'Introduction', in Cullmann, *Peter*, 11. For a brief but apt survey of the scholarly discussion on Peter since the time of F.C. Baur, see Bond, 'Introduction', in Cullmann, *Peter*, 11–13.

[4] M. Bockmuehl, *Simon Peter in Scripture and Memory: The New Testament Apostle in the Early Church* (Grand Rapids, MI: Baker Academic, 2012), 77.

[5] Recent studies on James include: J. Painter, *Just James: The Brother of Jesus in History and Tradition* (Columbia, SC: University of South Carolina Press, 2004) and B. Chilton and J. Neusner, *The Brother of Jesus: James the Just and His Mission* (Louisville, KY: Westminster John Knox, 2004).

therefore, seek to prove unequivocally the Petrine origin of the content of Mark and those sections in Acts attributed to Peter, our study supplies ample, indirect evidence in support of the *substantial thematic compatibility* of Mark, the Petrine sections in Acts, and 1 and 2 Peter; evidence which accords with the patristic notion that Peter is the source behind these documents. This compatibility encompasses at least Christology (in the context of Trinitarian theology with ensuing soteriology) and Christ-centered identity formation and character formation, that is, essential identity and personality traits which then drive integrity in morality and ethics. In other words, what we seek to shed light on in this study is the fact that this body of writings stands up to scrutiny as constituting the significant and central Petrine contribution to the general pool of early Christian witness to Jesus and his mission, a body of writings that even displays, at times, unique Petrine characteristics.

Essential Aspects of the Petrine Witness

Our study of Peter's canonical testimony leads to a surprising focus and confluence of witness to Christ (Christology) and core characteristics of discipleship (central aspects of Christian identity and character formation). While Christian maturity has many facets, it is refreshing to learn that, according to Peter's testimony, there are central building blocks of spiritual maturity. A focus on these Petrine core elements helps us build on a solid foundation of dependence upon Christ and to begin growth toward clear goals, both individually and corporately. We thus avoid both vague generalizations on the one hand, and on the other, a sense of feeling overwhelmed by the sheer number of character traits to be appropriated as maturing disciples.

Focus on the core elements does not imply, however, that one should neglect other aspects of following Christ (such as various further forms of spiritual discipline; personal development of skills; ethics; or social, political, economic, and cultural concerns). On the contrary, when we focus on—and grow in—core aspects of discipleship, we will develop in further areas with a sense of inner peace and a trusting confidence in God's guidance toward personal and communal growth. Even though complex societal issues are important and pressing, both during Peter's time and ours, we do well to follow Jesus to the crucial transformation of our inner beings in the hope—and with the goal—of serving as transformed and transforming members of our respective churches, cultures, societies, and nations. According to Peter's testimony, the heart of such transformation is turning from autonomy to God-dependence.

In part 1, we trace the historical portrait of Peter's striking growth as disciple, apostolic witness, and mentoring shepherd with particular focus on Mark, the Petrine portions of Acts, and 1 and 2 Peter (covering the non-transferable and semi-transferable aspects of Peter's formation). We explore how Jesus calls and shapes Peter (as a somewhat extended case study) in his identity, attitude, and inner character, thus laying the foundation for his moral conduct, ethics, and socially responsible ways of living (see the Gospel of Mark). Peter thus gains access to the facilitating source of and power for sustained and authentic transformation, affecting all areas of his personal and communal life. Under such tutelage, he becomes a highly motivated and motivating team leader. Subsequently, we discover that Peter arises, surprisingly, as a prophetic preacher of repentance to Israel and emerges as the 'witness and transformation rock', representing a key foundation upon which Jesus himself builds his worldwide community of disciples, accompanied by much suffering.

After laying this groundwork, parts 2 and 3 then seek to describe the meaning of Peter's foundational and unique witness and exemplary growth in terms of his witness to Christ (Christology) and in terms of the identity and character formation of a Christian disciple and leading mentor (in other words, the transferable aspects of Peter's character formation). We explore how Peter develops into a humble mentoring leader of suffering and struggling disciples of Christ in Palestine and Asia Minor (see Acts and 1 Pet). We thus seek to identify marks of spiritual maturity and characteristics of leadership by looking at transferable examples and teachings of Peter.

Technical, historical, and theological studies abound in treating various aspects of this material. Likewise, there are many popular books on Christian maturity. There is, however, a definite lack of a biblical-theological study that describes historically, exegetically, and biblically who Christ is in Peter's witness, what Christ-centered identity and character formation looks like according to Peter, and how it serves as the foundation of personal and communal change and transformation. We thus seek to explore a Petrine theological witness which is relevant for transformed life.

We are convinced that we conform to God's revealed approach to transformation and sustained change both personally and in community when we consider Peter's testimony to the dynamic between Christ (Christology) and the identity formation of the follower as crucial and central to Christian formation. It is biblically unconvincing to look merely at the work of Christ and then to consider directly our response to it in terms of our conduct. On the contrary, *we are incapable of responding in our conduct to God's work in Christ unless our inner being has been radically undone and 'reconfigured' at the hand of the chief physician.* In other words, a divinely initiated, orchestrated, and sustained heart-transaction and transformation (with ensuing identity formation) has to go hand-in-hand with a restorative conduct in our individual and communal lives. Such a heart-transaction can only be mediated and accomplished by God the Holy Spirit, who communicates the will of the Father and the atoning, substitutionary work of the Son. Our studies in the Gospel of Mark, the Petrine sections in Acts, and 1 and 2 Peter will thus display a tripartite understanding of Christian identity and formation, which, incidentally, echoes that of Paul. By looking at the tripartite impact of Christ, we mean that Christian maturity (discipleship in God's kingdom) addresses at least the following aspects and dimensions:

a) The *work and ongoing presence of the triune God*—the Father, Son, and Holy Spirit—focusing especially on the atoning work of the eternal Son, Jesus. We will often refer to this aspect as the christological, and thus Trinitarian, basis of discipleship and Christian maturity.
b) The corresponding transformation of the followers' *identity* in heart and mind. Transformation, according to Christian discipleship, addresses, above all, issues of individual and corporate *identity formation* as *character foundation* under the ongoing influence of Christ, mediated by the Holy Spirit. From this follows,
c) The resulting *character formation* as the essential makeup of a person or community, once again driven by Christ and mediated by the Holy Spirit. The consequences of such an impact are reflected in individual and societal behavior, morals, and ethics.

The aspect of ethics will not, unfortunately, be discussed in the present work, as important as it is for navigating personal decisions and conduct as well as public guidelines and cultural norms in contemporary culture. Far from speaking against keeping the law of God, however, we emphasize in this study that God's way of accomplishing Christ-centered, law-congruent godliness (see Rom 8:4; 10:4; 13:10; cf. Matt 5:17-20) arises from Christ's atoning and reconciling cleansing of the autonomous heart and will (Mark 7:22-23). He focuses on the transformation of the inner person that leads to a personal and purified, God-dependent identity and character. Only then can moral, ethical, and social issues in conduct and behavior, both individually and corporately, be addressed in a meaningful, God-empowered and sustained way (cf. 2 Pet 1:3). Only then will we be following Christ's priorities and his thoughtful and sustained approach to heralding God's royal and eternal rule on earth.

Definition of Concepts and Terms

Before we begin, let us define a few key concepts and terms that will play a significant role in what lies ahead.

Virtue. Part of this study pursues the question of what characterizes and marks the inner disposition and outlook (see 'Heart' below) of those who grow in a new identity in Christ. We are looking for marks of spiritual maturity and attitudes of the inner being that affect thinking, feeling, and behavior. In antiquity and modernity, the term 'virtue' was and is often used to describe such character formation (e.g., Pharisaic Judaism or Stoicism). The reason why we will not use this term much in our study is the fact that 'virtue', even in our contemporary usage, often implies the concept of self-generated excellence and autonomous perfection (Webster's definition is 'conformity to a standard of right'). This understanding is alien and antithetical to the biblical notion of a godly character and attitude of heart as a *consequence* of perpetual dependence upon God. We also question self-generated virtue due to the *pondus peccati* (i.e., the profound alienation of mankind from God outside the atonement provided by Christ)[6] and mankind's failure to live according to the standards of God. We thus prefer to speak of 'attitudes of the heart', 'marks of Christian maturity', 'mature discipleship' or the like, to describe these inner qualities of a person, which are based on a renewed identity and dependence upon Christ. Thus 'love', for example, is such a consequence rather than a 'virtue' (*pace* KJV for 1 Cor 13:1-7 or 2 Pet 1:5).

Character. Webster defines character as it applies to our subject as 'the complex of mental and ethical traits marking and often individualizing a person, group, or nation'. It furthermore pertains to the 'main or essential nature especially as strongly marked and serving to distinguish'. Finally, it represents 'moral excellence and firmness'. In addition to these definitions, we would like to add that in our study we will encounter the dimension of emotional maturity in terms of self-awareness, self-acceptance, and interpersonal adaptability. We will frequently use the terms *godly identity* and *character formation*. We caution the reader not to associate 'character' merely with principled conduct but rather with the deeper change of heart traceable in Peter's life and witness as a response to Jesus's person and teaching.

Heart. Webster defines the *figurative* use of the heart as 'one's innermost character, feelings, or inclinations', connected with personality and inner disposition. As we draw on passages from the Old and New Testaments, we will see that in addition to character, feelings, and inclinations, we must add inner thoughts, worldview, convictions, and volition to this list.

Ambiguities Between Heart Attitudes (Character Traits) and Expressed Character. A final word of clarification is necessary before we embark on our study: at times, we will discuss such heart attitudes and character traits as 'obedience', 'perseverance in persecution', 'courageous witness', 'prayerfulness', 'forgiveness', and 'living as alien sojourners'. It can be argued that these characteristics are not as much attitudes of the heart (and thus character traits) as they are *consequences* of heart attitudes; for instance, obedience as the consequence of the heart attitude of surrender, or perseverance in persecution as the result of faith, etc. While we acknowledge this ambiguity between heart attitudes (character traits) and expressed character, we have found in our texts that many of the aforementioned traits are deeply embedded in heart attitudes (for instance obedience embedded in surrender; courageous witness, prayer, and forgiveness embedded in faith), while at the same time *manifesting* themselves in the art of living. Our study suggests that these

---

[6] See C. Plantinga, *Not the Way It's Supposed to Be: A Breviary of Sin* (Grand Rapids, MI: Eerdmans, 1995).

characteristics could be identified as a 'heart of obedience', a 'heart of perseverance', a 'heart of witness', a 'heart of prayer', a 'heart of forgiveness', and a 'heart of living intentionally as sojourner in this world'. In other words, some of these forms of apparent conduct have so much become 'second nature' that they now characterize a follower of Christ in heart (character) *and* action.

PART ONE

The Apostolic Foundation:

Non-Transferable and Semi-Transferable Aspects of Peter's Work and Witness

By non-transferable aspects of Peter's work and witness we mean those elements of his early Christian work which are entirely unique to him and contain no hint of succession, continuation, or imitation. By semi-transferable aspects of Peter's work and witness we mean those elements of his work which are partially applicable to other followers of Christ.

CHAPTER 1

Peter's Development in the Setting of First-Century Palestinian Judaism[1]

The Names of Peter

Hengel rightly observes that the sheer fact that Peter is mentioned by name 181 times in the New Testament (75 times in the Synoptic Gospels and 35 times in John) indicates his prominence in early Christianity.[2] The New Testament features the following names for the Apostle Peter: (a) his original, 'native Greek'[3] name, Simon;[4] (b) the patronymic and Aramaic Simon Bar-Jonah[5] (=Simon, son of Jonah or John);[6] (c) the Aramaic nickname and common noun[7]

---

[1] Besides Cullmann, *Peter*, 19–33, more recent biographical sketches of Peter's life include: Bockmuehl, *Simon*, 153–76; L.R. Helyer, *The Life and Witness of Peter* (Downers Grove, IL: IVP Academic, 2012), 19–31; M. Hengel, *Saint Peter: The Underestimated Apostle* (Grand Rapids, MI: Eerdmans, 2010), 1–48; C.P. Thiede, *Simon Peter: From Galilee to Rome* (Exeter: Paternoster, 1986), 17–26; E. Dinkler, 'Petrus, Apostel', *RGG*, V, cols. 247–49; cf. R. Pesch, *Simon–Petrus. Geschichte und geschichtliche Bedeutung des ersten Jüngers Jesu Christi* (Stuttgart: Hiersemann, 1980); K.H. Rengstorf (ed.), *Das Petrusbild in der neueren deutschen Forschung* (Darmstadt: Wissenschaftliche Buchgesellschaft, 1964); R.E. Brown, Donfried, and K.P., Reumann, J. (eds), *Peter in the New Testament: A Collaborative Assessment by Protestant and Roman Catholic Scholars* (Eugene, OR: Wipf & Stock, 2002).

[2] Hengel, *Peter*, 10–11. Helyer, *Life*, 21, notes that Paul is mentioned 177 times in the NT.

[3] Cf. Helyer, *Life*, 19–20, and 20 n. 4. Cullmann (*Peter*, 19) states that Andrew and Philip (both from Bethsaida) likewise have Greek names.

[4] Often, the name 'Simon' occurs in conjunction with 'Peter': 10x in Matthew; 9x in Mark; 12x in Luke; 23x in John; 11x in Acts. Only in Acts 15:14 (cf. 2 Pet 1:1 in conjunction with 'Peter') the Semitic form of Symeōn is used.

[5] Matt 16:17; a relatively rare reference.

[6] John 1:42; 21:15-17. Yohana(n) can be transcribed as Iōna in Greek; thus 'Son of Jonah' and 'Son of John' are not necessarily at odds with each other; *pace* M. Bockmuehl, *The Remembered Peter in Ancient Reception and Modern Debate* (Tübingen: Mohr Siebeck, 2010), 145.

[7] See Bockmuehl, *Simon*, 22, who views the term 'Cephas' in the Aramaic-speaking churches of Palestine as 'a kind of dominical title of honor'. Cf. Cullmann, *Peter*, 21.

Cepha (or Cephas), given to him by Jesus (John 1:42)[8] and which means 'rock', 'stone', or 'cliff' and is translated into the relatively common Greek name of Πέτρος (*Petros*=rock; cf. Mark 3:16 and Matt 16:17); (d) Simon Peter, i.e., 'Simon Rock';[9] (e) Peter.[10] The name Simon occurred more frequently in Judaism subsequent to the Hasmonean uprising,[11] which included *Simon Maccabeus* (see below). Due to this name connection, it is possible, among other reasons, that Simon Peter might have taken special notice of the history of the Maccabean uprising during his early years in Galilee. Unlike the Maccabean Simon the 'hammer', however, Peter will arise as Simon the humbled and thus solid 'rock' for Christ. As our goal initially is to describe what type of person Jesus calls to be a disciple, a key witness and apostle, a brief sketch of Peter's life up to the time of his encounter with the Messiah is in order. Furthermore, our brief sketch will put into relief the life-lessons Peter internalizes in his particular life-setting *prior* to meeting the Messiah. By looking at formative elements in Peter's past, we will begin to see fundamental characteristics of Palestinian Jewish theology (from which his messianic expectations arose), teacher-pupil relationships, and patterns of leadership emerge. We will discover ostensible connections as well as distinct contrasts between his past and his radical formation under the tutelage of the Messiah.

Peter's Shaping Influences Prior to Becoming a Disciple of Jesus

The Place and Date of Peter's Birth

Peter lived in Galilee, in the context of revived Palestinian Judaism. However, according to John, Peter was born in the border-town of Bethsaida, perhaps

---

[8] John 1:42; 1 Cor 1:12; 3:22; 9:5; 15:5; Gal 1:18; 2:9, 11, 14. Cepha[s] (Aramaic כֵּפָא; Hebrew כֵּיפָא) is transcribed into Greek as Κηφᾶς=Kephas (or Cephas). Like the OT (Gen 17:5; 32:27-30; Isa 62:2; 65:15), Jesus gives nicknames to signal a particular characteristic of or divine purpose for some of his followers; see, e.g., Mark 3:17, regarding the sons of Zebedee; cf. Cullmann, *Peter*, 21. Bockmuehl, *Simon*, 59, argues that *hermēneutetai* in John 1:42 denotes '*meaning* rather than *naming*'.

[9] Cf. Cullmann, *Peter*, 21; 3x in Matthew, 2x in Mark, 2x in Luke, 17x in John, 5x in Acts.

[10] 'Peter' occurs 19x in Matthew, 17x in Mark, 17x in Luke, 12x in John, 49x in Acts, as well as in Gal 2:7-8, 1 Pet 1:1, 2 Pet 1:1.

[11] Bockmuehl, *Simon*, 21.

around 1 BC (cf. John 1:44).[12] According to Bockmuehl, Roman era Bethsaida Julias, east of the Jordan,[13] probably corresponds to the modern site of Et-Tell.[14]

When Peter grew up there, it was probably a small town or village (Mark 8:23, 26). It became a Roman *polis* in AD 30 (cf. Luke 9:10; John 1:44).[15] It was inhabited by both Gentiles and, to a lesser degree, Jews. Bockmuehl argues that Peter grew up bi-lingual (see below), given the fact that he initially lived in predominantly Gentile surroundings[16] and later in a place steeped in the renewed Jewish faith and nationalism (Capernaum).[17] His father's name was John (or Jonah), and his younger brother was Andrew, initially a follower of John the Baptist (Mark 1:29; John 1:40-42).

Sometime after his early childhood and a considerable time before his marriage (Mark 1:30; 1 Cor 9:5; cf. John 2:12), Peter moved to Capernaum (Mark 1:21, 29), perhaps for religious reasons,[18] and worked from there, together with his brother, as a 'middle-class' fisherman at the Sea of Galilee (=Lake Gennesaret; Mark 1:16; cf. Matt 4:18; Luke 5:2-3; John 21:3). Jesus's disciple Philip was also a resident of Bethsaida (John 1:44). Peter and his brother Andrew were, likewise, formally associated (μετόχοις, Luke 5:7; κοινωνοί, Luke 5:10), perhaps as business partners,[19] with the fishermen James and John, the sons of Zebedee (Mark 1:29).

---

[12] Bethsaida, upon which Jesus pronounces his woes (Matt 11:21/Luke 10:13), will be the site of the two-stage healing of the blind man, a pericope particular to Mark (Mark 8:22-26). Bockmuehl, *Simon*, 167, notes the symbolic connection between the blind man and Peter: both are from Bethsaida; both are coming to 'sight' in two stages; neither of them are permitted to return to the place of their birth.

[13] Bockmuehl, *Simon*, 168. Bethsaida lies technically in the tetrarchy of Trachonitis and not in Herod Antipas' Galilee. The phrase 'Bethsaida of Galilee' (John 12:21), as is the case with the 'Sea of Galilee', does not reflect strict political-geographic boundaries but rather the fact of Jewish settlements in the region adjacent to Galilee proper (Bockmuehl, *Simon*, 170).

[14] Bockmuehl, *Simon*, 22–23; 171–73; Helyer, *Life*, 21–24. For further detail on Bethsaida-Julias, see H.-W. Kuhn, *Betsaida/Bethsaida-Julias (et-Tell): Die ersten 25 Jahre der Ausgrabung (1987–2011—The First Twenty-Five Years of Excavation (1987–2011)* (Göttingen: Vandenhoeck & Ruprecht, 2014).

[15] Bockmuehl, *Simon*, 169.

[16] Bockmuehl, *Simon*, 175. See also Cullmann, *Peter*, 24.

[17] Bockmuehl, *Remembered Peter*, 186.

[18] Bockmuehl, *Simon*, 175.

[19] See details in Helyer, *Life*, 25 and n. 22, regarding the likelihood that we are dealing here with technical terms of financial partnerships.

Peter's Socio-Political Setting[20]

In order to understand the world in which Peter grew up and in which his convictions and perspectives on life developed, we briefly purvey the history of Israel (especially of Judea and Galilee) from approximately 164 BC onward.

It is highly probable that Peter was taught orally in both formal and informal ways to remember the recent Jewish history, especially spanning the preceding two hundred years prior to his adult life. Chief among these recollections was the Maccabean uprising against Syrian oppression (from 164 BC onward), subsequently commemorated in the annual Feast of Hanukkah (=dedication, cf. John 10:22).[21] Such commemoration was particularly significant on account of the renewed oppression by a foreign power (Rome) and due to strong messianic expectations (see the works of Josephus) during Peter's life. The Galilee in which Peter grew up and lived had also undergone a process of repopulation by Jews, especially in the wake of the Maccabean uprising (again, see below).[22]

Palestine During the Maccabean (Hasmonean) Period (164–63 BC)

Early Maccabean period (164–134 BC)
The highly offensive actions of the Seleucid (Syrian) ruler Antiochus IV (Epiphanes) against the Jewish people (cf. 1 Macc 2:4, 66; 2 Macc 6:1-5; 8:5, 16; 10:1, 16), as well as the increasing accommodation by Jewish leaders (especially Jason [2 Macc 4:7, 13, 22] and Menelaus [2 Macc 4:23-24, 26]) toward Antiochus IV, set the stage for the rise of a guerilla-type Jewish resistance movement.[23] The straw that broke the camel's back was Antiochus IV's order to desecrate the temple in Jerusalem in 167 BC.[24] This public provocation occurred after the attempt of inner-Jewish forces in Judea to reinstate the Zadokite Jason as high priest and to depose the first non-Zadokite high priest Menelaus, whose appointment in 171 BC had been sanctioned by Antiochus IV. In retaliation to such insubordination, Antiochus IV demolished the walls of the temple and looted the temple treasury.[25] The temple was partially destroyed, thus rendering

---

[20] For the following section on Peter's historical background, I thank my esteemed colleague, Prof. David Calhoun, who gave me his 1994 CTS lecture-notes on *New Testament Backgrounds*; some of his material is partially incorporated here. See E.M. Meyers and M.A. Chancey, *Alexander to Constantine: Archaeology of the Land of the Bible* (New Haven, CT: Yale University Press, 2014).

[21] See 1 Macc 4:36-59 and Josephus, *Ant.* 12.7.7. Significantly, John 10:22 refers to the 'Feast of Dedication' (τὰ ἐγκαίνια).

[22] See M.F. Bird, *Jesus and the Origins of the Gentile Mission* (New York, NY: Bloomsbury, 2007).

[23] See 1 Macc 13:43; 2 Macc 5:11.

[24] See also 2 Macc 6:1-5; 14:33.

[25] Cf. 1 Macc 1:16, 24.

temple worship impossible. Antiochus IV subsequently pursued the hellenization of Jerusalem as a means of controlling Judea. Between 167 and 164 BC, the temple became a center for Zeus worship and Dionysian observances as a substitute to the now forbidden Torah obedience.[26] Antiochus IV even had a pig slaughtered in the temple.[27] First Maccabees 1:54 calls this the 'appalling sacrilege' or the 'abomination of desolation'.[28] In the wake of this, many faithful and resisting Jews were martyred.[29]

These events spawned the Maccabean Revolt, characterized by loyalty to the Torah, martyrdom,[30] and military action based on the belief that God was with his people. In 167 BC, the rural priest Mattathias (1 Macc 5:62) led this Jewish Revolt with his five sons John, Simon, Judas, Eleazar, and Jonathan. They were known as 'Hasmoneans', named after their family patriarch, Hashman. Surprisingly, the Revolt resulted in the renewed purification of the temple in 164 BC (1 Macc 4:36-59; 2 Macc 10:1-8). Since Antiochus IV had greater plans of expansion eastward toward the Euphrates, he chose not to continue to do battle in Jerusalem. Nevertheless, further serious conflicts erupted between the Seleucid successors of Antiochus IV (from 164 to 143 BC) and subsequent Maccabean leaders, notably Jonathan, who became, with Syrian consent, high priest, governor, and military commander in 150 BC (1 Macc 9:28-31). Eventually, the Maccabeans attained independence for Judea in 142 BC,[31] thus ending a long and arduous struggle against Seleucid control.[32] Around 140 BC, Simon Maccabeus, the last surviving son of Mattathias, became governor (ethnarch) and, like his brother Jonathan, a *non*-Zadokite high priest (1 Macc 13:1-10; 14:35).[33]

Later Maccabean Period (134–63 BC)
The Hasmonean period lasted a little under one hundred years, extending from the Maccabean victory in 164 BC (with their rule commencing in 142 BC) to the

---

[26] During that time, Sabbath observances, circumcisions, sacrifices, and festivals were forbidden. C.J. Roetzel (*The World that Shaped the New Testament* [London: SCM, 1987], 12) notes that Antiochus IV makes the 'possession of a Torah scroll a capital offense'. See 2 Macc 6:10-11 (cf. 1 Macc 1:59-64) regarding reprisals for those disobeying Antiochus's orders.

[27] 1 Macc 1:41-59; cf. 2 Macc 6:3-9.

[28] See already Dan 9:27; 11:31; cf. Mark 13:14.

[29] See especially the mother's account concerning the martyrdom of her seven sons (2 Macc 7:1-41).

[30] Cf. 2 Macc 7; Heb 11:35b-38.

[31] Cf. 1 Macc 15:5-6; cf. also 1 Macc 13:43: 'The yoke of the Gentiles was removed from Israel'.

[32] 1 Macc 14:4-15.

[33] The hereditary, non-Zadokite priesthood (cf. 1 Macc 14:41) was justified 'until a true prophet arises'.

rise and direct rule of Palestine by Rome in 63 BC. While a great theocratic victory had been won in the second half of the second century BC for Jews in Palestine, dedicated leaders in the early Maccabean period were gradually replaced by weaker successors, sharing little concern for the initial Maccabean cause and displaying much greater interest in personal gain and power. Among them were John Hyrcanus, son of Simon (134–105 BC), and especially Alexander Janneus (103–76 BC). These latter Maccabean leaders attempted to limit aspects of Hellenistic influence and culture only for the sake of gaining power and access to the office of high priest, not in order to preserve the Jewish faith (and then ended up perpetuating Hellenistic practices nevertheless). In fact, Hellenistic life in aristocratic Jerusalem returned, at least partially, to the state it had been in during the pre-Maccabean compromise. The latter leaders also pursued an aggressive foreign policy.[34]

Eerily parallel to the earlier inner-Jewish strife over the high priestly appointment of the non-Zadokite priest Menelaus, which had been exploited by Antiochus IV, the 'civil war' between the last Hasmoneans Hyrcanus II and Aristobulus II led to Roman 'intervention'.[35] In 63 BC, the Roman commander Pompey occupied Syria. As part of the Roman province of Syria, Palestine's arduous subjection to Rome began in earnest, continuing the at times severe tax burden which had been levied against Palestine since the days of Seleucid dominance. Dodd aptly characterizes the time from 164 to 63 BC in this way: 'It began in the heroic resistance of the Maccabees, flourished for a time under their successors, the Hasmonean princes, and fizzled out in sordid squabbles among their last heirs, when a Roman takeover became inevitable.'[36] Nevertheless, the *memory* of Hasmonean resistance against foreign oppressors, believed to have been successful on account of God's intervention (cf. 2 Macc 3:22-34), continued to inspire tried Jewry for two hundred—and indeed for more than two thousand—years: the Feast of Hanukkah, commemorating the cleansing and rededication of the temple in 164 BC must have served as a telling testimony to this. The not-so-distant memory of the Maccabean uprising against Seleucid dominance would be crucial in forming Peter's view of Israel's past, marked by suppression, liberation, future hope (see Acts 1:6, 'restoration of the kingdom to Israel'; cf. Judg 6:13; Dan 2:44), and especially his expectation of a messianic liberator along the lines of a Maccabean leader (Mark 8:32b; Acts 1:6; cf. 2 Sam 7:14-16).

---

[34] Alexander Janneus, e.g., expands his realm of influence nearly to the extent of that of David (cf. Roetzel, *World*, 14).

[35] It is important to remember that the early Maccabean leaders had forged alliances with Rome (cf. 1 Macc 8:1-32; 12:1-4; 14:16-19, 24).

[36] C.H. Dodd, *The Founder of Christianity* (New York, NY: Macmillan, 1970), 6.

It is very likely that Simon Peter, together with a majority of his people, strongly identified with the sentiment and zeal of the early Maccabean uprising. During his early life, he must have longed for the reestablishment of a Jewish theocracy (see the national aspirations of the early Maccabeans described in 1 Macc 4:46–14:41; cf. Mark 13:3-4; 14; Acts 1:6), since Judea and Galilee had, again, been oppressed by foreign rule since 63 BC. The suffering of the Jewish people under Antiochus IV and the subsequent suppression under Roman rule must have been paramount in Peter's national and theological thinking, attitude, and hope. A free people have many hopes; a suppressed people have but one hope. The Maccabean uprising thus served as a blue print for sustaining faith in God as the liberator of Israel during renewed oppression. The martyrdoms described in 2 and 4 Maccabees would have a long-lasting impact upon Jews and early Christians.[37] As 2 Maccabees 6:12-17 makes amply clear, it is not that God had abandoned his people but that he was chastising them until the appointed time of redemption, which would be accomplished by guerilla-type uprisings (cf. Judg 6:13).

The Jewish Repopulation of Peter's Galilee

A significant development in the demographics of Galilee and Judea prior to and during the early life of Peter was the increasing resettlement of Jews in the former territory of the twelve tribes of Israel, including Galilee.[38] The beginning of postexilic resettlement of Jews goes back to the days of Ezra and Nehemiah but finds a new thrust in the wake of the Maccabean uprising and the later efforts of the Herodians.[39] The geographic areas which were being resettled[40] cover approximately the same territory as at the time of the Judges. A comparison of then predominantly Gentile areas (except for Judea and parts of Galilee) being resettled by Jews with those inhabited during the time of the Judges yields the following results:

---

[37] Cf. S.A. Cummins, *Paul and the Crucified Christ in Antioch: Maccabean Martyrdom and Galatians 1 and 2* (Cambridge: Cambridge University Press, 2001); J.W. van Henten, *The Maccabean Martyrs as Saviours of the Jewish People: A Study of 2 and 4 Maccabees* (Leiden: Brill, 1997); J.W. van Henten and A. Friedrich, *Martyrdom and Noble Death: Selected Texts from Graeco-Roman, Jewish and Christian Antiquity* (New York, NY: Routledge, 2002); R. Eyal, *Hasmoneans: Ideology, Archaeology, Identity* (Göttingen: Vandenhoeck & Ruprecht, 2013).

[38] Cf. R. Riesner, *Paul's Early Period: Chronology, Mission Strategy, Theology* (Grand Rapids, MI: Eerdmans, 1998), 238–39.

[39] E.J. Schnabel, *Early Christian Mission: Jesus and the Twelve* (Downers Grove, IL: IVP, 2004), I, 729–80; E. Schürer, *The History of the Jewish People in the Age of Jesus Christ,—175 B.C.–A.D. 135* (ed.) G. Vermes, F. Millar, and F. Black (Edinburgh: T&T Clark, 1973–87), II, 85–198 and III, 1–86.

[40] Schürer, *History,* I, 164–73; II, 86–97.

Time of Peter:	*Time of the Judges:*
Galilee	Zebulun, Naphtali, Issachar, and parts of Asher
Phoenicia	The southern part of this coastline region was part of Asher
Tetrarchy of Philip	Northern part of Manasseh in Transjordan and perhaps the new Dan
Decapolis	Eastern part of Gad; Manasseh in Transjordan
Perea	Reuben; western part of Gad
Samaria	Manasseh (west of the Jordan); Ephraim
Judea	Benjamin, Judah (including Simeon and the original Dan)

Especially since Aristobulus I (104–103 BC), the resettling of Jews in Galilee and in parts of the future Decapolis and Judea increased. Under Alexander Janneus (103–76 BC), the geographic region captured by Maccabean expansion extended in the north to Hazor, to the east into the future Decapolis, and included nearly all coastal cities from Egypt to Mount Carmel. The consequence was an increasing Jewish settlement. In the wake of the conquest of Pompey (63 BC), Jewish settlement receded for a time.[41] But especially the later king of Judea, Herod 'the Great' (37–4 BC), again welcomed returning Jews especially to the region east of the Sea of Galilee.[42] We can conclude that at the time of Peter the entire region of the former territory of Israel was again inhabited by pockets of Jewish settlers, albeit outside of Judea and parts of Galilee, in predominantly Gentile regions.

Such migration and resettlement, alongside the memory of suffering under Seleucid suppression and the Maccabean uprising, must have reinforced Peter's deep expectation for God to reestablish a theocracy (cf. 2 Sam 7:16), at least in Judea and Galilee, if not in the entire region of former Israel (cf. Acts 1:6). This expectation for God's intervention must have intensified subsequent to Roman oppression commencing in 63 BC. In what follows, we briefly focus on what happened in Judea and Galilee in the years prior to and during Peter's adult life.

The Impact of Roman Occupation in Galilee

The rise and reach of the Roman Empire occurred *gradually*, announcing itself in Palestine already with the subjugation of Seleucid powers in 190 BC and arriving with full force following the conquest of Palestine through Pompey in 63 BC. The time from 63 to 48 BC was marked by the inner-Roman transition from functioning as a republic to emerging as an empire headed by a 'Caesar'. The

---

[41] See Josephus, *Ant.* 11.301; 13.393–97 and *J.W.* 2.4; Strabo, *Geogr.* 26.2, 40. Schürer, *History*, I, 174–88; 209–28.

[42] Schürer, *History*, I, 304–20; II, 91–94, 136–37 and G.H. Dalman, *Sacred Sites and Ways: Studies in the Topography of the Gospels* (London: SPCK, 1935), 219–20.

centralized power in Rome and its systematic administration of the provinces (consolidated especially through the Emperors Augustus and Claudius) greatly affected life in Palestine. The respective emperor would shape the character of dominion over Palestine (and other regions), worsening or easing (in relative terms) the suppressive weight of Rome. The following succession of Roman rulers, from Caesar Augustus to Nero, would highlight these fluctuating but generally oppressive influences during Peter's life.

Life Under the Emperors Augustus, Tiberius, Caligula, Claudius, and Nero (31 BC to AD 68)

During Peter's life, a succession of Roman emperors shaped Jewish life in Judea and Galilee.

Caesar Octavian (=*Caesar Augustus*, 31 BC–AD 14) rose to power in 31 BC. With his ascendency, the former Roman republic underwent a thorough restructuring as a centralized empire, headed by one authoritative figure.[43] Such consolidated and immense power[44] strongly influenced the governance of the Galilee in which Peter grew up (especially regarding heavy taxes and suppression of uprisings), even though Herod Antipas served in Galilee as a Jewish client-ruler on behalf of Rome (4 BC–AD 39; see below).

During *Tiberius's* tenure (AD 14–37), the empire enjoyed relative peace (as seen from the perspective of Rome),[45] despite the fact that he tended to be increasingly antisocial, sexually perverse, suspicious, and anti-Judaic.[46] It was during Tiberius's reign that Jesus called Peter and others to be his disciples in Galilee, pursued his ministry and was crucified in Jerusalem AD 30 (or 33).

Gaius Caligula (AD 37–41) was incestuous, erratic, and despotic. He considered himself to be 'Zeus incarnate', and as such, he intended to have his cult-statue placed in the Jerusalem temple and to demand emperor worship (see below). Fortunately, Herod Agrippa's intervention in AD 40 and the assassination of Caligula in AD 41 precluded this offensive event and pacified

---

[43] During Caesar Augustus's rule, Jesus was born in 6–5 BC (cf. Luke 2:1). Extrabiblical references to Jesus include: Josephus, *J.W.* 2.174; 5.195 and *Ant.* 18.63–64; 20.200; Suetonius, *Nero* 16.2; Suetonius, *Claud.* 25.4; Tacitus, *Ann.* 15.44. See R.E. Van Voorst, *Jesus Outside the New Testament. An Introduction to the Ancient Evidence* (Grand Rapids, MI: Eerdmans, 2000).

[44] Suetonius, *Aug.* 47.

[45] Tacitus, *Hist.* 5.9, in J. van Bruggen, *Jesus the Son of God: The Gospel Narratives as Message* (Grand Rapids, MI: Baker, 1999), 22: '"*Sub Tiberio quies*" (Peace under Tiberius!)'.

[46] Caesar Tiberius's image was on a *denarius* handed to Jesus (Mark 12:16).

the resistance then concentrated in Tiberias.[47] Nevertheless, Caligula's provocative actions (including the temporary forfeiture of the Jewish faith as *religio licita*) contributed to a rising tension between Jerusalem and Rome, anticipating Rome's preemptive strike against Judea and Jerusalem in AD 66.

Under *Claudius's* rule (AD 41–54) many Jewish Christians were banished from Rome (AD 48).[48] The provinces were, however, administered with a higher degree of relative restraint.

Nero's (AD 54–68) first five years of (youthful) rule as Emperor stood in contrast to his capricious, sexually perverse, and malicious approach for the remainder of his rule. The ferocious fire that broke out on July 18 in AD 64 in the market area of the *Circus Maximus* in Rome is a telling example. When Nero was unable to rid himself of the persistent rumor that he had instigated the fire, he targeted Christians as scapegoats. Most likely, this occurred because the Roman Christians did not participate, for example, in immoral aspects of social and political life (cf. 1 Pet). Tacitus[49] describes the ensuing persecution of Christians: they were routed in large groups as wild dogs were let loose at them; some were crucified, some were burned at stakes. Later, Nero struck against the Jewish Revolt in Palestine instigated in AD 66. *It was under Nero's tenure that Peter and Paul were martyred in Rome around AD 67.* In the wake of Nero's suicide, Tacitus notes that people feared that 'the end of the empire was at hand'.[50]

The Oppressive Weight of Roman Governance, Emperor Worship, and Tax-Procurement

The political force of the Roman Empire at the time of Peter was particularly visible in the arena of the military, as well as in fiscal and administrative policy. It shaped public life in the areas of law-enforcement, and the development of extensive road systems, sports, and social life. In terms of philosophy and religion, Rome proved less innovative and essentially appropriated predominantly Hellenistic thought and religious disposition into many regions of its empire. Cicero observed: 'It was no little brook that flowed from Greece into our city, but a mighty river of culture and learning'.[51] Of particular influence on Rome was Stoicism with its centerpiece of strict self-control and ethical

---

[47] Josephus, *J.W.* 2.197 and *Ant.* 28.8.2–9; Tacitus, *Hist.* 5.9.

[48] See Suetonius, *Claud.* 25.4; Acts 18:2. This treacherous act landed Aquila and Priscilla in Corinth, where they met Paul (Acts 18:1-4). They returned to Rome following the death of Claudius in AD 54.

[49] Tacitus, *Ann.* 15.36-38, 44.4–5. Bockmuehl, *Simon*, 148, notes that the crucifixions occurred 'adjacent to the Vatican Hill', where Peter will later be crucified; cf. *1 Clem.* 6.

[50] Tacitus, *Hist.* 4.54.

[51] Cicero, *Resp.* 2.19.

discipline. Stoicism was the Hellenistic counterpart to the nomistic, Pharisaic Judaism that influenced Peter in his developing years. Later, Peter would encounter Stoicism in Asia Minor and Rome.

Especially from the Emperor Augustus onward, the Roman Empire was governed in regional divisions (especially provinces and colonies). The provinces were administered either by a *procurator* (or *legate*, or *prefect*; see, e.g., Judea[52]), who was directly answerable to the emperor or a *proconsul* (or *prosenator*), who was answerable to the Roman Senate. Other regions were governed by 'client kings' or rulers (such as, for example, Herod Antipas) who were in turn charged with keeping their subjects in order and procuring taxes for Rome. Their respective fates depended on it.

Judean and Galilean Life Under the Herodian Dynasty (4 BC–AD 68)

Herod the Great managed, against his Hasmonean opponents, to be confirmed in 40 BC by the Roman Senate as a 'client king' of Judea and ruled from then on until his death in 4 BC. He initiated the expansion of the second temple in Jerusalem.[53] Following Herod's death in 4 BC, Augustus divided Herod's realm into three 'client sovereignties', administered by Herod's three sons. The chief part went to Archelaus (Judea, Samaria, Idumea; 4 BC–AD 6).[54] The second section went to Herod Antipas (Galilee, Perea; 4 BC–AD 39),[55] who was a skillful ruler and an able builder.[56] He furthered Hellenistic culture and unlawfully married Herodias, the sister of Agrippa I, in AD 27, an act which John the Baptist condemned (Josephus, *Ant.* 18.116–19).[57]

Under Antipas's rule in Galilee, Peter grew up, became an adult, and began to follow Jesus. Jesus, also, spent his entire life as a Galilean subject of Herod Antipas (cf. Mark 8:15 [warning the disciples of the 'yeast of Herod']; Luke 9:9; 13:31, 32 ['that fox']; 23:6-12). Antipas was exiled in AD 39 for seeking to

---

[52] From AD 6 to 41, Judea was governed directly by a Roman *prefect* or *procurator*.

[53] The expansion began around 20 or 19 BC and was fully completed between AD 63 or 64. The temple was destroyed in AD 70; cf. John 2:20.

[54] Josephus, *J.W.* 2.94.

[55] Mark 3:8; cf. Matt 2:22. See Josephus, *J.W.* 2.94.

[56] Tiberias (AD 22), e.g., was a Gentile city. Antipas also rebuilt Sepphoris.

[57] According to the OT, it was an unlawful marriage (cf. Lev 18:16; 20:21), since Herodias was the wife of his half-brother, Philip (son of Marianne). See Matt 14:1-12 and Luke 3:19; 9:7-9.

be 'king'. The third section of Herod the Great's territory fell to the moderate Philip (Iturea, Trachonitis; 4 BC–AD 34).[58]

The Wider Religious Context of Peter's Life in Galilee

As mentioned above, Peter must have been deeply influenced during his younger years by the dramatic history of the Maccabean uprising, reinforced by the annual celebration of Hanukkah, going back some 180 years. While Peter was aware of the Roman endorsement, and, at times enforcement, of emperor worship, he was, as a law-abiding Jewish Galilean, committed to worshiping the Creator of the world, YHWH, the God of Abraham, Isaac, and Jacob, and the God who revealed his law to Moses. The strong commitment of Galilean Jews to this God arose particularly in the wake of the Maccabean uprising and was due, largely, to the conservative Pharisaic teaching in the many synagogue schools scattered across Galilee (and elsewhere).[59] Oppressive Roman policy only reinforced the memory of the Maccabean uprising against foreign powers in bygone eras.

Emperor Worship (Apotheosis) as a Means of Exercising Political Power[60]

As noted, Peter lived through the times of the Roman Emperors Augustus, Tiberius, Caligula, Claudius, and Nero. While it is unclear how seriously the different forms of emperor worship (especially the veneration of still living emperors) were taken by various Roman emperors in the first century AD,[61] it is clear that certain forms of veneration existed. This is partially due to the fact that the post-Republican Roman hierarchical worldview consisted of belief in the gods as the highest authority, then the practice of philosophy, below which autocratic emperors or 'divine men' governed the people (in contrast to this, the Greek hierarchical worldview subscribed to fate as a supreme law, then the gods or philosophy, below which the city-state was 'democratically' governed). From the time of Augustus to Nero, for example, priests in the Jerusalem

---

[58] Josephus, *J.W.* 2.94–95 and *Ant.* 17.189; cf. Luke 3:1.
[59] See M. Hengel, *Judaism and Hellenism: Studies in Their Encounter in Palestine During the Early Hellenistic Period* (London: SCM Press, 2012), 103–106, 255–309.
[60] M. Bernett, *Der Kaiserkult in Judäa unter den Herodiern und Römern. Untersuchungen zur politischen und religiösen Geschichte Judäas von 30 v. bis 66 n. Chr.* (Tübingen: Mohr Siebeck, 2007); F.F. Bruce, *New Testament History* (New York, NY: Galilee/Doubleday, reissue, 1983), 316; C.A. Evans, *Mark 8:27-16:20* (Nashville, TN: Nelson, 2001), lxxxii-xciii; Roetzel, *World*, 74; and Schnabel, *Mission*, I, 617-21.
[61] See, e.g., Schnabel, *Mission*, I, 617–21. Schnabel emphasizes that apotheosis is more likely demanded by the respective local population.

temple had to sacrifice *on behalf of* the emperor on a daily basis.[62] In the course of his rule, Augustus carried the priestly title *pontifex maximus*. Augustus's self-designation as *divi filius* was probably more politically than religiously motivated.[63] Starting in 27 BC, Augustus invited the designation *divus* but did not permit Romans to worship him. Nevertheless, Egyptians called him the 'god of the gods'. Following his death in AD 14, he was venerated as 'god, son of god' (see Virgil). His protective spirit (*genius*) was to be worshiped as *deus* (god) beside the other gods. The Emperors Tiberius and Claudius rejected the venerating epithets 'lord', 'savior', and 'god'.[64] The unpredictable Emperor Gaius Caligula, on the other hand, exacted the designation *dominus et deus* (lord and god), and liked to be celebrated as the bringer of good news (εὐαγγέλιον).[65] Nero's approach was similar to that of Caligula.[66]

The Jewish reaction during the time of Peter's youth was marked by resistance to emperor worship or veneration, since, once again, they distinguished clearly between the one God who created this universe and human beings who happened to hold political power (see Isa 26:13). It was for this reason that Jews negotiated special concessions from Rome to practice their religion and to be exempt from emperor veneration (see the somewhat debated status of Judaism as a *religio licita*).[67]

Taxation as a Further Means of Political Control

Besides conforming to Roman dictates pertaining to public order, a key factor in the administration of provinces was the procurement of revenue.[68] In the provinces, governors collected taxes for Rome. Tax rates were liable to be inflated and unjust by the time tax collectors (as tax leaseholders who charged

---

[62] After Julius Caesar's death, e.g., the Roman Senate attributed divine honors to him; a temple was built to his *genius*. Schnabel (*Mission*, I, 617–21) emphasizes, however, that individual emperors were not the object of direct worship, especially during their respective reigns.

[63] Schnabel, *Mission*, I, 618.

[64] See Roetzel, *World*, 74.

[65] Cf. Suetonius, *Vesp.* 7, and Philo, *Legat.* 357.

[66] Later, the Emperor Domitian (AD 81–96) followed the example of Caligula by expecting the populace to worship him and his family as *deus et dominus noster*. Domitian attempted to force Christians to worship him (see the executions in AD 93). Subsequent to Domitian, emperor worship was rigorously implemented.

[67] See Bruce, *History*, 316.

[68] Cf. J. Herrenbrück, *Jesus und die Zöllner: Historische und neutestamentlich-exegetische Untersuchungen* (Tübingen: Mohr Siebeck, 1990), as well as D.A. Fiensy and R.K. Hawkins (eds), *The Galilean Economy in the Time of Jesus* (Williston, VT: Society of Biblical Literature, 2013).

interest on the tax advance they rendered to their superiors), such as Matthew or Zacchaeus, lay their hands on the final profit margin. In cases of client rulers (such as Peter's Galilean ruler Herod Antipas), the tax collection system was administered through that intermediary.

The Socio-Religious Settings and Values of Palestinian Judaism

Parallel to the political and fiscal structures, we note the continued development within Palestinian Judaism of religious-cultural institutions, such as the Jewish court, the Sanhedrin, and, from about 200 BC onward, the rise of two significant parties within Judaism, the Sadducees and the Pharisees, the latter of which would be of great import during Peter's youth.

The Sanhedrin (from 198 BC onward)[69]

According to Bruce,[70] the Sanhedrin functioned as an aristocratic Senate, 'presided over by a Zadokite high priest' (at least until the non-Zadokite Menelaus [172–162 BC] took control). Bribing respective foreign rulers and the pursuit of wealth and power were common practices within the Sanhedrin. At a later stage, the court pursued anti-Hasmonean policies; still later, its very existence was dependent on Rome. The Sanhedrin favored accommodation of foreign rule over confrontation.

In terms of factions, the Sanhedrin court consisted of a majority of Sadducees and a minority of Pharisees. The authority of the Sanhedrin lay generally in limited legislative and judicial matters related to the Mosaic law. During the later Roman period, the Sanhedrin (whose high priest would then be appointed by the Roman governor) had the power to arrest and to try cases of those suspected of breaking Jewish law.[71] Generally speaking, however, only Roman authorities could execute a possible death sentence.[72]

The Sadducees and Pharisees[73]

Perhaps already during Seleucid rule but clearly during the Hasmonean period, two important factions (Josephus calls them 'sects') took form within Judaism which would significantly influence the political and religious life of the

---

[69] Cf. Josephus, *Ant.* 12.142.
[70] Bruce, *History*, 56.
[71] See, e.g., Jesus in Matt 26:47.
[72] See the informative overview by J. van Bruggen, *Christ on Earth: The Gospel Narratives as History* (Grand Rapids, MI: Baker, 1987), 220–41.
[73] Cf. Josephus, *J.W.* 2.119.

following decades and centuries. A third group, known as the Essenes, split off from the Pharisees at a later point (cf. 1 Macc 2:42).

The aristocratic and ruling Sadducees[74] were allegedly descendants of Zadok, one of David's high priests.[75] During the Maccabean period, they pursued a political policy of accommodation, or pragmatic acceptance of the political *status quo*, which was not popular with many Jews of lower rank. Publicly, they displayed formal devotion to and governance of the temple with its rituals.[76] Especially under Roman rule, Sadducees served as high priests (37 BC–AD 68). Given their political agenda, they resisted messianic agitation and political protest arising from within Judaism. On the other hand, the Sadducees did appeal to Rome in many cases to reverse unpopular policies of various Roman governors, especially prior to the outbreak of the Jewish War (AD 66–70). Theologically, the 'free will' Sadducees[77] considered the Torah to be authoritative, but not the Prophets or oral tradition; their interpretation of the Torah tended to be literal, and they denied various beliefs held by other members of Judaism (the resurrection of the dead, eternal life, the existence of angels or demons, and the like).

The Pharisees are of particular importance to our study, since Peter was taught in a synagogue school in Galilee shaped by the Pharisaic perspective on God's word, the world, and life. While the origin of their name is unclear, Pharisees[78] were definitely not of priestly descent. They, too, arose before or during the Hasmonean period.[79] Unlike the Sadducees, the Pharisees pursued, in an indirect way, a policy of political resistance.[80] Due to their focus on holistic life-conduct in the area of ethics, fasting, tithing, almsgiving, keeping the Sabbath, and ceremonial purity laws, a modest degree of resistance to Rome was typical as they sought to preserve their expression of religious life under the occupation.[81]

---

[74] A.A. Bell, *Exploring The New Testament World: An Illustrated Guide To The World Of Jesus And The First Christians* (Nashville, TN: Nelson, 1998), 32–33.

[75] Cf. 2 Sam 8:17, 15:27; 20:25; 1 Kgs 2:35. Their origin is historically unclear. They are documented during the Hasmonean period (from 167 BC onward). Cf. Eccl 51:12.

[76] Josephus, *J.W.* 2.166; *Ant.* 13.298.

[77] Josephus, *Ant.* 13.173.

[78] Cf. Bell, *Exploring*, 33–37.

[79] Cf. Josephus, *J.W.* 2.119, 2.162–63; *Ant.* 13.171-72.

[80] Cf. Josephus, *J.W.* 2.102.

[81] See, e.g., Mark 2:16 and Acts 23:9. See further, Josephus, *Life* 7-12; *Ant.* 13.284-89, 398-414; 18.11-25.

In the wake of E.P. Sanders's work,[82] much has been made of the somewhat hypothetical theological framework of 'covenantal nomism' in which Pharisaic Judaism before AD 70 supposedly functioned. Among other scholars, Deines and Hengel[83] demonstrate that Sanders' revised portrait of Pharisaic Judaism (particularly with regard to soteriology) does not hold up to historical scrutiny. Sanders' view is not representative of popular, 'on the streets' Palestinian Judaism, especially Pharisaic Judaism.[84] Nevertheless, van Bruggen[85] correctly adjusts the older (cf. the Protestant Reformation) portrait of Pharisees in the first century AD, which considered this movement to be merely 'legalistic, nationalistic, and hypocritical'.[86] Van Bruggen views Pharisees as a group of popular Jews, strenuously concerned with a law congruent 'lifestyle' in ethics and jurisprudence[87] and he wisely follows a close reading of Josephus[88] rather than, for example, the *Psalms of Solomon*.

Contrary, then, to such recent scholarly opinion, the Pharisees did subscribe to a strict *lifestyle*[89] of adherence to and zeal for the written *and* oral law (nomism) in all (especially ethical) areas of life, unlike the formalism of the Sadducees. They produced many lawyers, scribes, and teachers of the law as well as synagogue teachers, one of whom, as we shall discuss below, taught Peter from age seven to fourteen.

This explains the fact that while the Pharisees held little direct political power under Rome prior to AD 70, they nevertheless were more influential and popular among the general Jewish population as the 'party of the people'[90] than the distant and aristocratic Sadducees. Thus, their acceptance of the Torah and the Prophets, their theological beliefs of a balanced understanding of 'free will' and

---

[82] E.P. Sanders, *Paul and Palestinian Judaism* (London: SCM Press, 1981) and *Jesus and Judaism* (Minneapolis, MN: Fortress Press, 1985).

[83] M. Hengel and R. Deines, 'E.P. Sanders' "Common Judaism", Jesus and the Pharisees', *JTS,* 46 (1995): 17–41. R. Deines, *Die Pharisäer: Ihr Verständnis im Spiegel der christlichen und jüdischen Forschung seit Wellhausen und Graetz* (Tübingen: Mohr Siebeck, 1997).

[84] See, e.g., D.A. Carson, P.T. O'Brien, and M. Seifrid, *Justification and Variegated Nomism* (2 vols, Grand Rapids, MI: Baker Academic, 2004) and S.J. Gathercole, *Where is Boasting? Early Jewish Soteriology and Paul's Response in Romans 1–5* (Grand Rapids, MI: Eerdmans, 2002); cf. C.L. Quarles, 'The Soteriology of Rabbi Akiba and E.P. Sanders' *Paul and Palestinian Judaism*', *NTS* 42.2 (1996), 185–95.

[85] J. van Bruggen, *Jesus*, 18–19, 236–71.

[86] J. van Bruggen, *Jesus*, 18.

[87] J. van Bruggen, *Jesus*, 18 and esp. 250–53.

[88] See S. Mason, *Flavius Josephus on the Pharisees* (Leiden: Brill, 1991).

[89] Cf. van Bruggen, *Jesus*, 18.

[90] Josephus, *J.W.* 2.166 and *Ant.* 13.288, 18.15. Van Bruggen (*Jesus*, 18) speaks of their 'mildness and humanitarian' demeanor.

the 'sovereignty of God' (at times, lapsing into believing in fate), the resurrection, and eternal life, as well as their belief in demons and angels, shaped public opinion much more than those of the Sadducees. Together with the Sadducees and contrary to the Zealots and Essenes, the Pharisees pursued a policy of appeasement on the eve of the Jewish War. To a degree, they were more flexible than the Sadducees, which they demonstrated, for instance, in their ability to adapt to a new situation after the temple was destroyed in AD 70. The absence of sacrifice in the temple after AD 70 caused theological division among ensuing rabbinic schools, which grew out of Pharisaic Judaism. The Babylonian Talmud[91] reports rabbi Joshua as saying: 'Woe to us! For this house that lies in ruins, the place where atonement was made for the sins of Israel'. On the other hand, rabbi Johanan ben Zakkai, remarks: 'My son, be not grieved, for we have another means of atonement which is as effective, and that is, the practice of loving kindness, as it is stated, "For I desire loving kindness and not sacrifice"'.[92] While already popular during Peter's life, the Pharisees would shape rabbinic Judaism from AD 70 to about AD 500 and thus laid the foundation for elements of medieval and even modern Judaism.

Peter's Schooling in Jewish Centers of Learning

The Establishment of Synagogues

The blueprint for the establishment of synagogues in the wake of the Babylonian exile lies in the Mosaic command to 'teach the Torah' (Deut 6:7).[93] The earliest historically documented references to synagogues stem from the third century BC in Egypt.[94] By the time of Peter, however, the synagogue[95] was a well-established, highly significant institution,[96] both in the communities of the

---

[91] Cf. *'Abot R. Nat.* 20a.
[92] See T.R. Schreiner, 'Sacrifices and Offerings in the NT', *ISBE*, IV, 275. Schreiner correctly remarks that repentance, prayer, fasting, and the study of the Torah take the place of temple sacrifice in Judaism after AD 70 (with reference to *b. Ber.* 15a-b; 17a; *Sukkah* 49b; *B. Bat.* 9a; *Menaḥ.* 110a; *'Abot R. Nat.* 19a).
[93] Besides Deut 6:7 (family), see Deut 31:12 (theocratic nation) and Ps 74:8.
[94] See A.T. Kraabel, 'The Diaspora Synagogue', *ANRW* XIX/I, 500–10.
[95] See Josephus, *Ant.* 19.300 and *J.W.* 2.285; cf. Philo, *Opif.* 128. The synagogue is where Jesus and the apostles taught (cf. synagogue references in Acts 9:2, 20; 13:5, 16; 14:1; 17:1, 10, 17; 18:4-19, 26; 19:8; they were found in such places as Damascus, Cyprus, Iconium, Thessalonica, Athens, Corinth, Ephesus, Pisidian Antioch and Rome. It was the place of the earliest Christian converts. See also R. Riesner, *Jesus als Lehrer* (Tübingen: Mohr Siebeck, 1984), 123–37.
[96] See Acts 15:21. See Riesner, *Jesus*, 136–37.

Diaspora and in Palestine (cf. Acts 15:21).[97] After the destruction of the second temple in AD 70, the synagogue became the focal point of nascent rabbinic Judaism, absorbing some elements of the then abolished temple worship. Their establishment constituted a place of spiritual and sociological continuity for the Jewish community in the absence of the unifying temple and theocracy after AD 70. The synagogue as a house of prayer was an institution organized by lay leadership (requiring a *quorum* of ten Jewish men),[98] consisting of a ruler[99] and (an) attendant(s).[100] The services were open to all, including women, children, and Gentiles (proselytes and 'God-fearers').[101] The service consisted of non-sacrificial worship, and may have included the confession of faith, the reciting of the Shema and prayers. There was also a consecutive reading of the Pentateuch with a complementary reading from the Prophets (cf. Acts 15:21). Scripture was read in Hebrew, followed by an oral Aramaic translation (Targum) or Septuagint reading.[102] The reading from the Prophets was followed by an exposition.[103] The service ended with a benediction (cf. Num 6:24-26). Other than being a house of prayer and Scripture reading and of assimilating migrating Jews, the synagogue also served as an elementary school, a scribal center, a center for community discipline,[104] a hostel, and a place to collect revenue for temple tax in Jerusalem. In short, the synagogue in the first centuries BC and AD was the religious, political, and social haven and fortress, in which core elements of the Jewish faith were preserved against Hellenism.[105] Peter attended such a synagogue school, probably in Capernaum.[106]

Peter's Synagogue Schooling

Peter would have known about schools of prophets from the Old Testament. He would also have been aware of contemporary Pharisaic teachers of the law who instructed their pupils in institutions of higher learning (Torah schools) about

---

[97] Cf. Acts 6:9.

[98] Bruce, *History*, 119.

[99] Cf. the 'ruler of the synagogue', Jairus, in Mark 5:21-24, 35-43. It is possible that various heads of synagogues met in larger cities; cf. Roetzel, *World*, 69, who refers to Josephus, *J.W.* 7.47.

[100] Cf. Luke 4:20.

[101] Cf. Acts 10, 11, and Acts 18:7, regarding worshipers of God.

[102] See, e.g., Luke 4:14-30/Isa 61:1-2a; cf. *m. Meg.* 4:3-6.

[103] See, e.g., Luke 4:20; Acts 13:14-15, 16-41.

[104] Cf. Mark 13:9 and 2 Cor 11:24. See W.L. Lane, *The Gospel According to Mark* (Grand Rapids, MI: Eerdmans, 1978), 461 and n. 60. Lane refers to Deut 25:2-3, *m. Sanh.* 1.2, and *m. Mak.* 3.10; 3.12; 3.14.

[105] Cf. Roetzel, *World*, 67.

[106] Cf. Schnabel, *Mission*, I, 183–85; 188–89; 230–34; 750–52.

the law of Moses, oral tradition, and case law.[107] However, the former would have been merely a fact of history; the latter institution of learning would have been fairly removed from Peter's social sphere and life. His familiar setting would have been in elementary school education and being taught at home.

Various scholars[108] have presented illuminating details describing elementary educational patterns in first-century Palestine. One of the key findings is the focus on oral memorization in these synagogue schools. According to Dunn,[109] there are three models for understanding oral tradition in Palestine in the first century AD: Bultmann's 'informal, *un*controlled model';[110] Bailey's '*in*formal *controlled* tradition';[111] and Riesner's and Reicke's '*formal* controlled model'. Dunn states: '[W]e *must* endeavour to 'imagine the oral period' for the sake of

---

[107] Cf. M.J. Wilkins, *Following the Master: A Biblical Theology of Discipleship* (Grand Rapids, MI: Zondervan, 1992), 51–69 and C. Gambrell, 'The Portrayal of Discipleship in Mark 8:34' (MAET thesis, CTS, 2013), 12–32.

[108] See Matt 23:8. See Riesner, *Jesus*, 123–99; S. Byrskog, 'The Transmission of the Jesus Tradition', in T. Holmén and S.E. Porter (eds), *Handbook for the Study of the Historical Jesus* (4 vols; Leiden: Brill, 2011), II, 1465–94; A. Kirk, 'Memory Theory and Jesus Research', in Holmén and Porter (eds), *Handbook*, I, 809–42; R. Riesner, 'From the Messianic Teacher to the Gospel of Jesus Christ', in Holmén and Porter (eds), *Handbook*, I, 405–46; B. Gerhardsson, *The Origins of the Gospel Tradition* (Philadelphia, PA: Fortress, 1979); H. Wansborough (ed.), *Jesus and the Oral Gospel Tradition* (Edinburgh: T&T Clark, 2004); A.D. Baum, *Der mündliche Faktor und seine Bedeutung für die Synoptische Frage* (Tübingen: Francke, 2008); R.J. Bauckham, *Jesus and the Eyewitnesses: The Gospels as Eyewitness Testimony* (Grand Rapids, MI: Eerdmans, 2006); S. Byrskog, *Story as History–History as Story: The Gospel Tradition in the Context of Ancient Oral History* (Tübingen: Mohr Siebeck, 2000). See one of the many critiques of stereotype, oral tradition: R.K. McIver, 'Eyewitnesses as Guarantors of the Accuracy of the Gospel Traditions in the Light of Psychological Research', *JBL* 131.3 (2012), 529–46 (i.e., 20%, or less might be inaccurate in details of orally transmitted information).

[109] J.D.G. Dunn, 'Altering the Default Setting: Re-envisaging the Early Transmission of the Jesus Tradition', *NTS* 49 (2003), 139–75. The following quotations (with italics) stem from Dunn. See also J.D.G. Dunn, *Jesus Remembered: Christianity in the Making* (Grand Rapids, MI: Eerdmans, 2003); J. Schröter, 'Der erinnerte Jesus als Begründer des Christentums', *ZNW* 20 (2007), 46–61, and R. Stewart and G. Habermas, *Memories of Jesus: A Critical Appraisal of James D.G. Dunn's Jesus Remembered* (Nashville, TN: B&H Academic, 2010).

[110] See also G. Theissen and A. Merz, *Der historische Jesus. Ein Lehrbuch* (Göttingen: Vandenhoeck & Ruprecht, 2008), 200–206.

[111] K.E. Bailey, 'Informal Controlled Oral Tradition and the Synoptic Gospels', *AJT* 5 (1991), 34–54, as well as 'Middle Eastern Oral Tradition and the Synoptic Gospels', *ExpTim* 106 (1994/95), 363–67. Bailey displays proximity to the unsubstantiated, classical form-critical assumption of an *anonymous*, collective group that passed on the Christian tradition.

historical authenticity, to re-envisage how tradition was transmitted in an orally structured society; also that we *can* do so, or at least are more able to do so than has generally been realized. Here we are in the fortunate position of being able to call upon a wide range of research into oral tradition'.[112]

In what follows, we will argue in favor of the *formal controlled* model.

Riesner, especially, spearheaded the refinement of early investigations into oral tradition patterns conducted by Gerhardsson[113] and others in the early 1960s. Unlike Gerhardsson,[114] who initially studied oral transmission in the (often later documented) setting of rabbinic schools, Riesner analyzed educational principles which were more clearly documented for *first*-century Palestine. Furthermore, and also unlike Gerhardsson, Riesner looked especially at the milieu of elementary school education in the widespread Jewish synagogues, as both Jesus and his disciples clearly functioned *outside* the formal Torah schools.[115] To accomplish this, Riesner looked particularly at such varying sources as the Old Testament; selections from the Old Testament Apocrypha and Pseudepigrapha (including *1 Enoch*, esp. 72–83; *Jubilees*, e.g., 7:38-39; Ben Sira; 1 Maccabees, e.g., 1:13-14; 2 Maccabees, e.g., 4:9-12; *4 Maccabees*, e.g., 18:10-19); Josephus; Philo; Qumran (including 11QPs^a; 1QSa, e.g., 1, 4-5); and carefully selected rabbinic tradition (esp. that which contains incidental information or displays demonstrable echoes of older traditions), as well as Greco-Roman sources from Homer's *Iliad* to Quintilian. What follows is a brief overview of some of the elements which Riesner[116] and others have presented to illuminate the elementary educational pattern in first-century Palestine,[117] which focused on oral transmission and retention of predominantly written tradition (especially the Hebrew Bible).

These scholars argue further that oral and aural memorization also furnished the most convincing background for Jesus as a systematic teacher and thus for schematic and stereotyped oral transmission of the gospel witness (the *formal*

---

[112] Dunn, 'Setting', 139–75, 149.

[113] B. Gerhardsson, *Memory and Manuscript: Oral Tradition and Written Transmission in Rabbinic Judaism and Early Christianity* (Reprint. Grand Rapids, MI: Eerdmans, 1998 [1961]). See further refinements and modifications of Gerhardsson in Bauckham, *Eyewitnesses*, 240–89.

[114] See more recently again: P.W. Barnett, *Jesus and the Logic of History* (Grand Rapids, MI: Eerdmans, 1997), 138.

[115] Cf. Riesner, *Jesus*, 102–18, 137–51.

[116] Cf. Riesner, *Jesus*, 151–206.

[117] For this and the following, see Riesner, *Jesus*, 123–37; 189–98.

The Synagogue Schoolhouse

By the time Peter went to school (*bet sopher*) in Galilee, Pharisees (and their predecessors)[118] had long established schools adjacent to synagogues for the purpose of teaching the Hebrew Bible to young boys.[119] In Tiberias alone, some thirteen schools existed. The fort of Masada featured an archaeologically identified school, which was maintained and operated even during the Roman siege (AD 70–73).[120] The general pattern was to establish an elementary school as well as, at times, an advanced school (*bet Talmud*) for students of the Torah and oral traditions adjacent to each of the widely distributed synagogues.[121]

In New Testament times, two at times opposing factions of Pharisees existed,[122] consisting of the school of Hillel and the school of Shammai; while they shared much in common, some tendencies can be noted:

- the School of Hillel explored more the meaning and *intention* of the Torah; members belonged to the lower class; they were somewhat more 'lenient' regarding the application of the law and were a bit more conciliatory toward Gentiles.
- the School of Shammai followed a more literal interpretation of the Torah; members belonged to a higher class and there was more intolerance and stronger opposition to foreign rulers.[123]

For various reasons (e.g., his lower-class status) it is likely that Peter was trained in the Capernaum synagogue school by adherents of the school of Hillel.

The Teacher

Besides teaching, the elementary school teacher (especially in small cities) often

---

[118] See Riesner, *Jesus*, 189, 198.
[119] See Riesner, *Jesus*, 123–37 (and 136–37, regarding the wide geographic distribution of synagogues at the time of Jesus).
[120] Riesner, *Jesus*, 198–99, referring to *b. Ḥag.* 15b.
[121] Riesner, *Jesus*, 183.
[122] Bell, *Exploring*, 33–37.
[123] This wing supplies the majority opinion of the Pharisaic faction in the Sanhedrin. Both Pharisaic factions (as a whole) represent, however, the minority in the Sanhedrin.

served as the synagogue attendant as well as a scribe.[124] Usually these elementary teachers (*sopher*) received some recompense for their work, while the advanced teachers of the Torah (higher education) had begun the habit of refraining from pay several decades prior to Christ. In the eyes of advanced Torah teachers, elementary school teachers were thus inferior. This may have contributed to the trend in Jewish society to view elementary school educators as part of the lower spectrum of society.

The Student

At the time of Peter, most boys in Jewish Palestine began their formal education at age seven and ended it approximately at age fourteen.[125] School was held every day from sun-up to sun-down, except on the Sabbath.[126] Each Sabbath afternoon, however, fathers would examine their respective sons on material memorized during the previous week.

Contents to be Learned

Learning many sections of the Hebrew Bible by heart (especially the Torah) lay at the center of elementary school education.[127] Of great importance was the memorization of liturgically important sections of Scripture (such as the Shema YHWH and the *Hallel*),[128] as this became useful for both their life as Jews and as participants in synagogue services. Furthermore, learning rudimentary skills of reading and writing (by copying and dictation)[129] was likewise accomplished by

---

[124] Riesner, *Jesus*, 184–85.

[125] Cf., e.g., Josephus, *Life* 2.7–9, who apparently completed elementary education at age fourteen. Cf. *Gen. Rab.* 63:14 and *m. 'Abot* 5:21. See Riesner, *Jesus*, 187.

[126] Riesner, *Jesus*, 187.

[127] Riesner, *Jesus*, 189. Note that at least since Ben Sira 'wisdom' and 'law' represented virtually one concept; see E.J. Schnabel, *Law and Wisdom from Ben Sira to Paul: A Tradition Historical Enquiry into the Relation of Law, Wisdom, and Ethics* (Tübingen: Mohr Siebeck, 1985). Thus learning the Torah by heart was the key to wisdom. Cf. Riesner, *Jesus*, 188.

[128] Riesner, *Jesus*, 112.

[129] There is some debate about the degree and extent of literacy at the time of Jesus. While the society functioned predominantly on an aural level, reading (and some writing) literacy is still a factor to reckon with. Some scholars, such as Dunn, argue that literacy was less than 10 percent in Palestine at the time of Jesus (Dunn, 'Setting', 139–75, with reference to M. Bar-Ilan, 'Illiteracy in the Land of Israel in the First Centuries CE', in S. Fishbane and S. Schoenfeld, *Essays in the Social Scientific Study of Judaism and Jewish Society* (Hoboken, NJ: Ktav, 1992), 46–61; C. Hezser, *Jewish Literacy in Roman Palestine* (Tübingen: Mohr Siebeck, 2001). Riesner (*Jesus*, 110–18, 190–93) emphasizes, however, that reading and writing might have been learned already at home. See also A. Millard, *Reading and Writing*

the use of Scriptures.[130] Learning how to read often began with Leviticus, since it contained difficult texts and thus could not be 'read from memory'.[131] At times, Greek was taught in these schools as well. Tiberias and Sepphoris (some three miles north of Nazareth), for instance, had Greek-speaking members in their respective synagogues.

Methods of Instruction

As is the fact in many ancient cultures surrounding Judea and Galilee, learning by heart[132] constituted the focus of education.[133] Therefore, rote memorization was much more emphasized than creative, independent combination of facts or independent thinking and understanding. Proverbs 1–9, for instance, had to be memorized mechanically prior to understanding its hortatory and paraenetic message. The key to success was repetition.[134] Tradition holds that Hillel once remarked: 'He who repeats his passage one hundred times is not to be compared with him who repeats his passage a hundred and one times'.[135]

Many mnemonic aids, partially already present in the Hebrew text, were employed to reach the stated goal. Among them were preference of alliteration (cf. Prov 18:20-22), acrostic poetry (cf. Ps 119; Prov 31:30-31), paronomasia (wordplay), and cantillation (murmur).[136] Additional mnemonic devices, such as question and answer, or starting to recite a verse and letting the student finish, were common. All of this was carried out with strict discipline.[137] Riesner concludes that such relatively limited education led to a basic skill in reading and writing and the ability to retain large amounts of memorized material.[138] Peter was not only exposed to such an education, but it is likely that he grew up in a bi- (or tri-) lingual setting.

---

in the Time of Jesus (Sheffield: Sheffield Academic, 2000), 223–29; similarly, Schnabel, *Mission*, I, 631–32, and nn. 314–17.

[130] See Millard, *Reading*, 223–29.
[131] Riesner, *Jesus*, 191.
[132] Riesner, *Jesus*, 195–98.
[133] Riesner, *Jesus*, 193–95. Cf. Bauckham, *Eyewitnesses*, 319–57.
[134] Cf. Josephus, *Ag. Ap.* 2.178.
[135] Riesner, *Jesus*, 194, who refers to *b. Ḥag.* 9b.
[136] Riesner, *Jesus*, 195–96.
[137] See G. Baltes, *Hebräisches Evangelium und synoptische Überlieferung: Untersuchungen zum hebräischen Hintergrund der Evangelien* (Tübingen: Mohr Siebeck, 2011), 85–145. Cf. Riesner, *Jesus*, 197–98.
[138] Riesner, *Jesus*, 199.

Peter as a Bi- (or Tri-) Lingual Galilean[139]

Hebrew, Aramaic, Greek, and, to a degree, Latin, were read and/or spoken in Palestine at the time of Peter.[140]

Hebrew

The chief influence of Hebrew was the predominantly Hebrew Bible and its use both in synagogues and schools. While their main language was probably Aramaic, Jesus and Peter did speak Hebrew (cf. Luke 4:16-22).[141]

Aramaic

A Syrian Semitic dialect,[142] Aramaic was widely used in Galilee at the time of Peter. In this region it was also the spoken language of the synagogue,[143] where a synagogue service included an Aramaic translation of the Hebrew Scripture reading as well as an Aramaic homily. It remains open whether the New Testament[144] uses ἑβραϊστί (John 5:2; 19:13, 17) to refer to Aramaic or Hebrew.[145] Zahn adduces evidence to make it likely that Paul spoke Aramaic in one of his defenses (Acts 21:40; 22:2 states: ἑβραΐς διάλεκτος).[146] Aramaic did persist as a significant language long before and many centuries after the time of the New Testament.[147]

---

[139] Cf. J. Fitzmyer, 'The Languages of Palestine in the First Century AD', *CBQ* 32 (1970), 501–31.

[140] Latin came into wider usage (but mostly by non-Jews) on account of the political rise of Rome. Inscriptions on official buildings, signposts on roads, aqueducts, and tombstones document the presence of Latin in public, official life.

[141] See Baltes, *Evangelium*, 85–110.

[142] This includes various similar Semitic dialects, among them the Samaritan dialect, cf. T. Zahn, *Introduction to the New Testament* (Grand Rapids, MI: Kregel, 1953), I, 3–6; III, 326 n. 2.

[143] See, however, Baltes, *Evangelium*, 85–110, who argues that besides Aramaic, both Hebrew and Greek belong to the common languages of Palestine in the first century AD.

[144] See Aramaisms (and some Hebraisms) in the Gospels; e.g., Matt 5:22; 6:24; 11:9; 12:5; 12:25; 26:2; Mark 3:17; 5:41; 7:11,34; 14:36; 15:34 [cf. Matt 27:46]; Luke 11:51; John 1:42.

[145] Josephus, who calls עֲצַרְתָּא (=Pentecost) ἑβραῖος (*Ant.* 3.252), might refer to the Hebrew language; Baltes, *Evangelium*, 144–45.

[146] Zahn, *Introduction*, I, 11–14.

[147] Zahn, *Introduction*, I, 3–8.

Greek

The influence of the Greek language in Palestine began with eastward military campaigns by Alexander the Great (late fourth century BC). Parallel to this, the single most important witness to the influence of the Greek language upon Diaspora Judaism is the translation of the Hebrew Old Testament into Greek (the LXX from about 250 BC to about 50 BC). Greek was widely used in Palestine not only by visiting or returning Greek-speaking Diaspora Jews, but probably also by Palestinian Jews (including Galileans). According to Zahn, the most significant force behind the further spread of the Greek language was the Roman conquest of Palestine (from 63 BC onward).[148] Zahn portrays Palestine as an Aramaic (and Hebrew[149]) speaking region, which is *partially* penetrated by a Greek-speaking population.[150] The many Hellenistic cities, so-called πόλεις ἑλληνίδας (see Josephus, *J.W.* 2.97), testify to this. Among these cities were, for example, Gaza, Pella, Antipatris (Acts 23:31), Caesarea, Abila, and Gerasa.[151] Riesner argues that in such Galilean cities as Tiberias and Sepphoris the synagogue language was indeed Greek.[152] These and other predominantly Greek-speaking cities and towns in and around Palestine (replete with Hellenistic theaters, amphitheaters, gymnasia, etc.) had a majority of Hellenistic and a minority of Jewish inhabitants. From a Jewish perspective, however, Greeks remained βάρβαροι (=barbarians; cf. Josephus, *J.W.*, Prooemium 1).

Nevertheless, already in 170 BC, Greek names for Jews arose (see, e.g., Jason). The Maccabean Revolt was a temporarily successful resistance to Hellenistic power and thought, but *not* to the Greek language and some cultural infiltration.[153] Religious freedom became the dominant goal of the Jews, not complete freedom from Hellenistic influences, especially the Greek language. Thus we can say that the hellenization of Palestine was one issue, the spread of the Greek language in its territory, quite another.

Zahn observes that the rule of Judea and Samaria by Roman *procurators* stationed in Caesarea (AD 6–70, with brief interruptions) facilitated further infiltration of Greek in the Aramaic domain, since Greek was the official language when dealing with subjects.[154] Zahn has little doubt that tax collectors

---

[148] Zahn, *Introduction*, I, 34.
[149] Baltes, *Evangelium*, 85–110.
[150] Zahn, *Introduction*, I, 34–40. Cf. Hengel, *Judaism*, 58–64.
[151] See Mark 5:20, 7:31, and Matt 4:25.
[152] See also, Schnabel, *Mission* I, 201–206.
[153] Hengel, *Judaism*, 247–54.
[154] Zahn, *Introduction*, I, 36–43.

both in Roman-controlled territory (Judea and Samaria)[155] as well as in the Galilean territory controlled by Herod Antipas[156] had to speak Greek, regardless of whether they were Jews or not. Hasmonean and Herodian rulers in Palestine were more or less hellenized, and thus used the Greek language. Jerusalem, in particular, was both the center of Palestinian Judaism and of Hellenistic Judaism[157] (see the many Diaspora Jews, proselytes, and God-fearers). Diaspora Jews who had resettled in (and around) Jerusalem and who met in their own synagogues,[158] as well as regular pilgrimages of Diaspora Jews to Jerusalem and its temple (for tithes and sacrifices) brought the Greek language to the gates of the temple. Palestinian Jews, in turn, had to converse with those who spoke Greek. The Greek language (and with it, the LXX) thus made its way into the heart of Judaism long before the time of Christ.[159] Hengel thus considers the possibility that Peter, at least by the time of early Christianity, spoke Greek colored by his Semitic background.[160]

The persecution of the Christian 'sect' by Saul of Tarsus serves, on the other hand, as a good example of how strongly Jewish monotheism, based on the Old Testament and revived during the Hasmonean period, was upheld despite the long-standing exposure to the Greek language. Another piece of evidence for this fact is the returning Diaspora Jews who strengthened the most ardent branch of Judaism in Jerusalem. In this general milieu it is not surprising to find Greek documents with Aramaic and Hebrew coloring. While Jesus's teaching of a 'complex monotheism' clearly arose from the Old Testament in the context of Palestinian Judaism and not from the Hellenistic setting of culture and belief, we nevertheless have only Greek documents produced by

---

[155] Zahn, *Introduction*, I, 38–39, refers to Josephus, *J.W.* 2.284 and Luke 19:2-9.

[156] Zahn, *Introduction*, I, 39, refers to Matt 9:9 and Mark 2:14.

[157] Zahn, *Introduction*, I, 39–43, refers to Acts 6:1; 9:27.

[158] Zahn, *Introduction*, I, 43–44; cf. Acts 6:9.

[159] See, e.g., the painful history of the Maccabean Revolt and the many uprisings reported both in Acts 5:35-37 and Josephus, *Ant.* 18.23.

[160] See Acts 6:9 and the 'Theodotus Inscription', *CIJ* 2 1404. Cf. M. Hengel, 'The Origins of the Christian Mission', in M. Hengel, *Between Jesus and Paul: Studies in the Earliest History of Christianity* (Eugene, OR: Wipf & Stock, 2003), 56–57; M. Hengel, 'Christology and New Testament Chronology', in Hengel, *Jesus and Paul*, 33–47, arguing that some disciples were probably bi-lingual (e.g., Andrew, Philip, Barnabas [page 37], John Mark [page 40], as well as Silas/Silvanus, Peter, and Paul [page 40]). Hengel, 'Origins', 56, assumes that, e.g., Barnabas and John Mark, who originally spoke Hebrew/Aramaic in Jerusalem, joined Greek speaking missionaries. In rural areas of Galilee there was probably less Hellenistic influence since we are dealing with a degree of *xenophobia* (Hengel, 'Origins', 158–59 n. 15; cf. 174 n. 48). The exact description of the constellation of Galilean communities in terms of ethnicity and language is not easy; cf. Cullmann, *Peter*, 24; Str-B, II, 661–63.

followers of Christ, containing some transliterated and translated Aramaic words (see esp. in Mark's and John's Gospels).[161]

In conclusion, we can safely state that Peter spoke Aramaic, some Hebrew, and basic Greek even before he became a disciple of Jesus. Due to his early childhood in Bethsaida[162] and his extended geographical and socio-ethnic movements following his conversion[163] as a disciple of Jesus (esp. from ca. AD 42–44 onward), Greek would increasingly become a strong second language to him. He proclaimed the gospel in various communities in the Jewish Diaspora (see Acts 12:3, 17; Gal 2:9, 11-16; 1 Cor 9:5) before settling in Rome.

Peter's Marital and Economic Status

Mark 1:30 informs us that Peter was married (cf. 1 Cor 9:5). In terms of income, Peter can be described as a 'middle-class' fisherman,[164] since, according to Luke 5:3, Peter was the owner of at least one boat. He probably employed day-laborers (Mark 1:20). Helyer notes, however, that such ownership was still heavily dependent upon a 'state regulated, elite-profiting enterprise' associated with aristocratic families. Under Herod Antipas, taxes were levied on fishing licenses, on a catch of fish, and included harbor usage fees.[165] Finally, Peter's family owned a house (Mark 1:29), perhaps within a complex which might also have been occupied by the Zebedee family.[166] This house served as the home base of Jesus during his Galilean ministry (Mark 1:21, 29, 36; 2:1).

Peter as a Disciple of Jesus

According to John 1:40, Andrew had been attentive to John the Baptist's

---

[161] Zahn, *Introduction*, I, 41–42.

[162] Bockmuehl, *Simon*, 168; cf. Dalman, *Sites*, 161–63.

[163] See Bockmuehl, *Simon*, 155–63, who takes Luke 22:31-34 as a prediction of Peter's *conversion*, which is realized in Peter's experience of the death and resurrection of Jesus and which gives him renewed birth (ἀναγεννάω; 1 Pet 1:3, 23). Bockmuehl, *Simon*, 163, also notes that '[t]he rooster comes to symbolize the whole movement, marking the beginning of the end of darkness and heralding instead the beginning of dawn'.

[164] See Helyer, *Life*, 24–25, concerning the socio-economic importance of the fishing industry in Galilee, including fish-processing facilities (esp. by means of salting fish) near Capernaum and Bethsaida; he also mentions the fish trade between Galilee and Jerusalem (cf. the postexilic Fish Gate in Jerusalem, Neh 3:3).

[165] Helyer, *Life*, 25–26, with reference to K.C. Hanson, 'The Galilean Fishing Economy and the Jesus Tradition', *BTB* 27 (1997), 99–111. Helyer, *Life*, 26–27, conjectures that Matthew (Matt 9:9) would have collected these fees, besides tolls and duties.

[166] Helyer, *Life*, 28–29.

teaching and first spoke to Peter about having met Jesus through John the Baptist (John 1:41). Sometime after the first meeting between Jesus and Peter (John 1:42), Jesus calls Peter (Mark 1:16; cf. Matt 4:18-20). According to Luke 5:4-11, this call occurs in the context of Jesus's peculiar instruction to Peter to lower his nets (in the presence of James and John), which leads to an unusual catch of fish (compare this event with John 21:3-8 as a thematic and geographical *inclusio*).[167] We also note that even at this early stage, Peter's call echoes that of the Old Testament pattern of 'divine commission' (compare Luke 5:8 with Exod 3:5-6; cf. Isa 6:5; Ezek 1:28).[168] We shall have occasion to return to this important topic later.

Jesus as Teacher

Similar to synagogue education during his childhood, Peter underwent in his twenties a second three-year period of systematic memorization and training, this time under Jesus, in order to retain core elements of his teaching and actions.[169] Dissimilar to synagogue education, Jesus also gave Peter a grid for understanding the significance of the Messiah's identity and mission (see, e.g., Mark 10:45)[170] and confronted Peter with issues of the heart which are foundational to true learning, wisdom, and godly life (see below).[171]

Jesus as an Intentional Educator

The content of Jesus's 'curriculum' focused on a true, macro-biblical understanding of both God's rule and the identity and function of God's Messiah. This occurred in contradistinction to the narrowed parameters set by the familiar narration of the Maccabean uprising and political, Davidic-messianic expectations put forth by Pharisaic Judaism. Peter, who had already been trained biblically in his home and especially in his synagogue school during his childhood, initially learned from Jesus in a way similar to that of his

---

[167] It is unnecessary to entertain the question (as does Bockmuehl, *Simon*, 24) whether the Lukan call-narrative derives from John 21:3-8: the mosaic of the different Gospel accounts of Peter's call dovetail sufficiently.

[168] See M. Grant, *Saint Peter: A Biography* (New York, NY: Scribner, 1995), 106–107 and Helyer, *Life*, 33.

[169] See Byrskog, 'Transmission', II, 1465–94; Kirk, 'Theory', II, 809–42; Riesner, 'Messianic Teacher', I, 405–46. Cf. S. Hübenthal, *Das Markusevangelium als kollektives Gedächtnis* (Göttingen: Vandenhoeck & Ruprecht), 2014.

[170] H.F. Bayer and R. Yarbrough, 'O. Cullmanns progressiv-heilsgeschichtliche Konzeption', in *Glaube und Geschichte: Heilsgeschichte als Thema der Theologie* (ed., H. Stadelmann; Wuppertal: Brockhaus), 1998, 319–47.

[171] Cf. H.F. Bayer, *A Theology of Mark: The Dynamic between Christology and Authentic Discipleship* (Phillipsburg, NJ: P&R, 2012), 61–88.

synagogue schooling, namely, by memorization. In each case, memorization preceded understanding. While Jesus's teaching style connected pedagogically with that of the synagogue teachers, it also far exceeded it.

Similarities and Dissimilarities between Jesus's Pedagogy and That of Synagogue Schools

There are striking methodological parallels between elementary school education in the first century AD and the pedagogical approach of Jesus. The correlation suggests that Jesus as teacher did indeed utilize these existing and familiar methods of instruction as a primary foundation for training his disciples.[172] Riesner points especially to the following similarities:

1. Jesus employs similar methods of instruction and memorization in order to assure faithful transmission, especially *via* Peter and the other initial disciples. We point to Jesus's interpretation of Scripture, his use of summaries, and the rich use of *mašal* (various figures of speech). Jesus's particular teaching style includes brevity, imagery, and the use of vivid language; he uses parallelism, rhythm, rhyme, chiasm, pairs, alliteration, assonance, and aphorisms; he connects events and locations with instruction; he involves himself in memorable dialogues and controversial discussions. Examples of Peter's (and the apostolic group's) recollections, reflecting such teaching methods, are: Mark 8:18; 11:21; 14:72; cf. Matthew 26:75; Luke 22:19, 61; 24:6, 8; John *2:22*; *12:16*; *14:26* (the Holy Spirit will bring to remembrance); 15:20; *16:4*; Acts *11:16* (Peter remembers the word of the Lord Jesus); Acts 20:35; 1 Corinthians 11:24-25 (see 2 Pet 3:2 and Rev 3:3; cf. Matt 27:63 and John 2:17). In addition, Mary, the mother of Jesus, should be viewed as a significant transmitter of tradition. According to Luke 2:19 (see also Luke 2:51; cf. Luke 1:37, 66), she carefully preserves (συνετήρει; cf. Dan 7:28) what she has heard and experienced, pondering (συμβάλλουσα) it in her heart.[173]
2. The disciples, above all Peter, provide the personal tradition- and transmission-continuity[174] between Jesus's life and teaching and the beginnings of the messianic church. We note the development from Peter as

---

[172] See Riesner, *Jesus,* 357–407; cf. Matt 11:28-30; Mark 1:16-20.

[173] See R. Riesner, 'Die Rückkehr der Augenzeugen: Eine neue Entwicklung in der Evangelienforschung', *TBei* 38 (2007), 337–52, here 350, who also refers to James, the half brother of Jesus as a significant transmitter of tradition (Acts 12:17; 15:13-21; 21:18-26; see Josephus, *Ant.* 20.200–203).

[174] Riesner, *Jesus,* 19–20; 408–98; 499–502.

disciple (μαθητής) to apostle (ἀπόστολος).[175] The threefold denial and subsequent threefold confession of Jesus by Peter accentuates this continuity. All this (and more) focuses on facilitating *memorization, continuity, and faithfulness to learned tradition*.[176]

There are, however, also dissimilarities between Jesus's pedagogy and that of synagogue schools.[177] These dissimilarities *reinforce* the stereotyped memorization and transmission and *increase* learning and, especially, personal transformation:

1. The life-community Jesus develops with his disciples *surpasses* that of the (sometimes close) pupil-teacher relationships. Jesus pursues learning in the context of real-life settings and dialogues, life-on-life teaching, and mentoring.
2. Jesus *calls* his pupils *prophetically*;[178] they do not *come* to Jesus (as was especially the case in rabbinic schools). This factor emphasizes the *initiative* of Jesus as teacher from the start.[179]
3. Parallel to this, the unusual authority of Jesus (including his 'I am' and 'Amen' sayings) is without analogy in Judaism and lends further emphasis to his teaching,[180] embedding truths in the disciples' minds and hearts long before they truly understand.
4. The fact that Jesus sent out his disciples in pairs to teach and practice his instruction deepens learning and relationships, while the message is being spread (cf. Matt 28:19-20).[181]
5. A further factor in stereotyped memorization is the fact that the disciples *report* to Jesus what they had taught, accomplished, and failed in (see, e.g., Mark 6:30).
6. Jesus teaches as an *itinerant* teacher and prophet, thus exposing the disciples to frequent *repetition*, combined with innumerable slight variations.[182] John Wenham notes: 'It is inevitable that an itinerant preacher

---

[175] See H.N. Ridderbos, *Redemptive History and the New Testament Canon of Scripture* (Phillipsburg, NJ: P&R, 1988), concerning the kerygmatic, apostolic, and witnessing ministry of the disciples of Christ, which are all elements pointing back to the Christ of history.
[176] Riesner, *Jesus,* 422–53.
[177] For the following, see Riesner, *Jesus,* 297–496.
[178] Cf. Barnett, *Logic,* 140.
[179] Dunn, 'Setting', 139–75, 155.
[180] Cf. Barnett, *Logic,* 140, and n. 35.
[181] Riesner, *Jesus,* 453–75.
[182] A.D. Baum, *Lukas als Historiker der letzten Jesusreise* (Wuppertal: Brockhaus, 1993), 315–17.

must repeat himself again and again, sometimes in identical words, sometimes with slight variations, sometimes with new applications; sometimes an old idea will appear in an entirely new dress'.[183] Bengel states: 'Jesus ran an itinerant school. In this sort of school all occasions served as apt instructions for the disciples; much more so, than if they had sat comfortably on certain days at certain hours in a lecture hall, free from provocative challenges and temptations'.[184] This applies especially to sayings and dialogues, which are often securely embedded in their respective contexts,[185] as well as to mašal-sayings of Jesus. Excluded from this are those circumstances, which most likely could only occur once (see especially events during the passion week).

Part of the literary symmetry and variation of the canonical Gospels—e.g., Peter's testimony recounted in the Gospel of Mark—may thus be traceable to verbatim or near-verbatim *repetition* and *variation by Jesus himself*. The consequence of this consideration is that occurrences which are found in different contexts in Mark, Luke, Matthew (and John) must not *necessarily* mean that one account follows a historical sequence while the other follows a thematic approach; both may be thematic, both may be chronological.[186]

7. Jesus provides a *framework for interpretation* (see, e.g., Mark 10:45) which is important in any process of testifying and especially in the process of writing historical accounts.[187] This speaks against the unwarranted assumption that the canonical Gospels are to be viewed as faith-projections upon Jesus.

8. A further, very significant factor in maturing as a dependable witness is the fact that Jesus shapes the hearts and attitudes of his disciples in such a way that their mental processes find a profound echo in life and experience (see part 2 below). Such shaping of heart and character leads, among other factors, to embracing a God-intended point of view, as opposed to prejudice and slanted opinions. Jesus thus complements the memorization and learning process by means of exposing and shaping of the disciples' hearts. At a later point this will continue through the agency of the Holy Spirit (John 14:15-31; 16:4-15), who also assists the disciples in being able to

---

[183] J.W. Wenham, 'Synoptic Independence and the Origin of Luke's Travel Narrative', *NTS* 27 (1981), 507–15 [509] in Baum, *Lukas*, 315–16 n. 21.

[184] J.A. Bengel, *Gnomon Novi Testamenti: Auslegung des Neuen Testamentes in fortlaufenden Anmerkungen* (Leipzig: Heinsius, 1932), I, 61; trans. HFB.

[185] Baum, *Lukas*, 316.

[186] See Baum, *Lukas*, 316, who refers, e.g., to Luke 12:1 (cf. Matt 16:6) and Luke 12:16 (contrast with Mark 9:11-12 parr; cf. also John 2:18, 4:48; 1 Cor 1:22a).

[187] Cf. Bauckham, *Eyewitnesses*, 264–357.

recall what Jesus had previously taught them.
9. The possibility exists that some *resident disciples* of Jesus were *writing down* what they heard and saw of Jesus even prior to his passion and resurrection.[188]
10. The events of the death and resurrection of Jesus serve themselves as a profound learning and appropriation *catalyst* since the central message of Jesus has now become a God-vindicated reality before their very eyes (compare Mark 8:31 with Luke 24:25-27).

These reasons undergird the model of a '*formal controlled model*' presented above. As stated there, Dunn and others believe that the '*informal* controlled tradition' better reflects the situation of Jesus and his disciples, speaking of a relatively flexible[189] 'oral tradition' in and through community recitations (as a form of sustaining the tradition). Dunn states this in contrast to the supporters of the 'formal controlled model', who speak of, among other factors, the transmission of oral history through eyewitnesses.[190] Dunn fails to distinguish the disciples' retelling of events as 'originals' from frequent act and speech repetitions by Jesus *himself*, each time as originals, which in turn are narrated by witnesses. Dunn defines 'variation' and 'flexibility' predominantly in terms of the oral transmission ('performance') process,[191] rather than in terms of variant *selections* from the considerable body of material of Jesus's teaching which contains itself Jesus's own repetitions and variations.[192] There are thus multiple factors supporting the 'formal controlled model, suggesting structured stability in oral gospel transmission.

Peter's Character Formation as a Follower of Jesus
Under Jesus's tutelage, Peter was not only able to recall systematically memorized material, but he also experienced a radical, personal transformation from a deficient God- and self-perception (see John 8:19, 23-24) to a God- and self-perception revealed and shaped by Jesus.[193] Some of these deficiencies can be traced to early teaching Peter received concerning the history of the

---

[188] Riesner, *Jesus,* 487–98.

[189] Dunn, 'Setting', 139–75, 164.

[190] Dunn, 'Setting', 139–75, 151 n. 47. See aspects of agreement and critique of Dunn's and Bailey's approach in T.C. Mournet, *Oral Tradition and Literary Dependency: Variability and Stability in the Synoptic Tradition and Q* (Tübingen: Mohr Siebeck, 2005), 291–93.

[191] Dunn, 'Setting', 139–75, 164.

[192] See P. Chang, 'Repetition and Variation in John' (Ph.D. diss., Strassburg: Univ. of Strassburg, 1975).

[193] See Bayer, *Theology,* 61–88.

suffering of the Jewish people, the story of the Maccabean uprising, Pharisaic teaching in synagogues, etc. Other deficiencies go deeper and reach into the fabric of human nature since the fall of Adam and Eve (Gen 3:1-19; Rom 5:1-21).

As we proceed, we will see Peter's former personality of a 'sympathetically fallible man of resolve, eager to demonstrate commitment but slow to grasp the spiritual point at issue',[194] heal and flourish toward a surrendered follower of Christ, making Christ the object of his primary loyalty rather than himself (see the development from Mark 8:34 to 1 Pet 5:6-8). Peter is given a new identity and, through it, he appropriates various fundamental character traits, such as trust, obedience, surrender, forgiveness, watching over his heart, perseverance in trials, humility, and bold witness (see part 3 below). Peter also arises as one of the members of Jesus's inner circle and as a spokesperson of the Twelve (see below). Both the footwashing (John 13:2-11) and his restoration following his denial of Christ (John 21:15-19; cf. Luke 22:31-32) are crucial in the deeper formation of Peter. In fact, Jesus's call of 'follow me' forms a biographical *inclusio* in the life of Peter (compare Mark 1:17 with John 21:19). Prior to his conversion and transformation, Peter appears to have had rather opposing characteristics such as being resolute (Mark 10:28; cf. Matt 18:21-22), impulsive, courageous (cf. Matt 14:28-31), quick to speak and act,[195] while at other times fearing for his life, thus marked by both 'reluctance and zeal'.[196]

The fact that Jesus gives such a man the nickname 'Cephas' (=Peter, meaning 'rock'; John 1:42) from the very start, does *not* point to the great character or the promising potential of Peter as much as it anticipates who Jesus will shape him into (see, e.g., his calling as a 'fisher of men', Mark 1:17). It will be the *work of Jesus in Peter* which commends Peter to us (cf. Matt 16:13-19; Mark 8:29; John 6:66). On his own, Peter pursues what is human (Mark 8:32-33; 9:5-6). He follows Jesus closely and gives an oath-like affirmation of loyalty to him unto death (Matt 26:33-35; Mark 14:29-31; Luke 22:33-34; John 13:37-38). This is promptly contradicted by his Gethsemane slumber during Jesus's anguish, when he is admonished by Jesus three times (Mark 14:37-42),[197] and also by his previous denial of Jesus at the house of the high priest (see the three-fold denial predicted by Jesus during the Last Supper, Mark 14:26-31; cf. Luke 22:31-34). This denial will subsequently be narrated in self-disclosing detail (Mark 14:66-72; cf. Matt 26:40, 56, 69-72; Luke 22:45, 54-62; John 13:37-38; 18:15-18). Bockmuehl observes: 'As a truthful, if brutally honest,

---

[194] Bockmuehl, *Simon*, 66.
[195] See, e.g., John 13:6-10.
[196] Bockmuehl, *Simon*, 60.
[197] Cf. Helyer, *Life*, 60.

account of Peter's most spectacular failure, this story forms part of the core of Petrine memory in all three Synoptic Gospels'.[198] It may very well be true that Peter realizes that Jesus is indeed the Suffering Servant of Isaiah 53 (Mark 10:45) as Jesus turns to look at Peter during his trial at Caiaphas's house (Luke 22:61).[199] It is the unique prayer of Jesus on his behalf that makes Peter strong and predicts his future commission to 'strengthen the brethren' (Luke 22:31-34). Jesus restores Peter's relationship with himself in a threefold question/affirmation of Peter's love (John 21:15-17; cf. Luke 22:32). This encounter with the resurrected and vindicated Jesus may very well fortify Peter's realization that Jesus is indeed the Son of Man and future judge (Mark 8:38; 14:62; Dan 7:13-14).[200] As a consequence of the impact of Jesus, Peter displays Christ-likeness in his identity, character, and leadership style (see his admonition to 'watchfulness' in 1 Pet 1:13; 4:7; 5:8; cf. Mark 13:23, 32-37 and 1 Thess 5:6). His humility, servant-leadership,[201] and example stand in compelling contrast to the Peter we meet in the early sections of the four Gospels.

As Matthew and Mark report, besides his foundational calling as a disciple of Jesus, Peter and his brother Andrew were called to the particular work of being 'fishers of men' (Mark 1:16-17; cf. Matt 4:18-19). Furthermore, Jesus called Peter's confession and apostolic calling a 'rock' upon which he, Jesus, would build his church (Matt 16:17-18), accompanied by much suffering. Lastly, Peter is called to shepherd Jesus's sheep (John 21:15-19; cf. Luke 22:31-32). Much of what is briefly sketched here will be taken up in subsequent sections of this study.

Peter as *Primus Inter Pares* among the Disciples

We will demonstrate below specific aspects of the prominence of Peter as the spokesperson of the Twelve (see Matt 10:2-4; Mark 3:13-19; Luke 6:12-16; Acts 1:13-14; 2:14),[202] belonging, additionally, with John and James (cf. Acts 12:2) to the inner circle of Jesus's disciples (see Mark 5:37; 9:2-10/Matt 17:1-

---

[198] Bockmuehl, *Simon*, 83.
[199] A point observed by one of my students, Ben Burandt.
[200] Likewise suggested by Ben Burandt.
[201] Helyer, *Life*, 37–38, rightly observes that the primacy of Peter as well as the inner circle of three disciples indicates that Jesus did not oppose leadership among people, but rather 'the manner in which leaders exercise authority' (p. 38).
[202] For further details, see Cullmann, *Peter*, 25–31. See, likewise, F.J. Foakes-Jackson, *Peter: Prince of Apostles: A Study in the History and Tradition of Christianity* (London: Hodder & Stoughton, 1927), xii: 'the very fact that Peter was singled out by the unanimous voice of the writers of the New Testament for preeminence is sufficient reason why he should demand our serious attention'.

8; Mark 14:33/Matt 26:37; cf. Mark 14:33-36 and parr.; Mark 13:3-4 [with Andrew], and Gal 2:9 [albeit, that James is here the half-brother of Jesus]). The Gospel of Matthew and, to a lesser degree, that of Luke, stress Peter's prominence as 'the authoritative bearer of the Jesus tradition' and as the one 'concerned to understand Jesus's teaching'.[203] While the Gospel of Mark does not contradict this, it features Peter (as Peter's testimony) in less prominent ways by highlighting his weaknesses and omitting praiseworthy features mentioned by Matthew (e.g., that he walked on water, Matt 14:28-31)[204] and Luke (e.g., Luke 22:8; see below). According to John, Peter is the first among the Twelve to enter the empty tomb, even though John, the Apostle, arrives at the tomb first. (Note, however, that the women who had buried Jesus had seen the empty tomb [John 20:1-9; cf. Luke 24:1-12] and had already seen the resurrected Christ [Matt 28:9-10; John 20:14-17; cf. Mark 16:1-7]). According to 1 Corinthians 15:5, Peter is the first of the Twelve to become a witness of the resurrected Jesus (see Luke 24:34; cf. Mark 16:7).[205] Peter is the first to preach the gospel to Jews in Jerusalem (Acts 2:14-36; cf. 1:13), he will be involved in apostolically authenticating the mission to Samaria (Acts 8:14-25), and the first to preach the gospel to a Gentile group in Caesarea (Acts 10:34-43). Cullmann concludes: 'An examination of the passages . . . is sufficient to convince one that . . . each of the three Synoptic Gospels emphasizes in its own independent way the pre-eminent position of Peter'.[206]

Peter, nevertheless, does not appear in isolation. In earliest post-Easter times, he serves as the spokesperson[207] and representative leader of the Twelve, who arise as apostolic guarantors of the memorized Jesus tradition (see below).[208] During the earliest phase of nascent Christianity, Peter appears primarily in collaboration with the other apostles (see, e.g., Acts 2:14; 6:2), especially with John (see, e.g., Acts 4:1; 8:14-15; cf. Mark 9:2; 14:33).[209] Peter and John, for

---

[203] Bockmuehl, *Simon*, 73. See the rich material concerning Matthew in pages 67–85; he observes: 'Matthew, together with the Fourth Gospel, represents the most thoroughgoing Petrine portrait in the NT', 71.

[204] According to Bockmuehl, *Simon*, 25, the earliest extant picture of Peter on 'the wall of a Syrian house church at Dura Europos on the Euphrates' depicts Peter stilling the storm or walking on water.

[205] See Cullmann, *Peter*, 60–65.

[206] Cullmann, *Peter*, 26; Bockmuehl, *Simon*, 25.

[207] See early Petrine speeches in Acts, esp. Acts 2 and 3.

[208] Peter presides over the replacement of Judas Iscariot (Acts 1:15-26) and, most likely, the calling of deacons (Acts 6:2-5). For further details, see Cullmann, *Peter*, 34–38 and Bockmuehl, *Simon*, 124–26.

[209] R. Schnackenburg, *The Gospel According to St. John* (New York, NY: Crossroad, 1987), I, 28–30, lists various thematic connections between the Gospels of John and

example, are twice arrested and brought before the Sanhedrin; they boldly proclaim the gospel (Acts 4:7-22; 5:18-42).[210] Despite Peter's prominence, Clement of Alexandria (~AD 190) remarks: 'For they say that Peter and James and John after the ascension of our Saviour, as if also preferred by our Lord, strove not after honor, but chose James the Just bishop of Jerusalem'.[211] We shall return to this crucial and biblically supported (cf., e.g., Acts 12:17; 1 Cor 9:5) patristic statement[212] as we further discuss the character formation of Peter, especially in contrast to some of the statements of Irenaeus regarding Peter's supposed ecclesiastical prominence in Rome.

Peter After the Death and Resurrection of Jesus

After the death and resurrection of Jesus, Peter arose as a key witness of the resurrected Christ (John 21:14-24; Acts 1–10; 1 Cor 15:4; 1 Pet 1:3, 21; 3:21).[213] According to Acts, Peter, along the lines of an Old Testament prophet, announced the true Messiah of God. By now he also knew who he was in the eyes of God (loved and in constant need of the grace of God). As an irreplaceable and unique apostolic witness of Christ in the areas of Jerusalem, Lydda, Joppa, and Caesarea, he now had to learn the *extent* and *reach* of the gospel, breaking through innumerable barriers of ethnicity, religions, cultures, philosophies, political structures, languages, customs, etc. (see, e.g., Acts 10 and 11).

Mark, including: John 6:1-13 (Mark 6:34-44); John 6:16-21 (Mark 6:45-52); John 6:24-25 (Mark 6:53); John 6:30 (Mark 8:11); John 6:68-69 (Mark 8:29); cf. John 12:3-7 (Mark 14:3-6). According to J.A.T. Robinson, *The Priority of John* (London: SCM Press, 1985), 12, common material between Mark and John placed in *different contexts* include: John 1:40-42 (Mark 3:16); John 4:44 (Mark 6:4); John 6:67, 70 (Mark 3:16); John 9:6-7 (Mark 8:22-26); John 12:25 (Mark 8:35); John 12:39-40 (Mark 4:12); John 13:20 (Mark 9:37). Cf. John 5:19, 26-30 (Mark 2:1–3:6; 11:27-33); John 7:5 (Mark 3:31-35); John 10:19-20 (Mark 3:22-30).

[210] Cullmann, *Peter*, 40–41 n. 22, (with B. Reicke, 'Die Verfassung der Urgemeinde im Lichte jüdischer Dokumente', *TZ* 10 [1954], 95–112), entertains the possibility that the early church was initially led by Peter *and* the apostolic group, the latter in analogy to the 'council' of the Twelve at Qumran.

[211] Clement of Alexandria's sixth book of *Hypotyposes* (Eusebius, *Hist. eccl.* 2.1).

[212] See Tertullian, *Pud.* 21.

[213] It is noteworthy that Jesus first appeared to women, notably, Mary Magdalene (Matt 28:8; John 20:14-18; cf. Mark 16:9). Such statements carry the markings of authenticity since female witnesses, especially in a court of law, garnered little respect (cf., e.g., Josephus, *Ant.* 4.8.15). Peter was, however, the first of the Twelve to see the risen Lord (1 Cor 15:5; cf. Luke 24:34).

Following the intensive mentoring by Jesus and the impact of the outpouring of the Holy Spirit at Pentecost, Peter's work and witness was now marked by increasing consistency, clarity, focus, and courage. He had developed a deep faith in the uniqueness of Jesus as the eternal Son of God and recognized the fulfillment of Old Testament prophecy. He employed his apostolic anointing to heal and to exorcise and was willing to suffer. In short: he was a man of comprehensive, God-dependent integrity.

Despite all this, Peter was by no means finished with learning and growing. According to most plausible reconstructions, Peter's wavering exposed by Paul in Galatians 2:11-21 *preceded* the Jerusalem Council in Acts 15.[214] In the fundamental tenets of theology, Peter and Paul very much dovetailed (Gal 1:18 [Peter and Paul spent fifteen days together around AD 37]; 2:2, 9),[215] while Peter allowed pressure from the Judaizers[216] to temporarily sway his fellowship conduct in Antioch (Gal 2:12).[217] Paul was thus correct in challenging Peter (and Barnabas) regarding table-fellowship with Gentiles (cf. Acts 10 and 11, an event which probably predates that of Gal 2) now that God had provided purification for both Jews and Gentiles in the atonement of Christ. During his journey to Antioch (Gal 2:11-14 and, perhaps, Acts 12:17b[218]), Peter had to learn to consistently live out the ramifications of the gospel of Jesus, which he had already embraced (Acts 10),[219] by not making any distinction in table-

---

[214] See the detailed arguments in C.J. Hemer, *The Book of Acts in the Setting of Hellenistic History* (Tübingen: Mohr Siebeck, 1989), 244–307, esp. 278. Hemer reaches the convincing conclusion that Gal 2:1-16 predates Acts 15 and corresponds most likely to Acts 11:27. Cf. D.J. Moo, *Galatians* (Grand Rapids, MI: Baker Academic, 2013), 10–16; 118–20, and Bockmuehl, *Simon,* 91–92.

[215] Cullmann, *Peter,* 47–48, 52, 66; cf. J.J. Gibson, *Peter Between Jerusalem and Antioch. Peter, James, and the Gentiles* (Tübingen: Mohr Siebeck, 2013).

[216] The 'circumcision-faction', which is to be distinguished from James the Just (Acts 15:13-21), despite Gal 2:12.

[217] Cullmann, *Peter,* 48–49, 53, suggests that Peter's accountability to the Jerusalem church, with James as its leader, was much greater than Paul's; thus Peter's indecisive behavior, especially if one appreciates Peter's mediating function in the earliest church; see, e.g., Acts 6.

[218] See the various options of where Peter might have traveled, in Hengel, *Peter,* 48–49, 79.

[219] See Cullmann, *Peter,* 66–67, who stresses Peter's 'universalism' derived from Jesus (cf. Matt 8:11) and shared with Paul (Gal 2:11-14). By the time Paul wrote 1 Corinthians in AD 54–55, Peter was again the significant apostle and witness of the resurrection of Jesus (1 Cor 9:5; 15:5, 11; cf. Gal 1:18; 2:15-21). It is also possible that the *paradosis* of the Lord's Supper (1 Cor 11:23-26), characterized as παρέλαβον ἀπὸ τοῦ κυρίου (1 Cor 11:23), stems from Paul's encounter with Peter (Gal 1:18; so Bockmuehl, *Simon,* 144, and n. 62). On p. 144, Bockmuehl correctly observers: '[t]he complex evidence of Galatians and 1 Corinthians taken together

fellowship between Jews and Gentiles. During the subsequent Jerusalem Council (Acts 15, AD 49), Peter, with the support of James (the Just), spoke against the Judaizers[220] and in favor of the gospel of grace for both Jews and Gentiles (i.e., circumcision was not required for salvation).

According to some church fathers, Peter did probably work in the church in Antioch (cf. Gal 2:11).[221] According to Paul, Peter might have labored in, or at least visited, Corinth (1 Cor 1:12;[222] see also 3:22; 9:5; 15:5). He is said to have traveled later to Pontus, Galatia (cf. Gal 2:9), Cappadocia, Asia, and Bithynia (see 1 Pet 1:1),[223] before coming to Rome (see Clement of Rome, *1 Clem.* 5 and Ignatius, *Rom.* 4.2-3).[224] According to Eusebius and Jerome, Peter is said to have spent some twenty-five years of his life in Rome, a figure which is probably exaggerated.[225] On the other hand, the presence of Peter in Rome in the late 50s and early 60s AD is very likely. It remains unclear, however, who founded the church in Rome.

---

indicates that the rift at Antioch, though emotional and sharp, was a temporary disruption in an otherwise positive working relationship, if not friendship'.

[220] Judaizers are Pharisaic, law-abiding Jews who believe that Jesus is the Messiah.

[221] Concerning the unverifiable question whether Peter founded the church at Antioch (so Origen), see Cullmann, *Peter*, 54.

[222] See Cullmann, *Peter*, 55–57, regarding the fact that while Peter possibly visited Corinth, he was not involved in founding the church; see Bockmuehl, *Simon*, 104–105.

[223] See Jerome, *Vir. ill.* 1, who claims that Peter served in Antioch (cautiously, Bockmuehl, *Remembered Peter*, 65–66 and Bockmuehl, *Simon*, 30). He then labored in Pontus, Galatia, Cappadocia, Asia, and Bithynia. See the correspondence between Trajan and Pliny, AD 110–12, in which Pliny (*Ep.* 10.96) notes that the *Christiani* had been in Pontus/Bithynia for twenty years or longer. Peter then went on to Rome in the second year of Emperor Claudius (~AD 42). There is some speculation that Peter opposed Simon Magus in Rome (*Acts Pet.*, 32; cf. Acts 8:9-24 and 2 Pet 2:3 [Justin Martyr believes Simon Magus to be behind the false teaching rejected in 2 Pet 2:3]; cf. K. Beyschlag, *Simon Magus und die christliche Gnosis* [Tübingen: Mohr Siebeck, 1974]). Eusebius (*Hist. eccl.* 3.2.21), like Irenaeus (*Haer.* 3.3.1–2), the Apostolic Constitutions, and Rufinus, seem to regard Linus, not Peter, as the first bishop of Rome.

[224] Cullmann, *Peter*, 79–157.

[225] Eusebius, *Chron.* (AD 303), asserts the unverified scenario that Peter resided in Rome from AD 42 onward. See, however, Bockmuehl, *Simon*, 101–102, concerning possible evidence of an early visit of Peter to Rome. Besides 1 Pet 5:13 ('Babylon'), early church fathers, including the accounts of Eusebius, all affirm, however, Peter's presence in Rome and that he was martyred under Emperor Nero. See Clement of Rome (*1 Clem.* 5:1-4); Papias (Eusebius, *Hist. eccl.* 3.39.15); Dionysius of Corinth (*Letter to Pope Soter*, in Eusebius, *Hist. eccl.* 2.25.8); Irenaeus (*Haer.* 3.1.1); Jerome (*Vir. ill.* 1).

Irenaeus (*Haer.* 3.3.2–3) confusingly[226] identifies Peter and Paul as the founders and organizers of the church in Rome, referring to: 'bishops of the greatest and most ancient church known to all, founded and organized at Rome by the two most glorious apostles, Peter and Paul'. Rather, Acts 2:10 provides an indirect hint in favor of the fact that early Jewish converts to Christ returned to Rome after Pentecost in AD 33 (or AD 30).

Augustine (*Ep.* 102.8) states that the message of Christ was known in Rome already under Caligula (AD 37–41).[227] We also must take seriously the reference to Aquila and Priscilla coming from Rome around AD 49 on account of the Claudian expulsion (Acts 18:2).[228] Finally, Paul's Letter to the Romans makes it clear (Rom 1:15; 16:1-23) that he was not the founder of the church in Rome. On the other hand, the best historical evidence does place both Peter and Paul in Rome before they were both martyred under Nero.

We are arguing here that Peter receives a unique and unparalleled commission from Jesus as the 'rock' (see below), serving as the perpetual 'exhibit A' of Jesus's transforming work. In this regard, Paul simply serves as a complementary apostolic witness (see Acts, chs 9, 22, and 26, describing, for instance, the origin of Paul's gospel).[229] Despite his polemic in his Letter to the Galatians, Paul has to acknowledge Peter's witness and position (Gal 1:18): 'evidently Paul's gospel and apostolic identity cannot bypass Peter'.[230] Paul recognizes other (e.g., John) and subsequent leaders of the early church, such as James the half-brother of Jesus (see Acts 15 and Gal 1:19).

---

[226] See Cullmann, *Peter*, 116.

[227] See Bockmuehl, *Simon*, 100–101, for further detail.

[228] See also Paul's Letter to the Romans, written around AD 57. Despite the fact that Peter is not mentioned in Romans, he might be in Rome at that time; *pace* Cullmann, *Peter*, 113, who assumes on the basis of Paul's silence concerning Peter in *Romans* that Peter cannot have been in Rome at that time; see likewise, Bockmuehl, *Simon*, 102. Bockmuehl, *Simon*, 142, finds, however, an indirect hint to Paul's possible awareness that Peter was one of the apostolic workers in Rome: in Rom 15:20, Paul speaks of seeking to avoid building on another man's θεμέλιον, a term he uses elsewhere for describing the *apostolic* foundation of the church (1 Cor 3:10-12; Eph 2:20). See J.W. Wenham, 'Did Peter Go to Rome in A.D. 42?', *TynBul*, 23 (1972), 94–102. Differently, Hengel, *Peter*, 63, who assumes, unconvincingly, that Paul does not mention Peter because of ongoing divisions stemming from Gal 2:9-11.

[229] See S. Kim, *The Origin of Paul's Gospel* (Eugene, OR: Wipf & Stock, 2007).

[230] Bockmuehl, *Simon*, 75.

Likewise, Peter affirms Paul's position (2 Pet 3:15-16)[231] and even serves under the authority of James (Acts 15; cf. Gal 2:12).[232] Already Ignatius of Antioch (~AD 110) in his *Letter to the Romans* 4.3, hints at the special apostolic authority of *both* Peter and Paul by saying: 'I do not command you, as Peter and Paul did'.[233]

Peter's Martyrdom in Rome
John 21:15-18 (cf. 1 Pet 5:1 and 2 Pet 1:14) already casts an ominous shadow of a possible martyrdom over Peter's life.[234] Clement of Rome (AD 96) implies Peter's martyrdom in Rome by stating: 'Let us take the noble examples of our own generation. On account of jealousy and envy the greatest and most righteous pillars . . . were persecuted, and [came?] even unto death . . . Peter, [through] unjust envy, endured not one or two but many [labours], and at last, having delivered his testimony, departed unto the place of glory due to him'.[235] Clement identifies Peter and Paul as the outstanding heroes of the faith. Dionysius of Corinth (d. AD 171) also claims that both Peter and Paul faced martyrdom in Rome (see also Tertullian).[236] It is historically most plausible to posit that Peter and Paul were martyred in Rome around AD 67 (see Clement

---

[231] Bockmuehl, *Simon*, 32, believes that 2 Pet 3:15-16 'draws credibly on the relationship with Paul'.

[232] Cullmann, *Peter*, 229, frequently makes this point.

[233] In the present work we do not discuss later apocryphal materials associated with the name Peter, such as: *Acts of Peter, Gospel of Peter* (docetic), *Acts of Peter and Andrew, Acts of Peter and Paul, Acts of Peter and the Twelve, Preaching of Peter, Apocalypse of Peter* (gnostic), *Judgment of Peter, Letter of Peter to Philip* (Nag Hammadi library), and *Epistula Petri* (contained in some versions of the Clementine literature as an introductory letter ascribed to the Apostle Peter). In this context it is particularly noteworthy that Justin Martyr (*Dial.*) and Ignatius of Antioch (*Smyrn.* 3.1–3), connect 'a particular part of the gospel tradition . . . with Peter's authority and testimony' (Bockmuehl, *Simon*, 95–96). Regarding the ample second and third-century apocryphal documents pertaining to Peter, see Bockmuehl, *Simon*, 37–152.

[234] See S. Heid and R. von Haehling (eds), *Petrus und Paulus in Rom: Eine interdisziplinäre Debatte* (Freiburg: Herder, 2011), and Bockmuehl, *Simon*, 27.

[235] *First Clem.* 5:1-4. See the detailed arguments in Cullmann, *Peter*, 75, 91–123, especially regarding the fact that *1 Clem.* 5–6, in the context of chs 3–6, suggests Peter's martyrdom in Rome. Similarly, Bockmuehl, *Simon*, 109–11. Cullmann, *Peter*, 91 (see 87–91), is convinced that even the 'New Testament attests . . . the fact of the martyrdom of Peter'.

[236] Cf. Eusebius (*Hist. eccl.* 2.25.8); Irenaeus (*Haer.* 3.1–3); Tertullian (*Praescr.* 36; cf. *Scorp.* 15, *Marc.* 4.5); Clement of Alexandria (in Eusebius, *Hist. eccl.* 6.14 and 2.15); Origen (in Eusebius, *Hist. eccl.* 3.1).

of Rome and Ignatius, *Rom.*).[237] The rash promise made by Peter in Luke 22:33 (cf. John 13:37; Mark 14:31) thus finds its ultimate, somber fulfillment.[238] The Roman presbyter Gaius (~AD 210) asserts that the execution (or burial places; so Eusebius, *Hist. eccl.* 2.25.7) of Peter and Paul were at the Vatican Hill and on the Ostian Way, respectively.[239] Cullmann believes that the results of the Vatican excavations undertaken from 1939 onwards 'speak in favor of the report that the *execution of Peter took place in the Vatican* district'.[240] Bockmuehl believes 'that we almost certainly have under the Vatican the site identified by Gaius and still known in the time of Constantine as the tomb of Peter'.[241]

Conclusion

Peter's colorful development in the setting of first-century Palestinian Judaism, subsisting under an oppressive Roman rule, sets the stage for a most staggering calling: to serve as the unique, key witness to the most astounding person ever to live on earth.

---

[237] See Bockmuehl, *Simon*, 145, regarding the plethora of later references to places and items associated with Peter in Rome.

[238] See Bockmuehl, *Simon*, 121.

[239] See Cullmann, *Peter*, 117–18 and, with further and more critical details, Bockmuehl, *Simon*, 146–47.

[240] Cullmann, *Peter*, 156. See details in Bockmuehl, *Simon*, 148–49.

[241] Bockmuehl, *Simon*, 149, who also notes that there are no 'rival sites' for Peter's tomb. Peter's exact burial place can still be contested: see R.T. O'Callaghan, 'Vatican Excavations and the Tomb of Peter', *BA* 16 (1953), 70–87, and M. Guarducci, *The Tomb of St Peter: The New Discoveries in the Sacred Grottoes of the Vatican* (London: G.G. Harrap, 1960).

CHAPTER 2

Non-Transferable Aspects of Peter's Work and Witness

By non-transferable aspects of Peter's work and witness we mean those elements of his early Christian work which are entirely unique to him and contain no hint of succession, continuation, or imitation. These non-transferable aspects will serve as the crucial witness foundation for all future disciples of Christ.

Peter and His Confession as the Foundational 'Rock' of Jesus's Nascent Church (Matt 16:18-19)

The 'Rock' and the Problem of 'Apostolic Succession'

A first, non-transferable aspect of Peter's calling is found in the highly controversial passage of Matthew 16:18-19.[1] Contrary to the traditional Protestant view (e.g. Luther, Calvin, and Zwingli),[2] Cullmann argues in his influential work on Peter that Matthew 16:18-19 should indeed be viewed as pertaining to Peter as a person as well as to Peter's confession of Christ as 'Messiah' and 'Son of the living God'.[3] The traditional Protestant view holds that it is solely Peter's (Petros) *confession*, which is to be identified as the large rock (petra) on which Jesus builds his church. In Cullmann's view, however, Jesus commissions Peter himself as the foundation of the messianic church, built on the cornerstone, Jesus, not only by means of his confession but also as the continuing apostolic spokesperson (see below). Roman Catholic

---

[1] See Bockmuehl, *Simon*, 86.
[2] One of the most robust defenses of the traditional, Protestant view on the subject is: C.C. Caragounis, *Peter and the Rock* (Berlin: de Gruyter, 1990).
[3] Cullmann, *Peter,* 164–217. Besides Tertullian, Chrysostom already appears to have held that view (Cullmann, *Peter*, 167).

interpretation went wrong, Cullmann says, when it *added* apostolic succession[4] to Jesus's personal and partially unique commission of Peter. According to Cullmann, Peter is the rock of the church by virtue of his confession of Christ *and* by virtue of his unique person and calling (as apostolic spokesperson, eyewitness, and guarantor of Jesus-tradition in the early church; cf. Acts 1:21; 10:41).[5] Peter thus laid—and himself is—the irreplaceable and unique foundation of the church, which rests on Christ as the cornerstone (cf. 1 Cor 3:11). Bockmuehl notes: 'Peter alone of all the apostles is remembered as the founding figure of the church of Jesus *as a whole*'.[6] As a foundation, all followers of Christ are called to trust the apostolic witness, the *derivative* rock, Peter (see John 17:20). Once that unique apostolic foundation is laid, there is no need for someone to succeed Peter in a similar apostolic role or to guard its tradition and interpretation. Rather, there is the perpetual need, especially for those who serve as shepherds and watchmen of the apostolic witness-foundation, to point back to Peter.[7] *Apostolic succession* as such is impossible, since Peter's role is inseparably tied to his unique relationship to Christ, his personal and unique witness to the resurrected Christ, and his unrepeatable position as the spokesperson of the original apostles. Cullmann rightly observes that:

> it is quite remarkable that the apostle who later is regarded as the personification of organized church government in reality exercises such a function for only a short time at the beginning, and then exchanged it for missionary work. Peter was not the archetype of the church official but of the missionary.[8]

Tellingly, Cullmann's view seems to accord with that of Clement of Alexandria (AD 150–215),[9] Tertullian (AD 160–220),[10] and Origen (AD 182–254).[11]

---

[4] With many other scholars, Bockmuehl, *Simon*, 85–86, notes: 'The Matthean Peter per se has no application to the pope in Rome' (86). Contra Irenaeus, *Haer*. 3.3. Irenaeus is significant when *guarding* tradition; he is to be evaluated carefully when *creating* tradition.

[5] Similarly, Bockmuehl, *Simon*, 177 and Cullmann, *Peter*, 220–28.

[6] Bockmuehl, *Simon*, 77, referring also to U. Luz, *Matthew 8–20* (Minneapolis, MN: Augsburg Fortress, 2001, 469–70.

[7] Cullmann, *Peter*, 225.

[8] Cullmann, *Peter*, 41.

[9] See Eusebius, *Hist. eccl.* 2.1, quoting Clement of Alexandria's sixth book of *Hypotyposes,* on this issue; see also 1 Pet 5:1-4.

[10] *Pud.* 21. Tertullian applies Matt 16:17-19 *exclusively* to Peter: only Peter is the rock, only Peter holds the 'keys', and only Peter 'loosens' and 'binds'. Against the Roman

Cyprian (ca. AD 200–258) argues (against Pope Stephen, AD 254–57) that, as Bockmuehl phrases it, 'all bishops who confess the faith of Peter constitute the "rock" on which, according to Matt. 16, the church is founded'.[12]

Irenaeus (AD 130–202), on the other hand, attributes unfounded prestige, apostolic succession, and supreme significance to the church of Rome, that is, to the leadership in the church of Rome, based on the mere fact that Peter and Paul served there.[13] Unfortunately, Irenaeus *mixes* the succession of various bishops in Rome with a proto-Roman Catholic primacy-postulate for Rome and its respective bishops not found in the New Testament or among many other early church fathers; he speaks of the 'superior origin of the church of Rome', guarding the 'apostolic tradition'; '[t]he blessed apostles [Peter and Paul], having founded and built up the church [of Rome], they handed over the office of the episcopate to Linus . . . To him succeeded Anacletus, and after him, in the third place from the apostles, Clement was chosen for the episcopate. He had seen the blessed apostles and was acquainted with them'.[14] It was Pope Stephen who first applied Matthew 16:18-19 to the office of the bishop of Rome.[15] Contrary to Irenaeus, the following can briefly be mentioned here: first, it is *Peter* who is the rock, not a particular local church or its leader, even if that church or its leader is merely viewed as the guardian of Peter's work in that city. Second, Peter's simple and clear witness is not so much in need of being hermeneutically guarded as it is of being trusted and followed. Third, the particular church in Rome and its leader have, according to Jesus's teaching, no claim above any other church belonging to Christ in other cities; the significance of Rome derived exclusively from the fact that it was the center of the Roman Empire, not from any biblical or theological preeminence. The presence of Peter in Rome is on equal footing with Peter's previous presence in Antioch, Jerusalem, and elsewhere. If we properly understand Peter's unique witness to Christ, his utter surrender to Christ, his growing humility, including

---

Bishop Callistus (AD 217–22), Tertullian exclaims: 'what sort of man are you, subverting and wholly changing the manifest intention of the Lord, conferring (as that intention did) this [gift] personally upon Peter?' (quoted in Cullmann, *Peter*, 121 n. 5). Cyprian believes that Matt 16:17-19 applies to the subsequent *corporate* group of bishops (see Cullmann, *Peter*, 167 and n. 13).

[11] Origen, *Cels.* 6.77; *Comm. Matt.* 12.10–11.

[12] Cyprian, *Unit. eccl.* 4–5; Bockmuehl, *Simon*, 182. Likewise, the tone of *1 Clem.*, written by Bishop Clement of Rome in AD 96, is one of exhorting appeal, not one of papal, *ex cathedra* authority. See also Cullmann, *Peter*, 239.

[13] See Cullmann, *Peter*, 238–39, concerning other possible interpretations of Irenaeus' reference to the 'pre-eminent' position of Rome.

[14] Irenaeus, *Haer.* 3.3.2–3.

[15] Cf. Bockmuehl, *Simon*, 86.

his approach to leadership (for instance, leaving the leadership of the church in Jerusalem to James the Just; see Acts 12:17: 'he left and went to another place'; Acts 15; 1 Cor 9:5),[16] Irenaeus's notion diametrically opposes and *contradicts* what we know of Peter and his disarming and humble calling as a holistic 'rock-witness'. Based on our study, followers of Christ face a stark alternative: *either* they follow Peter's Christ-intended witness and person as the foundational, apostolic rock enshrined in Peter's canonical witness *or* they adhere to Irenaeus on this point; they cannot do both, since adherence to Irenaeus's view of Peter and the church of Rome will fundamentally *detract* from the witness of Peter as a humble, surrendered, servant-leader and his entire approach to individual and corporate discipleship (see 1 Pet 5:1-10; see also Paul as a 'gentle apostle', 1 Thess 2:6-8).

The biblical Peter leaves no room for the contradictory and distracting prestige of apostolic succession[17] or the political power of the church in Rome. It is true that considerable false teaching threatened the orthodox confession in the second and third centuries of the Christian church. The means of combating such heterodoxy are not, however, power and prestige; rather, it is the leaders' humility, teaching, writing (see *1 Clem.* as a stellar example), and orthopraxy. Above all, heterodoxy can be combatted most effectively by church leaders returning to and heeding Peter's unique apostolic and authoritative witness. We are, on the other hand, not arguing against the necessity of establishing church leaders in Rome and elsewhere. Pesch correctly points to this even in *1 Clement*.[18] However, the appointment of bishops,[19] elders, and deacons in Rome (and elsewhere) does not support apostolic succession but rather the necessity of godly leadership in the churches, which points to and builds upon the apostolic rock, Peter (as well as other apostles). Finally, what the early church did, indeed, is to *preserve* for posterity Peter's unparalleled, apostolic foundation.

In the present work, we further contend that Jesus's semi-transferable commission to Peter to *shepherd the flock of God* (see below) serves as an umbrella, under which his non-transferable, foundation-laying commission to serve as the rock of the apostolic church (Matt 16:18-19), based on Christ's finished work, finds ample room. One reason for this lies in the fact that the

---

[16] Cullmann, *Peter*, 39, states: 'from this point on Peter gives up his fixed residence in Jerusalem, and so also his position in the church there'.

[17] Cf. Bockmuehl, *Simon*, 65.

[18] R. Pesch, *Die biblische Grundlage des Primats* (Freiburg: Herder, 2001), ad loc.

[19] See A.C. Stewart, *The Original Bishops: Office and Order in the First Christian Communities* (Grand Rapids, MI: Baker Academic, 2014).

semi-transferable commission to shepherd God's sheep (John 21:15-19; Luke 22:31-32) is demonstrably realized in Acts and especially in 1 (and 2) Peter.[20] In contrast to this, the impact of Matthew 16:18-19 cannot be traced in Acts or 1 and 2 Peter, except in Peter laying the non-transferable, apostolic witness-foundation (see below). In other words, Peter does not build an ecclesiastical structure; rather, he lays the foundation of his authentic witness (Matt 16:18-19) and then he disciples and mentors others *based on that witness* (John 21:15-19; Luke 22:31-32). In Peter and the early corporate apostolic witness, we find no trace of laying the groundwork for any form of 'apostolic succession' or a focus on Rome as the 'mother church' (see also Clement of Alexandria *contra* Irenaeus). The apostolic authority vested in Peter as a witness and as a person (Matt 16:18-19) is kept as unique and irreplaceable (see, e.g., the criteria for belonging to the circle of the Twelve in Acts 1:21-22) throughout the New Testament. Peter is—and remains—the spokesperson for the twelve apostolic witnesses concerning the life, death, and resurrection of Jesus. As such, he is laying the groundwork for the messianic church, built and perpetually dependent on the one and only cornerstone, Jesus, the Messiah of God.

The only way to guard and preserve this apostolic deposit is to pay direct (not mediated) attention to it, to cherish it, and to let it impact mind and heart, individually and corporately, aided by the confirming and illuminating work of the Holy Spirit (see Acts 2:42a: 'and they devoted themselves to the apostles' teaching'). The separate hermeneutical issue of being able to understand Peter's witness properly is partially solved by the relative perspicuity of his simple *canonical testimony* and partially by a robust communal (i.e., truly catholic) process of learning from other interpreters of Peter and his unique apostolic witness. Such corporate learning must, in line with Jesus's impact upon Peter, include godly mind and character formation if it is to have the desired outcome of mature convictions of mind and heart. It is ironic that the Protestant tendency to overemphasize Paul, in whose inspired letters even Peter finds some elements hard to understand (δυσνόητά τινα, 2 Pet 3:16), has, at times, appeared to muddle the perspicuity of Scripture.

Analysis of Matthew 16:18-19[21]

The Matthean context of Peter's confession of Jesus as the Messiah (Matt 16:16) is similar to that of Mark's (Mark 8:29): Jesus confronts his disciples

---

[20] Helyer, *Life*, 105.

[21] Regarding the interesting history of interpretation of Matt 16:17-19, see Cullmann, *Peter*, 164–76. Concerning the authenticity of this passage, see Cullmann, *Peter*, 192–99.

with the danger of self-sufficiency and self-righteousness (Matt 16:5-12), as well as with his own identity. Peter rightly confesses Jesus as Messiah and 'Son of God' (Matt 16:16). While Jesus does eventually claim *ontological* sonship in Mark 12:1-12, the disciples do not understand this at least until that point;[22] during the public ministry of Jesus they adhere to the Jewish honorific 'son of God', signifying a human being who enjoys particular honor and familiarity with God (cf., e.g., 2 Sam 7:14-16; Ps 89:26-28). Cullmann aptly states that Peter did not grasp the 'essential meaning' of his confession that Jesus is the Messiah, because he could not conceive of a 'suffering messiah'.[23] In other words, Jesus causes a double-crisis of self- and God-perception among the disciples.[24] Part of the crisis of God-perception thus comes to a climax when Jesus does not only reinforce Peter's confession, but exposes Peter and the others to the stark reality that the Messiah of God must suffer, be killed, and be greatly exalted. While Peter did not understand the meaning of a suffering messiah, his confession can nevertheless be viewed as God-given and true; it is thus plausible that Jesus *confirmed* Peter's confession (Matt 16:17-19, going beyond Mark and Luke at this point) before strongly *challenging* Peter's diabolic resistance to a suffering messiah (so, the triple-tradition).[25]

Precisely between the two extremes of glorious messianic identity (Matt 16:16-17) and messianic humiliation (Matt 16:21-23) lie the 'Peter and the rock' as well as the 'Peter with the keys of the kingdom of heaven' sayings (Matt 16:18-19).[26] Jesus says to Peter (Matt 16:18): 'and I tell you, you are Peter, and upon this rock [fem.] I shall build my church [fem., i.e., people or community][27] and the gates of hades shall not be able to resist [or: overwhelm] her' (σὺ εἶ Πέτρος ['Peter'], καὶ ἐπὶ ταύτῃ τῇ πέτρᾳ [=rock] οἰκοδομήσω μου τὴν ἐκκλησίαν καὶ πύλαι ᾅδου οὐ κατισχύσουσιν αὐτῆς). Jesus calls Peter's

---

[22] *Pace* Helyer, *Life*, 42.
[23] Cullmann, *Peter*, 179. Contrast this lack of understanding with Peter's later affirmations, e.g., in 1 Pet 1:11. See also J.R. Edwards, *The Gospel According to Mark* (Grand Rapids, MI: Eerdmans, 2002), 252, and Grant, *Saint Peter*, 66.
[24] For details, see Bayer, *Theology*, 41-88.
[25] *Pace* Cullmann, *Peter*, 182-86, who is convinced that while Matt 16:17-19 is an authentic logion of Jesus, it was not originally uttered in the context of Peter's confession of Jesus as Messiah (Cullmann, *Peter*, 188-91, thinks of John 6:66 and esp. Luke 22:31).
[26] The strongly Aramaic character of Matt 16:17-19 has often been noted, especially: 'blessed are you'; 'Simon bar Jonah'; 'gates of hades'; 'flesh and blood'; 'bind and loose'; cf. Brown, *Peter*, 90-91.
[27] See Cullmann, *Peter*, 203, who refers also to Matt 26:31; Luke 12:32; John 10:1-16; 21:16-19.

confession (Matt 16:16) and Peter's apostolic person a 'rock'[28] (ἐπὶ ταύτῃ τῇ πέτρᾳ) upon which Jesus himself will build his messianic church (οἰκοδομήσω μου τὴν ἐκκλησίαν: '*I* will build *my* [emphatic position] church') as a visible expression of the inaugurated but not consummated messianic kingdom.[29] Whatever the precise interpretation of the 'Peter and the rock' passage will turn out to be, what we must hold fast is the fact that *Jesus does not hand over the building of his messianic fellowship and community to Peter.*[30] Jesus will remain the cornerstone, architect, and builder of *his* messianic, eschatological, and covenantal people of God (the church)[31] as part of the kingdom of heaven, based upon his work as a Suffering Servant and identity as Danielic Son of Man.[32] When we keep in mind that Jesus remains the eternal cornerstone, Bockmuehl rightly observes that 'Jesus *himself* is . . . the epitome of the wise man in Matt. 7:24-25 who built upon the rock . . . the . . . storms . . . cannot prevail against the house'.[33] Jesus thus remains 'pontiff' of his church, composed of the converted remnant of Israel (Isa 7:3; 10:21; Amos 9:9; Mic 5:3)[34] and converted Gentiles. He never cedes this authority and claim (see Matt 28:18-20); he only delegates responsibility.

---

[28] According to Cullmann (*Peter*, 167 and n. 18), Augustine (*Serm.* 76, 147, 149, 232, 245, 270, 295) unconvincingly identifies Jesus as the 'rock' (see also Cyril of Alexandria and, later, Luther). Note, however, the later rabbinic identification of Abraham as the rock upon which God builds: Str-B, I, 733; Cullmann, *Peter*, 193 n. 7.

[29] See C.E. Carlston and C.A. Evans, *From Synagogue to Ecclesia: Matthew's Community at the Crossroads* (Tübingen: Mohr Siebeck, 2014).

[30] F. Dostoyevsky also questions such ecclesiastical claims to autonomous authority in the *Grand Inquisitor* section in: *The Brothers Karamazov* (New York, NY: Penguin, 2003). Regarding the connection between messianic expectations and a messianic community, see, e.g., *1 En.* 38:1; 53:6; 62:8 (Cullmann, *Peter*, 195 n. 15).

[31] See Cullmann, *Peter*, 193–207, against the outdated fallacy of denying the authenticity of the Matthean saying based on the use of ἐκκλησία (used only one other time in the Synoptic Gospels, Matt 18:17). The term has deep OT roots (Num 16:3; Deut 7:6; the people of God=*qāhāl* [or *edhah*] YHWH; most of the approximately one hundred LXX occurrences of *ekklēsia* translate *qāhāl*; cf. also 1 Macc 3:13) and display a conceptual continuity in the NT (cf. Acts 7:38; Gal 1:22; 1 Thess 2:14). See D.A. Hagner, *Matthew 14–28* (Dallas, TX: Word, 1995), 465–66 and Bockmuehl, *Simon*, 73–75, with reference to 1QSa 2.4, where the Qumran community views itself as the eschatological people of God (73 n. 89).

[32] See Cullmann, *Peter*, 195–96, who rightly points to the fact that the Son of Man in Dan 7:13-14, 18, 27, represents the saints of the Most High.

[33] Bockmuehl, *Simon*, 76.

[34] Cf. Cullmann, *Peter*, 195 and Helyer, *Life*, 36. With many others, Helyer believes that the appointment of the twelve disciples (Matt 10:1-4; Mark 3:13-19; Luke 6:12-16) echoes the twelve tribes of Israel.

Matthew 16:18 states literally: 'you are Peter [masc., often a small but at times also a large rock³⁵] and upon this rock [ἡ πέτρα, fem.; large rock or boulder; a term used for Christ in 1 Cor 10:4] I, Jesus, will build my church and the gates of hades will not prevail against its expanse (or be victorious over it)'. The concluding 'it' (αὐτῆς) is feminine, thus referring either to τὴν ἐκκλησίαν (the church) or to τῇ πέτρᾳ (rock). Due to the proximity between τὴν ἐκκλησίαν and αὐτῆς, we take the phrase to mean primarily that the gates of hades (as the Underworld of death) will not be able to resist or oppress (cf. Ps 9:13; 107:17-20; Rev 19:19; 20:7-9) the expansive reach of Jesus's *church* based on the cornerstone, Jesus, and the foundation, Peter and his witness (cf. 1 Pet 1:4-5). Either the 'gates of hades' shall not be able to oppress³⁶ the church, or, more likely, the gates cannot resist—or remain closed to—the power of the church/rock which Jesus constructs. Because the dynamic thrust of this passage is that Christ *establishes* his *expanding* messianic rule via the church, it is most plausible that the church embodies the *offensive thrust* and not hades and death; ergo, the 'gates of hades' shall not be able to resist such dynamic expansion. Death will not be able to put an end to Christ's work. Only in a secondary sense does hades also oppress the church.

Hades (the primary Greek rendering of Sheol in the LXX) is essentially the place of the dead (Rev 6:8; 20:13-14), in contrast to gehenna (as the place of eternal condemnation (Mark 9:43, 45, 47; cf. Matt 18:9; 23:15; see 2 Pet 2:4). A careful analysis of the New Testament yields the insight that Jesus has conquered Hades (Acts 2:27, 31; cf. Ps 16:10) and that any Satanic forces associated with Hades are doomed (cf. Rev 19:19; 20:7-9).³⁷

A key argument against the older Protestant interpretation is that the name Πέτρος (Peter) as well as the word ἡ πέτρα (rock) in Matthew 16:18 are rendered in the Peshitta and the Old Syriac texts by the same word 'cepha'.³⁸ The reason for having to distinguish this same Aramaic word as 'Peter' and

---

[35] See Sophocles, *Oed. Col.* 1595.

[36] So W.D. Davies and D.C. Allison, *A Critical and Exegetical Commentary on the Gospel According to Saint Matthew* (Edinburgh: T&T Clark, 1988–97), II, 630. They refer to 1QH 14, which emphasizes that despite the threat of the gates of death there is shelter and fortification in God's truth.

[37] See T.R. Phillips, 'Hades', in *Evangelical Dictionary of Biblical Theology* (ed. W.A. Elwell; Grand Rapids, MI: Baker, 1996), 322–23; Philips, 'Hades', 323 continues: 'Jesus has promised that he will conquer Hades so that it will not defeat the church. Indeed, his resurrection establishes that this evil empire is already broken. Christ now holds the keys, the authority over death and Hades (Rev 1:18)!' *Pace* J. Jeremias, 'πύλη', *TDNT* VI, 924–28.

[38] Cullmann, *Peter*, 20, 192–93.

'petra' in the Greek of Matthew 16:18 is the fact that Cepha (or Kepha), rendered πέτρα as a feminine noun, could not be used as a proper name for a male; thus the need for Πέτρος. This, together with the fact that the two Greek terms Πέτρος (Peter) and ἡ πέτρα (rock) do not convey in Koine Greek significantly different semantic ranges, leads us to the conclusion that the exclusive identification of ἡ πέτρα (rock) with Peter's confession is not convincing.[39] Rather, the meaning of the entire phrase is that Jesus builds his invincible church upon Peter's confession *and* his transformed person as the primary, apostolic 'rock'-witness. In other words, the phrase 'and on this rock' does indeed point to the first rock, i.e., to Peter *and* his confession. Says Cullmann: 'here the name and the thing are exactly identical'.[40] Bockmuehl rightly combines John 1:42, 45 with Matthew 16:18 and notes: 'Simon is called Peter from the start, and Jesus then proceeds to say that he *is* Peter'.[41] In the present work we thus argue that both Peter as the apostolic spokesperson (in concert with other apostles) and his holistic confession of Christ are in view here.[42] In agreement with Cullmann there is, however, no warrant or justification for an apostolic (and church) succession in Jesus's statement, and even less so for the primacy of a Roman pontiff; says Cullmann: '[Roman Catholic exegesis] proceeds in an even more arbitrary way when it tries to find in this text a reference to "successors"'.[43] This accords approximately with the later positions of Chrysostom (the rock is Peter, his confession, and, by implication, the Twelve) as well as the Eastern Orthodox interpretation (with a simple focus on the apostolic faith).

The Apostle Peter with his confession (as a holistic witness) serves thus as a core building stone and rock, perpetually placed upon the foundational cornerstone, Jesus (see Mark 12:10-12; Acts 4:11; 1 Pet 2:4-8; cf. Matt 21:42; 1 Cor 3:11; 10:4; see also Ps 118:22-23; Isa 8:14; 28:16; Dan 2:34-35, 44-45

---

[39] See, however, Caragounis, *Peter*, 103–10, in favor of the interpretation that ἐπὶ ταύτῃ τῇ πέτρᾳ refers exclusively to Peter's preceding confession of Jesus as Messiah.

[40] Cullmann, *Peter*, 193; Helyer, *Life*, 44.

[41] Bockmuehl, *Simon*, 71; he concludes the paragraph by noting: 'Matthew here seems to preserve a sound Palestinian memory'.

[42] See S. Byrskog, *Jesus the Only Teacher: Didactic Authority and Transmission in Ancient Israel, Ancient Judaism and the Matthean* Community (Stockholm: Almqvist and Wiksell, 1994), 249.

[43] Cullmann, *Peter*, 213; Bockmuehl, *Simon*, 76. See also U. Luz, *Matthew in History: Interpretation, Influence, and Effects* (Minneapolis, MN: Fortress, 1994), 57–74, who argues that the view of apostolic succession is only attested from the third century onward and is particularly prominent in medieval and post-Reformation Roman Catholicism. My student, Alex Young, drew my attention to this.

[the messianic stone[44] growing into a kingdom, Luke 20:17-18]; Eph 2:20-22; Heb 10:21),[45] which will grow into the new and living temple of Christ's church (see the *house* of Israel, Num 12:7; Ruth 4:11; Amos 9:11; Acts 9:31).[46] The growth of this temple remains perpetually the direct and sustaining work of Jesus. Peter's holistic and foundational witness to Christ will continue to mark all other living stones built upon Christ. We cease to be truly 'apostolic' among God's people if we hold to any form of 'apostolic succession', since the 'person-and-witness' authority of Peter (and, by implication, the other eleven, together with James (Gal 1:19), the half-brother of Jesus, and Paul) is unique (see Acts 1:21-22), irreplaceable, and unrepeatable (cf. John 17:20; Rom 15:20; 1 Cor 3:10; Gal 2:9; Eph 2:20; Rev 21:14, 19). Cullmann states: '[i]n Matthew 16:18 Peter is addressed in his unrepeatable apostolic capacity'.[47] An irreplaceable aspect of such apostolic commission is the fact that he is a *direct* witness to the resurrection of Christ, as well as a witness to the life and death of Christ. Paul stands in some distance to these criteria: he is not a direct witness to the life and death of Jesus; and even his testimony to the resurrection of Jesus is expressed in a carefully nuanced way in Acts 13:31. Above all, it is the initial eyewitnesses who guarantee the fact of the resurrection of Jesus (chief among them, Peter). While Paul also encountered the resurrected Jesus, he does not consider himself on a par with the original eyewitnesses (cf. 1 Cor 15:5, 8). Peter as the apostolic spokesperson stands without parallel and cannot, on account of his uniqueness, be replicated. Peter, above all other apostles, is the appointed 'rock-witness' of Jesus's resurrection. As the leader of the collective witness, he vouchsafes that this witness is neither myth nor vision, but rather physical encounter with the resurrected Jesus. As such, the apostles are the foundation stones of the temple of Jesus, and chief among these stones is Peter. Any form of apostolic succession would thus detract authority from Peter's unique, ubiquitous, universal, and perpetually valid witness, which has been canonically encoded.

According to Cullmann,

> it is *only the work of building* which belongs to an unlimited future, *not the laying of the foundation of the rock* on which is built [sic]. In the future Jesus will build upon a foundation which is laid in the time of his

---

[44] Str-B, I, 877.

[45] See H.N. Ridderbos, *The Speeches of Peter in the Acts of the Apostles* (London: Tyndale Press, 1962), 11. Note the OT string of pearls in 1 Pet 2:6-8, focusing on the key term 'stone', which has its counterpart in the string of pearls in Mark 1:2-3, focusing on the key phrase 'prepare the way'.

[46] Cullmann, *Peter*, 199; cf. 1 Tim 3:15.

[47] See Cullmann, *Peter*, 215.

earthly career and in the time and person of the historical apostle, Peter.[48]

If someone wishes to follow Peter's primacy, he or she will need to adopt the binding faith-witness that Peter represented and embodied and refrain from unfounded claims to Roman apostolic succession and the primacy of the leadership of the Roman church. We posit that we can either hold to the apostolic authority of Peter as Jesus intended it to be *or* uphold him as the supposed founder of the Papal See in Rome from which apostolic succession is derived. We cannot do both. If we wish to be faithful to the Petrine apostolic tradition, especially as church leaders, we must ponder Peter's simple and clear apostolic witness and thus let Christ shape and form us.

As a point against Peter's life-and-faith witness, one could argue that Peter was initially a man of little faith (Matt 14:28-33) and that he denied Christ three times. While these events display weakness in Peter, we submit, however, that the 'rock' Jesus is referring to speaks of Peter's total witness and transformed person as a living stone-foundation in Jerusalem, Joppa, Antioch, Asia Minor, Corinth, and Rome.[49] Peter's apostolic witness and foundational testimony is the fruit of Christ's work in his life. Cullmann observes:

> Jesus knows better than anyone else the qualities of Peter, both the good and the bad ones, and he takes account of them in his view of the work he intends his disciples to do. On the other hand, however, the special distinction given this disciple as a rock-man rests on the Master's act of sovereign decision.[50]

In *this* way Peter also holds, together with other members of Christ's church, the 'keys' (as a metonymy for access to a building/temple)[51] of the kingdom of heaven (Matt 16:19; cf. Isa 22:22, as well as Gen 28:7; Ps 78:23). Here again, *Jesus continues to hold the keys in an ultimate sense* (see Rev 1:18, 'I have the keys of Death and Hades'; cf. Rev 3:7; 21:25).[52] Jesus is the one who is building his church and he is the one who holds its keys of entry (cf. 2 Pet 1:11). John 20:23 reinforces this: pronouncing or withholding forgiveness[53] is not absolutely in the hands of followers of Christ but it is always *derivative*:

---

[48] Cullmann, *Peter*, 214 (italics in the original).
[49] See Hengel, *Peter*, 49.
[50] Cullmann, *Peter*, 33.
[51] Cullmann, *Peter*, 209. Cf. M.P. Barber, 'Jesus as the Davidic Temple Builder and Peter's Priestly Role in Matthew 16:16-19', *JBL* 132.4 (2013), 935–53.
[52] See J.W. Bass, *The Battle for the Keys: Revelation 1:18 and Christ's Descent into the Underworld* (Milton Keynes: Paternoster, 2014), 36–44; 97–114.
[53] A.J. Köstenberger, *John* (Grand Rapids, MI: Baker Academic, 2004), 575.

Jesus remains the only one who forgives (Mark 2:5) and whose sacrifice atones (1 Pet 2:24). However, the apostolic witnesses, chief among them Peter, offer Christ's forgiveness by proclamation and conduct. Especially when we compare Matthew 16:19 with Matthew 18:18, it becomes apparent that the 'derivative keys' which Jesus gives to Peter are also given, to a lesser degree, to the church (see Isa 22:15-23, especially v. 22; John 20:23).

The 'loosening' which occurs in Matthew 18:18 is the mediated work of the Holy Spirit by members of the church in bringing a sinning person (Matt 18:15a) to repentance and to reconciliation (Matt 18:15b). 'Binding' (stating, prohibitively, the sinner's resistance to God's conviction, Matt 18:17b) and 'loosening' (e.g., permitting repentance, Matt 18:15b)[54] *affirm* what has happened in the heart of a rebelling person following exposure to the gospel's and thus the Holy Spirit's truth (Matt 18:15a). The meaning of 'binding' and 'loosening' is the authoritative forbidding, prohibiting, or banning ('binding') and authoritative permitting or acquitting ('loosening') of something.[55] While it is possible that Jesus's statements in Matthew 16:19 and 18:18 are similar in meaning to later rabbinic 'loosening' and 'binding' whereby various decisions especially of the Sanhedrin (interpreting the law; community exclusion/inclusion, *b. Ḥag.* 3b; *b. Šabb.* 31a–b, *Sipre* on Deut 32:25 [Isa 22:22]; *b. Sanh.* 38b) are viewed as subsequently *sanctioned* by God,[56] the efficacy of gospel transformation (e.g., the anticipated repentance in Matt 18:15-20) always safeguards that human decisions do *not* overrule what is God's own domain. In other words: Peter and the church 'bind' (forbid/ban) and 'loosen' (permit/acquit) what God has *already* bound and loosened, displayed, e.g., in repentance (see Matt 18:19; Rev 3:7; cf. John 6:44). Due to the overall *expansive thrust* of the entire passage, 'loosening' through Peter's authentic gospel witness is by far more emphasized than the concept of 'binding'. 'Loosening' (acquitting) and 'binding' (banning) through Peter (Matt 16:19; *and* other followers, Matt 18:18) does not refer to holding an authoritative office as a bishop or church leader but constitutes Peter's apostolic witness to Christ in word *and* in his transformed, Christlike person, in which regeneration, repentance, and conversion (thus community inclusion) happen, as worked by the Holy Spirit. 'Loosening' and 'binding' occurs under the direct authority of God, *mediated* by Peter and other followers of Christ.

---

[54] See the paronomasia אסר (bind) – שרא (loose).

[55] Cullmann, *Peter*, 211, distinguishes perhaps too sharply between 'prohibiting'/ 'permitting' and 'putting under the ban'/'acquitting'. Helyer, *Life*, 44, refers to 1QH 5:36; 1QM 5:3; CD 13:10. See also Köstenberger, *John*, 575–76, and n. 23.

[56] Cf. Hengel, *Peter*, 4–5.

This interpretation accords with both Matthew 16:19 and 18:18, as well as John 20:23.

The best answer to the question of how Peter is *holding the keys* entrusted to him by Jesus, as well as how he is 'loosening' and 'binding', is his public ministry described in the early chapters of Acts. Peter perpetually points in his word-and-life witness to the place where God provides forgiveness (see, e.g., Acts 2:38; cf. John 20:23),[57] namely, in Christ, through Spirit-led regeneration and repentance. His apostolic witness and transformed identity bring many thousands (Jews, Samaritans, Gentiles) into the kingdom of Jesus.[58] As Peter is faithful to his master, many people are 'loosened' and, in some cases, 'bound' by Peter's proclamation and transformed person. The Epistles of 1 and 2 Peter can serve as further illustrations of how Peter 'holds the keys' and 'loosens' and 'binds'. He serves as an admonishing and encouraging example, as a co-leader (1 Pet 5:1), witnessing to the reality of Christ, the chief shepherd (1 Pet 2:25),[59] thus binding and loosening in a *derivative* way among his hearers. While Peter's confession and person as the foundation-laying rock are irreplaceably unique in the life of Peter, 'loosening' and 'binding' are proclamation activities which also go beyond Peter's unique ministry and extend to the church at large, as it clings to the cornerstone, Jesus, and listens to his 'apostolic rock'.

It is our contention then that the most promising way of understanding the *purpose* of Matthew 16:18-19, besides the analysis of the text in its given context (see above), is to explore how Peter arises in both Acts and in 1 and 2 Peter as a fulfillment of Matthew 16:18-19. Our explorations in Acts and 1 and 2 Peter will thus serve as correctives for ill-guided interpretations of Matthew 16:18-19 and as reinforcements of appropriate interpretations. Given our analyses of these texts (see below), we believe that they indeed confirm our observations presented above. We do not encounter in Acts and 1 and 2 Peter a pontiff (in Jerusalem, Antioch, or Rome) who advocates the primacy of a particular local church or apostolic succession. Rather, we encounter an increasingly contrite and tested person who is strictly devoted to the apostolic witness-commission, reflecting a personal brokenness, humility, and Christ-likeness, which opposes the elevation of his ministry (see 1 Pet 5:1-3) and the

---

[57] Helyer, *Life*, 45, claims that beyond Peter's commission to announce 'the terms of admittance', Peter 'establishes the limits of acceptable behavior within that fellowship'. The latter is supported by Josephus, *J.W.* 1.111; *T. Levi* 18.12; *T. Sol.* 1:14. If the latter is present, it is much more a matter of testifying to Jesus's teaching and of ensuing communal decisions (cf. Acts 15).

[58] See, similarly, Helyer, *Life*, 69–82.

[59] See K.E. Bailey, *The Good Shepherd: A Thousand-Year Journey from Psalm 23 to the New Testament* (Downers Grove, IL: IVP Academic, 2014).

elevation of any local church. Rather, Peter gives Christ true honor and glory in the midst of the universal temple,[60] of which Christ is the cornerstone and in which Peter's apostolic witness is the foundation, laid once and for all. In Christ and through Peter's once-and-for-all life testimony, all disciples of Christ can access the one life that comes always and only from God, as mediated by his eternal Son (see Acts 3:6-7). It is in this sense, also, that the kingdom has been 'assigned' or 'conferred' (Luke 22:29-30, διατίθεμαι) to the disciples.

Peter's Apostolic Witness in Acts and Old Testament Prophetic Repentance Speeches

A second non-transferable aspect of Peter's calling is found in the surprising fact that Peter arises in Acts[61] as a prophetic repentance preacher using the format of Old Testament repentance speeches. As Jesus predicts that Peter will turn (ἐπιστρέφω) in his heart (Luke 22:32; cf. Luke 1:16-17), he now calls for the repentant turning of the hearts of his hearers (Acts 2:38; 3:19, 26; 5:31; 9:35; 15:19) to the Messiah of God (Luke 9:18-20).

Peter as Spokesman for the Collective Apostolic Witness of the Twelve

Cullmann observes:

> For the period following the death of Jesus the question concerning the unique position of Peter presents itself in another way. The disciple becomes the apostle of the crucified and risen Lord. In this capacity his unique position necessarily takes on another character.[62]

It is indeed important to understand the place and function Peter occupies in earliest Christianity. Acts 1–9 portray Peter not so much as an individual

---

[60] See Barber, 'Davidic Temple Builder', 935–53, in support of the motif of temple building, the priestly use of temple keys, and of 'binding' and 'loosing' as access to the temple in Matt 16:16-19.

[61] According to Jerome, *Vir. ill.* 7, Acts was written in Rome. See also Marcion's access to Luke's Gospel around AD 140 in Rome, as well as Justin Martyr, Hermas and Irenaeus. See Bockmuehl, *Simon*, 113–14, regarding Lukan hints of insider knowledge concerning the travel route of Paul to Rome.

[62] Cullmann, *Peter*, 33.

witness, but rather as the *spokesperson* of the collective apostolic witness group (see, e.g., Acts 2:14).[63] It has often been observed that whatever laudable and exposing descriptions we have of Peter in the Gospels and Acts, there is the conspicuous fact that he functions as the spokesman for the original apostles as he interacts with Jesus and especially as he arises as the key witness to Jesus's death and resurrection. Some historical-critical studies of Acts acknowledge this fact, attributing the phenomenon, however, virtually exclusively to Lukan composition,[64] while more conservative analyses tend to overlook the aspect of Peter as a spokesperson of the Twelve.[65] Without entering into the detailed argumentation, we can say with confidence that Luke certainly *intended* to portray Peter as the representative of the apostolic group (cf. Acts 2:14, 37, 42; 3:4, 12; 4:7-8, 13, 19, 24-30; [compare with 4:32]; 5:2-3, 29; 6:2; 8:14-25), thus emphasizing a collective witness to the resurrection of Jesus, led by Peter.[66] In significant contrast to this, Luke presents Peter from Acts 9:32 to 15:11, with a preliminary ending at 12:19, much more as an *individual* (cf., e.g., Acts 11:1; 15:6), while he still serves in the company of other believers (see, e.g., Acts 10:45; 11:12; 15:6). Once Peter sets out to witness beyond the confines of Jerusalem (see especially Acts 12:17; cf. 1 Cor 9:5),[67] the collective apostolic witness and leadership of Peter fades into the background in favor of Peter's missional ministry. When Peter works as an apostolic witness beyond Jerusalem, he is portrayed much more like Paul, Stephen, or Philip.

Given this telling *contrast* in the portrayal of Peter within Acts itself, it is safe to say that Luke wishes to emphasize the historical fact apparent in the *initial* stages of the early church (Acts 1:1–9:32 and prior to Peter's work *outside of Jerusalem*), namely, that Peter represents the collective witness of the Twelve and that the other apostles confirm and endorse the witness and leadership of Peter.[68]

---

[63] The significant theme of 'witness' in Acts has frequently been investigated; see, e.g., M.L. Soards, *The Speeches in Acts: Their Content, Context, and Concerns* (Louisville, KY: Westminster/John Knox, 1994), 283–86 and 302 n. 14.

[64] See, e.g., U. Wilckens, *Die Missionsreden der Apostelgeschichte* (3rd ed.; Neukirchen-Vluyn: Neukirchener Verlag, 1974), 193–207; cf. Soards, *Speeches*, 65–90.

[65] Foakes-Jackson, *Peter*, 75, is too simplistic; consequently, he cannot make sense, e.g., of the presence of John with Peter in Acts 3; see Foakes-Jackson, *Peter*, 78.

[66] See Cullmann, *Peter*, 34–38.

[67] Cullmann, *Peter*, 38–39. For a discussion on whether Peter did indeed visit Corinth (cf. 1 Cor 9:5), see Helyer, *Life*, 98–99.

[68] *Pace* Foakes-Jackson, *Peter*, 80. See H.F. Bayer, 'The Preaching of Peter in Acts' in I.H. Marshall and D. Peterson (eds), *Witness to the Gospel: The Theology of Acts* (Grand Rapids, MI: Eerdmans, 1998), 257–74 and P. Perkins, *Peter: Apostle for the Whole Church* (Edinburgh: T&T Clark, 2000), 95. In his analysis of second century data on Peter, Perkins (*Peter*, 151–67, esp. 159) makes the interesting observation

A more detailed look at Peter's Pentecost and temple speeches (Acts 2:14-36, 38-39, 40b; 3:12b-26) confirms what we have laid out above. Ridderbos points out that one of the literary features of the speeches in Acts within the unfolding narrative of the book is that many of them display a similar structural format concerning early Christian preaching (see especially, regarding Peter: Acts 2:14-36, 38-40; 3:12-26; 10:34-43; compare, regarding Paul: Acts 13:16-41),[69] thus implying the fundamental unity of the early Christian message.[70] The historical-critical work of such scholars as Dibelius, Wilckens, and Schneider has advanced the skeptical alternative to the above-mentioned view.[71] These scholars claim that the similarities among the speeches in Acts are evidence for Lukan composition.[72] It is at least clear that Luke *intends* to give the impression that the message was proclaimed with an abiding core shared by all preachers in Acts, allowing at the same time for unique emphases and telling particularities to surface at various points.[73]

We have argued elsewhere that the first three chapters of Acts lay the foundation and set the stage for the unfolding narrative.[74] This pertains, among other issues, to Christology, pneumatology, and eschatology. In other words, as Peter arises as the spokesperson for the Twelve, his early speeches may very well represent apostolic witness and *also* lay the foundation for the theological tone and framework of Acts, and by possible implication, earliest (even pre-Pauline) Christianity.

Based on the following observations it is possible to view Peter as a prominent, albeit not personally isolated and identifiable force behind the collective apostolic witness of earliest Christianity, shaping its theological tone which

---

that Peter figured for gnostic and orthodox Christians as 'the spokesperson for the understanding of Christian truth held by the majority of Christians'.

[69] Ridderbos, *Speeches*, 1–10.

[70] Soards (*Speeches*, 296) emphasizes 'repetition' as a unifying element in the speeches in Acts (e.g., 'witness', 'God's sovereignty', the 'centrality of Christ').

[71] It is apparent that Wilckens has considerably changed many of his views as evidenced in his more recent work (e.g., U. Wilckens, *Theologie des Neuen Testaments* [Neukirchen-Vluyn: Neukirchener Verlag, 2005]).

[72] The possibility of Lukan creative composition of the speeches must be considered. However, there are sufficient points of dissimilarity between the respective speeches to suggest that Ridderbos is handling the evidence essentially in a responsible manner. Ridderbos' *historical explanation* of the literary phenomenon is never seriously entertained even in the third ed. of Wilckens, *Missionsreden*, 193–207.

[73] See for further details on the following H.F. Bayer, 'Christ-Centered Eschatology in Acts 3:17-26', in J.B. Green and M. Turner (eds), *Jesus of Nazareth, Lord and Christ* (Grand Rapids, MI: Eerdmans, 1994), 236–50, here 237–41.

[74] Bayer, 'Preaching', 257–61.

Luke reflects in Acts (cf. Luke 1:1-4; see below for supportive evidence).

In a previously published study, we used the test case of eschatology to explore this supposition in some detail. We sought to demonstrate that Peter as a spokesperson for the apostolic group sets the tone of the eschatological framework for the entire book of Acts.[75] We noted that while the topic of eschatology fades after Acts 3, it provides the interpretive framework for the outpouring of the Holy Spirit[76] and the unfolding narrative of Acts.[77] The eschatological framework is that of Christ-centered, event-focused fulfillment of prophecy in the unfolding of redemptive history (cf. 1 Pet 1:10-12; 2 Pet 3:2), without conveying a strict time frame for outstanding eschatological events (cf. 2 Pet 3:8-10), most prominent among them: Christ's Parousia, associated with the Last Judgment and the resurrection of the dead.[78] Since so many of God's redemptive purposes have been realized through Christ's work, there is a deep and vivid anticipation of the Parousia, though not in terms of specific time frames.[79]

Detailed study of the test case of eschatology in Acts thus yields the result that the Petrine speeches (especially in Acts 2 and 3) neither contain an extreme near-expectation (see the contingent elements of 'delay' in Acts 3:18-26),[80] nor a distant far-expectation with regard to the timing of the Parousia of Christ (see

---

[75] Bayer, 'Eschatology', 236–41.
[76] See Isa 31:31-34; Ezek 36:25-35; Joel [LXX] 2:28-32; Zech 1:3-6; Mal 4:5-6; 1QS 55:20-21; *T. Levi* 8:14; *T. Benj.* 9:2; Luke 3:16. Cf. K. Giles, 'Present-Future Eschatology in the Book of Acts', 2 parts, *RTR* 40, 3 (1981) 65–71; *RTR* 41, 1 (1982) 11–18; here, part 2, 12.
[77] Isa 49:6; cf. Luke 21:24; 24:47.
[78] Cf. Acts 1:11; 2:17 and 3:20; Bayer, 'Eschatology', 239 n. 22.
[79] Giles, 'Eschatology', 2:18. Contra, P. Vielhauer, 'Zum "Paulinismus" der Apostelgeschichte', in P. Vielhauer, *Aufsätze zum Neuen Testament* (Munich: Chr. Kaiser, 1965), 9–27 and H. Conzelmann, *Die Mitte der Zeit: Studien zur Theologie des Lukas* (Tübingen: Mohr Siebeck, 1962), 87–127, who deny Luke a vital expectation of the Parousia on the basis of questionable and unsupported redaction-critical premises.
[80] See J.T. Carroll, *Response to the End of History: Eschatology and Situation in Luke–Acts* (Atlanta, GA: Scholars Press, 1988), 165–67. See also I.H. Marshall, *The Gospel of Luke: A Commentary on the Greek Text* (Grand Rapids, MI: Eerdmans, 1983), 783, who rightly considers it to be a false 'assumption that Jesus did not expect an interval before the parousia'. Cf. also H.F. Bayer, *Jesus' Predictions of Vindication and Resurrection* (Tübingen: Mohr Siebeck, 1986), 244–49. See, e.g., Luke 12:35-48 and Acts 1:6-8. The certainty of the sudden coming of Christ (Luke 21:34-35) constitutes the foundation of Luke's portrayed future expectation. See Luke 17:22-37; 21:24-28, 34-36; Acts 1:6-11; 3:19-26; see further Acts 10:42 and 17:31. Regarding near-expectation, see, e.g., Luke 18:1-8; 21:32.

elements of 'imminence' in Acts 2:16-21; cf. Luke. 21:29-36).[81] The future expectation of Christ's Parousia in Acts is cast by Peter in the context of both fulfilled (the outpouring of the Spirit at Pentecost) and yet anticipated redemptive-historical events (e.g., the *times of refreshment* and *restitution* of all things prophesied in the Old Testament; Acts 3:20-21). Open-ended time sequences take their place within this redemptive-historical framework.[82] The potential tension between far- and near-expectation is resolved by Peter's Christ-centered and event-focused approach. Peter thus may very well have shaped the entire outlook of future expectation in the early church, a notion which Luke reflects in his historical witness account of Acts. In particular, the Pentecost speech in Acts 2 addresses the *present fulfillment* of a central end-time event, while the temple speech in Acts 3 alludes to *past, present, and future* redemptive-historical events.[83] Regarding the past, Peter, as a spokesperson,[84] testifies to God's great, culminating deed in raising Jesus from death; regarding the present and future, the temple speech calls the Jewish audience to repentance which, in turn, anticipates sovereign acts of the resurrected and exalted Christ as a fulfillment of God's universal mission.[85]

In contrast to the historical-critical discussion driven by Conzelmann,[86] we can state that there is no convincing evidence that Luke sought to compensate for a supposed but unsubstantiated 'delay of the Parousia'[87] of Christ in early Christianity by highlighting present fulfillment (Luke 17:20-21; Acts 2:22-24). Rather, we can state that the early apostolically representative Petrine speeches recorded in Acts shape Luke's much more balanced eschatological outlook; an impression he, at least, wishes to create.[88]

---

[81] See also Marshall, *Luke*, 781; Soards, *Speeches*, 279. Cf. B.R. Gaventa, 'The Eschatology of Luke–Acts Revisited', *Enc* 43.1 (1982) 27–42, for an overview of current positions on Lukan eschatology.

[82] Cf. Bayer, 'Eschatology', 243–45; 249–50.

[83] Carroll, *Response*, 137–51. *Pace* Foakes-Jackson, *Peter*, 77–79, who can only detect near-expectation features in Peter's speeches in Acts 2 and 3.

[84] Bayer, 'Eschatology', 249–50.

[85] Cf. Soards, *Speeches*, 279.

[86] Conzelmann, *Mitte*, 87–127.

[87] See Carroll, *Response*, 166 and D.E. Aune, 'The Significance of the Delay of the Parousia for Early Christianity', in G.F. Hawthorne (ed.), *Current Issues in Biblical and Patristic Interpretation* (Grand Rapids, MI: Eerdmans, 1975), 87–109. Aune concludes: 'We found no evidence to suggest that the so-called problem of the delay of the Parousia was in fact perceived as a problem by early Christians' (Aune, 'Significance', 109).

[88] Bayer, 'Eschatology', 249–50.

Regarding the test case of eschatology in the early chapters of Acts, we thus stress that Peter, as the representative spokesperson of the collective witness group, presents eschatology as a Christ-dependent, redemptive-historical event sequence, thus guarding against heterodox extremes of a far- or near-expectation of the Parousia of Christ which Paul later exposes (see 1 Thess 4:13; 5:3; 2 Thess 2:3).

We will argue below that Peter arises as a preacher of repentance according to the pattern of prophetic Old Testament repentance speeches. In such speeches, the divine redemptive-historical acts and events likewise take central stage, not time frames. In other words, Peter understands that God's mission does not so much follow a precise time line as it is structured around sequences of redemptive-historical events, sovereignly executed by God. The presence of Christ as Messiah and Lord (Acts 2:36) is the most significant and central redemptive-historical event in God's unfolding mission. Peter provides the prophetic perspective in earliest Christianity, which reflects Jesus's redemptive-historical view of future events, including their present realizations. This balanced, Christ-centered, and event-focused future expectation accords generally with Jesus's eschatological discourse (Mark 13, parr), as well as the future anticipation expressed in 1 and 2 Peter (see below). It will become apparent that Peter proclaims in the early speeches in Acts an eschatological perspective learned from Jesus (compare Mark 1:14-15 with 14:25).[89]

We conclude that in Acts 1:1–9:32, Peter functions as the spokesperson of the collective group of apostolic witnesses. As such, he also presents a fundamental christological, pneumatological, and eschatological architecture, which may very well stem from Jesus's own systematic instruction. Furthermore, while his message is, broadly speaking, similar to that of other witnesses presented in Acts, particular *emphases* are visible, such as framing the Christ-centered, event-focused eschatological outlook of the early church.

Peter's Preaching as Patterned after Old Testament Prophetic Repentance Speeches

We now turn to one of the most surprising and exceptional apostolic functions of Peter. In the early chapters of Acts, Peter does not only arise as a spokesperson for the apostolic witness-group, but, more importantly, he arises as a prophetic repentance preacher patterned after Old Testament prophetic repentance speeches. This fact carries profound implications for our study,

---

[89] H.F. Bayer, 'The Eschatological Prospect in the Context of Mark', in D.W. Baker (ed.), *Looking into the Future: Evangelical Studies in Eschatology* (Grand Rapids, MI: Baker, 2001), 74–84.

since Peter thus arises as the prophetic 'rock' about which Jesus spoke to him (Matt 16:18-19).[90]

There is no doubt that early preaching in Acts was viewed as apostolic *witness* (μάρτυς; see Acts 1:8). A good case can be made that Old Testament prophets understood themselves as admonishing witnesses and that the witness-commission of Peter is thus closely associated with a prophetic self-understanding.[91] A first hint that Peter actually arises as a prophetic repentance preacher in earliest Christianity is given by the solemnity of his speeches. There is an emphatic and solemn tone of speech in Acts 2:14,[92] 21, 29, 36 (as well as in 4:10 and 10:34).[93] We further note a particular and repeated self-awareness in Peter as a personal witness of the resurrection (Acts 1:22; 2:32; 3:15; 5:32; 10:39-41; see Mark 16:7; cf. Luke 24:34; 1 Cor 15:5).[94] As such, Peter's obedience to God far surpasses his respect for man (Acts 4:19; 5:4, 29).[95]

---

[90] See Ridderbos, *Speeches*, 11.

[91] Regarding the connection between 'witness' and 'prophet', see O.H. Steck, *Israel und das gewaltsame Geschick der Propheten: Untersuchungen zur Überlieferung des deuteronomistischen Geschichtsbildes im Alten Testament, Spätjudentum und Urchristentum* (Neukirchen-Vluyn: Neukirchener, 1967), 162–65. See Isa 8:16; Neh 9:26; Zech 3:6-7; 1 Macc 2:56, and *Jub.* 1:12 where the prophetic call is understood as a witness ministry (cf. Deut 32:46). Likewise, the outpouring of the Holy Spirit can point to prophetic commissioning. In this sense, the apostolic commission of Peter was also a prophetic one (see Steck, *Israel*, 263–89; cf. the 3rd ed. of Wilckens, *Missionsreden*, 189). Similar research has been undertaken regarding Paul's apostolic and prophetic ministry; see T. Holtz, 'Zum Selbstverständnis des Apostels Paulus', *TLZ* 91 (1966), 321–30 (cf. Isa 39–62); cf. K.O. Sandnes, *Paul–One of the Prophets?: A Contribution to the Apostle's Self-Understanding* (Tübingen: Mohr Siebeck, 1991). See Rom 1:1-5; 10:14-18; 11:25-36; 1 Cor 2:6-12; 9:15-18; 2 Cor 4:6; Gal 1:15-16a; 1 Thess 2:3-8; cf. Acts 11:27-28; 21:10-14; 26:16-32; Eph 2:29–3:7.

[92] Cf. F.F. Bruce, *The Acts of the Apostles: The Greek Text with Introduction and Commentary* (Grand Rapids, MI: Eerdmans, 1986), 88–89.

[93] *Cf.* Soards, *Speeches*, 83.

[94] In support of Luke's careful reporting it is noteworthy that Paul's reference to 'witness' in Acts 13:31 *points away from himself* to the original collective group of apostolic witnesses. In Acts 22:15 and 26:16, Jesus declares Paul as a 'witness'. In Acts 22:20 Paul calls Stephen a 'witness'. Paul never refers to himself as a 'witness' in Acts (see, however, 1 Cor 15:8). There is thus a clear distinction both in Acts and 1 Cor between direct eyewitnesses of Jesus according to the definition given in Acts 1:21-22 and a witness like Paul, who did (merely) encounter the risen Christ at the gates of Damascus.

[95] See also Peter's emphasis that God is impartial (Acts 10:34; cf. 1 Pet 1:17).

A closer comparison between the pattern and content of Old Testament prophetic repentance speeches and Peter's speeches, especially in Acts 2 and 3, yields a most significant discovery regarding Peter in Acts: Peter's authority and claim is that of a 'prophet of repentance' before YHWH, assuming the well-established pattern and message of Old Testament (and intertestamental) prophetic repentance speeches. As such, Peter the prophet is calling the people of Israel to turn to YHWH on account of God's most recent deeds among them. The basic pattern (with many variations) includes the following elements:[96]

1. The unfaithfulness of Israel to God
2. God's faithfulness[97]
    a. *The description of the longsuffering of God with his people*[98]
    b. *His gracious and redemptive acts among his people,* which are sometimes connected with the
    c. *Fulfillment of prophecy;* therefore, Israel receives a
    d. *Prophetic admonition/call to repentance.*
3. *The hard-hearted persistence of Israel's ways against God, combined with the rejection of God's warning prophets* leads to[99]
4. Punishment, restoration, and final judgment through
    a. The announcement of impending punishment and, additionally, at times:[100]
    b. The promise that punishment is averted, if Israel *repents, and*
    c. *Salvation and restoration ensues,* or
    d. Final judgment ensues in the absence of repentance.

---

[96] The numbers and lower case letters in the above-given list correspond roughly to the following upper case letters and numbers assigned by Steck, *Israel*, 63, 68, 85, 117, 122–28, 133: 1=A; 2a=B; 2b=Ph; 2c=Pe; 2d=B1; 3=C; 4a=D; 4b=E; 4c=F and F1; 4d=F2. Steck uses the following abbreviations: A=history of unfaithfulness and rebellion of Israel; B=the long-suffering of God, displayed by prophetic warnings; B1=the call to repentance, embedded in the call; Pe=fulfillment of an OT prophecy; Ph=redemptive-historical prophecies which find their culmination in Christ; C=rebellion, despite the call to repentance; D=judgment on account of rebellion; E=repentance of Israel; F=salvation; F1=salvific restitution; F2=final judgment. See D.P. Moessner, 'Paul in Acts: Preacher of Eschatological Repentance to Israel', *NTS* 1.34 (1988), 97–101, who traces the motif in the Gospel of Luke (Luke 11:37-54; 13:34-35; 19:42-44; 21:8-36).

[97] The aspects which correspond especially to key elements in Peter's early speeches in Acts are set in *italics*.

[98] A good example for the combined motif of God's faithfulness and Israel's rebellion is Ps 78.

[99] See Mark 12:1-10; Luke 6:22-23; 11:47-54 and 13:34-35, regarding general references to the violent end of repentance preachers.

[100] Steck, *Israel*, 67–71.

Many variations to this basic pattern are visible throughout the ages. Especially the second and fourth segments display variations and additions in certain context and times (see below, on segment 2). At times, the fourth segment holds out either a conditional ('if you do not return or repent') announcement of judgment (followed by segments 4b and 4c), or the irreversible decision of God to mete out predicted judgment (segment 4d).

The Old Testament (and Intertestamental) Background for Peter as a Prophetic Repentance Preacher

What we have sketched above regarding this long-established motif has been extensively researched by O.H. Steck.[101] Steck traces a recurring and varying pattern of prophetic repentance speeches, often associated with the violent fate of God's prophets, spanning from the Old Testament and the intertestamental period through the Gospels and Acts to rabbinic Judaism, even to some apostolic and post-apostolic fathers.[102] Given this long-standing tradition, Steck notes: '[We have] a century-old conceptual and vital tradition . . . whose theological, tradition-historical . . . significance cannot easily be overestimated in intertestamental Palestinian Judaism, but also in early Palestinian Christianity.'[103] In the following paragraphs, we offer some details of this telling phenomenon.

From the times of the Old Testament until the time of Emperor Titus (AD 79–81) and beyond, there is in Judaism[104] an ongoing interest in and documentable literary trail of the variable motif of a call to repentance to Israel.[105] This motif serves as a prophetic interpretive framework to various redemptive-historical events in the history of Israel, but it does not exert itself as a corset. The different historical events in the tragic history of Israel

---

[101] See more recently, D.P. Moessner, *Lord of the Banquet: The Literary and Theological Significance of the Lukan Travel Narrative* (Minneapolis, MN: Fortress, 1989), 296–307, who asserts that Jesus is portrayed as the Prophet-like-Moses and that Peter, Paul, and Stephen arise in that framework. Cf. B. Rosner, 'Acts and Biblical History', in B.W. Winter and A.D. Clarke (eds), *The Book of Acts in its Ancient Literary Setting* (vol. I of *The Book of Acts in its First Century Setting;* ed. B.W. Winter; Grand Rapids, MI: Eerdmans, 1993) 65–82; esp. 71 and nn. 31–33.

[102] Steck, *Israel*, 60–214.

[103] Steck, *Israel*, 318.

[104] Diaspora Judaism does not seem to develop a motif separate and distinct from this. It is missing in Wis, 1–2 Macc; *3–4 Macc.*; cf. Steck, *Israel*, 184 n. 2.

[105] Steck, *Israel*, 191.

continuously offer new occasions for this motif to occur. The motif may very well be one of the key theological frameworks within which Old Testament prophets (and Palestinian Judaism) express and interpret Israel's challenging and, at times, confounding history.[106]

Among the key Old Testament texts for the above-mentioned pattern of prophetic repentance speeches are:[107] *Deut 4:25-31; 28:45-68; 30:1-10;* 1 Kgs 8:46-53; 17:7-20; 18:4, 13; 19:10, 14; *2 Kgs 17:13;* 22:17; *2 Chr 15:1-7; 29:5-11; 30:6-9; 36:14-16, 17-21*; Ezra 9:11; *Neh* 1:9, 11; *9:5-38*; Isa 63:7-10, 11-17; 64:1-4; *Jer 2:30; 3:12-14*, 15-16; *7:3-32; 14:7-9*; 25:3-14; 26:1-24 (2-6); 29:17-19; 35:13-17; 44:1-14; Lam 3:40-41, 64-66; 4:21-22b; *Ezek 14:6-7; 18:30-31*; Dan 9:6; Joel 2:12-20; Mic 7:7-20; *Zech 1:2-8; 7:4-14; 8:1-23; Mal 3:6-7*.[108]

A summary of the contents of the most significant Old Testament texts yields the following overall impression as outlined above: God's faithfulness, despite Israel's unfaithfulness, is pervasive (Neh 9:5-38). Israel's rebellion and idolatry lead to predictions of various forms of punishment and judgment, unless repentance occurs (Deut 4:25-31; 28:45-68; Ezra 9:11; 2 Kgs 17:13; 2 Chr 29:5-11; 36:14-21; Jer 2:30; 7:3-32; Ezek 14:6-11; Zech 7:4-14). At times, hope of restoration is in view (Deut 30:1-10; 2 Chr 15:1-7; 30:6b-9; Jer 3:12–4:14; Ezek 18:30-31; Zech 1:2-8; 7:4-14; Mal 3:6-7).

We might identify Nehemiah 9:5-38 as the paragon of a proper *response* to Old Testament repentance speeches (cf. also Jer 14:7-9). In the context of confession and worship, we find:

a. an acknowledgement of the majesty of the God of this universe;
b. a remembrance of redemptive history (Abraham, Moses, exodus);
c. a confession of the rebellion of the forefathers in the desert;
d. a confession of the rebellion of the generation that took the land of Canaan;

---

[106] Steck, *Israel*, 189.

[107] The most characteristic and significant texts are set in *italics*.

[108] Subsequent to the OT, there are many intertestamental texts continuing and developing the motif of prophetic calls to repentance, which are, at times, also associated with the motif of the violent fate of God's prophets: Tob 3:1-6; 4:12; 5:31; 13:1-6; *T. 12 Patr.* (Levi 10:2-5; 14:1-8; 15:1-4; 16:1-5; Jud. 23:1-5; Iss. 6:1-4; Zeb. 9:5-9; Dan 5:4-9; Naph. 4:1-5; Ash. 7:2-5); *1 En.* 90:6-26; 91:12-17; 93:1-10; *Jub.* 1:7-26; 7:20; 20:2; Bar 1:15–5:9; CD 1:1-13a; 4QDibHam^a 1:8; 5:12-14; 6:5-7; *Pss. Sol.* 2; 8; 9; 17; *As. Mos.*, 2–10; *L.A.B.* (Ps.-Philo) 3:9-10; 12:4; 13:10; 14:27-35; 19:2-7; 20:3b-4; 23:7; 30:1-3; *4 Ezra* 3; 7:1, 2, 7-9; 14, 27-35; *2 Bar.* 1:1-5; 4:1-6; 31:1-3; 32:1; 44:1-3, 7a, 14-15; 45:1; 77:1-2, 6a, 16. Intertestamental texts thus document that various repentance preachers understood themselves in the line of OT prophets (see esp. *Jub.* 1:12; *L.A.B.* [Ps.-Philo] 23:7; *4 Ezra* 7:1, 2, 9-10).

e. a remembrance of repeated rebellion, suffering, confession, and the mercy of God up to the Babylonian captivity; and
f. subsequent repentance and deliverance.

Two key aspects of the motif of prophetic Old Testament repentance speeches are of particular importance to our question of how the Petrine speeches in Acts can be characterized:

1. The occasional enlargement of the repentance speeches by the elements of the 'repentance of Israel', 'restitution', and 'final judgment in the absence of repentance' (segments 4b–4d), and
2. The fact that the motif of the violent death of God's prophets is often associated with these prophetic calls to repentance.

Regarding point 1, there are four varying perspectives surrounding the motif of repentance speeches which often call to following the law of Moses:[109]

a. Repentance speeches culminate in announcing the judgment by YHWH over all of Israel (Jer; Lam 1–2, and perhaps Ezra 9).
b. Repentance speeches holding out the possibility of repentance (Deut 4:25-31; 28:45-68; 30:1-10 and 1 Kgs 8:46-53)[110] as well as the possibility of restitution in case of repentance (Deut 4:31; 30:1-10; 2 Kgs 17:13; Neh 1:9; Ps 79:9, 11; 106:47; Isa 63:17; 64:1-4; Lam 3:22-33; 4:22; 5:21; cf. Tob 3:1-6; 13:1-6; Bar 2:34-35; 4QDibHam^a 6:11-15).[111] In case of repentance and restitution, Israel's enemies will be judged (Lev 26:32-42; Deut 4:25-32;[112] 30:1-3;[113] 1 Kgs 8:46-50; Ps 79:6, 10, 12; Isa 64:1-2; Lam 1:22; 3:64-66; 4:21, 22b; cf., indirectly, Neh 9:32, 36-37; Zech 1:2-3, 7-8; Mal 3:7; cf. Bar 2:33; 3:7; Tob 3:1-6; *T. 12 Patr.*; *Jub.* 1:7-26; Dan 9; Bar 1:15-17; 4QDibHam^a 5:12-14; 6:5-7).
c. Repentance speeches occur in the context of the *last times* where repentance is possible (cf. *1 En.*; *Jub.*; Bar 1:15-17; 4; *As. Mos.*; *Ps.-Philo*; *4 Ezra*; *2 Bar.*; 4QDibHam^a 1:8-10; cf. Acts 2). Those who

---

[109] Cf. Steck, *Israel*, 185–87.
[110] Steck, *Israel*, 139.
[111] Steck, *Israel*, 123 n. 3.
[112] Cf. Steck, *Israel*, 139–41.
[113] In Deut 28:45-68 and 30:1-10 we find expanded portrayals of the Deuteronomistic view of history, Steck, *Israel*, 141.

repent, receive blessing (*1 En.*; *Jub.*; CD 1:1-12;[114] *Pss. Sol.*; Ps.-Philo *[L.A.B.]*; *4 Ezra*; *2 Bar.*; Bar 4:1b). For those *Israelites* and enemies of Israel who do not repent, final judgment ensues (e.g., *T. 12 Patr.*). In other words: even unrepentant Israel will come under final judgment.[115]

d. At times, Old Testament repentance preachers include a future prophecy (see, e.g., Jer 3:12-16; 7:3-25; 14:6-7; Ezek 18:30-31; Zech 1:3; 7:8-10; Mal 3:7).

The pervasive motif of a call to repentance is not only found in prophetic speeches but can also appear in the following contexts:
- a prayer of repentance (Ezra 9:11; Neh 9; Dan 9:6; cf. 1 Kgs 8:46-53);
- an historical explanation (2 Kgs 17:7-20; 2 Chr 36:14-16, 17-21; Isa 63:7-10);
- a call of God (Jer 2:30);
- the proclamation of the law (Deut 4:25-31; 28:45-68; 30:1-10);
- a judgment call of God (2 Kgs 22:17; Jer 44:1-14), or
- the appeal of a king to repent (2 Chr 29:5-11; 30:6-9).

Regarding point 2, we note that the association between repentance speeches and the violent fate/death of God's prophets is conspicuous in Matthew 21:35; Mark 6:14-29; 12:1-10; Luke 11:49-51; 13:34-35 (cf. also Luke 19:41-44; Rom 11:3).

Given this rich background, Steck convincingly argues that the so-called 'mission speeches' addressed to Jews in Acts 2–5, belong, on account of striking similarities, to the group of Jewish-Christian repentance speeches which are patterned along the lines of Old Testament (and intertestamental) prophetic repentance speeches.[116] The preacher admonishes the hearers to turn from sin and guilt in the light of the recent and mighty eschatological works of God in and through his appointed Messiah (segment 2b). Peter as the spokesperson for the collective apostolic witness thus arises as YHWH's *prophetic preacher of repentance* in Jerusalem (see especially Acts 2:38, 40; 3:19b; 5:31b and, implicitly, Acts 8:22; 10:42-43; 15:8). Together with other preachers (see Stephen in Acts 7:2-53 and Paul in Acts 13:16-41),[117] he calls

---

[114] See H.-J. van der Minde, 'Geschichtliches Denken und theologische Implikationen', in G. Schneider; C. Bussmann, and W. Radl (eds), *Der Treue Gottes trauen* (Freiburg: Herder, 1991), 343–60.

[115] Steck, *Israel*, 187.

[116] Steck, *Israel*, 195, 267–68. See, e.g., Tob 14:5; *1 En.* 108:6; Sir 36:15b.

[117] D.P. Moessner ('Paul in Acts: Preacher of Eschatological Repentance to Israel'. *NTS* 1.34 [1988], 96–104) has demonstrated (esp. 101–103) that the same motif and prophetic self-understanding can be found in the preaching of Paul as 'preacher of

his fellow Jews to return to God in the light of his most recent sovereign, redemptive work (segment 2b; compare with segment 2c).

As can be easily demonstrated, the speeches of Peter in the early chapters of Acts aim at *repentance* and restoration (segments 2d, 4b, and 4c; see Acts 2:38; 3:19; 5:31) and initially only call Jews to return to the God of their fathers. Steck emphasizes that the main purpose of these early Petrine speeches is Israel's repentant return from a place of failure and guilt to renewed covenantal relationship with God, marked by his election.[118] These early speeches in Acts stand in noticeable contrast to the later speeches in Acts which address Gentiles (see, e.g., Peter in Acts 10:34-43; compare with 14:15-19; 17:22-31; regarding the speeches in Acts 7 and 13, see below) where this Old Testament motif is virtually absent.[119] Steck notes that the speeches in Acts 2–5 are thoroughgoing repentance speeches (note especially 2:38; 3:19; 5:31),[120] calling Israel to return to YHWH.[121] Gentiles are here only on the periphery. The call to repentance serves as a motivating exposure to acknowledging guilt before God[122] and is meant to usher in the possible turning of Israel (section 4b), with the associated hope of salvation (section 4c), or, in the event of hard-heartedness, divine rejection (cf. Acts 3:23). God's deeds of salvation and election are briefly mentioned (Acts 3:13; 5:30: the God of the Fathers; 2:39; 3:25: promise; see also Tob. 4:12; 5:31) but not as extensively as they are featured in Acts 7 and 13 (on these, see below).

Generally speaking, the most significant element in Peter's speeches, when compared with the Old Testament pattern, is that the call to repentance

---

eschatological repentance to Israel', when addressing Jews (see, e.g., Acts 13:40-46; 18:6; 28:25-28).

[118] Steck, *Israel*, 268. Concerning 4c, see Acts 2:39-40; 3:20-21; concerning 4d, see Acts 2:40.

[119] Cf. F. Hahn, *Das Verständnis der Mission im Neuen Testament* (Neukirchen-Vluyn: Neukirchener Verlag, 1963), 116–17, 385-87. See 1 Thess 1:9-10; Heb 5:11-14.

[120] Acts 4:8-12 does not contain a direct call to repentance. Peter does, however, mention the resistance of the people which issues in the rejection of Jesus (Acts 4:11). Furthermore, Peter emphasizes the necessity to find salvation before it is too late. In contrast to Acts 7 and 13, but similar to Acts 2, 3, and 5, there is no emphasis in Acts 4:8-12 on the redemptive-historical theme of judgment or fulfillment.

[121] See Steck, *Israel*, 268.

[122] Steck, *Israel*, 268.

(segment 2d) does not *end* in a pronouncement of irreversible judgment (contrast this with segment 4d; see Acts 3:23, when compared with 3:24-26).[123] Rather, his call to repentance is embedded in the offer of the grace of salvation in terms of receiving 'forgiveness of sins', 'peace', and being 'welcome to God' (segments 4b and 4c). This emphasis is conspicuous both in the Petrine speeches addressing Jewish people (Acts 2 and 3) as well as, surprisingly, Peter addressing Gentiles (Acts 10).

The following chart of speeches in Acts provides an overview of these phenomena:

2:14-36,38-40	*3:12-26*	*4:9-12*	*5:29-32*	*7:1-53*	*13:16-41*
(2c)[124] *15-21*	*	*	*	*(1) 1-36*	*
(2a) 22+24	*(2a) 12b-13a*	*(2a) 9-10a+c*	*(2a) [29]30a*	*(2b) 37-38*	*(2b) 17-25*
*	*	*	*	*	*(4c) 26*
(3) 23	*(3) 13b-15a*	*(3) 10b*	*(3) 30b*	*(3) 39-41*	*(3) 27-29*
(2c) 25-35	*(2a) 15b, (16)*	*(2b) 11*	*(2a) 31a,32*	*(2a) 45-50*	*(2a) 30-33a*
(2a) 36	*	*	*	*	*
*	*	*	*	*4a) 42*	*
*	*(3) 17*	*	*	*(3) 43-44*	*
*	*(2b) 18*	*	*	*	*(2b)33b-37*
(2d) 38	*(2d) 19a*	*	*(2d) 31b*	*	*
(4c) 39	*(4c) 19b-21a*	*(4c) 12*	*	*	*(4c) 8-39*
*	*(2b) 21b-25a*	*	*	*	*(2c) 40-41*
*	*[(4a) 23]*	*	*	*	*
(2d) 40	*	*	*	*	*
*	*[(4c) 25b, 26)]*	*	*	*	*
*	*	*	*	*(2a) 45-50*	*
*	*	*	*[(3) 33]*	*(3) 51-53*	*

The speech-format of Acts 2–5 thus belongs most probably to a very early Jewish-Christian stage in Christian tradition.[125] According to Steck, the early

---

[123] Peter's differentiated accusation of the Jewish authorities/audiences (Acts 2:36; 3:13-14; 4:10; 5:30), including the 'ignorance motif' (Acts 3:17; cf. 17:30 and 1 Pet 1:14), further support this fact.

[124] The abbreviations follow the numbered sequence given above.

[125] Steck, *Israel*, 268. Cf. Mark 12:1b-9 and 1 Thess 2:15-16. Acts 7 emphasizes the repeated disobedience of God's people throughout the ages. In the key speeches in Acts 2–5, however, merely the resistance to Jesus as the last messenger of God is in view. Especially the Jewish leadership is made responsible for this: Acts 2:23, 36; (cf. 4:10; 3:13-17; see also 5:30 and 10:39. While it is true that in contrast to Acts 7, the speeches in Acts 2–5 do not take up the theme of the rejection of the message of the OT prophets, Steck does not pay sufficient attention to the fact that with the rejection of the prophesied Jesus, a rejection of OT prophets is implied. The abbreviated speeches in Acts 2–5 imply an argument *a maiore ad minorem*: he who rejects Jesus rejects those who prophesied him.

Christian Christology[126] and the key concept of calling Israel back to YHWH[127] before the mission to the Gentiles commences, vouchsafe for this conclusion. Tracing the relationship between Christianity and Judaism in the first century AD, Dunn observes in general terms what we will seek to demonstrate in specific terms regarding Peter's ministry in Jerusalem. Dunn states: 'Christianity began as a movement of renewal breaking through the boundaries first within and then round the Judaism of the first century.'[128] This sentiment takes up what Schlatter observed in 1927 regarding the function of Peter in the early parts of Acts: 'The ultimate goal of the apostle was not to place Christianity alongside Judaism, but to bring forth the Christian church from Judaism.'[129] At least during the initial stages of Peter's work in Jerusalem, repentance and belief in YHWH's acts through his appointed Messiah (segment 2b) was preached *within* the ancient Jewish and prophetic framework of calling the chosen covenant people of God to return to the God of their Fathers (segment 2d).

Parallel to the tradition of prophetic repentance speeches, Steck notes the long-standing motif of the *violent fate* of God's prophets. Early Jewish Christianity combines these two motifs, before and parallel to Pauline emphases along the same lines (see Acts 13 and, regarding Stephen, Acts 7).[130] Steck assumes that early Palestinian Jewish-Christian tradition passed on the *combination* of the violent fate of God's prophets and the prophetic repentance speech.[131] We see evidence that Peter adopted and spearheaded this tradition in Christian circles. According to Steck, the most conspicuous difference between the intertestamental tradition and the presentation of the repentance speech and the violent fate of God's prophets in the Jewish-Christian speeches of Peter lies in the fact that Jesus is now the most recently killed prophet of God and at the same time the representative of the last great salvific act of God (see Jesus's teaching in Mark 12:1-10).

We are thus dealing with a dynamic perspective which goes back to the Old Testament, spans the intertestamental time, reaches into earliest Petrine and

---

[126] Cf. Hahn, *Verständnis*, 116–17, 385–87.

[127] Steck, *Israel*, 268.

[128] J.D.G. Dunn, *The Parting of the Ways: Between Christianity and Judaism and their Significance for the Character of Christianity* (London: SCM, 1991), 258–59 (italics in the original).

[129] A. Schlatter, *Die Geschichte der ersten Christenheit* (Gütersloh: Bertelsmann, 1927), 53–54 (trans. HFB).

[130] Steck, *Israel*, 278.

[131] Steck, *Israel*, 289.

Pauline Christianity (see also Philip[132]), and continues into rabbinic Judaism, as well as the apostolic and post-apostolic fathers.[133] This tradition is by no means formulaic and uniform, but it maintains a constant basic thrust in all its variability. This means that a Palestinian, Jewish-Christian provenance of the Petrine speeches in Acts 2–5, closely associated with the Old Testament motif of prophetic repentance speeches, is certainly likely.

Other Expressions of the Prophetic Speech Pattern
While Stephen's speech (Acts 7:1-53) and the Pisidian Antioch speech of Paul (Acts 13:16-41) take up and *emphasize* the motif of the violent fate of the prophets of God,[134] they do not focus as explicitly on repentance, as do the early Petrine speeches. Especially Stephen's speech focuses on the hard-heartedness and rebellion of God's people against the Holy Spirit and the law (see Neh 9:30; Isa 63:10; Zech 7:12; compare with Mark 12:1-12; Heb 1:1-2). The death of Jesus is presented in the context of the rebellious killing of God's prophets who were sent to Israel from the times of Moses to the present (cf. Mark 12:1-12).[135] Acts 7:52 climaxes in the theme of rebellion against God's Spirit despite the presence of yet another prophet (see Steck's segment 3): Jesus stands as a last prophet in the long line of prophets who were violently rejected by God's people.[136] What is missing in Stephen's speech is the explicit mention of a call to repentance. While it is possible to imply such a call,[137] it is perhaps an indication that this speech is already addressing a less Palestinian and a more Hellenistic-Jewish and proselyte audience. Among these Diaspora Jews the focus of Stephen's speech is simply on the redemptive-historical fact of the rejection of the prophets of God. Stephen's speech might demonstrate, therefore, that the close connection between a prophetic call to repentance *and* the violent fate of God's prophet(s) in Peter's early speeches (see especially Acts 2, 3 and 5) gradually fades in the Diaspora Jewish settings in favor of the emphasis on a redemptive-historical review, listing the hard-hearted rebellion of God's people which issues in the violent fate of God's prophets.[138] Specifically, Stephen's speech focuses on God's many messengers, while

---

[132] Cf. F.S. Spencer, *The Portrait of Philip in Acts: A Study of Roles and Relations* (Sheffield: JSOT Press, 1992), 273–74.

[133] Steck, *Israel*, 317–18.

[134] Steck, *Israel*, 266.

[135] Steck, *Israel*, 267.

[136] Steck, *Israel*, 266–67.

[137] Steck believes that Stephen's speech implies such a call to repentance (*Israel*, 267, and n. 3).

[138] See H.-W. Neudorfer, *Der Stephanuskreis in der Forschungsgeschichte seit F.C. Baur* (Giessen: Brunnen, 1983), 322–23, 330–31, 338.

Paul's Pisidian Antioch speech zeroes in on Jesus as the rejected and vindicated Messiah of God (Acts 13:16-41).

It is noteworthy that in the unfolding narrative of Acts the characteristic Jewish element of the call to repentance from hard-heartedness *in the context of YHWH's redemptive acts* fades even more. In this regard, the speeches in Acts 7 and 13 may constitute a modest transition[139] into the Gentile world, in which the ongoing theme of repentance will have to be conveyed differently. There, the theme of repentance will arise especially *in view of the future judgment of all mankind* (see Acts 10:42; 17:30-31).[140]

As we compare the early Petrine speeches in Acts 2–5 with later speeches addressed especially to Diaspora Jews (Acts 7 and 13), we conclude that the focus on Jesus as God's most recent and culminating act of redemption and the call to repentance with promised salvation, is more prominent in Peter's early speeches. In fact, only Acts 7:51-53 concerns itself with the *present* circumstances, while the majority of Stephen's speech addresses the long *history* of rebellion against God's prophets (see Steck's segment 3).[141] The early Petrine speeches may thus be viewed as more deeply grounded in *Palestinian* Jewish tradition than the speeches in Acts 7 and 13 (Diaspora Judaism) due to their telling combination of the violent fate of God's prophets with the prophetic call to repentance. The conspicuous call to repentance in Acts 2, 3, 4, and 5 places these speeches in a unique Palestinian Jewish-Christian milieu in contrast to the 'mixed' speeches in Acts 7 and 13.

Those who argue that Luke must have created the early Petrine speeches[142] may thus have to consider the following: the early Petrine speeches fit well historically and rhetorically into the longstanding Old Testament Palestinian-Jewish admonitions regarding the violent fate of God's prophets and the equally ancient motif of prophetic repentance speeches.

---

[139] Cf. Wilckens, *Missionsreden*, 221.

[140] The significant relationship between Acts 2, 3 and 5 and the circumstance of Jesus sending out his disciples in Galilee (Mark 6:7-13) supports our thesis.

[141] Wilckens, *Missionsreden*, 221. While Wilckens did modify his view somewhat from the second to the third edition of his *Missionsreden*, he nevertheless could not fully accept the notion that the motif-historical evidence presented by Steck was sufficiently conclusive to demonstrate that Luke's report in Acts reflected historical fact. Wilckens did accept, however, that the pattern of these repentance speeches did stem from a pre-Lukan source (compare Wilckens, *Missionsreden*, 2nd ed. [1963], 100 and 186 with his 3rd ed., 205 and 221).

[142] It is likely that Luke was well acquainted with forms of Hellenistic historiography (see the technical terms in his prologue, Luke 1:1-4). See, e.g., D.W. Palmer, 'Acts and the Historical Monograph', *TynBul* 43.2 (1992), 373–88. But Luke nearly exclusively quotes from the LXX with its Semitic tone and its Jewish faith.

This long tradition spans many centuries and includes especially prophets, but also kings and priests. The Petrine speeches which Luke transmits convey in form and content the milieu of the Old Testament repentance speeches. From our vantage point there are but two options: either Luke composes these speeches according to the pattern of Old Testament repentance speeches, or he reports that once again a prophetic repentance preacher, in this case Peter, arose to proclaim the important call to the people of Israel.[143] The latter is indeed likely.

As we briefly look at the broader New Testament witness, it is undeniable that John the Baptist arose as a prophetic repentance preacher and that he was persecuted for it (cf. Luke 3:3, 7-9, 17).[144] Jesus introduces his announcement of the imminent kingdom of God with a prophetic call to repentance (Mark 1:15; cf. Luke 11:37-54; 12:32; 13:34-35; 15:3-7; 19:42-44; 21:8-36) and will subsequently find himself in the line of the *passio iusti* (Mark 8:31; 9:31; 10:32-34, 45; 12:1-12).[145] What, then, should we expect historically from the witnesses who were trained by Jesus to go to the towns of Israel with the message of repentance (Mark 6:12; cf. Luke 9:2; 10:5-11 par.),[146] except that they would continue to call all of Israel to repentance, following the unparalleled, culminating, and mighty deeds of God in Christ?[147] It stands to reason that this ongoing Old Testament phenomenon arises especially at a time when God has acted so majestically through his eternal Son, Jesus, to whom the chief spokesperson and key witness, Peter, testifies. If we consider the unparalleled recent event of the death and resurrection of the promised Messiah, as well as the long-anticipated outpouring of the Holy Spirit on people of different walks of life, a sufficient catalyst is provided for a renewed period of prophetic repentance speeches to Jews in the light of the mighty

---

[143] See similarly, M. Wilcox, 'A Foreword to the Study of the Speeches in Acts', *SJLA* 12.1 (1975), 206–25, 216; M. Kähler, 'Die Reden des Petrus in der Apostelgeschichte, sprachlich untersucht', *TSK*, 3, (1873), 516.

[144] Besides the canonical Gospels, see Josephus, *Ant.* 18.5.2 and 1 QS 8:13-16; 10:20.

[145] See Bayer, *Predictions*, 54–61, 239–42; R. Pesch, *Das Markusevangelium* (Freiburg: Herder, 1980), II, 13–14, 24–25. Regarding Mark 12:1-12, see K.R. Snodgrass, *The Parable of the Wicked Tenants* (Tübingen: Mohr Siebeck, 1983), 80–87; 95–110. Peter, as a mediator between Palestinian and Hellenistic Jewish Christians (Acts 6) is a good candidate for such speeches. See also the statements concerning the intent to kill Jesus (Mark 12:1-12 par.; Luke 4:24 par.; 13:31-33) as well as general statements concerning the violent fate of repentance preachers (Luke 6:22-23 par.; 11:47-54 par.; 13:34-35).

[146] See Wilckens, *Missionsreden*, 205.

[147] See 1 Thess 2:15-16. See the informative overview in Wilckens, *Missionsreden*, 200–208.

deeds of God.[148] The Spirit-filled Peter (Acts 2:1-4) thus arises as a prophetic repentance preacher to Israel. Furthermore, the ominous shadow cast by the violent death of God's prophets, including the death of John the Baptist and of God's Messiah (Mark 12:1-10), is now cast upon Peter as well (see John 21:18-19; cf. Mark 10:30; 13:13; Luke 6: 22-23; 11:47-48, 49-51; John 10:11, 13:36; 2 Pet 1:14-15).[149]

The provenance of the prophetic and now Christ-centered repentance speeches in which the God of the Fathers remains always the initiator is thus conceivable at *any* stage in early Christianity. Because of its long history and the present deeds of God, the form and content of the prophetic repentance speech 'is in the air', so to speak. Since the well-established phenomenon of repentance preachers can surface at any time in Israel (especially in Jerusalem), the Lukan report of the systematically trained, Spirit-filled, and prophetic witness Peter captures the historical motif and the historical potential of the times. Additionally, there is sufficient evidence to claim that the followers of Jesus are aware of their potential rejection in line with prophetic preachers of repentance of old (see Mark 10:35-44, the suffering of Peter in Acts, and his teaching on suffering in 1 Pet; see below).[150]

Conclusion

Surprisingly, a relatively simple Galilean fisherman arises, under the tutelage of Jesus, as an unequivocal, solid, and prophetic witness to God's redemptive deeds in and through the resurrected person of Jesus, the Messiah.

---

[148] Cf., similarly, 1 Sam 12:6-7.
[149] See Wilckens, *Missionsreden*, 204–205.
[150] Cf. Bayer, *Predictions*, 54–61.

CHAPTER 3

Peter's Non-Transferable Contributions to the Content and Formation of the New Testament Canon

Peter as Key Guarantor and Transmitter of Oral Jesus-Tradition in the Form of the Earliest Gospel Witness[1]

Recent research has bolstered the likelihood that Peter, together with the other apostolic witnesses, bridges between Jesus's ministry, the early post-Easter oral witness,[2] and the written fixation of this testimony (cf. Luke 1:2-4). Bockmuehl suggests that Peter is

> positioned at the center of the Jesus tradition, as an eyewitness transmitter of the oral history that became the story of Jesus . . . it is highly unlikely that this narrative feature is a mere literary fiction or post-Easter retrojection, but it is more likely based on genuine memory of the historical Peter.[3]

In the following, we submit a possible description of this important and crucial process, in the beginning of which we find Jesus as the *initiator* (see above). He arises as prophet (he calls to God; predicts; teaches with authority),[4] as priest (he propitiates and atones for sins), and as kingly Son of God incarnate (he ushers in the eternal reign of God).

---

[1] Bauckham, *Eyewitnesses*, 264–89; 319–57 and, cautiously, Bockmuehl, *Simon*, 132: 'Peter as the guarantor of Mark's Palestinian story of Jesus for a Roman readership'. See Barnett, *Logic*, 133–58, 159–61, who presents a similar model without explicitly referring to Riesner or Reicke. Regarding the Pauline emphasis on reliable tradition, see Barnett, *Logic*, 142–44. Cf. P. Stuhlmacher, *Biblische Theologie des Neuen Testaments* (Göttingen: Vandenhoeck & Ruprecht, 1992), I, 179–96, 197–203, and M.F. Bird, *The Gospel of the Lord: How the Early Church Wrote the Story of Jesus* (Grand Rapids, MI: Eerdmans, 2014), 57, 100–104, 190, 214.
[2] Bockmuehl, *Remembered Peter*, 3–30.
[3] Bockmuehl, *Simon*, 88, referring also to Byrskog, *Story*, 71–73.
[4] Riesner, *Jesus*, 251–53.

Besides much else, Jesus acts as an authoritative teacher (see Mark 13:31 par.: 'heaven and earth will pass away, but my words will not pass away'; Matt 5:18: 'until heaven and earth pass away, not an iota, not a dot, will pass from the Law until all is accomplished').[5] This unique person calls pupils above all, Peter, whom he personally teaches, mentors, and shapes. With the systematic training of his disciples (see above), Jesus thus lays the foundation for a unique transmission as his disciples will: witness the life, work, teaching, death, and resurrection of Jesus; bear witness to this in the early church; and be involved in the recording of such testimonies in the form of ancient *bioi*. As Jesus systematically trains his disciples by memorization and impact-rich relationships, he thus shapes what is to follow (cf. Acts 1:15-26). The stereotyped oral form of memorization and the memorable, heart-transforming life lived in company with Jesus serve the purpose of laying the foundation for remembering all that Jesus entrusts into his disciples' care and for reflecting Christ-likeness.[6] The careful collection and systematic transmission (partially already in writing) of apostolic tradition sets the framework for the genesis of the written gospel documents (see, e.g., Acts 20:35; 1 Cor 7:10; 11:23-25).[7]

It is thus historically plausible to envisage a pre-Easter oral (and partially written) phase in which the disciples memorize a considerable body of material related to the actions and teachings of Jesus. Since Jesus himself frequently repeats and slightly varies his relatively narrow body of teaching and actions, a

---

[5] See J.W. Wenham, *Christ and the Bible* (Grand Rapids, MI: Baker, 1994), 69–87.

[6] Herein lies one of the core criticisms of Riesner (*Jesus*, 20) concerning classical form criticism (esp. R. Bultmann, *History of the Synoptic Tradition* [New York, NY: Harper, 1968]): classical form criticism replaces the historically plausible continuity of persons (*Personalkontinuität*; Jesus's original disciples become witnesses in Acts) by means of a historically unfounded, collective transmission in which the early church is the creative genius of the Jesus kerygma. Westcott states: 'As long as the first witnesses survived, so long the tradition was confined within the bounds of their testimony; when they passed away, it was already fixed in writing.' (B.F. Westcott, *An Introduction to the Study of the Gospels* [Cambridge: Macmillan, 1881], 211–12).

[7] Cf. E.E. Ellis, 'Preformed Traditions and Their Implications for Pauline Christology', in D. Horrell and C.M. Tuckett (eds), *Christology, Controversy, and Community* (Leiden: Brill, 2000), 303–20, esp. 310. Bauckham, *Eyewitnesses*, 264–89; 319–57. Dunn, 'Setting', 139–75. There is a considerable difference between the above-presented view of an oral phase of learning and transmitting the words and deeds of Jesus and the view of classical form criticism. Classical form criticism virtually rejects the historical continuity of the original disciples in the post-Easter community. It also postulates without historical support the theological and historical (historicizing) creativity of the early church. This postulate contradicts the tenor of the canonical Gospels which claim that the creative impulse came from Jesus.

stable deposit of memories is placed in the minds (and hearts) of the disciples, which is further deepened by Jesus's sending them out to preach and live out the same message. All of this provides a rich source for reliable oral witness. Further reciprocal learning is enhanced by the fact that Jesus calls a *group* of learners to follow him, sends them out and continues to train them.[8] Additionally, Millard demonstrates that at least some disciples were capable of writing.[9]

Complementing this learning process, we have noted elsewhere (see also below)[10] that Jesus begins a profound process of radical heart transformation that runs in concert with and reinforces the memorization process. As it relates to the faithful transmission of tradition, this heart-transformation is particularly important regarding the formation of accurate perspectives, attitudes, and approaches of the disciples to Jesus's teaching concerning the overall, missional purpose of God both globally and individually. They have to understand that it is not only their memories (i.e., knowledge and wisdom) which must be formed, but also their inner outlook on and worldview of life: that is, their self- and God-perception, their approach to the *pondus peccati* of noetic and moral autonomy from God, and so on. This will provide the interpretive framework for their knowledge and memorized content in the years to come. In a real way, the atonement of Christ also resets their perspective on life so that their testimony is Christ-congruent.

The stereotyped oral phase occurs at least in a bi-(tri-) lingual fashion (Aramaic, Hebrew, and Greek; see above). This provides the assurance that Jesus's 'curriculum' is safely transmitted from Semitic languages to Greek. Already during his earthly life, Jesus had taught with authority. Just as his true identity becomes increasingly apparent to the disciples, so the authoritative impact of his teaching increases as well. Now that Jesus has been divinely vindicated from shameful crucifixion by physical resurrection (thus also

---

[8] See Bauckham, *Eyewitnesses*, 264–89; 319–57. See further the assertion that the resurrected Jesus continues instructing his disciples (Luke 24:13-49). The Holy Spirit is promised as the one who assist in the process of remembering (see John 14:26 and 16:12-15; cf. Rom 16:26). These factors connect the historical witness with the claim of inspiration and the fact of the canonization of the canonical Gospels as part of the reliable and authoritative revelation of God.

[9] Millard, *Reading*, 223–29. See Barnett, *Logic,* 140–42 and C.P. Thiede and M. D'Ancona, *Eyewitness to Jesus* (New York, NY: Doubleday, 1996), 135–36, concerning the likelihood that Matthew had a working knowledge of *tachygraphy* (a form of ancient stenography). Cf. R.E. Brown, *An Introduction to the New Testament* (New York, NY: Doubleday, 1997), 151 and n. 66, concerning the coexistence of oral and literary cultures in the Greco-Roman world.

[10] Bayer, *Theology,* 41–88.

divinely authenticating the entire body of teaching that was systematically entrusted to the disciples), every word he uttered and every act he performed takes on even greater significance and importance. This is all the more true as the God of Abraham, Isaac, and Jacob so uniquely confirms the messianic claims of Jesus that he had to be humiliated and vindicated by death and resurrection (Acts 3:13-21). His authoritative teaching goes even beyond this: whatever Jesus taught the disciples regarding eternal life and future judgment at the hand of the vindicated Son of Man now possesses the divine seal of approval (see, e.g., Mark 8:34-38; 13:31). The chief witness of all of this is Peter, spokesperson of the Twelve.

Regardless of the particular explanation of how the canonical Gospels came about, it is historically plausible that the disciples individually and collectively had access to and command of a significant body of systematically memorized material from which they were able to draw according to the witness-needs of a given situation (cf. John 20:30; 21:25).[11]

Peter and the Provenance of the Gospels' Narrative Framework

We turn now to the question of whether Peter might have initiated the shaping of the Gospels' particular framework and overall narrative sequencing. It is likely that Peter's post-Easter witness concerning Jesus focuses initially on the immediate past of the passion and resurrection of Christ (see the conspicuously close proximity of the synoptic accounts). In the further progression of early Christian witness, the additional systematically memorized body of material, now verified and reinforced by Jesus's resurrection, will gradually be connected with the vividly recalled passion and resurrection account. Pesch, echoing Kähler,[12] speaks of an initial composition of the Markan passion account which was then extended toward the beginning of Jesus's ministry.[13] Pesch views this as the genesis of the characteristic format of the Gospels.

Prior to considering the evidence in Acts 10:34-43 in more detail, we must briefly note that there is considerable debate over the historicity of Peter's spearheading the Gentile mission. Hengel surmises that Peter turned increasingly toward mission among Gentiles as his mission among Jewish people became more and more difficult. However, he identifies Acts 10:1-11, 18 as a 'missions-legend', because Peter is presented as the founder of the mission to Gentiles.[14]

---

[11] See also Baum, *Faktor*, 400–402.
[12] M. Kähler, *Der sogenannte historische Jesus und der geschichtliche, biblische Christus* (Leipzig: Deichert'sche Verlagsbuchhandlung, 1892), 60.
[13] Pesch, *Markusevangelium*, I, 1–40; II, 1–27.
[14] Hengel, 'Origins,' *Jesus and Paul*, 170 n. 26.

Since, however, Paul is known to Luke as the 'apostle to the Gentiles' (Acts 9:15; 13:47; 22:21; Rom 11:13; 1 Tim 2:7) it is all the more striking that *Luke* narrates the fact that Peter is the *first* gospel messenger to a group of Gentiles (Acts 10:45; 15:7, 12-14). Cullmann suggests that Peter and the other initial apostles took on a mediating role between Greek-speaking and Hebrew or Aramaic speaking Jewish Christians.[15]

A significant piece of evidence regarding the provenance of the Gospels' narrative framework might be found in Peter's often discussed speech in the house of the God-fearing Gentile, Cornelius (Acts 10:34-43).[16] Surprisingly, a key section of the speech in Acts 10:34-43 mirrors, *in nuce*, the narrative sequence and framework of the Gospel of Mark.[17] In other words, Acts 10:34-43 can be identified as a skeletal precursor to the account of Mark (as well as the other canonical Gospels).[18] The Petrine speech (note also Peter's comments in Acts 1:21-22; cf. also Acts 2:22-36; 3:11-26) displays a similar format to Mark, especially regarding the *sequencing* of the material. It provides a simple *selection* and outlines key elements of the life and work of Jesus. Westcott had already observed that the so-called *kērygma Iēsou* presented by Peter in Acts 10:34-43 points to the origin of the selection of gospel material, further details of which Peter later conveys to John Mark.[19] A comparison of Acts 10:34-43 with the format of the Gospel of Mark yields the following results:

Acts	Mark
10:34-36	1:1
10:37-38a	1:2-11
10:38b	1:12–9:50
10:39a	10:1–15:20
10:39b	15:21-47
10:40	16:1-8 (compare with Mark 9:9)
[10:41	Luke 24:36-43 (see Mark 9:9)]

---

[15] Cullmann, *Peter*, 37. See Rom 10:3, 16; 11:6-7; 1 Cor 9:5 (context of missions); cf. Acts 15:7 and 1 Cor 1:12; 3:10-23.

[16] K. Berger, *Formen und Gattungen im Neuen Testament* (Tübingen: Francke, 2005), 408–10. Berger, *Formen*, 390, identifies this gospel-*précis* as part of the genre of a summarizing 'base account . . . which represents the successful work of missionaries' (Berger, *Formen*, 388; trans. HFB). Cf. Bauckham, *Eyewitnesses*, 155–182 and Riesner, *Jesus*, 22.

[17] See R.A. Guelich, *Mark 1–8.26* (Dallas, TX: Word, 1989), 11–12; P. Stuhlmacher, *Theologie*, I, 50–57, 163–64. Against this notion, see, e.g., Schneider's discussion of Acts 10:34-43 (G. Schneider, *Die Apostelgeschichte* [Freiburg: Herder, 1980/82], II, 61–64) in which he concurs with Wilckens and Conzelmann that the speech in Acts 10 reflects Lukan composition and lacks any decisive evidence for a kerygmatic structure associated with the Gospel of Mark.

[18] Compare with Baum, *Faktor*, 400–402.

[19] Westcott, *Introduction*, 211–12; cf. Riesner, *Jesus*, 22.

[10:42   (see Mark 8:38; cf. Matt 28:19-20; Acts 1:8)]
[10:43   (see Mark 1:8; 10:45; cf. Luke 24:44-49)]

While this correspondence does not provide conclusive evidence in support of the Petrine genesis of the particular arrangement and general sequencing of gospel material, it is certainly plausible, especially if Papias (AD 120) is taken seriously, that Peter is not only the key *source* of the Gospel written by John Mark,[20] but also that he might have crafted and orally transmitted the basic narrative sequencing of that account.

Another consideration might solidify the above-stated connection between Acts 10:34-43 and the narrative sequencing of the Gospel of Mark. We have stated above that Peter must have been strongly inspired by the theocratic fervor of the Maccabean uprising prior to and into his involvement with Jesus. It is at least possible to think that Peter, now a follower of Jesus with a growing universal perspective of the mission of God, uses a format of historical narration similar to that of 1 and 2 Maccabees. The preface to 2 Maccabees (2 Macc 2:19-32) might very well describe Peter's approach, not as a 'professional historian' (2 Macc 2:30) 'but the man who is making an adaptation . . . to aim at brevity of expression and to omit detailed treatment of the matter' (2 Macc 2:31; see the entire section of 2:24-32) and thus to provide a 'summary outline' (2 Macc 2:28) and 'adaptation' (2 Macc 2:31).[21] While 2 Maccabees is a summary of a five-volume work written by Jason of Cyrene (2 Macc 2:23), where the precise connection to the historical events is open to discussion, Mark's account represents the Petrine summary of personally memorized content of very recent events, spanning a period of three momentous years. These considerations lead us to the next section.

Peter's Possible Contribution to Casting the Gospel Narrative in the Form of Ancient *Bios*

Mark describes his narrative and argumentative discourse in 1:1 as εὐαγγέλιον (=good news).[22] In the following discussion, we will seek to identify the

---

[20] See Irenaeus (*Haer.* 3.1.1, 10; 3.3.1–3), concerning the relationship between Peter and Mark.

[21] Part of the motive for this was to be able to commit the content to memory (2 Macc 2:25).

[22] In the Greco-Roman world the term conveys an imperial proclamation, e.g., of a military victory.

literary genre of this 'good-news-account'[23] and ask whether Peter was instrumental in casting the account in such a genre.

It is now held with greater certainty than in the past that the Synoptic Gospels (and, to a degree, John) are most likely cast in the genre of ancient *bios*,[24] based on its specific literary and historical characteristics.[25] If that were the case, it would mean that Mark claims to present a biographical sketch (*bios*) of a hero, containing descriptions of historical events and commensurate messages as good news. In contrast to classical form criticism, which operates within a naturalistic philosophy of history[26] and an unfounded, historical-critical, and nearly exclusively literary approach to the Gospels, the good news accounts in the form of *bios* are both historically reliable witness-accounts and challenging proclamation (kerygma). Dahl correctly observes: 'if one draws too sharp a distinction—either the gospel message or the 'recollection of the apostles'— one introduces an opposition that early Christianity did not know.'[27]

It would be wrong to compare such an ancient *bios*-account with the literary form of a modern comprehensive biography. What the ancient genre indicates is that Mark functions within Greco-Roman conventions of his time which intend to give reliable biographical excerpts while not providing an exhaustive

---

[23] See J.A. Kehlhoffer, *Conceptions of 'Gospel' and Legitimacy in Early Christianity* (Tübingen: Mohr Siebeck, 2014).

[24] For a detailed discussion of the gospel genre as ancient *bios*, see R.A. Burridge, 'About People, by People, for People: Gospel Genre and Audiences', in R.J. Bauckham, ed., *The Gospels for All Christians: Rethinking the Gospel Audiences* (Grand Rapids, MI: Eerdmans, 1997), 113–45; R.A. Burridge *What are the Gospels?: A Comparison with Graeco-Roman Biography* (Grand Rapids, MI: Eerdmans, 2004); M. Hengel, 'Kerygma oder Geschichte? Zur Problematik einer falschen Alternative in der Synoptikerforschung', *TQ* 151 (1971), 323–36; J.D. Kingsbury, 'The Gospel of Mark', *Int* 47 (1993), 341–409; B. Reicke, *The Roots of the Synoptic Gospels* (Philadelphia, PA: Fortress, 1986), 24–33; Riesner, *Jesus*, 29–32; W.R. Telford, *Mark* (Sheffield: Sheffield Academic Press, 1997, 96–98; D.E. Aune, *The New Testament in Its Literary Environment* (Philadelphia, PA: Westminster John Knox, 1987).

[25] Genre can be defined in simple terms as *a recurring, recognizable rhetorical pattern*. See Berger, *Formen*, 403–404, regarding arguments against those who question the ancient biographical character of the canonical Gospels.

[26] See G.E. Lessing, *Über den Beweis des Geistes und der Kraft*, in P. Rilla (ed.), *G.E. Lessing, Gesammelte Werke* (Berlin: Aufbau Verlag, 1968), VIII, 10–16; in contrast to A. Schlatter, *Die philosophische Arbeit seit Cartesius* (Giessen: Brunnen, 1981).

[27] N.A. Dahl, 'Anamnesis: Memory and Commemoration in Early Christianity', in N.A. Dahl, *Jesus in the Memory of the Early Church* (Minneapolis, MN: Augsburg, 1976), 27. Dahl, however, comes close to the traditional form-critical error by stating that the recollections of the apostles reflected *their views of Jesus* and do not necessarily constitute a reliable *testimony* to the person of Jesus.

life-story (see 2 Macc 2:28). Unlike historical-critical scholarship which often denies that much of Mark's account is historically authentic, both the term 'good news' and especially the *genre* of Mark's Gospel account point toward historical authenticity in support of its message. The genre of *bios* thus portrays itself as proclamation through reliable (albeit for the Greco-Roman reader potentially foolish) historical witness.[28]

In an extensive study, Burridge analyzed ten differently dated Greco-Roman biographies and concluded that the Gospels conform to the (rather flexible) literary genre of (religious) *bioi*[29] rather than to alternate genres such as 'philosophical treatises',[30] 'deeds of heroes', 'memoirs of heroes', fictitious stories, a novel, an aretalogy,[31] a biographical sketch,[32] a 'Jewish apocalyptic drama', or an account of 'divine men'.[33]

Accounts of 'divine men', for example, narrating their miracles, martyrdoms, and metamorphoses into divine beings, display significant differences from the canonical Gospels. Among these differences are the facts that: (1) the genre of these accounts is difficult to determine; (2) many of these collections post-date the canonical Gospels; and (3) parallels to the canonical Gospels are limited to superficial analogies.[34] While Jesus also performs miracles, his kingdom-mission provides a firm context and purpose for his miracles. This aspect is conspicuously missing in the accounts of 'divine men'.

Bioi in antiquity primarily describe the mature lives of key persons who are mentioned at the beginning of the accounts.[35] The format includes a brief introduction (with an optional infancy section), then proceeds to give select anecdotes (stories, dialogues, special events, and characteristic statements (i.e., *chreiai*; see below) depicted from the mature years of the main character, and

---

[28] See M. Hengel, *Crucifixion in the Ancient World and the Folly of the Message of the Cross* (Minneapolis, MN: Fortress Press, 1977), 1–10.

[29] Burridge, *Gospels*, 233–47; Burridge, 'About People', 113–45. See also Barnett, *Logic*, 136–37.

[30] See, however, the proximity to biographies of philosophers, Berger, *Formen*, 404.

[31] Against identifying the canonical Gospels as aretalogies, see H.C. Kee, 'Aretalogy and Gospel', *JBL* 92/3 (1973), 402–22 and B. Blackburn, *Theios Aner* (Philadelphia, PA: Coronet Books, 1990).

[32] See, e.g., Justin, *Dial.*, 103.8, who identifies the Gospels as 'memoirs of the apostles'. Cf. Bockmuehl, *Remembered Peter*, 84–86.

[33] See Burridge, 'About People', 113–45. Cf. Berger, *Formen*, 403–15 and Telford, *Mark*, 96–98.

[34] See Telford, *Mark*, 97, and especially Blackburn, *Aner*, 13–72. See for further details, Berger, *Formen*, 404–405.

[35] Berger, *Formen*, 404. Some biographies do, however, contain the so-called *genethliakon*, i.e., predictions over a child's life (405).

ends with a description of how the main character died. A simple chronological sequence, noticeable at the beginning and end of an account, is complemented by various thematic insertions in the middle section.[36] *Bioi* rely on oral and written sources concerning the hero's actions and words to provide an anecdotal (*chreiai*), characterizing biographical sketch of the hero.[37]

Berger defines a *chreia* as an 'instigated . . . speech or act in the life of a significant person' and states that a *chreia* constitutes an important building block of an ancient biography.[38] Berger notes that 'the written collection of *several chreiai* concerning the *same* person has demonstrably the greatest significance for the development of ancient biographies'.[39] A *chreia* can possess 'a regulative character for a multitude of people who feel accountable to the respective authority'.[40] Berger emphasizes that 'the decisive step toward composing a biography occurs when *chreiai* are collected exclusively surrounding one authority'.[41] Such biographical descriptions are mostly serious in tone and display respect for the protagonist.[42] Finally, it is significant to report *how* the hero dies, together with the last words of that person (*ultima verba*).[43] This provides clues about the character of the hero: will the way the hero dies confirm his life's conduct or question it?[44]

A unique element in the type of *bios* Mark (and the other canonical Gospels) represents is the innocent death of the main character as his *life's goal*.[45] Barnett, in particular, refines Burridge's conclusions by stating that the canonical passion accounts run, to a degree, counter to the broader *bios* genre. While classical *bios* accounts observe the way in which an important figure dies,[46] nowhere besides the canonical Gospels is there the notion that the *purpose* of the main character's life was, in fact, to die. Nor is there a reference

---

[36] Berger, *Formen*, 404.
[37] Among other sub-genres of *chreiai*, which all display a biographical character (Berger, *Formen*, 151), we find, e.g., *apothegms* and *expanded chreiai*, such as the *dramatic chreiai* (148–52).
[38] Berger, *Formen*, 142, as well as 143–52. The following quotes were translated by HFB.
[39] Berger, *Formen*, 142–43.
[40] Berger, *Formen*, 143.
[41] Berger, *Formen*, 144.
[42] Berger, *Formen*, 408, points out the fact that the eschatological prospect in Mark 13 displays structural analogies to Deut 32–33, Tob 14, and *Did.* 16, containing a *peroratio* which seeks to motivate present behavior by reference to God's future plans.
[43] Berger, *Formen*, 406.
[44] Cf. Burridge, *Gospels*, 140–49 and Berger, *Formen*, 405, 414.
[45] Barnett, *Logic*, 159–61.
[46] Burridge, *Gospels*, 142–49, 174–75, 202, 212, 337–39.

in comparable ancient *bios* accounts of the most shameful and offensive form of execution by crucifixion. Finally, there is no parallel in other *bios* accounts to the uniquely liberating and reconciling effect or significance of the hero's death. Barnett's observations also support the notion that the Gospel account as *bios* is, inseparably, both historical witness and proclamation. As stated above, the witness account is the consequence of stereotyped memorization and the proclamation is the consequence of learned interpretations given by Jesus himself. We note, for example, Mark 10:45, where Jesus teaches the disciples how to *interpret* the meaning of his impending death.[47]

Burridge further suggests that the mere fact of telling the story of Jesus in the form of the Greco-Roman *bios* genre might have christological ramifications. He aptly states:

> it is significant that this biographical 'shape' is a Graeco-Roman genre . . . [a]nd yet . . . contain[s] stories . . . sayings and dialogues which are very Jewish . . . [W]e can find many parallels within rabbinic literature to these gospel passages. What is striking, however, is that no one ever brought them together to compose an account of the life of a particular rabbi . . . despite there being ample material so to do. As Philip Alexander comments, 'There are no rabbinic parallels to the Gospels as such'. . . He concludes that this is because no rabbi held 'the central position that Jesus held in early Christianity.' The point of preserving and passing on . . . accounts of questions and answers within the rabbinic tradition is to remember what different rabbis have said about this or that point of the law. When, however, the evangelists collect their material into the form of an account of Jesus, they are revealing that the focus on the Torah has been replaced by a focus on Jesus . . . Thus, writing a bios out of a Jewish context is itself a christological claim . . . In writing a biographical account of Jesus, they redirect our attention to the foundation, Jesus of Nazareth and his words and deeds . . . and all that happened to him in his life and death and afterwards.[48]

While Burridge might overstate some of his observations on account of the fact that at least short biographical sketches outside the category of rabbinic anecdotes can be found in Jewish literature (for example in 1 and 2 Macc), his key point of a shift from focus on the Torah to a biographical sketch of Jesus is certainly noteworthy.

---

[47] See J. Frey and J. Schröter, *Deutungen des Todes Jesu im Neuen Testament* (Tübingen: Mohr Siebeck, 2012).
[48] R.A. Burridge, *Imitating Jesus: An Inclusive Approach to New Testament Ethics* (Grand Rapids, MI: Eerdmans, 2007), 156–57; referred to the author by D. Gleich.

A final, important observation regarding *bios* is that the character of its hero is often intended to be imitated by the reader/hearer.[49] This raises the intriguing question as to what degree the very genre of Mark's account hints that Jesus's person and actions are to be imitated by his followers. We will argue below that Jesus teaches, exemplifies, and, above all, enables 'pattern-imitation' among his followers rather than calling for a simplistic, self-generated 'copying of Christ'.[50] But the connection between *bios* and pattern-imitation is significant.

Regardless of whether the Gospel of Mark, a Hebrew proto-Matthew,[51] or a Greek Matthew was written first, it appears to be historically plausible to connect Peter, above all others, with the gospel genre of *bios* into which he cast the particular selection and arrangement of oral material noted in the previous section. Extrabiblical support for this possibility comes from a surprising source.

More recent analysis of Papias's description concerning the origin of Mark's Gospel has provided support for the connection between Peter and the *bios* genre.[52] According to Bauckham, the well-known Papias section (see below) is best understood as saying that John Mark accurately recorded the remembrances of Peter, in which Peter rendered the teachings of Jesus (i.e., the words and deeds of Jesus) as *chreiai* (ὃς πρὸς τὰς χρείας ἐποιεῖτο τὰς διδασκαλίας).[53] While Peter did not give these *chreiai* in exact order, he recounted what the Lord said and did. Older translations of the Papias section[54] read that Peter adjusted his teaching to the 'needs' (τὰς χρείας) of his hearers. This understanding is now seriously questioned by the alternative rendering that Papias may have used the technical literary term of χρεία to characterize the literary form of Peter's teaching. If Bauckham's interpretation of Papias's reference to Peter is correct,[55] it would mean that Peter cast the memory of

---

[49] D.B. Capes, 'Imitatio Christi and the Gospel Genre', *BBR* 13.1 (2003), 1–19; cf. Burridge, *Imitating Jesus*, 29, 55, 78.

[50] Cf. C.D.J. Agan, *The Imitation of Christ in the Gospel of Luke: Growing in Christlike Love for God and Neighbor* (Phillipsburg, NJ: P&R, 2014), 1–20, and H.D. Betz, *Nachfolge und Nachahmung Jesu Christi im Neuen Testament* (Tübingen: Mohr Siebeck, 1967).

[51] Baltes, *Evangelium*, 597.

[52] See Bauckham, *Eyewitnesses*, 202–39, and Riesner, 'Rückkehr', 344. It is noteworthy that the Gospels of Mark and Luke display both Palestinian and Gentile 'local flavor'; see R. Riesner, 'Das Lokalkolorit des Lukas-Sonderguts: Italisch oder Palästinisch-Juden-Christlich?', *LASBF* 49 (1999), 51–64.

[53] See Bauckham, *Eyewitnesses*, 214–39, who refers, e.g., to Theon of Alexandria, *Progymnasmata*, 3.2–3 (p. 215), for a definition of a *chreia* as a 'short discourse'.

[54] Eusebius, *Hist. eccl.* 3.39.15.

[55] See Riesner, *Jesus*, 22; cf. Westcott, *Introduction*, 211–12.

Jesus's words and deeds into various *chreiai*, the combination of which, together with the focus on one protagonist, characterizes ancient *bios*. In other words, Peter not only would have generated a simple *outline* of the life of Jesus as a basis of a narrative gospel sequence (see above, concerning Acts 10), but would also have cast his recollections in the genre of *bios*. The fact that, according to Papias, the various *chreiai* of Peter were not strictly ordered simply means that various stories, beside the rather structured and fixed Passion Narrative, were not bound by a specific sequence, but were always placed within the general Petrine framework (see above) of the life of Jesus.

Considering all factors, we submit that Peter might very well have adopted and communicated via John Mark the genre of predominantly Hellenistic *bioi*, but in a way which draws on Old Testament and intertestamental (see 1 and 2 Macc) historical writings. The central impact for such an undertaking arises from the authoritative acts and deeds of the key figure, Jesus, who 'came to die' as the foundation of transformed lives which are shaped by him.

We never question that Felix (AD 52–59 or 60), a former slave, rose to the rank of *procurator* of Judea,[56] but we routinely tend to question whether a Galilean fisherman with an elementary school education could rise, in the span of some thirty years, to testify in Greek to an extraordinary person, casting his broadly sequenced account in a relatively simple format of *bios* and remembering, after systematic training for some three years, a fair amount of details about that person's life, words, and deeds.

Peter and the Need for Written Documents

Groups of many new converts formed in Judea, Samaria, Galilee, and Syria as the gospel message spread, which rapidly increased the need for authentic apostolic witness to the Jesus who transforms lives (see, e.g., Acts 8:14). These converts would soon be asking what else this saving Jesus said and did. This gave the impetus and drove the need for written fixation of the apostolic witness. The systematically trained and transformed disciples, and now experienced witnesses, were well-prepared to pass on what they had received. Peter, as their spokesperson, functioned as a central figure in this setting.

The process of how the Synoptic Gospels came about can be most convincingly explained either by means of a modified tradition hypothesis or a modified two-source hypothesis.

---

[56] See Tacitus, *Ann.* 12.54, and *Hist.* 5.9.

Peter and the Rise of Four Written Gospel Accounts in the Framework of a Modified Tradition Hypothesis[57]

The modified tradition hypothesis operates on the assumption of the literary independence between the Synoptic Gospels.[58] Before we discuss this modified hypothesis, it must be emphasized against the opinion of many scholars that *both* literary dependence and literary independence hypotheses have their strengths and weaknesses.[59]

Among various discussions of this issue, Linnemann's work concerning the Synoptic phenomenon[60] has at least demonstrated that literary independence is a defensible option in comparison with the literary dependence alternatives. Especially her 'representative cross-sectional analysis' of Synoptic data[61] demonstrates that merely ~22 percent of triple attestations feature *totally identical wording*. For identical wording of material common to Matthew and Mark that figure rises to (merely) ~41 percent, and to (merely) ~34 percent of material common to Luke and Mark. When identical wording does arise, it rarely extends to a sequence of words, let alone to a verse or a pericope.

---

[57] See Bailey, 'Informal', 34–54; Bailey, 'Middle Eastern', 363–67; A.D. Baum, 'Experimentalpsychologische Erwägungen zur synoptischen Frage', *BZ* 44.1 (2000), 37–55; P. Head, 'The Role of Eyewitnesses in the Formation of the Gospel Tradition', *TynBul*, 52.2 (2001), 275–94; J.D. Harvey, 'Orality and Its Implications for Biblical Studies: Recapturing an Ancient Paradigm', *JETS* 45/1 (2002), 99–109; Reicke, *Roots*, 9–11, 45–67, 155–90; H. Riesenfeld, *The Gospel Tradition and its Beginnings: A Study in the Limits of 'Formgeschichte'* (London: A.R. Mowbray, 1957), 3–30; Riesner, *Jesus*, 474–75, 481–87; R. Riesner, 'Jesus as Teacher and Preacher', in Wansborough, *Jesus*, 185–210; cf. J.D.G. Dunn, *A New Perspective on Jesus: What the Quest for the Historical Jesus Missed* (Grand Rapids, MI: Baker Academic, 2004); B. Gerhardsson, *The Gospel Tradition* (Lund: Gleerup, 1989); F. Godet, *Commentary on St. Luke* (New York, NY: Funk & Wagnalls, 1887); E.A. Havelock, *The Muse Learns to Write: Reflections on Orality and Literacy from Antiquity to the Present* (New Haven, CT: Yale University, 1986); contra oral tradition, H.C. Kee, 'Synoptic Studies', in E.J. Epp and G.W. MacRae (eds), *The New Testament and Its Modern Interpreters* (Atlanta, GA: Scholars, 1989), 245–69; W.H. Kelber, *The Oral and the Written Gospel: The Hermeneutics of Speaking and Writing in the Synoptic Tradition* (Bloomington, IN: Indiana Univ. Press, 1996); see the critique of Riesner in D.L. Balch, 'The Canon: Adaptable and Stable, Oral and Written. Critical Questions for Kelber and Riesner', *Forum* 7.3-4 (1991), 183–205.

[58] See, e.g., Westcott, *Introduction*, 201–207, and Baum, *Faktor*, 400–402, in support of literary independence.

[59] See Dunn, 'Setting', 139–75; cf. R. Thomas (ed.), *Three Views on the Origins of the Synoptic Gospels* (Grand Rapids, MI: Kregel, 2002), and D.A. Black, *Why Four Gospels? The Historical Origins of the Gospels* (Grand Rapids, MI: Kregel, 2001).

[60] E. Linnemann, *Is There a Synoptic Problem? Rethinking the Literary Dependence of the First Three Gospels* (Grand Rapids, MI: Baker, 1992).

[61] Linnemann, *Problem*, 109–29. Linnemann investigates 35 parallel pericopes.

With regard to *word choice*, Linnemann observes that Matthew and Luke share only ~62 percent of Mark's vocabulary (in triple attestation cases).[62] It is especially significant to ponder the fact that of the 830 words shared by Matthew, Luke, and Mark 'a large number belong to the basic word stock necessary for verbal communication' and to 'the distinctive vocabulary of the NT in general'.[63] The narrow subject-matter addressed in the Synoptic Gospels may create the *impression* of literary dependence when in fact common constraints naturally limit word usage. While we cannot discuss here all aspects of literary independence, it does, when sufficiently considered, arise as a legitimate alternative to the *opinio communis* of literary dependence.

As stated above, the chief objection to the classical tradition hypothesis is its failure to account for the *verbal correspondence of parallel Greek texts in the Synoptic Gospels* (which, as we suggested above, is not as strong as often presented) as well as the clearly established sequence pattern embedded in all three Gospels. Addressing these concerns, the *modified* tradition hypothesis suggests a mix of stereotyped oral transmission, written fragments, and early written gospel compositions clustered around the Passion Narrative.[64] Additionally, the modified tradition hypothesis counts on the possibility that some of the authors, while writing independently of each other,[65] later 'compared' their respective Gospels with each other.[66]

The *modified tradition hypothesis* is particularly associated with the Scandinavian School (e.g., Riesenfeld, Gerhardsson, Nyberg, Byrskog,), as well as Riesner, Reicke, Ellis, and, more recently, Dunn, Bauckham, and Baum.[67] It

---

[62] Linnemann, *Problem*, 132.
[63] Linnemann, *Problem*, 134.
[64] See Baltes, *Evangelium*, 586–92, who argues that each Synoptic Gospel writer drew on a common, Semitic (written or oral) *Vorlage*. See J. Jay, *The Tragic in Mark: A Literary-Historical Interpretation* (Tübingen: Mohr Siebeck, 2014), ad loc., regarding the possibility that the narrative plot-development in Mark might be akin to motifs and moods of ancient tragedy. See also Bayer, *Theology*, 19–32.
[65] See D. Dungan, 'Dispensing with the Priority of Mark', in Holmén and Porter (eds), *Handbook*, II, 1313–42.
[66] Reicke, *Roots*, 180–90; see also A. Schlatter, *Einleitung in die Bibel* (Stuttgart: Calwer, 1923), 276–80, 300–301.
[67] Riesenfeld, *Tradition*, 3–30; Gerhardsson, *Memory*, 324–35; Riesner, *Jesus*, 408–98; Reicke, *Roots*, 22; E.E. Ellis, 'Preformed Traditions and Their Implications for the Origins of Pauline Christology', in E.E. Ellis (ed.), *History and Interpretation in New Testament Perspective* (Leiden: Brill, 2001), 133–50; Bauckham, *Eyewitnesses*, 240–89; Baum, *Faktor*, 387–402, and A.D. Baum, 'Der semitische Sprachhintergrund der Evangelien und die Urevangeliumshypothese: Überlegungen im Anschluss an Guido Baltes', *TBei* 44 (2013), 306–23.

also draws on insights gleaned from earlier researchers such as B.F. Westcott,[68] F. Godet, and A. Schlatter. The common denominator of these scholars is the attempt to explain the Synoptic Phenomenon by recourse to historical (in this case predominantly the study of stereotyped oral transmission of tradition) as well as to literary analysis. Furthermore, the above-mentioned scholars seriously consider the patristic testimony to the effect that the authors of the canonical Gospels are either eyewitnesses (Matthew and John)[69] or followers of eyewitnesses (Mark follows Peter; Luke follows Paul, and, for his Gospel, he consults various apostolic eyewitnesses). The chief modification (and substantiation) of the classical tradition hypothesis lies thus in the more specialized historical investigation of the question of the origin and transmission of the Gospels (i.e., the study of the mode of formation and transmission; see above). This investigation thus focuses on the circumstances and guiding principles of early oral collection and transmission of apostolic witness accounts (see above; cf. Acts 1:21-22 and the 'micro-gospel' in Acts 10:36-42), chief among them those of Peter.[70] The question concerning the exact relationship between the Synoptic Gospels is thus *coupled* with the question of *how* the Gospels came into existence not only in a literary, but also in a historical setting, requiring text-based, historical analyses, supplemented by socio-historical study. Finally, the apostolic validation or rejection (Luke 1:1) of written Gospel accounts must be kept in view.

Peter and Luke 1:1-4 as Support for the Modified Tradition Hypothesis

An indirect support for the above-mentioned scenario—moving from Jesus to the disciples to early Christian writings and finally to the canonical Gospels—comes from Luke's prologue (Luke 1:1-4), since he claims to have accessed apostolic eyewitnesses. Godet's careful analysis of Luke's prologue is significant in regard to the fact that Luke himself claims to know various written accounts of witness to Jesus (Luke 1:1).[71] In principle, this could include the *written* accounts of Mark and Matthew, and perhaps even John. Luke himself, however, claims to rely exclusively on *oral* apostolic eyewitnesses, that is, he appears *not* to have used any written accounts. The pool of apostolic eyewitnesses from which Luke draws could include Peter, John, and Matthew.[72] We thus believe that Luke 1:1-4 contributes important

---

[68] Westcott, *Introduction*, 165–68, 174–84, 192–209, 211.
[69] See Byrskog, *Story,* 48–91, esp. concerning eyewitness accounts.
[70] See already Westcott, *Introduction*, 212.
[71] Godet, *Luke*, 35.
[72] See M. Hengel, 'Der Lukasprolog und seine Augenzeugen: die Apostel, Petrus und die Frauen', in S.C. Barton, L.T. Stuckenbruck, and B.G. Wold (eds), *Memory in the*

complementary perspectives and aspects to our claim that Peter serves as a key guarantor in the move from oral tradition to written documents.

We thus now explore in further detail the significance of the Lukan prologue. In our view, Luke makes the following claims regarding the historical (and thus theological) trustworthiness of his account:[73]

a. Writing reliable history is a matter of great importance to Luke: investigative recourse to eyewitnesses, writing accurately[74] and in order, embeds the message in a reality framework and guards against possible docetic teaching or imaginative embellishment.

b. Luke *knew* of the written work of his predecessors[75] but he probably did not make *use* of their work.

c. Careful investigation of tradition probably sets Luke apart from his (now probably unknown) predecessors. Luke accesses and uses apostolic witness. He thus investigates personally carefully guarded tradition.

d. Luke's clear composition purports to undergird the reliability of the account and ultimately the compelling nature of the message, which focuses on the reality of salvation in Christ.

In support of these four points, we submit the following details:

It has long been observed that the Hellenistic-Jewish historian Josephus features a significant parallel to Luke–Acts in his two-part work *Against Apion*. The preface to Josephus's first volume states (*Ag. Ap.* 1.1-4, λόγος πρότερος):

Bible and Antiquity: The Fifth Durham-Tübingen Research Symposium (Durham, September 2004) (Tübingen: Mohr Siebeck, 2007), 195–242.

[73] See A.D. Baum, 'Lk 1, 1–4 zwischen antiker Historiografie und Fachprosa: Zum literaturgeschichtlichen Kontext des lukanischen Prologs', *ZNW* 101/1 (2010) 33–54. Baum convincingly demonstrates against the thesis of L. Alexander (*The Preface of Luke's Gospel: Literary Convention and Social Context in Luke 1:1-4 and Acts 1:1* [Cambridge: Cambridge University Press, 1993]; i.e., that Luke's prologue represents a technical or scientific manual) that Luke's prologue formally represents conventions of ancient historiography (recounting a 'story of history'), both in terms of Greco-Roman literary convention (key terms used and syntax) and anonymity in Jewish historical books. See also T. Callan, 'The Preface of Luke–Acts and Historiography', *NTS* 31.4 (1985), 576–81; Marshall, *Luke*, 39–44; Hengel, 'Lukasprolog', 195–242.

[74] Cf. Luke 7:21, and Acts 1:3 ('many proofs').

[75] The process of writing down is attested early; cf. Godet, *Luke*, 40.

> In my history of our *Antiquities*, most excellent Epaphroditus, I have . . . made sufficiently clear . . . the extreme antiquity of our Jewish race . . . That history . . . was written by me in Greek on the basis of our sacred books. Since, however, I observe that a considerable number of persons . . . discredit the statements in my history concerning our antiquity . . . I consider it my duty to devote a brief treatise to all these points; in order . . . to correct . . . to instruct all who desire to know the truth . . . As witnesses to my statements I propose to call the writers who, in the estimation of the Greeks, are the trustworthiest authorities on antiquity as a whole.[76]

Josephus's preface to his second volume states (*Ag. Ap.* 2.1-2, λόγος δεύτερος):

> In the first volume . . . my esteemed Epaphroditus, I demonstrated the antiquity of our race, corroborating my statement by the writings of Phoenicians, Chaldaeans, and Egyptians, besides citing as witnesses numerous Greek historians; . . . I shall now proceed to refute the rest of the authors who have attacked us.[77]

Among other factors, this parallel supports the fact that Luke sets out to write a *public narrative* within formal conventions of ancient historiography[78] and that the phenomenon of a two-part work is not unique to Luke–Acts. Much discussion focuses on the initial question of whether Luke's prologue pertains to *both* parts of his work. Godet argues that Luke 1:1-4 can only be the prologue to his Gospel.[79] He notes that 'us' in the expressions 'among *us*' (Luke 1:1) and 'handed down to *us*' (Luke 1:2) refer to the circle of believers (with the apostles) only, especially its use in verse 2 (believers without the apostles). While this holds true for verse 2, it is by no means clear that verse 1 is equally exclusive. Godet himself acknowledges that 'among us' would make more sense if Acts (even with Godet's limited interpretation for v.1) were in view as well. Be that as it may, Godet refers above all to παράδοσις in verse 2 and κατήχησις in verse 4 as strong indications that Acts *cannot* be in view.[80]

---

[76] Josephus (*Ag. Ap.* 1.53-54) states that he who transmits reports of trustworthy historical deeds and events must ascertain exactly (ἀκριβῶς) what happened, either by following the events himself or by finding out from those who were present.

[77] Cf. also the preambles to Herodotus and Thucydides (see Godet, *Luke*, 33). Cf. Marshall, *Luke*, 39.

[78] See Baum, 'Historiografie', 33–54 and S. Uytanlet, *Luke–Acts and Jewish Historiography: A Study on the Theology, Literature, and Ideology of Luke–Acts* (Tübingen: Mohr Siebeck, 2014).

[79] Godet, *Luke*, 36.

[80] Godet, *Luke*, 36.

Godet acknowledges, however, that 'becoming ministers of the word' also hints at Acts. To us, this is more significant than Godet permits. The παράδοσις clearly *includes* accounts of God's deeds among the earliest Christian communities. The instruction (κατήχησις) mentioned in verse 4, which Theophilus received, is nothing else than *explained* παράδοσις mentioned in verse 2 (see Acts 2:42). The prologue thus refers most plausibly to both the Gospel *and* Acts and serves as an introduction to both.[81]

In his prologue, Luke presents the historiographical purpose of his two-part work and explains both the (re-)sources utilized and methods employed.[82] Furthermore, the author declares that he is *not* an eyewitness of Jesus. The structure of the prologue is simple. It consists of two parts (vv. 1 and 2 as subordinate clauses and vv. 3 and 4 as the main clauses), molded in three matching phrases. We here offer an explanation of key statements in Luke 1:1-4.

- *Luke 1:1.* It is important to observe that composing a narrative of the events surrounding Jesus is nothing new from Luke's point of view (πολλοί refers to predecessors). Godet argues convincingly that the term διήγησις does not denote, as Schleiermacher mistakenly took it, 'recitals of isolated facts.'[83] Rather, the term here refers to the fact that predecessors composed *historical narratives* or *written arrangements*.[84] That Luke's predecessors undertook this task (ἐπεχείρησαν) is not mentioned in a condescending way, but is kept in a neutral tone (note 'just as' in v. 2 and 'it seemed good also to me' in v. 3). The focus lies on deeds of God (πραγμάτων) which have left a lasting effect.[85]

- *Luke 1:2.* The content of the message has been handed down carefully. Παραδίδωμι in this context is a *terminus technicus* implying that the contents are 'formally guarded,' 'carefully transmitted,' and faithfully 'taught'.[86] The message has been transmitted by eyewitnesses (αὐτόπτης) 'from the beginning'[87] who are also identified as 'servants

---

[81] W.C. van Unnik, 'The "Book of Acts"–the Confirmation of the Gospel', *NovT*, 4.1 (1960), 26–59, presents significant arguments in support of Luke 1:1-4 serving as the key preface to the entire two-volume work.

[82] Similarly, Godet, *Luke*, 33.

[83] Godet, *Luke*, 34.

[84] Cf. LXX Hab 1:5. See Brown, *Introduction*, 227.

[85] Note that the culminative perfect (πεπληροφορημένων) implies generally a conclusion with ongoing effect; cf. 2 Tim 4:5, 17.

[86] See Mark 7:13; 2 Pet 2:21; cf. 1 Cor 11:2-23, 15:3). See Riesner, *Jesus,* 440–98.

[87] Cf. Acts 1:21-22; 10:37.

of the word'[88] (ὑπηρέται[89] τοῦ λόγου). The transmitters of this tradition are thus not innovators but rather faithful communicators of what was entrusted to them. The expression 'servant of the word' is only found here in the New Testament. The analogous expression 'ministry of the word' (διακονία τοῦ λόγου) in Acts 6:4 (see Acts 6:2)[90] pertains to the preaching ministry of the apostles. In their calling, therefore, the apostles are not only 'witnesses' but they also bear the responsibility of 'servants' (following the ascension of Jesus).

- *Luke 1:3.* Luke emphasizes that he engaged in *investigation* (an abstract and technical use of παρακολουθέω) prior to passing on this apostolic witness and teaching. 'Investigation' conveys (together with ἄνωθεν[91]) the retracing of the subject matter, going back to its sources (eyewitnesses) [92] by following up on *each aspect* of the tradition.[93] This work was executed 'accurately' (or 'with precision', ἀκριβῶς) and in orderly (temporal or local) fashion (καθεξῆς). The story of Jesus thus 'makes sense' and 'hangs together,' not necessarily in an absolutely chronological order but as a reliable narrative and in generally historical sequence.[94] This may very likely indicate that Luke went beyond his predecessors with regard to investigative effort. Luke drafts his conscientious work from the apostolic witness bedrock, checks and/or compares (apostolic) sources, and orders his material. It thus becomes evident that Luke wishes to be taken seriously as a responsible historian of his time.[95]

---

[88] Cf. the word-group of ἀπόστολος and διάκονος.

[89] The term occurs 9x in Luke–Acts, 9x in John, 1x each in Matt and Mark, and in 1 Cor 4:1. In Luke 4:20, e.g., the term is used to describe a *synagogue attendant*; in Acts 5:22, 26 the term is used for *jail officers*; in Acts 13:5, John Mark is the *attendant* of Barnabas and Saul. Generally, therefore, the term denotes assistance or help. Acts 26:16 is significant (but not semantically different) in that the ministry of Paul is identified as being a *servant* and witness of Christ.

[90] Cf. the only other similar expression in Col 1:25: Paul, the servant (διάκονος), is to present the word of God.

[91] The term ἄνωθεν (Acts 26:5) means: 'from the beginning'/'go back to beginning or roots, in each section of his account' or: 'at length'.

[92] Godet, *Luke*, 37, refers to Demosthenes, *Cor.* 53, as a parallel.

[93] Cf. Godet, *Luke*, 37, who refers also to 2 Tim 3:10.

[94] *Pace* Godet, *Luke*, 38, who argues in favor of a chronological sequence.

[95] Cf. Marshall, *Luke*, 38. See Hemer, *Acts*, 63–243, who argues that Luke ranks among the conscientious historians of his time.

- *Additional Thoughts on Luke 1:1-3.* Riesner comments aptly that the Lukan prologue shares at least three significant terms with Josephus (*Ag. Ap.* 1.53)[96] and Papias (Eusebius, *Hist. eccl.* 3.39.15):[97] all three authors seek to present true events (conveyed by the stem πραγ-); the events are to be presented ἀκριβῶς; and in order to achieve this, the writer has to have been present himself (eyewitness; Josephus, as well as Peter, according to Papias) or he has to have accessed eyewitness reports (Luke). Such 'following of events' is expressed by παρακολουθέω. Riesner concludes that Luke intends to write as an historian.

  Verses 1–3 thus describe Luke's investigation of *primary* (oral/written) *sources* (i.e., eyewitnesses, see v. 3), while acknowledging awareness of written *secondary sources*. It is thus impossible that Luke 1:1 refers to the Gospels of Matthew or John (assuming apostolic authorship), since the written secondary accounts mentioned by Luke are *not* composed by apostolic eyewitnesses. If any canonical Gospel account could be in view as a source for Luke, it would be that of Mark only. However, Godet convincingly rules out the Gospel of Mark as well, since ἐπεχείρησαν implies 'research,' a term hardly applicable to Mark's account, if we take Papias seriously.[98] This does not mean, however, that Luke could not have contacted Peter or John Mark (especially when arriving with Paul in Rome, Acts 28:16),[99] or compared Mark's account with his own;[100] but he does not make explicit *mention* of it.

- *Luke 1:4.* Luke thus wishes to compose an account which meets all necessary conditions for accuracy (ἀσφάλεια), stated at the *conclusion* of his prologue for emphasis. Accuracy may refer to 'firmness' (see Acts 5:23), 'safety,' 'security' (see 1 Thess 5:3), 'certainty,' or 'irrefutable reliability' of the content. The patron Theophilus is given certitude concerning that which he already knows and believes at least

---

[96] Riesner, 'Rückkehr', 348, also notes that there are correspondences to Josephus, *J.W.* 1.1-13 and *Ant.* 1.1-4.

[97] Riesner, 'Rückkehr', 348.

[98] Godet, *Luke*, 33. Godet believes that 'the works to which Luke alludes are . . . unknown and lost' (p. 35).

[99] See Phlm 24; Col 4:10, 14; 2 Tim 4:11. John Mark and Luke may have contact with each other during Paul's imprisonment in Caesarea, and later, in Rome. Reicke surmises that certain verbal agreements between Matt and Mark as well as between Mark and Luke stem from such contact (cf. Reicke, *Roots*, 180–90).

[100] See Reicke, *Roots*, 183–84.

to a degree.[101] It is thus unwarranted when Brown wishes to identify this assurance as the 'saving value of what is narrated, not primarily about history or objective reporting'.[102] It is exactly the intimate connection between fact, report, *and* salvation message that *characterizes* the prologue and Luke–Acts. Brown promulgates a long-standing, unfounded, and anachronistic dichotomy between reliable history and salvation which has neither served to elicit the intent of Luke (affirming historical reliability) nor the life of the church.[103] Brown[104] himself concedes that Luke was convinced of the fact that the 'original eyewitnesses and ministers of the word' accomplished what they were commissioned to do in Luke 24:47-48, namely, to bear (reliable) witness to Jesus's deeds, words, passion, and resurrection. According to Godet,[105] λόγων (Luke 1:4) refers to both fact and interpretation (see 1 Cor 15:1-4).

The above-mentioned modified tradition hypothesis thus dovetails well with the main emphases and claims of Luke's prologue to Luke–Acts with its emphasis on the testimony of eyewitnesses. Peter stands in the center of such reliable, apostolically transmitted tradition.

We shall not spend much time discussing the alternative of a modified two-source hypothesis.[106] Suffice it to say that, for example, Guthrie[107] and Carson/Moo[108] have presented modified versions of the classical two-source hypothesis[109] by carefully considering patristic and socio-historical factors in the

---

[101] See κατηχέω; cf. Acts 2:36; 21:34; 22:30; 25:26; 2 Pet 1:16, 19; cf. Marshall, *Luke*, 43–44 and Godet, *Luke*, 39: 'to give certitude concerning (περὶ) the instruction which'.

[102] Brown, *Introduction*, 227.

[103] Brown, *Introduction*, 227, claims that Lukan theology is 'dramatized in history and geography' while in fact Luke claims that theology *arises* from historically reliable witness.

[104] Brown, *Introduction*, 262.

[105] Godet, *Luke*, 39.

[106] See Brown, *Introduction*, 151, and 152 nn. 66–67.

[107] D. Guthrie, *New Testament Introduction* (Leicester: IVP, 1978), 234–36. See, to a certain degree, R. Morgenthaler, *Statistische Synopse* (Zürich: Gotthelf Verlag, 1971), 305–306.

[108] D.A. Carson and D.J. Moo, *An Introduction to the New Testament* (Grand Rapids, MI: Zondervan, 2005), 85–103.

[109] For a representative presentation of the classical two-source hypothesis, see, e.g., W.G. Kümmel, *Introduction to the New Testament* (Nashville, TN: Abingdon, 1975).

genesis of the Synoptic Gospels, which lead them to substantially different conclusions than those of many adherents of the classical two-source hypothesis.

Regardless of these two most viable models of the genesis of the Synoptic Gospels, we have sought to demonstrate that Peter functions centrally in the transmission of pre-Easter tradition, the shaping of the format of the canonical Gospel accounts, and the choice of the *bios* genre. This holds true especially for the Gospel of Mark, but it also applies to the other three canonical Gospel accounts. This means that while the Gospel of Mark may not necessarily have been written as the first of the canonical Gospels,[110] the initial oral gospel message and gospel format (and, perhaps, its *bios* genre) most likely go back to Peter. In this sense, he and his apostolic testimony are, to a large degree, the rock upon which the universal and messianic church of God is built (Matt 16:18-19).[111]

Peter as the Source of the Gospel of Mark, the Petrine Sections in Acts, and as the Author of 1 and 2 Peter

Peter as the Source of the Gospel of Mark[112]

Widespread patristic evidence affirms that John Mark, companion of Peter[113] (Acts 12:12, 25; 1 Pet 5:13) and Paul (Acts 13:2-13; [cf. 15:37-40]; Col 4:10; 2 Tim 4:11; Phlm 24), wrote the Gospel attributed to him.[114] Nevertheless, various scholars have argued that we simply do not know who wrote the Gospel of Mark.

---

[110] See, e.g., Baltes, *Evangelium*, 220–573, 597, who argues in favor of a Hebrew proto-Matthew.

[111] See our discussion of Matt 16:18-19, above.

[112] See J. Dewey, 'The Historical Jesus in the Gospel of Mark', in Holmén and Porter (eds), *Handbook*, III, 1821–53; M. Hengel, *The Four Gospels and the One Gospel of Jesus Christ: An Investigation of the Collection and Origin of the Canonical Gospels* (Harrisburg, PA: Trinity Press, 2000).

[113] See Papias, Justin Martyr, Irenaeus, (*Haer.* 3.1.10; 3.3.1-3), Clement of Alexandria, Tertullian, Origen, and Jerome, as well as the *Muratorian Canon* and the Anti-Marcionite Prologue. For details, see Bockmuehl, *Simon*, 102–11.

[114] See A.D. Baum, 'Papias als Kommentator evangelischer Aussprüche Jesu', *NovT* 28.3 (1996), 257–75; A.D. Baum, 'Der Presbyter des Papias', *TZ* 56 (2000), 21–35; Brown, *Introduction*, 159; M. Hengel, *Studies in Early Christology* (Edinburgh: T&T Clark, 1998), 47–64; Hengel, *Peter*, 36–48; J. Kürzinger, 'Papias von Hierapolis: Zu Titel und Art seines Werkes', in *Papias von Hierapolis und die Evangelien des Neuen Testaments* (Regensburg: Pustet, 1983), 69–87; Reicke, *Roots*, 163; Riesner, *Jesus*, 20–24; Schlatter, *Einleitung*, 302–303; C.-J. Thornton, 'Justin und das Markusevangelium', *ZNW* 84 (1993), 93–110; R. Yarbrough, 'The Date of Papias: A Reassessment', *JETS* 26.2 (1983), 181–91.

It is true that the *inscriptio* ΚΑΤΑ ΜΑΡΚΟΝ ('According to Mark') was added to the Gospel at a later stage.[115] Technically speaking, the Second Gospel is thus an anonymous[116] work. In this context it is possible that Peter and John Mark were aware of 2 Maccabees, which adopted some Greek conventions but refrained, in line with the Old Testament Historical Books, from giving the author's name. To take the 'agnostic route' based on this fact alone means, however, to ignore significant and ancient external (and internal) evidence in support of Markan authorship and Peter as the Gospel's source.

External Evidence

As stated, nearly all patristic authors consider John Mark to be the writer of the Second Gospel.[117] Of particular significance are the brief extant statements by Papias, bishop of Hierapolis (~ AD 120), preserved by Eusebius of Caesarea (AD 260–340).[118] Papias[119] states that he received oral tradition[120] from the presbyter (and apostle) John.[121] Concerning the Gospel of Mark, Papias notes[122] several key points concerning Mark:

---

[115] At the latest at the end of the second century AD. Concerning an earlier date, see M. Hengel, 'The Titles of the Gospels and the Gospel of Mark', in *Studies in the Gospel of Mark* (Philadelphia, PA: Fortress, 1985), 64–84.

[116] Regarding the overall issue of anonymity among the Historical Books of the NT, see A.D. Baum, 'Anonymity in the NT History Books: A Stylistic Device in the Context of Greco-Roman and Ancient Near Eastern Literature', *NovT* 50 (2008), 120–42; See Bauckham, *Eyewitnesses*, 183–201, regarding the possibility of deliberate anonymity to protect an author writing during times of persecution (e.g., the Gospel of Mark or *1 Clem.*).

[117] See Pesch, *Markusevangelium*, II, 4–11, regarding an extensive discussion of this issue. Only Hippolytus (~ AD 200) differentiates between the cousin of Barnabas (John Mark) and an evangelist, Mark, author of the Gospel of Mark.

[118] See Baum, 'Papias', 257–76, who argues that Papias sought to give in his (now mostly lost) work explanations of canonical, dominical sayings and deeds. See also M.A. Shanks, *Papias and the New Testament* (Eugene, OR: Pickwick Publishing, 2013).

[119] Eusebius, *Hist. eccl.* 3.39.1-7.14-17; cf. *Hist. eccl.* 2.15. See U.H.J. Körtner, *Papias von Hierapolis* (Göttingen: Vandenhoeck & Ruprecht, 1983); Yarbrough, 'Date', 181–91; Reicke, *Roots*, 7–8, 155–66; Kürzinger, *Papias*, 69–87; Baum, 'Papias', 257–75. Cf. C.C. Black, *Mark: Images of an Apostolic Interpreter* (Columbia, SC: University of SC, 1994).

[120] See J. Becker, *Mündliche und schriftliche Autorität im frühen Christentum* (Tübingen: Mohr Siebeck, 2012).

[121] Eusebius, *Hist. eccl.* 3.29.15. It is most plausible that the 'Apostle John' is also the 'presbyter John' (both mentioned in one phrase: Eusebius, *Hist. eccl.* 3.39.4), especially since Papias states there that the 'presbyter John' was a 'disciple' of the Lord. Papias calls the (twelve) apostles 'presbyters.' Papias's reference to the otherwise unknown 'disciple' Aristion is awkward but does not falsify the above

1) *Mark was a writer for Peter* (Μάρκος μὲν ἑρμηνευτὴς Πέτρου γενόμενος),[123] that is, Peter passed on reports of the words and deeds of the Lord to his attendant (ὑπηρέτης,[124] see Acts 13:5) Mark. It is less likely that ἑρμηνευτής denotes 'translator' here, so that the meaning would be that John Mark translated from Aramaic/Hebrew to Greek.[125]

The interpretation of 'translator' is favored, by Bauckham,[126] for example, partially because the lexical evidence favors this view. Most likely, however, the term denotes more technically 'writer', 'transmitter', 'conveyor', 'reporter', or 'recorder', since the specific emphasis in Papias's report lies on *Mark writing down* what Peter remembered (ὅσα ἐμνημόνευσεν, twice applied to Peter).[127] Bauckham's[128] arguments against Kürzinger[129] do not convince, especially since Bauckham concedes himself that Kürzinger's arguments in favor of *hermeneutēs* being a technical rhetorical term 'certainly [are] coherent with the general tenor of what Papias says about Mark—that he reproduced

---

statements. Irenaeus (*Haer.* 5.32) also supports the identification of John as 'apostle' and 'presbyter'. Differently, Bauckham, *Eyewitnesses,* 16–21; 32–35; 412–37.

[122] Eusebius, *Hist. eccl.* 3.39.15: 'Mark having become the interpreter of Peter, wrote down accurately whatsoever he (Peter) remembered. It was not, however, in exact order that he related the sayings or (and) deeds of Christ. For he neither heard the Lord nor accompanied Him. But afterwards, as I said, he accompanied Peter, who put his instructions into 'chreiai', but with no intention of giving a chronological (regular) narrative of the Lord's sayings. Wherefore Mark made no mistake in thus writing (some) things as he (Peter) remembered them. For of one thing he took especial care, not to omit anything he had heard, and not to put anything false (fictitious) into the statements' (cf. also Eusebius, *Hist. eccl.* 3.39.1-7.14-17).

[123] Eusebius, *Hist. eccl.* 3.39.15.

[124] According to Acts 13:5, John Mark was known as an assistant (ὑπηρέτης). Some scholars believe that this term represents the title of a synagogue attendant. It is, however, more likely that the term refers to the fact that John Mark was, in this instance, at Paul's and Barnabas' disposal for service (perhaps as a secretary).

[125] So, e.g., Josephus, who originally wrote his *History of the Jewish War* in Aramaic before translating it into Greek himself, probably with the help of a certain Epaphroditus (cf. *Ag. Ap.* 1.50). Josephus notes that translating the work into a foreign language was difficult.

[126] Bauckham, *Eyewitnesses*, 205–208 and Baum, 'Presbyter', 21–35.

[127] Eusebius, *Hist. eccl.* 3.39.15. In support of this, see Riesner, 'Rückkehr', 337–52 and Riesner, *Jesus*, 20, who also refers to Kürzinger, *Papias*, 47, as well as Brown, *Introduction*, 160. See also Bockmuehl, *Simon*, 170, and n. 9; Pesch, *Simon-Petrus*, 11–12, and Hengel, *Peter*, 12, 37.

[128] Bauckham, *Eyewitnesses*, 207. Bauckham assumes that the mature Peter, while bilingual, still preferred to use a 'translator' in Rome (p. 206).

[129] Kürzinger, *Papias*, 45–47.

exactly what Peter said'.[130] Given these factors, Kürzinger's view that Mark serves as one who 'records' what Peter remembers, is most convincing. This interpretation also seems to be supported by Justin Martyr, who considers Mark to be the writer of what Peter remembered (ἀπομνημονεύματα αὐτοῦ).[131] Justin refers to Mark 3:16-17 as a section of the 'memoirs' of Peter.[132] Finally, it is unlikely that *hermeneutēs* means 'expounder' or 'interpreter' of what Peter said or that Mark served as an *amanuensis*, since the work never carried the title '*Gospel of Peter*'.[133] Regardless of the precise definition of *hermeneutēs*, the main emphasis of Papias is to testify to a reliable transmission of tradition from Jesus to Peter, and eventually to the Gospel of Mark via John Mark.

2) *Mark wrote down accurately* (ἀκριβῶς ἔγραψεν)[134] *the remembrances of Peter* (ἐμνημόνευσεν; twice mentioned),[135] in which Peter rendered the teachings (τὰ ὑπὸ τοῦ κυρίου λεχθέντα ἢ πραχθέντα; i.e., the words *and* deeds) of Jesus in the form of biographical *chreiai* (ὃς πρὸς τὰς χρείας ἐποιεῖτο τὰς διδασκαλίας), albeit not in order (οὐ μέντοι τάξει; twice mentioned). According to Papias, however, the lack of precise chronological order vouchsafes for the Gospel's authenticity as stemming from Peter and thus confirms the Gospel of Mark as a reliable apostolic document.

3) *Mark was not an eyewitness of Jesus*, nor a disciple (οὔτε γὰρ ἤκουσεν τοῦ κυρίου οὔτε παρηκολούθησεν αὐτῷ).

4) *Mark did not intend to omit or misrepresent anything.*

According to Papias, the Gospel of Mark gains its apostolic and reliable character on account of these factors.

It is historically plausible to identify the 'Mark' of Papias with 'John Mark' of the New Testament, attendant of both Peter and Paul. A careful reconstruction of John Mark's life yields the following results: John Mark began his early Christian years in the company of Barnabas and, at times, Peter; later he accompanied Paul and experienced temporary tension with him; toward the end of Paul's life, Mark was restored to Paul. Simultaneously, around AD 63, John Mark was once more in Peter's company (1 Pet 5:13) in Rome. Around AD 64,

---

[130] Bauckham, *Eyewitnesses*, 207.

[131] Justin Martyr, *Dial.* 106, 3.

[132] Justin, *Dial.* 106.3. See the Anti-Marcionite Gospel Prologue (AD 160–80).

[133] See, e.g., Josephus, *Ant.* 2.72, who uses *hermeneutēs* to describe Joseph 'interpreting' dreams; see, convincingly, Bauckham, *Eyewitnesses*, 205.

[134] Cf. Josephus, *Ag. Ap.* 1.53.

[135] Cf. Justin Martyr, *Dial.* 106, 3. See further Irenaeus (*Haer.* 3.1.2) and Tertullian (AD 160–222; *Marc.* 4.5) concerning the fact that Peter is the main source of the Gospel of Mark.

John Mark may have been in Ephesus (2 Tim 4:11 [he joined Timothy to see Paul in Rome]). Besides his associations with Peter and Paul, John Mark appears frequently in the company of Demas and Luke (see Col 4:10-14; 2 Tim 4:11-12; Phlm 24). The following overview summarizes a simple itinerary of John Mark:

AD 44   In Jerusalem with his mother, Mary; contact with Peter and Barnabas; Acts 12:12
AD 45   Goes with Paul and Barnabas to Syrian Antioch; Acts 12:25
AD 46   Joins Barnabas and Paul on Paul's first missionary journey; Acts 13:5
AD 46   Departs prematurely from Barnabas and Paul and returns to Jerusalem; Acts 13:13
~AD 47/48 Paul challenges Peter; Gal 2:11-14
AD 49   Travels with Barnabas to Cyprus following the 'Antiochene conflict'; Acts 15:36-40; see Acts 13:13
AD 61   Is with Paul in Rome; serves, perhaps, as missionary in Asia Minor; Col 4:10; Phlm 23-24
AD 63 (?) Serves as attendant of Peter in Rome (from 'Babylon'); 1 Pet 5:13
AD 64   Serves as attendant of Paul; John Mark's sojourn in Ephesus (?); 2 Timothy 4:11

As a relative of Barnabas, John Mark grew up in the setting of Hellenistic Judaism. Through Barnabas, he was intimately acquainted with the Apostles Peter and Paul and their teaching (see Acts 4:36-37 and 9:26). Schlatter aptly states: 'Mark thus held from the beginning a central place in the church. He witnessed how the Jewish and Greek churches took shape; he enjoyed extended times of personal contact both with Peter and Paul, and thus became a special witness to the apostolic preaching. Furthermore, he himself engaged in an extensive teaching ministry in the church.' [136]

There is only a faint possibility that Mark was an eyewitness of events described at the end of Mark. Mark 14:51-52 may be a personal reminiscence. It is true that the omission of these two verses would facilitate narrative continuity. The detail in Mark 15:21 (Simon of Cyrene, father of Alexander and Rufus[137]) may reflect personal eyewitness reporting.[138] However, patristic evidence is divided on this question.

---

[136] Schlatter, *Einleitung*, 293 (trans., HFB).

[137] Rufus has been identified with the Rufus mentioned in Rom 16:13. This may be a hint that Mark is writing from Rome. Nevertheless, not too much should be made of this possibility.

Papias[139] speaks against Mark as an eyewitness of Jesus, while the later Muratorian Canon (~AD 200)[140] identifies John Mark as an eyewitness. Papias may be seen as simply defending the correct view that John Mark was neither a disciple nor a witness of the life of Christ. This does not necessarily preclude that John Mark may have become a personal witness at the end of Jesus's life. Regardless of this issue, we conclude that John Mark had direct access to the eyewitness Peter, leader of the early Christian disciples and eyewitness of Jesus and his teaching. Our biblical findings thus dovetail with Papias's portrait. Later patristic tradition relates that Peter sent John Mark to Egypt as a missionary where he planted the church in Alexandria and became its first bishop. John Mark is said to have met martyrdom in Alexandria around AD 68. His remains are said to have been transferred to Venice.

What appears to cast doubt on the independent value of Papias's report is the fact that he also refers to 1 Peter 5:13.[141] This means for Pesch[142] and others that Papias was exclusively dependent on New Testament documents for his (thus conjectured) information on Mark. While there is little doubt that Papias knew 1 Peter 5:13, it is by no means justified to assume (especially in the light of Papias's expressly stated case to the contrary) that he had no *separate* access to oral information concerning the authorship of Mark.[143] It is indeed Papias who considers terse oral information drawn from authentic sources (in this case, the presbyter and Apostle John, around AD 95–100)[144] to be more significant than written documentation.[145] Papias may not be robbed that easily of his ostensible access to extra-biblical oral information, especially since his testimony is congruent with other patristic voices (see, e.g., the Anti-Marcionite Prologue and Irenaeus). It is also important to keep in mind that a relatively unknown, non-

---

[138] See also Mark 15:39.

[139] Eusebius, *Hist. eccl.* 3.39.

[140] See, e.g., E. Hennecke, *Neutestamentliche Apokryphen* (Tübingen: Mohr Siebeck, 1968), I, 19. It is likely that Mark (Second Gospel) is in view in this incomplete fragment. This can be inferred by the next line, which speaks of the 'Third Gospel' as that of Luke.

[141] Eusebius, *Hist. eccl.* 3.39.17. See the discussion in Riesner, *Jesus*, 21–22.

[142] Pesch, *Markusevangelium,* I, 4.

[143] See J.W. Wenham, *Redating Matthew, Mark and Luke* (Downers Grove, IL: IVP, 1992), 137–38, 141.

[144] Yarbrough ('Date', 181–91) dates Papias around AD 110. If this information is taken seriously, a date of AD 85–100 for the *provenance* of the oral information from John is reasonable (see Bauckham, *Eyewitnesses*, 204).

[145] See especially A.D. Baum, 'Papias, der Vorzug der *Viva Vox* und die Evangelienschriften', *NTS* 44.1 (1998), 144–51.

apostolic person is consistently, and without controversy, identified as the author of the Gospel of Mark.[146]

A further point of criticism against the validity of Papias's statements is that he appears to speak *apologetically* in favor of Mark. First, it must be noted that the apologetic aim does not pertain to Mark as author (which is a significant factor, considering the fact that Mark was not an apostle and eyewitness), as much as it pertains to the content of his report. One may surmise from Papias's statement that some contemporaries held that the Gospel of Mark did not conform sufficiently to the narrative sequence of the 'primary' and popular[147] Gospel of Matthew. Furthermore, Papias's apologetic by no means automatically speaks against the credibility of what he affirms. An apologetic motif can reflect dedication to truth (e.g., in order to offset denial or error)[148] or it may cover up truth.[149] In Papias's case, therefore, none of the presented arguments against the validity of his statements stand up to scrutiny.

While it is historically true that especially in the first five centuries AD Mark's Gospel was much less popular than that of Matthew,[150] the evidence does not support an inference that therefore Mark was not seen as standing in close proximity to Peter. The predominant reason why Mark's Gospel was less popular than that of Matthew was the fact that Mark was long viewed as giving an abbreviated version of the content of Matthew (see, e.g., Augustine[151]), not that the source of Mark was seen as any less apostolic than that of Matthew. External patristic evidence thus makes a strong case for John Mark having written the account and for Peter being primarily responsible for its contents.

Internal Evidence

We have some internal indications[152] which support the patristic testimony that Peter stands behind the Gospel of Mark.[153] In general terms, the Markan account

---

[146] Brown, *Introduction*, 159, remarks: 'If someone was inventing a tradition about authorship, why attribute the Gospel to such a minor Christian figure?'

[147] Bockmuehl, *Simon*, 70.

[148] See Hemer, *Acts*, 63–100, regarding the various ambitions and motives of ancient historians.

[149] It is possible that Papias defends the difference in sequence of the material presented in Mark in comparison with Matthew. Schlatter assumes that the presbyter John was asked by Papias regarding the non-apostolic Gospel of Mark. The ensuing answer by John is to endorse the apostolic authenticity of Mark (*Einleitung*, 302–303).

[150] H.F. Bayer, *Das Evangelium des Markus* (Wuppertal: Brokhaus, 2013), 91–94.

[151] Augustine, *Cons.* 1.2.

[152] See Bauckham, *Eyewitnesses*, 155–82; H.-J. Schulz, *Die apostolische Herkunft der Evangelien: Zum Ursprung der Evangelienform in der urgemeindlichen Paschafeier* (Freiburg: Herder, 1997), 125–86; R. Feldmeier, 'The Portrayal of Peter in the

is vivid when recounting incidents involving Peter in a *special* way,[154] presents vividly certain features of *weakness* of Peter, and *omits*, at times, *praise worthy* or noticeable references to Peter reported in Matthew and Luke.

Regarding the first of these, Brown[155] is correct in observing that Peter is at any rate the unquestioned leader in earliest Palestinian Christianity, thus making a particular proximity of the Gospel of Mark to Peter rather difficult to prove. But in Mark's vivid report, Peter occupies a significant and central place, which goes beyond that which Matthew and Luke report (see the synoptic parallels to Mark 1:36; 5:37; 8:29; 9:2; 11:21; 13:3; 14:33). At times, Mark also displays Peter's point of view. We note the following: Mark 1:16-20 (calling of disciples); 1:29 (Jesus in the house of Peter and Andrew); 5:21 (Jairus's daughter); 9:2-10; 14:54, 72 (Jesus and Peter); 16:7 (report concerning Jesus's resurrection). In each instance Peter is the central figure. Furthermore, the directness of an eyewitness report is especially noticeable in all these same passages, as well as in 14:33-42.

Regarding the second aspect (Peter's weakness), we especially mention telling (self-) critical features in Mark 8:33; 9:5; 14:30-31, 37, 54-72 (cf. 1 Pet 5:1-6).[156]

Regarding the third feature noted above, it is of considerable significance that praise-worthy or noticeable references to Peter are conspicuously missing in the Markan account. Mark does not feature (1) the report of Peter walking on water (contrast Mark 6:45-52 with Matt 14:28-31); (2) the pericope concerning temple tax, in which Peter figures prominently (Matt 17:24-27; no Markan parallel); (3) Jesus's prayer for Peter in Gethsemane (no Markan parallel; see Luke 22:31-32); or (4) Peter as the 'rock' (no Markan parallel; see Matt 16:18). Occasionally, Peter is not mentioned by name in Mark, when Matthew, Luke, or John do so (compare, e.g., Mark 7:17 with Matt 15:15; Mark 14:13 with Luke 22:8; Mark 14:47 with John 18:10-11).

Synoptic Gospels', in M. Hengel (ed.), *Studies in the Gospel of Mark* (London: SCM, 1985), 59–63; J. Jeremias, *Neutestamentliche Theologie* (Berlin: Evangelische Verlagsanstalt, 1973), I, 95; Lane, *Mark*, 11–12; V. Taylor, *The Gospel According to St. Mark* (Grand Rapids, MI: Baker, 1981), 26–32.

[153] For details, see Bockmuehl, *Simon*, 132–41.

[154] Riesner, *Jesus*, 22. See, e.g., Mark 1:16; 4:1; 4:38, regarding cast-net fishing, the acoustics of a fishing-boat on water, and the cushion in the stern of the boat (Bockmuehl, *Simon*, 133; on p. 134, Bockmuehl speaks of 'privileged access to private episodes of Jesus' life and ministry'; cf. Mark 5:37; 9:2-13 [2 Pet 1:16-18]; 11:14, 21; 14:29-42, 54-72). See also Mark 1:30-31; 8:27-33; 14:33, 37, 54 (cf. 1 Pet 5:1; 2 Pet 1:16); 14:61 (cf. 1 Pet 2:23).

[155] Brown, *Introduction*, 159. See also Taylor, *Mark*, 130–31, 148–49.

[156] Bockmuehl, *Simon*, 140, rightly points to the parallel in Paul (cf., e.g., 1 Tim 1:15) who 'explicitly highlights and disowns his previous enmity to Christ'.

Even Mark 14:13, 72 can be understood as portraying modesty or shame by an eyewitness. In Mark 14:13 (compare with Matt 26:17) Peter is not named as one of the two disciples who are to prepare the Passover meal (contrast this with Luke 22:8-13, where Peter and John are mentioned by name). Mark 14:72 omits πικρός as a description of the severity of Peter's remorse (contrast this with Matt 26:75 and Luke 22:62). Would Peter really want to 'shine', when it comes to the tale of deep remorse following his denial of Christ? The tendency is clear: where Peter occupies a praiseworthy or prominent position, Mark's account is clearly more muted than that of Matthew or Luke. Despite these factors, it is especially significant that Mark still reflects the general prominence of Peter as the spokesperson of the Twelve (compare, e.g., the Matthean and Lukan parallels to Mark 1:36; 5:37; 8:29; 9:2; 11:21; 13:3; 14:33).[157]

While such internal evidence is at best corroborative in nature, we note that there is an *unforced* and *consistent* convergence between patristic evidence (John Mark, author of the Second Gospel and companion of Peter), and internal indicators in the Gospel of Mark, insofar as Peter is a likely source behind the Markan account.

Bockmuehl aptly concludes: 'Mark's is . . . the earliest and most influential account in a whole tradition of Peter as the chief witness to the memory of Jesus'.[158] Peter, as the spokesperson of the Twelve, passes on to John Mark what he considers to be an important cross-section of Jesus's teaching. In this transmission, Peter not only passes on memorized material, but also hints at the *impact* on his heart, caused by Jesus, in terms of his God- and self-perception, the mission of the Messiah and thus the mission of God, and the true purpose and aim of the Old Testament and the reach to the Gentile world as part of the living and witnessing temple of God.

Peter as a Key Source of the Petrine Sections in Acts[159]

A central question surrounding Peter in Acts is how Luke, a companion of Paul, would have had access to testimony information about Peter during the early stages of the nascent messianic church (see Acts 1–9, 12, 15). As noted above, Luke claims to have accessed directly apostolic eyewitnesses in order to compose his two-volume account (Luke 1:1-4).

---

[157] Brown, *Introduction*, 159, underestimates the simultaneous prominence of Peter and the reticence noticeable in the Gospel of Mark regarding the portrait of Peter. *Pace* Pesch, *Markusevangelium*, I, 10.

[158] Bockmuehl, *Simon*, 135. Bauckham's arguments (*Eyewitnesses*, 124–82) support the likelihood that Peter is the unnamed but evident source of the Gospel of Mark.

[159] See E.J. Schnabel, *Acts* (Grand Rapids, MI: Zondervan, 2012), 38–41.

According to Hengel and Bauckham, Peter is a very significant candidate as one of the Lukan eyewitnesses.[160] Luke most likely visited Antioch (and perhaps Jerusalem) before and during Paul's imprisonment in Caesarea (AD 57–59; cf. Acts 21:18; 27:1), which would have given him access to the apostolic witness of tradition and events in, or pertaining to, Antioch (Acts 6:1-6, 6:8–8:4, 11:19-30) and Jerusalem. Since Peter definitely visited Antioch (Gal 2), it is possible that Luke encountered Peter there. It is also likely that Luke had *direct* access to Peter (via John Mark) in Rome, while tending to Paul following their arrival (~AD 60; see Acts 28:16) and awaiting the trial of Paul in Rome (Acts 28:30). This is conceivable due to the contact between Luke and John Mark (2 Tim 4:11) at a later stage in Paul's life. All of this would have given Luke access to much of the material mentioned in Acts 1–12.[161]

A further, historically likely source for Luke's reliable presentation of Peter's acts and speeches in Acts 1–12 and 15 is Silas/Silvanus who was associated with Peter and Paul in a similar way as was John Mark (see above).[162] Silas is known as a leading disciple (Acts 15:22, 27, 32), a Roman citizen (Acts 16:37-38), and Paul's attendant (Acts 15:40; 2 Cor 1:19; 1 Thess 1:1; 2 Thess 1:1). On the other hand, he is also a companion of Peter (1 Pet 5:12). There are certain parallels between Silas and John Mark: first, they both accompany Peter; then, on various Pauline missionary journeys, they accompany Paul (John Mark on the first and Silas on the second missionary journey; see Acts 15:37-40; 16:3, 17-19, 25, 29, 40; 17:4, 10, 14-15; 18:5).[163] Toward the end of Peter's life, both John Mark and Silas seem to be accompanying him once

---

[160] Hengel, 'Lukasprolog', 239; Bauckham, *Eyewitnesses*, 116–24, 124–27. Eyewitnesses (Luke 1:2) consulted by Luke for his two-volume account most likely include Peter and the other apostles, as well as female disciples, all of whom followed Jesus 'from the beginning' (cf. Luke 1:2; Acts 1:21-22; 10:36-37). Riesner, 'Rückkehr', 349–51, adds to this list, that the natural family of Jesus, chief among them Mary (Luke 2:19, 51; Acts 1:13-14) and Jesus's half-brother James (Acts 1:13-14; 12:17; 15:13-21; 21:18-26) may also serve as significant sources.

[161] Note the Semitic influence in 1:6–2:40, 3:1–4:31, 4:36–5:11, 5:17-42, 8:5-40, 9:32–11:18, 12:1-23. See R.A. Martin, 'Syntactic al Evidence of Aramaic Sources in Acts i-xv', *NTS* 11.1 (1964–65), 38–59, and M. Black, *An Aramaic Approach to the Gospels and Acts* (Peabody, MA: Hendrickson Publishers, 1998).

[162] Concerning the likelihood that Silas is also known as Silvanus, compare 2 Cor 1:19 (Silvanus and Timothy) with Acts 17:14 and 18:5 (Silas and Timothy). Note the association between Silas/Silvanus and John Mark in 1 Pet 5:12-13.

[163] Regarding the connection between Luke and Silas, see Thornton, *Zeuge*, 79–80, 87–90, 99.

again and, notably, in Rome (1 Pet 5:12-13).[164] Silas does not seem to accompany Paul on his journey to Rome. The parallel between John Mark and Silas (compare Acts 13:5 with Acts 15:40), serving as attendants to both Peter (e.g., Acts 12:12; 1 Pet 5:12-13) and Paul (e.g., Acts 12:25; 15:40; 2 Cor 1:19) supports the view that a somewhat 'untidy' historical reconstruction is closer to the truth than a one-sided, simple, and smooth explanation concerning John Mark's and Silas's associations either with Peter or Paul.

An additional possibility, entertained by Hengel, is that Luke contacted further apostles during the two-year house arrest of Paul in Caesarea (Acts 24:27) when he was awaiting trial, first under the *procurator* Felix (AD 52 [?]–59), then under Festus (AD 59–62). If we date the trial under Festus around AD 59–60, Luke could have traveled between ~AD 57–59 to Jerusalem, or, more likely, to his home town of Syrian Antioch to speak with apostles. While contact with other apostles is plausible, it is unlikely that Luke would have been able to meet Peter at that time in either Jerusalem or Antioch, as Peter was probably already in Rome.

Peter as the Author of 1 and 2 Peter[165]

First Peter 1:1 (see also 2 Pet 1:1) uses the term ἀπόστολος, conveying the meaning of a *delegated authority* with a mission or message given by the sending authority (cf. Gal 1:18; John 13:16).[166] The claim of 1 Peter is thus to

---

[164] See J. Becker, *Paulus, der Apostel der Völker* (Tübingen: Mohr Siebeck, 1989), 154 n. 349, who considers the possibility that Silas, once again, joins Peter's mission. See Bockmuehl, *Simon*, 30.

[165] See the discussions in support of and against Petrine authorship in 1 Pet: I.H. Marshall, *1 Peter* (Downers Grove, IL: IVP, 1991), 21–24 (favorable); E.G. Selwyn, *The First Epistle of St. Peter* (London: Macmillan, 1969), 7–38 (favorable); J.R. Michaels, *1 Peter* (Nashville, TN: Nelson, 1988), lxii–lxvii (favorable) and P.J. Achtemeier, *1 Peter* (Minneapolis, MN: Fortress, 1996), 1–23 (skeptical; see his discussion of unlikely literary links to Jude and various Pauline Epistles). See D. Wenham, 'Jesus Tradition in the Letters of the New Testament', in Holmén and Porter (eds), *Handbook*, III, 2041–58.

[166] See the use of ἀπόστολος (=*shaltach*) in contemporary Koine Greek (cf. K.-H. Rengstorf, ἀποστέλλω, ἀπόστολος, in G. Kittel, *TDNT* I, 398–447), such as an invoice, a military expedition, a travel document, a political delegation, etc. (see, e.g., POxy 3.522.1; 9.1197; 10.1259. Prior to the Koine period, the usage is sparse, but it does, at times, occur in the sense of a *delegated commission* (Herodotus 1.21; 5.38). The few Greek OT occurrences of ἀπόστολος are rendering the Hebrew term *šāliaḥ* (LXX, 3 Kgdms 14:6; Aquila, 3 Kgs 14:6; Symmachus, Isa 18:2). Josephus, *Ant.* 17.300, uses the term in the sense of a *delegation*. Luke–Acts is consistent in attributing the term to the Twelve (cf. Gal 1:17), defining an original apostle in Acts

have been written by Peter, the emissary of Jesus, implying a derivative authority to speak in the place and name of Jesus. The author also claims to be 'a witness of the sufferings of Christ' (1 Pet 5:1). It is debated whether 'witness' should be taken as someone who personally witnessed Christ's sufferings or someone who merely testifies *to* Christ's sufferings.[167] In support of the former (and considering 1 Pet 1:1 and 5:1), Bockmuehl argues that since the author of 1 Peter does not state that he is a 'fellow witness', it points to the self-designation as an 'apostolic witness' in accordance with Acts 1:8, 22; 2:32; 3;15; 5:32; 10:39; 13:31; cf. Luke 24:48.[168] This is further supported by apparent witness reports in 1 Peter 1:7 (cf. Luke 22:31, tested by Satan); 1 Peter 1:10 (cf. Mark 16:7, renewed commission); 1 Peter 2:25 and 5:2, 4 (cf. Mark 14:27 and John 21:15-17, metaphor of shepherd and sheep), as well as 1 Peter 5:5-6 (cf. John 13:4-16, humble service).

The author also may have used an *amanuensis* (i.e., Silas/Silvanus, 1 Pet 5:12),[169] indirectly supporting the claim made in 1 Peter 1:1. For why should an author writing under the pseudonym[170] of 'Peter' refer to a 'Silvanus'? It is also noteworthy that the author 'does not trade on his status as an apostle but prefers to identify himself as a fellow elder and shepherd of the flock'.[171] Finally, the patristic attestation of 1 Peter having been written by Peter is significant: Clement of Rome (AD 96) quotes from 1 Peter (*1 Clem.* 30:2/1 Pet 5:5; *1 Clem.* 49:5/1 Pet 4:8), as does Polycarp (*Phil.*, AD 135). Early church fathers

---

1:15, 22-26, namely as one who was with Jesus from the time of the execution of John the Baptist until the death and resurrection of Jesus. Note the qualified addition of Paul (cf. 1 Cor 9:1-2; 15:9; 1 Thess 2:6; 1 Tim 2:7; 2 Tim 1:11) and James, the half-brother of Jesus (1 Cor 15:5, 7; Gal 1:19). The two exceptions in Acts are found in 14:4, 14, where the term is attributed to Barnabas (and Paul). This may signal the later patristic usage where an *apostolos* is simply one sent out from a church to evangelize or to plant a church (*Did.* 11:3-12, 14-16; Justin, *Dial.*, 75.3). See K. Haacker, 'Verwendung und Vermeidung des Apostelbegriffs im lukanischen Werk', *NovT* 30.1 (1988), 9–38.

[167] Cf. Helyer, *Life,* 107 and n. 3.

[168] Bockmuehl, *Simon,* 31.

[169] Bockmuehl, *Simon,* 127, rightly emphasizes that Peter wrote 'through' rather than 'with' Silvanus. Some scholars take this reference to mean that Silvanus merely 'carried' the letter.

[170] Concerning the question of early Christian pseudonymity and pseudepigraphy, see D.A. Carson, 'Pseudonymity and Pseudepigraphy', *DNTB* 857–63 and E.J. Schnabel, 'Paul, Timothy, and Titus: the Assumption of a Pseudonymous Author and of Pseudonymous Recipients in the Light of Literary, Theological, and Historical Evidence', in J.K. Hoffmeier and D.R. Magary (eds), *Do Historical Matters Matter to Faith?: A Critical Appraisal of Modern and Postmodern Approaches to Scripture* (Wheaton, IL: Crossway, 2012), 383–403.

[171] Helyer, *Life,* 109; Bockmuehl, *Simon,* 130.

consistently identify Peter as the author of 1 Peter.[172] Note also that 2 Peter 3:1 endorses 1 Peter.

Key arguments casting doubt on Petrine authorship,[173] however, include that 1 Peter: (a) uses a rather elevated form of Koine Greek; (b) reflects a good knowledge of the Greek translation of the Old Testament (LXX), (c) contains some echoes of Paul's letters, and (d) apparently implies widespread persecution, which only began some fifteen years subsequent to Peter's martyrdom in AD 67.[174] Possible answers to these critical questions and arguments in support of Petrine authorship of 1 Peter are as follows.

Regarding (a): Peter probably learned Greek during his Galilean, bi-lingual upbringing[175] (see details above) and was able to perfect it during his subsequent thirty-years of travel and work in the Greco-Roman world of Asia Minor, Greece, and Rome.[176] The often repeated reference to Acts 4:13 must, finally, be laid to rest. The two terms ἀγράμματοι and ἰδιῶται, describing Peter and John, merely state the obvious: they were not formally trained in an advanced Torah school.[177] Furthermore, some scholars argue that 1 Peter displays elements of Semitic syntax, a factor which would fit the Palestinian Greco-Roman profile of Peter.[178]

---

[172] See Papias (Eusebius, *Hist. eccl.* 3.25.2) and Irenaeus (*Haer.* 4.9.2; 5.7.2; 16.5). Bockmuehl, *Simon*, 30 n. 18, also refers to Tertullian and Hippolytus.

[173] See also Helyer, *Life,* 109–13.

[174] Further questions include: (1) was there a Christian presence in 'North-Galatia' during the life of Peter? While there is indeed no extrabiblical evidence of a significant Christian presence in 'northern Galatia' prior to Pliny the Younger's letter to Trajan (*Ep.* 10.96; ~AD 115), the early work of Paul in 'South-Galatia' (AD 48–52) certainly opens the possibility of a Christian (Petrine?) mission into 'North-Galatia' (2) Does 1 Peter display early Catholic church governance? The arguments that the form of church governance presented in 1 Pet displays early signs of *Frühkatholizismus* are unconvincing in the light of the humble and hortatory tone of leadership (see, e.g., 1 Pet 5:1-7).

[175] Bockmuehl, *Simon*, 127.

[176] For examples see Helyer, *Life,* 110.

[177] J. Murphy-O'Connor, 'Fishers of Fish, Fishers of Men: What We Know of the First Disciples from Their Profession', *BR* 25.3 (1999), 22–27, 48–49. Cullmann, *Peter*, 24, and n. 30, who also mentions the view of Foakes-Jackson, *Peter*, 55, namely that the description refers to 'contempt for the Galilean accent' (n. 30). Note the *pairing* of John, son of Zebedee, with Peter in Acts 1:13; 3:1, 3-4; 4:13, 19; 8:14; cf. John 13:32-35; 20:2-10; 21:7, 20-22.

[178] N. Turner, *A Grammar of New Testament Greek* (Edinburgh: T&T Clark, 1976), 124, 130; K.H. Jobes, *1 Peter* (Grand Rapids, MI: Baker Academic, 2005), 325–33.

Regarding (b): Because the LXX was so widely used among Jews living in the Greco-Roman world, Peter and Silas had no choice but to acquaint themselves in depth with this Greek translation of the Old Testament.

Use of the LXX might already have been practiced in Galilee and was certainly prominent among Jews in the Diaspora, including Rome.

Regarding (c): There was indeed a common pool of catechetical and liturgically relevant truth shared by both Peter and Paul (see, e.g., 1 Cor 11:23-26; 15:3; cf. Acts 15:1-21).[179] Affinities between 1 Peter and Ephesians are best explained this way rather than postulating genealogical dependence.[180] As stated above, Silvanus, the carrier of Peter's letter and possible *amanuensis* of Peter (1 Pet 5:12),[181] is most likely also the companion of Paul (2 Cor 1:19; 1 Thess 1:1; 2 Thess 1:1; cf. Acts 15:40; 18:5). He was thus fully capable of assisting Peter in the writing of 1 Peter.[182]

Regarding the persecutions described in 1 and 2 Peter (d): These could have occurred before AD 81. No empire-wide persecution (such as under Domitian, AD 81–96, or Trajan, AD 111 or later) must be postulated to account for the various forms of suffering described in 1 and 2 Peter.[183] See the description below of the various forms of suffering in Acts and in 1 Peter (e.g., slander and abuse), which could have occurred at any time following the rise of the messianic movement surrounding Jesus. See also Paul (e.g., 2 Cor 1:8-11; 4:7-12; 6:1-10 (suffering in Asia); 1 Thess 2:14-16), regarding his own suffering in Asia Minor and elsewhere before AD 60.

Concerning the connection between 1 and 2 Peter, we can note that while the letters were not written in similar Greek, they could derive from one author if one keeps in mind that they were probably penned by different *amanuenses*: 1 Peter was likely written by Silas/Silvanus, under the guidance of Peter, while 2 Peter was probably written by an unnamed amanuensis under the auspices of Peter (see below).[184]

---

[179] See Bockmuehl, *Simon*, 93, who observes that '1 Cor 11:23-25 and 15:3-7 relate to narratives in which all four Gospels assign Peter a prominent role'.

[180] See Helyer, *Life*, 110–11.

[181] See, cautiously, Jobes, *1 Peter*, 6, 319–21. On the connection between Peter and Silas see Thornton, *Zeuge*, 79, 226. While Bockmuehl, *Simon*, 30–31, questions the *amanuensis* hypothesis, he attributes historical significance to the fact that 1 Pet 5:12-13 mentions 'Babylon' as the author's location *in conjunction* with John Mark and Silvanus.

[182] See the fact that Peter uses John Mark as the writer of his gospel testimony.

[183] See T.B. Williams, *Persecution in 1 Peter* (Leiden: Brill, 2012), 327–35; cf. Bockmuehl, *Simon*, 128.

[184] See, however, R.J. Bauckham, *Jude, 2 Peter* (Dallas, TX: Word, 1990), 43–46, who believes that 2 Peter was written by a member of the Petrine school, conveying Petrine reminiscences, following Peter's death.

The historical circumstances of stereotyped oral memorization and transmission described above contribute substantially to a reliable tradition of Jesus's teaching. Conservative collection and systematic transmission through oral and written means thus marks the general attitude toward Jesus's teaching (see Acts 20:35; 1 Cor 7:10; 11:23-25).[185] What Jesus says is confirmed by signs and wonders (compare with Deut 18:20). Jesus also fulfills Old Testament prophecy, which is witnessed to by the disciples (see, e.g., Luke 24:25-27). What the apostles testify to is confirmed, once again, by signs and wonders (Acts 2:43; 5:12; 14:3; 15:2; 2 Cor 12:12; Heb 2:4; see also Acts 2:22; 4:30; 6:8; Rom 15:19). The historical circumstances in which the canonical Gospels arose (modified tradition hypothesis) point to a reliable connection between the earthly life of Jesus, the stereotyped memorization, and the written fixation of the tradition in the Gospels in which Peter operates as the 'rock'.[186] Athanasius (AD 325) is thus correct when he states: 'this is no Ecclesiastical Canon; nor have we had transmitted to us any such tradition from the Fathers, *who in their turn received from the great and blessed Apostle Peter*'.[187]

Peter as a Foundation-Laying Contributor to the New Testament Canon[188]

Concerning the genesis of the New Testament canon, we note that the four canonical Gospels, Acts, and the major Pauline letters, as well as 1 Peter and 1 John, were circulated, read, and accepted widely as a substantial core

---

[185] See Ellis, 'Traditions', 303–20, esp. 310.

[186] Note Hengel's apt comment: 'The mere fact that the Gospels were written on the basis of earlier Jesus-tradition, forces us . . . to investigate . . . the "history of Jesus" as the ἀρχὴ τοῦ εὐαγγελίου. The key aim of such historical investigation is . . . Jesus himself' (Hengel, 'Kerygma', 336, trans. HFB).

[187] Athanasius, *H.Ar.* 5.36 (emphasis HFB). A. Szabados, drew my attention to this quote.

[188] See C.E. Hill, *Who Chose the Gospels?: Probing the Great Gospel Conspiracy* (Oxford: Oxford University Press, 2010) and especially M. Kruger, *Canon Revisited: Establishing the Origins and Authority of the New Testament Books* (Wheaton, IL: Crossway, 2012). G. Maier (ed.), *Der Kanon der Bibel* (Wuppertal. Brockhaus, 1990); B.M. Metzger, *The Canon of the New Testament: Its Origin, Development and Significance* (Oxford: Clarendon, 1987/88); J.W. Wenham, *Christ*, 128–68; B.F. Westcott, *A General Survey of the History of the Canon of the New Testament* (Grand Rapids, MI: Baker, 1980); H.M. Conn (ed.), *Inerrancy and Hermeneutic* (Grand Rapids, MI: Baker, 1988); J. Schröter, *From Jesus to the New Testament: Early Christian Theology and the Origin of the New Testament Canon* (Waco, TX: Baylor Univ. Press, 2013). T. Zahn, *Grundriss der Geschichte des neutestamentlichen Kanons* (Leipzig: Deichert'sche Verlagsbuchhandlung, 1901).

canon from a very early stage onward.[189] Metzger judiciously observes: 'What is really remarkable . . . is that, though the "fringes" of the NT canon remained unsettled for centuries,[190] a high degree of unanimity concerning the greater part of the NT was attained within the first two centuries among the very diverse and scattered congregations not only throughout the Mediterranean world but also over an area extending from Britain to Mesopotamia.'[191] Bruce contends that at least at the beginning of the second century 'two collections of Christian writings' already existed.[192] According to more recent studies by J. Wenham, Kruger, Schröter, and Hill,[193] such a substantial core canon can be shown to have existed around AD 110 and consisted of: the four canonical Gospels (see, e.g., the *Didache's* [AD 120] reference to the Gospel(s); Ignatius [~AD 115], speaks of the gospel [=4 witnesses] as authoritative writ; the allusions to gospel material in *1 Clem.*); Acts; the thirteen Pauline Epistles (cf. the explicit reference in *1 Clem.* to Paul's 1 Cor and the early endorsement of a *corpus Paulinum* in 2 Pet 3:15b-16), with the possible addition of 1 Peter and 1 John, even at that time.[194]

As we have seen above, the root and central catalyst of the canonical Gospels and Acts is Jesus himself, transmitted especially via Peter (as well as other apostolic witnesses). We have also noted above that Peter lays foundations in terms of the particular format and possibly even the *bios* genre of the canonical Gospels. He provides the content for the Gospel written by John Mark and lays the foundation of earliest Christian witness (Peter as a key oral source of Acts 1–9, 12 and 15), reliably recorded by Luke and aided by Silas/Silvanus. We note especially Acts 1:13-14, where the core group of the early church is identified: the Twelve (with Peter as *primus inter pares*); the women; Mary, mother of Jesus, and Jesus's half-brothers.

Furthermore, Peter acknowledges the leadership of James, the half-brother of Jesus, in Jerusalem (Acts 12:17; 15:1-21) and Luke presents James also favorably in Acts 15:13-21 and 21:18-26.[195]

---

[189] See, e.g., Schröter, *Jesus*, 249–71, who does not clearly describe, however, how the 'early Christian faith convictions' (271) arose.

[190] This does not relegate the so-called 'uncertainty fringe' to a second-class canon. It merely acknowledges the historical fact that some canonical writings belonging to this second group were not as straight forward in their canonical inclusion as was the early core canon.

[191] B. Metzger, *Canon*, 254.

[192] F.F. Bruce, *The New Testament Documents, Are They Reliable?* (Grand Rapids, MI: Eerdmans, 1987), 23.

[193] Cf. Kruger, *Canon*, 231, and Hill, *Who Chose the Gospels?*, 132–35; 149–50; 195–203; 225; 231–33; 249–50.

[194] Cf. J.W. Wenham, *Christ*, 151–64.

[195] See Riesner, 'Rückkehr', 350 and Hengel, 'Lukasprolog', 195–242.

In other words, Peter contributes substantially to the *foundation* of the core canon and thus functions as the foundational 'rock' upon which Jesus himself builds his church using irreplaceable apostolic witness as canon-tradition. In addition to these contributions, it is very possible that Peter serves as the living, eyewitness guarantor for major parts of Luke–Acts (if written ~AD 62) prior to his martyrdom (~AD 67).

We will thus now only ask how the two epistles attributed to Peter also became part of the New Testament canon. For the basic content and argument of our study, the authenticity and canonicity of 1 Peter is of particular and central importance. The complex discussion of the canonicity of 2 Peter will thus not be pursued in detail in what follows.[196]

Regarding the canonicity of 1 Peter, we can state with certainty that 1 Peter (as well as 2 Pet) was confirmed as belonging to the New Testament canon[197] by AD 397 (Council of Carthage). Shortly prior to this date, the Council of Hippo (AD 393) also recognized the 27 books of the New Testament. The thirty-ninth Festal Epistle of Athanasius (AD 367) likewise listed the 27 books as canonical. This is especially important as this is a product of the Eastern church. The Council of Laodicea (AD 363) requested that only Old and New Testament books be read in the churches. All New Testament books except for Revelation are mentioned therein.[198]

Eusebius (AD 270–340)[199] most likely represents the view of a wide spectrum of the church when he states that the New Testament documents belonging to the group of *homologoumena* (i.e., canonically recognized or conferred books) include the four canonical Gospels, Acts, thirteen letters of Paul, 1 Peter, 1 John, Hebrews, and Revelation (this roughly comports with the core canon mentioned above). According to Eusebius, there exists a second category of canonical writings, called *antilegomena* (i.e., somewhat disputed,

---

[196] Regarding this issue, see, e.g., the skeptical analysis by Bockmuehl, *Simon*, 32, 89–91.

[197] Bruce (*Documents*, 22), states regarding the origin of the concept of a NT canon: 'Marcion's list . . . does not represent the current verdict of the Church but a deliberate aberration from it'. This goes against A. v. Harnack, who claimed that we owe the concept of canon to Marcion. Marcion, in fact, challenged the nascent NT canon, at least the existence of a 'core canon' and rejected the present canon of the OT.

[198] See, similarly, Cyril of Jerusalem, AD 315–86.

[199] Eusebius, *Hist. eccl.* 3.25.1-7.

but well known and recognized as canonical by most),[200] including James, 2 Peter, Jude, and 2–3 John.[201]

The scholar and traveler[202] Origen (AD 185–253) presents a similar list to that of Eusebius. Like Eusebius, he was interested in reflecting *widespread* views of his day on the canon. Similar to Eusebius, Origen grouped the New Testament into *homologoumena* (the four canonical Gospels, thirteen letters of Paul, 1 John, Acts, 1 Pet, and Rev) and *antilegomena* (Heb, 2 Pet[203], 2–3 John, Jas, and Jude). Origen adds to this list Barnabas, the Shepherd of Hermas, the *Didache*, and the Gospel of the Hebrews. Irenaeus (AD ~125–202), a pupil of Polycarp,[204] already confirms the four canonical Gospels, Acts, 1 Peter, 1 John, all of Paul's Epistles,[205] and Revelation as belonging to the canon. The historical evidence thus indicates that 1 Peter was considered to be part of the canon at least since ~AD 180.[206] Kruger believes that 1 Peter was part of the core canon by 'the middle of the second century'.[207]

Based on the early Christian criteria of apostolicity, orthodoxy, and catholicity, no one raised questions regarding 1 Peter's place in the canon at any stage of the process. Based on the evidence, it is reasonable to assume that 1 Peter as part of the early core canon blazed its own path in the early church (see John 14:26; 15:26-27; 16:13).[208]

---

[200] The so-called 'disputed books' (*antilegomena*) were questioned primarily on *internal* grounds, not on the basis of *external* evidence, such as authorship (see the exception regarding Hebrews).

[201] In a *third* group of writings, Eusebius lists those which are spurious (*notha;* i.e., not included in the canon but, among some, useful for reading), including the *Apoc. Pet.* A *fourth* group is identified by Eusebius as *heretical*, including the *Gos. Pet.* and the *Gospel of Thomas* (see Kruger, *Canon*, 266–67).

[202] He was probably aware of canonical views held in Alexandria, Arabia, Antioch, Rome, and Caesarea.

[203] Which Origen personally considered to being canonical.

[204] Polycarp died in AD 155.

[205] With the exception of Philemon.

[206] Whether the mention of 1 Pet may have been accidentally omitted by scribes copying the so-called *Muratorian Fragment* remains uncertain. T. Zahn, *Geschichte des neutestamentlichen Kanons* (Hildesheim, Zürich: Olms Verlag, 2013), II, 143, assumes a scribal error; similarly, Bockmuehl, *Simon*, 30 n. 18 and Kruger, *Canon*, 230 n. 179. Among early papyri of 1 Pet, we find *P* 125 and *P* 72 (including 2 Pet), both dated 3rd/4th century.

[207] Kruger, *Canon*, 231.

[208] The 'criterion of apostolicity' in the early church must have *included* trusted associates of apostles (John Mark and Luke), since these two writers were known as non-apostles but their writings were never questioned, because their association with apostles (Peter and Paul, respectively) were known.

An additional serendipitous factor in support of the early canonical inclusion of 1 Peter arises in the work of Zahn.[209] Zahn traces patristic evidence in support of the early church's *reading* of various sacred texts in public Christian services. He argues that to a very high degree these sacred texts converged especially with the core canon of the New Testament, which arguably included 1 Peter.[210] The church essentially acknowledged those writings which were being read in Christian services for edification and teaching, despite the fact that there were some differences in frequency and regularity of reading some of the texts. However, Zahn observes: 'Despite all uncertainties of exact terminology and related vacillations and developments, the identity of what constituted canonical writings and writings that were read in the churches was *retained* during all the centuries in which the canon underwent development'.[211] Zahn aptly notes: 'According to our knowledge of extant, literary evidence, the early, ante-Nicene church possessed no historical testimony concerning the question of *who* gave the church these books as Holy Scripture and introduced them for use in public services'.[212] Zahn adduces detailed and early, ante-Nicene evidence for the public reading of Scripture, implying proto-canonical authority. When official lists/texts of lectionaries were drafted (see esp. Jerome, *Comes Hieronymi,* after ~AD 470), it was assumed and known that these lists included texts which had been read in public worship services all along. Regarding the reading of 1 Peter in church services, bishop Serapion of Antioch (AD 191–211, in Eusebius, *Hist. eccl.* 6.12.3) exposes the falsehood of the *Gospel of Peter* and states: 'For we, brethren, receive both Peter and the other apostles as Christ; but we reject intelligently the writings falsely ascribed to them, knowing that such were not handed down to us'. Irenaeus (*Haer.* 1.27.2; 3.1.1; 3.11.9; 4.34.1; cf. Eusebius, *Hist. eccl.* 2.15.2) assumes that the apostolic Epistles were to be read not only in the cities to which they were originally sent, but everywhere.[213] Given the arguments we presented regarding the AD 110 core canon above, to which 1 Peter probably belonged soon thereafter, Zahn's research implies that 1 Peter was received as an authentic apostolic letter to be read in church services as

---

[209] Zahn, *Grundriss*, 11–14.

[210] The following comments draw heavily on Zahn, *Grundriss*, 11–14.

[211] Zahn, *Grundriss*, 13 (our emphasis; trans., HFB).

[212] Zahn, *Grundriss*, 13 (our emphasis; trans., HFB).

[213] See Justin, *Apology* 1.67: 'On the day called Sunday, all who live in cities or in the country gather together in one place, and the memoirs of the Apostles or the writings of the prophets are read . . .; then, when the reader has ceased, the president (presiding minister) verbally instructs and exhorts to the imitation of these good things'; in A. Roberts and J. Donaldson (eds), *The Ante-Nicene Fathers (*New York, NY: Christian Literature, 1906), I, 186.

Scripture a good time before it appears in second and third-century canonical lists.

Conclusion to Chapters 2 and 3

Peter, who was shaped by Christ, drives and contributes both directly and indirectly to the genesis of the New Testament canon, especially regarding the Gospel of Mark, the Petrine sections in Acts, and 1 and 2 Peter. Furthermore, Peter provides the narrative framework for the canonical Gospel accounts, and, most likely, the Gospel genre of *bios*. In addition, he functions, until his death around AD 67, as a chief guarantor and witness, able to *discredit* (cf. 2 Pet 1:16) or *affirm* (cf. 2 Pet 3:15-16) apostolic traditions.

Our emphasis in chapters 2 and 3 on non-transferable aspects of Peter's calling might give rise to the false impression that our findings have no relevance for today and that they are mere relics of a bygone age. To the contrary, what we have encountered in Peter's calling serves as the enduring foundation for everything we will unearth in Peter's ministry that is directly relevant and applicable to our modern lives as disciples of Christ. Peter's foundational work includes the commission to serve and to confess as a 'rock' (Matt 16:18-19) in his *bios* gospel testimony. He is to serve, furthermore, as God's witness in earliest Christianity (Acts) in the pattern of an Old Testament prophet and repentance preacher and as an apostolic letter writer. In this sense, Ephesians 2:19-22 represents a direct commentary on our findings, namely that the original apostles, chief among them Peter, are the enduring foundation of the eternal temple of God. Significantly, Jesus remains as the perpetual cornerstone of this living structure,[214] both according to Paul (Eph 2:20) and Peter (Acts 4:11; 1 Pet 2:4, 6-8). Such a foundation is irreplaceable and unique. Cullmann rightly states: 'he [Peter] does remain for us the rock, the foundation; he remains such in the Gospels and in a derived way in the book of Acts and the letters, which rest entirely upon the first apostolic witness'.

We have thus unearthed concrete historical and theological elements which Paul calls the 'foundation of the apostles'. Our lives as followers of Christ are based on that foundation (see John 17:20) and we benefit from Peter's Christ-intended, unique, and irreplaceable functions at least in the following ways:

Christ appointed Peter as the 'rock' (Matt 16:18-19) in order that our faith and our transformation in Christ might not be self-guided or self-generated, but guided by the Christ-shaped person and witness of Peter. Peter points us reliably to the true Christ, who is the perpetual source of faith. Cullmann makes

---

[214] See H. Krämer, 'γωνία', *EDNT* I, 268, who notes that the cornerstone (rather than the capstone) sets the orientation and direction of the site. Helyer (*Life*, 137–38) correctly notes that due to Peter's reference to Isa 8:14-15 it is likely that a stone of stumbling (i.e., cornerstone) rather than a capstone is in view.

the important point that Peter's rock-testimony to Jesus as the Suffering Servant lays the foundation for Christian theology upon which Paul later builds.[215] Cullmann rightly notes that 'it is perverse to wish to be content, for example, with the Apostle Paul, as often happens in Protestant churches . . . In reality every church needs also the Apostle Peter, because he as "first" among the twelve apostles has to guarantee the continuity with the incarnate Jesus'.[216]

Christ appointed Peter as a repentance preacher along the lines of an Old Testament prophet. This occurred so that Jews and Gentiles might turn to the God of Abraham, Isaac, and Jacob and embrace the propitiating and atoning work of his eternal Son, Jesus Christ. Peter who is aligned with the Old Testament history of repentance preachers thus singularly and reliably points to the redemption from sinfulness through Jesus Christ (cf. 2 Pet 1:21). While Peter's prophetic ministry is initially aimed at the covenant people of Israel, it is apparent in the Gospel of Mark, Acts 10 and 11, as well as in 1 and 2 Peter, that this ministry is extended to Gentiles as well (Mark 13:10; cf. Matt 28:18-20) on account of the stated mission of God (see, e.g., Gen 12:3; 22:16-18; Ps 22:27-29; Isa 49:6; Rev 5:9; 7:9; 13:7; 14:6).

Christ appointed Peter as an apostolic letter-writer (1 and 2 Peter) in order to continue the ministry of transformation which Christ worked in Peter and accomplishes in us. Such an historically based, theologically formed apostolic witness and transformation-foundation (i.e., Peter) points us reliably and perpetually to Christ (see even Paul's acknowledgement of this fact in Acts 13:31). Peter's witness is corroborated by other apostles and especially by Paul, as well as other prophets.[217] Jesus thus intended to create an authentic, personally transformed cadre of truth-witnesses, with Peter as the central spokesperson and guarantor.

Jesus sets out on his eternal and universal mission by revealing himself to Peter (and others around him), by transforming Peter (and others), and thus establishing his 'sculpture' as the authoritative witness-foundation and lasting *martys*, witness, *eo ipso*. It is not, however, Peter the hero that we are to focus

---

[215] Cullmann, *Peter*, 69.

[216] Cullmann, *Peter*, 227.

[217] The terminological pair 'apostles and prophets' in Eph 2:20 is best taken as a reference to the twelve apostles as well as to other *NT witnesses* ('prophets') who taught and witnessed to Christ. Based on Eph 3:5 and 4:11 (see Luke 11:49) it is incongruent to identify 'prophets' in Eph 2:20 as OT prophets (cf. H.W. Hoehner, *Ephesians: An Exegetical Commentary* [Grand Rapids: MI, Baker Academic, 2002], 397–404). In contrast to this, see, however, 2 Pet 3:2 where 'prophets' clearly refers to OT heralds. At times, 'prophets and apostles' may refer to the entire canon of the Old and New Testaments.

on. It is the amazing sculpturing of Peter *at the hands of Jesus* that we are to marvel at both in terms of Peter's confession and his character. The concept of a foundation (Peter) designed from the cornerstone (Jesus) readily anticipates a structure, a *corporate entity*, namely the universal temple made of living stones.[218] The great goal of this, initially, individual transformation around the true, triune God of this universe is the corporate temple or city of God, consisting of many living stones crafted by God (Eph 2:21-22; 1 Pet 2:4-10; see below).[219] Cullmann observes: 'The foundation that is laid in Peter thus has to support a building that means victory over death'.[220]

Everything we will explore in the subsequent chapters thus *rests* on the witness foundation and bedrock of apostolic tradition described above. Peter's witness to Christ (Christology in the context of the Trinity), identity, and character formation is apostolically secured and scripturally engraved (γέγραπται).[221] There is thus no need for an apostolic succession. Peter himself gave the leader's office in Jerusalem to James the Just (Acts 12:17).[222] As one who lays the foundation, he traveled and served as the apostolic witness wherever he was, thus staying true to his particular calling.[223] His focus was not on an office but on serving as a unique apostolic witness. As such he enduringly bears witness to Christ and his ways. As a result, we are the living stones, *based* on the cornerstone, Jesus, and built on the foundation of Peter's (and others') enduring, apostolic witness.

---

[218] See P. Vielhauer, *Oikodome, das Bild vom Bau in der christlichen Literatur vom N.T. bis Clemens Alexandrinus* (München: Chr. Kaiser, 1986).

[219] See N. Perrin, *Jesus the Temple* (Grand Rapids, MI: Baker Academic, 2010) and G.K. Beale, *The Temple and the Church's Mission: A Biblical Theology of the Dwelling Place of God* (Downers Grove, IL: IVP Academic, 2004).

[220] Cullmann, *Peter*, 209.

[221] See E.J. Schnabel, *Inspiration und Offenbarung: Die Lehre vom Ursprung und Wesen der Bibel* (Wuppertal: Brockhaus, 1986), 109–27, concerning the biblical concept of γραφή.

[222] It is true that Peter's mysterious 'departure' from Jerusalem (Acts 12:17) occurred partially on account on the threat to his life, cf. Cullmann, *Peter*, 42.

[223] Cullmann, *Peter*, 39–57.

CHAPTER 4

Semi-Transferable Aspects of Peter's Work and Witness

So far we have focused on unique apostolic functions of Peter which are not transferable in any way. We now turn to his semi-transferable roles. By 'semi-transferable' we mean those aspects of Peter's work in early Christianity that contain unique but also generally applicable features. They are unique in that Peter is commissioned with particular responsibilities tailored to his particular life; they are generally applicable in that many other disciples of Christ will be commissioned with similar responsibilities of witnessing and shepherding.[1] This transferability arises from the respective texts and contexts, in which we find reference to these characteristics.

Peter as a 'Fisher of Men' (Mark 1:16)

Besides his foundational calling as a follower of Jesus, Peter, as reported by Mark (and Matthew), was called along with his brother, Andrew, to the particular commission of serving as 'fishers of men' (Mark 1:16-17; see also 3:14; 6:7, 30, and Matt 4:18-19).[2] Bockmuehl notes that Peter's birthplace, Bethsaida, means '"place of fishing" (or ". . . hunting")'.[3]

Becoming a 'fisher of men' grows out of being 'fished', mentored, and commissioned by Jesus and develops as a consequence of primary dependence upon him (Mark 1:14).[4] The life-on-life relationship with Jesus results in his disciples calling other people to return to the gracious lordship of the triune God, facilitated by Jesus (see Mark 6:7-13; 8:34-38; 10:45), prior to the Last Judgment of all creation. Such a message is to reach, initially, the covenant

---

[1] Similarly, Bockmuehl, *Simon*, 65.
[2] Pesch, *Markusevangelium*, I, 111.
[3] Bockmuehl, *Simon*, 170.
[4] Cf. Schnabel, *Mission*, I, 275–77. See the apt comments by B.E. Wassell and S.R. Llewelyn, '"Fishers of Humans", the Contemporary Theory of Metaphor, and Conceptual Blending Theory', *JBL* 133.3 (2014), 627–46; their exclusive 'synchronic' reading of the metaphor in the narrative of Mark prevents them, however, from seeing the *additional* background of Jer 16:14-21.

people of Israel. For this purpose Jesus commissions his disciples, chief among them Peter, to 'fish' fellow Jews in Galilee and Judea, alongside Jesus. The call to become a fisher of men is thus initially, at least, not directly transferable. Rather, we have to appreciate the fact that this is a particular calling of Peter (and other initial disciples of Christ) to a unique ministry in Galilee and Judea, aimed at addressing Jews in fulfillment of a particular task pursued and given by Jesus.

In the Old Testament we occasionally encounter people as 'suppressive fisher[s] of men' (Hab 1:14-17).[5] At times, God is referred to as a fisher of men, or he sends messengers as fishers of men, mostly in the context of imminent redemption or judgment. God's judgment is in view in Ezekiel 29:4-5; 38:4, and Amos 4:2. Redemption, in the context of judgment, is apparent in Jeremiah 16:14-21.[6]

Even though we do not find a direct reference in Mark 1:16 to any Old Testament text,[7] the *concept* of 'fishers of men' in the Markan context is nevertheless most akin to that of Jeremiah 16:14-21,[8] the literary context of which—that is, Jeremiah 1:1–16:13—speaks of the imminent judgment of Israel through the Babylonian exile. The immediately preceding section of the core verse in Jeremiah 16:16 ('Behold, I am sending for many fishers, declares the LORD, and they shall catch them') refers in a proleptic way to the restoration of the people of God (Jer 16:14; see 16:18) *following* the Babylonian exile (Jer 16:14-15). Subsequent to this punishment (Jer 16:15, 18), God will, in the context of thorough cleansing and purification, send messengers to 'fish' his people back to himself. Jeremiah 16:14-21 thus conveys the following sequence of events:

Warning of imminent and certain judgment →

Subsequent restoration ('fishers of men', including purification)[9] →

True worship in the absence of idolatry.[10]

---

[5] See Lane, *Mark*, 67.
[6] Bockmuehl, *Simon*, 71, and n. 80.
[7] See Schnabel, *Mission*, I, 275–76, who adds that this also applies to Hellenistic and rabbinic texts. See Schnabel, *Mission*, I, 275–76, for other explanations of the phrase.
[8] See Pesch, *Markusevangelium*, I, 111 and Schnabel, *Mission*, I, 276, who refers to 1QH 3, 26; 5, 7–8.
[9] Cf. Jer 33:8.
[10] See analogies to this, e.g., in Jer 30:3, 8-9, 11; 31:8, 10, 28; 32:8-15, 37-38, 42; 33:10-11.

The figurative use of 'fishing' people in Jeremiah 16:16 refers thus to the gracious restoration and purification (the latter is implied in Jer 16:17) of God's people, following judgment. According to Jeremiah 16:14-21, God's fishers of men will have a grace-filled commission to call the people back to the promised land, to purify his people (including Gentiles, cf. Jer 16:19) from idolatry (perhaps even to chastise), and to restore them to a heartfelt devotion to God.

It is conceivable that Jesus fills the phrase 'fishers of men' with his own figurative sense, without any reference to the Old Testament.[11] On the other hand, we can trace the following natural correspondence between Jeremiah 16:14-21 and Mark 1:16 in the context of the entire Markan storyline:

Parallel to Jeremiah 16:14-21, the imminent and certain judgment is borne by Jesus (see, e.g., Mark 14:1–16:8)[12] →

Followed by restoration of God's people to God (Mark 10:45) through the proclamation of his disciples as 'fishers of men' (Mark 13:10), including purification through Jesus (Mark 9:42-50; 10:35-44) →

And a return to true worship (Mark 11:17), including Gentiles (Mark 11:17).

The concept of fishers of men, restoring Israel (and, later, Gentiles) to God following judgment, dovetails with the wider motif of a second exodus in which people from all nations are restored to God, both individually and collectively. In this view, final judgment (both in Mark 1:16-17, 8:38, and Jer 16:16) is never ignored. However, in both cases, a time of *temporary* judgment (the Babylonian exile and the substitutionary atonement of Christ, respectively), with subsequent restoration and purification, is also in view.[13] Due to the reference to Gentiles in Jeremiah 16:19 and the fact that Jesus's kingdom-mission extends to the entire world (cf. Gen 12:1-3; Mark 11:17; 13:10), we can state that Jesus's allusion to Jeremiah 16:14-21 places the fishing of men in the context of the universal and messianic mission of God.

We thus conclude that in an analogous way to Jeremiah 16:14-21, God's judgment of his eternal Son and Jesus's substitutionary death (Mark 10:45; 14:36) is followed by sending out the disciples as fishers of men to restore,

---

[11] See Schnabel, *Mission*, I, 276.

[12] The judgment pronounced over Jesus is a proleptic, eschatological aspect of the final judgment.

[13] See Schnabel, *Mission*, I, 276. *Pace* Pesch, *Markusevangelium*, I, 111.

once again, a people unto himself in the context of purification and cleansing (Mark 13:10).[14] Significantly, Jesus's initial disciples are themselves in need of salvation (Mark 10:45; 14:36) and purification by fire (Mark 9:42-50; 10:35-44). As such they call others in word and deed to restoration and purification on the basis of Jesus's atoning and God-satisfying sacrifice for their own lives. They thus participate in Jesus's universal mission. While the commission is a corporate undertaking, Peter, as the disciples' spokesperson, thus serves as a fisher of men, initially sent to God's covenant people of Israel, and eventually to Gentiles as well. Peter lives himself within a judgment-redemption continuum whereby he is 'passed-over' in judgment on account of the ultimate paschal lamb (see Mark 10:35-44; 14:22-24) but not exempt from the purifying fire of God's Spirit (Luke 3:16-17). His 'fishing' will reflect these varied components as well. Such an unusual commission becomes even more compelling when we consider the evidence in favor of Peter arising as a prophetic repentance preacher aligned with the Old Testament in the book of Acts (see above).

In a derivative way, however, all other disciples also become fishers of men, since the call to proclaim the gospel (Mark 13:10) is subsequently entrusted to all followers of Christ (see Matt 28:18-20).

Peter as Shepherd of God's Jewish and Gentile People (John 21:15-19 and Luke 22:31-32)

It behooves us, once again, to explore Jesus's call (John 21:15-19) as initially applying to Peter only. As it turns out, only in a secondary way is Jesus's appointment of Peter to shepherd God's flock applicable to other shepherds. While we cannot go into details here, it is indeed possible that John assumes that his readers were already acquainted with one of the Synoptic Gospels.[15] If this is the case, we can view the passage in question as a Johannine complement to what we know about Peter's call from the Synoptics.

The encounter between Peter and Jesus, narrated in John 21:15-19 (cf. Luke 22:31-32), follows the resurrection accounts in which Peter (and John) find the tomb empty (John 20:7), and where Jesus appears to Mary Magdalene, the ten disciples, Thomas (John 20:11-29), and seven disciples (John 21:1-14). Prior to the encounter between Peter and Jesus, Peter sees the risen Christ ('Jesus was revealed [ἐφανερώθη] to the disciples') on three different occasions (John 21:14). While the disciples recognize the resurrected Jesus, they nevertheless

---

[14] Bockmuehl, *Simon*, 117 n. 29, notes that Tertullian, Jerome, Lucinius, and Gregory of Nazianzus understood Jesus in this way.
[15] Cf. R.J. Bauckham, 'John for Readers of Mark', in Bauckham, *Gospels*, 147–71; Bockmuehl, *Simon*, 58.

are in awe of him as he is the same but also different (John 21:12). There are many memorable echoes to Peter's meeting with Jesus. For instance, the scene in John 21:1-6 echoes Peter's initial call while fishing (Luke 5:1-11).[16] Tellingly, Jesus approaches Peter once again with a question (John 21:15; see Mark 8:27, 29). The threefold question redresses Peter's threefold denial of Jesus, quite similar to Luke 22:31, when Jesus prays ἵνα μὴ ἐκλίπῃ ['fail'] ἡ πίστις σου. After Jesus had predicted Peter's impending denial (Mark 14:29-31; ἀπαρνέω is used twice), both Peter (Mark 14:66-72, ἀπαρνέω) and the leaders of Israel (Acts 3:13-14; twice ἠρνήσασθε) had *denied* Jesus. In sharp contrast to this, Jesus had called Peter to deny *himself* (ἀπαρνησάσθε ἑαυτόν, Mark 8:34). Peter's primary loyalty is to be trained on Jesus, not on himself.[17]

Jesus's threefold question (John 21:15, ἀγαπᾷς με; 21:16, ἀγαπᾷς με; 21:17, φιλεῖς με;) and Peter's threefold affirmation of a love that is known to Jesus (John 21:15, φιλῶ σε, 21:16, φιλῶ σε, 21:17, φιλῶ σε, John 21:17) serves initially, then, as the antidote to Peter's past denial of Christ and marks his restoration.[18] Most importantly, however, it conveys a future call upon Peter's life, namely, to *feed* (βόσκε; cf. Luke 22:32, στηρίζω, 'strengthen') the chief shepherd's (John 10; 1 Pet 5:1-4) lambs (John 21:15c), to *tend* Jesus's sheep (John 21:16c, ποίμαινε τὰ πρόβατά μου), and, again, to feed Jesus's sheep (John 21:17d, βόσκε τὰ πρόβατά μου).[19]

Cullmann notes that the *Damascus Document* identifies its leader as the 'shepherd of the flock' who 'is to proclaim the word, explain the Scripture, and exercise community discipline'.[20] As a strong echo to Peter as the rock, upon which Jesus builds his church, as well as to the 'derivative key' which Peter (and the binding and loosening church) is given, we see again that Jesus does *not* separate himself from Peter or simply transfer responsibilities upon Peter. Rather, Peter (and other shepherds of Christ's flock), holding delegated authority, will always have to be directly dependent upon the master who remains the chief shepherd (1 Pet 5:4), the one who continues to hold the key (Rev 3:7), and the one who ultimately 'loosens' and 'binds' (Matt 18:15-20; John 20:23) as his work of atonement is proclaimed and lived out. While Peter holds a prominent position, 'he always appears as their spokesman in the

---

[16] For further echoes, see Helyer, *Life*, 64–65.
[17] Cf. Gambrell, 'Mark 8:34', 42–43.
[18] G.J. Wenham, *The Book of Leviticus* (Grand Rapids, MI: Eerdmans, 1979), 131–32, considers the possibility that the reinstatement and commissioning of Peter echoes the eventual ordination of Aaron to the high priestly office (Lev 8–10; cf. Exod 29) which had been interrupted by the production of the golden calf.
[19] The various terminological variations found in this pericope are primarily due to stylistic nuance rather than to semantic differences.
[20] Cullmann, *Peter*, 65. Cf. Matt 10:6; John 10:1-18.

"dialogue with Christ"; apart from this relation to Christ he never plays, as he does in the later literature, a leading role'.[21] Bockmuehl rightly notes that in the Old and New Testaments God merely delegates authority to human 'shepherds' (Jer 23:1-5; Ezek 34:2-24; Zech 11:3-17; 1 Pet 5:2).[22]

Peter is to serve at Jesus's behest in a continuous way (note the durative aspect of the shepherding verbs in John 21:15-17). He is entrusted with what belongs eternally to Jesus (note the pronouns' possessive genitives, governing the sheep and lambs in John 21:15-17; see 1 Pet 2:25: 'For you were straying like sheep, but have now returned to the Shepherd and Overseer of your souls'). The feeding and tending of Christ's flock (see 1 Pet 5:2 ποιμάνατε τὸ ἐν ὑμῖν ποίμνιον τοῦ θεοῦ; also 1 Pet 5:4; cf. Luke 22:32; Rev 7:17) points in one direction: Peter is to assist in Jesus's mission among his worldwide disciples. For Peter, that includes: serving obediently as the unique apostolic and holistic witness; bringing people to Christ (see the Petrine speeches in Acts and 1 Pet 3:18); nurturing people in dependence upon Christ (cf. Luke 22:32);[23] exhorting people, individually and corporately, toward godliness as being the holy temple of God, purified in suffering; encouraging among God's people the testimony which this growth will have in the world; and being prepared for the second coming (Parousia) of the Lord (1 Pet 1:13). The first call to Peter in Mark 1:17 (δεῦτε ὀπίσω μου) and the last word to Peter in John 21:19, 22 (v. 19: ἀκολούθει μοι; v. 22: σύ μοι ἀκολούθει) form a thematic *inclusio*: at the beginning and the end, Jesus summons Peter to 'follow me' (cf. Mark 1:16 and 16:7).[24] This simple call permeates all non-transferable, semi-transferable, and transferable aspects of Peter's life. The commission displays Jesus's profound mercy to Peter by including him in the grand mission of God despite his previous denial of Jesus.

The formation of Peter during Jesus's earthly life is now complete. He is on the path where he is 'to follow his master all the way as a shepherd laying down his life'.[25] Peter's identity and character formation through the exalted Lord by means of the Holy Spirit will, however, continue (see Acts 1–12 and 15). Peter's primary allegiance is now unwaveringly trained on Jesus and thus on the triune God. The outpouring of the Holy Spirit (temporarily, in John

---

[21] Cullmann, *Peter*, 28.
[22] Bockmuehl, *Simon*, 65.
[23] The plural pronoun in this verse probably refers to Peter in the form of a formal 'thou'.
[24] Bockmuehl, *Simon*, 132, draws attention to the fact that in Mark 'Peter is virtually the only member of the Twelve with whom Jesus converses individually, and he is the only one addressed by name (14:37)'.
[25] Bockmuehl, *Simon*, 66.

20:22,[26] and then permanently in Acts 2:2-4; 4:31) reinforces this. Furthermore, Peter's future call focuses squarely on tending the flock of Jesus (1 Pet 2:5; cf. Luke 22:32). We are convinced that 'feeding' the sheep of Christ includes what Luke will record in Acts concerning Peter (i.e., proclamation, prayer, and leadership) and what Peter wrote in 1 and 2 Peter (i.e., witnessing, mentoring, admonishing, and encouraging the followers of Christ). The best commentaries on Peter's execution of John 21:15-22 (cf. Luke 22:32) are thus both the Petrine sections in Acts and 1 and 2 Peter. We emphasize that the commission of Peter includes personal obedience to love of and maturing in Christ ('Do you love me?') as well as care for people ('feed', 'tend'), teaching, prayer, and leading (cf. Mark 3:14).

Jesus's call upon Peter to shepherd *his* flock is semi-transferable since the exclusive elements encountered with regard to Peter being the apostolic 'rock' are missing here. While Peter's shepherding is intertwined with his laying the unique apostolic foundation, it is, insofar as it is the continuation of nurturing disciples of Jesus, now transferable, at least to those among God's people who are particularly called to shepherding the flock themselves (see especially Peter's admonition to elders in 1 Pet 5:1-4).

We suggest that Jesus's call of Peter to shepherd *his* sheep (John 21:15-19; Luke 22:31-32) serves as the umbrella under which the unique commission to serve as the holistic and apostolic rock (Matt 16:18-19) finds its place. While the former commission is semi-transferable in the sense that other disciples of Jesus will shepherd (part of) his flock, the latter commission is unique and irreplaceable, devoid of any possibility of succession or continuation. On the other hand, Peter's commission to shepherd Christ's people includes the initial situation of establishing the once-and-for-all apostolic 'rock-witness'.

The pastoral function for Peter's future ministry (John 21:15-19) *interprets* Jesus's preceding claim that he, Jesus, will build his church on the foundation of Peter's confession and transformed person as the 'rock' (Matt 16:18-19). In other words, the pastoral commission of Peter in John 21 *clarifies* and *directs* the long-term implications and consequences of the identification of Peter as the rock in Matthew 16.

---

[26] John 20:22 is best viewed as a *temporary* bridging between the physical departure of Jesus and the definitive outpouring of the Holy Spirit as narrated in Acts 2 (i.e., not a 'Johannine Pentecost'). See D.A. Carson, *The Gospel According to John* (Grand Rapids, MI: Eerdmans, 1991), 649–55; A. Köstenberger, *John* (Grand Rapids, MI: Baker Academic, 2004), 574–75, and n. 16. Differently, Schnackenburg, *John,* III, 325–26, who believes that the disciples now 'receive' the promised Holy Spirit; the Holy Spirit is not yet, however, given as the emboldening Paraclete (see Pentecost in Acts 2).

Conclusion

In this chapter we have traced the few semi-transferable aspects in Peter's calling. While the non-transferable aspects serve to cement his apostolic foundation, the transferable aspects (see the following chapters) readily point to Christ-centered transformation. Between these two poles, the semi-transferable aspects are both unique to Peter (John 21:15-19; or are at least unique to the original apostles, Mark 1:16-17), but they do simultaneously contain patterns that are indeed transferable to other disciples.

While the commission to Simon Peter and Andrew to become fishers of men (Mark 1:16-17) contains unique features (their particular kingdom-ministry during Jesus's earthly life in Judea and Galilee), it implies simultaneously an ongoing commission of calling human beings back to God (Mark 13:10; see the Great Commission, Matt 28:19-20).[27] And while Peter is uniquely reinstated in John 21:15-19 after denying Christ three times prior to his passion, the commission to 'feed' or 'tend' Christ's sheep extends at least to those followers of Christ who are called to shepherd or to pastor in one form or another (1 Pet 5:1-4).

As we subsequently explore the apostolic ministry of Peter in Acts, and 1 and 2 Peter, we will learn that, in the end, Clement of Alexandria (AD 190) was right: Peter did not arise as an ecclesiastical authority seeking high office in Jerusalem or in Antioch or in Rome.[28] Rather, following his master's specific commission, he set out to lay the irreplaceable and unique foundation of his apostolic witness and person while personally shepherding Jews and Gentiles to the point of martyrdom.

---

[27] Matt 28:19-20 is arguably not only intended for the initial disciples, since Jesus's commission is universal and implies an extended time-frame until the end of this aeon.

[28] See Eusebius, *Hist. eccl.* 2.1, who quotes Clement of Alexandria's sixth book of *Hypotyposes.* Clement of Alexandria (Eusebius, *Hist. eccl.* 2.15.2) is reported to have said that Peter wrote his first letter from Rome and 'used a cryptic word in designating the city of Rome by the name Babylon' (quoted from Cullmann, *Peter*, 117).

PART TWO

Transferable Aspects of Peter's Witness Embedded in his Apostolic Functions

By the phrase 'transferable aspects of Peter's witness', we mean those aspects of Peter's formation and work which readily and explicitly apply to all disciples of Christ. Peter, like all followers of Christ, undergoes a transformation into Christ-likeness which is intended for all members of God's messianic and eternal kingdom.

The following chapters focus on Peter's canonical testimony (i.e., the Gospel of Mark, the Petrine sections in Acts, and 1 and 2 Peter). By maintaining the canonical sequence in the following explorations, we are not overlooking the fact that these documents can be roughly dated around the same time (Mark ~AD 65; Acts ~AD 62–63; 1 and 2 Peter ~AD 65).[1] Nevertheless, they purport to reflect a historical development of Peter that spans from the testimony of Peter's beginnings as a disciple in the Gospel of Mark (approximately from AD 27 onward), continuing with his growth and development in Acts (approximately from AD 30 [33] to 49), and culminating in the mature stage of an elder leader and shepherd in 1 and 2 Peter. The justification for comparing Christology, identity, and character formation in Peter's entire canonical testimony arises from the following claims:

a. the patristic assertion that Peter serves as the source of the Gospel of Mark (see above);
b. Luke's claim that he presents apostolic witness in Acts (cf. Luke 1:1-4; see above), and
c. the authorial claim in 1 and 2 Peter (see above).

Given the fact that these claims are more substantial than what is often presented in scholarly debate, it is therefore reasonable and promising to

---

[1] See Carson and Moo, *Introduction*, 179–82 (Mark), 296–300 (Acts), 646 (1 Peter), 663 (2 Peter).

compare these works associated with Peter regarding their particular Christology, identity formation, and characteristic elements of Christian character formation. Should we be able to isolate considerable material connections within Peter's canonical testimony, especially regarding Christology, identity, and character formation, then the Petrine sections in Acts and 1 and 2 Peter would, e.g., serve to demonstrate that Peter did indeed answer Jesus's call to shepherd Christ's flock *by displaying characteristic christological emphases and engendering a new identity and aspects of Christian character to which he had been brought by Christ himself.* John 21:17, 19, 21 (cf. 1 Pet 5:13) states that Peter is commissioned by Christ to pass on what he had learned and who he had become under Jesus's direct tutelage. The Gospel of Mark, on the other hand, would testify to the fact that Jesus had engendered a proper understanding of himself and characteristics of Christ-like identity and character formation in Peter (and others) in the first place. While we seek to trace Peter as the source of his canonical testimony, we also bear in mind that the direct author of the Gospel of Mark is John Mark (see above); the author of Acts is Luke, the physician (see above); and the writer of 1 Peter is Silas/Silvanus (see above).

In Part Two, we thus seek to focus on the following elements within Peter's canonical testimony:
1. the compatibility of various characteristic, christological emphases;
2. the similarity of identity formation;
3. similar emphases of Christlike character traits, exemplified by Peter (cf. 2 Pet 3:15-16). This becomes particularly manifest in the setting of suffering and adversity in a godless society (i.e., various regions of the ancient world in Acts, Asia Minor for 1 Peter, and the larger Roman Empire for Mark).

In short, we seek to determine whether a compatible and coherent connection between Christology, identity, and character formation exists throughout Peter's canonical testimony. If this can be demonstrated, we would be able to state that the patristic and authorial claims in the various canonical writings associated with Peter (Peter's canonical testimony) are reinforced and supported by our findings. On the other hand, such a demonstration would not conclusively demonstrate by itself that Peter was indeed the source of the canonical testimony attributed to him.

In order to avoid unnecessary repetition, the discussion on Christology, identity and character formation derived from the respective documents of Mark, the Petrine sections of Acts, and 1 and 2 Peter will be more detailed (Chapters 5–7) than the composite presentation of these areas of investigation in the entire canonical Petrine testimony (Chapter 8). The details presented in Chapters 5–7 are necessary in order to demonstrate the particularities and unique characteristics of each book associated with Peter; the relatively brief syntheses in Chapter 8 merely seek to demonstrate the concept-compatibility within Peter's canonical testimony.

CHAPTER 5

Christology, Identity, and Character Formation in the Gospel of Mark

Christology[1]

In the following pages, we try to characterize Mark's, and indirectly, Peter's testimony to the complex and intriguing figure of Jesus. Jesus's proclamation of the kingdom rule of God means that God is, more than ever before, proceeding to take up his own *direct* rule over his people. Jesus's teaching marks the comprehensive fulfillment of Old Testament prophecy by means of a human and divine messiah who will govern the people of God together with the Father and the Spirit. Mark testifies that Jesus is the eternal Son of God who dies a substitutionary death by crucifixion, thus inaugurating his eternal kingly rule. Jesus's ultimate purpose is to rule over his people based on his humiliation, sacrifice, and reconciling work (cf. 1 Pet 3:18) in the context of his creation.

---

[1] Elements of the following chapter represent a recapitulation and further development of Bayer, *Theology*, 41–60. Mark features especially the following OT quotations: 1:2-3/LXX Isa 40:3 (cf. Exod 23:20; Mal 3:1); 4:12/Isa 6:9-10; 4:32/LXX Ps 103:12; 6:34/Num 27:17; 7:6-7/LXX Isa 29:13; 7:10/Exod 20:12 and 21:17; 8:18/Jer 5:21; 9:11/Mal 3:23; 9:48/Isa 66:24; 10:6-8/Gen 1:27 and LXX Gen 2:24; 10:19/LXX Deut 5:16-20; 11:9-10/Pss 118:25-26 and 148:1; 11:17/Isa 56:7 and Jer 7:11; 12:10-11/Ps 118:22-23; 12:19/Deut 25:5-6 and Gen 38:8; 12:26/Exod 3:6, 15-16; 12:29-31/Deut 6:4-5 and Lev 19:18; 12:32/Deut 6:5; 12:36/Ps 110:1; 13:14/Dan 12:11; 13:24-26/Isa 34:4 and 13:10; 13:26/Dan 7:13-14, 14.27/Zech 13:7; 14:34/Ps 42:6, 12; 14:62/Dan 7:13 and Ps 110:1; 15:24/Ps 22:19; 15:34/Ps 22:2. See particularly the allusion to Isaiah 53 in Mark's passion account: 14:24-25/LXX Isa 53:11-12; 14:48/Isa53:7; 14:61/Isa 53:7; 15:27/Isa 53:12. Cf. D.L. Bock and M. Glaser (eds), *The Gospel According to Isaiah 53: Encountering the Suffering Servant in Jewish and Christian Theology* (Grand Rapids, MI: Kregel, 2012). See B.D. Chilton et al. (eds), *A Comparative Handbook to the Gospel of Mark: Comparisons with Pseudepigrapha, the Qumran Scrolls, and Rabbinic Literature* (Leiden: Brill, 2010), concerning connections between Mark's Gospel and extrabiblical Jewish sources.

As Jesus pursues his purposes, a serious religious-historical conflict arises, in which the disciples are caught up as well. Elsewhere, we have argued in detail that the self-revelation of Jesus in Mark does not conform to the messianic expectation of the disciples, nor, for that matter, of most Palestinian Jews in the first century AD.[2] The conflict between opposing messianic expectations is the religious-historical setting for Jesus's self-disclosure of his mission and identity. We noted above that especially the Maccabean uprising delimited and shaped the prevailing messianic expectation at the time of Jesus, including that of Peter. This narrow expectation will now constitute a great liability in welcoming the true Messiah of God.

Jesus's Challenge of the Prevailing Messianic Expectation Among his Jewish Contemporaries[3]

Most factions in popular Judaism at the time of Jesus expected a Davidic political messianic ruler who would liberate the Jewish people from Roman suppression and religious defilement. This popular expectation is primarily driven by Pharisaic Judaism and its focus on 2 Samuel 7:13-14, 16 (and context).[4] This even applies to Qumran, where we find 2 Samuel 7:11-14 connected with a messianic interpretation of Amos 9:11 (4QFlor 1:11-13). Further support for similar connections is found in 1QSa 2:11-14; 4QFlor (2 Sam 7); 4QCommGen A (Gen 49:10), and CD 7:16 (cf. *b. Sanh.* 96b, 97a). Zimmermann explores various parallels between Pharisaic messianic expectations and those of Qumran. He states that the core of various messianic expectations was centered on a Davidic royal liberator, even at Qumran, with the particularity that Qumran used partially unique terminology.[5] Luke–Acts reflects such political Davidic expectations (e.g., Luke 24:21) as the liberation from enemies[6] and in Acts 1:6; 15:16-17, regarding the messianic restoration of

---

[2] Cf. Bayer, *Markus*, 68–88; 101–102; 313–33.

[3] M.V. Novenson, *Christ among the Messiahs: Christ Language in Paul and Messiah Language in Ancient Judaism* (Oxford: Oxford University Press, 2012).

[4] J.J. Collins, *The Scepter and the Star: The Messiahs of the Dead Sea Scrolls and Other Ancient Literature* (New York, NY: Doubleday, 1995), 209–10. Regarding Qumran, see J. Zimmermann, *Messianische Texte aus Qumran: Königliche, priesterliche und prophetische Messiasvorstellungen in den Schriftfunden von Qumran* (Tübingen: Mohr Siebeck, 1998), 23–34, 230–311, 470–80. See M.F. Bird, *Jesus Is the Christ: The Messianic Testimony of the Gospels* (Downers Grove, IL: IVP Academic, 2013). M.F. Bird, *Are You the One Who Is to Come? The Historical Jesus and the Messianic Question* (Grand Rapids, MI: Baker Academic, 2009).

[5] Zimmermann, *Texte*, 480.

[6] Marshall, *Luke*, 895.

the house of David.⁷ Pesch adds to this that Pharisees most likely react to the non-Davidic Hasmonean rule with a particular emphasis on the *Davidic* descent of the expected Messiah.⁸

While the Davidic political expectation holds true for popular, general Judaism, we find on the periphery of Palestinian Judaism additional and different expressions of messianic expectations. Collins observes that parallel to widespread Davidic messianic expectations of a king who restores Israel, there are, in certain circles, expectations of a priestly messiah (1QS 9, 11; 4QTest; CD 7), an anointed prophet (*Pss. Sol.* 17-18), or a heavenly Son of Man figure (*1 En.* 37–71). Collins remarks:

> Jewish ideas of messianism were not uniform. There was a dominant notion of a Davidic Messiah, as the king who would restore the kingdom of Israel, which was part of the common Judaism around the turn of the era. There were also, however, minor messianic strands, which envisaged a priestly messiah, or an anointed prophet or a heavenly Son of Man.⁹

These peripheral expectations can be documented partially in contemporaneous Qumran, as well as other writings (esp. *1 En.* and *Pss. Sol.*) which might be, according to some scholars, contemporaneous to the New Testament as well. Other scholars date the latter two documents after AD 70 (see below).

Qumran

In addition to the expected prophet,¹⁰ the Qumran community awaited by means of rigorous implementation of the Mosaic law a priestly (1QS 9, 11; 4QTest; CD 7) and especially a kingly messiah (1QSa 2, 11-13; 4QFlor; 4QCommGen A).¹¹ Even though these expectations are to be differentiated and distinguished (see *T. 12 Patr.*), they nevertheless represent aspects of the anticipation of a messianic figure in which the Davidic expectation

---

[7] See Zimmermann, *Texte*, 23–34, 46–229, 470–80 and Lane, *Mark*, 435 n. 58.
[8] Pesch, *Markusevangelium*, II, 252.
[9] Collins, *Scepter*, 209–10; see J.H. Charlesworth, H. Lichtenberger and G.S. Oegema (eds), *Qumran-Messianism: Studies on the Messianic Expectations in the Dead Sea Scrolls* (Tübingen: Mohr Siebeck, 1998).
[10] There is debate whether the expected prophet is indeed the 'teacher of righteousness' in Qumran; see Zimmermann, *Texte*, 312–417, 455–57.
[11] See 1QS 9, 9–11; cf. CD 19, 10–11 and Num 24:17. Cf. Zimmermann, *Texte*, 23–34, 230–311, 312–417, 470–80, and K. Berger, 'Die königlichen Messiastraditionen des Neuen Testaments, *NTS* 20.1 (1973), 1–44.

dominated.[12] The expected priestly messiah assumed a significant but secondary role.[13] This means that Qumran, which criticized and separated itself from the temple service in Jerusalem, nevertheless shared with it the Davidic-royal expectation of a messiah while at the same time expecting the restoration of a purified sacrificial system in Jerusalem.[14] In this regard, Qumran takes up an important aspect of divine messianic restitution (see also 4QMessAp; see Mark 11:17; Luke 7:18–23)[15] which found only secondary consideration in popular Judaism.

First Enoch 37–71 and Psalms of Solomon 18

Besides Qumran, we note on the periphery of Palestinian Judaism further messianic expectations regarding a Danielic 'Son of Man' figure (*1 En.*) and a messianic 'Lord' (*Pss. Sol.* 18). It remains unclear, however, whether these texts reach into the time of Jesus or should be dated later (see below).

First Enoch 37–71

Scholars debate whether the relevant section of *1 Enoch* 37–71 is of post-Christian provenance. Milik, Knibb, and Lindars date the text between the end of the first century AD and the middle of the second century AD. Isaac dates the text toward the end of the first century AD.[16] Black, on the other hand, dates the section before AD 70. It is often emphasized that the section 37–71 is conspicuously missing in the Enoch text of Qumran. Some have argued that Jewish scribes at Qumran might have intentionally omitted the section because of the Christian identification of Jesus as the Son of Man (see below).

Further issues pertain to the question of whether the text is Jewish (Isaac, Riesner, Berger[17]) or Jewish-Christian (Milik). In this regard the Jewish

---

[12] See Zimmermann, *Texte*, 463–66, 478.

[13] Zimmermann, *Texte*, 480. Similarly, R.D. Rowe, *God's Kingdom and God's Son: The Background to Mark's Christology from Concepts of Kingship in the Psalms* (Leiden: Brill, 2002), 217–18.

[14] Qumran connects this with the expected messianic banquet (cf. 1QSa 2, 11-21).

[15] Helyer, *Life*, 35, and n. 12.

[16] Cf. J.T. Milik, *Books of Enoch: Aramaic Fragments of Qumran Cave 4* (Oxford: Oxford University Press, 1976), 1–135, B. Lindars, *Jesus Son of Man: A Fresh Examination of the Son of Man Sayings in the Gospels* (London: SPCK, 1983), 5, 158 (with reference to Knibb) as well as Riesner, *Jesus*, 323. See Bayer, *Predictions*, 230, and n. 40.

[17] K. Berger, *Die Auferstehung des Propheten und die Erhöhung des Menschensohnes: Traditionsgeschichtliche Untersuchungen zur Deutung des Geschickes Jesu in frühchristlichen Texten* (Göttingen: Vandenhoeck & Ruprecht, 1976), 142.

provenance is more convincing.[18] There is thus still much uncertainty concerning this text, especially regarding the precise date of the text.[19]

In *1 Enoch* 49:2-4 and 62:1-4, the Anointed and Elected is filled with the Spirit of God. The Son of Man figure is associated with the messianic Servant of Isaiah 53 and seen as a human being (see *1 En.* 90:14, 17, 20) and as 'my son' (*1 En.* 105:2). Riesner (referring also to 4QMessAp 1:7-8) highlights the close connection in *1 Enoch* 37–71 between the Davidic Messiah, the Danielic Son of Man, the Servant of YHWH, and preexistent Wisdom.[20]

We can conclude that *1 Enoch* 37–71 demonstrates, at the most, a peripheral concept in Palestinian Judaism in which various messianic Old Testament concepts, *ostensibly* connected by Jesus, are apparent.

Psalms of Solomon 18

Wright identifies the 18 *Psalms of Solomon* as pre-Christian pseudepigraphic psalms, probably from the first century AD.[21] According to Wright, the messianic figure is primarily a Davidic royal ruler (see especially *Pss. Sol.* 17:23-37).[22] This figure, however, restores Israel and its temple by spiritual means (see *Pss. Sol.* 17:33-34, 37). The messianic figure purifies the people and achieves victory over Gentile oppression. A further characteristic featured herein is the fact that this messiah is called 'Lord Messiah' (*Pss. Sol.* 18:7), albeit as a mere *human* mediator (see *Pss. Sol.* 18:7-9), who brings his people back to the fear of God.

We conclude that the popular first-century AD expectation of a messiah does indeed focus on 2 Samuel 7:13-14, 16.[23] Driven by popular Pharisaic Judaism, the majority of Jews expected a Davidic figure, a royal liberator and ruler[24] in Jerusalem.[25] Texts such as *1 Enoch* and the *Psalms of Solomon*, as well as some particular expectations found in the Qumran community, find their place on the periphery of Palestinian Judaism at the time of Jesus. Furthermore, the exact

---

[18] Berger, *Auferstehung*, 142. Cautiously, Isaac, *Enoch*, 7–8.
[19] The consensus dates it in the first century AD.
[20] Riesner, *Jesus*, 323–24, here 324.
[21] R.B. Wright, 'Psalms of Solomon', in J.H. Charlesworth (ed.), *The Old Testament Pseudepigrapha* (Garden City, NY: Doubleday, 1985), II, 639–50. See R.B. Wright, 'Psalms', 640–41, regarding details for dating the document.
[22] R.B. Wright, 'Psalms', 645.
[23] Rowe, *Kingdom*, 217. See even *Pss. Sol.* 17. Different, Berger, 'Messiastraditionen', 1–44.
[24] See, e.g., Zimmermann, *Texte*, 480.
[25] Collins, *Scepter*, 24–27, 49–73; 204–10.

date, provenance, and specific theological concepts of *1 Enoch*, 37–71 and *Psalms of Solomon*, remain, in various ways, obscure. While these less prominent messianic expectations at the time of Jesus are historically possible, none of them represent a widespread popular view that would have been taught in Pharisaic synagogue schools or presented in synagogue services.

As it turns out, Jesus challenges precisely this most popular messianic expectation which the disciples also held. Incrementally, he advances a messianic portrait that encompasses much more of the Old Testament than the narrow, politicized messianic expectation surrounding 2 Samuel 7:12-14, which had been shaped by the momentous experiences of the Maccabean uprising in the second century BC. In contrast to the popular expectation, Jesus conveys a complex messianic spectrum of humiliation and exaltation (Ps 110:1; Isa 53:1-12; Dan 7:13-14) largely unique to himself and in accord with divergent Old Testament messianic expectations. Even 2 Samuel 7:13, 16 will be taken, in a way, more seriously by Jesus since he will, following the resurrection, reign on the throne of David forever (see Acts 2:30; cf. Luke 1:32-33).

The danger of or temptation to forcing Jesus into the role of a narrowly defined political, quasi-religious guerrilla leader against the Roman Empire, like those of the Maccabean uprising, was real (see Mark 8:32-33; Luke 24:21; Acts 1:6). Surprisingly, John's Gospel conveys the serendipitous and highly significant remark that 'Jesus, knowing that they intended to come and make him king by force, withdrew again to a mountain by himself' (John 6:15).

We will seek to demonstrate below that Jesus introduces a corrective[26] element to the popular messianic expectation of the disciples and Palestinian (especially Pharisaic) Judaism in general. Jesus picks up the messianic strand of the Servant of God (*Ebed YHWH;* see Mark 2:20; 10:45; Isa 53:8) as well as the theme of the rejection, humiliation, suffering (e.g., Mark 8:31; 10:45; 14:25), and exaltation of the Messiah of God as Son of Man and Lord (Mark 8:38; 12:35-37; 14:62; Ps 110:1, 5; Dan 7:13-14). The prevailing political-messianic expectation in first-century Palestinian Judaism does not have a framework for a suffering, serving, dying, and highly exalted messiah who exists as the divine Son of God.

This clash, then, makes it historically necessary for Jesus to shroud himself in his own 'messianic secret', whereby he must give injunctions to silence to the disciples until his resurrection (Mark 9:9; see details below). In other words, Jesus has to navigate the difficult and perilous path of rejecting narrow political messianic expectations while at the same time affirming *all* biblical

---

[26] See J.D. Kingsbury, *The Christology of Mark's Gospel* (Philadelphia, PA: Fortress Press, 1983), 25–45.

messianic truths which include his death, resurrection, and universal rule 'on the throne of David' (Acts 2:30; cf. Luke 1:32-33).

The Messiah of God according to Jesus's Self-Disclosure and Comprehensive Old Testament Foundation

Jesus the Messiah of God as a Human Being

Far from presenting Jesus as an oblique figure, Mark describes Jesus as a real human being who is compassionate and merciful (Mark 1:41; 6:34; 8:2). He can display righteous indignation (Mark 3:5;[27] 8:33; 10:14). He can be distressed in suffering (Mark 14:33-34), experience fatigue (Mark 7:34; 8:12) and hunger (Mark 11:12), be in need of sleep (Mark 4:38) and be, at times, astonished (Mark 6:6).

Jesus the Messiah of God as a Divine Being

The disciples are confronted, however, by a person who exhibits not only human but also increasingly divine characteristics and attributes. This is all the more perplexing as the report pertains to a Galilean Jew (Jesus) in a post-Maccabean, Palestinian Jewish testimony (Peter). The divine nature of Jesus becomes apparent in his extraordinary power over nature (e.g., Mark 4:35-41) and demons (e.g., Mark 3:11-12); in his claim to forgive sins directly (Mark 2:10); in his transfiguration; in his claims to be the 'Son of Man' (Mark 8:31; 38) and 'Lord' (Mark 12:35-37); and not least in his authoritative, sovereign call to discipleship.

The transfiguration narrative (Mark 9:2-8) offers a striking example of the divine self-revelation of Jesus as the Son of God. Mark 9:1 presents the imminent transfiguration as a proleptic anticipation of the future kingdom of God and thus also as a proleptic anticipation of the Parousia of Christ (of which Pentecost is a down payment). It is important to note that the three witnesses of the transfiguration belong to Jesus's 'inner circle', one of whom, Peter, will later refer to the event (see 2 Pet 1:16-18). There, Peter will interpret the

---

[27] See the text-critical debate whether Mark 1:41 represents Jesus as feeling 'compassion' or 'anger' when healing a leper. In favor of 'anger', see, e.g., B. Ehrman, 'A Leper in the Hands of an Angry Jesus', in *New Testament Greek and Exegesis: Essays in Honor of Gerald F. Hawthorne* (Grand Rapids, MI: Eerdmans, 2003), 77–98. See also D. Wallace, *Revisiting the Corruption of the New Testament: Manuscript, Patristic, and Apocryphal Evidence* (Grand Rapids, MI: Kregel Academic, 2011). Regardless of this issue, there is no question that Jesus expressed, at times, righteous indignation.

transfiguration 'as the expression of Jesus's divine glory and the anticipation of his glorious return at the *Parousia*'[28] (see 2 Pet 1:16). He will also identify the voice at the transfiguration as the voice of God attributing honor and glory to Christ (2 Pet 1:17; regarding the phrase, 'This is my Son, my beloved one, with whom I am well pleased', see Ps 2:7; cf. Gen 22:2; Isa 42:1). Finally, Peter will state that the transfiguration makes the anticipated Old Testament prophecies about Christ 'all the more reliable'.[29]

For a brief time, Jesus displays his full glory to the three disciples present on the Mount of Transfiguration. We see here the future messianic king illustrated by the meeting between him, Moses, and Elijah. Moses represents the Torah and Elijah the prophets: Moses revealed God's law, the prophets called God's people back to the Torah of God. Here, both of them look to Jesus as the fulfillment of both the Law and the Prophets (cf. Matt 5:17). As Jesus's divine nature is revealed, he radiates as a source of light[30] from the inside out,[31] in contrast to the *reflective* radiance of Moses when he receives the Ten Commandments (Exod 24:15-18; 34:29-30, 33, 35; cf. Dan 7:9-10).[32] The description is also marked by humorous realism: 'And his clothes became radiant, intensely white, as no one on earth could bleach them' (Mark 9:3). We see a human being radiating divine glory with supremacy over the great mediator of the Law (Moses) and over the prophetic heritage (Elijah). In the midst of this supernatural occurrence Peter intends to build three tabernacles. He still views Moses, Elijah, and Jesus as equals. Peter is slow to realize who God's Messiah really is (see Acts 1:6).[33] The divine voice declares: 'This is my beloved Son. Listen to Him'' (Mark 9:7), echoing Deuteronomy 18:15: 'God will raise up . . . a prophet like me . . . listen to him'.[34]

The Father of Jesus helps shape the understanding of Peter, John, and James regarding the full identity of his eternal Son. He is the only One who receives such divine affirmation as the eternal Son.[35] The Mount of Transfiguration thus opens a unique window into the divine nature of him who calls to discipleship.

---

[28] D.J. Harrington, *Jude and 2 Peter* (Collegeville, MN: The Liturgical Press, 2003), 256.
[29] See the convincing arguments of Harrington, *Jude and 2 Peter*, 257.
[30] See Ezek 1:22-28 and Rev 21:23.
[31] See Phil 2:5-7.
[32] Moses *reflects* the glory of God when the Jews see him (cf. Matt 17:1-13).
[33] Note, however, Peter's recollection of this event in 2 Pet 1:16-17.
[34] Cf. D.L. Bock, *Luke* (Grand Rapids, MI: Zondervan, 1996).
[35] See Mark 1:11; 9:7 (Ps 2:7); cf. Gen 22:2; Isa 42:1.

Jesus as the Messianic Son of God[36]

The transfiguration of Jesus displays and confirms his divine nature. Tellingly, the heavenly voice identifies Jesus as the 'beloved Son' and calls the disciples to 'listen to him'. Unmistakably, the term 'Son of God' in this context is meant in its full ontological sense, not merely as a phrase of adoption or as a figure of speech. Jesus is eternally Son of the Father, sharing in his divine nature.

According to V. Taylor and others, the title Son of God constitutes a central phrase in Mark. Taylor notes the bracket verses of Mark 1:1 and 15:39. Conspicuously placed references to '[my beloved] Son' at Jesus's baptism (Mark 1:11), his transfiguration (Mark 9:7), and the parable of the Wicked Tenants (Mark 12:6-8) are noteworthy as well, as is the fact of Jesus's self-identification as the 'Son' (Mark 13:32). Demons refer to Jesus as 'the Son of [the Most High] God' (Mark 3:11; 5:7), and the high priest links the Messiah with 'the Son of the Blessed' (Mark 14:61-62). The high priest's statement toward the end of the trial is probably based on reports about Jesus's own filial claims in Mark 12:1-12.[37] Finally, exclusive references to his Father (Mark 8:36; 13:32; 14:36) are very significant for understanding Jesus's self-understanding.

Jesus as the Messianic Son of Man

The phrase 'Son of Man'[38] is found nearly exclusively in sayings of Jesus and constitutes a unique phenomenon in early Christianity, since Son of Man is virtually absent from the New Testament outside the Gospels.[39] More specifically, the phrase Son of Man is a unique self-designation of Jesus.[40] He

---

[36] D.A. Carson, *Jesus the Son of God: A Christological Title Often Overlooked, Sometimes Misunderstood, and Currently Disputed* (Wheaton, IL: Crossway, 2012).

[37] Taylor, *Mark*, 120–22; for details see Bayer, *Markus*, 101–102.

[38] It occurs about 72 times in the Gospels. See J.J. Collins, 'The Son of Man in Ancient Judaism', in Holmén and Porter (eds), *Handbook*, II, 1545 68.

[39] Besides some references in Rev, which draw on Ezekiel's use of 'Son of Man' to describe a prophet, the only exception outside the canonical Gospels is the stoning of Stephen in Acts 7:56.

[40] Various historical-critical scholars have tried to separate Jesus from the concept of the suffering and exalted Son of Man, but this key phrase turns out to be historical bedrock. See the time-honored and robust arguments in I.H. Marshall, 'The Synoptic Son of Man Sayings in Recent Discussion', *NTS* 12 (1965–66), 327–51. The phrase thus affords us deep insight into Jesus's unique self-understanding as Messiah of God.

associates three distinct but related ideas with this phrase:[41]

First, Jesus uses the term to refer to his humble human state.[42] As such, it may simply reflect the Aramaic phrase *bar enash,* which can be used as a simple circumlocution for the first person personal pronoun.[43]

Second, Jesus's frequent references to the divine necessity of the Son of Man's suffering and rejection (Mark 8:31 [δεῖ]; 10:32 [μέλλω]; 10:45; 14:21, 36) have given rise to much debate. Doubtless, there are historical circumstances which point to the intention of opponents to execute Jesus. In Mark 1–12 alone, there are no less than fifteen conflict discourses. Not only does the fate of John the Baptist cast an ominous shadow over Jesus's work, but all accounts also agree that opposition increases in proportion to Jesus's expansive claims. There are thus good historical reasons for Jesus to anticipate suffering and rejection.[44]

Given these historical factors, Jesus plausibly employs the relatively uncommon and, for his purposes, useful phrase 'Son of Man' to *correct* popular messianic, Davidic-political expectations.

He uses the phrase to emphasize that God's Messiah must suffer on behalf 'of many' (Mark 10:45; compare with 2:10 and 8:31). Thus, divine necessity and human opposition converge in the death of the Son of Man. In Mark 10:45, Jesus interprets his suffering as the Son of Man in terms of ransom (λύτρον).[45] We have here a most exceptional self-identification of Jesus. Many scholars agree that Jesus alludes thereby to Isaiah 53:8 ('stricken for the transgression of my people' [LXX: ἀπὸ τῶν ἀνομιῶν τοῦ λαοῦ μου ἤχθη εἰς θάνατον]; cf. λυτρωθήσεσθε, Isa 52:3) and Isaiah 53:12.[46]

---

[41] For more detail, see Bayer, *Predictions,* 154–76; 211–13; 229–36; Marshall, 'Son of Man', 327–51.
[42] This aspect is prominent in Matt and Luke, e.g., Matt 8:20.
[43] See Lindars, *Son of Man,* 8–9.
[44] See Bayer, *Predictions,* 29–148; 221–56.
[45] See S.H.T. Page, 'The Authenticity of the Ransom Logion (Mark 10:45b)', in R.T. France and D. Wenham (eds), *Gospel Perspectives* (Sheffield: JSOT Press, 1980), I, 137–61. See J.C. Edwards, *The Ransom Logion in Mark and Matthew: Its Reception and Its Significance for the Study of the Gospels* (Tübingen: Mohr Siebeck, 2012) and W. Haubeck, *Loskauf durch Christus* (Giessen: Brunnen, 1985).
[46] See, e.g., O. Cullmann, *The Christology of the New Testament* (Philadelphia, PA: Westminster, 1959), 51–82; R.E. Watts, 'Mark', in G.K. Beale and D.A. Carson (eds), *Commentary on the New Testament Use of the Old Testament* (Grand Rapids, MI: Baker, 2007), 203–206.

While Isaiah 53 speaks of the 'Servant of Yahweh' (*Ebed YHWH*) and not of the Son of Man, Cullmann has demonstrated in detail that Jesus *connects* the concepts of *Ebed YHWH* with that of the Son of Man in Mark 10:45.[47] Above all other arguments, Jesus's entire demeanor supports his identification with the Servant of Isaiah 53. Jesus *lives the life* of the *Servant* of YHWH as the rejected and humble Son of Man. Jesus's actions and his explicit references to the suffering Son of Man (Mark 8:31; 10:45) point to the double theme of rejection and substitutionary suffering of the Servant of YHWH (Isa 52:13–53:12).

One of the reasons for considering the Servant Song in Isaiah 52:13–53:12 in more detail is the fact that we are dealing with a particularly emphasized *Petrine* Old Testament allusion and reference, surfacing again, for example, in *Acts 3:13-15* and *1 Peter 2:21-25*.

Isaiah 52:13–53:12[48] is both unusual and exceptional in its own context. On the surface, a major interpretive problem arises with the Servant Songs of Isaiah 42–53 when we compare Jewish and Christian commentaries on these texts. The prevailing Jewish interpretation of the Servant of YHWH songs in these chapters is that the *Ebed YHWH* is *always* to be identified as the people of Israel. The understanding of the persecuted people of Israel is that as the collective *Servant* of YHWH they endure much suffering and humiliation. In fact, many sections in Isaiah 42:1–52:12 can—and should be—interpreted in this manner; they may very well represent Israel as a suffering people (see especially Isa 44:1-2, 21; 45:4; 48:20; 49:3). Some Jewish interpreters identify the *Ebed YHWH* as: (a) the Messiah; (b) the Prophet like Moses; (c) Cyrus; and (d) the city Zion.[49] However, it is very difficult to apply this interpretation to Isaiah 52:13–53:12, because here an *individual* Servant of YHWH suffers *on behalf* of his people Israel (Isa 53:4-6, 8).[50] If we consistently defined 'Servant of YHWH' as referring collectively to Israel, then Israel would suffer in Isaiah 52:13–53:12 on behalf of Israel, effectively atoning for itself. This contradicts the very tone of Isaiah 42–53, where it is God who saves and redeems (see especially, Isa 42:6; 43:3, 14; 44:6, 22, 24; 45:17, 22; 47:4; 48:17, 20; 49:6, 8, 26; 50:2; 51:5-6; 52:3, 7, 10).

---

[47] See Cullmann, *Christology*, 51–82 (esp. 65), 137–192; Stuhlmacher, *Theologie*, 128–30; *Pace* M.D. Hooker, *The Gospel According to Saint Mark* (London, A&C Black, 1991), 247–51.

[48] See, e.g., W.H. Bellinger and W.R. Farmer, *Jesus and the Suffering Servant: Isaiah 53 and Christian Origins* (Harrisburg, PA: Trinity Press, 1998).

[49] Rowe, *Kingdom*, 70–84.

[50] Stuhlmacher, *Theologie*, I, 128–30.

Targum Isaiah 53 (part of which may be contemporaneous to Jesus)[51] sees in Isaiah 52:13–53:12 at least partially a messianic figure, while the suffering of the *Ebed YHWH* may still refer to the people of Israel.[52]

There is, however, a more fitting explanation for the identity of the 'Servant of YHWH' in the context of Isaiah 42–53. The *Ebed YHWH*, which may very well be collective Israel, suffers much. However, it is the royal leader and representative head of the people who will ultimately suffer and give his life as an atonement on behalf of the people (Isa 52:13–53:12), just as Mark tells us in 10:45 (see 1 Pet 2:21-24). The pre-Christian Qumran scroll 1QIsa[a] reads for Isaiah 53:8, 'he was stricken for the transgression of my people' (cf. 1QIsa[a] 53:6). The suffering people of God are thus purified and healed by their royal leader and head, Jesus, the divine Messiah of God.[53] Further study of Isaiah 52:13–53:12 reinforces a *representative* interpretation and points simultaneously to a kingly figure who suffers.

Rowe observes the following motifs arising in the fourth Servant Song (Isa 52:13–53:12):[54] The section is closely connected with psalms of suffering (see especially Pss 22 and 69) and psalms of *kingly suffering* (Pss *89:39, 44* and 118). The fourth Servant Song likewise contains hints of further kingly functions, such as enthronement (Isa 52:13), the exaltation of other kings (Isa 52:15), and victory (Isa 53:12; cf. 1QIsa[a] 53:11 which reads, in conjunction with the LXX, 'out of the suffering of his soul he will see *light,* אוֹר, φῶς). These elements echo Psalms 2:2, 6, 8-10 and 110:1-2, 5-6. Furthermore, the references to 'root' (Isa 53:2) mirror Isaiah 11:1, 10. Isaiah 53:6 might furthermore point to the motif of a royal shepherd (Ps 78:70-72; Isa 40:11; 44:28; Ezek 34) who takes upon himself the punishment of lost sheep. The lengthening of the days of the Servant (Isa 53:10) may echo 2 Samuel 7:12-13 (see also Ps 132:11-12). The Davidic covenant is connected with the Servant (Isa 53:10), and the people find life in the Servant's substitutionary suffering

---

[51] J. Kim, 'Targum Isaiah 53 and the New Testament Concept of Atonement', *JGRChJ* 5 (2008), 81–98 (regarding the date, cf. 83–85); *pace* Stuhlmacher, *Theologie*, I, 129–30.

[52] See Lane, *Mark,* 303. Kim, 'Targum', 81–98, argues that *Tg. Isa.* 53 speaks more broadly about a messianic and atoning figure, compatible with NT emphases of Jesus as the atoning mediator and as the one who establishes a new covenant.

[53] At the beginning of his public ministry, Jesus goes to the Jordan in communal repentance. While he has nothing personally to repent of, he acts as an intercessor for the people of Israel, who go to the Jordan to be baptized in their repentance. He offers pure repentance to God on behalf of the people by identifying fully with them. As Daniel prays on behalf of the sins of his people (Dan 9:5), so Jesus, being pure in heart and without sin, already begins to suffer on behalf of his people.

[54] Rowe, *Kingdom*, 76–79.

(Isa 53:11).⁵⁵ Just as Isaiah 24:16 identifies Yʜᴡʜ as the 'Just One', so is the Servant in Isaiah 53:11 'righteous' (see the righteous rule of the Messiah in Ps 72:1-2; Isa 9:7; 11:4-5; 32:1). The nation is found righteous based on his sacrifice.

Rowe concludes that a messianic individual must be in view in the fourth Isaianic Servant Song that unites in himself both *royal dignity* and *sacrificial humility* (cf. Heb 10:12-13). This messianic figure serves the community of the people of God.⁵⁶

Third, the phrase 'Son of Man' is also known in an apocalyptic context, based on Daniel 7:13-14, where the exaltation and authority of a 'Son of Man' before the 'Ancient of Days' is highlighted. It is Jesus as the honored Son of Man who forgives sins directly (Mark 2:10; a prerogative reserved for God alone), who is the Lord over the Sabbath (Mark 2:28), and who ultimately judges humankind (Mark 8:38; 13:26; 14:62). In Daniel 7:13-14 (cf. Dan 7:15-27) the Son of Man receives honor and worship from people of all nations⁵⁷ together with the Ancient of Days and rules, as king, over the people of God together with the Ancient of Days (see the exaltation of the Servant of Yʜᴡʜ in Isa 53:10-12). The people of God, in turn, will co-reign with the Ancient of Days and the Son of Man (Dan 7:27). As we saw already in Isaiah 52:13–53:12 (in the context of Isaiah 42–53), Jesus likewise functions in Daniel 7:15-27 as the *representative* head of his people, co-ruling with the Ancient of Days.⁵⁸ Finally, the universal mission of God shines through Daniel 7:13-27, whereby people from *every nation* serve the Ancient of Days and the exalted Son of Man (Dan 7:14, 27).

Excursus: The Worship of the Son of Man in Daniel 7:13-14

Daniel 7:13-14 makes the surprising claim that the Ancient of Days *shares* his divine glory with a Son of Man⁵⁹ (see Mark 8:38, ἐν τῇ δόξῃ τοῦ πατρός αὐτοῦ; compare 2 Pet 1:17, λαβὼν γὰρ παρὰ θεοῦ πατρὸς τιμὴν καὶ

---

⁵⁵ Rowe, *Kingdom*, 79.
⁵⁶ Rowe, *Kingdom*, 77–78.
⁵⁷ See Bayer, *Markus*, 84–85.
⁵⁸ Regarding the messianic interpretation of Dan 7:13-14 at the time of Jesus, see, e.g., 11QMel 2, 18. See D.L. Bock, *Blasphemy and Exaltation in Judaism and the Final Examination of Jesus* (Tübingen: Mohr Siebeck, 1998), 223, who refers to 4Q 491; *1 En.* 46–71. Bock, *Blasphemy,* 223 n. 95, also refers to W. Horbury, 'The Messianic Associations of the "Son of Man"', *JTS* 36 (1985), 34–55, 42.
⁵⁹ C.F. Keil, *Commentary on the Old Testament in Ten Volumes: Vol. IX, Ezekiel, Daniel* (eds, C.F. Keil and F. Delitzsch, Grand Rapids, MI: Eerdmans, 1983), IX, 234–37, notes that this formulation describes a divine being in human form.

δόξαν), by ascribing to him (ἐδόθη) eternal power, rule, and even glory (δόξα, LXX; τιμή, Theodotion). Furthermore, *all* peoples, nations, and languages will *worship* him (LXX λατρεύουσα=worship[60] (see MT Dan 7:14, יִפְלְחוּן). The old-Aramaic term פלח is used in biblical texts exclusively to express *worship* (of God or of idols; see, besides Dan 7:14, Dan 3:12, 14, 17-18, 28; 6:17, 21; *7:27* and Ezra 7:19, 24).[61] In contrast to this, Theodotion renders יִפְלְחוּן in Daniel 7:14 with the less apt δουλεύσουσιν (=will serve). It is noteworthy in this context that the saints of the Most High, who will co-rule with him and the Son of Man[62] in the coming kingdom (Dan 7:18, 22, 27),[63] will themselves receive dominion and kingdom (Dan 7:27), but not the *glory* and *worship,* a privilege reserved exclusively for the Son of Man (and the Ancient of Days; Dan 7:14). Daniel 7:27 also raises the question of whether the sg. masc. suffix to 'kingdom' (מַלְכוּתֵהּ) and the sg. masc. prep. suffix לֵהּ must be taken as referring to the holy people (masc. sg.) or, more convincingly, as a reference to the Most High or the Son of Man (cf. LXX, as well as KJV, ERV, NIV). It is clear that the primary association with the eternal kingdom is the Most High (also masc. sg.) and his Son of Man (see, besides Dan 7:27, Dan 3:33; 4:31; 6:27; cf. Dan 2:44[64]).[65] Given this primary association, it is indeed more likely that the suffix and the pronoun (*'his* kingdom' and *'he'*) in Daniel 7:27 either refer to the Most High (and, by implication, to the Son of Man; cf. Dan 7:14). If this alternate interpretation of Daniel 7:27 is seriously considered, we can state that every authority and power in the world will *worship* the Most High/Son of Man (Dan 7:14, 27). The LXX uses in Daniel 7:27 ὑποταγήσονται for יִפְלְחוּן (as well as πειθαρχήσουσιν), a term which was rendered in LXX Daniel 7:14 by means of λατρεύω (Theodotion renders for יִפְלְחוּן in Dan 7:27, as in Dan 7:14, δουλεύσουσιν=serve). We thus note the conspicuous parallel of the *worship* of the Son of Man by *all* peoples and tongues (Dan 7:14) and the *worship* of the Most High (with the Son of Man) by every authority and power (Dan 7:27).

---

[60] Cf. J.P. Louw, E.A. Nida, *Greek-English Lexicon of the New Testament Based on Sematic Domains* (New York, NY: UBS, 1988/89), I, 533.

[61] See Keil, *Daniel*, 237, regarding Dan 7:14 and 7:27. Cf. BDB, 1108b.

[62] Keil, *Daniel*, 234–37.

[63] Cf. J. Wehnert, 'Die Teilhabe der Christen an der Herrschaft mit Christus', *ZNW* 88.1 (1997), 81–96, regarding analogous NT themes.

[64] There appears to be an exception in Dan 7:18, unless the saints are merely perpetual coregents.

[65] See Keil, *Daniel*, 244–45. My colleague, C. John Collins, made me aware of the Israeli commentary on Daniel by Y. Kiel, *Sefer Daniel* (Jerusalem: Mossad Harav Kook, 1994) *ad* Dan 7:27, who calls the reference to לֵהּ in Dan 7:27 'messianic'.

Jesus as the Messianic LORD

The significant identification of Jesus as κύριος (Lord) has its origin in Jesus's own interpretation of Psalm 110:1, 5. The key text for the identification of 'Jesus as Lord' is Mark 12:35-37 (cf. Mark 2:28). There, Jesus identifies the messianic 'son' of David as the 'Lord of David' (cf. Mark 10:47-48). Psalm 110:1 is thus taken by Jesus as a reference to the Messiah, i.e., himself as the *Adonai* (Lord) to whom YHWH speaks (cf. also Mark 14:62). The exaltation of *Adonai* to the right hand of YHWH (Ps 110:1) and subsequent subjugation of *Adonai's* enemies with the aid of YHWH point to the fact that Jesus as Lord is exalted to coregency with God the Father and thus shares in the divine glory and power with the Father (compare Phil 2:9-11 with Isa 45:22-23).[66]

Jesus thus establishes the crucial link between Psalm 110:1-5 and the exalted Messiah as Lord in Mark 12:35-37 and reinforces it during the hurried trial before the high priest (Mark 14:62). In Jesus's answer to the high priest's question about whether he is the Messiah, the Son of the Blessed, he combines in an unparalleled way references to Daniel 7:13-14 and Psalm 110:1. Both passages appear to challenge a basic tenet of the Old Testament, namely, that God will not share his glory with another (Isa 42:8; 48:11). Surprisingly, Daniel 7:13-14 and Psalm 110:1-5 explicitly state that YHWH does indeed share his glory with someone. In Daniel 7:13, God, as the Ancient of Days, shares his glory with a 'Son of Man' to the point of endorsing the worship of the Son of Man. In Psalm 110:1, 5, YHWH shares his glory with *Adoni/Adonai*, the 'Lord of David'. Both passages have been interpreted in a messianic way before the time of Jesus.[67] The two passages offer a glimpse into the Trinitarian complexity of the one (Deut 6:4) God. Only in a Trinitarian fashion do these messianic passages make sense in the consistently monotheistic context of the Old Testament. According to Bock, there is little evidence that a messianic hopeful before or around the time of Jesus claimed to be either the fulfillment of Daniel 7:13-14 or that of Psalm 110:1-5.[68] Most importantly, there is virtually no evidence that a messianic figure before Jesus claimed to be the fulfillment of *both*.

Mark 14:62, therefore, represents a singularly bold combination of these two Old Testament texts. So bold, in fact, that the high priest, as God's official representative, feels justified in accusing Jesus of most blatantly blaspheming the very person and identity of YHWH. Either Jesus directly challenges the exclusive glory of the true God and must rightly be executed for blasphemy

---

[66] See N.T. Wright, *Jesus and the Victory of God* (Minneapolis, MN: Fortress, 1996), 624–29; see the allusion to Isa 45:23 in Phil 2:9-11.
[67] Bock, *Blasphemy*, 220–24.
[68] See Bock, *Blasphemy*, 230–33.

according to Jewish law, or he is indeed an eternal member of the one triune God, deserving the unique honor of the eternal Father (Dan 7:13-14; Ps 110:1-5).

The recorded affirmations of Jesus by the heavenly Father are thus highly significant. God the Father is 'pleased' in his Son (Mark 1:11), he endorses him as his 'beloved Son' (Mark 9:7), glorifies him (Acts 3:13), and raises him from the dead (Acts 3:26; cf. 1 Cor 15:3-11). This also means that God the Father stands behind the humiliation and exaltation of his eternal Son (Acts 3:13, 26). Even though the Father curses Jesus by crucifixion on account of our sinfulness (cf. Mark 10:38-39), he exalts him and thus endorses and confirms Jesus's claim that his death effects ransom (Mark 10:45; see Isa 53:4-6, 8-10, 12).[69] The human trial and divine judgment of Jesus only make historical sense if Jesus, indeed, makes such a lofty and dangerous claim; a claim which is divinely vindicated by his physical resurrection from death to eternal immortality.

The Messiah of God and the Kingdom of God

It is important to notice that toward the end of his public ministry, Jesus did connect the coming kingdom of God with his own mission. A fitting paraphrase of Mark 14:25 might be: 'As surely as I am now not any more drinking from the fruit of the vine, so surely will I drink it again in the [future] kingdom of God.' In this statement, Jesus anticipates an interim period between his death and the messianic banquet. In the messianic banquet (cf. 1QSa 2:11-15) the motifs of 'victory', 'celebration', the 'presence of the Messiah', 'judgment', and 'pilgrimage of the nations' (cf. 1 Chr 12:38-40; Isa 25:6-8; 34:5-7; 54:5–55:5; Joel 2:24-26; Zech 9:15; Matt 22:1-10; Mark 2:18-20; Rev 19:7-9) converge. As soon as Mark 14:25 and 14:62 are seen together, there remains no doubt that the vindicated Son of Man (Dan 7:13-14, 22, 27), as well as the enthroned Lord of David (Ps 110:1, 5) rules presently over his universal kingdom (Acts 2:30), awaiting ultimate culmination (Mark 14:25).[70]

In the course of Mark, the initial messenger of the kingdom (Mark 1:14-15) turns out to be its king. While there remain many detailed questions regarding the exact nature of this messianic kingdom, it is now certain that he who died a substitutionary death determines the character of the kingdom, including the question of who enters it. On account of Mark 14:25 and its context, it becomes clear that the future messianic kingdom is inseparably linked with the present rule of Christ over his people (Acts 2:30; 1 Pet 2:9; 2 Pet 1:11; cf. Acts 28:31; Rom 14:17; 1 Cor 6:10; 15:24, *25*; Eph 5:5; Col 1:13). Christ-driven

---

[69] Stuhlmacher, *Theologie*, I, 125–43, esp. 128–30.
[70] See Bayer, 'Prospect', 74–84.

transformation will affect character and conduct, e.g., in political, socio-economic and educational areas of life.

The Historical Necessity for Jesus to Give Various Injunctions to Silence

Cullmann, Kingsbury, and others[71] have offered an historical explanation for the necessity of a messianic secret in the life of Jesus: in general terms, Jesus had to be discreet and delay full revelation (see Mark 7:24, 8:30, 9:9, 30) due to the fact that God's Messiah had to die and be raised from death in order to be enthroned as the eternal Messiah-ruler (Acts 2:36; see John 6:15). While Jesus lived and taught, there was, thus, an anticipation of an impending culmination regarding his messianic self-disclosure (see Mark 9:9).[72]

More specifically, Kingsbury[73] has convincingly argued that there is a corrective element found in Jesus's messianic self-disclosure vis-à-vis the messianic expectation of the disciples and Palestinian Judaism in general. The intense expectation of a political messiah among Jews (especially the Pharisees; see, e.g., Acts 5:36-37) in the first half of the first century, narrowed Old Testament messianic expectations along the lines of the Maccabean uprising (see above, regarding the focus on 2 Sam 7:12-14, 16 in Palestinian Judaism; cf. 4QFlor 1,11-13). The danger of inciting a form of guerilla warfare against Rome was very high. In general terms, the people of Israel thus had a fixed plan for their expected messiah (cf. John 6:15). Such a narrow anticipation naturally clashed with the messianic identity and mission of Jesus (see above). When we insert the very different picture of God's Messiah, Jesus, into the historical framework of the political messianic expectation of Palestinian Judaism, we encounter a nearly impossible situation. As soon as Jesus acts even remotely like the expected political-messianic figure, he might become the spark which could cause a political uprising. While the contemporary atmosphere is filled with a particular expectation of political liberation, Jesus, as the eternal Son of God, is sent for a broader messianic purpose that includes the totality of the Old Testament anticipation of liberation by God. We might call this the 'great exodus'. That plan does not ignore the

---

[71] Cullmann, *Christology*, 60, 65, 79–82, 113–33; R.P. Martin, *Mark: Evangelist and Theologian* (Carlyle: Paternoster, 1972), 107–39; J.D.G. Dunn, 'The Messianic Secret in Mark', *TynBul* 21 (1970), 92–117.

[72] Simon Bar Kokhba, e.g., as a messianic contender had to be confirmed by his life. While rabbi Akiba was convinced of his messianic claims, quoting Num 24:17 and Hag 2:21-23 (cf. *b. Sanh.* 97b), Bar Kokhba failed miserably.

[73] Kingsbury, *Christology*, 11–15, 21, 136, 147.

oppressed plight of the Jewish people at the time of the New Testament, but it has a much deeper and more universal perspective of God's purposes.

Given this precarious historical setting, it was thus necessary for Jesus to issue injunctions of silence to his disciples until they would grasp what the mission of God's Messiah was, including his suffering and death. We note, however, the apparently greater openness of Jesus regarding his messianic identity in John's Gospel. It is indeed possible that Jesus was more self-disclosing about his messianic identity (John's testimony; cf. Mark 5:19-20) when appropriate. The Synoptic Gospels narrate a very *public* dimension of Jesus's ministry where he would have been particularly cautious about his messianic identity for fear of being misunderstood. John 6:15 tellingly testifies to such misunderstanding.

Conflicting messianic views also go a long way to explain the phenomenon of the disciples' lack of understanding. As stated above, and in contrast to Wrede (see below), various other categories of injunctions to silence have to be clearly distinguished from the injunctions to silence issued to the disciples. The former injunctions include: a. the injunctions to the demons (which are necessary on spiritual grounds as the demons misuse, twist, and deny the truth); and b. the injunctions to healed persons (which are necessary on political grounds and also affect Jesus's freedom of movement).[74] In contrast to these injunctions, Jesus forbids his disciples to speak about his messianic identity until the Messiah of God has achieved his goal of death and resurrection (Mark 9:9).

The above-stated historical need for a messianic secret on the part of Jesus is thus plausible because of the religious-political danger in which God's Messiah found himself (John 6:15). It is also necessary because the disciples (together with Palestinian Judaism) did not understand God's Messiah on account of a politicized narrowing of Old Testament messianic promises along Maccabean lines. This lack of understanding persists despite the fact that Jesus repeatedly spoke to his disciples about this (e.g., Mark 8:27-33; 9:31; 10:32-34).

We thus conclude that we are dealing with a profound clash between Jesus's perspective of the suffering, atoning, and highly exalted Messiah of God on the one hand, and a relatively fixed political messianic expectation in first-century Palestinian Judaism, initially shared by Jesus's disciples, on the other hand. This necessitates, for a limited time, Jesus's own 'messianic secret'. In the

---

[74] According to Mark, these injunctions are often not obeyed. An exception lies in Jesus's initial work in the Decapolis (a non-Jewish, Gentile area to the east of the Sea of Galilee) where he tells the healed person to go tell everyone (Mark 5:19-20). At a later stage in Jesus's work in the Decapolis, he issues an injunction to silence to another person healed there (Mark 7:36).

midst of such a tension-laden setting, Jesus's temporary injunctions to silence are not only plausible but necessary.

Excursus: The Messianic Secret as Mark's Invention: W. Wrede's Unconvincing Hypothesis

The messianic secrecy motif in Mark became a major topic of discussion after the influential publication of Wrede's *The Messianic Secret* in 1901.[75] Without sufficient justification, Wrede bundles under the heading of the messianic secret (which was supposedly invented by Mark) three distinctive and separate Markan motifs:

1. Jesus's injunctions to silence issued to demons (see, e.g., Mark 1:23-24; 3:11-12; 5:6-7), to healed people (see, e.g., Mark 1:43-44; 5:43; 7:3b; 8:26), and to his disciples (see, e.g., Mark 8:30; 9:9);
2. Secrecy surrounding Jesus's messianic identity (see, e.g., Mark 7:24; 9:30); and
3. The disciples' lack of understanding (see, e.g., Mark 8:17-21; 8:31-33; 9:9-13; 9:31-32; 10:35-44).

Wrede's brilliant but equally flawed hypothesis was that 'Mark', an unknown creative theologian at the end of the first century AD, linked the messianic faith of the early church[76] with the supposed non-messianic tradition of Jesus[77] by means of his own messianic secrecy idea. 'Mark' was thus able to retain both the integrity of the rather limited historical tradition (Jesus as a non-messianic prophet) handed down to him as well as the church's rather developed messianic faith. In this scenario, Jesus is primarily viewed as the *object* of early Christian, messianic projections.[78] Wrede held that it was merely necessary for 'Mark' to historicize the secrecy motif into the life of the historical Jesus as a narrative link between the two (essentially incompatible) strands of tradition and Christian faith. For instance, injunctions to silence were placed by 'Mark' (8:30) in order to link Jesus's non-messianic life (8:27-28) with the confession of the early church (8:29).

However, Wrede fails to explain the origin and development of the early church's messianic faith in Jesus, especially in sharp contrast to popular messianic expectations of Palestinian Judaism (see above). Even though the physical resurrection (which Wrede did not consider a historical fact) *confirms*

---

[75] W. Wrede, *The Messianic Secret* (Cambridge, MA: Attic Press/James Clarke, 1971).
[76] Wrede does not explain *how* that post-Easter faith arose.
[77] Wrede does not *demonstrate* that such a tradition ever existed.
[78] See Wrede's classic statements in *Secret*, 4–7.

Jesus's messianic claims, it does not *constitute* his messianic identity. We thus ask: how did the faith in Jesus as *suffering* and exalted Messiah arise, if not through his own teaching and the ensuing, dramatic events?[79] Wrede never answered this question from a historically plausible standpoint; he was satisfied with merely postulating that only the early church began to believe in Jesus as Messiah. Furthermore, Wrede never proved the existence of a non-messianic, pre-Markan Jesus tradition.[80] Finally, Wrede did not pay attention to the fact that the three motifs listed by him as belonging to the 'messianic secret' are to be sharply distinguished, since they represent very different causes and rationales.

Since it can be shown that there exists a plausible historical explanation for the need of a messianic secret in the public life of Jesus (see above), Wrede's hypothesis has lost its key pillar, namely, that the messianic secrecy motif had to be a later literary construction by 'Mark'.

The existence of historically conflicting messianic expectations in the life of Jesus provides a basic historical rationale and need for Jesus's own messianic secrecy motif. In specific terms, the following answers can be given to Wrede: The injunction to silence issued to his disciples (e.g., Mark 8:30; 9:9) means that Jesus must first fully communicate and demonstrate who the Messiah of God is in contrast to popular, political expectations, before his disciples testify that he is, indeed, God's Messiah. The injunction to silence issued to demons (e.g., Mark 1:23-24; 3:11-12; 5:6-7), on the other hand, is necessary because the Son of God will not tolerate demons in their twisted attempt to exercise power over him. The injunctions to silence issued to healed people (e.g., Mark 1:43-44; 5:43; 7:3b; 8:26), finally, are necessary in order to maintain Jesus's physical freedom of movement. Since these latter injunctions are, understandably, often not honored by the healed people, Jesus experiences certain limitations in mobility (compare, e.g., Mark 5:19-20 with 7:36). The secrecy surrounding Jesus's identity (Mark 7:24; 9:30) is further necessary since he has not yet been confirmed as the divinely established Messiah (cf. Acts 2:36). Finally, the disciples' ongoing and conspicuous lack of understanding (Mark 8:17-21; 8:31-33; 9:9-13; 9:31-32; 10:34-44) is most plausibly explained on account of their mentally fixed messianic expectation as taught in Pharisaic Judaism (see, e.g., Mark 8:32) as well as their hardness of heart (see, e.g., Mark 8:17-18).

---

[79] It is astonishing how uncritically Wrede's theories have been accepted by historical-critical scholarship from R. Bultmann and H. Räisänen to B. Ehrman.

[80] Toward the end of his life, Wrede wrote a letter to Adolf von Harnack dated Jan. 2, 1905, stating that he was now more inclined to believe that Jesus considered himself to be the Messiah (see H.-J. Rollmann and W. Zager, 'Unveröffentlichte Briefe William Wredes zur Problematisierung des messianischen Selbstverständnisses Jesu', *Zeitschrift für neuere Theologiegeschichte* 8 [2001], 274–322).

Conclusion

God's Messiah, Jesus of Nazareth, the Son of God, the Son of Man, and Lord, thus embodies many apparently divergent aspects of the Old Testament messianic expectations. As such, he displays great humility as well as supreme power and authority. He has power over natural forces (e.g., Mark 4:35-41; 6:45-52), demons (e.g., Mark 1:23-26; 3:11-12), and sickness (e.g., Mark 1:29-32; 2:3-12). He interprets the Torah authoritatively (e.g., Mark 1:21-22; 2:23-28; 7:1-13; 10:1-9; cf. Matt 5–7) and forgives sins (Mark 2:10). He is the inaugurator of the eternal kingdom of God (Mark 14:25). The consequence of this reality for his authoritative call to discipleship and character formation cannot be overstated. The call occurs as the triune God involves himself directly with the disciples by means of the incarnate Son of God. No other than God himself thus calls to discipleship (Mark 1:16-17; 9:2-8) and transforms his followers. While Jesus appears as a mere human being, ready to suffer, he turns out to be God, the Son as well. The call to discipleship and character formation is thus encompassed by the humility and greatness of the one who calls. Identity and character formation in discipleship is thus primarily a function of the imprint of such an eminent, sacrificial master.

Identity and Character Formation

Identity Formation

In a previous study on the Gospel of Mark,[81] we argued that Jesus intentionally causes a double crisis of self- and God-perception among his disciples, implicitly asking them the questions: Who do you perceive God to be? and Who do you perceive yourself to be? Jesus's goal is to resolve this double crisis by means of his substitutionary atonement, which reconciles human beings with their Creator by atoning for the guilt and shame of autonomous living. By this, he also heals their brokenness and sickness (see Isa 53:5c), which are consequences of a rebellious existence. The outcome of such restoration is a renewed, life-giving relationship with the true God. It is characterized by ongoing dependence and the truthful reckoning with our human identity as deeply loved by God but profoundly broken and in radical need of fundamental, transformational, and progressive restoration. A simple way to describe the Christ-centered character foundation in Mark is thus to understand discipleship as a radically renewed dependence upon God facilitated by the atonement of Jesus (Mark 10:45). Such discipleship serves as the ultimate

---

[81] Bayer, *Theology*, 61–88.

antidote to autonomy and resistance and thus constitutes the beginning of the ultimate reversal of the effects of the fall of mankind. This means that identity and character formation always rest on the foundation of a radical, interminable dependence upon the Redeemer-king in all areas of life. God's Messiah arises as the eternal king, presiding over a rule that will never end (see, e.g., Mark 14:25). Jesus's call to discipleship marks the beginning of a transformative process in which disciples ultimately will reign with the triune God (see Dan 7:15-27).

A more comprehensive way of describing identity formation as the foundation of character development in Mark is that the Messiah of God shapes the foundational realities (a new identity) necessary for kingdom-congruent character formation in his followers. He accomplishes this by means of teaching, exemplifying, and by his substitutionary atonement. He employs these means in such a way that his followers reflect him in analogous patterns of character (pattern-imitation). At the outset of transformational discipleship, Jesus launches a process of honest self-disclosure of the state of the disciples' hearts. The reason why identity formation and character formation are always Christ-centered lies in the fact that Jesus intends a radical reshaping of his disciples' attitudes, minds, and perspectives. The identity shaping answer to the double crisis of self- and God-perception lays the foundation for Christ-centered formation of character.

The Double Crisis of Self-Perception and God-Perception

While Jesus never explicitly poses these two questions associated with the double crisis, we will demonstrate below[82] that the two questions *underlie* much of what Jesus teaches his disciples, especially in Mark 4 and 7–8.[83] The double crisis caused by Jesus among his disciples removes misconceptions, false attitudes, and projections about self and God,[84] thus laying the foundation for true discipleship as holistic and enduring dependence upon the triune God. Whoever avoids Christ's double crisis is liable to subscribe to a false concept of identity and discipleship, which most often deteriorates either into pursuing a well-meant set of rules or disciplines (autonomous legalism and an additive

---

[82] For details, see Bayer, *Theology,* 61–98.
[83] J. Calvin states: 'We are ruined statues in which we can still trace outlines of our former glory'. Elsewhere Calvin says: 'look to the image of God in them, an image which, covering and obliterating their faults, should by its beauty and dignity allure us to love and embrace them' (J. Calvin, *Institutes of the Christian Religion* [1536; repr., 2 vols; London: James Clarke, 1953], I, 3.7.6).
[84] The biblical restoration mission of God answers, according to C.J.H. Wright (*The Mission of God* [Downers Grove, IL: IVP], 2006, 55), the four essential questions of existence: 1. Where are we? 2. Who are we? 3. What's gone wrong? 4. What's the solution?

approach to spirituality) or into falling for 'cheap grace'[85] (autonomous and licentious antinomianism). Becoming—and being—followers of Christ thus occupies the center of the overarching redemptive-historical purpose of God, individually and corporately, issuing in the universal, missional, living temple of God.

The Crisis of Self-Perception
Jesus challenges his disciples with searching and radical questions. We find this focus particularly in Mark 4, as well as in Mark 7–8. The questions uncover the DNA of man's fundamental human nature both in its ugly brokenness and its original glory and God-given purpose.[86]

We can point to various aspects of Jesus's teaching in support of this contention. The parable of the Sower (Mark 4:1-20) conveys Jesus's fundamental challenge for knowing which type of soil (attitude of heart) a person is. Is the inner heart like a 'hospitable soil' to God's word and mission, or is it comparable to 'inhospitable soil'? In Mark 4:1-20, Jesus thus confronts his disciples (and others) with the question of the state of their inner being ('he who has ears to hear, let him hear'). Besides Mark 4:1-20, we point especially to four text clusters in Mark 7 and 8, in which Jesus pursues the crisis of self-perception.

1. *The defilement of the heart (Mark 7:14-23).* Especially the defilements listed in Mark 7:20-22 are of such profound weight that their successful removal has exercised Stoics, ascetics, and earnest Pharisees alike.[87] Although Jesus does not, surprisingly, provide in this context an answer to the question of how these serious heart-defilements might be overcome, he confronts his disciples with their stark reality and leaves them to dwell on this.[88]
2. *Jesus's prophetic deeds of mercy as heuristic tools (Mark 7:31-35 and 8:22-26).* The macro-context of Mark 7 and 8 is telling: As a form of *inclusio*, Jesus heals a deaf-mute person in 7:31-35 and a blind person in 8:22-26. Both of these healings are at the same time acts of mercy and figurative prophetic warnings to his disciples. Again, the implied searching

---

[85] See D. Bonhoeffer, *Discipleship* (Minneapolis, MN: Fortress Press, 2001), IV, 3–5; 43–44, 50–55, 67–69.
[86] See, e.g., Benner, *Gift*, 47–107.
[87] See Paul's critique of the doomed Stoic, ascetic, and Pharisaic attempts at removing the defilements of the inner person, i.e., the power of sin in Col 2:23.
[88] It is therefore short-sighted, to point too quickly at Pharisees and teachers of the law as those who are defiled (Matt 23:1-39). The very issues Jesus exposes in the Pharisees, he also exposes in his disciples.

question posed to the disciples is whether they are able to 'hear' and to 'see', given their inner heart-condition, especially described in Mark 7:20-22. It is important to ask why Jesus heals the blind man of Mark 8:22-26[89] in *two* stages, especially since Jesus is elsewhere reported to have healed blind persons at once (cf. Mark 10:46-52 and John 9:1-41). The most convincing answer to this question is that Jesus probably heals the blind man intentionally in two stages simply to confront his disciples with their hardness of heart,[90] while still acting in messianic mercy toward the blind man. We can therefore say that Jesus does not only warn his disciples directly (Mark 7:20-22), but also instructs them by means of prophetic acts of exhortation (as did, e.g., Isaiah, Jeremiah, and Hosea) in order to get his point across. Jesus thus heals the blind man in two stages (Mark 8:22-26) in order to confront his disciples with two significant facts about their own inner selves. Their inner darkness is hindering: (1) their proper awareness of what they harbor in their own hearts (see Mark 7:20-22) and (2) their ability to see who Jesus really is (see, e.g., Mark 8:31-33; 9:2-8). While they capture *aspects* of who they really are and who Jesus really is (see e.g., Mark 8:29), they do not see clearly yet. Seeing clearly requires radical change of heart through the work of God. All of this echoes the prophetic warnings in Jeremiah (5:21-22; see below) and Isaiah (6:9-10; see Mark 4:10-12) to a people with hard hearts.

3. *Figurative 'blindness' and 'deafness' (Mark 8:17-21).* Mark 8:17-18 states: 'Do you not yet perceive or understand? Are your hearts hardened? Having eyes do you not see, and having ears do you not hear?' (cf. Jer 5:21-22; 6:10).[91] 'Hearing' and 'seeing'[92] are to be understood in a figurative sense.[93] Mark 8:17-21 directly challenges the disciples to take a closer look at themselves; otherwise they will not recognize who Jesus really is. Given what Jesus says to his disciples in Mark 4:10-12, they might be tempted to view themselves in a privileged and right relationship with God. In Mark 4:10-12, Jesus applies the warning of Isaiah 6:9-10 concerning a hard heart to those 'outside' (see, e.g., Mark 12:1-12). Isaiah 6:9-10 indicates hardening for judgment. In the Markan context, Jesus

---

[89] Mark 8:22-26 is Markan *Sondergut*.

[90] On the literary level, there are eight words for 'seeing' in these five verses. Repetition occurs for emphasis, and in this case it points to exaggeration, thus pointing to the disciples' figurative lack of 'seeing'.

[91] In Mark 4:1-20, we find the word 'hear' thirteen times; see further J. Coody, 'The Motif of Hearing and Seeing in Mark 4-8: Contributions to a Missional Reading of the Second Gospel' (Th.M. Thesis, CTS, 2011), 31, 51–61.

[92] Cf. Eph 1:18.

[93] See the prophetic OT background to the figurative use of 'seeing' and 'hearing', e.g., Isa 6:9-10; Jer 5:21-22; 6:10.

speaks in parables as a severe warning, while still offering the possibility of repentance (see especially Mark 4:33-34). In Mark 8:17-21, however, Jesus warns those 'inside' of that very hard-heartedness of those 'outside', alluding to Jeremiah 5:21 (see Isa 42:18-19; 43:8; Ezek 12:2).

4. *Jesus's figurative reference to 'yeast' (Mark 8:15).* Among first-century Jews, the figurative use of 'leaven' or 'yeast' usually referred to defiled Gentiles. Jesus, however, refers to a different kind of defilement, since he is speaking of Jews. Luke 12:1 uses 'yeast' figuratively in terms of 'hypocrisy', 1 Corinthians 5:6-8 uses it in the sense of 'self-praise', and Galatians 5:9 uses it to denote 'self-righteousness'. It is significant that later rabbinic Judaism interprets the metaphor 'yeast' or 'leaven' as the evil inclinations in all human beings (*yetzer ha-ra*).[94] Jesus strongly implies the following vis-à-vis his disciples: the Pharisees, Herod Antipas, and the disciples deem themselves 'well' and 'healthy'. He implicates his own disciples and warns them of the deceptive, self-righteous attitude (i.e., 'yeast') of Herod Antipas and the Pharisees (Mark 8:17-21; cf. Jer 5:21-22 and Mark 7:20-23), which he first uncovers in those on the 'outside' (Mark 4:10-12; Isa 6:9-10), before confronting his disciples with the same problem. Their only hope is that they continue under Jesus's influence, which will lead them to the place of Christ's atonement, purifying healing, and example.

The Crisis of God-Perception

Jesus not only confronts his disciples with the truth about their deficient self-perception, but also with their blinded perception of God. We believe that the second crisis concerning their God-perception is set off by Jesus's startling question in Mark 8:29: 'Who do you say that I am'? In addition to the expanding *exousia* of Jesus described in the first half of Mark, this question further drives a 'crisis of theology' among the disciples. While they deem themselves thoroughly cognizant of God, they resist YHWH's self-revelation in and through his Christ, and thus YHWH's mission.

During his last journey to Jerusalem (Mark 8:27–16:8), Jesus confronts his disciples more directly with the question of who God's Messiah really is and thus, by implication, who God really is. As a divine and human being (see the discussion on Christology above), God's Messiah is called to die an atoning death. In the minds of the disciples, however, their expected messiah is neither

---

[94] See *b. Ber.* 17a (2nd or 3rd century AD). See C.G. Montefiore and H. Loewe (eds), *A Rabbinic Anthology* (New York, NY: Schocken, 1974), 295–314, 362, 578; cf. M. Borg, *Conflict, Holiness, and Politics in the Teachings of Jesus* (Philadelphia, PA: Trinity Press International, 1998). See Exod 12:15-17, where literal 'yeast' is to be avoided in the bread-baking process on account of imminent judgment and deliverance.

divine nor must he die. The Gospel of Mark describes the disciples' serious lack of understanding as a problem of the mind (preconceived views) and the heart.[95] Jesus has to clarify for Peter's mind and heart how to distinguish his culturally conditioned messianic ideas (Mark 8:32-34) from the truth of God's Messiah (Matt 16:17).

The 'crisis of theology' deepens when Jesus confronts his disciples with the divine necessity of the suffering (Mark 8:31) and exaltation of the Son of Man (Mark 8:38; 9:2-8). In other words, the crisis of theology is only resolved by acknowledging the divine nature of the Messiah who atones as the Suffering Servant. This, in turn, directly affects the disciples' identity formation.

A new identity (and character) only grows as the disciples enter into the crisis of self-perception,[96] in order to see the need for the justifying and healing atonement of the incarnate Son of God. Likewise, identity (and character) only develop as the disciples enter into the crisis of God-perception (Mark 8:31-33) in order to see the depth of who God really is. Jesus's call to discipleship thus leads to both a radical self-assessment and a radical review of God-perception. Elsewhere, we concluded the following:

> If we do not see ourselves as Christ sees us—as self-sufficient and broken as well as exceedingly loved and precious to God—we will be disciples who miss Jesus' core call . . . If we do not see our true selves, we will be disciples who do not really need the Jesus of the Gospels. All we really need is a wise teacher of some aphorisms.[97]

We will argue below that the very challenging issues Peter wrestles with as a young disciple have clearly been resolved in 1 Peter, both with regard to the question of who Jesus really is and who he, Peter, is in the eyes of God. The book of Acts will display a state in Peter's development where he securely grasps the divine and human nature of Jesus as well as his own dire need for the substitutionary atonement of Christ (see Acts 15:10-11). In Acts, however, Peter has not yet grasped the extent to which God brings his mission to all peoples of the earth (see, e.g., Acts 10 and 11), nor has he fully appropriated the purifying work of the Holy Spirit (Gal 2:11-12) in the midst of pursuing God's mission.

---

[95] See N. Farelly, *The Disciples in the Fourth Gospel: A Narrative Analysis of Their Faith and Understanding* (Tübingen: Mohr Siebeck, 2010). According to Farelly, discipleship in John moves from trust to understanding, not *vice versa* (219–29).

[96] Benner, *Gift*, 63.

[97] Bayer, *Theology*, 82.

Character Formation

We have seen that followers of Christ cannot avoid facing the double crisis that fundamentally challenges everything on which they base their lives. One consequence of Jesus's double question is that each of his followers has to accept his or her inability to mend the broken relationship with the Creator and its effect on self-perception and other human relationships. Jesus's coming provides reconciliation and restoration with God (see 1 Pet 3:18: 'For Christ also suffered once for sin . . . that he might bring us to God'; cf. Luke 5:8), thus answering both fundamental questions. Because of reconciliation with God, the disciples can know who God really is and, consequently, who they are in the eyes of God. The Father identifies himself so closely with Jesus (Mark 1:11; 9:7; Acts 3:13, 15) that to deny one is to deny the other (John 17:5, 24). In short, the new identity which Jesus gives his disciples serves as the foundation for their new character.

Eight Core Characteristics of Jesus That Are Applicable to All Disciples

As Jesus lives with his disciples, he shapes them, individually and corporately, toward a new character that reflects Christ. We thus speak of discipleship as transformation toward Christlike character. Thus, 'being conformed to Christ', 'seeking pattern-imitation of Christ', and 'sharing in union with Christ' are all results of the same cause: by means of the atonement, Jesus enables and facilitates the accomplishment of what he teaches, calls for, and exemplifies.

Here we present and rank character traits applicable to all disciples of Christ as presented in the Gospel of Mark.[98] These core characteristics arise by asking a simple question: which character traits in Mark are explicitly given by Jesus as binding for *all* present and future followers of Christ?[99] In our list of criteria we look especially for general statements in Mark beginning with such formulations as 'whoever', 'anyone', 'everyone', and 'whosoever'. Among other functions, we discover that these statements often serve as introductions to generally applicable statements of discipleship.[100] The answer to this question

---

[98] Square brackets refer to the frequency of occurrence. In Bayer (*Theology*, 89–124), we identified eight core characteristics in Mark as 'fruit' of Christ's work in the disciples which are applicable to all followers of Christ: (a) surrender; (b) trust; (c) prayer; (d) watching over the heart; (e) being humble; (f) forgiving; (g) withstanding temptation and persecution, and (h) confessing Christ to all humanity.

[99] Certain elements of discipleship are, however, unique to the original disciples of Christ: (a) their calling as unique apostles (cf. Mark 3:14 in contrast with Acts 1:21–22); (b) their being sent out in Israel two by two to preach, cast out demons, and heal while under a set of restrictive travel stipulations (see Mark 6:7, 12).

[100] See especially general statements in Mark beginning with: ὅς . . . ἄν; τὶς; ὅς . . . ἐάν; ὅταν; πᾶς; ὅς + finite or auxiliary verb; ὁ + participle or

yields eight core characteristics which are fundamental to the development of Christlikeness in Mark. Our analysis yields the following character traits in Mark.

Going beyond our previous study,[101] we are especially asking the question here of what emphasis (relative to the entire account of Mark) is attributed to each of the eight core character traits in the unfolding narrative of Mark's Gospel. The following ranked list thus features approximate results of the frequency and length of occurrence, that is, the total amount of verses used in all relevant occurrences of each of the eight topics relative to the entire narrative.[102]

1. *Surrendering and following Christ* (unconditionally/obediently): [10:28]; 10:29-30; 12:44; regarding money 10:21 [23-27]; denying yourself: 8:34-35; bearing your cross:[103] 8:34, and following: (being at Jesus's disposal) 1:17; [2:14]; 4:23, 25; 8:34; 10:11; thus doing God's will: 3:35 (including the fulfillment of God's law). Total [12-13 vv.]
2. *Believing*: [neg. 4:40]; 10:27; 11:22; 13:11; [16:6]; and *trusting/faith*: 1:15; [2:5]; [5:34]; [neg. 6:6]; 7:28-29; 9:19, [24]; 11:23-24 [see 16:16]. Total [8-9 vv.]
3. *Watching over and guarding the heart* (so as to beware of hardheartedness and lack of understanding): [3:29; 4:1-20; neg. 6:52; 7:14-21]; 7:22-23; 8:17-21; [9:42-47; 14:38]. Seeking the purification of the heart: 9:49; [10:35-44]. Total [8 vv.]

οὐδείς ἐστιν ὅς . . . ἐὰν μή, the English equivalents of which are primarily 'whoever' (KJV 'whosoever'), 'anyone', and 'everyone'. The most relevant references in the following lists are given in italics: a) ὅς . . . ἄν: *3:29, 35*; 6:11; *8:35; 9:37, 41-42; 10:11, 15, 43-44; 11:23*; b) τὶς (we offer the relevant occurrences only): *4:23; 8:34; 9:35*; c) ὅς . . . ἐάν: *8:35, 38*; d) ὅταν: *11:25*; e) πᾶς: *9:49*; f) ὅς + finite or auxiliary verb: *4:25; 9:40*; g) ὁ + participle *7:10; [16:16]*; h) οὐδείς ἐστιν ὅς . . . ἐὰν μή: *10:29-30*. The ESV (supplemented by KJV and NIV) references are as follows (the most relevant ones for our topic are given, again, in italics): 'Whoever': *3:29, 35; 7:10; 8:35, 38; 9:37, 41-44; 10:11, 15, 43-44; 11:23; [16:16]*. 'Anyone': 1:44; *4:23*; 7:24; *8:34*; 9:8, 30, *35*; 11:3, 16, *25*; 13:21; 16:8. 'Everyone': 1:37; 5:20; *9:49*. 'There is no one . . . who will not' 10:29-30. The KJV adds 6:11 'whosoever' (in addition to ESV 'whoever'/'anyone' occurrences). The NIV reads 'whoever' (in addition to ESV) in *4:25; 9:40*. Additionally, we note less direct statements in Mark 2:17 (call to sinners); 7:28-29 (faith); 9:23 (all things are possible with God); 10:14 (let the children come to me); 10:23-27 (it is difficult for a rich person to enter the kingdom of God); 11:17 (prayer); 13:33 (be watchful).

[101] See Bayer, *Theology*, 89–124.
[102] Unless otherwise indicated, references pertain to the Gospel of Mark.
[103] See S. Böe, *Cross-Bearing in Luke* (Tübingen: Mohr Siebeck, 2010).

4. *Being humble:* 10:13-16; [neg. 12:38-40]; being teachable: [2:17a; 8:4-7]; and expressing a servant's heart: 9:35, especially when holding authority [10:42-44]. Total [7-8 vv.]
5. *Withstanding temptation, suffering, and persecution:* 10:30, 37; 13:9-13 [13:33; 14:38]. Total [6-7 vv.]
6. *Confessing Christ/witness to all humanity:* 8:38; preaching/proclaiming: [3:14-15]; 13:10. Total [2-3 vv.]
7. *Praying:* [9:29; 11:17]; 11:24-25. Total [2-3 vv.]
8. *Forgiving:* 11:25 (in the context of prayer and worship). Total [1 v.]

From this follows a ranked and simplified list of character traits in Mark:

1. Surrender and following Christ
2. Faith
3. Purity of heart (watching over heart)
4. Humility
5. Withstanding temptation/persecution (and witness)
6. Confessing Christ
7. Prayer
8. Forgiveness

Christ-centered character formation rests on the fact that Jesus atoned for and healed (see 1 Pet 3:18) followers who have been exposed to the existential double crisis of self-perception (autonomous alienation) and God-perception (no openness to the triune God). On the basis of forming in his disciples a new self-perception (identity formation), the earthly and then the exalted Jesus, teaches, exemplifies, and facilitates, according to the Gospel of Mark, eight core character traits in every disciple throughout the ages. As a consequence of radical transformation effected by Christ and mediated by the Holy Spirit, each follower will increasingly: (1) surrender to God and do his will; (2) believe and trust; (3) watch over and guard his/her heart; (4) be humbly serving and teachable; (5) withstand temptation and persecution; (6) confess Christ to all humanity; (7) remain in prayer, and (8) practice forgiveness.

The Dynamic between Christology, Identity, and Character Formation in Mark's Gospel

Peter's personal testimony to Jesus's person and impact is particularly reflected in the Gospel of Mark. Significant connections between Christology, identity and character formation arise (see the ranked list above). We have noted that Jesus asks nothing of his disciples which he does not facilitate in them (atonement) and exemplify for them (in his teaching and person). We cannot easily overstate the fact that the intimate causal connection between Christ and the identity and character formation of his followers is the key to godliness. The humbled and exalted Messiah of God draws his followers into the double-crisis of God- and self-perception in order to restore them to live as God-dependent human beings, expressing the consequence of their dependence in identity (loved and purified, while deeply broken) and character. As the Messiah had to humble himself prior to being vindicated, so his followers will undergo much humbling as they trust, likewise, in God's vindication.

Chapter 6

Christology, Identity, and Character Formation in the Petrine Sections of Acts

In Acts, the crisis of God-perception and self-perception which Jesus caused in the initial years with his disciples[1] is overcome, based on Christ's death and resurrection as well as the outpouring of the Holy Spirit at Pentecost (Acts 2). Additionally, as we have argued above, Peter arises with great integrity in Acts as the leading spokesperson for the Twelve[2] and as a prophetic repentance preacher along the pattern of Old Testament repentance speeches. As always, a prophet of God focuses on worshiping the true God and on character formation and maturity as he proclaims his message (cf. Luke 3:2-14). During his earthly ministry, Jesus has shaped Peter in his identity and character to arise as a personally credible prophetic voice in Jerusalem. Initially, this call addresses Palestinian and Diaspora Jews, as well as proselytes. Subsequently, this call goes out into the entire world (Acts 1:8; 10:15; 15:7-11; cf. Mark 13:10).

Petrine Material in Acts

Luke features Peter in Acts 1:1–6:7; 8:1, 14-25; 9:26–11:18; 12:1-19; and 15:1-29. We have argued above that this material may very well derive from Peter as a source, aided by the witness of such early apostolic companions as Silas/Silvanus. Initially, we will ask what christological emphases we encounter in these sections and then explore which aspects of identity formation can be isolated. Finally, we will seek to extract various ensuing dimensions of character formation which arise in those sections of Acts where there is a particular focus on Peter or where Peter is present among the apostolic leaders.

---

[1] See Bayer, *Theology,* 61–88.
[2] Cullmann, *Peter,* 34–41, mentions various elements of Peter's leadership during the initial years of the nascent church in Jerusalem, prior to Peter's apostolic mission and handing over leadership in Jerusalem to James. Cf. Bockmuehl, *Simon,* 27–28.

As we seek to distinguish Petrine speech-material from narrative discourses pertaining to Peter in Acts, the following picture arises:

1. Luke's report of Peter's *statements* and *speeches*:

    Acts 1:16-22; 2:14-36, [37], 38-40; 3:4, 6, 12-26; 4:8-12, 19-20; 5:3-4, 8-9, 29-32

    Acts 8:20-23; 9:34, 40; 10:14, 21, 26, 28-29, 34-43, 47; 11:5-17; 12:11, 17b

    Acts 15:7b-11

2. Luke's report of *acts/events* involving or surrounding Peter:[3]

    Acts 1:13-15, 23-26; 3:1-5, 7-11; 4:1-7, 13-18, 21-23; 5:15

    Acts 8:14-19, 24-25; 9:32-43; 10:1-33, 44-46, 48; 11:1-4, 18; 12:1-10, 12-19

    Acts 15:1-7a, 12-29

We have argued that Peter initially functions in Acts as the spokesperson (e.g., Acts 2:14), temporary leader (e.g., Acts 5:1-11), and key miracle worker (e.g., Acts 3:1-10) for the Twelve (Acts 1:1–6:7; 8:1-25).[4] Only at a later stage does Peter arise as an *individual* who participates and serves in God's expanding mission (Acts 9:26–11:18; 12:1-19; 15:1-29). We have also mentioned that Peter arises as a repentance preacher along the lines of Old Testament prophets.

For a characterization of Peter as a group member and leader in Acts, it is important to notice that he is now, in many ways, a different person. His apprentice time with Jesus until Pentecost can be identified as a critical time of 'incubation'. Now, Peter steps into his calling as a single-minded, God-trusting person who courageously testifies to the challenging teaching of and facts about Jesus, chief among them the bodily resurrection of Jesus following his crucifixion and death at the hands of the Romans. Connected with this is a Christology fueled by the conviction of the divine nature of Jesus: he is indeed part of the God of Abraham, Isaac, and Jacob. Together with the Father and the Holy Spirit, he is YHWH (see below). Additionally, Peter arises as a person of true God-dependent identity and character—a boldly witnessing, apostolic disciple of Christ. Despite all this, we will also learn in which ways Peter still has to develop (see, e.g., Acts 10 and 11), particularly in adversity. Finally, as Peter is caught up in the *missio dei* in Acts, his identity and character are further shaped and purified.

---

[3] Excluding the acts or events surrounding Peter *as part of the apostolic group* (see, e.g., Acts 1:1-12; 2:1-13, 42-47; 4:24-37; 5:1-2, 5-7, 10-14, 16-28, 33-42; 6:1-7; 8:1; 9:1, 26-27).

[4] See Bockmuehl, *Simon*, 27–28.

Peter's Apostolic Witness to Christ

Peter's preaching in the initial chapters of Acts is marked by a strong focus on the God of Abraham, Isaac, and Jacob. Christology is always presented within a Trinitarian framework and never as a monistic 'Jesus only' message (see, e.g., Acts 1:4-5; 3:13-15, 33; cf. 7:55). According to Peter, the *'Echad'* (='one') of Israel's foundational confession in the Shema (Deut 6:4) has not changed by any means; it has simply been explained more deeply and in its fuller complexity. God is still *one* and *unified* (see John 14–16). Characteristic for such a Shema-embedded Christology is Peter's statement in Acts 3:13: 'The God of Abraham, the God of Isaac, and the God of Jacob, the God of our Fathers, glorified his Servant (ἐδόξασεν τὸν παῖδα αὐτοῦ; cf. Isa 53:1-12) Jesus'. In other words, Peter fully expresses himself in the theological, monotheistic context of the Old Testament and Palestinian Judaism. This is particularly significant for Peter's predominantly Jewish hearers. No other than the 'God of our Fathers' vouchsafes the past, present, and future identity and deeds of his beloved Messiah-Servant-Son.

God as the *initiator* of the redemptive-historical unfolding of the life of Jesus can be demonstrated especially in Peter's speech recorded in Acts 3:12-26. In addition to what we just mentioned concerning verse 13, it was God who raised Jesus from the dead (ὃν ὁ θεὸς ἤγειρεν, v. 15), thus fulfilling his word (ὁ θεὸς . . . ἐπλήρωσεν οὕτως, v. 18). God (ἀπὸ προσώπου τοῦ κυρίου) also sends times of refreshment and eventually sends Jesus once again (v. 20); Christ's presence in heaven accords with God's will (see the divine δεῖ) and God ultimately fulfills all he has spoken (v. 21); God raises (double *entendre*?) up a Prophet like Moses (ἀναστήσει . . . ὁ θεός, v. 22); God made a covenant (διέθετο ὁ θεός, v. 25), and God raised his Servant and sent him (ἀναστήσας ὁ θεὸς τὸν παῖδα αὐτοῦ . . . ἀπέστειλεν αὐτόν, v. 26).

Besides a clear foundation in the Trinity and the obvious focus on Christology (for details, see below), Peter, perhaps as the source of the theological thrust of Acts, highlights the work of the Holy Spirit (e.g., Acts 2:38; 5:32) as the agent of Christ (see especially Acts 2:33). In other words, the exalted Christ, as the *executor* of the Father's promise (Gal 3:18; 4:6),[5] *continues*[6] his Father's work through the Holy Spirit.

---

[5] See T.R. Schreiner, *Paul, Apostle of God's Glory in Christ: A Pauline Theology* (Downers Grove, IL: IVP, 2001), 73–85.

[6] It is most convincing to take ἄρχομαι in Acts 1:1 in the full sense of the verb (i.e., what Jesus *'began* to do') rather than as complementary to 'doing' (i.e., 'what he *set out* to do'); cf. I.H. Marshall, *The Acts of the Apostles* (Leicester: IVP, 1980), 56.

The Significance of Pentecost

Characteristic for this Petrine emphasis is the fact that the outpouring of the Holy Spirit has a dual purpose and effect: he is given toward purity of heart *and* boldness in witness (see the analogy in Deut 4:1; Israel is to 'keep the law' and to 'take possession of the land'). This dual purpose arises from the fact that Jews who celebrated Pentecost at the time of Jesus remembered not only God's blessing in harvest (harvest thanksgiving) but, tellingly, the giving of the Mosaic law as covenant renewal.

In order to shed light on our subsequent reflections on Petrine Christology, identity and character formation, it is important to pay attention to this historical background of Pentecost:[7] besides the Old Testament meaning of Pentecost (=Feast of Weeks) as a harvest-thanksgiving of firstfruit (Exod 34:22),[8] a further commemorative association arises over time, namely, that of the giving of the law of Moses in the context of covenant renewal. There is some debate on whether this additional meaning of Pentecost was already prevalent during the time of Christ or whether it only arose in the second century AD.[9] A good number of contemporary voices such as Philo and Josephus do not mention a possible second meaning of Pentecost. However, there are indications in *Jubilees* (second or first century BC)[10] that Pentecost was already associated with the giving of the Mosaic law.[11]

---

[7] Cf. Exod 34:22; Lev 23:15-16; Num 28:26; Deut 16:9-12; 2 Chr 8:13; Josephus, *Ant.* 3.252. See Marshall, *Acts*, 72. Regarding rabbinic literature, see Str-B, II, 597–602.

[8] The significance of a feast of harvest remains in the intertestamental time; cf. E. Lohse, πεντηκοστή, *TDNT*, VI, 47.

[9] Rabbis after AD 70 are certain that 50 days after the exodus the Mosaic law was given. Compare Exod 19:1 (the Mosaic law was received in the third month following the exodus) with Deut 16:9 (seven weeks following the Passover the people of Israel are to celebrate the Feast of Weeks). See RJose bChalaphta (ca. AD 150); cf. Str-B, II, 601. The report concerning the giving of the law (Exod 19:1-25) and Deut 16:9-15 (instructions for the Feast of Weeks) were read at Pentecost starting latest with the second century AD (cf. Lohse, πεντηκοστή, *TDNT*, VI, 47 n. 19). In the third century AD, R Eleazar states that the Torah was given at Pentecost.

[10] The midrash narrative and pre-Christian book of *Jubilees* re-narrates events spanning from Genesis 1 to Exodus 12 (cf. Wintermute, 'Jubilees', in: J.H. Charlesworth, *The Old Testament Pseudepigrapha*, II, 40). It also mentions the circumstances surrounding the receiving of the law of Moses (Exod 24:18; cf. Wintermute, 'Jubilees', 39). Concerning the proximity between *Jubilees* and Qumran, see Wintermute, 'Jubilees', 43–44. See also 1QapGen as an example of re-narrating biblical texts. Qumran appears to have at least read *Jubilees* (cf. CD 16, 2–4).

[11] See also 1QapGen and 4QFlor. More hesitant, see E. Lohse, *Die Texte aus Qumran: Hebräisch und Deutsch* (Munich: Kösel, 1986), 291 n. 103; more certain, see Wintermute, 'Jubilees', 50.

The central concern in *Jubilees* is to exhort Jews to return to the Mosaic law and to resist the pressure of compromising faithfulness to God's law by succumbing to a Gentile way of life. Part of this paraenesis is found in *Jubilees* 6:17-22. In this section we encounter several indications that Pentecost was associated with the receiving of the Mosaic law and with covenant renewal. According to Jubilees, *Shavuot* (Pentecost) has already a double meaning (see *Jub.* 15:1-16; 22:1): it is the Feast of Firstfruits (*Jub.* 6:21) *and* the feast of covenant renewal and its laws (*Jub.* 6:17), especially a covenant renewal on 'this mountain' (cf. *Jub.* 6:19). The giving of the law on Sinai is herewith viewed as an event of covenant renewal, since the Feast of Pentecost goes back to creation, extends from Noah to Abraham, Isaac, and Jacob, and finally reaches 'this mountain'.[12] Due to the fact that the patriarchs have been mentioned prior to this reference, the identification of 'this mountain' with Sinai is plausible. This means that, according to Jubilees, Pentecost is a time of remembering the giving of the law to Moses as a covenant renewal. *Jubilees* 6:20b, 21 states: 'One day per year in this month they shall celebrate the feast, for it is the feast of shebuot and it is the feast of the firstfruit. This feast is twofold and of two natures'.[13]

The double factor mentioned in *Jubilees* is already indirectly hinted at in the Old Testament (cf. esp. Lev 23:15-21 and Deut 16:1-17). The explicit connection between exodus and Passover (*Pesach*, Deut 16:1-8) lays the foundation for identifying the two further feasts of pilgrimage, namely, the Feast of Weeks or Pentecost (*Shavuot*) and the Feast of Booths or Tabernacles (*Sukkot*), as *subsequent* to Passover and the commencement of the exodus (*Pesach*). In Leviticus 23:42-43 the Feast of Booths (*Sukkot*) is clearly connected with the memory of sojourn in the desert following the exodus. This means that the Feast of Weeks (or Pentecost) must be placed, according to Leviticus 23:1-21 and Deuteronomy 16:1-12, *between* Passover (*Pesach* and the commencement of the exodus) and the Feast of Booths (*Sukkot*=sojourn in the desert).

Since Pentecost as the Feast of Weeks (*Shavuot*) is to be celebrated fifty days (Deut 16:9; see Exod 19:1: in the third month after *Pesach*) after Passover, the association of Pentecost with the giving of the Mosaic law falls naturally together, even if the event and the celebration are not explicitly

---

[12] See the text in Wintermute, 'Jubilees', 67.
[13] See the texts in Wintermute, 'Jubilees', 67. Wintermute (67) assumes that the 'two natures' reflect the ambiguity of the Hebrew root of *Shavuot* (=week or oath). That would mean that in the second and first century BC this feast was already associated with celebrating firstfruits *as well as* remembering the oath of God (covenant renewal). In addition, echoes to the covenants with Noah and Abraham can be discerned (cf. *Jub.* 15:1-16: God makes the covenant with Abraham at Pentecost).

connected. Together, the three historical events (exodus; receiving the law at Sinai; sojourn in the desert) are thus mirrored by the three pilgrimage feasts of Passover (*Pesach*), Pentecost/Weeks (*Shavuot*), and Booths (*Sukkot*).

This background for the particular Pentecost narrated in Acts 2 is highly significant.[14] Jews were presently celebrating *Shavuot* as a Feast of Firstfruits and as a feast of commemorating the giving of the law of Moses as a covenant renewal. The background of the giving of the law of Moses in the context of covenant renewal combined with the outpouring of the Holy Spirit (see Gal 3:14; cf. Gen 12:3)[15] thus carries great significance (see especially Joel 2:28-32; compare with Isa 59:21; Jer 31:31-34; Ezek 37:26; 39:29). At the particular Pentecost narrated in Acts 2, Jeremiah 31:31-34 thus finds its fulfillment (see Heb 8:8-12; 10:16-17). The grand outpouring of the Holy Spirit[16] means that God is writing the law on the hearts of his Messiah-believing covenant people, having cleansed them by the substitutionary atonement of Christ, which together with the anointing by the Holy Spirit, serves as the *foundation* for godliness (Luke 3:16b). The more obvious second consequence of the outpouring of the Holy Spirit at Pentecost is to embolden to Christian witness (Acts 1:7-8).

This dual effect of Pentecost—the purification of the heart (Luke 3:16b) and emboldened witness (Acts 1:7-8)—is embedded in a momentous missional thrust[17] in which the early church finds itself due to God's presence and the unfolding of his eternal purposes. Furthermore, as stated above, Peter takes up the longstanding form of prophetic repentance speech which presents salvation accomplished by the covenant-keeping God to both Jews and Gentiles (see Jer 16:19). The witness to the person and work of Jesus is thus presented in the context of the current redemptive-historical deeds of God, which drive the urgency for the call to repentance, leading to a life devoted to God and his purposes.

The Universal Reach of the Message

In his Pentecost speech Peter already hints at a global offer of salvation (Acts 2:21, 39), even though his audience is Jewish. The same can be said for Peter's temple speech (cf. Acts 3:25). The speech at Cornelius's house, finally, displays explicit (and implicit) references to the salvation of Gentiles. Above

---

[14] C.S. Keener, *Acts: An Exegetical Commentary* (Grand Rapids, MI: Baker Academic, 2012), I, 784–87.

[15] See Schreiner, *Paul*, 78–82 regarding the promise of the Holy Spirit as the fulfillment of Gen 3:12 (see Gal 3:14).

[16] According to John, Jesus might be teaching that the Holy Spirit was *with* the people of Israel. Now, however, he is *in* them (see John 14:16-17).

[17] See C.J.H. Wright, *Mission*, 514–16; Schnabel, *Mission*, I, 389–405.

all, Acts 10:34-35 (cf. 10:45 and 11:18) states that there are Gentiles who are δεκτός (=welcome) to an impartial God (see 10:28).[18] This is reinforced by the statement that Jesus is Lord of all (πάντων κύριος, Acts 10:36) and that the prophets predicted forgiveness of sins through the name of Jesus to *all* who believe (πάντα τὸν πιστεύοντα εἰς αὐτόν, Acts 10:43).[19] Such forgiveness of sins by repentant faith in Christ (2:38; 5:31; 8:22; 10:43; see Mark 11:25) is an aspect of salvation (see, e.g., Acts 2:14-36; 4:12; 11:14). It issues in peace with God, various times of refreshment, and eventual restoration of all that has been prophesied throughout the ages (see below).

Peter as a Preacher of Christ: The Christology of the Collective Apostolic Witness with Some Petrine Emphases[20]

We believe that Peter's early speeches represent collective apostolic witness. They are presented in the form of authoritative prophetic repentance speeches along Old Testament patterns. Christological particularities thus primarily reflect the collective witness, which Peter, as spokesman, conveys and names. The driving force for such collective witness is Jesus himself. *Within* this general framework, we can, at times, isolate several prominent emphases which might allow a glimpse of Peter himself, despite the fact that Paul and others testified similarly in Acts. Various scholars, such as Wilckens,[21] are skeptical regarding the authenticity of Peter's speeches in Acts because they display, among other factors, no 'characteristic Petrine' elements. We simply note at this point that unique 'Petrine theology' is not to be expected here. The question to ask at this point is only whether Peter is a convincing candidate for having given these (abbreviated) speeches to a Jewish audience as a

---

[18] Δεκτός does not imply that God is gracious to these Gentiles *because* they are God-fearing. Instead, Peter merely states that God's grace *also* extends to the sociological group of God-fearers. Acts 17:30 finally extends the call to repentance to Gentiles who are not even God-fearers.

[19] Cf. Soards, *Speeches*, 83, and 183 n. 179.

[20] Regarding the OT usage in Luke-Acts, see D.L. Bock, 'The Use of the Old Testament in Luke-Acts: Christology and Mission', *Society of Biblical Literature 1990 Seminar Papers* (Atlanta, GA: Scholars Press, 1990), 494–511; see further M. Rese, 'Die Funktion der alttestamentlichen Zitate und Anspielungen in den Reden der Apostelgeschichte', in J. Kremer (ed.), *Les Actes des Apôtres: traditions, rédaction, théologie* (Leuven: Université, 1979), 61–79. See also D.W. Pao, E.J. Schnabel, 'Luke', in Beale/Carson, *Commentary*, 251–414. Peter arises as an authoritative, prophetic interpreter of God's revealed word by applying it unequivocally to concrete situations.

[21] Wilckens, *Missionsreden*, 193–207.

representative of the corporate apostolic witness. Petrine particularities may, on the other hand, be present (1) when these emphases *continue* beyond Acts 1:1–9:32 into the Petrine sections in Acts 10–15, and (2) wherever the Petrine Epistles (as well as the Gospel of Mark) corroborate characteristic concepts identified in Acts (see below). In the final analysis, it might very well be true that Peter, as the apostolic representative, shapes the theological outlook of persons and events narrated in the unfolding account of Acts, including that of Stephen (Acts 6:2, 5; 7:58); James, the future leader of the Jerusalem church (Acts 1:14; 15:7-21); Paul (Gal 1:18; cf. Acts 13:28-31); and Luke (Luke 1:2-3; Acts 28:16).

We have argued above that Peter arises as a prophetic repentance preacher, who declares that the acts of God through Christ occurred for the initial purpose of bringing the chosen, covenant people back to God. In doing so, Peter combines narrative and (partially unique) titular Christology. Various Petrine *emphases* within these broadly sketched theological perspectives include:

1. an emphasis on the sovereign purposes of God the Father (see above);
2. characteristic, titular Christology such as *Ebed YHWH* (see Isa 53), as well as *Prince/Author of life*;
3. Christ-centered eschatology; and
4. Old Testament-patterned repentance preaching.

Jesus as the Fulfillment of Old Testament Prophecy

A general emphasis in Peter's early speeches lies on Jesus as the fulfillment of Old Testament prophecy (cf. 1 Pet 1:10-12). Peter often refers in *general* terms to such prophecy (see, e.g., Acts 3:18, 21, 23-25). Jesus is vindicated through the resurrection, in which God turns the scandal and curse of crucifixion on a cross (see Deut 21:22-23) into victory and vindication. He thus ushers in a new era of salvation for mankind. This fact is announced by Old Testament prophets and is confirmed by the eyewitness accounts of the disciples who now serve as apostles.

In the Pentecost speech, for example, we observe that the Petrine citations from the Old Testament respect their natural meaning and display the tendency to apply them legitimately to Christ *for lack of any more fitting application in the original context* (see the case of Pss 16:8-11 and 110:1, neither of which can ultimately refer to King David).[22]

---

[22] See I.H. Marshall, 'Acts', in Beale/Carson, *Commentary*, 532–43. The speech at Cornelius' household contains, in accordance with a different audience, no direct

The reference to Psalm 118:22 in Acts 4:11 also displays a noteworthy Petrine element. The focus on divine vindication in Acts 4:11 draws on one aspect of the total spectrum of meaning of the psalm. Similarly, Jesus refers to the aspect of divine judgment and vindication in Mark 12:10-11, a notion in turn echoed in 1 Peter 2:7. There, Psalm 118:22 serves as the *climax* of various citations beginning in 1 Peter 2:6.[23]

Peter's Proclamation of Jesus

The propelling catalyst and dynamic force of the narrative in Acts is the person of Jesus (see especially the speeches in Acts testifying to him; Acts 2–5; compare with Acts 7, 13, 17). As stated above, Jesus, as the Son of God, acts in concert with the Father and the Holy Spirit, driving forward the universal *missio dei*.

In the Jesus-kerygma, Peter testifies to the deeds and words of Christ with the purpose of showing that Jesus is *Christ* and *Lord,* in fulfillment of Scripture (see below). It calls to repentance those who hitherto have not honored God's will through Christ despite the fact that Jesus was affirmed and vindicated by no other than the God of Abraham, Isaac, and Jacob (Acts 3:13). Particularly concentrated christological statements are found in Acts 2:24-36 and 3:12-33 regarding Jesus as: (a) the 'Messiah' (Acts 2:31); (b) the 'Lord' (Ps 110:1, 5; Acts 2:34); (c) 'Messiah and Lord' (Acts 2:36); (d) the 'Holy One' and 'Righteous one' (Acts 3:14; cf. John 6:68-69; 1 Pet 1:19; 2:22); (e) the 'Prince/Author of life' (Acts 3:15; cf. 1 Pet 1:3, 23; 2:2); and (f) the 'Prophet like Moses' (Acts 3:22-33).[24]

Christological Focus and Foundation in Acts 2 and 3

Some of the christological differences between the Acts 2 and Acts 3 speeches are:

- In Acts 2, the focus on the death of Jesus is weaker than in Acts 3. Rather, the focus lies on Jesus's work prior to his death.
- In Acts 3, more details surrounding Jesus's death are mentioned, climaxing in the statement that even though Pilate was prepared to free Jesus, some of Peter's listeners insisted on having the *Prince of life* killed.

---

reference to the OT (see, however, Acts 10:43). Regarding Peter's apt handling of the OT in 1 Pet, see Jobes, *1 Peter*, 292.

[23] See Selwyn, *Epistle*, 33–36 and 268–77. In contrast, Paul does combine Isa 8:14 with Isa 28:16 in Rom 9:33 without, however, referring to Ps 118:22 (cf. Matt 21:42; 1 Pet 2:6).

[24] See Bayer, 'Eschatology', 236–50.

- It is also noteworthy that the Pentecost speech exclusively refers to texts derived from Joel and the Psalter (Acts 2:17-21/Joel 2:28-32 [MT]; Acts 2:25-28/Ps 16:8-11; Acts 2:30/Ps 132:11; Acts 2:31/Ps 16:10; Acts 2:34-35/Ps 110:1).[25] In contrast to this, the temple speech contains exclusively texts from the Pentateuch (Acts 3:13/Exod 3:6, 15; Acts 3:22/Deut 18:15-16; Acts 3:23a/Deut 18:19; Acts 3:23b/Lev 23:29; Acts 3:25/Gen 22:18; 26:4).

The most significant parallel between the two speeches lies in the fact that the exalted Christ *continues* his work: in Acts 2:33, Jesus pours out the promise of the Holy Spirit (cf. Gal 3:14); in Acts 3:16, Jesus continues to heal through the Apostles Peter and John (note the echo to Jesus's baptism and exorcism in Luke 3:21-22 and 4:33-35).[26]

The Specific Work of Christ

Peter speaks repeatedly of the *forgiveness of sins* (Acts 2:38; 3:19; 5:31; 10:39; 10:43; see 1 Pet 2:7, 10; 3:21).[27] Even though Jesus's propitiation and atonement are not presented explicitly, it is clear that salvation, following repentance,[28] is provided in the *name* (i.e., in the person) of Jesus (Acts 4:9-12; 10:36). We are, after all, in a historical setting of the *general* proclamation of the good news of Jesus, not in the setting of Christian catechism. This may be sufficient to explain the relative paucity in Acts of references to the substitutionary atonement of Christ. Peter refers explicitly to *being saved* in Acts 2:40; 4:9, 12; 11:14 (see also: 'to turn from this wicked generation' in Acts 3:26; compare with 2:21 and 15:11).

Repentance and forgiveness are connected with various 'times of refreshment' and the 'restoration of everything prophesied' (Acts 3:19-21). Elsewhere, we have sought to demonstrate (see also below) that 'times of refreshment' refer to intermittent divine interventions, 'which relieve and refresh from this world's bonds and burdens',[29] while 'restoration' refers to

---

[25] See the quote from Ps 118:22 in Peter's speech in Acts 4:8-12 (v. 11). The prayer of the church, perhaps led by Peter, in Acts 4:24b-30 includes a quote from Ps 2:1-2 (vv. 25-26).

[26] See R.C. Tannehill, *The Narrative Unity of Luke–Acts: A Literary Interpretation* (Minneapolis, MN: Fortress Press, 1990), II, 53–58.

[27] See Paul in Acts 13:38. In Acts 26:18, Jesus announces to Paul that he will proclaim forgiveness of sins to the Gentiles. Cf. Soards, *Speeches*, 87.

[28] See M. Kim-Rauchholz, *Umkehr bei Lukas: Zu Wesen und Bedeutung der Metanoia in der Theologie des dritten Evangelisten* (Neukirchen-Vluyn: Neukirchener Verlag, 2008).

[29] Bayer, 'Eschatology', 245; for further detail see pp. 236–50.

God bringing Jews and Gentiles to himself and fulfilling the totality of his promises.[30] Throughout, the assumption is that the death and resurrection of Jesus as the suffering and exalted Messiah carries with it the means for forgiveness of sins and new life.

Key Aspects of Peter's Titular Christology: Jesus as Christ, Lord, and Ebed YHWH

Concurrent with the entire thrust of Acts, Peter emphasizes in his early speeches the often discussed[31] twin titles of κύριος[32] and χριστός.[33] These titles are central to the collective apostolic witness given by Peter. Significantly, both christological references have their provenance in Jesus's own teaching (see, e.g., Mark 8:29, 31; 10:45; 12:36-37; 14:62). It is thus very conceivable that Peter's christological witness *carries over* what Jesus taught him in a systematic fashion and *focuses* the early Christian testimony of Christ, including the subsequent account of Acts.

In the summary statement of Acts 2:36, Peter conspicuously combines the two major titles of κύριος and χριστός in one expression (see, similarly, Mark 14:61-62). It is significant here that Peter intertwines theology and history in a most striking way.[34] The confession of Jesus as *Christ* and *Lord* breaks through the confines of our existence and declares that Jesus is greater than space and time. Yet, at the same time, Peter maintains that this exalted Jesus is the one who was crucified in Jerusalem. It is the same Jesus who is today enthroned at the right hand of God. Peter thus testifies to the deep connection between the earthly life of Jesus and the ongoing truth about the resurrected and enthroned Jesus. The death of Jesus is inseparably connected with his eternal exaltation as Christ and Lord. Peter serves as witness to both (cf. Heb 10:12).

---

[30] Bayer, 'Eschatology', 247–48.
[31] See, e.g., the concise and informative overview by Schneider, *Apostelgeschichte*, I, 331–35.
[32] See especially Acts 2:36 and Acts 10:36 ('Lord of all'). The κύριος thread extends from the OT (Ps 110; cf. Dan 7:13-14; exalted Son of Man) via Jesus (Mark 12:36-37; 14:62) to the early church (Acts 2:21, 36; 4:12; *Acts 26:11*; cf. 9:5, 'calling on the name of the Lord', i.e., YHWH=Jesus to be saved; see 1 Cor 16:22: *maranatha*: '*Lord* come quickly'; cf. God as κύριος, Acts 2:39; 3:22, and frequently).
[33] The χρίστος thread extends from the OT (see messianic interpretations of 2 Sam 7:13-16 and Ps 16:10-11), via Jesus (Mark 8:29-31) to the early church (see among many instances, Acts 2:36; *Acts 9:22*; cf. Acts 3:20).
[34] See, e.g., A. Schlatter, *The Theology of the Apostles* (Grand Rapids, MI: Baker, 1998), 33–37.

Christ. In Acts, the frequently used term Messiah/Christ is still mostly employed as a title rather than a name or honorific[35] (see especially, Acts 2:36; 3:20; 4:26). The *suffering* of the Messiah is particularly emphasized (see especially, Acts 3:18; compare with Acts 17:3, 18:5, 28; 26:22-23; Luke 24:26, 46). Peter states that Jesus has been appointed as the anointed eternal ruler (Acts 2:30). Now, following Jesus's teaching and Pentecost, Peter proclaims the Messiah of God in sharp contradistinction to the popular expectation of a political Davidic messiah. Peter now realizes that the Messiah of God had to die and be raised from death in order to take up his eternal reign after making atonement for sin and sinfulness (cf. Mark 8:31; 10:45). The Christ who is confirmed and appointed as the Messiah of God (Acts 2:36) is not the one who was expected in popular Palestinian Judaism, but rather he who Jesus claimed to be all along. In Acts 1:6, the disciples, with Peter, still ask when Israel will be restored and thus when the throne of David will be reestablished in Israel. While imminent political restoration was, in Peter's mind, still one of the expected functions of the Messiah, Peter subsequently realizes that the Messiah of God operates according to an even greater plan (see below). After Pentecost, Peter arises as a witness to that which Jesus had taught him all along concerning the Messiah of God: he is both the suffering, messianic Son of Man (Mark 8:31; 10:45; cf. Isa 52:13–53:12) and the exalted messianic Son of Man and Lord (Mark 8:38; 14:62-63; see Dan 7:13-14/Ps 110:1; Mark 12:35-37; Ps 110:1, 5). Peter realizes more fully that Jesus, the Messiah of God, had to be humbled and exalted according to the Father's purpose (Acts 3:13-15). Peter thus confesses now the very Messiah of God about whom he had learned from Jesus: the exalted Messiah of God is now enthroned as the anointed eternal ruler on the throne of David (Acts 2:30-31; cf. Luke 1:32-33).

Lord. Besides Jesus as the appointed Christ, the title of κύριος (Lord) is highly significant in Acts. Sometimes it refers to God the Father and sometimes to Jesus.[36] In Acts 2:21, Peter says: 'Everyone who calls on the name of the LORD (YHWH) shall be saved' (cf. Joel 2:32, MT; cf. Zeph 3:9).[37] Likewise, Peter

---

[35] See Novenson, *Christ*, 87–97, regarding Paul's possible use of *Christos* as neither titular nor as a name but as honorific (paying homage to Jesus as Messiah).

[36] There are about 41 references in Acts which associate 'Lord' with God and about 60 referring to Jesus. The Gospel of Luke contains 96 references to 'Lord'. Together, Luke–Acts contain 29 percent of all references to 'Lord' in the NT.

[37] We are convinced that the unconverted Saul, persecutor of the church, knew that Christians were claiming that 'Jesus is Lord' and thus worshiped him (cf. Acts 26:11; see the phrase 'calling on the name of Jesus', Acts 9:14; see 2:21); see R.N. Longenecker, 'Some Distinctive Early Christian Motifs', *NTS* 14.4 (1968), 526–45, and A.B. McGowan, *Ancient Christian Worship: Early Church Practices in Social, Historical, and Theological Perspective* (Grand Rapids, MI: Baker Academic, 2014).

states in Acts 4:12 (with clear references to Jesus, Acts 4:11): '[a]nd there is salvation in no one else, for there is no other name under heaven given among men by which we must be saved.' If we consider Acts 2:21, 3:15-16, and 4:12 together, we have an early Christian confession of *worshiping* Jesus as YHWH (Acts 2:21), as κύριος (Lord), as the one who has been exalted to the right hand of God the Father, and as the one who saves. The Father is pleased with the worship of his eternal Son.

As we observed in our discussion of the Christology in Mark, it was Jesus who spawned the early Christian confession of 'Jesus as the exalted Lord'. The key lies in Mark 12:36-37, where Jesus intentionally refers to Psalm 110:1. In this passage, Jesus implies what he claims in Mark 14:61-63 explicitly, namely, that he is David's messianic Lord who is to be (re-)exalted to the right hand of God, thereby giving rise to the confession 'Jesus is Lord'. In the early speeches in Acts, Peter thus draws the natural conclusion from Jesus's former teaching on Psalm 110:1 (Mark 12:36-37; 14:62) and Daniel 7:13-14 (Mark 8:38; 14:62). In Acts 2:21, he quotes Joel 2:32 (MT) with reference to the outpouring of the Holy Spirit and with reference to Jesus: he is part of YHWH, the Adonai of David, and the only name (i.e., person) by which to find salvation (Acts 4:12; see 1 Pet 3:18). Furthermore, Acts 2:34 and the citation of Psalm 110:1 identify Jesus as the Lord[38] of David.[39]

A further note is in order regarding Acts 2:36, where Peter refers to Jesus as 'Lord and Christ'. Contrary to the position of some, we are here not dealing with an 'adoptionist confession'. Luke 1:43, 76; 4:18-21; 9:35; 19:31, 34, and Acts 2:22 already portray the earthly Jesus as Lord and Christ. Thus, according to Luke, no ontological change is to be associated with Acts 2:36. Rather, the declaration in Acts 2:36 is a statement of enthronement and affirmation (see Ps 2:2).[40] The term 'make' (ποιέω) is thus to be taken in the sense of 'establishing' or 'enthroning', as it is used in Mark 3:14, 16, in the context of the appointment of the twelve disciples.[41]

---

[38] See 1 Cor 16:22, μαράνα θά (=our Lord come) as a very early Christian confession. See M. Hengel, 'Christology and New Testament Chronology', in *Between Jesus and Paul: Studies in the Earliest History of Christianity* (London: SCM Press, 1983), 41; N.T. Wright, *Victory*, 507–509.

[39] See Acts 2:30 and 13:23: Jesus as 'Son of David'; cf. Rom 1:3.

[40] See the messianic interpretation of Ps 2:2, 7 in *Pss. Sol.* 17:36.

[41] Contra J. Zmijewski, *Die Apostelgeschichte* (Regensburg: Pustet, 1994), 147, who pits this section against 'Lukan' tradition, which affirms that Jesus is Lord and Christ *prior* to exaltation. Zmijewski does not explore the 'both/and' possibility implied by ποιέω: Jesus was already Lord and Christ prior to his exaltation, but he is *enthroned* and affirmed as such at the point of resurrection and exaltation.

Christ's exaltation is a source of great comfort to the apostles. The Lord they worship and serve has been given a place of authority that cannot be taken from him. In this way, the Messiah of God far exceeds the political messiah expected in Palestinian Judaism. The Messiah of God has been enthroned in the highest place, sharing glory with the Father, and there is no one who can gain victory over him. The struggle of ensuing subjugation that is described in Psalm 110 is echoed, for example, in Philippians 2:6-11 (cf. Isa 45:22-23 and Ps 110:1). The Father exalts the Son, and the enemies are put under the feet of Christ (Mark 12:36-37; Ps 110:1, 5). The worship of the entire world is, in the end, rendered to God the Father, together with the Son and the Holy Spirit. Thus the entire process of regaining a people unto himself is ultimately for the glorification of the Father, Son, and Holy Spirit. As we study Petrine Christology in Acts, we are thus catching a glimpse of the beauty and mystery of the Godhead.

As mentioned above, we believe that herein lies a (or, rather *the*) key element of the early Christian zeal to missional witness and sacrifice. This mission is so unlikely to succeed because the message of crucifixion, resurrection, and exaltation is so scandalous for Jews and foolish to Gentiles (cf. 1 Cor 1:18-25).[42] Despite this, there is an inner conviction among the early Christians, above all, Peter, that this is true and therefore to be confessed. This zeal is the result of two aspects: (1) Jesus taught and shaped his disciples systematically, and his teaching was authenticated by his resurrection; and (2) the confirmation of the Spirit of God gave the disciples liberty and assurance to testify to this truth. While the above-mentioned emphases on Jesus as Lord and Christ are not unique to Peter's early apostolic witness, there is good evidence to viewing them as germane to earliest Petrine witness, thus shaping subsequent Christian confessions, including that of Paul (see the second half of Acts).

Ebed YHWH. The references to the *Servant of God, Ebed YHWH* (Acts 3:13/Isa 52:13; Acts 3:26; 4:27, 30 [a Peter-led prayer of the early church?]; cf. Acts 8:32/Isa 53:7-8) are rare and do not arise often elsewhere in the New Testament. Here we might indeed be dealing with a Petrine emphasis (see below). As stated above, the major allusion to this representative 'Servant' is found especially in Isaiah 52:13–53:12, which probably saw a degree of messianic interpretations already at the time of Christ.

---

[42] Among Jews, the message of Christ as divine Lord is blasphemy (Acts 26:11); among Romans, the message of Jesus as *dominus* (Lord) can be viewed as a direct affront to Caesar's imperial claims.

We briefly note additional christological concepts which Peter, in particular, refers to:[43]

1. Besides Acts 3:15 and 5:31, the New Testament contains the reference to *Prince/Author* (of life) only in Hebrews 2:10 and 12:2. While ἀρχηγός could mean 'source' or 'origin' in Acts 3:15, it is probable that 'leader' or 'head' is implied here. This is likely so, because the material proximity of this usage to Acts 5:31 (the functional context of Acts 5:31 suggests the meaning of *leader* or *prince* in conjunction with *savior*) and the fact that the context of Acts 3:15 permits both interpretations.
2. While salvation is a significant theme in Luke–Acts, the noun *Savior* as a title of Jesus only occurs twice in Acts (Acts 5:31; see Acts 13:23). Salvation implies different aspects, such as forgiveness of sins (Acts 5:31) and deliverance from oppression (Acts 13:23, as suggested by the context).
3. Unique to the New Testament is the identification of Jesus as the *Prophet like Moses* (Acts 3:22-23; cf. Acts 7:37 and Luke 7:16), referring to Deuteronomy 18:15, 18. The context of Deuteronomy 18 is that the Israelites are not to practice sorcery in order to ascertain the will of God; rather, God will raise up a Prophet like Moses, to whom the people are to listen. Qumran features a messianic interpretation of Deuteronomy 18:15 in 4QTest 5-7, thus documenting the messianic expectation of such a prophetic figure.[44]
4. The phrase 'Holy One' may connote divine prerogatives (Acts 3:14).[45] Note the emphasis on the righteousness of a messianic king in Isaiah 32:1 (see 2 Sam 23:3). *First Enoch* 38:2 uses the honorific 'the Righteous' to describe the messiah. In *1 Enoch* 46:3, the Son of Man is *righteous*. We may state, tentatively, that these two terms are christological titles with possible divine implications.
5. The title *Nazarene* (Acts 2:22; 3:6; 4:10; 6:14; see also Acts 22:8; 26:9) primarily refers to Jesus's town of origin (see Acts 10:38).[46]
6. Jesus as *Judge* (Acts 10:42; see 1 Pet 4:5 and Acts 17:31).
7. Jesus as *Son of David* (Acts 2:29-31).[47]

---

[43] Paul refers to Jesus as *Son of God* (cf. Ps 2 and *Pss. Sol.* 17:36 [βασιλεὺς αὐτῶν χριστὸς κύριος]) in Acts 9:20 and 13:33 (cf. Ps 2); see also Mark 1:11; 9:7. Only once in Acts is Jesus referred to as 'Son of Man' (7:56). See Soards, *Speeches*, 73, and n. 22.

[44] See also 1QS 9, 10–11 concerning the messianic expectation of a 'Prophet like Moses' (Deut 18:15, 18).

[45] Besides Acts 3:14, a *Righteous One* is mentioned in Acts 7:52 and 22:14.

[46] Connected with this is the fact that Christians are known as 'Nazarenes' (Acts 24:5).

[47] See Paul in Acts 13:23.

Key Aspects of Peter's Narrative Christology

As a complement to titular Christology, we find many narrative christological elements in Peter's speeches. The life and work of Jesus encompasses the following trajectory:

- It commences with John the Baptist (Acts 1:22), continues with his earthly ministry, and culminates in his death and resurrection (Acts 1:22; 2:23; 2:32; 3:15; 4:10; 5:30; 10:38-41).
- It continues with his ascension (Acts 1:22), exaltation (Acts 2:33; 5:31), and glorification (Acts 3:13), issuing in his outpouring of the promised Holy Spirit (Acts 2:33; see also 11:16).
- Jesus' exalted rule is demonstrated by his works (Acts 3:6, 16 [healing]; Acts 3:20 [refreshment]; Acts 3:21 [restoration of all things]) and climaxes, finally, in his Parousia (Acts 3:20) with the associated day of judgment (Acts 10:42).[48]
- The events are seen as fulfillment of Scripture (Acts 2:31; 3:18; cf. 13:33-37).[49]

Given this framework, Peter declares that:

- God affirmed Jesus by means of 'signs and wonders' (see, e.g., Acts 2:22; 3:26; 10:38) and enthroned him as Lord and Christ (Acts 2:36), despite rejection (Acts 2:36; 3:13-15).
- God planned to give Jesus into the *hands* of lawlessness (Acts 2:23; compare with Mark 9:31) in order to achieve his goal of providing salvation to mankind.

Once again, a notable Petrine *focus* upon God's sovereign will is apparent. While Soards is right that this theme is *assumed* and prominent throughout Acts,[50] it is, nevertheless, clearly emphasized in Peter's speeches. As stated above, the sovereignty and initiative of 'the God of our Fathers' (Acts 3:13, 18; 4:24; 11:9), is particularly manifested through Jesus (Acts 2:22-36; 3:13, 15, 18, 20-21, 26; 4:12, 27-28;[51] 10:38, 40, 42[52]). As noted, the theme of God's

---

[48] See also Schneider, *Apostelgeschichte*, I, 334.

[49] See E. Lövestam, *Son and Saviour: A Study of Acts 13, 32-37* (Lund: Gleerup, 1961). Note that Ps 2:7, Isa 55:3 and Ps 16:10 (see also Acts 2:30-31) are all cited in Acts 13:33-35 as references to Jesus's resurrection.

[50] Soards, *Speeches*, 273.

[51] See Soards, *Speeches*, 276.

[52] See similarly, Schneider, *Apostelgeschichte*, I, 334 and Soards, *Speeches*, 85.

foreordination recurs repeatedly.⁵³ Since he was raised from death,⁵⁴ Jesus was not left in hades and his flesh did not see corruption (Acts 2:31; see also Acts 2:27 and 1 Pet 3:18). Jesus appeared to his chosen witnesses (Acts 10:40) and was exalted (Acts 2:33; 5:31). This happened because God was and is 'with Christ' (Acts 10:38; see 2:22).

Characteristic for Peter's speeches is finally that the Holy Spirit is sent as a divine promise⁵⁵ (Acts 2:33, 39: the Holy Spirit is poured out by Jesus; cf. Acts 26:6) and gift (Acts 2:38; 8:20; [10:45]; 11:17; [15:8]). Schneider, following Lohfink, aptly summarizes the narrative Christology in Acts for which Peter is a key witness and, perhaps, key catalyst for Luke–Acts:

> God sent Jesus as Savior, anointed him at his baptism with the Holy Spirit, had him preach peace and work miracles, handed him over according to his plan, raised him from the dead, had him appear, exalted him to his right hand, had him pour out the Holy Spirit, glorified him through the miracles of the apostles, appointed him as judge, and decreed that he should return at the Parousia to judge the earth.⁵⁶

*The Temple Speech in Acts 3 as a Unique Combination of Titular and Narrative Christology*⁵⁷

Titular and narrative Christology intersect in Acts 3 in the following way:

1. God validates and vindicates Jesus (Acts 3:13, 15, 18, 20-22, 25-26). Peter develops this repeated motif in a rhetorically circumspect fashion by referring first to the *present* deeds of Christ (vv. 12, 13a, 16) before reviewing *past* events (vv. 13b-18) and outlining *future* deeds of Christ (vv. 19-21) following the repentance of Jewish listeners.
2. While verse 13 contains primarily functional Christology (the present activity of Christ), verses 14-15 are rich in titular Christology. Associated with these descriptions we find the challenging and, for Jewish hearers,

---

⁵³ See Acts 2:22-23, 36; 4:28; 10:41-42 (compare with *1 Pet 1:2, 20*); Acts 15:7 (compare with 1 Pet 1:1 and 2:9).

⁵⁴ The reference to God *raising Jesus* appears to be more generic to Acts (Acts 2:24, 32; 3:15, 26; 4:10; 5:30; 10:40; cf. Acts 10:29-33; regarding Paul, see 13:30, 33-34, 37; 17:31).

⁵⁵ See Schreiner, *Paul*, 79–82, on the connection to Gen 12:3.

⁵⁶ Schneider, *Apostelgeschichte*, I, 334 (summarizing paraphrase and trans., HFB).

⁵⁷ For more details, see Bayer, 'Eschatology', 241–43 and 'Preaching', 272–73.

offensive reference to Jesus as the *object* of faith (v. 16).[58] For a Jewish audience this comes dangerously close to identifying Christ as God, a notion which we believe Peter was fully convinced of.[59]

We conclude that Peter's apostolic witness points to Christ as preeminent and as a member of YHWH as Godhead. As such, Jesus also shapes the present and future salvation or perdition of mankind. In this sense, Peter as a person and as a witness holds, in a God-dependent, derivative way, the keys to the kingdom (see above).

The Relationship between Christology and Eschatology in Peter's Temple Speech

Given the preeminence of Christ, we briefly explore here the relationship between Christology and eschatology in Peter's early preaching, with particular reference to his temple speech in Acts 3.[60] We pursue this motif because both Mark (esp. Mark 13) and 1 Peter will display a similar eschatological framework and focus in which the future coming of Christ reaches into the present as a *future indicative*, shaping the followers' character parallel to Jesus's *past* life and work, as well as his *present* work through the Holy Spirit.[61]

The climactic redemptive-historical events of Jesus's death and resurrection, and especially his continuing deeds as the exalted Christ in Acts (see especially Acts 2:33), spawn future expectations promised in the Old Testament, which Jesus himself reinforces.[62] Peter's early preaching in Acts is so realistically and

---

[58] See the emphatic repetition of the *name* (v. 16) and of *faith* (v. 16). Grammatically, Peter's faith could also be in view, but the faith of the one administering the healing is never emphasized in Luke (cf. D. Hamm, 'Acts 3:12-26: Peter's Speech and the Healing of the Man Born Lame', *PRSt* 11.3 [1984], 199–217, 204).

[59] See Peter's reference to Christ as judge of the living and the dead before a Gentile audience, Acts 10:42; cf. 1 Pet 4:5.

[60] For more detail, see Bayer, 'Eschatology', 236–50.

[61] See Isa 31:31-34; Ezek 36:25-38; LXX Joel 2:28-32; cf. Luke 3:16; Acts 1:5-8; 2:1-11 and 1QS 55:20-21. See Giles, 'Eschatology' (part 2), 12, who points to the general outpouring of the Holy Spirit as prophesied for the end times: Joel 2:28-29; Zech 1:3-6; Mal 4:5-6; *T.Levi* 8:14; *T.Benj.* 9:2.

[62] Gaventa, 'Eschatology', 27–42, presents various positions concerning future expectations in Luke: (1) Because of a persistent delay of the Parousia, Luke develops his salvation-historical concept as a 'solution' (Conzelmann). (2) Luke expects the imminent Parousia (Mattill). (3a) Luke expects the Parousia rather soon: There is, however, no imminent expectation (Ellis, Marshall). (3b) Luke reflects both a near- and far-expectation of the Parousia (S.G. Wilson). (3c) The delay of the Parousia is merely a problem of the community Luke addresses. Luke himself

stringently Christ-centered that potentially competing expectations of the future (a near- or far-expectation of the Parousia of Christ) are 'resolved' in the matrix of a redemptive-historical continuum, in which Christ is actively Lord of future event-sequences.[63]

In the macro-text of Luke–Acts we observe a coexistence of salvation-historical sequences (with a potential delay motif) as well as an expectation of the near end (compare, e.g., Luke 21:5-9 with 21:32). In another essay, we stated:

> If we can explain the compatibility of this coexistence from the viewpoint of Luke, we may have accomplished historically more than what tradition-historical hypotheses have produced by way of separating . . . one strand from the other to produce a 'Lukan' (salvation-historical) and a 'traditional' (near-expectation) line of transmission . . . Luke . . . was able to *live* with these seemingly incompatible factors and views . . . The outpouring of the Holy Spirit and the mission among the Gentiles[64] [is] viewed in Acts as fulfilled (or in the process of being fulfilled) eschatological prophecy. Merely the expectation of the parousia with its related events remains. As surely as the outpouring of the Holy Spirit and the mission among the Gentiles . . . is in the process of occurring, the parousia is to be expected.[65]

Like the Pentecost speech, the temple speech looks back and especially forward.[66] The speech describes the dynamic between repentance and anticipated eschatological events. In Acts 3:12b-26 we encounter highly Christ-centered eschatology, commencing with the healing of the lame and the account of the 'Jesus-kerygma'. As noted, the close interconnection between Christology and eschatology in the temple speech aims at a piercing call to repentance. There is a lively assurance that Christ is the divinely and uniquely confirmed leader for all times. The eschatological prospect with the call to repentance (Acts 3:17-21) is further embedded in a preceding Jesus-kerygma and a following confirmation by Scripture. The urgency for repentance is

---

attempts to offset this by maintaining a sure near-expectation (Franklin). See also Giles, 'Eschatology', (part 1), 65–66.

[63] See the important contribution to this topic by O. Cullmann, *Salvation in History* (Norwich: SCM Press, 1967).

[64] Isa 49:6. See Matt 24:14; Luke 21:24; 24:47; Acts 11:18; cf. Matt 24:14; 28:19-20; Mark 13:10; Luke 1:32; 3:6; 4:25-28; Acts 8:4-40; 10:10-34.

[65] Bayer, 'Eschatology', 239. See Acts 1:11; 2:17; 3:20, and possibly 7:55-56. Cf. Giles, 'Eschatology' (part 1), 67. The expectations of full restoration, the resurrection of the dead (Luke 14:11-14; 20:35-36; Acts 4:2; 17:32; 24:15; 26:3), and final judgment (Acts 4:23; 10:42; 13:41; 17:31; 24:25) are essentially related to the Parousia.

[66] Carroll, *Response*, 141–51.

heightened by the eminence of Christ. As stated above, no less than the God of Abraham, Isaac, and Jacob affirms Jesus in all that he is, teaches, and does. The Father initiates, the Son mediates, and the Holy Spirit communicates the unfolding eschatological events in Acts and beyond. Peter presents Christ in the nexus of the God of their Fathers.

Jesus's Ongoing Ontological and Functional Eminence. In Acts 3:13, Peter identifies the healing of the lame man as one consequence of the raising of the 'Righteous One' from death. This signals that Christ's influence is by no means merely a matter of the past. Verse 16 implies that the resurrection and exaltation of Christ ushered in a new thrust of the deeds of Christ. Peter bridges here the two known factors of present healing and past death of Jesus with the hitherto unknown (or denied) fact of Jesus's resurrection (v. 15) as the 'missing link'. Without the witness (μάρτυς,[67] v. 15b) to the resurrection of Christ, the two known facts[68] remain unrelated events. Now, however, the known factors (the death of Jesus and the healing of the lame man) and the resurrection are related to the same person. There is thus a marked Christ-centered connection of events which also applies to yet unfulfilled redemptive-historical occurrences. Because of who Jesus is as divinely authenticated, future salvation-historical events are fundamentally shaped in terms of content and time frame by Christ himself. In verse 16, Peter prepares the appeal (see vv. 17-26) to repent and to trust this God-affirmed, eminent leader.

Christ Shapes Future Expectations and the Fulfillment of Old Testament Prophecy. Peter's main concern and aim of the speech, namely, the call to repentance[69] is surrounded by 'supportive motivations'[70] as appeals to the

---

[67] This term is particularly important in Luke: of a total of 35 occurrences in the NT, thirteen appear in Acts, two in his Gospel.

[68] The severity of denial (ἀρνέομαι) is emphasized by double reference (vv. 13 and 14).

[69] The call to repentance (Acts 2:38) consists of two imperatives: μετανοήσατε (cf. Acts 26:18) and ἐπιστρέψατε. These terms hint at the fact that repentance is not only turning away from the old ways but also *toward* Christ. The consequence is the forgiveness of sins (Acts 2:38). See G. Delling, 'Die Jesusgeschichte in der Verkündigung nach Acta', *NTS* 19.4 (1972–73), 373–89, who notes that repentance (Acts 2:38; 3:19; 5:31; 17:30) and forgiveness of sins (Acts 2:38; 5:31; 10:43; 13:38) are mentioned in nearly every missional speech (374).

[70] See R.C. Tannehill, 'The Functions of Peter's Mission Speeches in the Narrative of Acts', *NTS* 37.3 (1991), 400–14, here 405. The reference to 'ignorance' (Acts 3:17; cf. Luke 9:45; 18:34; 24:16, 31; Acts 17:30) as a 'supportive motivation' is not a general excuse and dismissal of guilt but rather an expression of hope in the context of the possibility and *necessity* of repentance. Thus far their ignorance paradoxically furthered God's unsearchable ways regarding Christ. It is part of God's wisdom (Acts 2:23; cf. Delling, 'Jesusgeschichte', 382, and Hamm, 'Acts 3:12-26', 207).

hearers.[71] A partial motivation for repentance is the fact that the divinely affirmed and eminent Christ will surely act in the future. This implies that the question of time frames is secondary. Rather, repentance prior to future *deeds* of Christ is the central concern, coupled with the assurance that Christ will *act* in the future as surely as he has in the past[72] and present.[73] Once again, all of this occurs in a Trinitarian framework where the 'God of our Fathers' is the *initiator* of everything mentioned in this speech. Based on the will of the Father and mediated by Jesus, there will be 'times of refreshment' (Acts 3:20).[74] These 'times of refreshment' precede[75] the restoration[76] of all things which God has spoken of. They are as of yet unfulfilled prophecy (Acts 3:21). It is therefore legitimate and necessary to take note of the broad spectrum of prophecies of and references to restoration (both in the OT and NT), which do not exclusively focus on Israel as a nation (see already the *progression* from Acts 1:6 to 1:8).[77] Already some relevant Old Testament references point to a *universal restoration*, which the New Testament reinforces. Among various Old Testament passages,[78] Isaiah 49:6-7;[79] 66:18-22; Ezekiel 37:21-28;[80]

---

[71] Tannehill, 'Functions', 406, rightly calls this speech a 'repentance speech *par excellence*'.

[72] This also holds true for the Pentecost speech where the *event* of the outpouring of the Spirit marks the inauguration of end times.

[73] References to OT prophecy underline this: v. 18 (prophesied suffering of the Messiah); v. 21 (prophesied expectation of future restoration).

[74] By bringing, e.g., occasional release from suppression and establishing justice and righteousness, Isa 32:15-20.

[75] See Acts 20:6, where ἄχρι ἡμερῶν πέντε covers the time-span necessary to sail from Philippi to Troas, with the emphasis placed upon the arrival occurring *after* five days; cf. W. Kurz, 'Acts 3:19-26 as a Test of the Role of Eschatology in Lukan Christology', *Society of Biblical Literature 1977 Seminar Papers* (ed. P.J. Achtemeier; Missoula, MT: Scholars Press, 1977), 309–23, 311 and nn. 12–13.

[76] The diachronic and synchronic spectrum of ἀποκατάστασις includes 'restoration'. An eschatological context is possible, but the term is not limited to it (cf. Heb 13:19, of Christian fellowship). Although there are no occurrences of the noun in the LXX, the term is used by Philo and Josephus in the Jewish, redemptive-historical sense of 'deliverance', 'return' (e.g., Philo, *Her.* 293), or 'restoration' (of the temple after the Babylonian exile, Josephus, *Ant.* 11.63; cf. A. Oepke, ἀποκατάστασις, *TDNT*, I, 389–90). Later rabbinic evidence (*Gen. Rab.* 12; cf. Str-B, I, 19) mentions that messiah Ben Perez was to restore six items, which man had lost since the fall of Adam.

[77] Cf. Isa 1:26-28; 61:1-5; Amos 9:11-15. See Tannehill, 'Functions', 406.

[78] See I.H. Marshall, 'Acts', in Beale/Carson, *Commentary*, 528.

[79] The chosen Servant of Y<small>HWH</small> serves as (a) the restorer of Israel and (b) a saving light to the *nations/Gentiles* ('to the ends of the earth'; cf. the terminological proximity to Acts 1:8), and as (c) the highly exalted servant-ruler (cf. Luke 2:32; Acts 13:47 and 26:23).

Daniel 7:13-27 (compare with Jonah 4:2) convey the end-time expectation of a *general* and *universal* restoration[81] whereby Jews and Gentiles are being reconciled with God through a Redeemer[82] and, at a future point in time, inherit the earth (see Rom 4:13: Abraham as 'heir of the world', fulfilling Deut 1:8 and especially Gen 17:7; cf. Matt 5:5).[83]

Additionally, Acts 2:25-36 serves as one of the crucial turning points in the understanding of the connection between the throne of David and Jesus (see Mark 12:35-37) whereby Jesus, the Messiah of God, is now indeed the eternal and exalted ruler *on the throne of David* (Acts 2:30; cf. Luke 1:32-33).[84] The exalted Christ thus constitutes the fulfillment of Abrahamic and Davidic promises regarding an eternal messianic rule (and possession of land). Parallel to this, Peter emphasizes a general resurrection of the dead (Acts 4:2; see also 17:32; 24:15; 26:3) and a universal Last Judgment (Acts 4:23; 10:42; cf. 13:41; 17:31; 24:25). The general reference to restoration of all unfulfilled prophecy thus points well beyond Israel, now that the Messiah of God is enthroned and establishes his eternal rule. We believe that Jesus, via Peter, issues the following perspective: the 'small wave' of expected fulfillment of outstanding promises regarding Israel and its land (see Acts 1:6) will be overtaken by the 'greater wave' of God's future fulfillment of *global* promises regarding repentant Jews,[85] Gentiles and the entire earth (see Acts 1:8).

Old Testament Israel thus serves as a real but preliminary blue print of God's universal purposes concerning his rule (see Acts 1:3[86]) and realm (see Acts 1:8: 'the ends of the earth'), inaugurated with the coming and enthronement of the Son of God (Acts 2:36), culminating in its full establishment (Acts 3:21; cf.

---

[80] Cf. Isa 37:25-28.

[81] See, e.g., Jer 31:31-38: Israel receives a new covenant, forgiveness, and restoration of Jerusalem. However, Heb 8:8-10 and 10:16 applies Jer 31:31-34 to all those who are cleansed by the atoning blood of Jesus (Jews and Gentiles alike).

[82] In the NT we find *one* eschatological people of God, consisting of Jews and Gentiles (1 Pet 2:4-10; Eph 2:11-19).

[83] See ἐν τῇ παλιγγενεσίᾳ in Matt 19:28 (cf. Rev 21:1-2). See Rom 8:20-21 and the rabbinic reference to creation in *Gen. Rab.* 12.

[84] As anticipated in 2 Sam 7:13-16 and already in the promise to Abraham, Gen 22:18. See H.F. Bayer, 'Das Hauptmotiv der südphönizischen und ostjordanischen Reisen Jesu bei Markus', in W. Hilbrands (ed.), *Sprache lieben–Gottes Wort verstehen: Beiträge zur biblischen Exegese* (Giessen: Brunnen, 2011), 205–15, and G.M. Burge, *Jesus and the Land: The New Testament Challenge to 'Holy Land' Theology* (Grand Rapids, MI: Baker Academic, 2010), 25–42; 58–72.

[85] See Rom 11:5, 14, 21, 23, 26: God has never rejected Israel, or broken his promises, since he (always) preserves a remnant.

[86] See further Acts 8:12; 14:22; 19:8, 20, 25; 28:23-31.

Heb 12:22; Rev 21:2, 10, 22, 24, 27). God does not abandon his promises to his people Israel, but he envelops them in his greater universal mission (cf. Jonah 4:2).

Events leading up to the Parousia commence with the present healing of the lame man, the proclamation of repentance, and the remission of sins. Various times of divine relief from suppressing burdens follow. Finally, a worldwide restoration of repentant Jews and Gentiles culminating in their inheriting the earth under God's rule is in view.[87] Without Christ, *nothing* of the Father's will occurs, in the past, now, or in the future. Christ's mediating *eminence* dynamically permeates present and future events and expectations. *Time frames* operate relative to this nexus.

According to Peter, not many salvation-historical *conditions* have to be met before the end may come. A delaying factor may be in view only regarding the possible lack of repentance on the part of the hearers, understanding 'delay' as God's active mercy (see 2 Pet 3:9). There is thus a dynamic tension between repentance and unfolding eschatological events. As soon as Christ is confessed and preached (see, e.g., Mark 12:35-37; 14:62; compare with Phil 2:4-11) as clearly as in Acts 2:36 and 3:17-21, Christ- and event-centered eschatology, as outlined above, is near at hand.

Peter's Witness to Christ-Centered Identity and Character Formation

Now that we have presented rough outlines of Peter's testimony to Christ in the context of a Trinitarian confession and the work of the Holy Spirit, we turn to the fact that the work of God the Father through Christ, the Son, mediated by the Holy Spirit, *directly shape the new identity and character of his followers.*

---

[87] In the above-mentioned essay we give the following reasons: (a) the close parallelism in v. 20 between times of *refreshment* and the sending of Christ Jesus suggest that refreshment likewise is being *administered* by Jesus; (b) in the same way as the healing of the lame (see v. 13) and forgiveness of sins (v. 19 and 26) are Christ's 'refreshing' deeds (see v. 13), further refreshment will follow; (c) divine release and refreshment may be connected with the work of the Holy Spirit and, according to Acts 2:33, it is Christ who sent the Holy Spirit as his agent; (d) just as Christ's death has been prophesied, likewise prophesied *restoration* is bound up with him, since universal restoration is a uniquely messianic act and connotes reinstating justice and proper ownership (see, e.g., Luke 4:18-19; cf. Isa 61:1-2); (e) in line with the consistent emphasis on the 'God of our Fathers' as the initiator and Christ as the one who administers and mediates, it is most plausible that here too Christ *executes* the fulfillment of this prophecy.

The impact of Christ's teaching, his past deed of atonement, his resurrection and his sending the Holy Spirit (see John 14:16-17) is radically transformative, both individually and corporately. In other words, who Jesus is and what he did and still does as the eternal Son of God impresses itself as a salvific foundation and as a shaping pattern upon his followers. The painful path of Jesus becomes, to a degree, the challenging path of his followers. Far from simply conveying theological truths as a mere mental activity, Peter speaks of Christ (and thus the Father and the Holy Spirit) as the transformative reality *eo ipso,* as a theology-in-transformation (compare with Paul in Phil 2:1-14 and Col 1:12-21). For example, what struck his heart (Mark 14:72 parr) now strikes his hearers (Acts 2:37). Peter never separates the dimensions of theology, identity, and character formation. Without the presence of Christ, no sustained identity and character formation occurs. Likewise, Christ is not holistically manifest without the reality of identity and character transformation. According to Peter, Jesus did not come to make his followers merely more theologically astute; he also came to transform them in a radical way by means of restoring them to an ongoing dependence upon the atoning God who shapes them, individually and corporately, toward kingdom character. In other words, the resolution of the double crisis of self- and God-perception now issues in the twin realities of knowing Christ and his transformative impact on his redeemed followers.

Peter's Adversity and Suffering as a Key Setting and Catalyst for Character Formation

Before we explore specific aspects of Petrine identity formation and character development in Acts, we must recognize that the main thematic thrust of Acts sets the framework for the expression of discipleship characteristics, both in terms of identity and character formation. We believe that the thematic thrust of Acts is as follows: *the unstoppable mission of God leads to external growth and internal maturity despite external opposition and internal tensions.* In other words, Peter's expression of discipleship characteristics in word and deed are displayed in Luke's account within the context of this fourfold, individual and corporate matrix. For example, as Peter grows in and calls others to faith, he does so in the context of external and internal tensions and adversity. Faith operates in the coordinates of 'external and internal growth despite external opposition and internal tensions'. This applies to all specific identity and character traits enumerated below. Regardless of the precise understanding of the ending of Acts, the *unhindered* nature of gospel growth in Acts is apparent.[88] God is on a mission and nothing will be able to oppose or hinder it

---

[88] See T. Troftgruben, *A Conclusion Unhindered. A Study of the Ending of Acts within its Literary Environment* (Tübingen: Mohr Siebeck, 2010). Troftgruben argues that the surprising ending of Acts serves as a literary, historical, and thematic 'linkage' (177–78): (a) there is a literary convention in antiquity to end with such an 'open

(cf. Matt 16:18; 28:18-20; Mark 13:10).[89] The Old Testament tells of anticipatory redemptive acts which culminate in God's redemptive acts of the New Testament.[90] The thematic thrust of Acts (see above) becomes apparent by considering a simple literary and geographical outline of the book:

Introduction   1:1-26
I. *Witness to Jerusalem* [1:8]   2:1–8:4
    Summary #1   2:42-47   (internal growth statement)
                                 [additional growth statement, 4:4]
    Summary #2   4:32-37   (growth statement; testimony)
    Summary #3   5:12-16   (internal and external growth statement)
    Summary #4   5:42   (growth statement; preaching)
    Summary #5   6:7   (external growth statement)
                                 [additional growth statement, 8:4 (preaching)]
II. *Witness to Samaria and Judea* [9:31]   8:5–9:31
                                 [additional growth statement, 8:25; preaching]
                                 [additional growth statement, 8:40; preaching]
    Summary #6   9:31   (internal and external growth statement)
III. *Witness to Phoenicia, Cyprus and Antioch* [11:19]   9:32–12:24/25
                                 [additional growth statement, 11:19–21, 24 (as a 'retrospective hinge', cf. 8:1, btw. 11:1-18 and 11:22-24)]
    Summary #7   12:24   (external growth statement)
IV. *Witness to Phrygia and Galatia* [16:6]   13:1–15:35
                                 [additional growth statement, 13:49]
    Summary #8   15:35   (growth statement; preaching)
V. *Witness to Macedonia and Asia* [cf. 16:9]   15:36–19:20/21
    Summary #9   16:5   (internal and external growth statement)
                                 [additional growth statement, 19:10]
    Summary #10   19:20   (external growth statement)

---

conclusion', i.e., the adverb 'unhindered' (ἀκωλύτως); (b) the end of a narrative, telling the story in such an open-ended way, is not unfamiliar to ancient ears; (c) God's role is emphasized in the movement of the witness going forward, i.e., the witness will continue in an unhindered manner. It is conceivable that the arguments of Troftgruben (i.e., Acts, as 'volume two', is 'finished') are compatible with the historical possibility that Luke wrote his account shortly after the end of what he recounts in Acts. In other words, it remains open whether Luke still intended to write 'volume three' (following the outcome of Paul's trial in Rome) while stating in his 'second volume' that the gospel went out *unhindered*, regardless of the outcome of the trial of Paul.

[89] See C.J.H. Wright, *Mission*, 350–56.
[90] See, e.g., Gamaliel's advice in Acts 5:38-39 (v. 39: 'but if it is of God, you will not be able to overthrow them. You might even be found opposing God'; literally: 'lest you be found also as a God-fighter', μήποτε καὶ θεομάχοι εὑρεθῆτε).

VI. *Witness to Rome via Macedonia, Achaia and Jerusalem* [28:14] 19:22–28:31
                                    [additional growth statement, 21:20b]
        Summary #11   28:31   (growth statement; preaching)

God's manifest mission in Acts leads to *external growth* and *internal maturity* of the church despite *external opposition* and *internal tensions*. In order to understand the setting in which Peter arises as apostolic witness, we must therefore identify these four elements as the coordinates of Peter's own formation. In a real sense, the Petrine sections in Acts fulfill Jesus's prediction to Peter (and the other disciples) of adversity and fruitful growth in God's mission; he prepared them for external persecution (e.g., Mark 10:30; 13:9, 13, 19-20), internal opposition (e.g., Mark 13:12; Luke 12:49-53), and internal and external growth (e.g., Mark 4:20; 8:35; 10:29-30; 13:10). We will argue that Peter develops in character both through adversity and by seeing the mission of God advance in and around him. The fact that these themes continue throughout the non-Petrine sections of Acts, especially in the ministry of Paul, might not reflect Lukan redaction; it may simply indicate that the mission of God into which Jesus brought Peter and which Peter now *proclaims and lives out*, was subsequently shouldered by Paul, following his conversion.

We begin with Peter's exposure to *external opposition* and challenges.[91] External opposition[92] arises on account of political (Acts 12:1-6, 19) and religious reasons, which often are ignited over the person of Jesus (Acts 2:13[15]; 4:1-3, 5-7, 18, 21, 29[93]), occasionally giving rise to jealousy (Acts 5:17-18, 21b-28, 33, 40[94]) and disputes (Acts 6:9, 11-15[95]). At times there is also satanic opposition (e.g., demonic powers, Acts 8:7, 9-13, 18-24[96]).

The disciples' response to these forms of external oppositions, at times led by Peter, include:[97] prayer (Acts 4:24-30[98]); rejoicing (Acts 5:41);[99] acknowledging the sovereignty of God in the midst of challenges (Acts 5:29); preaching (Acts 8:4);[100] willingness to suffer (Acts 4:3; 5:18);[101] exorcism; and

---

[91] References and topics mentioned in the following are representative, not comprehensive.
[92] Cf. also Acts 16:16, 19-24 (economic opposition); 16:21 (cultural-legal opposition); and 17:18, 32 (philosophical opposition).
[93] Cf. also Acts 14:2, 5, 11-13.
[94] Cf. also Acts 13:45, 50; 17:5-9.
[95] Cf. also Acts 7:54, 58; 8:1.
[96] Cf. also Acts 13:6-8; 16:17; 19:13-16.
[97] Cf. also Acts 13:10-11; 16:35-40.
[98] Cf. also Acts 12:5, 12; 14:23.
[99] Cf. also Acts 16:25; 21:5.
[100] Cf. also Acts 11:19; 17:22-31.

healing (Acts 8:7). These responses indicate how Peter practices, together with other disciples, watchful (Mark 13:9, 18, 23, 33, 35, 37) and surrendered trust in God and his mission in the midst of adversity and resistance.

Reasons for *internal tensions* and challenges often faced by Peter include:[102] diversity of backgrounds[103] (see, e.g., Acts 2:40; 6:1);[104] socio-ethnic divisions and discrimination (Acts 6:1, including ministry overload); human depravity and impurity (e.g., dishonesty and deception, Acts 5:1-10; see Achan's sin in Josh 7:10-26);[105] different religious views (Acts 11:2-3; 15:1-2, 5, 7);[106] and physical sickness (Acts 9:36-41).

The disciples' response to these internal divisions and challenges, most often led by Peter,[107] include:[108] prayer (Acts 1:14, 24; 6:4, 6; 9:36-41); engaging in the ministry of the word (Acts 6:4; cf. John 17:20); electing deacons (Acts 6:3-6); and calling a council (Acts 15:3-29). These responses indicate how Peter and other followers of Christ trustingly and prayerfully look to God's Holy Spirit to guide and direct them in resolving internal challenges by aligning themselves with God's mission.

Forms of *external growth*, especially through conversions[109] (associated with prayer, singing, trust, and a willingness to suffer)[110] occur (in the presence of Peter) by means of: personal evangelistic messages, conversations, or small gatherings[111] which are, at times, associated with healings (Acts 5:14-16) or an exorcism and healing (Acts 9:32-35, 36-42); household gatherings (Acts 10:9-48, accompanied by visions);[112] public speeches (e.g., Acts 2:14-36, 38-39; 3:4-6, 12-26; 4:8-12; 10:34-48), as well as public hearings and trials (Acts 4:8-12, 19-20; 5:20-21, 29-32). We watch Peter follow Jesus's call to testify to the world (Mark 13:10) while not allowing external or internal adversities to hinder that call. In doing so, Peter closely aligns himself with God's mission and grows in boldness, courage, and trust, despite much opposition.

---

[101] See Rom 8:31-39; 2 Cor 6:1-10.

[102] Two initial challenges are quickly overcome: the physical departure of Jesus (Acts 1:9, 11) and the replacement of Judas Iscariot (Acts 1:16-26).

[103] Cf. also Acts 9:13-14, 21, 26-28; 16:3.

[104] Cf. also Acts 9:13-14; 15:1-5.

[105] See also not-yet confessed sins (Acts 19:18).

[106] See also 'deficient doctrine' (Acts 18:26).

[107] Cullmann, *Peter*, 34–41, identifies many elements which mark Peter as the temporary leader of the early church.

[108] See also Acts 9:27 (building bridges); 18:26 (engaging in gentle instruction); 15:37-40 (going separate ways in non-essentials); 19:18-19 (confessing past, evil practices).

[109] See, above, the '*growth* statements' in the narrative of Acts.

[110] Cf. also Acts 7:2-53, 56, 59-60; 8:30-38; 9:1-19, 28-29; 16:6-14.

[111] Cf. also Acts 8:5-8, 12; 9:20-22; 13:2-3, 5.

[112] Cf. also Acts 20:20; 28:23-28.

It appears that various expressions of *internal maturity* and growth occur especially in response to internal and external challenges as a means of growth. Such growth is displayed in Peter's life by means of: [113] prayer (Acts 1:14, 24; 2:42; 3:1; 4:24, (25-30); 6:4; 12:5, 12);[114] apostolic witness and teaching (Acts 2:42; cf. 2 Pet 2:1, 12-21; 3:1-2, 15-18); fellowship ('koinonia'; Acts 2:42; 5:12); sharing of possessions (Acts 2:44-46; 4:32, 34-37); breaking of bread (Acts 2:42, 46); rooting out evil by divine judgment over dishonesty (Acts 5:1-4, 9, 11); exhortation regarding a false heart (Acts 8:21); a call to repentance (Acts 8:22); mercy ministry (Acts 6:1); appointing deacons (Acts 6:1-6); giving testimony (Acts 11:1-18); and holding a council (Acts 15:1-21).

The presence of the Holy Spirit is a significant factor in the elements of external growth and internal maturity despite external opposition and internal tension. As stated above, Pentecost (Acts 2:1-4) commemorates, besides firstfruits of harvest, the giving of the Ten Commandments. The outpouring of the Holy Spirit upon the followers of Christ has a dual purpose and effect. Besides empowering for witness (Acts 1:8), it is, as we have noted above, a means of implementing the purification[115] effected by Christ's atonement (Acts 2:2-4, 38; 15:8-9). The giving of the law of Moses and the outpouring of the Holy Spirit are thus intimately connected (Jer 31:31-34). Pentecost, following the death and resurrection of Christ, makes it possible that the Holy Spirit now also comes upon Gentiles, 'having cleansed their hearts by faith' (Acts 15:8-9). Now, God writes his law on their hearts (Jer 31:31-34) combined with many tribulations which have a purifying effect upon the follower. The effect of the presence of the Holy Spirit is much prayer (Acts 1:14; 4:24-30; 12:5, 12) and fasting (Acts 14:23), as well as the exposure of the impurity of the heart.[116]

A conspicuous aspect in the unfolding drama of Acts is thus the motif of *growth through suffering and testing* that arises in the pursuit of the mission of God.[117] It occurs through both internal tensions and external opposition.[118] Peter is thus shaped by the taxonomy of the setting of early Christianity to mature as a disciple of Christ in the midst of these challenges (cf. Mark 10:29-

---

[113] Cf. also Acts 8:2; 11:23, 26-30; 12:25; 13:10; 14:20, 22-23, 28; 16:40; 19:18-19; 20:7, 18-35; 26:18; 28:30.

[114] Cf. also Acts 10:2, 4.

[115] Cf. Luke 3:16.

[116] See the exposure of *motives*: e.g., of dishonesty and deception, Acts 5:1-11; exhortation over a false heart, Acts 8:23; cf. Paul in Acts 13:10.

[117] Regarding suffering as a motif in Acts, see P.R. House, 'Suffering and the Purpose of Acts', *JETS* 33.3 (1990), 317–30.

[118] See E. Graf, *Durch Leiden geprägt: die gegenwärtigen Leidenserfahrungen der indischen Nathanja-Kirche mit einem Blick auf die paulinischen Gemeinden* (Ph.D. diss., Dortmund: Technische Universität Dortmund, 2012).

30). Acts 14:22b summarizes this reality: 'to remain in the faith because through many tribulations it is necessary that we enter the Kingdom of God' (cf. Mark 13:5-27; Luke 3:16). As Peter follows Jesus's call into God's mission, his identity and character are increasingly based on Christ-dependence, leading to Christ-likeness.

Identity and Character Formation according to Peter's Witness in Acts

Identity Formation

As we have seen, Peter grows through suffering and testing. He 'follows' Jesus into the *missio dei* (Matt 16:18-19; Luke 22:31-32; John 21:15-19) rather than pursuing his own agenda. This reinforces his newfound identity in Christ and thus forges solid character formation. Not surprisingly, the increasingly Christ-centered life of Peter is demonstrated by the close proximity between Peter's testimony to Christ and his self-perception and identity. For instance, Peter counters the false accusation of being intoxicated by his sober Christ-witness (Acts 2:15, 16-36). The modest lifestyle of Peter (and John)[119] in Acts 3:6 is naturally connected with his trust in the provision and power of Christ who manifests himself particularly to confirm the apostolic witness to the resurrection. His conviction that obedience to God is more important than civil obedience (Acts 4:19-20) naturally arises from his trust in the supreme and vindicated Christ who revealed himself as the Son of God. Peter directly connects the dishonesty of Ananias and Sapphira (Acts 5:9) with lying to the Holy Spirit. Thoroughgoing honesty is a precious and purifying gift of Christ, subsequent to faith in the atoning work of Christ. We thus find an uncompromising, steady person resting in the assurance of Christ.

There is thus no doubt that character formation naturally arises from the *salvific impact* of Jesus upon Peter, radically transforming his God- and self-perception, moving him from an anthropocentric to a God-dependent approach

---

[119] Cullmann, *Peter*, 34–35, gives a somewhat one-sided view in which John appears merely as 'an extra' in Acts. Cullmann sees in Luke's portrait of John a parallel to the Gospel of John in which he sees a certain rivalry between Peter and John (Cullmann, *Peter*, 28–31; contrast with Luke 22:8-13). As Bockmuehl, *Simon*, 27, notes, however, in a more balanced fashion, the momentous reinstatement of Peter (John 21:15-18) is found in the notable context of an account in which Peter 'has repeatedly come second to the Beloved Disciple in attentiveness, access, and proximity to Jesus'. What is historically noteworthy is the fact that John and Peter belong to Jesus's inner circle during Jesus's earthly ministry (also in the Gospel of John), they appear together in the initial chapters of Acts, and they are mentioned as apostolic pillars by Paul (Gal 2:9).

to life.[120] Without such a newfound Christ-centered identity, the following character traits would merely be copies of Stoic or Pharisaic 'virtues'. Now, however, they are the *consequence* and *fruit* of ongoing and trusting dependence upon Christ in terms of his atoning work, example, and teaching. Peter's character traits described in Acts will reflect the transformative presence of Christ, mediated by the Holy Spirit.

Character Formation
Now that we have analyzed christological emphases and aspects of identity formation in the Petrine sections in Acts, we are in a position to ask, which aspects of character formation are frequently emphasized in the Petrine sections of Acts.[121] The following traits arise in a particularly conspicuous fashion:

- *Courageous witness* (also in the midst of opposition, prison, persecution): Acts 4:3; 5:18, 26, 33, 41; 8:1; 10:39, 41; 12:1-5; to Christ and his resurrection, Acts 1:8, 22; 4:20, 33; 5:42; 6:4; *bold proclamation* (see all 'prophetic repentance speeches'): Acts 2:14-36; 3:12-26; 4:8-12; 5:29-32; [9:26–11:18], cf. Mark 1:14-15; 13:9-13, regarding 'witness and perseverance'. Acts 10 and 11 narrate a significant challenge to Peter, namely, that his theological attitude toward Gentiles, based on God's stated mission (e.g., Gen 12:3; Matt 28:19-20), must radically change.
  [Total: ~ 68 vv.]
- *Faith:* Acts [2:36, 44]; 3:16; 8:13; 10:43, which leads to forgiveness of sins, cf. Acts 11:17; 15:7-9. A clean and God-dependent heart will lead to the right approach to the Mosaic law, Acts 15:10-11.[122] The close 'sister' of faith is *prayer*: Acts 1:14, 24; 2:42; 4:31; 6:4, 6; 8:15; 9:40; 10:9.
  [Total: ~10 vv., plus 9 vv. re: prayer]
- *Surrendered obedience*: Acts 4:19; 5:29, 32 (obedient to the faith, Acts 6:7b; cf. Mark 8:34, 38 and Acts 9:26–11:18). [Total: ~4 vv.]
- *Guarding/Watching the heart.* This is often contrasted by the absence of a pure heart: Acts 5:3-4, 7-11; 8:17-24, and especially Acts 8:21-23. Peter will not eat ceremonially unclean food (Acts 10:14; 15:8-9, 'God, who knows the heart'). [Total: ~13 vv.]
- *Humility and service*: Acts 10:25-26 (see the entire context of 10:21-48, as Peter enters the house of a Gentile; 10:28; 11:3). [Total: ~6 vv.]

---

[120] See Bayer, *Theology*, 41–132.

[121] That is, the *approximate* number of verses dedicated to the respective themes relative to the *entire* sections devoted to Peter.

[122] Peter's emphasis in Acts 15:10-11 may sound like that of Paul, but it is based on Acts 10 and 11, as well as his own training (Mark 4, as well as 7–10) issuing in his need for the cross of Christ (Mark 10:45; 14:22-24), despite being circumcised and a law-abiding Jew.

- *Overcoming* in adversity and persecution, including Satan: Acts 2:13 (15); 4:1-3, 5-7, 18, 21, 29; 5:17-18, 21b-28, 33, 40; 6:9, 11-15; 8:7, 9-13, 18-24; 12:1-6, 19. [Total: ~39 vv.]

A ranked list of these character traits in Acts yields the following results:

1. Witness
2. Overcoming in trials and persecution
3. Faith (with prayer)
4. Watching the heart
5. Humility and service
6. Surrendered obedience

Certainly, the thematic thrust of Acts (see above) is unique as it focuses on the *public* presentation of holistic witness in earliest Christianity. Consequently, the featured and ranked character traits will echo this Lukan emphasis. As such, it is not surprising that *witness* and *overcoming in trials* rank at the top of the list. The courageous witness to God and his mission trigger political, cultural, and satanic *opposition*. Witness and overcoming in trials thus go hand in hand in Acts. Wherever the gospel of God's expanding kingdom is holistically proclaimed, a bewildering array of opposition will be encountered (cf. Matt 16:18). Since, however, God is building his living temple in the context of such missional witness, *faith*, *watching* over the *heart*, *humility*, and *surrender* reflect the character of members of the growing kingdom, *even* in Acts.

Significant Consequences of Such a Heart Attitude

The Christ-centered character traits we have noted open the door to many further character traits, such as transparent honesty, dependability, willingness to acknowledge faults and mistakes, self-control, and a teachable attitude. In addition, we find at least the following *corporate* expressions of faith in Christ mentioned explicitly: sharing of goods (Acts 2:44-45; 4:32-37; 5:3-4, 8-9, [cf. Luke 14:33]); devotion to the apostles' teaching (Acts 2:42); fellowship (Acts 2:42); and breaking of bread (Acts 2:42).

The Dynamic between Christology, Identity, and Character Formation in Acts

The eminence of Christ as the Father's eternal Son is paramount in Acts. Christ, mediating the will of the Father, communicates by means of the Holy Spirit the ongoing unfolding of God's global mission in terms of emboldening witness, overcoming in adversity, and other character traits. Pentecost serves as a catalyst both toward an inner maturity ('writing the law on their hearts') and an emboldened holistic witness to a watching world. By his atonement, example, and teaching, Christ, by means of the Holy Spirit, shapes a people who increasingly reflect characteristics of his eternal covenantal kingdom (cf. Acts 28:31). Peter spawns this forward thrust, embodies it, and motivates others in the process. As stated above, the thoroughly Christ-centered nature of character formation is the consequence of the indissoluble union between Peter's testimony to Christ and his newfound identity and character as a disciple of Christ. A significant feature in Peter's growth is the fact that adversity and suffering serve as a catalyst for character formation: as Christ suffered in obedience, so Peter is exposed to adversity which issues in an increasingly cruciform character.

Surprisingly, a considerable number of core character traits which we first isolated in Mark (see above) surface, once again, in Peter's speeches and actions as portrayed by Luke in Acts. Since Luke focuses on the spread of the public apostolic witness and growth of the messianic church, he particularly features Peter's call to be an apostolic witness (corresponding to the core characteristic of courageous witness isolated in Mark). This apostolic witness spreads in the setting of serious adversity and opposition, coming from within and without the nascent church. Such adversity, in turn, facilitates further growth of Peter (and others) especially regarding *faith*, *watching over the heart*, *humility*, and *surrendered obedience*.

CHAPTER 7

Christology, Identity, and Character Formation in 1 and 2 Peter

Introduction

The longstanding, ill-perceived view that 1 Peter represents an early catholic, moralizing diatribe, devoid of the grace focus found in the canonical Gospels and in Paul's Epistles, has gradually been laid to rest, especially in the second half of the twentieth century. It is now widely held that 1 Peter represents a significant, profound, and insightful theological and paraenetic discourse, the likes of which is hard to duplicate.

As we review our journey thus far, we see that Peter has come a long way. Both Mark and Acts (and, to a degree, Matthew, Luke, and John) display in a disarming and transparent way everything that Peter has to learn and appropriate as he increasingly trusts Jesus and becomes willing to follow him all the way. In Mark, this growth focuses on the necessity of radical transformation from self- to God-dependence as well as on learning basic elements of identity and character formation which arise from Jesus's impact. In Acts, Peter's growth focuses on his bold witness (Acts 2–5) as the result of accepting God's will, which issues in the courage to bring the gospel to the Gentile world (Acts 10); on faithfulness to his calling in the midst of much adversity and suffering; and on growth in trust, learning to watch over his heart, humility, and surrendered obedience. His faithfulness to Christ's call invites many external and internal challenges and problems, all of which further contribute to the purifying formation of his character.

Subsequent to the report in Acts, Peter most likely took his holistic apostolic witness to Asia Minor. There, he probably worked among followers of Jesus to whom he later wrote the Epistle of 1 Peter (cf. 1 Pet 1:1: Pontus, Galatia, Cappadocia, Asia, and Bithynia), before working in Greece and Rome.

As we turn to 1 Peter, it becomes apparent that the above-mentioned factors of growth have been lived out and now deeply mark him. He is seasoned and formed in suffering (cf. 1 Pet 1:7, δοκιμάζειν, tested in fire and approved). As such, Peter comes both as an emissary (ἀπόστολος) of Jesus (1 Pet 1:1) and as a witness (μάρτυς) of the suffering of Christ (1 Pet 5:1) in order to encourage

Christians in Asia Minor in their own suffering. At this stage in his life, Peter is a wise, tested, and seasoned witness, encourager, and humble mentor (1 Pet 5:1-10).

The Circumstances for the Composition of 1 Peter

It is most plausible that Peter wrote 1 Peter from Rome ('Babylon', 1 Pet 5:13; compare with Rev 17:18).[1] The typological use of a geographical name is well documented (Gal 4:26; Heb 12:22; Rev 11:8).[2] Cullmann notes: '[S]ince the greeting must have a definite city in mind, there could have been in the time of the writer no other place but Rome to which this figurative meaning of the ancient Babylon was applied'.[3] Bockmuehl argues that this designation also 'makes sense' *before* AD 70 and 'does in fact pre-date the year AD 70'.[4]

Even though there are no recorded empire-wide persecutions[5] prior to the times of Domitian and Trajan, Peter must have been aware, for instance, of Claudius's expulsion of Jewish-Christians from Rome (AD 48), the Neronian persecution of Christians in Rome in AD 64 (cf. Tacitus, *Ann.* 15.44.17-20), as well as the multiple forms of personal and public suffering experienced by Christians in Asia Minor and elsewhere (see our discussion above regarding external opposition in Acts). As a leader who knows suffering, Peter writes to scattered Christian sojourners (παρεπιδήμοις διασπορᾶς) in the five Roman provinces of Asia Minor in order to encourage them to stand firm in Christ as they face localized opposition from Jewish and/or pagan quarters (1 Pet 4:12-19). Regardless of the exact nature of political persecutions in the first century AD, 1 Peter focuses on societal (e.g., legal) and personal suffering and ostracization (see below) and does not dwell on politically organized and empire-wide persecutions of Christians.

Key Themes in 1 Peter[6]

The central theme of 1 Peter may be presented in the form of an exhortation: live personal and public lives of uncompromising devotion to Christ, bearing the fruit of moral purity, and seek sincere, non-retaliatory godliness in the

---

[1] See, e.g., G.W. Forbes, *1 Peter* (Nashville, TN: B&H Academic, 2014), 2–4.
[2] See also *Ap. John* 14:8; 16:19; *Sib. Or.* 5.159–60; *2 Bar.* 11:1; *4 Ezra* 3:1-3; 28:31. Cf. Cullmann, *Peter*, 84–87.
[3] Cullmann, *Peter*, 85.
[4] Bockmuehl, *Simon*, 31, with references to Dan 9, Mark 13:14; Josephus, *Ant.* 10.79, as well as various Qumran sources (p. 128).
[5] Schnabel, *Mission*, II, 1533–38.
[6] See L. Goppelt, *A Commentary on 1 Peter* (Grand Rapids, MI: Eerdmans, 1993), 18–20.

midst of undeserved public and personal suffering.[7] Within this general admonition, we can isolate the following characteristic features: the, mostly Gentile[8] recipients of 1 Peter experience various forms of suffering (1 Pet 1:6; 2:11-12, 19-24, 25; 3:13-18; 4:12-16, 17 [cf. Jer 25:15-29]; 5:10) as *aliens and strangers* (1 Pet 1:1, 17; 2:11; see Abraham, Gen 12:1-3, 7, as well as Israel in Egypt, Heb 11:13-16; 13:14), because of their godly conduct in society by word (1 Pet 3:15; 4:14) and deed (1 Pet 3:13-17). According to 1 Peter, civil society is endowed with God-given institutions (e.g., rulers, such as a Roman emperor: 1 Pet 2:13-14; see Rom 13:1). Simultaneously, much injustice and arbitrary actions on the part of members of civil society and of God-given institutions and structures (1 Pet 2:18; 5:13) exist. As a tender plant in harsh winds, so to speak, Peter develops the motifs of holiness, godliness (1 Pet 1:15-16, 2:11-12; 3:8-9), and hope (in Christ's return, 1 Pet 1:3; 3:5, 15) amidst slanderous and oppressive adversity as the fruit of the presence of God among his people as the living temple. In 1 Peter 2:13-14 (cf. Rom 13:1-7) there is implicit room for civil disobedience when God-given authority-spheres deviate from their limited competence or demand that the church contradict the moral and ethical law of God (cf. Acts 5:29, 32). Peter often speaks of the future consummation of salvation as a 'future indicative' of the Christian life, in addition to the 'past indicative' of the atoning work of Christ. Between these redemptive-historical poles, Peter envisions growth in peace and holiness in the midst of much unjust suffering and adversity (1 Pet 1:6, 8; 2:9; 4:13; 5:10).[9]

First Peter and the Old Testament

We find the following direct Old Testament quotations (either MT or LXX) in 1 Peter:[10]

- Pertaining to holiness and the word of God (1 Pet 1:15-16/Lev 11:44-45; 1 Pet 1:24/Isa 40:6, 8, the word of God as an imperishable seed).

---

[7] See Goppelt, *1 Peter*, 18–19. Helyer, *Life*, 17, notes that πάσχειν occurs in 1 Pet eleven times out of a total of forty in the NT. Helyer, *Life*, 128, believes in a somewhat reductionist way that the central theological motif in 1 Pet is 'undeserved suffering'.

[8] Helyer, *Life*, 113–16.

[9] This is similar to Paul's past (Romans 1–8) and future indicatives (1 and 2 Thess), used as motivations for growth in maturity.

[10] Christological interpretations of the OT include 1 Pet 2:3-4, 6-10, 22-25; 3:12-15; 2 Pet 3:8-13.

- Pertaining to the messianic stone metaphor (*1 Pet 2:6*/*Isa 28:16*; *1 Pet 2:7*/*Ps 118:22* [LXX Ps 117:22], cf. Acts 4:8-12; *1 Pet 2:8*/*Isa 8:14*).
- Pertaining to the messianic *Ebed Yhwh* (1 Pet 3:10-12/Ps 34:12-16; 1 Pet 4:18/Prov 11:31).
- Significantly, we encounter various additional *allusions*, especially to Isaiah 53 (1 Pet 2:22 [1:11]/Isa 53:9;[11] 1 Pet 2:23/Isa 53:6, 12; 1 Pet 2:24d/Isa 53:5; 1 Pet 2:25a/Isa 53:6).

These Old Testament references demonstrate that the messianic stone metaphor and Jesus as the *Ebed Yhwh* is of paramount significance to Peter's Christology (see below).

Characteristic Christological Themes

As noted above, the broader context of Christology in Mark is the *coming kingdom of God*. The wider context of Christology in Acts is *the unfolding mission* of God to the 'end of the world' whereby Jesus, with the Father and the Holy Spirit, mediates the unfolding purposes of the rule of God over his Jewish and Gentile people. The broader context of Christology in 1 Peter is the *ongoing, sovereign purpose* (1 Pet 1:5, 10-12, 20-21, 2:8-10; 3:18-22, 4:12, 17; 5:4, 10-11) of the living, triune God (1 Pet 1:2-3, 17 [God as the Father of Jesus]; cf. 1 Pet 1:19-21; 2:22; 3:18-19) who leads his people home to himself in the midst of adversity (the *victory* of the kingdom of God).[12] God the Father is the faithful Creator (1 Pet 2:3; 4:19). God the Father *elects* with a destining foreknowledge (1 Pet 1:1-2; 2:9-10) which leads to and calls for worship (1 Pet 1:17, 2:5, 12; 3:4) and obedience (1 Pet 1:21-22); he causes *rebirth* (1 Pet 1:3; cf. John 1:13; 3:3, 7-8; Titus 3:5) through his word and the good news (1 Pet 1:23, 25) in order to *gather* his covenant people (1 Pet 2:9-10), and *judges* the deeds of all (1 Pet 1:17; 4:5-6, 17). As a guidepost to God-given life, Peter is convinced (1 Pet 1:23, 25) that the word of God (here as the inspired Scriptures of the Old Testament and the gospel proclamation) is an imperishable seed (see Isa 40:8). Such a focus is akin to the christological emphasis isolated in the Petrine section of Acts.

Peter dwells much on the death and resurrection of Jesus (see, e.g., 1 Pet 1:18-19; 2:4, 6-8, 21-22, 24; 3:7, 9-12, 18-22).[13] First Peter 1:11 and 2:21 state

---

[11] The MT of Isa 53:9d states: וְלֹא מִרְמָה בְּפִיו: 'And there was no deceit in his mouth'; the LXX supplies *ad sensus* εὑρέθη before δόλος. The LXX corresponds to 1 Pet 2:22.

[12] See esp. Jobes, *1 Peter*, 261–83 and Marshall, *1 Peter*, 53–57, 91–98.

[13] Helyer, *Life*, 128–29, claims that the christological core found in 1 Pet 1:18-21; 2:21-25; 3:18-22, belongs, together with Phil 2:5-11; Col 1:15-20 and 1 Tim 3:16, to the 'earliest and formative stages of "the apostles' teaching"' (Helyer, *Life*, 129).

that the Old Testament prophets prophesied by means of the Spirit of Jesus concerning the necessary (cf. Mark 8:31) suffering and death of Christ (see, e.g., Isa 52:13–53:12 and Dan 9:26; cf. Acts 10:43). The events surrounding Jesus are seen in profound continuity to God's self-revelation and the people of God. Specifically, 1 Pet 1:11 and 2:22 (see 5:1) identify Jesus with the suffering *Ebed YHWH* (Isa 52:13–53:12). 1 Peter 1:18-19 speaks of the death of Jesus ('blood of Christ') as propitiation. He dies silently and 'unjustly abused' (Mark 14:61)[14] as an *innocent* man (1 Pet 2:22-24). 1 Peter 2:24 and 3:18 note that Christ bore our sins on the cross (cf. Isa 53:4a, 5d, 12). Guthrie aptly notes: 'Christ in his suffering becomes an example because he has first become a substitute'.[15] He is the chief example of submission to God's will in the midst of suffering and shame (see 1 Pet 5:6).

First Peter 2:19-21, 23 identifies Jesus's suffering and death as a 'passion'. The sacrificial suffering of Jesus atones in a vicarious, substitutionary fashion (1 Pet 1:18; cf. 1 Pet 2:21-25; cf. Mark 14:22-24). Helyer notes: 'The confession of Jesus as the sinless Lamb of God who takes away the sin of the world lies at the core of apostolic doctrine and runs like a scarlet thread through NT literature'.[16] First Peter 1:3, 21, and 3:21 speak of the resurrection of Jesus and 1 Peter 3:22 with 4:11 mention the exaltation of Christ to the right hand of God (see Acts 2:33-34 and Mark 8:38; 14:62). Given God's exceeding power, demonstrated in Christ, the suffering followers must not fear. Peter expects the Parousia of Christ (ἐν ἀποκαλύψει Ἰησοῦ Ξριστοῦ; 1 Pet 1:5, 7, 11, 13; 4:7, 13, 17; 5:4, 10; see παρουσία in 2 Pet 1:16; 3:4, 12; cf. 2 Pet 1:19; 2:9) and looks forward to the glory of Jesus (1 Pet 1:21). In conjunction with the Parousia, Peter expects Jesus to return as judge (1 Pet 4:5; see Mark 8:38 and Acts 10:42).

As a conspicuous echo to Mark 12:1-12 and synoptic parallels,[17] 1 Peter refers to Jesus's self-reference as the *Living Stone* (1 Pet 2:4, 6-7; see Acts 4:11; cf. Ps 118:22; Isa 8:14; 28:16; Rom 9:33; Eph 2:20). Jesus, the living stone, was rejected by some, but accepted by others. Pre-Christian tendencies of the messianic interpretation of Isaiah 28:16 can be found in the LXX translation of the MT (adding 'in him' to 'he who believes shall not be ashamed') as well as in the *Tar. Jonathan* on Isaiah 28:16 (speaking of the

---

[14] Bockmuehl, *Simon,* 31, notes the possible 'biographical touch' found in the connection between Mark 14:61 and 1 Pet 2:23-24.

[15] D. Guthrie, *New Testament Theology* (Downers Grove, IL: IVP, 1981), 474, referred to by Helyer, *Life,* 135 n. 15.

[16] Helyer, *Life,* 131.

[17] See Bayer, *Markus,* 411–20.

appointment of a king in Zion). Josephus likely identifies Isaiah 28:16 as referring to the Messiah (*Ant.* 10.210).[18]

A further motif in 1 Peter is Jesus as *shepherd* and *overseer* (ἐπίσκοπος) of 'souls' (1 Pet 2:25; 5:2-4 [ἀρχιποίμενος]; cf. Mark 6:34 par.). In the Old Testament, the metaphorical use of 'shepherd' applies, at times to God (e.g., Gen 48:15; Ps 23; 80:1; Jer 31:10). God's kings were to lead as shepherds (2 Sam 5:2; 7:7; Ezek 34:11-23, the messianic shepherd 'David'; Mic 5:2-4; *Pss. Sol.* 17:39-40; cf. John 10:1, 15, 17-18) and not as self-serving rulers (Ezek 34:1-10; Zech 11:16-17; cf. John 10:11-13). According to Mark 14:27, Jesus serves as the stricken shepherd (Zech 13:7), which leads to the temporary scattering of his 'sheep' (Mark 14:43-50 par.). As indicated above, Peter's emphasis that Jesus's death fulfills Isaiah 53 (1 Pet 1:11 and 2:22; cf. 2:18-25) echoes Mark 10:45 and Acts 3:13-15. Besides the messianic stone metaphor and the shepherd motif, this connection to Isaiah 53 is highly significant for Peter's entire canonical testimony.

Peter thus stresses in 1 Peter that dependence upon Christ is unequivocally the foundation of any spiritual growth and ethics.[19] In our view, this represents the resolution of the crisis of self- and God-perception isolated in the Gospel of Mark (see above). Peter implies that Christ's atonement was *necessary* because of the severe human condition of alienation from and enmity toward God. This becomes particularly evident when he states, similarly to Paul in Romans 1:17–3:26, that Christ, the Righteous one, suffered for the unrighteous (implying Jews and Gentiles) and that thus 'he might bring us to God' (1 Pet 3:18).[20] If Jews and Gentiles alike have to be brought (back) to God at such extraordinary cost (1 Pet 3:18), it follows that unregenerate man's alienation from God is, indeed, most severe; without Christ human beings were like scattered sheep (Isa 53:6) but now they have returned to their souls' shepherd (1 Pet 2:25). The triune God is supreme in revealing himself in Christ and addressing mankind's universal alienation by Christ's atonement.

Identity and Character Formation

We have already noticed significant christological connections between Mark, Acts, and 1 and 2 Peter. As it turns out, we will also find in 1 and 2 Peter a set

---

[18] See D.A. Carson, '1 Peter', in: Beale/Carson, *Commentary*, 1023–30. Helyer, *Life*, 137 notes that the Qumran community (1QS 8, 7) viewed itself as the 'stone' of Ps 118:22.

[19] See the important work by J. Dryden, *Theology and Ethics in 1 Peter: Paraenetic Strategies for Christian Character Formation* (Tübingen: Mohr Siebeck, 2006), 48–49, and esp. 177–91.

[20] See Bayer, *Theology*, 98–124.

of identity and character traits that are naturally compatible with what we isolated in Mark and the Petrine sections of Acts.

Identity Formation

Based on the resolution of the crisis of God- and self-perception[21] (see 1 Pet 2:25; 3:18), a regenerate disciple's identity and self-perception is defined in 1 Peter by his state in and relationship to Christ (1 Pet 2:11). The following elements of identity are to be grasped against the background of first-century AD values of honor and shame.[22] On account of the ostracism which the Christians in Asia Minor, and for that matter, Jews,[23] experienced (1 Pet 2:12; 3:16; 4:4), their honor could not be found in acceptance by the Greco-Roman culture surrounding them, but by the dignity conferred upon them by their new master who loved them sacrificially (1 Pet 2:11). Jesus's work provides them with:

- new life through an imperishable new birth ('born again', 1 Pet 1:3, 23; cf. 1 Pet 1:14, 17) into a new 'family' (1 Pet 2:17; ἀδελφότης, i.e., born from the same 'womb'[24]; cf. 1 Pet 1:14; 2:2);
- an individual and corporate, imperishable inheritance (1 Pet 1:4) as the consequence of the resurrection (1 Pet 1:3; 3:21), glory and dominion of Christ (1 Pet 1:7-8, 21, 24; 4:11, 13-14; 5:1, 4, 10; cf. 2 Pet 1:3, 17; 3:18); and
- the anticipation of the future culmination of salvation (1 Pet 1:5, 9) and the future reality of the Parousia (1 Pet 1:13).

In particular, followers of Christ are:

1. a 'chosen' and 'elect' race, people/nation, and flock,[25] consisting of Jews and Gentiles (1 Pet 1:14; 2:9-10; 5:2; cf. Deut 7:6; Hos 2:23; Mark 6:34; Acts 10:1–11:26; 15:1-29). It is noteworthy that 1 Peter does not use the term *ekklēsia*. However, the *concept* of the new people of God, the new Israel, is paramount in 1 Peter. A characteristic mark of the people of God is the fact that before him there is no partiality, since there is equal access

---

[21] See also Bayer, *Theology*, 61–98.
[22] Cf. Helyer, *Life*, 184, who refers to D.A. deSilva, 'Honor and Shame', *Dict. of NT Background* (ed. Evans and Porter, 2000), 518–22.
[23] Cf. Helyer, *Life*, 186.
[24] Cf. Helyer, *Life*, 189, quoting W. Günther, 'brother', *NIDNTT*, I, 255.
[25] Helyer, *Life*, 184–85.

to his kingdom, based on repentance and receiving the atonement of Christ (1 Pet 1:17, ἀπροσωπολήμπτως; see Gal 2:6);
2. ransomed ('sprinkled') in the blood of Jesus (1 Pet 1:2, 18-19; cf. 2:21-25; 3:18-22); note here the covenantal language and echoes of the exodus and Passover;[26]
3. his people, the 'possession of Christ' (1 Pet 2:9-10);
4. 'living stones' and 'a holy priesthood', being fitted into and serving in a spiritual temple (1 Pet 2:5, 9; cf. Exod 19:6; Rom 12:1). We find here the priesthood of all true disciples who offer 'spiritual sacrifices acceptable to God', i.e., prayerful godliness in word and deed (cf. 1 Pet 2:9; 4:7, 11). In their dependence upon Christ (1 Pet 2:21), they are called to loving (1 Pet 1:22; 3:8; 4:8) 'pattern-imitation' (1 Pet 2:21-23; 4:1, 13) and to be, in turn, 'examples' to the flock of God (1 Pet 5:2-3). This applies especially to leaders. Jesus in his divine majesty and human perfection should not and cannot be copied; however, we are called to reflect Christlike characteristics in our dependence upon him (i.e., pattern-imitation; see, e.g., 1 Pet 2:21). God equips his followers with strength (1 Pet 4:11; 5:10) and facilitates growth, sanctification, and perseverance in suffering by the Holy Spirit (1 Pet 1:2, 11-12; 4:14).

Further details can be pointed out regarding the identity (self-perception) and life-circumstance of the disciples according to 1 Peter: followers of Christ are elect *sojourners*, scattered like seed (1 Pet 1:1). As such they:

- abstain from defilement (1 Pet 2:11) and (thus) suffer as the people of God (1 Pet 1:1, 17; 2:11; 4:4); while such suffering (1 Pet 4:12; 5:14) is not outside the bounds of the will of God (1 Pet 2:15; 3:17; 4:2, 19; cf. Mark 10:28-30), they will be vindicated (1 Pet 5:6);
- live in battle (1 Pet 1:22; 2:1; 4:3-4, 15) while pursuing purity of heart (see especially 1 Pet 2:1);
- have 'returned to the shepherd and guardian [ἐπίσκοπος] of their souls' (1 Pet 2:25; 5:4; see John 21:15-17; cf. Pss 77:20; 78:52; 80:1; 95:7; Isa 40:11; Zech 10:3).[27]

Character Formation

Based on such a rich foundation of identity formation provided for the followers of Christ, we now turn to an exploration of the traits of character

---

[26] See Helyer, *Life*, 129, 185; cf. Exod 24:6-8.
[27] Cf. Helyer, *Life*, 196.

formation that arise from such a new identity. First Peter yields the following character traits in which the disciples grow:

- *surrendered obedience* to do the will of God (1 Pet 1:2, 14; 2:21);
- *trust* and *faith*, especially by facing suffering as well as trials in exile (1 Pet 1:6, 8; 2:9, 19-20; 4:12-13, 16, 19; 5:10), filled with hope (1 Pet 1:7, 21) and without worry (1 Pet 5:7);
- sober and *watchful* resistance to the destructive aims of Satan, awaiting the Parousia in the midst of adversity (1 Pet 1:7; 5:4, 8-11) and being ready to render praise and glory to Jesus at his Parousia;
- *watchfulness* over their hearts with a view toward godliness, pursuing a new life by overcoming old ways (1 Pet 1:14), realizing that the flesh wars against the soul (1 Pet 2:11);
- being ready for *holistic witness* of Christ, proclaiming the glory of God (1 Pet 2:9; 4:11), being a faithful witness to Christ (1 Pet 3:15), and pursuing an honorable conduct among Jews and Gentiles (1 Pet 2:12, 15);
- growth in *humility*; submitting to authority (1 Pet 2:13); pursuing God-trusting, tender-heartedness, and love (1 Pet 3:8; 4:8-19; 5:5-6); and being good stewards (1 Pet 4:10-11) in servant-leadership (1 Pet 5:2; cf. John 21:15-17).

Taking account of the frequency of occurrence and emphasis of each of these themes in 1 Peter,[28] our study yields the following ranked character formation characteristics:[29]

1. *Faith and trust* (with surrender) in God's (future) salvation [10x]; as hope in God [5x]; as worship [4x] (especially 1 Pet 3:15), without fear [2x, e.g., 3:6]; see especially 1 Pet 1:3, 4, 7, 8, 13, 21; 2:7, 23; 3:5, 14; *5:7, 9*
   [Total ~21 vv.]

2. *Humility* (honor, respect) of heart [4x] and demeanor (1 Pet 5:3; see Mark 10:42); submission [8x] and a gentle and quiet attitude [4x]; see especially 1 Pet 2:13-17, 19; 3:1, 4, 7-8, 15-16; 4:10-11 [humble service]; 5:2-3, 5-6; cf. 3:8 [harmony], and 4:9 [hospitality]
   [Total ~17 vv.]

3. *Witness* in word and *deed* (life-style) [2x], especially through good deeds ('good doing') and sober action [13x], including the context of hospitality; see especially 1 Pet 1:12, 25; 2:9, 12, 15; 3:1, 15; 4:14; cf. 4:5
   [Total ~15 vv.]

---

[28] That is, the *approximate* number of verses dedicated to each characteristic relative to the entire Epistle.

[29] Numbers in square brackets represent frequency of occurrence.

4. *Watchfulness* regarding *purity of heart* (overcome evil passions [4x]), since the believers were ransomed from futile ways. They are to be holy [1x], a priesthood [1x], a people of God [1x], watchful [1x], vigilant over heart-attitudes, with a purified heart [2x], die to sin and live to righteousness [1x or 2x], having moved from darkness to light [1x]; see especially 1 Pet 1:14-16; 2:1-2, 11, 24; 3:1, 4, 10-11 (cf. Ps 34), 15-16; cf. 1:22; 4:3 and 5:8 [Total ~12 vv.]

5. *Perseverance and overcoming* in the midst of (unjust) *suffering* and trials, based on exemplary conduct: 1 Pet 1:6-7; 2:20-21, 23; 3:13, 16 [no shame], 17; 4:12, 16, 19; 5:9, 10, 12 [cf. Christ's suffering, 1:11]
[Total ~11 vv.]

6. *Obedience* [6x] and *fear of God* [2x]: 1 Pet 1:2, 8, 13-15, 22; 2:16, 21, 25; 3:2; 4:10; see 'strangers' 1:1, 17;[30] [cf. 2:8, 11, 13, 18; 3:6] [Total ~9 vv.]

7. *Prayer*: 1 Pet 1:17; 2:5, 9; 3:7, 12 [Total 5 vv.]

Additional emphases *particular* to 1 Peter which do not arise explicitly in Mark and the Petrine sections in Acts include the following important characteristics:

- A *Dispersion mentality*—as the elect and chosen, they are scattered sojourners (life style) [5x]: 1 Pet 1:1, 17; 2:11; 5:13 [cf. Mark 10:29-31 and Luke 14:33] [Total 5 vv.]
- *Love* of the 'brotherhood' [4x]: 1 Pet 1:2, 9; 3:8; cf. 1 Pet 1:18 [redeemed]; 1 Pet 1:22; 2:10 [love from the heart]; 1 Pet 4:8 [received mercy]
[Total ~4 vv.]
- *Joy*: 1 Pet 1:6, 8; 4:13 [Total 3 vv.]

A simplified ranked list of traits of character formation in 1 Peter thus looks like this:[31]

1. Faith
2. Humility
3. Witness in word and deed
4. Purity of heart (watching over heart)
5. Perseverance and overcoming in suffering and trials
6. Obedience

---

[30] Compare with the possible ninth core characteristic in the canonical Gospels (Luke 14:33).

[31] The following is ranked according to approximate frequency of occurrence (i.e., the approximate number of verses alluding to a given character trait).

7. Prayer *and* a Mentality of scattered sojourners (tied at #7)
8. Love of the brotherhood
9. Joy[32]

We shall further explore these character traits in Chapters 8 and 9. In order to round out the picture, we now take a brief glance at 2 Peter.

Peter's 'Farewell' in 2 Peter as Encouragement and Warning to Continue in Christ-Dependent Character Formation

Christology

Second Peter represents most likely a 'farewell letter',[33] in which hope in God's ultimate transformative purposes, the Parousia of Christ, and the certainty of God's judgment over those who deny his call in Christ are prominent.[34] In 2 Peter 1:3-11, the author presents a summary of his message, reflecting much common ground with early Christianity.[35] The transfiguration is as central to 2 Peter as is the suffering of Christ in 1 Peter.[36] The divine sonship of Jesus is emphasized (2 Pet 1:1, 11, 17-18; 2:1, 10; 3:18). Even here, we encounter some Christ-centered core characteristics of identity and character formation, especially in the context of shepherding (see, e.g., 2 Pet 3:1-2).

Christ-Centered Identity Formation

The following elements of identity formation are conspicuous:

a. Disciples are privileged to participate in the present and future eternal kingdom of the Lord and Savior Jesus (2 Pet 1:11; 3:18; cf. Mark 1:14-15; 14:25). God ushers in the new heaven and new earth in righteousness (2 Pet 3:13);[37]

---

[32] Additionally, one time each: 'love of Jesus' and 'stewards of gifts'.

[33] The literary proximity of 2 Pet to a 'last testament' is not sufficiently compelling. See G.L. Green, *Jude and 2 Peter* (Grand Rapids, MI: Baker Academic, 2008), 165; *pace* R.J. Bauckham, *Jude, 2 Peter* (Waco, TX: Word, 1983), 160–62.

[34] Helyer, *Life*, 18. See, however, some cautionary remarks in G.L. Green, *Jude and 2 Peter*, 207.

[35] See Bauckham, *Jude, 2 Peter* (1983), 160.

[36] Bockmuehl, *Simon*, 178.

[37] See the discussion in Helyer, *Life*, 269–71.

b. The righteousness of Christ as our God[38] and Savior (2 Pet 1:1) as well as his glory (2 Pet 1:17-18: the glory of Christ was briefly revealed on the Mount of Transfiguration) are paramount to Christian living;
c. Disciples are cleansed from former sins (2 Pet 1:9);
d. The master 'bought' his followers (2 Pet 2:1, 9; cf. Mark 8:34-37);
e. God rescues his godly people from trials (2 Pet 2:9); and
f. God is patient with sinners in order to lead them to repentance (2 Pet 3:9).[39] Note the connection between the Parousia of Christ and repentance both in Acts 3:19-20 and 2 Pet 3:12.[40]

Christ-Centered Character Formation

Peter's farewell letter reinforces his testimony in Mark, the Petrine sections in Acts, and 1 Peter. Highlighted features include:

- *Godliness (purity of heart)*: Since the followers of Christ have been cleansed from their former sins (2 Pet 1:9), Peter admonishes them toward *godliness* (εὐσέβεια, 2 Pet 1:3, 6-7; 2:9; 3:11; cf. Acts 3:12) as those living in the light of the 'prophetic word' (2 Pet 1:19 [including but not limited to OT prophets, 2 Pet 1:20]). They are to pursue peace and *purity* (2 Pet 3:14) in the light of the Last Judgment (2 Pet 3:10-11, 'the Day of the Lord will come like a thief'; see Mark 13:32-37; cf. Matt 24:43; Luke 12:39; 1 Thess 5:2; 5:4; Rev 3:3; 16:15). Peter often contrasts this new life with the old way of living in lust, passions, ungodliness, despising authority, and living as scoffers (2 Pet 1:4; 2:2-3, 7-8; 2:10-19; 3:3-7, which is very similar to 1 Peter).
- Such godliness is enabled by divine power (2 Pet 1:3) and by being able to partake of the divine nature, i.e., by receiving the Holy Spirit (2 Pet 1:4).
- In order to bear fruit (2 Pet 1:8), we must pursue godliness, which includes virtue, knowledge, steadfastness, brotherly affection, and love (2 Pet 1:5-7).[41]

---

[38] See Helyer, *Life*, 124–25, and esp. M.J. Harris, *Jesus as God: The New Testament Use of Theos in Reference to Jesus* (Grand Rapids, MI: Baker, 1992), 229–38.

[39] Based on 2 Pet 1:10, there is no conditional salvation implied in 1:11 and 2:20; cf. Phil 2:12-13.

[40] See, however, R.F. Zehnle, *Peter's Pentecost Discourse: Tradition and Lukan Reinterpretation in Peter's Speeches of Acts 2 and 3* (Nashville, TN: Abingdon, 1971), 73, who demonstrates that this type of connection is *not* unique to Acts and 2 Peter.

[41] The compact list in 2 Pet 1:5-7 describes *consequences* of the impact of Petrine core characteristics, since 2 Pet 1:3 states that God's power (i.e., to transform hearts) provides everything that is necessary for 'life and godliness'.

Besides seeking godliness, other core characteristics that we highlighted in Mark's Gospel, the Petrine sections in Acts, and in 1 Peter arise, such as faith (2 Pet 1:8), obedience in self-control (with brotherly love), witness in a decaying and sinful world, and overcoming in suffering and temptation (steadfastness).

Peter stirs up the believers by means of reminding, admonishing, and encouraging (2 Pet 1:13-14; 3:1-2). He motivates them especially by reminding them about the foundation of their faith in the person of Jesus.[42]

The Dynamic between Christology, Identity, and Character Formation in 1 and 2 Peter

We encounter a rich interplay between Christology, identity, and character formation in 1 and 2 Peter. We note the following explicit connections between Christology, identity, and character formation, especially in 1 Peter:

1. *Suffering and witness of godliness:* Christ's suffering is foundational and serves as a basis for—and as an example of—submission to God's will in the midst of suffering and shame (1 Pet 2:21, 23; 4:1, 13-14; 2 Pet 1:9; 2:1; cf. Heb 11:25-26). As Jesus did not revile in suffering (1 Pet 2:23-24), so his followers, loved and precious (e.g., 1 Pet 2:9-10), should bear insult, slander, and hatred for Christ's sake (see especially 1 Pet 4:13-14, 16).[43] Disciples must follow in Christ's footsteps (ἴχνεσιν) even into suffering (1 Pet 2:21; 4:1) and thus spread the good news (1 Pet 1:12; cf. 2 Pet 3:13).
2. *Rejection by opponents of God*: Jesus, the living stone, is rejected by some and accepted by others (1 Pet 2:4, 6-7; Acts 4:11; cf. Ps 118:22; Isa 8:14; 28:16). The disciples are, likewise, rejected or accepted living stones, built into a spiritual house (1 Pet 2:5).
3. *Honored by God*: The disciples are honored by God through believing and confessing the vindicated and honored Jesus (1 Pet 2:7).
4. *Judged/chastised by God:* Judgment begins with the house of God; Jesus had to drink the cup of judgment first (Mark 10:38); the disciples are subsequently chastised (1 Pet 4:17-18; see Mark 10:39; cf. Ezek 9:6).

---

[42] G. Green, *Jude and 2 Peter* (Grand Rapids, MI: Baker Academic, 2008), 206, 210–13, 309–13. See Helyer, *Life,* 162–83. The connections between Acts and 2 Peter are as follows: Acts 2:14-21/2 Pet 3:7-14 (eschatology); Acts 3:12-16/2 Pet 1:3 (*dynamis*/*eusebeia*); Acts 3:21-21/2 Pet 3:9. See 2 Pet 1:16-18 as characteristic Petrine tradition. Cf. Thiede, *Simon Peter,* 64, 112–13.

[43] See Helyer, *Life,* 163, on further details of the nature of suffering portrayed in 1 Peter.

5. *God sustains in adversity:* God's strengthening presence in adversity is seen both for Christ and his followers (1 Pet 5:10-11; 2 Pet 2:9).
6. *Hope and the coming of Christ:* The disciples are called to prayerful and hopeful sobriety at the imminence (but not immediacy) of the Parousia of Christ (1 Pet 4:7; 2 Pet 3:12; cf. Acts 3:19-20).

Surprisingly, we encounter in 1 and 2 Peter many christological emphases as well as identity and character traits which are very compatible with those isolated in Mark's Gospel, and, to a somewhat lesser degree, in Acts. We can thus state that *a specific cluster of christological, identity, and character formation features are identifiable in Peter's canonical testimony.* We will discuss this cluster of characteristics further in Chapters 8 and 9.[44]

---

[44] Even if we found that Paul emphasized similar traits of character formation, we content that he would have received such emphases from Peter (Gal 1:18) and other, early apostolic witnesses.

CHAPTER 8

Characteristic Dynamics between Christology, Identity, and Character Formation in Peter's Canonical Testimony

In the previous three chapters we have sought to identify specific and characteristic elements of Christology, identity, and character formation in Mark, the Petrine sections of Acts, and in 1 and 2 Peter, respectively. Now we seek to determine whether these respective marks are thematically compatible or fundamentally at odds with each other. As we draw on the results of the previous three chapters, a coherent synthesis will arise that demonstrates, above all, the *thematic axis* between 1 Peter and the Gospel of Mark, but also the further Petrine emphases isolated in the Petrine sections of Acts and 2 Peter.

The Thematic Cohesion of Peter's Testimony Despite the Virtual Absence of Literary Indicators[1]

It is readily apparent that a connection between the Gospel of Mark and 1 Peter cannot be demonstrated by means of *literary* (especially lexical, grammatical, and stylistic) evidence.[2] Direct literary connections between Mark and 1 Peter are found only between Mark 10:42/1 Peter 5:3 and Mark 16:16/1 Peter 3:21. There may be literary (or oral) connections between 1 Pet 4:14/Mark 3:28-30

---

[1] See R. Gundry, 'Verba Christi in 1 Peter: Their Implication Concerning the Authorship of 1 Peter and the Authenticity of the Gospel Tradition', *NTS* 13.4 (1966–1967), 336–50; E. Best, '1 Peter and the Gospel Tradition', *NTS* 16 (1969–1970), 95–113. See Gundry's response to Best in R. Gundry, 'Further Verba on Verba Christi in First Peter', *Bib* 55 (1974), 211–32.

[2] See the detailed discussion in Michaels, *1 Peter*, xli–xlii. Selwyn, *Epistle,* 27–33 does present, however, a significant list of literary connections between Mark and 1 Peter. Helyer, *Life,* 17, notes, e.g., that σταυρός neither occurs in the Petrine sections of Acts nor in 1 and 2 Peter, while σταυρόω does occur eight times in Mark's Gospel.

and 13:11, 1 Pet 5:8/Mark 13:37 and 14:37-38, 1 Pet 1:18/Mark 10:45, and 1 Pet 2:13-17/Mark 12:13-17. Generally speaking, there are stronger literary connections between 1 Peter and the writings of Matthew,[3] Luke, and John than between 1 Peter and the Gospel of Mark.[4] Michaels thus draws the following conclusion in his discussion of literary connections between the canonical Gospels and 1 Peter: 'The preceding examples demonstrate that, for the most part, the parallels in 1 Peter to the Gospel tradition are of the same type as in the letters of Paul'.[5] The paucity of literary connectors between Mark and 1 Peter is partially responsible for the fact that historically skeptical arguments could not be redressed in a convincing way. This pertains both to the patristic notion that Peter provided the content for Mark and the claim that 1 Peter was authored by the Apostle Peter. It is noteworthy, however, that we do have a number of *literary* connections between the Petrine sections in Acts and 1 Peter: compare Acts 4:11-13 with 1 Peter 2:4, 7 (the rejected stone metaphor, cf. Ps 118:22), and Acts 10:42 with 1 Peter 4:5-6.[6] See further Acts 2:36; 4:28; 10:41-42/1 Peter 1:2, *20*; Acts 3:5, 16; 4:10, 12; 5:41; 10:43/1 Peter 4:14, 16 (focus on the 'name of the Lord'); Acts 1:10/1 Peter 3:22; Acts 2:22-23/1 Peter 1:2, 20; Acts *3:14*/1 Peter 3:18; Acts 3:18/1 Pet 1:10-12 (fulfillment of OT messianic prophecies); Acts *5:32*/1 Peter 5:1; Acts *5:41*/1 Peter 4:13-14; Acts 10:34/1 Peter 1:17 (God shows no partiality); Acts *11:26*/1 Peter 4:16; Acts *12:12*/1 Peter 5:13-14; Acts 15:7/1 Peter 1:1; 2:9.[7]

---

[3] R. Metzner, *Die Rezeption des Matthäusevangeliums im 1. Petrusbrief: Studien zum traditionsgeschichtlichen und theologischen Einfluss des 1. Evangeliums auf den 1. Petrusbrief* (Tübingen: Mohr Siebeck, 1995).

[4] See details in Michaels, *1 Peter*, xli–xlii, Goppelt, *1 Peter*, 33–35 and Marshall, *1 Peter*, 20–21, 25–27. See, however, Selwyn, *Epistle*, 30.

[5] Michaels, *1 Peter*, xlii.

[6] See R.P. Martin, *New Testament Foundations* (Grand Rapids, MI: Eerdmans, 1987), I, 330–31.

[7] See Selwyn, *Epistle*, 33–38, regarding such possible *literary* connections between the Petrine material in Acts and 1 Pet. Selwyn argues that the evidence points toward a literary independence but a *commonality of person* writing in 1 Pet and speaking in Acts. Contrast this, e.g., with Schneider, *Apostelgeschichte*, I, 334, who considers much of the Petrine material in Acts to be Lukan redaction. Similar to Selwyn, see Thiede, *Simon Peter*, 64, 112–13, who lists further thematic similarities and parallels between the Petrine sections of Acts and 1 Pet. Connections between Acts and 1 Pet, not directly associated with the Petrine sections in Acts, are: Acts 7:52/1 Pet 1:11; Acts 14:15/1 Pet 1:18; Acts *15:27*/1 Pet 5:12; Acts *16:5*/1 Pet 5:9; Acts 16:34/1 Pet 1:8; Acts 17:30/1 Pet 1:14; Acts 20:28/1 Pet 5:2; Acts *23:1*/1 Pet 3:16, 21; Acts 25:16/1 Pet 3:15; Acts 26:18/1 Pet 2:9. From a redaction-critical standpoint this may be interpreted as evidence for Lukan composition. From a historical standpoint this may indicate that Peter's early Christian testimony framed and affected the Pauline witness, faithfully reflected by Luke (cf. Gal 1:18).

Here we seek to demonstrate, however, that despite the paucity of *literary* connections between the Gospel of Mark and 1 Peter, as well as a limited amount of literary connection between the Petrine sections in Acts and 1 and 2 Peter, the *thematic* cohesion (concept connections) in Peter's canonical testimony is, nevertheless, notable and compelling and thus substantially supportive of the patristic testimony.[8]

The Complementary Portraits of Peter

Before we trace characteristic dynamics between Christology, identity, and character formation in Peter's canonical testimony, a few comments on the portrait of Peter in the *testimonium* are in order. We note that, essentially, the portrait of Peter in the canonical Gospels dovetails with the portrait of Peter in Acts and in 1 and 2 Peter. Within the various portraits, we can discern a progressive movement toward maturity (from the Gospel of Mark, via Acts, to 1 and 2 Peter). This pertains especially to:

1. Peter as the *apostle*[9] of Jesus: Mark 3:14, 16; 6:30 (see also Luke 6:13; 9:10; 11:49-51; 17:5; 22:14; 24:10); Acts 1:2, 25-26; 2:37, 42-43; 4:33, 35-37; 5:2, 12, 18, 29, 40; 6:6; 8:1, 14, 18; 11:1; 15:2, 4, 6, 22-23; 1 Pet 1:1; 2 Pet 1:1; 3:2 (cf. 1 Cor 9:5; 15:5; Rev 21:14). As such, Peter 'watches' over himself and the people of God (1 Pet 5:8; contrast with Mark 14:37).
2. Peter as a key *witness*, especially of the suffering of Christ: Mark 14:1–16:8 (compare with Luke 24:48 and Acts 10:39, 41); Acts 1:8, 22; 2:32, 40; 3:15; 5:32; 10:39, 41; 1 Pet 5:1 (cf. Acts 13:31; Heb 2:4).
3. *Peter as the rock*: Matthew 16:18-19 (see 1 Pet 2:4-5); arising temporarily as an apostolic leader in Acts (Acts 2–5; 10; 11:16; 15:7-11),[10] and as a teacher in 1 and 2 Peter.
4. Peter as the *undershepherd of Christ's flock*:[11] Mark 9:33-37; 10:35-44; John 13:1-20; 21:15-17; 1 Pet 2:25; 5:1-4.
5. Peter as the *object of Satan's attack* (Mark 8:32-33), enduring much adversity (cf. Luke 22:31-32)[12] and opposition (concerning Acts, see above; 1 Pet 5:8).[13]

---

[8] Cf. Helyer, *Life*, 17.
[9] See A. Bash, *Ambassadors for Christ. An Exploration of Ambassadorial Language in the New Testament* (Tübingen: Mohr Siebeck, 1997).
[10] See Ridderbos, *Speeches*, 11.
[11] Michaels, *1 Peter*, xlii.
[12] Part of suffering includes the possibility of being 'sifted' by Satan (cf. Amos 9:9; 11QtgJob 10.2); cf. Bockmuehl, *Simon*, 120.
[13] See Michaels, *1 Peter*, xlii.

Characteristic Christological Connections in Peter's Testimony

We have already noted the fact that the *literary* connection, especially between Mark and 1 Peter is weak at best. It is noteworthy, however, that we are discovering, in support of Selwyn's suggestions, strong *thematic* connections between the Gospel of Mark, the Petrine sections in Acts, and 1 Peter with regard to Christology, identity, and character formation. Selwyn observes: 'The connexion . . . is not literary but historical: the common ground lies in the mind of St. Peter who gave, and was known to have given, teaching along these lines and to a great extent in these terms.'[14] This does not mean that the thematic connections to Matthew, Luke, and John are less so, since Peter experienced and learned what these three additional accounts testify to as well. What we are emphasizing is the *compatibility* between Mark and 1 Peter, *not the exclusive (especially literary) connection between them*. As we have already noted, these observations do not *prove* the Petrine origin of Mark's Gospel, the Petrine sections in Acts, or Petrine authorship of 1 and 2 Peter. Rather, our findings dovetail very well with the patristic and *canonical assertions* that Peter serves, in one way or another, as the source of the Gospel of Mark (written by John Mark), the Petrine sections of Acts (written by Luke), as well as 1 and 2 Peter (written respectively by Silas/Silvanus and probably an unnamed *amanuensis*; cf. 2 Pet 1:1; 3:1). We believe that our findings demonstrate the deep compatibility of material in the New Testament which is, according to patristic evidence, associated with Peter. In other words: we find strong *material* support for Peter as the source of canonical testimony[15] attributed to him, despite meager to modest literary evidence.

Before we begin the discussion of christological connections in Peter's canonical testimony, it is important to stress that Peter, along with all New Testament witnesses, subscribes to a redemptive-historical framework within which God's grand mission with his creation is realized. Be it his testimony to Jesus via John Mark, or his speeches in Acts or 1 and 2 Peter, the backdrop of Peter's teaching is always God's creation and redemption, pursued with Israel and now continued with his redeemed people, consisting of Jews and Gentiles. Christology, identity, and character formation always operate within this framework. Peter would have learned aspects of this framework in synagogue

---

[14] Selwyn, *Epistle*, 33–38. See G. Maier, 'Jesustradition im 1. Petrusbrief?', *Gospel Perspective* (Sheffield: JSOT Press, 1984), V, 85–128, regarding gospel material in the Petrine Epistle.

[15] The proximity between Peter and the content of Mark's Gospel in no way excludes the likelihood that Matthew, e.g., adds much reliable information about Peter; cf. Bockmuehl, *Simon*, 88.

school and from the Old Testament; it would have been reinforced by his teacher and master.

In the following section, we will pay particular attention to christological connections in Peter's canonical testimony. We note the following christological motifs:

- Peter's Christology is thoroughly rooted in a *monotheistic (Deut 6:4) and Trinitarian (cf., e.g., Mark 1:10-11; 9:7; Acts 3:13; 1 Pet 1:2)* framework. God is the Father of Jesus: Mark 1:11; 9:7; 13:32; Acts 2:22-32; *3:13-14*, 15-26; 4:24; 11:9; 1 Pet 1:3; *3:18*.[16] The Holy Spirit is promised by the Father (Joel 2:32 MT/Acts 2:21) and mediated by the Son (Mark 1:8; Acts 2:33; 3:16, 20). The Spirit of Christ worked through the Old Testament prophets and the Holy Spirit now works in the gospel proclamation of its fulfillment (1 Pet 1:11-12; see also 2 Pet 1:21 and see below). Jesus is the exalted (Acts 2:33; 5:31) mediator of the Father's will (Mark 9:2-8; Acts 2:22; 3:13, 15, 18, 20-21, 26; 4:12, 27-28; 10:38, 40, 42; 1 Pet 1:10-12, 20).

- *Prophecies* concerning the rejection and suffering of Christ which were given in the Old Testament by the Spirit of Christ (Acts 3:19-21; 10:43; 1 Pet 1:11; see also 1 Pet 2:21) are taken up by the earthly Jesus (Mark 8:31; 9:31: 10:32-34, 45 [Isa 53/Dan 9]; Mark 14:1–16:8; see Acts 2:24-31, 39, and especially Acts 10:43).[17] Jobes emphasizes regarding Peter's approach to the Old Testament in 1 Peter that a guiding principle is that the (implied) preexistent Christ (Spirit of Christ) was operative in the Old Testament prophets (1 Pet 1:10-12).[18] This unites God's work as narrated in the Old Testament with God's ongoing mission since the incarnation of Christ: in 1 Peter there is thus a theological continuity from the Old to the New Testament in the agency of the person of Christ, before, during, and after his earthly life. Old Testament Scriptures, as prophecy, are being fulfilled (compare Acts 1:16, 20 [Ps 118:22 in Acts 4:11; Mark 12:10-11] with 1 Pet 2:6-7) and the patriarch David is identified as a prophet (Acts 1:16; [cf. 2:16, 18]; Acts 2:29; Acts 2:30-31; [see 4:25]; compare with Acts 2:25-28/Ps 16:8-11; Acts 2:31/Ps 16:10; Acts 2:34-35/Ps 110:1; see Acts 3:18).

---

[16] See Maier, 'Jesustradition', 97, 105; Selwyn, *Epistle*, 33–36; 72–81; E. Lohse, 'Paränese und Kerygma im 1. Petrusbrief', *ZNW* 45.1 (1954), 70; A.M. Stibbs, *The First Epistle General of Peter: An Introduction and Commentary* (Grand Rapids, MI: Eerdmans, 1988), 35.

[17] D.A. Carson (ed.), *The Scriptures Testify about Me: Jesus and the Gospel in the Old Testament* (Wheaton, IL: Crossway, 2013).

[18] Jobes, *1 Peter*, 52.

This emphasizes God's foreknowledge and foreordination. The significance of Scripture as the word of God is highlighted throughout and thus continues its Old Testament emphasis (cf. Deut 8:3; Pss 19:7-14; 119:9-11).

- Cullmann rightly observes that Peter *'was the first one to grasp'* the atoning significance of Jesus's death: 'I think that here too he should be given a place of honour at the beginning of all Christian theology'.[19] Christ, the innocent one, bore our sins on the cross (Mark 14:1–16:8; Acts 2:11 [mighty works of God]; Acts 1:10-12; [2:18]; 2:21-24; 3:18; 1 Pet 2:22-24). His flesh did not see corruption (Acts 2:31; see also 2:27; 1 Pet 3:18). Especially 1 Peter's characteristic emphasis on Isaiah 52:13–53:12 (see esp. 1 Pet 2:21-25, but also 1 Pet 1:11; 3:18; 4:13) is strikingly compatible with the λύτρον-saying in Mark 10:45. There the Son of Man gives his life as a ransom for many, reflecting Isa 53:10-12 (esp. v. 11, suffering 'for many'). Contrast this with Peter's initial rejection of the necessity of Jesus's death in Mark 8:32 (see 1 Pet 1:18-19; Mark 14:22-24). Note the Petrine Suffering Servant references (*Ebed YHWH*=παῖς θεοῦ) in Acts (Acts 3:13/Isa 52:13; Acts 3:26; Acts 4:27, 30/Isa 53:11b; cf. Peter's statements in Acts 2:23, 32-33, 36; 3:13, 18; 4:27-30). Many of the most significant New Testament references to Isaiah 53 are thus, at least indirectly, associated with Peter: besides Mark 10:45, see Mark 9:12/Isa 53:3; Mark 14:24/Isa 53:11-12; Mark 15:27/Isa 53:12; *1 Pet 2:21-25/Isa 53:4-6, 9, 12*; cf. Acts 3:13/Isa 52:13). Even the reference to Isaiah 53:12 in Luke 22:37 (being counted among the lawless) is also found in 1 Peter 2:24.[20] See also 1 Peter 3:10-12/Ps 34:12-16 and 1 Peter 4:18/Proverbs 11:31. Cullmann notes regarding the *unique* Suffering Servant passages in the early chapters of Acts: 'This confirms the existence of a very early Christology on the basis of which Jesus was called *ebed Yahweh*';[21] '[T]he Christology of the apostle Peter . . . was quite probably dominated by the concept of the *ebed Yahweh*'.[22] Jobes[23] emphasizes that 'Peter exegetes Jesus' death in light of Isa. 53 – and not vice versa'. However, Jesus

---

[19] Cullmann, *Peter*, 67.

[20] Additional, important allusions to Isa 53 are found in Luke 24:25; John 12:38; cf. Matt 8:17/Isa 53:4; Acts 8:30-35, esp. v. 32/Isa 53:7-8; Rom 10:16/Isa 53:1; Rev 14:5/Isa 53:9).

[21] Cullmann, *Peter*, 68.

[22] Cullmann, *Peter*, 69.

[23] Jobes, *1 Peter*, 51, with reference to Selwyn, *Epistle*, 91, Achtemeier, *1 Peter,* 193, and Goppelt, *1 Peter*, 211. See also B. Janowski and P. Stuhlmacher (eds), *Der leidende Gottesknecht: Jesaja 53 und seine Wirkungsgeschichte mit einer Bibliographie zu Jesaja 53* (Tübingen: Mohr Siebeck, 1996).

already 'exegetes' his own death in light of Isaiah 53 (see Mark 10:45). Salvation and forgiveness of sins (Acts 2:14-36, 38, 40; 3:19; 4:12; 5:31; 8:22; 10:39, 43; 11:14; see Mark 11:25) have a universal reach (Mark 13:10; Acts 3:25; 4:12; 10:34-35, 43, 45; 11:18; 1 Pet 2:7, 10; 3:18, 21). Jobes aptly notes: '(i)ronically, the suffering of Christ has become central to the Christology of the apostle who most strongly objected to Jesus's predictions of his death (Mark 8:31-33)'.[24]

- We find *vivid predictions and descriptions of the resurrection of Jesus* (Mark 8:31; 9:31; 10:32-34; 16:1-8; Acts 1:22; 2:23-32; 3:15; 4:10; 5:30; 10:38-41; 1 Pet 1:3, 21; 3:21).[25] The fact of the resurrection of Jesus (1 Cor 15:5) necessitates that his crucifixion take on a new meaning for the 'judgment of God', that is, substitutionary judgment.
- The *Parousia of Jesus* is emphasized (Mark 8:38; 13:26; Acts 1:11; 1 Pet 1:13; 4:7; see also 2 Pet 1:16). As we have seen in Peter's early speeches in Jerusalem (Acts 2 and 3) as well as in Mark 13, Peter does not subscribe to a form of near-expectation; rather, he reinforces Jesus's perspective of the redemptive-historical progression of event-sequences, which, due to the death and resurrection of Jesus, give rise to an expectation of imminence without leading to the heterodox fallacy of temporal immediacy (cf. 2 Thess 2:3-4). Ever since the death and resurrection of Jesus, the end is near (1 Pet 4:7); simultaneously, it could take a long time before Christ returns (2 Pet 3:8).
- There is the *assurance of seeing the radiant glory* of Jesus (Mark 8:38; 9:2-8; 12:35-37; 14:62; Acts 3:13; 1 Pet 1:21).
- The *word of God as the 'imperishable seed'* is emphasized (Mark 4:1-20; 13:31; Acts 4:31; 6:2, 4; 1 Pet 1:23-25; compare with Isa 40:8).
- Jesus, the living stone, *was rejected by some and accepted by others* (Mark 12:10-12; Acts 4:11; 1 Pet 2:4, 6-8 [Ps 118:22; Isa 8:14; 28:16]; compare with Eph 2:20).
- Christ was *exalted at the right hand of God* (Mark 8:38; 12:35-37; 14:62; Acts 2:30; 1 Pet 1:7, 11, 21; 2:6-7; 3:22; 4:5, 11, 13; 5:1, 4, 6, 10; 2 Pet 1:11, 16-18; 3:10, 18). The fact that Jesus now sits on the throne of David (Acts 2:30-31; cf. Luke 1:32-33) accords with Mark 11:17 and 13:10 (the universal reach of the gospel; compare with Mark 7:27) and dovetails well with 1 Peter's emphasis that the followers of Christ are dispersed sojourners (see below). The exaltation of Christ is the source of great hope for the disciples (Acts 2:33-36; 1 Pet 3:22; 4:11).

---

[24] Jobes, *1 Peter*, 192.
[25] See Jobes, *1 Peter*, 51–52.

- Jesus will come *as judge* (Mark 8:38; Acts 4:23; 10:42; 1 Pet 4:5 [God?]).
- Pentecost marks the *beginning of the end times* (Acts 2:17, 21, 38; 1 Pet 1:10-13; 2:12; 4:5, 13; 5:1, 4, 6, 10; 2 Pet 1:19; 3:1-15; cf. Mark 13:11, 14, 31).

Titular Christology focuses on the following:

a. Jesus as Lord (κύριος): Mark 12:36-37 and 14:62-63 (note the mixed reference to the Son of Man and the Lord of David [Ps 110:1/Dan 7:13-14]); Mark 12:35-37 (cf. Ps 110:1, 5); Mark 8:38 (note the exalted Son of Man [Dan 7:13-14]); Acts 2:21, 36; Acts 26:11; 1 Peter 1:3; 3:15; 2 Peter 1:2, 8, 11, 14, 16; 2:20; 3:2, 18. See the phrase 'calling on the name of the Lord', i.e., calling on YHWH=Jesus, in order to be saved: Acts 2:21; 4:12 (cf. Acts 9:5).

b. Jesus as Messiah, Christ (χριστός): see especially Mark 8:29-31; Acts 2:36; 3:20; 9:22; 1 Peter 1:1-3, 7, 11, 13, 19; 2:5, 21; 3:15, 18; 4:1 (and often).[26]

c. The New Testament references to the *Servant* (παῖς) *of God* (*Ebed YHWH*) are relatively rare. Since Peter, however, frequently speaks of Jesus in this way we are probably dealing with Petrine bedrock (see above). As stated above, the Servant of YHWH section in Isaiah 52:13–53:12 was probably interpreted in a messianic way, at least to a degree, at the time of Christ.[27] See also, indirectly, 1 Peter 2:22-25.

d. Besides Acts 3:15 and 5:31, the New Testament contains the reference to *Prince* or *Author* (of Life) only in Hebrews 2:10 and 12:2. While ἀρχηγός could mean *source* or *origin* in Acts 3:15, it is probable that *leader* or *head* is implied here on account of the material proximity of this usage to Acts 5:31 (see above). See also 1 Peter 3:7 and 2 Peter 1:3.

e. While salvation is a highly significant theme in Luke–Acts, the noun *Savior* as a title of Jesus only occurs twice in Acts (Acts 5:31; cf. 13:23). Salvation has different consequences, such as forgiveness of sins (Acts 5:31) and deliverance from oppression (Acts 13:23, as suggested by the context).

f. Unique to the New Testament is the identification of Jesus as the *Prophet like Moses* (Acts 3:22-23; cf. Acts 7:37 and Luke 7:16), referring to Deuteronomy 18:15, 18. The context of Deuteronomy 18 is that the Israelites are not to practice sorcery to divine God's will. Rather, God will raise a Prophet like Moses, to whom the people are to listen. Qumran features a messianic interpretation of Deuteronomy 18:15 in 4QTest 5-7

---

[26] Cf. Helyer, *Life*, 143–46, regarding details on Jesus as Messiah in 1 Pet. According to Helyer (p. 144), the following occurrences in 1 Pet display the use of 'Messiah' as a title: 1 Pet 2:21; 3:15, 18; 4:1.

[27] See Cullmann, *Peter*, 68–69.

(see also 1QS 9:10-11), thus documenting the messianic expectation of such a prophetic figure. See Mark 6:4, 15; 1 Peter 1:11 (the Spirit of Jesus as the supreme origin of OT prophetic speech).

g. The phrase *Holy One* may connote divine prerogatives (Acts 3:14). Note the emphasis on the righteousness of a messianic king in Isaiah 32:1 (see 2 Sam 23:3). See Mark 10:45 and 1 Peter 1:19; 2:22-24.[28]

h. The title *Nazarene* (Acts 2:22; 3:6; 4:10; 6:14; 10:38; see Acts 22:8; 26:9) primarily refers to Jesus's town of origin. See Mark 1:9, 24; 10:47; 14:67; 16:6.

i. Peter also refers to Jesus as *Judge* (Mark 8:38; 14:62; Acts 10:42; 1 Pet 4:5; compare with 1 Pet 1:17; Acts 17:31), as well as *Son of David* (Mark 10:47-48; 11:10; see 12:35-37; Acts 1:16; 2:25, 29-31, 34; see Acts 4:25).

Characteristic, Christ-Centered Identity and Character Formation according to Peter's Testimony

In the previous chapters we have asked which elements of identity and character formation are particularly emphasized in Mark, the Petrine sections of Acts, and 1 and 2 Peter respectively. We are now in a position to compare our results to see how they complement—or differ from—each other.

On account of the lack of literary evidence in support of the axis of Mark–1 Peter, as well as other elements of Peter's canonical testimony, even conservative studies on this issue have focused nearly exclusively on historical and christological aspects linking Peter's canonical testimony (see, e.g., Selwyn). Regarding historical aspects, scholars present various arguments in support of the reliability of patristic claims that Peter is indeed the source of the Gospel of Mark[29] and the author of 1 Peter[30], and that he is reliably represented in Luke's account in Acts. At times, christological observations concerning Peter's canonical testimony supplement such studies (see our own arguments presented above). While these historical and thematic (Christology) connections are indeed very significant, we argue in the present study that the additional thematic connections within Peter's canonical testimony, especially

---

[28] *First En.* 38:2 uses the honorific *the Righteous* to describe the messiah. In *1 En.* 46:3, the Son of Man is *righteous*.

[29] See Bayer, *Theology*, 159–80, Bauckham, *Eyewitnesses*, 93–154, and esp. 155–201; Riesner, 'Rückkehr', 337–52.

[30] Compare Jobes, *1 Peter*, 6–19 and Marshall, *1 Peter*, 21–25 with Selwyn, *Epistle*, 7–38.

with regard to identity and character formation, are conspicuous and can thus complement historical and christological studies.

Most surprisingly, the similarities of marks of Christian identity and character are not apparent on the surface of Peter's canonical testimony, especially between Mark and 1 Peter. These characteristics only arise in their significance when intentionally and systematically researched. Once Petrine characteristics of identity and character formation are considered in *conjunction* with the important historical and christological indicators noted above, *a considerable thematic bond* within Peter's canonical testimony arises. On the other hand, we stress, once again, that the observations presented in this study do not unequivocally prove that Peter is the source of the canonical testimony attributed to him. This holds true because the christological, identity, and character formation characteristics isolated in the present study are sufficiently generic that they do not demonstrate an exclusive link within the canonical testimony attributed to Peter.[31] On the other hand, notable inter-connections between Christology, identity, and character formation, complemented by historical evidence in support of Peter's canonical testimony, strongly suggest that the historical person of Peter does indeed lie behind it.

Identity Formation in Peter's Canonical Testimony

Before we present a synthetic view of identity formation according to the canonical testimony of Peter, we need to pursue the initial question of what 'following Jesus' means to Peter. Obviously, being a 'follower' of Jesus is a rudimentary identity marker in its own right.

'Following Jesus' in Mark, Acts, and 1 Peter

In a simple comparison between Mark, the Petrine sections of Acts, and 1 and 2 Peter concerning the question of what it means to follow Jesus, Peter has no apparent difficulty in moving from a literal sense of following/walking behind Jesus (e.g., Mark 1:17) to a different framework of 'following' the exalted Jesus (see 1 Pet 2:21: 'so that you might *follow* in his steps', ἵνα ἐπακολουθήσητε τοῖς ἴχνεσιν αὐτοῦ; compare with Acts 5:29, 32; 1 Pet 4:17; cf. Zeph 1:6). Bockmuehl notes: 'Christ's suffering as exemplary . . . has repeatedly been linked to the Synoptics and, interestingly, perhaps also should be linked to the Petrine speeches in Acts'.[32] In 1 Peter 2:21, Peter emphasizes

---

[31] Note the various common theological threads linking Peter, John, and Paul, as presented, e.g., by Helyer, *Life*, 199–203, and I.H. Marshall, *New Testament Theology: Many Witnesses, One Gospel* (Downers Grove, IL: IVP, 2004), 695–98.

[32] Bockmuehl, *Simon*, 31.

one aspect of following Jesus, namely, the pattern-imitation of the suffering of Christ (see 1 Pet 1:19-20). This phenomenon is already present, e.g., in Mark 9:33-37; 10:35-44; cf. John 13:1-20. One reason for this apparently easy transition lies in the fact that 'following Jesus' in Mark—that is, during Jesus's earthly life—already goes far beyond a literal walking behind/with Jesus. As we have argued elsewhere,[33] following Jesus in Mark encompasses a radical transformational process involving the whole person which affects personal identity and the relationship with God, self, and others, as well as decisions in concrete ethical circumstances. The catalyst for such transformation is always Jesus, either during his earthly life or as exalted Lord. *Following Jesus* in Mark thus already leads to thinking, feeling, and behaving in utter dependence upon Jesus, whether he is physically present or not (see 'following the Lord' in the wilderness, Deut 1:32-33, and esp. 1:36, regarding Caleb's entry into the promised land: διὰ τὸ προσκεῖσθαι ['utterly cling to'] αὐτὸν τὰ πρὸς κύριον).[34]

Since Jesus *continues* his work subsequent to his resurrection and exaltation (see Acts 1:1; 2:33; 3:16) by means of the presence of the Holy Spirit, it follows that Jesus's transformational impact on his disciples continues as well. We could, to a degree, argue that following Jesus after his ascension is 'easier' than during his earthly life (see John 16:7) for the following reasons: at a certain point, disciples of Jesus will have the scriptural accounts (in the form of the NT, supplementing the OT), pointing them comprehensively to who Jesus is; after Pentecost, the disciples have the *residing* gift of the Holy Spirit (John 14:15-28; 16:7-15), affirming Jesus, his word, and his mission and applying his mission to the disciples' hearts. The blueprint of radical and holistic discipleship encountered in Mark thus continues in the work and purposes of the exalted Christ until his Parousia. In other words, the transition from literally walking behind Jesus to a comprehensive dependence upon the exalted Jesus, mediated by the presence of the Holy Spirit, is not insurmountable for Peter: the same person who literally 'followed behind the master' (Gospel of Mark) now speaks of 'following in the footsteps of the master' (1 Pet 2:21; cf. Deut 1:36), although the master is no longer visible.

Identity Formation of the Disciples

We begin by comparing various references to the identity formation in Peter's canonical testimony, since identity formation always serves as the foundation for character formation in Jesus's call to discipleship. In such a synthetic view,

---

[33] Bayer, *Theology*, 61–124.
[34] See Wilkins, *Following*, 51–97, regarding 'following the Lord' in the OT and 'discipleship-patterns' in extrabiblical documents.

Acts will contribute less to the issue of identity formation than will Mark and 1 and 2 Peter, since Peter is publicly communicating and exemplifying in Acts the fundamental tenets of the Christian faith. Peter's canonical testimony displays the following emphases concerning the identity formation of the disciples of Jesus.

Foundational is the fact that *Jesus causes a double-crisis of self- and God-perception in his followers* (see esp. Mark 4–8). Jesus 'deconstructs' various fixed perspectives of his disciples which oppose the redemptive purposes of God (see above). In the book of Acts we encounter a God-trusting and God-dependent person in Peter, who witnesses boldly to who Christ claimed to be in the face of death. Peter displays a dependable character, increasingly tested and purified through suffering and opposition. He attributes greater importance to obedience to God than to civil authorities. Particular aspects include:

a. The disciples are scattered *sojourners*: Mark 8:34-37; 10:29-31, 35-44; 13:9, 11, 13, 19; Acts 4:25-30 (incl. Ps 2:1); 5:41; 12:11 (rescued from the hand of Herod); 1 Peter 1:1, 6-7, 17; 2:1 (see below the 'purifying suffering of the sojourning people of God'; cf. Mark 10:35-44).
b. The disciples are people who *hope in the future culmination* of (present) salvation: Mark 10:45; 13:13, 20; Acts 2:21; 1 Peter 1:5, 9.
c. The disciples are *ransomed people* through the blood of Jesus: Mark 10:45; 14:22-25; Acts 2:21, 38, 40; 3:19; 4:12; 5:31; 10:43 (focus on 'saved' and 'forgiven'); 15:8-9, 11 (v. 9, 'God . . . having cleansed their hearts by faith'; v. 11, 'we will be saved through the grace of the Lord Jesus'; cf. Jer 31:31-34); 1 Peter 1:2, 18-19; cf. Luke 5:8. As such, they have been *rebirthed imperishably* (1 Pet 1:3, 23), they have received an *imperishable inheritance* (1 Pet 1:4), and they are now members of a *new family* (1 Pet 2:17).
d. The disciples exist in the midst of a *battle* between purity of heart on the one hand and impurity and immorality on the other: Mark 4:1-20; 7:1-22 (compare especially 1 Pet 2:1 with Mark 7:22-23); Mark 8:17-21; Acts 5:3; 1 Pet 1:22; 2:1, 11; 4:3-4, 15.
e. The disciples are *living stones*, being built into a spiritual house as a holy and royal priesthood (1 Pet 2:5, 9). This is already implied in Mark 11:1-25; see Acts 1:5; 2:4, 38; 5:32; 10:45; 11:17, 18 ('repentance that leads to life'); 15:8 (see Eph 2:21-22; they have the gift of Holy Spirit; note the connection between the temple motif and the presences of the Holy Spirit). As such, they are a witness to Christ (Acts 1:8, 22; 4:13, 20, 33; 1 Pet 2:5).
f. The disciples are a *chosen, elect race*: Mark 4:10-12; 6:34; 13:20, 22, 27; Acts 3:25-26 (blessed 'sons . . . of the covenant' [Abrahamic], Gen 12:3; 22:18); see Acts 1:2; 10:41 ('chosen' as apostles); 1 Peter 1:14; 2:9-10.
g. The disciples are a *possession* of God: Mark 8:34-37; compare with Acts 4:19; 5:29, 32 (we must obey God rather than men); 1 Peter 2:9; 3:1, 20; 4:17.

h. The disciples constitute *God's* Jewish (and, later, Gentile) *people*; Mark 3:33-35 (the messianic family of God); Mark 13:10; Acts 15:7-11, 14 (Gentiles are included [no distinction, Acts 15:9], based on faith alone [Acts 15:11], without circumcision, see Amos 9:11-12); 1 Peter 2:10.
i. *Without Christ* the disciples were like *scattered sheep*: Mark 14:27; see Acts 8:32, as well as Acts 8:1, 4; 11:19. Now, they have returned to the shepherd and guardian of their souls (1 Pet 2:25; 5:4).

We have noted that Jesus intentionally leads his disciples into a double-crisis of self- and God-perception (see especially Mark 4 and 6–8) in order to confront them with reality from the vantage point of God. Jesus resolves this double crisis by means of his substitutionary atonement, which reconciles his disciples (and all believing followers of Christ) with their Creator and restores them from autonomy to God-dependence (see 1 Pet 3:18) in all crucial relationship dynamics. We have argued that Peter implies in Acts and in his first Epistle that Christ's substitutionary atonement was crucial because of the severe human condition of alienation from and enmity toward God (Acts 2:38, 40; 3:19; 5:31; 1 Pet 2:21-25; 3:18). Out of this restoration grows a life-changing and healing involvement with the true God. This is expressed in ongoing obedience and a realization of our human condition and existence as deeply loved by our Creator but seriously broken and thus in profound need of transformation and character formation. In our analyses of the Petrine sections of Acts and of 1 Peter, we found that Peter bases identity formation squarely on Christ's atoning work. In this sense, he reflects the resolution of the double crisis of self-perception and God-perception, which we already found in the Gospel of Mark. In Acts and 1 Peter, such dependence upon Christ serves as the irrevocable foundation of any spiritual growth. Especially according to 1 Peter, the identity of a regenerate disciple (1 Pet 1:3) is now shaped by his dependence upon and relationship with Christ and subsequently guided especially by Jesus's power and example. Additionally, all of this occurs in the context of facilitative and purifying suffering, as is apparent in Mark, the Petrine sections of Acts, and in 1 Peter (see below).[35]

Character Formation in Peter's Testimony

Followers of Christ receive a new identity both individually and communally. As such, much of maturing in character formation occurs in the nexus of community and relationships. The community and various relationships serve as the framework of shaping and growth.

---

[35] See C.H. Talbert, *Learning Through Suffering: The Educational Value of Suffering in the New Testament and in Its Milieu* (Collegeville, MN: Liturgical Press, 1991).

We now bring together key elements of character formation as found in Peter's canonical testimony.[36] The composite list represents the calculated, approximate ranks derived from our respectively ranked lists of character traits isolated in Mark, the Petrine sections in Acts, and 1 Peter (see the three previous chapters). Surprisingly, there is a high degree of compatibility between these respectively ranked lists. As we compare and combine the lists of character formation traits in ranked form,[37] we gain the following overall results for the *testimonium Petrinum*:

1. *Faith (and trust)*[38]   rank 2-3-1[39] (ø 2)
2. *Witness*   rank 6-1-3 (ø 3.33)
3. *Seeking purity of heart (watching over temptation)*   rank 3-4-4 (ø 3.66)
4. *Humility*   rank 4-5-2 (ø 3.66)
5. *Overcoming in suffering, trials, and persecution*   rank 5-2-5 (ø 4)
6. *Surrender and obedience*   rank 1-6-6 (ø 4.33)

The additional significant characteristics of prayer,[40] forgiveness,[41] love, and being prepared for Jesus's Parousia[42] are present in Mark, the Petrine sections of Acts, and 1 and 2 Peter as well, but they are less emphasized. As we stated above, we are not seeking to isolate *all* character traits highlighted by Peter. Rather, we seek to *focus* on the most frequently mentioned characteristics in

---

[36] The gift of *repentance* is a precondition of growth in character formation. See, e.g., Acts 2:38; 3:19, 26; 5:31; 8:22; 11:18 (repentance that leads to a godly, honest life; cf. Mark 1:14-15).

[37] We ranked according to the respective frequency and *approximate* amount of verses used in each occurrence, regarding Mark, the Petrine sections in Acts, and 1 Peter. For the present purpose, we consider 2 Peter as reinforcing the characteristics isolated in 1 Peter.

[38] In this study, we encounter *prayer* as the *vade me cum* of faith. Where there is the character trait of faith, there is likewise the expression of prayer. The gift of faith also assumes the gift of *repentance* with ensuing forgiveness in Christ (Acts 10:43), *surrender* and obedience (1 Pet 1:2; cf. Rom 1:5; 6:16; 16:26).

[39] The first rank-number pertains to Mark, the second to the Petrine sections of Acts, the third to 1 Peter, respectively; for instance, 'faith (and trust)' is ranked '2-3-1', i.e., it has rank #2 in Mark's ranked list, rank #3 in the Petrine sections of Acts, and rank #1 in 1 Peter's ranked list. The ø is 2, thus rendering 'faith' the top ranked category (#1) in the composite, canonical Petrine testimony. The resulting figures are *approximate*.

[40] See, e.g., Acts 1:14, 24; 2:42; 3:1; 4:31.

[41] See, e.g., Mark 11:25; Acts 2:38.

[42] See, e.g., Mark 8:38; 13:26; 33-37; 1 Pet 1:7, 13; 4:7; 5:4, 10-11.

order to gain a fundamental orientation for character formation in individual and communal discipleship.[43]

While we are indeed surprised by the amount of compatible connections between the Gospel of Mark, the Petrine sections in Acts, and 1 and 2 Peter (and, to a degree, by the other canonical Gospels),[44] we also note some differences in emphasis. A particular characteristic of 1 Peter, not found as much in Mark or the Petrine sections in Acts, is the emphasis on living and suffering as *dispersed sojourners* (see, however, the important parallel in Mark 10:29-30 and Peter's missional mobility in Acts). On the other hand, *surrender* and radically *following Christ* are particularly emphasized and developed in Mark, while not missing in 1 Peter and the Petrine sections of Acts. Finally, we encounter in Acts, as would be expected, a significant focus on *witness* and *overcoming in trials*.

The surprising echo in 1 Peter of Mark's eight core characteristics and those found in the Petrine sections of Acts regarding aspects of character formation lends profound emphasis to these particular characteristics, shaping disciples of Christ individually and corporately. These traits of character formation arise from a new, developing identity marked by an individual and communal, reconciled relationship with God through Christ's unique atonement, example, and teaching. Such a conspicuous convergence between Mark, the Petrine sections in Acts, and 1 Peter highlights the common foundation of spiritual maturity and the six characteristics of character formation. As already stated, the connection is not so much literary as it is content-driven. It gives us a focused answer to the question of which traits of character formation in a disciple and, thus, in a Christian community, are highlighted in Peter's canonical testimony.

---

[43] From there, we would need to further examine other character traits mentioned in 2 Pet, as well as, e.g., the Sermon on the Mount (Matt 5–7), the entire Pauline *corpus*, and James.

[44] Most of these character formation elements also arise in Matthew (with a focus on ethical consequences), Luke (with a focus on social consequences), and John (with a focus on life and relational consequences). These Gospels generally appear to reinforce the eight core characteristics isolated in Mark. However, Luke appears to add a further core characteristic of radically sharing (renouncing?) resources and/or possessions in dependency upon God (Luke 14:33; cf. Matt 19:16-29; Mark 10:17-30; Luke 10:25-28; 18:18-30). This character trait requires a particularly careful exploration, especially when compared with similar statements in 1 Pet (and James). See, e.g., C. Blomberg, *Neither Poverty nor Riches: A Biblical Theology of Possessions* (Downers Grove, IL: IVP, 2001).

The Dynamic between Christology, Identity, and Character Formation according to Peter's Testimony

We note some explicit *connections* between Christology, identity, and character formation between Mark, Acts, and 1 and 2 Peter.

1. *A comprehensive theology of the cross*, including its effect on soteriology, serves as the foundation for a godly life. Jesus died on our behalf; the personal ramifications arise in 'dying to sin', very similar to Mark 10:35-44; Jesus came to serve and to atone (Mark 10:45); the disciples are to 'bear their daily cross' by surrendering their primary loyalty to self in exchange for loyalty to Christ[45] (Mark 8:34; 1 Pet 2:21; 4:1) and serve as a consequence (Mark 9:33-37; 10:35-44; see both Peter's demeanor in the Petrine sections of Acts and 1 Pet 2:18-25).

2. *Christ's suffering is atoning and serves as an example*; as he suffered, he did not revile (Mark 10:35-45; 13:13; 1 Pet 4:14 [insulted/hated for Christ's sake]); followers of Christ are called to walk in Christ's footsteps, also into suffering (Mark 8:34-37; 10:38-39; 13:7-13, 14-23; Acts 4:27-30; 1 Pet 2:21, 23; 4:1, 13-14). Helyer observes that Peter's testimony to discipleship is 'cruciform in nature'.[46] Cullmann observes: 'he who tried to turn Jesus from the way of suffering, and denied him at the decisive moment of the Passion story, was the first one who, after Easter, grasped the necessity of this offence'.[47]

3. Like Jesus (Mark 1:14-15), the disciples are to *spread the good news* (Mark 6:7-12 [sending out the disciples]; 10:13; see the speeches of Peter in the Petrine section of Acts and the pastoral Letter of 1 Peter).

4. Jesus, the living stone, is *rejected by some, accepted by others* (Mark 12:10-12; Acts 4:11; 1 Pet 2:4, 6-8). Likewise, the disciples are living stones being purified in suffering and built into a spiritual house (implied in Mark 11:1-25; Acts 4:27-30; see especially 1 Pet 1:12; 2:4, 6-7 [Ps 118:22; Isa 8:14; 28:16]; see Eph 2:20-22).

5. As Christ is honored (Mark 1:11; 9:7), so the disciples are *honored by God through believing and confessing* (Mark 8:38; Acts 5:41; 1 Pet 2:7).

6. The disciples' closeness to Christ is expressed by *prayerful sobriety at the imminence (but not immediacy) of the Parousia of Christ* (Mark 8:38; 13:29, 35-37; Acts 3:19-21; 1 Pet 1:13; 4:7). Mark 9:1 is most likely proleptically fulfilled in Mark 9:2-8 (cf. 2 Pet 1:16).[48]

---

[45] See Gambrell, 'Mark 8:34', 42–43.
[46] Helyer, *Life*, 17.
[47] Cullmann, *Peter*, 69.
[48] Bockmuehl, *Simon*, 134.

7. *Judgment begins with the household of God*: Jesus had to drink the cup of judgment first (Mark 10:35-38, 45; 14:36 [Isa 51:22; Jer 25:15-17]); the disciples drink, subsequently (Mark 10:39; Acts 5:41; 1 Pet 4:17-18), the ('commuted') cup of chastening and purification.

8. Both for Jesus and the disciples, *God's strengthening presence is a reality in adversity* (Mark 1:13 [Matt 4:11]; 13:11; 14:36; Acts 5:18-20; 1 Pet 5:10-11).

Six of the eight core characteristics marking *all* who would follow Christ, which we isolated in Mark's Gospel in a previous study, reappear amply and conspicuously in the Petrine sections of Acts and in 1 and 2 Peter. They include trust, witness, purity of heart, humility, overcoming in trials, and surrendered obedience. Especially in 1 Peter, they are applied to concrete, pastorally[49] significant circumstances. Based on a possible additional core characteristic of carefully stewarding (or renouncing) possessions (Luke 14:33; contrast with Luke 8:1-3 and Acts 5:4; 12:12),[50] 1 Peter's characteristic emphasis on living as alien sojourners is highly significant (see, e.g., 1 Pet 1:1, 17). The Petrine sections in Acts take up a considerable number of the Markan core character traits, again in the setting of adversity and suffering, sustained by the power of the Spirit of God, manifesting Christ's continuing work.

---

[49] See Dryden, *Theology*, 43–54, 117–42, 190–91.
[50] See, e.g., C.M. Hays, *Luke's Wealth Ethics: A Study in Their Coherence and Character* (Tübingen: Mohr Siebeck, 2010).

PART THREE

Universal Watermarks of Jesus:
Contours of Christ-Driven Character Formation
According to the Apostle Peter

CHAPTER 9

Essential Christ-Driven Character Traits Derived from Identity Formation

The Foundation of Christ-Driven Identity

In the present chapter we explore thematically each of the six core characteristics ('watermarks of Christ') which we isolated especially in Mark and 1 Peter, but also in the Petrine sections in Acts and in 2 Peter. In doing so, we also draw, at times, on ancillary and complementary characterizations found in Matthew, Luke, and John. The following exploration represents, to a degree, a biblical-theological treatment of these six marks of Christian maturity, with an intentional focus on Mark's Gospel, the Petrine sections of Acts, and the two Petrine Epistles. Since these documents also draw on the Old Testament, we will also need to keep this background in mind, since it clearly serves as a significant theological context of Peter's canonical testimony.[1]

According to Peter's testimony, Christ shapes the character of his followers in the process of their increasing dependence upon him. Such formation issues from a God-given new identity. The person of Christ and the disciple's developing identity are thus inseparable and interrelated realities. The fundamental reason for this lies in the fact that God created and intended mankind to exist as God-dependent creatures, not as autonomous entities (see the OT motif of 'walking with God', e.g., Gen 5:22, 24; 6:9; 17:1; Mic 6:8). According to Peter, an autonomous human being lives against the creation design. Jesus, the eternal Son of God, came to earth to bring human beings, Jews and Gentiles alike, back into relationship with God (1 Pet 3:18). Without a new identity in Christ (see above), character formation degenerates into self-improvement and ceases to be a fruit of the Spirit.

The six emphases of Petrine character formation are, first of all, character traits found in Jesus himself.[2] They are then to be expressed as 'fruit' in and

---

[1] See especially Beale and Carson, *Commentary*, 111–250; 513–81; 1015–63.
[2] See Mark 10:45; 14:36.

among all disciples of Jesus; it is the consequence of Christ's transformative impact in the form of identity and character formation.

Taking Mark, the Petrine sections in Acts, and 1 and 2 Peter together, we see that Jesus leads his transformed people like a sojourning tabernacle through the desert of suffering and adversity, always remaining in their midst (Mark 10:29-31; 13:10; cf. Matt 28:20). As he must suffer, so must his followers. One central effect of the crucible of suffering and adversity is purification ('salted with fire', Mark 9:49) for the glory of God (Mark 11:17; Isa 48:10-11). In other words, individual and communal character formation does not occur for its own sake but as part of the calling of being crafted into the new temple of God as the presently sojourning people of God: disciples are to reflect their master's character and thus their redefined, godly loyalties to a watching world. Character formation is thus not merely a personal affair; it is, rather, embedded in the master plan of the triune God to shape a pure people according to his own heart which worships in truth and Spirit (Mark 11:17; 12:1-12; John 4:24) and glorifies the one true God by its individual and corporate life, actively pursuing his universal mission (Mark 13:10). Various forms of suffering and adversity thus ultimately serve God's purposes. In it, the disciples progressively appropriate the significance and reach of the substitutionary atonement of Christ (Mark 10:45) as a basis and means of purification (i.e., progressive sanctification; see Mark 10:38-39). God thereby achieves his comprehensive mission of having a purified and missional people reflect his radiance (Mark 11:17; 1 Pet 3:15; 2 Pet 1:16) amidst a watching and often hostile world.

Prominent Christ-Driven Character Traits

In this section we take up the six ranked core character traits that have particularly arisen in our study of Peter's canonical testimony to Christ's universal call to all disciples. While these characteristics are *prominent* in 1 Peter, Mark, the Petrine sections in Acts, and in 2 Peter, we do not claim that they encompass the total range of character traits that Christ works in all those who follow him. Rather, they represent the *focus* of Peter in earliest Christianity, so far as we can determine it. We also do not claim that these characteristics are *unique* to Peter. Elsewhere in the Old and New Testaments, we encounter various aspects of these six traits. What we do claim, however, is that these character traits *reflect Peter's focus*. It behooves us, therefore, to pursue our own formation in Christ along the lines of the foundation laid by Peter at the behest of Christ.

A final comment is necessary before we embark on our exploration. As mentioned, we view *repentance* as a precondition for reconciliation with God through Christ (Mark 1:14-15; Acts 2:38). Repentance is a gift of God (Acts 11:18, 'may God grant repentance that leads to life'; cf. 3:19, 26 [God gives repentance]; 5:31; 8:22; 11:18). Following Christ involves constant repentance as a reconciled disciple of Christ, resting in the once-and-for-all covenantal assurance of the substitutionary atonement of Christ. If we counted repentance among the core character traits of a follower of Christ, it would constantly run in concert with all other character traits, especially faith and surrender.

Trait 1: Growth in Faith and Trust[3]

According to Mark's Gospel as Peter's report, faith is initially a trusting disposition toward God's presence and purpose. It calls for personal involvement on a practical basis. It presupposes that we acknowledge a fundamental resistance to God and that we turn away from such rebellion and self-sufficiency (Mark 1:14-15). In Mark, faith often simply means counting on Jesus's (and with him, the entire Godhead's) power to work his will into our lives (see the concept of entrusting ourselves to God in 1 Pet 2:23; 4:19; 5:6). The essence of faith is to put personal, childlike, and God-given trust in God's existence, presence, and sovereign will (Mark 2:5; 5:34; 9:42; 10:52; compare with 10:27; Acts 15:11; see 1 Pet 1:8-9). Such trust is closely intertwined with prayer (Mark 11:24; see below) and worship (1 Pet 3:15).

Such a new disposition involves a trust in Jesus in the midst of various struggles with unbelief (see Mark 9:24). Principal doubt must be distinguished from a struggling faith that encounters various forms of doubt. In such 'struggling' doubt, we humbly wrestle with the challenge of not being able to trust Jesus wholeheartedly. In principal and skeptical doubt we persist in a distanced, intentional posture toward God (cf. Rom 5:10). Principal autonomous doubt and resistance to God's self-revelation in and through Christ is very serious (Mark 9:19; [16:16]). Furthermore, we must draw a sharp distinction between true faith in God and speculative, subjective credulity (Mark 13:21). Genuine faith is based neither on complete, unequivocal proofs (Mark 15:32; see Heb 11:1-2) nor on fideism, or, worse, fictitious myth (see 2 Pet 1:16). Instead, it is based on credible witness (μάρτυς, e.g., 1 Pet 5:1) to Jesus (Mark 16:1-8; see the entire witness-cluster in Acts, esp. Acts 1:8; cf. Heb 11:1). As a witness, Peter can clearly distinguish between a *vision,* a myth, and physical reality (see the contrast between ἀληθές and ὅραμα [=vision] in Acts 12:9). Regarding an ὅραμα, see Acts 10:17; 11:5 (Peter's vision of food; cf. φάντασμα, Mark 6:49).[4] Regarding myths, Peter claims: '[f]or we did not follow cleverly devised myths (μῦθοι)[5] when we made known to you the power

---

[3] Faith also assumes surrender (Mark 8:34) and obedience. See A. Schlatter, *Der Glaube im Neuen Testament* (Stuttgart: Verlag der Vereinsbuchhandlung, 1905, 75–78; 180–92; 293; cf. C.D. Marshall, *Faith as a Theme in Mark's Narrative* (Cambridge: Cambridge Univ. Press, 1989).

[4] Cf. Acts 7:31; 16:9-10.

[5] Cf. 1 Tim 1:4; 4:7; 2 Tim 4:4; Titus 1:14.

and coming of our Lord Jesus Christ, but we were eyewitnesses (HL: ἐπόπται) of his majesty' (2 Pet 1:16; cf. ἐποπτεύω, 1 Pet 2:12; 3:2; cf. Acts 10:41). He thus identifies himself as a careful observer and witness.

Entrusting ourselves to God thus always includes a form of surrender (Mark 8:34-37). In Mark, Jesus reinforces what John the Baptist had already proclaimed (Mark 1:4), namely, that the people of Israel (and thus humankind) do not start life from a neutral state of heart, perspective, and morality. Rather, they find themselves in serious noetic, personal, and moral alienation from God which requires God-given repentance (see Lam 5:20-21) as a prerequisite for renewed trust in God. Peter reinforces this especially in 1 Peter 3:18, where *everyone*, be he a law-abiding Jew or a Gentile, is in need of being 'brought back to God'. There, Peter finally concedes that even he, as a circumcised covenant member of the people of Israel, needed to be brought back to God by Christ's substitutionary atonement. Above all else, the divine necessity of Christ's crucifixion for reconciliation (cf., e.g., Mark 8:31) reveals the severity of this alienation (*pondus peccati*). In the end, repentance and appropriating the substitutionary atonement of Christ are the exclusive and appropriate means by which to redress such alienation from God and to find enduring forgiveness (Mark 10:43; Acts 10:43; 1 Pet 3:18). Thus Peter is convinced that Gentile believers have indeed 'cleansed their hearts by faith' (Acts 11:17; 12:5, 11) and that, as a member of the Jewish people, he can only 'be saved through the grace of the Lord Jesus, just as they will' (Acts 15:9-11; see also Acts 3:16; 8:13; 10:43; 11:17; 1 Pet 1:6-7, 21; 2:19-20; 4:12, 16, 19; cf. Eph 2:8-10).

Jesus teaches Peter that faith's greatest enemy is not doubt but fear (Mark 4:40; 5:36; see also Mark 6:50; 1 Pet 3:6). Trust and fear cannot coexist in one heart (Mark 4:40; see 6:50) since ongoing fear is a form of practical atheism. Trust in the living and powerful God fends off the temptation to become intimidated and overwhelmed by idols, suffering, opposition, and persecution (Mark 8:38; 13:3, 9-14, 16-17; 16:6; see 1 Pet 3:9-14, 16-17; 4:19; 5:6, 9-10) or the temptation to revile in persecution (Mark 13:9, 11, 13; Acts 3:4-7, 12, 16; 8:13; 9:34, 40; 1 Pet 2:21-23; 3:16; 4:1, 12-19). Weakness in faith, however, is a correctable form of doubt (Mark 9:24; [16:11, 13]), and does not stand in direct antithesis to God's gift of faith. Rather, growth in faith (and a decrease of doubt) can be facilitated by repentance and petition (Mark 9:24).

Trust as the opposite of self-sufficiency reflects an ever-growing assurance in God's will, purposes, and mission. To 'claim God's promises' ('name-and-claim'), however, in a self-determined fashion is spiritually and emotionally dangerous. In Mark 11:22-24, faith in God's purposes and mission leads to the removal of idols among human beings and the restoration of true worship. In this way, the proper relationship between faith and a right approach to God's law is at least suggested by Peter. A heart cleansed by faith in Christ's atonement will resist trying to keep the law by self-effort (Acts 15:10-11) or worse yet, to seek purity of heart by trying to keep the law (Mark 7:1-23). On the other hand, a follower of Christ will not live against the intent and purpose of the Mosaic law (see Christ's fulfillment and *abrogatio* of the ceremonial law, implied in Mark 7:18-19 and in Acts 10 and 11) through his atonement. Godliness (εὐσέβεια), as a fruit of faith which accords with the moral tenets of the Mosaic law, is paramount (see, e.g., 1 Pet 1:14-19). For followers of Christ, Jesus lives the example of ongoing dependence upon and trust in God, his Father (Mark 14:32-36). In 1 Peter, Peter encourages his beleaguered letter-recipients to do likewise (1 Pet 4:19).

Finally, faith always contains the elements of anticipation, hope, and obedience. Living by faith does not cleave to the perceived phenomena (Heb 11:2); rather, it acts upon God's redemptive deeds and word in confidence that he will bring about what he promises (Mark 4:1-20; 1 Pet 1:8-9; 2:9; 5:4; see also Heb 10:36 and 11:39). For the life of faith, as being born again, it is crucial to let the word of God flourish as the 'imperishable seed' planted in the followers (Mark 4:1-20; 1 Pet 1:23-25).

Closely related to faith is *prayer*. In fact, prayer is faith's mouthpiece. Judging from the perspective of God's creation design, prayer should become for the disciple the most natural and fundamental form of communion with God. Prayer in Mark means helplessly counting on God's (Jesus's) ability to intervene in human affairs. It implies surrender to God's purposes. It means putting our declared will consciously under God's will and care (Mark 11:22-25; see Acts 4:24-30).[6] Prayer includes watchfulness, resistance to the subtle temptation to follow self, joyful solitude with God, and worship of God (Mark 11:17; see Acts 1:14, 24; 6:4, 6). It is also a key tool in exorcism (Mark 9:29; see Acts 9:32-35) and is closely associated with forgiveness of others and with fasting (as a sign of particular availability to God).

In Mark 11:22-25, the important character traits of faith, prayer, and forgiveness are interconnected. The context of this section concerning the cursing of the fig tree and the cleansing of the temple points to one simple purpose: Jesus calls God's people to true and universal worship and prayer (cf. Mark 11:17). As the Son of the owner of the vineyard (i.e., God's Israel, Isa 5:1-7), Jesus is rightfully seeking the fruit of worship (see Mark 12:1-12). He illustrates this by means of the harsh and figurative treatment of a fig tree (Mark 11:12-14). Faith that moves mountains (a phrase clearly intended to be understood figuratively)[7] is faith that willingly conforms to God's stated mission and prays along that mission in contrast to our own aspirations. The obstacles to true worship (the existence of Satan and human sinfulness, expressed, e.g., in rationalism, militant Islamism, corruption, moral and intellectual compromises of Christians) are formidable. We are thus called by

---

[6] See O. Hallesby, *On Prayer* (Minneapolis, MN: Augsburg Fortress, 1937).
[7] Bayer, *Markus,* 405–409.

God to pray *humbly and confidently* toward the divine removal of everything that hinders true worship of the one true God. Such bold prayer for removal of all idolatry begins, not surprisingly, with ourselves and focuses on pursuing forgiveness (Mark 11:25). It involves the call to let the unmerited grace of God affect our identity in redemptive character transformation. This means there will be a heartfelt readiness to pass God's unmerited forgiveness on to others. On yet another level, prayer is dedication and appeal to God that he will manifest his unparalleled power over evil (Mark 9:29; thus overcoming fear; see above).

In Mark, Jesus seeks intimate, prayerful fellowship with his heavenly Father (Mark 1:35; 6:46; 14:32-36). By his example, Jesus draws his disciples into the same attitude and habitual conduct of prayer. If Jesus, the Son of God, seeks communion with his Father, then we, too, need to—and are invited to—seek such communion with God as foundational to our lives. Through the Holy Spirit our eyes are gradually opened to our fundamental and ongoing need for God's presence, wisdom, and strength.

Trait 2: Becoming a Courageous Witness[8]
Our ongoing relationship with Christ becomes increasingly significant as we mature in following him; it determines our identity, our way of living on this earth, and eternal life with God. Being ashamed[9] of Christ before a watching world (Mark 8:38) is commensurate with persistent and ongoing denial of our defining identity in word and deed (cf. Matt 16:27).[10] A natural consequence of being impacted by Christ's loving pursuit of us is that we will naturally speak to others about who he is and what he means to us (Mark 5:20; see Acts 18:9-10), especially due to his death and resurrection (Acts 1:8, 22; 4:20, 33; 5:42; 6:4). This conforms to Christ's declaration that 'the gospel must . . . be proclaimed to all nations' (Mark 13:10; cf. 1:17; 16:15). We will proclaim the glory of God (Mark 8:38; 11:22-25; 13:10; Acts 3:15) in faithful witness to Christ (Mark 8:38; Acts 2:12, 15). By means of the Holy Spirit, we are led to

---

[8] See Bauckham, *Eyewitnesses*, 472–508, regarding the philosophical, historical (historiographical), and theological (biblical) issue of (eye-) witness reporting, with particular reference to P. Ricoeur, *Memory, History, Forgetting* (Chicago, IL: University of Chicago Press, 2004).

[9] The term ἐπαισχύνομαι (Mark 8:38, par. Luke 9:26: 'ashamed' in the sense of 'denying') also occurs in Rom 1:16 (feeling shame; cf. 2 Tim 1:8, 12, 16). The less emphatic αἰσχύνομαι occurs in 1 Pet 4:16 (shame in suffering as a Christian; cf. 2 Cor 10:8; Phil 1:20; 2 Thess 3:14; 2 Tim 2:15; 1 John 2:28; cf. Heb 2:11, 16).

[10] Peter denied Christ, albeit under life-threatening circumstances (Mark 14:30, 72). He did, however, not persist in denial but repented deeply (Mark 14:72; cf. Luke 22:32: ἐπιστρέψας).

bold proclamation (see all 'prophetic repentance speeches' in Acts: Acts 2:14-36; 3:12-26; 4:8-12, 20; 5:29-32; cf. Mark 1:14-15; 1 Pet 2:9; 4:11; see also Acts 15:21; 18:9-10 and Mark 13 regarding witness and perseverance). Part of this proclamation will be the pursuit of an honorable conduct among Jews and Gentiles (Mark 13:9-13; cf. Matt 5:16). Note the lifestyle witness of good deeds and sober actions encouraged in 1 Peter, including the practice of hospitality (1 Pet 1:12, 25; 2:9, 12, 15; 3:1, 14-16; 4:14; see also 4:5). Paradoxically, our good conduct can incite external opposition. We will thus bear witness to Christ not only in welcoming settings, but often in adverse (opposition, persecution, prison: Acts 5:19, 22, 25; 12:5-6;[11] cf. Luke 22:33) circumstances (see, e.g., Acts 1:8, 22; 2:11, 32, 41; 3:15; 4:3, 13, 20, 33; 5:18, 26, 32-33, 41-42; 6:4; 8:1; 9:32; 10:39, 41-42; 12:1-5, 19).

The public proclamation is aimed at the entire world (Mark 13:10; cf. 7:27). This corresponds to the universal nature of the kingdom of God and the universal sufficiency[12] of Jesus's substitutionary atonement. It clearly implies that Jesus not only intended for his disciples to be with him, to depend upon him, and to reflect basic kingdom character traits and become Christlike (Mark 3:14; 5:20). He also intended for them to continue, by their example and speech, the proclamation and restoration mission that he began (Mark 8:38).[13] Such proclamation includes the fact that Jesus identifies himself as Isaiah's Servant of YHWH (Isa 52:13–53:12) in terms of the humiliated Son of Man (Mark 10:45) who suffers on behalf of his people.[14] Likewise, such proclamation includes the fact that Jesus claims to be the exalted Son of Man who shall, at a future point, preside as judge over every soul in this universe (Mark 8:38; see Ps 110:1, 5; Dan 7:13-14; cf. Acts 10:42; 1 Pet 1:13; 5:4).

Again, Jesus serves by teaching, exemplifying, and facilitating. In Mark, Jesus openly 'confesses' the Father (Mark 1:14-15, 38-39; 2:2; 14:36). Jesus came to proclaim the eternal, messianic rule (kingdom) of God (Mark 1:14-15, 38; 4:1; 6:2, 34; 8:31; 12:14) and inaugurated that rule by his substitutionary atonement (Mark 10:45; 14:25). The subsequent testimony of his followers is thus so intimately connected with dependence upon Jesus that eternal ramifications are associated with it (Mark 8:38; John 5:27). While eternal salvation is provided solely on the basis of the substitutionary atonement of Jesus (Mark 10:45; 1 Pet

---

[11] This occurred in AD 41, shortly after Caligula died and Claudius permitted Herod Agrippa to govern Judea.

[12] While the work of Christ is *sufficient* for all humankind, it is *efficient* for those who believe (John 3:16; 5:23; 6:29), who are, according to John, the elect (John 6:37, 44; cf. Rom 8:29-30). This truth may be contained in the oblique statement of 'many' in Mark 10:45; cf. Isa 53:11-12.

[13] Compare the keyword connection 'gospel' in Mark 1:14 (-15) and 13:10.

[14] See Phil 2:5-8.

3:18), public confession of that reality is a necessary and natural outgrowth of it. But this does not mean that individual instances of denying Christ forfeit salvation (see, e.g., Peter's denial of Jesus in Mark 14:30-31, 72).

A widespread way of reading Romans 10:14-15 is that the word of the gospel, the good news of salvation in and through Christ, must be communicated exclusively by preaching (especially in the pulpit), teaching and evangelism through particularly called persons. While it is true that the word must be proclaimed in such a way, it is also necessary that the gospel message be preached and taught, not just by preachers, evangelists, teachers, elders, and deacons (see 1 and 2 Tim, as well as Titus), but by everyone in a given congregation (1 Pet 3:15). All disciples are called to such individual and corporate proclamation and must take care that this happens in a holistic way. In holistic confession, speech is embedded in the totality of our lives, which proclaims the gospel, reflecting and confessing Christ. Our lives and our speech together confess who Jesus is and what he accomplishes in the reversal of the universal collapse of God-dependent relationships. Disciples of Christ are thus called to be holistic 'living letters' (2 Cor 3:3).

Such holistic confession invariably is met with different responses. At times this leads to trials and persecution. As noted above, following the *missio dei* implies the potential of much external opposition and oppression (Mark 10:30; 13:9-13; Acts 2:13, [15]; 4:1-3, 5-7, 18, 21, 29; 5:17-18, 21b-28, 33, 40; 6:9, 11-15; 8:7, 9-13, 18-24; 12:1-6, 11, 19; 1 Pet 5:10-11). Paradoxically, persecution and opposition intensifies communion among Jesus's followers (Acts 2:42-47; 4:26-30; 1 Pet 4:14, 16). The satanic world also opposes such proclamation which therefore calls for discerning resistance to suffering inflicted by Satan (Mark 4:15; cf. Acts 5:3; 1 Pet 5:8-9).

Holistic confession will, at times, result in a change of heart of the one who 'confesses'. Acts 10 and 11 serves as a significant illustration for such progressive transformation. Here, Peter's theological attitude toward Gentiles, based on God's stated mission (e.g., Gen 12:3; Mark 13:10; cf. Matt 28:19-20), must radically change in order that the mission of God may go forward.

Trait 3: Pursuing Purity of Heart

When Simeon holds the baby Jesus, the Anointed of the Lord, in the temple of Jerusalem, he turns to Mary in the presence of Joseph and predicts that Jesus will cause the 'thoughts from many hearts' to be brought to light (Luke 2:35; see 6:45).[15] Paul admonishes Timothy to 'keep a close watch on yourself' (1

---

[15] One of the last works painted by Rembrandt depicts Simeon as a virtually blind man, 'seeing' with his heart.

Tim 4:7b, 15-16; see Phil 4:9). Jesus declares to hypocritical Pharisees: 'First clean the inside of the cup and the plate, that the outside also may be clean' (Matt 23:26).[16] The heart is the fountain of sin (Matt 15:19) and the place where purification must commence.[17] Expressions such as these have a long history in the Old Testament, in which the 'heart' is the center of a person's thought, will, and feeling (Deut 8:2; Jer 23:20; see Acts 11:23). Thus, a defiled heart is of grave concern to God. Jeremiah warns doomed Judah that 'they dress their wounds lightly' (Jer 6:14; 8:11, NIV), meaning that they do not really take the depth of their rebellion against God to heart and deal with it in a radical way. Jeremiah often addresses the sickness and deceitfulness of the heart (e.g., Jer 6:7; 17:9-10, 16; cf. Hos 5:13). Ezekiel speaks of the idolatry of the heart (Ezek 14:3-4, 7), meaning that in the inner being of a person there is worship of someone or something other than God. We hear of a hard heart (Exod 4:21; cf. Eph 4:18) and the duplicity of the heart (Ps 12:2). Given the defilement of the heart, God tests the heart (1 Chr 28:9); in other words, he seeks to reveal to us what is in the heart (Pss 7:9 and 17:3; see Rom 8:27). Proverbs 4:25 thus admonishes us to 'watch over your heart' (see Prov 4:23, 24-27). The Psalms encourage the readers to talk to themselves (Ps 42:6, 12; 43:5). Ezekiel 36:26-27 speaks of the Spirit of God who gives life to the heart (cf. Jer 31:31-34). Psalm 19:14 is a prayer toward purity of the heart. We hear of the goodness of a steadfast heart (Ps 57:7; 73:26; Prov 14:30) and the benefit of an enlarged heart (Ps 119:7; Isa 60:5; cf. Mark 12:30), since the heart is the wellspring of life (Prov 4:23).

It is no accident, therefore, that God is particularly focused on the heart as the sacred and powerful center of his highest creation. Since the heart represents the inner center of the human being as a physical, emotional, and spiritual being, God delights exceedingly in its purity and is intensely active in restoring it to a right relationship with him and others, due to its severe defilement. Not that we are to play the heart against the whole person, but the entire person (body, soul, and spirit) *follows* its inner center of thought, will, and feeling,

---

[16] The entire pericope of woes (Matt 23:1-36) exposes the defilement of the heart as the core problem. See, e.g., vv. 25, 27-28, 34.

[17] Regarding the *impurity* of the heart, see, e.g., Mark 7:20-22; 2 Pet 2:14, cf. 1 Pet 3:8 (εὐσπλάγχνος). See C.J. Miller, *The Heart of a Servant Leader: Letters from Jack Miller* (Phillipsburg, NJ: P&R Publishing, 2004); E.H. Peterson, *The Pastor: A Memoir* (New York, NY: HarperOne, 2012); R. Saucy, *Minding the Heart: The Way of Spiritual Transformation* (Grand Rapids, MI: Kregel, 2013); H.T. Armerding, *The Heart of Godly Leadership* (Wheaton, IL: Crossway, 1992). Regarding Jesus, see Heb 5:7. True holiness is based on Jesus's atonement; it is applied to us by God, and mediated through baptism in the 'Holy Spirit-and-fire' (Luke 3:16; cf. Mark 1:8 and Rom 8:9).

as Jesus said: 'where your treasure is, there your heart will be also' (Matt 6:21; Luke 12:35; cf. Matt 12:35; Luke 6:45; Col 2:23). In other words, once the heart is (re)captured for God, the entire person follows suit. It is therefore no surprise that Jesus speaks much about the heart as the inner place of will, thought, and emotion (Mark 7:20-23).[18]

As we analyze what Jesus teaches Peter about watching over the heart, we call to mind Augustine's reflections on knowing the heart:

> The strength of self-deceivers is not that strength that well people enjoy, but like those in delirium. They are like those out of their minds, who imagine themselves in such good health that they do not consult a physician, and even fall upon him with blows as if he were an intruder![19]

The disciple is called to focus on God, reliably revealed and represented in Christ. He is receptive to the purposes of Christ. In peripheral vision, the follower keeps a watchful eye on the condition of his/her heart as the inner center of his/her being. This includes, like a rhythm of breathing, perpetual surrender, trust, and prayer. Jesus lays the foundation for watching over our hearts in his fundamental challenge of the disciples and us (cf. Mark 8:15, 17-21). As we continue to follow Christ, we must identify our personal areas of a hard, autonomous heart attitude (Mark 6:52; 8:17-21) which persists in self-reliance. None of us know the full truth about our inner self (Mark 10:35-44; cf. Jer 17:9-10). We must recognize more and more what resides in and proceeds from our hearts (Mark 7:14-23, especially vv. 21-22; cf. Mark 7:6).

Not surprisingly then, Peter speaks of God as the 'knower of the heart' (καρδιογνώστης; only twice in the NT: Acts 1:24 [perhaps a prayer by Peter]; 15:8 [Peter]; cf. 1 Chr 28:9). Note Peter's frequent but not unique reference to the heart (καρδία; Acts 5:3-4; 8:21-22; 15:8-9; cf. Acts 2:26-27, 37; 1 Pet 1:22; 3:4, 15; 2 Pet 1:19; contrast with 2 Pet 2:14) as the *locus* of repentance. As the gospel message is taken to the nations, we are not surprised that Peter often emphasizes the absence of a pure heart (Acts 5:3-4, 7-11; 8:17-24). We must be radical in naming, condemning, and rejecting idols, sin patterns, and particular sins when tempted (Mark 8:33; 9:43-47). According to God's purposes, it is absolutely necessary for us to be purified by the blood of Christ (Mark 9:49; see 1 Pet 1:15). This also means watching out for principal doubt (Mark 11:23; see above). We must take care not to mislead others (Mark 9:42). Instead, we

---

[18] In John 9:35-41 (especially 9:39), we encounter the paradox that those who are physically blind may see spiritually and those who see physically may be spiritually blind.

[19] Augustine, quoted in: T.C. Oden and C.A. Hall (eds), *Mark* (Downers Grove, IL: IVP, 1998), 31.

must know our specific personality weaknesses and particular temptations of the heart, since Jesus describes the inner being of a person (heart) by means of the metaphor of the soil (Mark 4:13-20; see there the references to figurative 'hearing'). As concrete examples, this means watching over our attitudes toward our parents (Mark 7:10) and shunning blasphemy (Mark 3:29).

Without a proper self-understanding, growth in Christlike attitudes and actions is impossible (Mark 7–8; see Luke 21:34-36). As stated above, Mark 8:17-21 plays a crucial role in confronting the disciples with their true hearts before God. They are exposed in their fundamental self-sufficiency, i.e., hard hearts (Mark 6:50-52; 10:35-44; [16:14]), not unlike those of Jesus's opponents (see Mark 3:5, 29; 9:42-49; 10:5). The parable of the Sower (Mark 4:1-20) provides the disciples (and others) a mirror for analyzing their hearts: will they be hospitable to Jesus's word and thus to Jesus as the Word? Will they be open to the purposes and the fruit of Jesus's mission? This will continue into Acts. As a law-abiding Jew, Peter will not eat unclean food (Acts 10:14; 15:8-9, 'God, who knows the heart'). However, what God declares clean, is clean. Peter has to continue to depend upon God's purpose and mission and allow God, in a progressive way, to purify him.

Peter will continue this theme and expound upon it in 1 Peter. He exhorts his listeners toward watchfulness regarding purity of heart in order to overcome evil passions, die to sin, and live to righteousness, since they are ransomed from such futile ways. They are to be a holy priesthood, a people of God who are vigilant over heart attitudes, since they have been brought from darkness to light (1 Pet 1:14-16; 2:1-2, 11, 24; 3:1, 4, 10-11 [Ps 34], 15-16; 5:8-9; see also 1:22; 4:3). They must face this battle of overcoming sin, temptations, and old ways in the pursuit of a new life, since godlessness wars against a healthy soul (Mark 8:34-37; 1 Pet 2:11). They are called to die to God-alien passions and live instead to righteousness and the will of God (1 Pet 2:24: 4:2; see Mark 3:35; 8:34-37; see the repentance cluster in Acts [Acts 2:38; 3:19, 26; 5:31; 8:22; 11:18, repentance that leads to godly, honest life]; cf. Mark 1:14-15). They thus pursue a pure heart (Mark 4:13-20; 7:20-22; 8:17-21; Acts 5:3-4, 7-9; 8:20-23; 10:14; 11:8; 15:8-9; 1 Pet 1:14, 22). They are to 'watch and pray'; that is, to guard their hearts in prayer, so they can endure temptation and persecution (Mark 14:38).

In Mark 7:20-22, Jesus confronts his disciples in a particular way with the defilement of their hearts. Not that the disciples' personhood itself is sinful; they remain image-bearers of God. Rather, their personhood is deeply marred and infected by the disease of autonomy, idolatry, and self-satisfaction. Jesus confronts them with the fact that they do not possess in themselves the power and resources to address and reverse such defilement of their core being (see Col 2:23). Only the divine Son of God can remove the guilt of their defilement, cleanse them, reconcile them with God, and progressively heal their illnesses (see 1 Pet 2:24-25, as a reversal of their separation from God, Isa 59:2). Elsewhere, we have suggested in more detail possible reversals of the defilements pointed out in Mark 7:20-22, reversals caused and facilitated by Christ.[20] They include:

- thoughts aligned with God's perspective and purpose;
- inter-gender reverence and appreciation without exploitation;
- reverence for the possessions and abilities of others;
- reverence for the sanctity of life;
- contentment and faithfulness in marriage;
- gratitude and generosity in all areas of life;
- godly desires;
- rejoicing in what is good and true; friendliness; shunning evil in any form; mercy;
- a transparent, honest life;
- moderation, with healed affections and needs;
- rejoicing in the success of others; looking at others as God looks at them; generosity in thought of others;
- speaking well of others;
- readiness to admit weakness and faults; healthily deflecting attention to God and others; admitting need for God; and
- seeking wisdom for life; being teachable and willing to grow.

In Mark, Jesus maintains a pure heart in the midst of severe temptation (Mark 8:33; 14:36; see 1 Pet 2:22-23; Heb 7:5). He thus serves as the example *par excellence*.

As noted, ongoing forgiveness[21] is closely connected with purity of heart. Without watching over our hearts, the need to forgive might either be ignored or remain hidden. When disciples become aware before God of what is really stirring in their hearts, they might, for the first time, be confronted with the profound challenge to forgive and to seek forgiveness.

The impact of Christ's atonement enables, enlarges, and deepens our capacity for true and lasting forgiveness. We must first be recipients of forgiveness before we can extend it to others. Forgiveness has nothing to do with 'condoning wrongdoing'. Forgiveness means *releasing* someone, since valid accusations against us were released (covered) by Christ. Profound, costly forgiveness is what each disciple receives when coming to Christ. Such a disciple learns to forgive by passing on the atoning, pardoning deed of Christ to someone else. As disciples, we love because we have been loved (compare 1

---

[20] Bayer, *Theology*, 110–12.
[21] See, e.g., T. Hägerland, *Jesus and the Forgiveness of Sins: An Aspect of his Prophetic Mission* (Cambridge: Cambridge University Press, 2012), 75–82; 89–103.

Pet 5:7 with 1:22); we forgive because we have been forgiven (compare 1 Pet 3:18 with 3:16-17). The *costliness* of forgiveness is thus *always* present. Forgiveness is especially difficult if we have been very deeply wounded, abused, or hurt. This requires repeated and ongoing contemplation and existential appropriation of Christ's atonement and costly sacrifice on our behalf. To the degree to which we are captivated by his loving sacrifice, to that degree we mature in the capacity to forgive such deep wounds. Concurrently, we also develop a deeper sense of our own sinfulness, aided by the Spirit of God.

A follower of Christ who has received forgiving atonement for sins (Mark 10:45; see 2:7, 10; 14:23-24; Rom 3:20-26; Col 1:21-22) is then strongly exhorted to forgive others (Mark 11:25). If such a person is not moved to forgive, he/she is met with a real but not realized[22] warning concerning God's withheld forgiveness (Mark 11:25; cf. Matt 18:35). Prayer for the softening impact of the Holy Spirit is sorely needed. Repentance and forgiveness (Mark 1:4) are closely connected. Due to the atonement of Christ (Mark 10:45; 14:22-24), repentance is not the cause of or reason for our forgiveness but rather a condition of our receiving unmerited forgiveness. Since the Holy Spirit leads to repentance and conveys salvation in Christ, damning the Holy Spirit rejects God's chosen means of bringing salvation and forgiveness (Mark 3:29).

Once again, we observe that Jesus exemplifies and facilitates what he teaches. In Mark Jesus freely forgives (Mark 2:5, including the accusations of his adversaries, Mark 2:5-10) by giving his life as a substitutionary atonement (Mark 10:45; 14:36; 1 Pet 2:24). Early on in Jesus's public ministry, he begins to address the human need for the removal of sin. Jesus identifies himself with the people of Israel (Mark 1:9), thus affirming that the call to repentance issued by John the Baptist is indeed from God. Simultaneously, Jesus begins to speak of his mission to atone for his people. Already in Mark 2, Jesus asserts the unparalleled authority to forgive sins as only God does (Mark 2:7, 10; contrast this with the way the prophet Nathan declares forgiveness to David, 2 Sam 12:13).

A further hint of this unique mission is found in Mark 2:19-20, where Jesus points to the fact that the messianic bridegroom will be 'taken away', ἀπαρθῇ ἀπ' αὐτῶν (see LXX Isa 53:8, ἤρθη and αἴρεται). He will provide substitutionary atonement in order to ratify lasting forgiveness with God (Mark 10:45; 14:36; 15:25, 37; cf. 1 Pet 3:18). Following his atonement, Jesus baptizes with the Holy Spirit (Mark 1:8; Acts 2:33).

The sinfulness of all human beings is so severe that John the Baptist calls even the people of Israel, who are privileged in having the patriarchs, adoption, the covenants, the law, the temple, and the promises (see Rom 9:4-5), to repent

---

[22] This occurs on account of the Holy Spirit's softening a disciple's heart.

in order that they may receive forgiveness of sins (Mark 1:4). If this call to repentance applies even to the covenant people of Israel, how much more does it apply to Gentiles? By what means this forgiveness is attained, however, remains undefined in John the Baptist's ministry, until the one arises to whom the Baptist points (Mark 1:7-8; Rom 9:5). He who will baptize each disciple with the Holy Spirit (Mark 1:8) will provide cleansing from sin as the condition for receiving the pure Holy Spirit. Those who blaspheme against the Holy Spirit, however, cannot be forgiven (Mark 3:29), since they resist the very agent who makes the forgiving atonement of Christ efficient. Providing forgiveness for alienation from God is thus the unique privilege of Jesus.

As stated above, trust, prayer, and forgiveness are intimately connected in Mark (see Mark 11:22-25). Those who confidently pray for the removal of everything that resists the true worship of God must begin with their own hearts. They must especially begin with the very challenging issue of forgiving those who wronged them. Having received unmerited, divine forgiveness by means of the substitutionary atonement of Jesus, the disciples are to pass this on to those who have wronged them.[23] If this new reality, which was set in motion by God's sovereign act and grace, does not grow in and among the disciple(s), God himself will withhold forgiveness (Matt 18:21-35). Ultimately, however, God will cause his disciples to come to repentance and willingness to surrender to God's forgiveness-causing power.

Trait 4: Growth in Humility and Service[24]

Humility has nothing to do with being a soft marshmallow or an abused doormat. Neither is a humble person strong in a self-assured fashion. Rather, a humble person actively depends on God's strength, will, wisdom, and power (1 Pet 2:23; 4:19; 5:6; see Isa 66:2, 'but this is the one to whom I will look: he who is humble and contrite in spirit and trembles at my word'; cf. Eph 4:2; Phil 2:3; Col 3:12; Titus 3:2). The fruit of humility is tenderness and respectfulness (1 Pet 3:16) but it is undergirded by persistent boldness (meekness), unwavering tenacity in patience, and obedience to God (Acts 4:19; 5:29; cf. Zeph 3:12-13). Humility opens many doors to a deeper life, to deeper relationships and experiences, which otherwise would remain closed. It is

---

[23] Cf. 1 John 4:19.
[24] See A. Murray, *Humility and Absolute Surrender* (Peabody, MA: Hendrickson, 2011), 1–56; cf. J. Dickson, *Humilitas: A Lost Key to Life, Love, and Leadership* (Grand Rapids, MI: Zondervan, 2011); J.I. Packer, *Weakness Is the Way: Life with Christ Our Strength* (Wheaton, IL: Crossway, 2013); and R. Feldmeier, *Macht – Dienst – Demut: Ein neutestamentlicher Beitrag zur Ethik* (Tübingen: Mohr Siebeck, 2012).

surprising to discover that true surrendered humility before God can lead to strength in perseverance and courageous witness, especially when humility is combined with faith, as it so often is (see the speeches of Peter in Acts 2, 3, 4, and 5). Such humility can be the gate to growth in godliness, love, and boldness.

There is thus great strength in humility since such surrendered persons do not rely on their own limited resources (see the ironic and convicting statements regarding small, self-generated 'lights' in Isa 50:10-11, in contrast to the light of God), but entrust themselves and their good cause into the mighty hand of God (1 Pet 2:23; 4:19; *5:5*; Phil 2:5-11; cf. Ps 22:1; Zeph 3:12-17). Contrary to self-abuse, or being abused, such a surrendered state, even if it is accompanied by suffering, is full of healthy, God-given strength. Furthermore, it is God's powerful presence which then becomes a more real (but always uncontrollable) factor.

We can thus speak of a healthy form of humility and suffering and distinguish it from pathological suffering and false humility whereby the person is hurt, compromised, damaged, abused, or hypocritical. We submit that Christ's suffering was always 'healthy' in the sense that he was always true to God, to himself, and to his mission, even in the midst of great rejection and being utterly despised (see 1 Pet 2:22-23). He thus never compromises truth, his identity, calling, and purpose. What he did give up on our behalf was privilege, honor, and recognition, and he took our place of condemnation and shame, motivated by love (see Phil 2:5-11).

During his life, and especially at the time of his passion, Jesus suffered much accusation, misrepresentation, maligning, criticism, opposition, even physical abuse (compare with Peter's suffering described above; see also Paul's suffering described in 2 Cor 6:4-10; 11:16-29). But in his inner life, he was never 'given over' to his opponents' skewed ways of thinking, their distorted perspectives and deficient worldviews, their twisted or deceptive arguments, crooked hearts, and false attitudes. Rather, Jesus kept himself pure in the sense of trusting his heavenly Father whole-heartedly and single-mindedly (1 Pet 2:23). In other words, Jesus maintained an inner health and strength in the midst of great external injustice.[25] This pattern should hold true for us as well. Murray observes concerning humility that '(h)ere is the path to the higher life. Down, lower down . . . Just as water ever seeks and fills the lowest place, so the moment God finds the creature . . . empty, his glory and power flow in to exalt and to bless'.[26]

---

[25] We are not advocating that it is healthy to remain in abusive situations. If possible, it is right to seek shelter from it.
[26] Murray, *Humility*, 20.

Humility is expressed in submitting to human authority (Mark 12:17; 1 Pet 2:13-14, 17; 2 Pet 2:10), but always in the context of obeying God more than people (Acts 4:19; 5:29; cf. Zeph 3:12-13). In Christ, the disciples are *free* to live as servants, (Mark 9:33-37 and 10:35-44; 1 Pet 2:16, 18; 4:10). They are God-trusting, tender-hearted, and loving people (Mark 9:37 and 10:43-44; 1 Pet 2:13; 3:8; 5:5-6; see Acts 10:21-48 [esp. vv. 25-26, 28]; 11:3; cf. Zeph 3:13).

As we delve more deeply into the topic of humility as testified to by Peter, it becomes apparent that humility is probably one of the most misunderstood character traits of discipleship. In the Roman Empire, including its prevalent philosophy of Stoicism, humility represented weakness, indecision, and lack of will. In contrast, ancient (and modern) societies project the ideal of self-sufficient strength. According to Peter, however, Christian humility means letting go of a self-sufficient agenda because of a greater trust in the supreme purpose, power, and wisdom of the redeeming God of this universe (1 Pet 5:6). Humility is the display of courageous surrender of self-sufficiency because of a greater confidence in the power of God. Humility, according to Peter, always looks to God's presence and greatness. It neither gives up on self nor does it focus on self; rather, it gives *over* to God by seeking his ways and his strength. According to Peter, humility represents a shift of confidence from self to God. While various world religions feature a form of humility as an important character trait, Peter testifies to a uniquely Christian form of humility. The characteristic Petrine element of humility in discipleship is that the master, Jesus, is not only Peter's example, but that he himself takes Peter down with him, down into the recesses of heart-humility which have little to do with self-generated humility or false contrition. It is rather a trusting surrender of control toward dependence upon the master.

According to Peter, humility is a relational consequence of following Christ, not a self-generated virtue. Jesus guides Peter to places of humility he could never have reached by himself, nor would he ever have wanted to. In the following, we briefly trace the dynamic of Peter having to follow Christ into deeper levels of humility. Christ-generated humility is a fundamental posture of the heart which corresponds to the original pre-fall attitude of human beings and conforms to total reality.

Peter's 'Downward Mobility' into True and Healthy Humility

According to Peter's testimony in Mark, Jesus focused heavily on teaching his disciples the nature and central importance of humility. According to Jesus, humility involves serving others in a comprehensive way (Mark 1:31; 9:35; cf. Acts 10:25-26; see the entire context of Acts 10:21–11:3), as Christ serves us in a unique and unparalleled way (Mark 10:45).[27] Jesus gives many examples to illustrate what humility means. When welcoming a person who seems to be unimportant (e.g., children who were unimportant in the ancient world) into our presence, we welcome Jesus and with him God the Father (Mark 9:37). Serving someone (in whatever form) who belongs to Christ is particularly emphasized (Mark 9:41). If we are—or aspire to become—leaders or are already important in the eyes of others, we must become a servant and slave of all (Mark 10:4-44), just like Jesus (Mark 10:45). As leaders, we must not be heavy-handed, oppressive, exploitative (Mark 10:42), or ostentatious (Mark 12:38-40). Since coming under the rule of God happens by way of childlike simplicity, humility will always be a characteristic mark of kingdom life. Once again, we see the characteristic of humility exemplified in Jesus as the kingdom's ruler. In Mark, he embodies the greatest extremes of humility and service by dying a God-cursed, substitutionary death as *Ebed YHWH* (Mark 10:45; 14:36). Prior to his death, his healings are, among other things, acts of service (see, e.g., Mark 1:31). The statement in Mark 10:45 concerning Jesus's substitutionary atonement is the most climactic example for advocating service, humility, and sacrifice. Mark 10:45 forms a sort of *inclusio* with the third prediction of Jesus's death and resurrection (Mark 10:32-34), in the midst of which is found the audacious ambition of James and John to be 'great' (Mark 9:31-50 and 10:35-44; see below).

The child whom Jesus calls to himself (Mark 9:37; cf. also 10:16) serves as a further example of childlike humility (cf. also Mark 9:41). The attitude of simple and pure humility is further illustrated in Mark 10:13-16, where Jesus does not say that we are to become children (falsely interpreting Mark 10:14 without looking at Mark 10:15), but rather that we are to become childlike in our attitude toward the things of God (Mark 10:15). This humble approach is necessary for entry into the kingdom of God (repentance; see Mark 1:14-15) and serves as a characteristic trait in that kingdom.

Let us now look at how Jesus embeds the character trait of humility in Peter's life.

1) First, around AD 30,[28] Peter lives under the teaching and influence of Christ in Galilee, where he begins to learn that one of the core characteristics of following Christ is humble service and humility (Mark 9:31-50 [esp. v. 35];

---

[27] Luther observed: 'True humility does not know that it is humble. If it did, it would be proud from the contemplation of so fine a virtue' (*Martin Luther's Christmas Book*, ed. R.H. Bainton and W.L. Jenkins [Philadelphia, PA: Westminster Press, 1948], 20).

[28] Peter's age may roughly correspond to the dates given below.

10:35-44 [esp. vv. 43b-44]). Jesus enlarges Peter's heart for such an attitude toward all of life.

Immediately following Jesus's second prediction of his death and resurrection (Mark 9:31), the disciples discuss among themselves 'who was the greatest' (Mark 9:34). A similar scenario arises after the third prediction of Jesus's death and resurrection (Mark 10:32-34), when James and John request places of honor in Jesus's messianic rule (Mark 10:35-37). In both cases, Jesus turns the situation into a teaching moment by paradoxically inverting the human attitude and cultural approach to greatness: 'If anyone would be first, he must be last of all and servant of all' (Mark 9:35; cf. also 10:42; 12:38-40, as well as 1:31). We find a similar statement in Mark 10:43-44: 'But whoever would be great among you must be your servant, and whoever would be first among you must be slave of all'.

Concerning Mark 9:31-50: Preceding this important section on humility, the divine nature of Jesus has been revealed to Peter and two other disciples on the Mount of Transfiguration, followed by Jesus healing a boy with an unclean spirit (Mark 9:2-30). Both episodes display the power of Jesus, in sharp contrast to the following section on humility. In the second prediction of Jesus's suffering, death, and resurrection (Mark 9:31), Jesus repeats that his path is one of humiliation (cf. Phil 2:5-11). Jesus then involves Peter in a lesson in humility. He presents the memorable paradox: 'If anyone would be first, he must be last of all and servant of all' (Mark 9:35). Peter must not overlook apparently unimportant people (Mark 9:36-37) and must enter the kingdom in childlike humility and simplicity of heart (Mark 9:43-50). Jesus teaches Peter to put himself last and to serve all in such contrite simplicity (see Jesus's footwashing in John 13:1-20).

Concerning Mark 10:35-44: The contextual setting for this second key section on humility in Mark is the motif of earthly possessions. Riches can be a form of autonomous and proud self-protection, hindering entrance to the kingdom of God. Jesus emphasizes that anything which jeopardizes a dependent union with God (e.g., idols) must be removed (Mark 10:29-30). Once again, Jesus predicts his own impending humiliation (i.e., the third prediction of Jesus's suffering, death, and resurrection, Mark 10:32-34). Against this background, the sons of Zebedee seek to secure places of honor and recognition (Mark 10:37). Such ambitions are analogous to the rich young ruler seeking security in possessions. Jesus confronts Peter and the other disciples with the paradox that suffering loss of self-sufficient security is the path to life (Mark 8:35-37; cf. John 12:24-26). While Jesus must suffer judgment first (Mark 10:38; see esp. the metaphors of the cup of judgment in Isa 51:17, 22; Jer 25:15, 17, 28; 49:12;[29] 1 Pet 4:17), Peter and the other disciples will undergo the fire of purification (see Jer 16:13-16 and Luke 3:16), without the guarantee of a place of honor (Mark 10:40).

In contrast to the oppressively heavy-handed approach of Gentile leaders (see κατακυριεύουσιν and κατεξουσιάζουσιν, Mark 10:42) Peter and the other disciples are to become servant-leaders (Mark 10:43b-44; cf. 9:35). Evidence for the enduring impact of Jesus on Peter's approach to servant-leadership is found, e.g., in 1 Peter 5:1-3 (see below). Jesus concludes this time of instruction in discipleship by making the most startling announcement: not only does he teach about such humility in leadership, not only is he *the* example of servant-leadership, but also he will *make it possible* for Peter and others to become servant-leaders by being reconciled to God through his atonement (Mark 10:45; 1 Pet 3:18). Being shaped by purifying suffering is a necessary means of letting go of pride and a means of cleansing in order to learn God-surrendered humility. While Jesus saves through his substitutionary atonement, our non-salvific service is meant to be of benefit to others.

Concerning the footwashing in John 13:1-20: Jesus knows that Peter has not yet really appropriated the implications of his teaching and the necessity of his impending atonement. The footwashing testifies to Jesus's deepening challenge of Peter to let go of self-protective attitudes in exchange for a God-dependent approach. Peter must *let* Jesus wash his feet (John 13:8-9, 20).[30] Peter must surrender any form of self-defensiveness and putting up barriers of the heart in exchange for ever-deepening surrender. Additionally, he is to follow Jesus's example (John 13:14-16). Significantly, Peter later states that the 'Spirit of Christ' inspired the Old Testament prophets to announce the necessary suffering of Christ (1 Pet 1:1-11). This stands in stark contrast to Peter's initial resistance to the necessity that the Messiah of God would have to suffer, also for him (Mark 8:32-33).

2) Around AD 34, Peter endures a further step of 'downward mobility' in Joppa/Caesarea. As he seeks to follow Christ *and* to uphold the entire Mosaic law, he is led to 'defile' himself by being in the company of Gentiles. God declares: 'What God calls clean, you shall not call unclean' (Acts 10:15; 11:9; cf. 15:9). In the account of Acts 10:1-48, Peter increasingly defiles himself in ceremonial terms: he stays with a ceremonially unclean tanner; he is to eat unclean food; he is to go to unclean Gentiles; he is to enter the unclean house of a Gentile. As a paradoxical climax he witnesses, however, that the Holy

---

[29] See Bayer, *Predictions*, 54–89.
[30] See Bockmuehl, *Simon*, 60, regarding Passover purity. For some reflections on Jesus's footwashing as a key instrument of shaping Peter, see Bayer, *Theology*, 77–78; 120.

Spirit falls on these seemingly unclean Gentiles (Acts 10:44; cf. Acts 15:7-9). Peter must be humbled so that Gentiles can hear of God's purifying mercy in Christ's atonement, affecting the people of God regarding the breaking down of barriers of race, ethnicity, and gender.[31]

3) Around AD 48, Peter encounters yet another humbling experience, this time in Antioch. Paul has to oppose Peter 'to the face' (Gal 2:11),[32] because he temporarily[33] succumbed to the pressure of Judaizers (who insist that Gentile converts must be circumcised, Acts 15:1) to avoid ceremonially defiling table-fellowship with Gentile Christians.[34] Peter has to realize that fear of men caused him to compromise the grace-based reach of the gospel (Gal 2:6).[35] This humbling experience must have served as one of the bridges from Jesus's teaching on humility, via the footwashing, Peter's denial of Christ, his restoration by Jesus, and the events surrounding Acts 10–11, to the humility permeating 1 Peter. Acts 15:10-11 affords a further glimpse into Peter's cumulative humbling when he openly acknowledges his inability to bear the yoke of the law and his utter dependence on the grace of Christ for salvation (cf. Acts 10:15; Gal 2:11). Helyer notes: 'Christian church history is littered with too many leaders unwilling to acknowledge errors and repent of misdeeds'.[36] The outcome of such humbling is true fellowship among diverse groups; the community of God grows beyond barriers of race and ethnicity with uncounted, beneficial ramifications.

---

[31] See the book of Jonah. Cf. A. Bradley (ed.), *Aliens in the Promised Land: Why Minority Leadership Is Overlooked in White Christian Churches and Institutions* (Phillipsburg, NJ: P&R, 2013).

[32] See, however, Bockmuehl (*Remembered Peter*, 61–70) concerning the false dichotomy between Peter and Paul ever since the Tübingen School. See 1 Cor 1:12, 22; 9:5; 15:5; Gal 1:8, and 2:9, where Paul endorses Peter's ministry. Bockmuehl argues that even in Gal 2:11-17, the sharp difference between Peter and Paul is not over the foundation of the gospel but rather over its consequence in Jewish-Gentile fellowship (pp. 61–62); cf. Acts 15:7.

[33] See Hengel, *Peter*, 59, who cautions to overemphasize this incident.

[34] According to the circumspect arguments of Hemer, *Acts*, 278, it is historically most convincing to date the Letter to the Galatians *prior* to the Jerusalem Council reported in Acts 15, which took place around AD 48–49.

[35] See Gal 2:6-14, especially vv. 11-14: Peter is called a hypocrite (2:13) together with Barnabas and others. See also 2 Pet 3:15-16, where Peter expresses great respect for Paul, despite the incident recorded in Gal 2:6-14. Gal 2:6 is best taken to mean that Peter and others did have the reputation of leaders in Jerusalem; but before God everyone is equal (cf. 1 Pet 1:17), given the one truth of the gospel (cf. 1 Cor 2:2; 3:21). For further details, see Helyer, *Life*, 94–96.

[36] Helyer, *Life*, 96.

4) Around AD 63, we find Peter, who has by now long resided in Rome, as a humbled, steadied, God-trusting and leading mentor, full of integrity and God-dependent character (see especially 1 Pet 5:1-11; compare with 2:23; 3:8, and 4:19). Despite the fact that he is the foundation-laying apostolic witness of Christ, he does not employ heavy-handed authority in this Epistle. He has been humbled toward dependence upon God over the past thirty-five years. He has a settled heart, settled in Christ, partially in the wake of facing his many failures. In many a trial he has been tested and approved (1 Pet 1:7; cf. Deut 8:2, 5, 16). He serves as a natural authority, full of real and sustained humility. Helyer aptly comments: 'Peter's denial can never be taken back. It happened, and he had to live with the painful memory. But rather than letting his failure cripple him spiritually and emotionally, he used it as a means of building up the flock of God'.[37] Authority structures are important and remain in the redeemed and new humanity, but they all have to be transformed and filled with Christlike humility. Humility is expressed in honoring and in respecting. In 1 Peter, there is a demeanor of submission, with a gentle and quiet spirit and attitude (1 Pet 2:13-17, 19; 3:1, 7-8, 15; 4:10-11; 5:2-3, 5-6; see 3:8, regarding harmony, and 4:9, regarding humility and hospitality; cf. Mark 10:42).

We now turn to exploring the significant text on humility found in 1 Peter 5:1-11. The key transition to this passage (and a possible summary of 1 Peter) is found in 1 Peter 4:19: 'Therefore let those who suffer according to God's will entrust their souls to a faithful Creator while doing good'. This sets the tone for the remainder of the Epistle. The larger context of 1 Peter 5:1-11 is one of suffering, especially in the form of persecution and being excluded from society on account of being a follower of Christ (1 Pet 4:12-19; cf. 3:8-22 and 4:1-11, which speaks of godliness expressed in the midst of such suffering). It is the suffering of the wandering, sojourning people of God, visualized as the moving tabernacle with the presence of God in its midst.

Initially, Peter challenges church leaders toward humility *as peers* and connects leadership with suffering and future hope (1 Pet 5:1-4). As a fruit of Jesus's teaching and example (Mark 9:33-37; 10:35-44; John 13:1-20) and other stages in Peter's 'downward mobility' into humility, servant-leadership is now described as voluntary and selfless. Contrary to a domineering and prideful approach, it entails much exemplary shepherding (see Ezek 34:4; Mark *10:42*; cf. Acts 3:6; 10:1-48) in the awareness of serving before the chief shepherd, Jesus. Peter then turns to younger people. One of their opportunities toward humility is to respect the leadership of elders (1 Pet 5:5a).

Peter subsequently reinforces the profound interplay between humility and suffering (1 Pet 5:5b-11; cf. 5:1) for all followers of Christ, since 'God opposes

---

[37] Helyer, *Life*, 61.

the proud but gives grace to the humble'.³⁸ We have here a reciprocal humility as the antidote to self-defensive pride. As such, humility is a fundamental seedbed for the multi-faceted fruit of the Spirit (Gal 5:22; cf. Zeph 3:12-13). The concept of 'clothing oneself' in the context of paraenesis aims at adopting a new inner attitude and does not merely speak of external appearance. It is not a veneer.³⁹

The *locus classicus* for Peter's teaching on humility is found in 1 Peter 5:6-7. The passive voice of the imperative (ταπεινώθητε; cf. Jas 4:10 and ὑποτάγητε, Jas 4:7), often rendered by modern translations in a reflexive as 'humble yourself', may very well convey the passive sense of 'being humbled' as in: 'let God humble you [pl.] under his mighty hand',⁴⁰ that is, under his powerful agency.⁴¹ God's care for his people (pl.; v. 7) is 'second nature' to God's heart and character.⁴² The logical precedent (v. 6)⁴³ of 'having cast all your anxieties on him' states that surrender of anxiety and worries is a prerequisite or form of letting God humble you. We will not be able to allow God to humble us while still actively nourishing anxieties and worries, as if God were not present (cf. Matt 6:25-34; Mark 4:19). To be 'humbled under the mighty hand of God' can be understood as taking refuge in his strength (cf. Isa 50:10; Zeph 3:9, 12, 15, 17) rather than insisting on our meager resources and abilities (cf. Isa 50:11). Such an interpretation coheres well with the following section, where Peter warns of the opposing power of Satan (v. 8). When a person or a community abandons self-assurance and moves toward existential God-dependence, it also gains—and only then—power over Satan. Humble faith is *the* shield against satanic attack and against capitulating in suffering (cf. 1 Pet 5:9). In his sovereign grace, God is the one who restores, confirms, strengthens, and establishes toward participation in Christ's glory (v. 10; cf.

---

[38] Peter paraphrases LXX Prov 3:34 in 1 Pet 5:5b, as does James (Jas 4:6, 10). Instead of 'grace' in Prov 3:34, one can also read 'favor'.

[39] See, similarly, Col 2:23.

[40] Or, be 'humbled by God's mighty hand'; or: 'cooperate with being humbled by God'. Regarding 'God's mighty hand', see the frequent references to humbling surrounding the exodus from Egyptian slavery (e.g., Exod 13:9; Deut 3:24; 4:34); see Jobes, *1 Peter*, 311.

[41] A foundational connotation of the stem ταπ- is to 'level' or to 'make plane.' See, e.g., Isa 40:3-11, concerning pride and being downcast; see also the Magnificat in Luke 1:46-55.

[42] God's care (נתן) is often noted in the OT (cf., e.g., Gen 1:29; 17:16; 24:35; 30:6; Exod 12:36; Lev 17:11). Concerning God's love, see Jesus's affirmation of Peter in John 21. See Pss 37:5; 40:17; 55:22, and Matt 6:25.

[43] *Epiripsantes* (ἐπιρίψαντες) in v. 6 is an aorist participle (with imperatival force) and thus logically precedes the imperative of the main verb ('having cast . . . let yourselves be humbled').

Zeph 3:17-18). The dominion of God becomes a mercy because we cease to be strong in ourselves and count rather on being 'strong' in the God we trust (v. 11; cf. 1 Pet 3:22 and 4:11).

Humility, especially among leaders, engenders a peer mentality which moves toward godly authority structures. The humble leader, as a follower of Christ, walks under the mighty hand of God and serves as an example, an encourager, and an exhorter and thus motivates others to growth in like manner.[44] There is a fundamental willingness to suffer opposition while being inspired by hope that comes from the promise of future splendor, purity, and communion with Christ. Humility also engenders a community of reciprocal deference, especially toward elders. It is the practice of faithfully counting on God's powerful and caring strength, filled by a peaceful confidence in God's love and restoration.

The strength of humility lies in the fact that God is now central to life's circumstances. The humble person does not act in an oppressive fashion. Conversely, a humble person is not unhealthily pushed around. Rather, by surrendering control to God, God is existentially and directly called upon in his wisdom, power, mercy, and love, to act as central agent. Derivative responsibilities, such as, for example, family, other relationships, calling and work, and finances, ensue for such a humble person. In other words, such a person might carry heavy and great responsibilities. However, such responsibility is held in an attitude of stewardship, based upon a principal and existential dependence upon God.[45]

---

[44] Contrast this with the second century messianic claimant, Simon Bar Kokhba, who was known to be extremely forceful with his troops and failed miserably.

[45] The Old Testament figure of Joseph exemplifies someone who moves from 'pits' to 'peaks' while trusting in the goodness and faithfulness of God. Joseph's unseen confidence was that 'the LORD was with him'. Note Joseph's various 'descents': he was despised and thrown into a pit by his brothers; he was sold into slavery; he was falsely accused for seducing Potiphar's wife; he was unjustly imprisoned and forgotten. But all along he trusted in the living God. Note Joseph's various 'ascents': from pit to survival; from slave to respected man of the house; from prisoner to 'prime minister'. He thus became a blessing to many. He forgave and reconciled with his brothers and was restored to his father and the rest of his family. Genesis 50:19b-20a summarizes Joseph's attitude: 'Do not fear; for am I in the place of God? As for you, you meant evil against me, but God meant it for good'. A further exhortation toward true humility is found in Deuteronomy 8:14. When their wealth might increase, God warns the people of Israel not to 'raise up' (LXX ὑψωθῇς τῇ καρδίᾳ) or 'boast in' (MT) their heart by focusing on the work of their hands at the expense of acknowledging God's provision (Deut 8:17-18). Boastful pride as the antithesis to humility deceptively loses touch with reality; such self-deceived persons are rich in their seemingly independent self, forgetting that they needed liberation from slavery.

One of the benefits of Peter's growth in humility is healthy and exemplary leadership for the building up of the body (temple) of Christ. In a comprehensive way, humility facilitates an authentic and godly walk with God in the face of fears, oppression,[46] and Satan (cf. Zeph 2:3; 3:12-13).

5) Around AD 66–67, Peter is martyred under Emperor Nero (AD 54–68).[47] The consequence of Peter being led toward such a 'descent' is surrendered humility, a teachable posture, and increasingly counting on the triune God alone. In the process, Peter learns to entrust himself to God's vindication and to let go of self-sufficiency and ubiquitous control. Peter's 'downward mobility' into true humility may be illustrated by the following graph:

AD 30
  Mark 9–10 + John 13
  Undergoes personal growth
    AD 34
      Acts 10
      Learns ethnic equality before God
        AD 48
          Gal 2
          Must grow in humility to facilitate true fellowship among diverse believers
            AD 63
              1 Pet 5
              Displays exemplary leadership in humility
                AD 66-67
                  1 Clement
                  Martyrdom

The Purpose and Importance of Humility

Humility is an essential imprint and gift of God in the context of obediently following Christ. The aim of Christ-centered humility is to afford God as much room as is due to him in his majesty and as is needed in restoring us to himself, to each other, and the world around us (cf. 1 Pet 3:15). God thus employs us as his servants and manifests himself in his goodness and greatness. In this process, the God-given attitude of humility serves as the perpetual entry to

---

[46] Peter might have fled Rome in AD 64 during Nero's persecution of Christians; cf. *Acts Pet.*, 9.35.6; see Bockmuehl, *Simon*, 140.

[47] See John 21:18-19. See especially Clement of Rome (*1 Clem.* 5:1–6:4): 'Peter, who by reason of wicked jealousy . . . frequently endured suffering and thus, bearing his witness, went to the glorious place which he merited' (5:4) . . . 'To these men [i.e., Peter and Paul] who lived such holy lives there was joined a great multitude of the elect who by reason of rivalry were victims of many outrages and tortures and who became outstanding examples among us' (6:1).

aligning ourselves with all truth and reality. This holds true for both the individual and the community. The benefits of humility, affording us to know God and others, is immeasurable and life-necessary; the loss of such benefit through pride (cf. also 'quenching the Spirit', 1 Thess 5:19) suffocates real life.

Trait 5: Overcoming in Purifying Trials and Persecution[48]

While guarding our hearts is directed toward the inner life of followers (Mark 8:15), watchfulness is also directed toward the external issues of life, including temptation and persecution, as well as the expectation of the second coming of Christ. Some forms of external persecution or trial are to be expected as followers of Jesus (Mark 4:17; 10:30; 13:9-13; cf. Acts 2:13, 15; 4:1-3, 5-7, 18, 21, 29; 5:17-18, 21b-28, 33, 40; 6:9, 11-15; 8:7, 9-13, 18-24; 12:1-6, 19), partially brought on by exemplary conduct (1 Pet 1:6, 7; 2:20-21, 23; 3:13, 16-17; 4:12, 16, 19; 5:9-10, 12; see above, on 'courageous witness'). Watchfulness is needed as we face temptations and trials, in which we will be enticed to deny our undivided dependence upon Christ. Alertness also pertains to the Parousia of Christ (Mark 13:33-37; cf. 1 Pet 4:12-19). We must conduct ourselves in the light of the nearness and suddenness of his coming to final consummation and judgment (1 Pet 1:7). This future reality should order our priorities in our present life and assist us in living out surrender and obedience (i.e., living under the influence of the 'future indicative').[49]

The disciples will progressively surrender to God to such a degree that external opposition, persecution (Mark 10:30), and temptation will not easily shake them (contrast with Mark 4:17; see Acts 4:1-14 and often; 1 Pet 5:1-8). Part of the reason for this is that Jesus explicitly spoke about it (Mark 13:9, 10-13). Growth in this area is further facilitated by watching and praying (Mark 14:34, 37-38). Persecution also intensifies communion among Jesus's followers (Acts 2:42-47; 4:26-30; 1 Pet 4:14, 16). The disciple is to reckon with persecution (Mark 13:9-13) and to be watchful for the signs of the culmination of the end

---

[48] P.C. Zylla, *The Roots of Sorrow: A Pastoral Theology of Suffering* (Waco, TX: Baylor Univ. Press, 2012). C.S. Lewis, *A Grief Observed* (San Francisco, CA: HarperOne, 2009). On lament, see O. Bayer, 'The Theology of Lament', *Jahrbuch für Biblische Theologie*, 16 (2001), 298–301. N. Wolterstorff, *Lament for a Son* (Grand Rapids, MI: Eerdmans, 1987). We also possess musical lament: after J.S. Bach's first wife, Maria Barbara, had suddenly died in 1720 at age 35, leaving him with five children, he composed the so-called *Chaconne* for solo violin; the piece is marked by deep grief over his sudden loss, but it does also contain consolation in Christ.

[49] Cf. P.H. Davids, *A Theology of James, Peter, and Jude: Living in the Light of the Coming King* (Grand Rapids, MI: Zondervan, 2014).

times (Mark 13:33, 37). All of this points to the fact that spiritual battles are part of the disciple's reality. Both the satanic world (Mark 4:15; see Acts 5:3; 1 Pet 5:8-9) and human forces (see above on external and internal opposition in Acts) which are opposed to the expanding rule of God will seek to obstruct dedicated and consistent service to God. Prayer is the only means by which to navigate these obstacles. Jesus, together with the Father and the Holy Spirit, is our victor (1 Pet 5:8); we have no strength, wisdom, or strategy apart from him. By following the *missio dei* we will, likewise, encounter much external opposition and oppression (Mark 10:30; 13:9-13; Acts 2:13, [15]; 4:1-3, 5-7, 18, 21, 29; 5:17-18, 21b-28, 33, 40; 6:9, 11-15; 8:7, 9-13, 18-24; 12:1-6, 11, 19; 1 Pet 5:10-11).

As we have seen in other character traits emphasized by Peter, Jesus arises as the example, teacher, and facilitator for overcoming in suffering, trials, and persecution. Jesus withstands temptation and persecution (Mark 1:12-13; 2:1-10; 3:6; 14:8, 32-41; cf. 1 Pet 1:11). Both satanic and human forces are opposed to his mission. Ultimately, both are rendered powerless in Christ's resurrection power.

The Theological Context of Suffering: Peter's Emphasis on Living as Alien and Scattered Sojourners[50]

In 1 Peter 1:1, 17, and 2:11, Peter characterizes the recipients of his letter as 'sojourning aliens'. His reference to διασπορᾶς (='of the Diaspora', 1 Pet 1:1) is best taken metaphorically as 'sojourning aliens who are dispersed', alluding less to the Jewish Diaspora (as in LXX Deut 28:25; Isa 49:6; Jer 15:7; Jdt 5:19; 2 Macc 1:27; John 7:35) than to the fact that the persecuted, elect sojourners of God are sown and *scattered* as seed in Asia Minor (see, in the context of persecution, Acts 8:1, διεσπάρησαν; cf. Jas 1:1).

Jobes[51] suggests that the 'dispersed sojourning aliens' were Jewish-Christians from Rome who had been expelled under Claudius (AD 41–54) to the five provinces in Asia Minor mentioned in 1 Peter. In conjunction with this literal meaning, Jobes also accepts a secondary metaphorical meaning for the dispersed in analogy to previous Jewish Dispersions. It is most likely, however, that the primary recipients of 1 Peter were Gentiles (cf. 1 Pet 4:3; see also 1 Pet

---

[50] C.S. Lewis, *The Problem of Pain* (San Francisco, CA: HarperOne, 2001), 91 said: 'Pain insists upon being attended to. God whispers to us in our pleasures, speaks in our conscience, but shouts in our pain: it is His megaphone to rouse a deaf world'. Cf. J.A. Kehlhoffer, *Persecution, Persuasion and Power: Readiness to Withstand Hardship as a Corroboration of Legitimacy in the New Testament* (Tübingen: Mohr Siebeck, 2010).

[51] Jobes, *1 Peter*, 28–41.

1:14, 18) and that the Gentile Christian mission expanded into North-Galatia subsequent to AD 52. The 'dispersed sojourning aliens' are thus suffering Christians (not only dispersed from Rome).[52] The people of God, redeemed by Christ, *do not look toward returning to the land of Israel* or Judea (Heb 11:15), but rather to entering God's eternal kingdom (1 Pet 1:4-5, 7; 2:12; 4:7; Heb 11:8-10, *13-14* [ὁμολογήσαντες ὅτι ξένοι καὶ παρεπίδημοί εἰσιν ἐπὶ τῆς γῆς], *16a*). There is a forward movement in sojourning more in analogy to the sojourn of Abraham (Heb 11:14-15; cf. Lev 25:23) than a hope to *return* from Jewish exile (unless it is the reversal of exile from the garden of Eden). If there is an echo to the Babylonian exile of the Jewish people, it is the fact that as Daniel pursued God's ways in adverse geo-political and cultural settings, so Christians do now in Roman occupied Asia Minor.

Peter emphasizes that our individual and corporate lives on this earth are to be incarnate, concrete, settled, and specific. However, we are to live in such a way as to be people on pilgrimage toward a life of trust in God and his purposes. Our life and our suffering are real but penultimate in the light of God's present and future work (cf. Acts 3:19-21). Especially in 1 Peter 1:1-2, 17, and 2:11, Peter stresses that we are elect sojourners who have been born again to live out the newness of life in a foreign land and in a sinful and decaying world. In this new existence, we are faced with the question of true belonging: we are to be associated with but not dependent upon this 'land' and this 'world'. By living in such a way, we must build on what will never change.[53] In doing so, we are exhorted to avoid two extremes: to live either as virtually bodiless saved spirits in the presence of God or to live exclusively in this changing world, with a faint sense of God's ongoing pursuit of his stated end. Neither of these extremes is Petrine.[54]

Peter's emphasis on living as elect sojourners should not be confused with a post-modern tendency to 'keeping options open'. To the contrary, Peter calls for a true and covenantal commitment to God and his call of living as sojourning aliens in this world, focused on God's provisions and ways.

---

[52] Likewise critical of Jobes' suggestion, see Bockmuehl, *Simon*, 127 n. 43.

[53] See M.D. Williams, *Far as the Curse Is Found: The Covenant Story of Redemption* (Phillipsburg: P&R, 2005), 271–302. The ultimate place of existence is envisioned as God living among his people, the entire world being redeemed as mankind's inheritance.

[54] Helpful Old Testament examples are: Abraham journeying to Canaan (Gen 15:13; 23:4); Gershom: 'I have been a sojourner in a foreign land' (Exod 2:22); 'Israel sojourning in Egypt' and the desert (Deut 8:1-7); the Psalms of Ascent and Sojourn; Daniel in Babylon; another Gershom, descendant of Phineas, who returned from Babylonian exile (Ezra 8:2), and, finally, pilgrimage as foreigners (Heb 11:13-16; 13:14; cf. Lev 25:23). See Peterson, *Pastor*, 9–11, seeking a sacred place in God's nature.

A person who wants to 'keep options open' achieves exactly that: open options, and nothing more. This is not human, since human existence is meant to be marked by commitments to particulars (e.g., the local people of God, marriage and family, profession, location, a particular mission), all, however, held in a *penultimate* place vis-à-vis the ultimate devotion to God and his purposes (cf. 1 Cor 7:29-31). Along the way of sojourning, God purifies his people to become living stones who reflect the impact of his presence, individually and corporately.

Purifying Testing and Suffering in Peter's Canonical Testimony

With reference to 1 Peter, McCartney states that suffering represents a necessary 'proving ground of faith' (1 Pet 1:6-7).[55] Peter, together with many Old Testament prophets, compares God's benevolent testing in faith (cf. Abraham) with refining gold or silver. When purifying a precious metal, the refiner uses a fired clay container called *crucible* (often laced with enamel) that can withstand high temperatures. The precious metal is heated in the crucible to the point of burning off its impurities. According to Peter, God uses a metaphorical *crucible* to purify the faith of his sojourning, scattered people. It is a covenantal 'testing by fire'[56] (cf. 1 Pet 4:12). The Old Testament background is rich (cf., e.g., Deut 8:2, 5, 16; Isa 1:25-26; 48:10-11; Jer 16:14-21; *Zech 13:9*; cf. Heb 12:3-11). The important passage in Malachi 3:2b-4 is found in the context of Mal 3:1-15, which speaks of the messenger who *prepares* the way of the Lord (cf. Isa 40:3). In the New Testament, this messenger is identified as John the Baptist who comes in the 'spirit of Elijah'. It is clear in Malachi that the one who subsequently comes suddenly to visit *his* temple is no other than YHWH, *represented* by the 'messenger of the covenant'.[57] The 'messenger of the covenant' who represents the *coming of the Lord* brings purification through the fire of cleansing to those who are being purified (Mal 3:2b-4; cf. Zeph 1:7) and judgment to those who are being judged (Mal 3:5; cf. 3:6-15). In the New Testament adaptation of this motif, the fire of

---

[55] D.G. McCartney, 'Suffering in the Teachings of the Apostles', in C.W. Morgan and R.A. Peterson (eds), *Suffering and the Goodness of God* (Wheaton, IL: Crossway, 2008), 108–14, here, 108. Cf. G.S. Smith, *The Testing of God's Sons: The Refining of Faith as a Biblical Theme* (Nashville, TN: B&H Academic, 2014).

[56] See Lane, *Mark*, 349, and M. Dubis, 'First Peter and the "Sufferings of the Messiah"', in D. Baker (ed.), *Looking into the Future: Evangelical Studies in Eschatology* (Grand Rapids, MI: Baker, 2001), 85–96, here, 87.

[57] Cf. C.F. Keil and F. Delitzsch, *Commentary on the Old Testament in Ten Volumes, Volume X, The Twelve Minor Prophets* (Grand Rapids, MI: Eerdmans, 1983), X, 458: 'The coming of the Lord to His temple is represented as a coming of the covenant angel'.

cleansing is benevolent; it is grace-filled and not damning because of Christ's atonement (cf. Luke 3:16).

Additionally, suffering matures the believer(s) in appropriating the merits of Christ's finished work.[58] In other words, suffering as a consequence of following Christ is one of the catalysts toward growth in godliness,[59] as long as the disciple practices humble surrender to God's provisions in the midst of adversity. The form of suffering encountered by the Christians to whom Peter writes, ranges from verbal abuse and slander (1 Pet 2:12; 3:16; 4:14) to physical abuse and persecution (1 Pet 4:12).[60] Their isolation from various aspects of popular culture and society is implied by the reference to being 'strangers and exiles' (1 Pet 1:1; 2:11). McCartney aptly states that 'suffering is the key connection between the believer and Christ. Christ, by suffering, identified with his people; Christians, by suffering, are identified with Christ'.[61]

While the forms of suffering enumerated in 1 Peter initially point to being externally ostracized and rejected, 1 Peter 4:17 suggests that suffering goes as deep as the human heart. Being born to a new life (1 Pet 1:22-23) requires the surrender of familiar and temporarily gratifying passions and patterns (2 Pet 2:11) and the challenge to love sacrificially him whom we do not see (1 Pet 1:8), each other (1 Pet 1:22; 4:8), and those who oppose us (1 Pet 2:12, 15, 21).

As mentioned above, Christ's atoning suffering is conspicuously featured in the witness account of 1 Peter (1 Pet 5:1; see Mark 10:45; 14:22-24), especially by echoing Isaiah 53 (1 Pet 2:24).[62] His suffering is the key to atoning for sinfulness and thus liberating toward godliness (cf. 1 Pet 1:11). Part of the purifying theme in 1 Peter is, furthermore, that 'judgment begins with the household of God' (1 Pet 4:17; cf. Prov 11:31; Ezek 9:6; Zech 13:9; Mal 3:1-3; see also Amos 3:2). Peter finally understands what Jesus taught in Mark 1:16-17, 9:49, and 10:35-44 (see below; compare with Isa 51; Jer 25:29; Ezek 9:6). The judgment (τὸ κρίμα either refers to 'judgment' or to the 'action of a judge')[63] which Peter refers to in 1 Peter 4:17 is eschatological judgment, a foreshadowing of the Last Judgment.[64] This means, that *final judgment has already begun*, along the pattern of Old Testament forms of judgment which often begin with the people of God (cf. Jer 25:29; Amos 3:2; Zech 13:9; Mal

---

[58] McCartney, 'Suffering', 108.
[59] See the purifying suffering of Abraham when God tested him (Gen 22:1) by directing him to sacrifice his only son of promise (Gen 22:1-12).
[60] Jobes, *1 Peter*, 291.
[61] McCartney, 'Suffering', 108. See Isa 63:9.
[62] See Marshall, *1 Peter*, 91–98 and Jobes, *1 Peter*, 192–96.
[63] See Jobes, *1 Peter*, 293.
[64] On the theme of the 'messianic woes', see Dubis, 'First Peter', 85–96.

3:1-5). This eschatological final judgment has already impacted Jesus, the chief representative of his people; it is now extended to God's people who trust in Christ, and it will eventually issue in the future, final judgment of all mankind. The eschatological judgment is thus connected with condemnation. The judgment of Christ, satisfying the wrath of God, the Father, has, however, changed the consequence of the condemnation of the people of God, since Christ already bore the judgment and wrath of God (see below, on Mark 10:38-39).

Surprisingly, the eschatological condemnation is *commuted* to chastisement and purification of his people (i.e., the fire of purification) on account of the substitutionary work of Christ, who satisfied the wrath of God, atoned for our sins, and ransomed us from the slavery of Satan, sin, and death. Those who are, however, not 'passed over' for lack of seeking shelter in Christ's atoning blood, will face final judgment and condemnation at a future point. In other words, eschatological judgment presently affects the people of God by means of 'God's fiery presence' (Zech 13:9; Mal 3:1-3; cf. Luke 3:16b),[65] as an experience of chastisement, partially at the hands of the enemies of God (persecution).[66] Note here the echo to Deuteronomy 8:3, where God leads his stubborn people through the desert in order to humble them and reveal their heart to them, all the while providing manna.

Jobes notes correctly that in the midst of persecution 'God will begin his process of judging humanity with his own people, to see which are truly Christ's' (1 Pet 4:16-17b; i.e., 'the sorting out of humanity').[67] Perhaps Jobes does not emphasize enough that the *commuted* eschatological judgment of those who now follow Christ also serves the goal of *purifying* the covenant people of God who have already been passed over by the blood of Christ (purification in suffering as part of the 'messianic woes').[68]

The sojourning disciples suffer for the sake of Christ (1 Pet 4:14, 16; cf. Deut 8:1, 7) and as a consequence of doing good (1 Pet 2:20b).[69] As they gradually overcome sinful patterns they mature and grow toward godliness in the setting

---

[65] See Jobes, *1 Peter,* 291, referring to D.E. Johnson, 'Fire in God's House: Imagery from Malachi 3 in Peter's Theology of Suffering (1 Pet 4:12-19)', *JETS* 29 (1986), 285–94; here, 292. Jobes, *1 Peter,* 291, also quotes Seneca, *Ep.* 5.10, who states that 'fire tests gold, affliction strong men'.

[66] Dubis, 'First Peter', 85–96.

[67] Jobes, *1 Peter,* 293.

[68] Dubis, 'First Peter', 87.

[69] See T.B. Williams, *Good Works in 1 Peter: Negotiating Social Conflict and Christian Identity in the Greco-Roman World* (Tübingen: Mohr Siebeck, 2014). Peter also notes that we suffer because of our own folly and wickedness (1 Pet 2:20; 3:17; 4:15).

of opposing societal values and laws. In the midst of this process, the suffering disciples, be it as slaves, as servants (1 Pet 2:18), or otherwise (1 Pet 2:21; 5:9), cling to the unique atonement of Christ (1 Pet 2:24). Furthermore, they see Christ's encouraging example as a path for themselves (i.e., 'pattern-imitation', 1 Pet 2:21) and trust God for a purified life ('die to sin and live to righteousness'; cf. 1 Pet 4:17-19) and ultimate vindication (1 Pet 2:24-25; see 3:14-18; 4:13).[70] Helyer aptly notes: 'suffering for the sake of Christ demonstrates one's membership in the fellowship of the cross'.[71]

It is certainly possible that Peter looked at Christian suffering against the background of Jewish suffering. We already noted above that Peter probably learned of the suffering of the Maccabeans in their struggle against Seleucid forces. He probably heard of a form of suffering in which human beings seek to be faithful to God in the midst of adversity and persecution.[72] However, Peter's theology of purification in adversity and suffering arises, above all, from *experiencing* Jesus: *his* teaching (Mark 10:45; 14:22-24; cf. Matt 5:10-12, 21-26, 38-48; 7:1-5) *his* humility, *his* dedication to the Father, *his* suffering, *his* substitutionary death, *his* resurrection, and *his* exalted presence through the Holy Spirit (cf. 1 Pet 2:21, 23; 3:9).

A problem we encounter here is Peter's claim that the one who has suffered (judgment) will 'cease from sin' (1 Pet 4:1).[73] Jobes notes in a clarifying way that the intent of 1 Peter 4:1 is to say: 'those who suffer unjustly . . . have demonstrated that they are willing to be through, or done, with sin by choosing obedience'.[74] McCartney lays out the following contrast between Peter and Paul: According to Paul, we progressively cease from sin because we have 'died' to sin. According to Peter we progressively cease from sin because we have suffered chastisement (and because Jesus suffered the judgment). Paul emphasizes that Christ *died* an atoning death. Peter states that Christ *suffered* an atoning death (but see Phil 3:10). McCartney concludes: 'In a unique way then, the believer's actual experience of suffering links him or her to Christ. The believers, the 'house of God,' thus undergo, as it were, the judgment of God but in Christ, not alone, and so can entrust themselves to their faithful Creator by doing good ([1 Pet] 4:19)'.[75] While McCartney points in the right direction, further clarification of what it means to 'undergo . . . the judgment of

---

[70] Peter's humble embrace of facilitative suffering is akin to Paul's view expressed in Acts 14:22; 2 Cor 1:8-11 (esp. v. 9), and 2 Tim 3:12.
[71] Helyer, *Life*, 174. Cf. Lane, *Mark*, 372.
[72] See the account of the persecution and eventual martyrdom of the mother and her seven sons in 2 Macc 7:1-41.
[73] See McCartney, 'Suffering', 112–13 and Helyer, *Life*, 174–78.
[74] Jobes, *1 Peter*, 265.
[75] McCartney, 'Suffering', 113 (square brackets added).

God . . . in Christ' is possible if we consider more deeply Jesus's message both in Mark 10:38-39[76] and Mark 9:49, while keeping the above-stated reflections on eschatological judgment in mind.

Peter's Recollection of Jesus's Teaching on Purification

As part of a central text on humility and servant-leadership (Mark 10:35-45; see above), Mark 10:38-39 alludes to both shared and distinct circumstances befalling Jesus and his followers. Both Jesus (Mark 10:38-39; 14:36; Luke 12:50) and his followers (Mark 10:39) have to undergo a form of judgment (compare with Jer 49:12). The metaphors of the cup and of baptism speak of such judgment (see especially Isa 51:17, 22; Jer 25:15, 17-18, 29).[77] However, there is a marked difference in the *nature of judgment* befalling his followers, since Jesus, the innocent one (Mark 10:45; 1 Pet 2:22-24), takes judgment *first* upon himself.[78] Mark 10:38 (cf. Mark 10:45; John 19:30; 1 Tim 2:6) thus implies what is explicitly stated elsewhere in the New Testament, namely that the judgment of Jesus completely satisfies God's wrath (Rom 3:25; Heb 9:5). Jesus thus functions as the *representative* of God's people. We have noted above, that both Isa 52:13–53:12 and Dan 7:13-14 imply *representation*: in Isa 52:13–53:12, the *Ebed YHWH* suffers *on behalf* of God's people (Isa 53:4-6, 8, 10-12); in Dan 7:13-14, the Son of Man comes into the presence of the Ancient of Days in order to receive honor, glory, and rule over 'all peoples, nations, and languages' (Dan 7:14). The saints, however, will co-reign with the Son of Man (and, implied, with the Ancient of Days; Dan 7:18-27). By drinking the cup *first* (Mark 10:38), Jesus, as the pure substitute (Isa 53:9-10), takes the *entire* judgment and punishment for all the sins of his people upon himself (Mark 10:45; Isa 52:13–53:12). When the cup of judgment is subsequently passed on from Jesus to his followers (Mark 10:39; cf. Jer 25:15, 29), the wrath of God, the Father, has already been satisfied. Justice has been reestablished between God and his people through the innocent representative. The subsequent (temporary) judgment which still befalls his people (Mark 10:39; 1 Pet 4:17) is therefore *commuted* to the crucible of covenantal chastisement and a fire of purification (see Luke 3:16b, baptism with the Holy Spirit and fire[79] and Acts

---

[76] For details, see Bayer, *Predictions*, 54–89.

[77] Bayer, *Predictions*, 54–84.

[78] In the OT, God judges his own people *first* (cf. Isa 10:12; Jer 25:29; Ezek 9:6), before he exacts judgment upon the oppressors of his people.

[79] See J.D.G. Dunn, *Baptism in the Holy Spirit: A Re-examination of the New Testament on the Gift of the Spirit* (Louisville, KY: Westminster John Knox, 1977), 8–14, 18–21), who convincingly argues that the term 'fire' does not refer to final judgment but to grace-driven purification.

14:22b, 'through many tribulations we must enter the kingdom of God'). We noted above that both Pentecost and the concept of 'fishers of men' (Mark 1:16; Jer 16:16) also communicate aspects of purification.

A further key to understanding Jesus's teaching on the purification of his disciples lies in Mark 9:49. There, Jesus makes a seemingly opaque statement that the disciples must be 'salted with fire' (i.e., dedicated in purity).[80] Followers who belong to God will be 'salted', i.e., sacrificially dedicated to God (Rom 12:1).[81] This dedication, i.e., 'being salted', occurs by means of purification ('fire') and overcoming of sin. Salt serves as a metonymy of the entire process of purification of the sacrifice, both in the Old Testament (especially animals; cf. Lev 2:13; Ezek 43:24)[82] as well as in the New Testament (the offer of a 'living sacrifice', Rom 12:1).[83] The crucible of trial, tribulation, and persecution (1 Pet 1:7; 4:12), is to have a purifying effect upon all disciples (cf. Mark 1:16/Jer 16:14-21). To 'salt with fire' is thus a compact statement for a progressively purified dedication to God.[84] The additional phrase, 'have salt among you' (Mark 9:50; cf. Matt 5:13 par.) continues the same thought. Again, 'salt in sacrifice'[85] serves as a metonymy of surrendered and purified dedication and consecration. Reconciled peace ensues when such dedication through purification (fire) increases (it becomes 'spicy'; see Job 6:6). Inner purification is the condition for growth in humility.

The followers of Jesus are thus graciously 'passed over' by the atoning blood of Jesus (Mark 10:45; 14:22-24).[86] Nevertheless, and now especially, God purifies his redeemed people by means of the crucible of suffering (cf. Mark 1:16-17/Jer 16:16; Mal 3:2b-4), albeit safe in the atonement of Christ which has put them in a right and covenantal relationship with God (1 Pet 3:18).

---

[80] The context of Mark 9:49-50 (Markan *Sondergut*) sets out a sharp contrast: either a person enters into life and the kingdom of God, or into gehenna (hell) and fire: Jesus strongly emphasizes humility, service, and the radical removal of any 'cause for sin'.

[81] The text-critically debated addition 'and every sacrifice is salted with salt' (see B.M. Metzger, *A Textual Commentary on the Greek New Testament* [Stuttgart: Deutsche Bibelgesellschaft, 1994], 102–103) points toward the correct interpretation of the text-critically unquestioned, preceding verse.

[82] See Lane, *Mark*, 349. C.S. Keener, *The IVP Bible Background Commentary* (Downers Grove, IL: IVP, 2014), 152, refers to *Jub.* 21:11.

[83] See Lane, *Mark*, 349 and, to a degree, Pesch, *Markusevangelium*, II, 116–17.

[84] See Titus 2:14; Heb 1:3; 9:13-14, 22; Jas 4:8, and 1 John 3:3.

[85] In later rabbinic Judaism, the figurative meaning of 'salt' was used to refer to 'Torah' or 'wisdom'; see P. O'Brien, *Colossians, Philemon* (Waco, TX: Word, 1982), 242–43, regarding Col 4:5.

[86] In the Lord's Supper, disciples thus drink from a 'cup of blessing' (1 Cor 10:16). It is a cup of fellowship and commemoration of having been 'passed over' (Mark 14:23 parr.).

Followers of Christ thus 'drink' from two distinct cups: a 'cup of blessing' in the Lord's Supper (Mark 14:23-24), celebrating the 'pass-over' in the real, spiritual presence of Christ, as well as a 'cup of purification' (Mark 10:39; cf. Mark 9:49; Luke 3:16; Acts 14:22b; 1 Pet 1:7; 4:12, 17). Suffering is thus a weighty catalyst for growth in maturity.[87]

Purification and the Living Temple of God

Associated with the Petrine themes of sojourning and purifying suffering is the motif of the living, eternally established messianic *temple* of God. Peter emphasizes that followers of Christ are living stones (1 Pet 2:5), thus alluding to the messianic temple which Jesus builds (cf. 1 Cor 3:16-17; 6:19; 2 Cor 6:16; Eph 2:21). Jesus himself became the stone who was rejected by men, but was affirmed by God to become the foundation stone of the eternal temple (Mark 12:10-12 [Ps 118:22; Isa 8:14; 28:16; 37:25-28]; Acts 4:11; 1 Peter 2:4, 6-8; cf. Eph 2:20 and also Matt 7:24-25).[88] His disciples, likewise, are rejected by men (i.e., suffering sojourners) but are becoming living stones of God's messianic temple (1 Pet 2:5). The reflections on purification above dovetail closely with the temple motif, as God's presence is inseparably and perpetually connected with purity. The temple motif, with its deep roots in the Old Testament, has been taken up by Jesus (see Mark 11) and passed on to Peter.[89]

The temple motif always conveys a particular presence of God: 'temple' is where God resides. He is *perpetually* present in the heavenly temple where he dwells (Isa 6:1-6; Jer 17:12; Heb 9:23-24). Subsequent to the creation of his magnificent universe and world and prior to the fall of mankind, God is said to have 'walked' among men (Gen 3:8; Lev 26:12). While God's glory fills the heavens and the earth and is not confined to a particular space (Isa 66:1; Acts 7:48-50; 17:24), he condescends, as an anticipation of the future, to be present in a particular locality (1 Kgs 8:27; 2 Chr 6:18). First we find God 'dwelling' some 400 years in Israel's tabernacle (Exod 40:34-35; see Num 17:13). At times, God abandons this dwelling (Ps 78:60-61). Following the period of sojourn, God 'dwells', again condescendingly, in the first (2 Chr 7:9-11) and

---

[87] Helyer, *Life*, 177, speaks of 'an aid to spiritual maturity'. Referring to J.H. Elliott, *1 Peter* (New York, NY: Doubleday, 2000), 13–14, Helyer (*Life*, 177) notes that 1 Peter frequently echoes Proverbs regarding 'disciplinary suffering': 1 Pet 2:17/Prov 24:21; 1 Pet 3:6c/Prov 3:25; 1 Pet 4:8/Prov 10:12; 1 Pet 4:18/Prov 11:31; 1 Pet 5:5/Prov 3:34.

[88] See McCartney, 'Suffering', 110.

[89] See G.K. Beale, *A New Testament Biblical Theology: The Unfolding of the Old Testament in the New* (Grand Rapids, MI: Baker Academic, 2011), 592–650.

the second temple (Ezra 6:16), totaling some 1000 years (950 BC–AD 70).[90] Both the tabernacle and the temple point beyond themselves to a future anticipation of God dwelling among his people.[91] With Jesus, God incarnate (Immanuel) dwells among his people (John 1:14, σκηνόω=I tabernacle; see 2:19-21).[92] While he is rejected by the spiritual leaders of Israel (Mark 9:31), Jesus is established by God as the cornerstone of the eternal, messianic temple (Mark 12:9-12; see Mark 14:58: 'I will build another, not made with hands' [ἀχειροποίητον])[93] which is part of the true, eternally existing temple in the presence of God (Heb 9:11). The universal people of God, purified by the blood of the innocent lamb, are being built into and given access to the eternal temple of God (1 Pet 2:5; cf. Zeph 1:7). Part of this 'access'-imagery identifies Jesus, the Son of Man, *as* Jacob's ladder (compare Gen 28:12 with John 1:51). At the culmination of all things, where there will be no earthly temple (Rev 21:22), God will dwell in the midst of his purified people (Rev 21:3; see 2 Cor 6:16-18 [Lev 26:11-17]; cf. Isa 37:25-28; Zeph 1:7), bringing the temple of living stones together with the eternal, heavenly temple of God on earth.

Jesus Prepared Peter and the Other Disciples to Anticipate the Messianic Temple of God (Mark 11:1-25)[94]

Surprisingly, Jesus's entry into Jerusalem (Mark 11:1-11) sparks popular, messianic expectations (Mark 11:10) which he does not squelch. Zechariah 9:9 carries messianic and divine overtones (i.e., YHWH as the entering king):[95] 'Rejoice greatly, O daughter of Zion! ... behold, your king is coming to you; righteous and having salvation is he, humble and mounted on a donkey...'. On

---

[90] Helyer, *Life*, 192 n. 17, observes that the Qumran community viewed itself as the priestly successor to the sons of Zadok (1QS 5:1-10; 8:4-6; 9:3-5; 1QpHab 12:1-3; CD 3:21–4:3).

[91] As an example of a misguided, Christian expectation of a future temple to be built in Jerusalem, see J.W. Schmitt and J.C. Laney, *Messiah's Coming Temple: Ezekiel's Prophetic Vision of the Future Temple* (Grand Rapids, MI: Kregel, 2014).

[92] Perrin, *Temple*, 106–13; J. Ådna, 'Jesus and the Temple', in Holmén and Porter (eds), *Handbook*, III, 2635–76.

[93] Cullmann, *Peter*, 205, rightly notes that Jesus would not have said, 'I will destroy'; rather, he would have said that it will 'be destroyed' (cf. Mark 13:2).

[94] Cf. T.C. Gray, *The Temple in the Gospel of Mark: A Study in its Narrative Role* (Tübingen: Mohr Siebeck, 2008) and R.H. Stein, *Jesus, the Temple and the Coming Son of Man: A Commentary on Mark 13* (Downers Grove, IL: IVP Academic, 2014).

[95] See W.H. Rose ('Zechariah and the Ambiguity of Kingship in Postexilic Israel', in *Let us Go up to Zion: Essays in Honour of H. G. M. Williamson on the Occasion of his Sixty-Fifth Birthday* [Leiden: Brill, 2012], 219–32), who argues that the 'king' in Zech 9:9 refers to YHWH.

the one hand, Jesus enters Jerusalem in humility and zeal for true worship of God from people of all nations. On the other hand, Jesus's entry into Jerusalem and his cleansing of the temple must be viewed as God 'visiting' his city and temple (see Mal 3:1 and the purification and rededication of the temple in the wake of the Maccabean uprising).[96] Rather than finding true worship, he encounters commerce, greed, and self-interest.[97] Jesus juxtaposes the fruitless, earthly temple, signified by cursing the fig tree and cleansing of the temple, with sincere trust in God. Only through faith in God and his work, do followers bear acceptable fruit of worship, prayer, and godliness (Mark 11:12-25).

Jesus zealously seeks true worship and prayer in and among his people (see Isa 61:11), since they are becoming, after being brought into it, the new and eternal temple of God (Mark 12:10-11; 14:58; 15:29, 38; 1 Pet 2:5; see also Matt 12:6; John 2:19; 1 Cor 3:16-17; 6:19; 2 Cor 6:16; Eph 2:21; Rev 21:22; cf. Luke 20:9-19; 22:54-55, 63-71; 23:26-43, 44-49). The untimely cursing of the fig tree which cannot bear fruit out of season makes sense only if it is seen as representing the fruitless temple, which should bear fruit at any time (Mark 11:12-14; cf. 11:20-21). What befalls the fig tree will befall the fruitless temple (see the destruction of the temple in AD 70; cf. Mark 13:2).

The disciples of Christ are called to bear the fruit of godliness (e.g., worship and prayer) in all areas of life, as well as holistic testimony to others. Jesus cleanses the temple (see 2 Chr 29:16) because the temple is meant to display the fruit of true worship, not commerce (Mark 11:15-19; cf. 1 Chr 29:10-19; 2 Chr 6:14-42). The temple is meant to draw people from all nations to purity and worship of God (see 2 Chr 7:1, 3). Prayer is for 'all nations' (Mark 11:17; cf. 2 Chr 6:32-33; Isa 56:7). God gives his disciples the Spirit of fire (cf. Luke 3:16). The mercy and grace of God has a purifying effect in their lives as living stones of his eternal temple (Eph 2:21; 1 Pet 2:4-5).

True worship of God is foundational to a reality-congruent, healthy, and God-designed life (Mark 11:22-25). Above all, it is the right response to the character and nature of God. Followers of Christ pray boldly and confidently (with faith) toward the end that God would remove all hindrances (the figurative meaning of 'mountain') to true worship of the triune God. However, this boldness can never be manipulative before God or coercive toward other human beings. The focus lies always on surrendered trust in God's sovereign power, ability, and will.

---

[96] We must bear in mind that according to Mark, Jesus already displayed his divine nature (see especially Mark 2:5-12; 9:2-7; 12:1-9; 14:62).

[97] See 1 Chr 29:10-12; God is king over all things and all things come from God (2 Chr 29:14b-15). See J. Ådna, *Jesu Stellung zum Tempel: Die Tempelaktion und das Tempelwort als Ausdruck seiner messianischen Sendung* (Tübingen: Mohr Siebeck, 2000).

Suffering on Account of Satan and Other Opposing Powers

Both in the Gospels (Mark 1:13; 4:15; Luke 10:18; 13:16; 22:31) and in 1 Peter and Acts, Christ's victory is not only over sin, but also over Satan and other opposing powers (1 Pet 3:18-22;[98] see Acts 5:3; 26:18, and 1 Pet 5:8-9; cf. Rom 16:20). In 1 Peter the suffering of the people of God can be on account of the adversary, Satan, or due to opposing powers in the physical world (see above, regarding 'external opposition' in Acts, and Col 1:15-17).

A similar dimension in the unfolding drama of Acts is the motif of *suffering* and *testing*. It occurs by means of *internal* tensions and *external* opposition. Peter is *shaped* by the taxonomy of the setting of early Christianity to grow as a disciple of Christ in the midst of these challenges (see Mark 10:29-30). Acts 14:22b summarizes this reality: 'to remain in the faith because through many tribulations it is necessary that we enter the Kingdom of God'. Such suffering and opposition drives the disciples to remember the substitutionary sufferings of Christ (see the metaphors of the cup and baptism in Mark 10:35-44) and his atoning liberation from sin and Satan (Mark 10:45; cf. Acts 11:16). Jesus's example gives us a model for persevering in suffering and the acceptance that suffering works God's purification into our hearts toward the ultimate hope of vindication of the exiled and sojourning people of God (1 Pet 5:10).[99]

The reality of a new life in Christ (his atonement and forensic justification and purification) is progressively applied to our hearts and lives, among other means, through various forms of suffering, including that inflicted by Satan and other opposing powers.

Trait 6: Progressing in Surrender and Obedience[100]

Disciples cannot be captains of their own surrender to Christ. Rather, the essence of surrender is yielding control to the one who calls, with legitimate authority, to surrender (Mark 8:34). Surrender means transferring the primary

---

[98] See Helyer, *Life*, 148–60, for a detailed discussion of this difficult text. Helyer convincingly states (*Life*, 154–55) that, in its creedal form, 1 Pet 3:18-22 affirms Jesus's atonement, burial (implied), resurrection, victory over 'rebellious spirits', ascension to heaven, exaltation to the right hand of God, and installation as Lord (cf. Rom 8:34; 1 Cor 15:1-5; Eph 1:20-22; Phil 2:5-11; Col 1:13-20; 2:9-15; 3:1-4) .

[99] See McCartney, 'Suffering', 113–14.

[100] D. Bonhoeffer, *Discipleship*, 63–70. The 'Theological Declaration of Barmen' (1934) states in article 8.11: 'Jesus Christ, as he is attested for us in Holy Scripture, is the one Word of God which we have to hear and which we have to trust and obey in life and in death' (A.C. Cochrane, *The Church's Confession Under Hitler* [Philadelphia, PA: Westminster, 1962], 237–42).

allegiance from self to Christ[101] (and, with Christ, to the Father and the Holy Spirit). This is why Acts 6:7b speaks of 'obedience to the faith' (see Mark 8:34, 38; 9:26–11:18; Acts 4:19; 5:29, 32; cf. Rom 1:5; 16:26). Christ himself will serve as the master who leads into ever deepening surrender, peeling off one layer of self-sufficiency after the other. Surrender is not self-destruction but rather the act of relearning human responsibility in God-dependence as opposed to self-sufficiency.

True surrender involves the cessation of the disciples' deepest loyalty to all ties and dependencies (especially idols and addictions) that obstruct full availability to Christ and thus obedience to God's will. It means surrendering control of self-determination. The result is a perpetual dependence upon Christ, expressed in love of God, of others, and of self (Mark 12:30-31). Peter expresses this especially in the way of fearing God above all else (Acts 4:19; 1 Pet 1:1, 2, 8, 13-15, 17, 22; 2:16, 25; 3:2; 4:10; cf. 1 Pet 2:8, 11, 13, 18; 3:6). Surrender and obedience to the will of God are closely related concepts (Mark 3:35; 8:34-37, 38; Acts 4:19; 5:29, 32; 6:7b; 9:26–11:18 [esp. 10:28]; 1 Pet 1:2, 14). Jesus's initial call of his disciples (Mark 1:17; 2:14) includes at least two elements. First, he calls them to 'be with him' (Mark 3:14) and to follow him. Second, he calls them to participate in his mission (esp. in the case of the initial disciples this involves becoming 'fishers of men'). 'Following Christ' initially means to 'leave behind and to go along with Christ' (Mark 1:17; 2:14; 5:37; see also 10:28-30; 14:13; cf. Deut 13:4; 2 Kgs 23:3). This implies 'to let go of all that which hinders full availability and service to Christ' (see, e.g., Mark 4:23, 25; 10:11, 21; 12:44), to appropriate Christ's provisions and example in communion with him, and to follow his instructions (e.g., Mark 8:34-38).

The core passage for our purposes here is Mark 8:34-37 (especially v. 34), which is found near the beginning of the second half of Mark (beginning with Mark 8:27). The literary structure of that section of Mark (Mark 8:27–10:45) is particularly conspicuous since each major prediction of Jesus's passion (Mark 8:31; 9:31; 10:32-34) is followed by an instruction on discipleship (Mark 8:34-37; 9:33-37; 10:35-44). This very structure tells us that there is an interconnection between what befalls Jesus and what happens to his disciples (cf. 1 Pet 2:21). He imprints his patterns on them. Mark 8:34 expands the call to discipleship to *all* who would follow Christ and serves as the heading for the following three verses. However, its meaning has often been obscured. As noted above, Jesus summons us essentially to surrender our primary loyalty to self in exchange for our primary allegiance to Jesus;[102] it is a surrender of

---

[101] Gambrell, 'Mark 8:34', 16, 26, 42–43, 53.
[102] See Gambrell, 'Mark 8:34', 42–43.

control.[103] As a paraphrase, Jesus says: 'If anyone would follow me on an ongoing basis, let him surrender all self-sufficiency to me, live a sacrificial life as pardoned by my death, and continually follow me into true life.' Much of this echoes the Old Testament comprehensive motif of 'walking' with God (see, e.g., Gen 5:22, 24, 33; Deut 10:12; Josh 22:5; 2 Kgs 10:31; Jer 7:23; Mic 6:8; cf. 2 Cor 6:16). Once again, we find such surrender exemplified, taught, and facilitated by Jesus himself who yielded fully to the Father and obeyed his will (Mark 14:36; cf. 1 Pet 2:23 and John 6:38).

Conclusion

Christ-driven identity formation spawns a rich array of character traits which lay at the center of sustained transformation and are the basis of engaged political, ethical, and social engagement. Such a Christ- and identity driven character leads to individual and corporate integrity, at the heart of which lies Christ-representation in the form of increased prayerful trust in God, holistic witness, purity of heart, serving and life-giving humility, endurance and maturing in suffering and adversity, and surrendered obedience. Such Christ-representation takes individual and corporate forms, issuing in the ultimate goal of a purified, living 'temple' and 'city' of followers of Christ, manifesting hope to a despairing, alienated world, and awaiting the ultimate renewal of all things.

---

[103] Augustine's *Confessions* and T. à Kempis's *Imitation of Christ* rightly focus on surrender to God. However, both tend to have too negative a view of the value of God's physical world, which is to be embraced and enjoyed so long as a person lives in dependence upon God and seeks to worship God in all areas of life.

Conclusions

In this book we have explored the function of Peter as a unique apostolic witness to the life, saving work, and impact of Christ. Peter, as the rock, guarantees authentic and reliable witness, both in word and in personal, Christ-centered transformation. As such, Peter is *the* living letter of Christ (cf. 2 Cor 3:3). Like no one else, Peter vouchsafes for the faithful representation of Jesus, his person, teaching, and kingdom mission. Peter secures, uniquely, the reliable transfer of learned and experienced Jesus-tradition to a central and crucial section of the New Testament canon, thus serving as the enduring apostolic *rock*. Such stable transfer of tradition does not only concern witness to the truth of Christ but also to the authenticity of Christ-centered transformation of a disciple's identity and character. We have traced the impact of Christ upon Peter and its ensuing consequence for all followers of Christ. It is thus not surprising that Christology, identity, and character formation are so profoundly reflected in Peter's direct (1 and 2 Peter), semi-direct (Mark) and indirect (Acts 1–12, 15) witness. The lasting imprint of Peter's witness is that the person and work of Christ (Christology) and identity and character formation (discipleship) go hand in hand and reinforce each other. Never do we encounter in Peter's witness a separation of these factors and realities.

Initially, we considered non-transferable aspects of Peter's calling and found that they provide the enduring witness foundation for trust in Christ. They serve as the unshakeable deposit upon which faith in the triune God can grow. Peter's calling to testify to Christ, his witness in Acts like an Old Testament prophetic repentance preacher, and his apostolic letter-writing all serve as a most significant foundation (see the 'rock', Matt 16:18-19) for everything vital to a follower of Christ. We have noted that this aptly echoes Paul's statement in Ephesians 2:20. Accordingly, the original eleven apostles, chief among them Peter, are the foundation (through their witness and appointment as unique messengers) for the eternal temple of God. Jesus is the perpetual cornerstone of this 'structure' (Mark 12:10-12; Acts 4:11-12; 1 Pet 2:4-10; cf. Eph 2:20-22). Our lives as followers of Christ are squarely based on that witness foundation. In John 17:20, Jesus prays for us as we put trust in the witness of his original disciples. Particularly, our trust in Christ is informed by Peter's person and witness. We note the following conclusions:

- Peter is the source of the Gospel of Mark.

- Peter's early Christian *message* provides the foundational gospel *format* for Mark's, Matthew's, and Luke's Gospel accounts. This holds true even if it is correct that a proto-Matthew was written in Hebrew before the composition of the Greek Gospel of Mark.[1]
- Additionally, Peter may have spearheaded the use of the *bios* genre for such a narration of Jesus's life and words.
- Peter's early speeches in Acts represent authentic Petrine repentance speeches, patterned after Old Testament prophetic repentance preachers. Christ appoints Peter as a repentance preacher along the lines of an Old Testament prophet (Acts 1–5) so that our repentance and turning to the God of Abraham, Isaac, and Jacob and the embrace of the atoning work of his eternal Son, Jesus Christ, might be in response to one of God's latter prophets, Peter. He is aligned with the Old Testament history of repentance preachers, who foundationally point to the redemption from sinfulness through Jesus Christ (see 2 Pet 1:21).
- Christ appointed Peter as an apostolic letter-writer (1 and 2 Peter) in order to continue in us the ministry of transformation that Christ worked in Peter and is accomplishing in us. We conclude that on such a historically based, theologically formed witness and transformation-foundation (i.e., Peter) rests our full trust in Christ (see Paul's acknowledgement of this fact in Acts 13:31). As is apparent throughout the New Testament, Peter's personal witness is corroborated by other apostles (cf., e.g., John and Matthew) and by Paul.[2]

Overall, Peter contributes substantially to the genesis of the New Testament canon, thus fulfilling his commission to be the apostolic rock calling others to faith in Christ. Christ thus appointed Peter as the 'rock' (Matt 16:18-19) in order that our faith and our transformation in Christ might not be self-guided, but guided by the Christ-shaped person and witness of Peter. At any point we might say that a particular word, phrase, concept, or emphasis associated with Peter is not unique to Peter but can be found, at times, in John, James, or Paul as well. To this we reply: yes, indeed. According to the overall evidence concerning Peter's role and impact, he was, however, the overall core transmitter of such words, phrases, concepts, and emphases, as gleaned from his master.

---

[1] Baltes, *Evangelium*, 590–99.
[2] Bockmuehl, *Simon*, 19–36.

We noted above that Jesus intends to create an authentic, personally transformed cadre of truth-witnesses, with Peter as the central spokesperson. Jesus sets out on his eternal and universal mission by revealing himself to Peter (and others around him), by transforming Peter (and others), thus establishing his 'sculpture' as the apostolic foundation *eo ipso*. Obviously, it is not Peter as a hero that we are to focus on; rather, it is the amazing sculptor, Jesus, and with him the Father and the Holy Spirit, to whom our adoration and worship belong. Peter thus uniquely and reliably testifies to the Triune God.

We have argued above that Peter's witness and transformation as 'foundation' is not meant to exist in isolation; rather, it intrinsically points beyond itself. The concept of a foundation (Peter and the other apostles), designed from the cornerstone (Jesus), readily anticipates a dynamic *building*, a corporate entity. The great goal of the individual transformation, around the one and true, triune God of this universe, is the corporate and communal temple or city of God, consisting of many living stones crafted by God (1 Pet 2:4-10; cf. Eph 2:21-22; Rev 21:3, 22). In this image, there is no need for a Roman Catholic 'apostolic succession', since recourse to the apostolic foundation (especially set by Peter) will open or lock access to God's presence. What needs to be guarded then is not a community under the ecclesiastical office of a successor of Peter, but rather the apostolic foundation itself ('rock'), which 'opens' or 'closes' the gates of heaven. Simultaneously, this foundation is not only Peter's witness to Christ but also his transformation by Christ. It is in this way that we hope to have supplied further evidence in support of the fact that Peter is a formidable factor and catalyst of Christian origins. Says Bond:

> Peter was the one historical person to play a significant role in the ministries of both Jesus and Paul and in many ways provides a bridge between the two. An accurate assessment of his contribution is surely foundational to our ongoing attempts to reconstruct Christian origins.[3]

Peter, as the unique witness and spokesperson for the Twelve, outlines the theological landscape in which Paul and others develop their apostolic commission.

Built on this 'non-transferable' foundation, we explored various 'semi-transferable' aspects in Peter's function. While the semi-transferable aspects are unique to Peter (John 21:15-19) or are at least unique to the original apostles (Mark 1:16-17), they simultaneously contain patterns that are transferable to other disciples.

---

[3] Bond, 'Introduction', in: Cullmann, *Peter*, 16.

We noted the following:

1. While the commission to Simon Peter and Andrew to become 'fishers of men' (Mark 1:16-17) contains unique features (their particular kingdom ministry during Jesus's earthly life in Judea and Galilee), it implies simultaneously an ongoing commission of drawing human beings back to God (see, e.g., Matt 28:19-20, which extends to the end of the present aeon).
2. While Peter is uniquely reinstated in John 21:15-19 after denying Christ three times, the commission to 'feed/tend my sheep/lambs' continues at least to all followers of Christ who are called to shepherd or pastor in one form or another.

Furthermore, we have discovered a natural Christological compatibility in Peter's witness in Mark, the Petrine sections of Acts, and 1 and 2 Peter, uniquely clustered around Jesus as *Ebed YHWH*. As soon as we explore in some depth aspects of Peter's Christology (as witness to Christ's self-disclosure), especially Jesus as κύριος, as *Ebed YHWH* (Isa 52:13–53:12), as the temple, and as the universal temple builder, we find ourselves challenged to let these Petrine witness-truths about Christ impact our identities and lives in such a way as to be molded in pattern-imitation. According to Peter in Mark, the Petrine sections of Acts and 1 and 2 Peter, Jesus is the rescuing master who draws our entire individual and corporate lives into a pattern analogous to that of Christ. In doing so, Peter always acknowledges the unparalleled uniqueness of Christ (e.g., 1 Pet 5:4 [Jesus as the chief shepherd]; 1 Pet 5:1 [Peter as witness to the sufferings of Christ]). Nevertheless, time and again, Peter's witness to Christ invariably leads to Christlike transformation of himself and of his listeners. Peter thus does not convey merely abstract truth-knowledge of Christ. Rather, he personally knows the depths of the person of Christ, his profound humiliation in suffering (1 Pet 5:1-7) and his exalted majesty (2 Pet 1:16-18) as they relate to the follower's own humiliation and vindication. The effect of Christ's atonement on his followers is therefore always radical identity and character transformation based on reconciliation with God, individually and corporately. Such transformation is thoroughly Christ-centered and patterned after Christ's own humiliation (with varied forms of suffering) and vindication (see Paul in Phil 2:1-12). With Peter, there is no limit to exploring Christology. His witness to the extraordinary uniqueness of Christ is very lively (1 Pet 5:1; 2 Pet 1:16; cf. Luke 1:2), but it always carries the embedded message that such truth must radically transform identity and character.

Throughout the remainder of the study we explored various readily transferable aspects of identity and character formation. According to Peter, our new identity is intimately connected with the master's unique work on our behalf and, consequently, his approach to and perspective on us. According to the triune God, we are severely broken but beloved and redeemed people, purified by his sacrifice. The ensuing six most prominent and ranked Petrine characteristics found in Mark, the Petrine sections in Acts, and 1 and 2 Peter include:

1. faith and trust
2. courageous witness
3. pursuing the purity of heart
4. humility and service
5. overcoming in suffering, trials, and persecution
6. surrender and obedience

These characteristics never function as autonomous 'virtues'. Rather, they are consistently imprints of Christ upon the followers. They are consequences of a relational dependence upon the rescuing master, marking and expressing the new identity being formed in the disciples. Specifically, courageous witness is a natural consequence of the transforming power of Christ; overcoming in suffering and trials is a consequence of Jesus's suffering for us; the gift of faith ensues when Christ reveals the depth of autonomous, sinful rebellion against God; purity of heart ensues in the wake of Christ's purity, exposure of our defilement, and purifying atonement; humility ensues as a consequence of Jesus's own humble approach to our rebellion and his taking us with him into humility; surrendered obedience follows the profound and unmerited love Jesus brings to us in his substitutionary atonement and ongoing pursuit.

Peter, as the apostolic rock and holistic witness, encapsulates such truth and reality once and for all: Christology, identity, and character formation, both individually and corporately, are always meant to progress in a coherent dynamic. Truth and transformation are forever meant to have a cause-and-effect relationship (see discipleship in John). In following Christ, we are thus restored to the original creation design in which the values of truth, understanding, wisdom, identity, relationship, character, and community are carefully interrelated in beautiful harmony. Such individual and corporate identity and character formation makes the reality of Christ discernible in a hurting, yearning, and rebellious world.[4] In the end, the sojourning, suffering community of the followers of Jesus Christ grows in a living Christ-representation and temple formation (e.g., in the form of authentic humility), based on a constant recourse to the unique, holistic, authentic, and authoritative Christ-witness of the apostles, chief among them Peter.

We find that the Petrine watermarks of Christ express a God-caused, God-dependent, and God-glorifying, comprehensive integrity and character which reflects restoration of the original creation design. The majesty of the triune God, seen in the astounding salvific and atoning work of Christ as the center of

---

[4] See Bayer, *Theology*, 133–56.

his mission, becomes paramount and anticipates the new, living, and eternal rule, 'city', and 'temple' of God. From such transformed individual and corporate identity and character, concrete personal, communal, and social ethics must arise.

Peter, the rock for Christ, vouchsafes for such ultimate hope.

Author Index

Prepared by Alissa Rockney

Achtemeier, P.J., 113, 216
Ådna, J., 263, 264
Agan, C.D.J., 92
Alexander, L., 97
Allison, D.C., 57
Armerding, H.T., 236
Aune, D.E., 67, 88
Bailey, K.E., 27, 40, 62, 94
Bainton, R.H., 245
Balch, D.L., 94
Baltes, G., 31, 32, 33, 92, 95, 103, 269
Barber, M.P., 60, 63
Bar-Ilan, M., 30
Barnett, P.W., 28, 38, 82, 84, 89, 90, 91
Bash, A., 213
Bass, J.W., 60
Bauckham, R.J., 27, 28, 31, 39, 82, 83, 84, 86, 88, 92, 95, 104, 105, 106, 108, 109, 111, 112, 116, 128, 207, 219, 234
Baum, A.D., 27, 38, 39, 85, 86, 94, 95, 97, 98, 103, 104, 105, 108
Bayer, H.F., 17, 36, 40, 55, 64, 65, 66, 67, 68, 80, 81, 84, 95, 109, 135, 136, 138, 143, 144, 147, 150, 155, 156, 160, 161, 162, 165, 173, 174, 175, 181, 182, 183, 186, 194, 201, 202, 203, 219, 221, 233, 240, 246, 247, 260, 272
Bayer, O., 253
Beale, G.K., 124, 144, 171, 172, 185, 202, 229, 262
Becker, J., 104, 112
Bell, A.A., 23, 29
Bellinger, W.H., 145
Bengel, J.A., 39
Benner, D.G., 13, 157, 160
Berger, K., 86, 88, 89, 90, 137, 138, 139

Bernett, M., 20
Best, E., 211
Betz, H.D., 92
Beyschlag, K., 46
Billerbeck, P., 23
Bird, M.F., 12, 82, 136
Black, C.C., 104
Black, D.A., 94
Black, M., 112, 138
Blackburn, B., 89
Blomberg, C., 225
Bock, D.L., 135, 142, 147, 149, 171
Bockmuehl, M., 2, 9, 10, 11, 18, 35, 36, 41, 42, 43, 45, 46, 47, 48, 49, 50, 51, 52, 53, 56, 58, 63, 82, 89, 103, 105, 109, 110, 111, 112, 114, 115, 116, 119, 120, 125, 126, 128, 130, 165, 166, 193, 198, 201, 207, 213, 214, 220, 226, 247, 248, 252, 255, 269
Böe, S., 162
Bonhoeffer, D., 157, 265
Borg, M., 159
Bradley, A., 248
Brooks, D., 13
Brown, R.E., 9, 55, 84, 99, 102, 103, 105, 109, 110, 111
Bruce, F.F., 20, 21, 22, 26, 69, 118, 119
Bruggen, J. van., 17, 22, 24
Bultmann, R., 27, 83, 154
Burge, G.M., 186
Burridge, R.A., 88, 89, 90, 91, 92
Byrskog, S., 27, 36, 58, 82, 95, 96
Callan, T., 97
Calvin, J., 156
Capes, D.B., 92
Caragounis, C.C., 50, 58
Carlston, C.E., 56
Carroll, J.T., 66, 67, 183

Carson, D.A., 24, 102, 114, 131, 133, 143, 144, 171, 172, 185, 202, 215, 229
Chancey, M.A., 12
Chang, P., 40
Charlesworth, J.H., 137, 139, 168
Chilton, B.D., 2, 135
Cochrane, A.C., 265
Collins, J.J., 136, 137, 139, 143
Conn, H.M., 117
Conzelmann, H., 66, 67, 86, 182
Coody, J., 158
Cullmann, O., 1, 2, 9, 10, 11, 34, 42, 43, 44, 45, 46, 47, 48, 49, 50, 51, 52, 53, 54, 55, 56, 57, 58, 59, 60, 61, 63, 64, 86, 115, 122, 123, 124, 129, 130, 132, 144, 145, 151, 165, 183, 191, 193, 198, 216, 218, 226, 263, 270
Cummins, S.A., 15
D'Ancona, M., 84
Dahl, N.A., 88
Dalman, G.H., 16, 35
Davids, P.H., 253
Davies, W.D., 57
Deines, R., 24
Delitzsch, F., 147, 256
Delling, G., 184
Dewey, J., 103
Dickson, J., 242
Dinkler, E., 9
Dodd, C.H., 14
Donaldson, J., 121
Donfried, K.P., 9
Dostoyevsky, F., 56
Dryden, J., 202, 227
Dubis, M., 256, 257, 258
Dungan, D., 95
Dunn, J.D.G., 27, 28, 30, 38, 40, 77, 83, 94, 95, 151, 260
Edwards, J.C., 144
Edwards, J.R., 55
Ehrman, B.D., 141, 154
Elliott, J.H., 262
Ellis, E.E., 83, 95, 117, 182
Evans, C.A., 20, 56

Eyal, R., 15
Farelly, N., 160
Farmer, W.R., 145
Feldmeier, R., 109, 242
Fiensy, D.A., 21
Fitzmyer, J., 32
Foakes-Jackson, F.J., 42, 64, 67, 115
Forbes, G.W., 198
France, R.T., 144
Frey, J., 91
Friedrich, A., 24, 15
Gambrell, C., 27, 129, 226, 266
Gathercole, S.J., 24
Gaventa, B.R., 67, 182
Gerhardsson, B., 27, 28, 94, 95
Gibson, J.J., 45
Giles, K., 66, 182, 183
Glaser, M., 135
Godet, F., 94, 96, 97, 98, 99, 100, 101, 102
Goppelt, L., 198, 199, 212, 216
Graf, E., 192
Grant, M., 36, 55
Gray, T.C., 263
Green, G.L., 207, 209
Guarducci, M., 49
Guelich, R.A., 86
Gundry, R., 211
Guthrie, D., 102, 201
Haacker, K., 114
Habermas, G., 27
Haehling, R. von, 48
Hägerland, T., 240
Hagner, D.A., 56
Hahn, F., 75, 77
Hall, C.A., 238
Hallesby, O., 233
Hamm, D., 182, 184
Hanson, K.C., 35
Harrington, D.J., 142
Harris, M.J., 208
Harvey, J.D., 94
Haubeck, W., 144
Havelock, E.A., 94
Hawkins, R.K., 21
Head, P., 94

Heid, S., 48
Helyer, L.R., 9, 11, 35, 36, 41, 42, 54, 55, 56, 58, 61, 62, 64, 114, 115, 116, 122, 129, 138, 199, 200, 201, 202, 203, 204, 207, 208, 209, 211, 213, 218, 220, 226, 248, 249, 259, 262, 263, 265
Hemer, C.J., 45, 100, 109, 248
Hengel, M., 9, 20, 24, 33, 34, 45, 47, 60, 61, 85, 88, 89, 96, 97, 103, 104, 105, 109, 111, 112, 113, 117, 119, 177, 248
Hennecke, E., 108
Henten, J.W. van, 15
Herrenbrück, J., 21
Hezser, C., 30
Hill, C.E., 117, 118
Hoehner, H.W., 123
Holtz, T., 69
Hooker, M.D., 145
Horbury, W., 147
House, P.R., 13, 192
Hübenthal, S., 36
Hunter, J.D., 15
Janowski, B., 216
Jay, J., 95
Jenkins, W.L., 245
Jeremias, J., 57, 110
Jobes, K.H., 115, 116, 172, 200, 215, 216, 217, 219, 250, 254, 255, 257, 258, 259
Johnson, D.E., 258
Kähler, M., 80, 85
Kant, I., 14
Kee, H.C., 89, 94
Keener, C.S., 170, 261
Kehlhoffer, J.A., 88, 254
Keil, C.F., 147, 148, 256
Kelber, W.H., 94
Keller, T., 15
Kiel, Y., 148
Kim, J., 146
Kim, S., 47
Kim-Rauchholz, M., 174
Kingsbury, J.D., 88, 140, 151
Kirk, A., 27, 36

Körtner, U.H.J., 104
Köstenberger, A.J., 60, 61, 131
Kraabel, A.T., 25
Kruger, M., 117, 118, 120
Kuhn, H.-W., 11
Kümmel, W.G., 102
Kurz, W., 185
Kürzinger, J., 103, 104, 105, 106
Lane, W.L., 26, 110, 126, 137, 146, 256, 259, 261
Laney, J.C., 263
Lessing, G.E., 88
Lewis, C.S., 253, 254
Lichtenberger, H., 137
Lindars, B., 138, 144
Linnemann, E., 94, 95
Llewelyn, S.R., 125
Loewe, H.M.J., 159
Lohfink, G., 181
Lohse, E., 168, 215
Longenecker, R.N., 176
Lövestam, E., 180
Luz, U., 51, 58
Maier, G., 117, 214, 215
Marshall, C.D., 231
Marshall, I.H., 66, 67, 97, 98, 100, 102, 113, 136, 144, 167, 168, 172, 182, 185, 200, 212, 219, 220, 257
Martin, R.A., 112
Martin, R.P., 151, 212
Marx, K., 14
Mason, S., 24
Mattill, A.J., 182
McCartney, D.G., 256, 257, 259, 262, 265
McGowan, A.B., 177
McIver, R.K., 27
Merz, A., 27
Metzger, B.M., 117, 118, 261
Metzner, R., 212
Meyers, E.M., 12
Michaels, J.R., 113, 211, 212, 213, 214
Milik, J.T., 138
Millard, A., 31, 84
Miller, C.J., 236

Minde, H.-J. van der, 74
Moessner, D.P., 70, 71, 74
Montefiore, C.G., 159
Moo, D.J., 45, 102, 133
Morgenthaler, R., 102
Mournet, T.C., 40
Murphy-O'Connor, J., 115
Murray, A., 242, 243
Neudorfer, H.-W., 78
Neusner, J., 2
Novenson, M.V., 136, 176
O'Brien, P.T., 24, 261
O'Callaghan, R.T., 49
Oden, T.C., 238
Oegema, G.S., 137
Packer, J.I., 242
Page, S.H.T., 144
Painter, J., 2
Palmer, D.W., 79
Perkins, P., 64
Perrin, N., 124, 263
Pesch, R., 9, 53, 80, 85, 104, 105, 108, 111, 125, 126, 127, 137, 261
Peterson, E.H., 236, 255
Phillips, T.R., 57
Plantinga, C., 6
Quarles, C.L., 24
Reicke, B., 27, 44, 82, 88, 94, 95, 101, 103, 104
Rengstorf, K.H., 9, 113
Rese, M., 171
Reumann, J.H.P., 9
Ricoeur, P., 234
Ridderbos, H.N., 38, 59, 65, 69, 213
Riesenfeld, H., 94, 95
Riesner, R., 15, 25, 27, 28, 29, 30, 31, 33, 36, 37, 38, 40, 82, 83, 86, 88, 92, 94, 95, 99, 101, 103, 105, 108, 110, 112, 119, 138, 139, 219
Roberts, A., 121
Robinson, J.A.T., 44
Roetzel, C.J., 13, 14, 20, 21, 26
Rollmann, H.-J., 154
Rose, W.H., 263

Rosner, B., 71
Rowe, R.D., 138, 139, 145, 146, 147
Sanders, E.P., 24
Sandnes, K.O., 69
Saucy, R., 236
Schlatter, A., 77, 88, 95, 96, 103, 107, 109, 175, 231
Schmitt, J.W., 263
Schnabel, E.J., 15, 20, 21, 26, 30, 31, 33, 111, 114, 124, 125, 126, 127, 170, 171, 198
Schnackenburg, R., 44, 131
Schneider, G., 65, 74, 86, 175, 180, 181, 212
Schreiner, T.R., 25, 167, 170, 181
Schröter, J., 27, 91, 117, 118
Schulz, H.-J., 109
Schürer, E., 15, 16
Seifrid, M.A., 24
Selwyn, E.G., 113, 173, 211, 212, 214, 215, 216, 219
Sen, A., 13
Shanks, M.A., 104
Smith, G.S., 256
Snodgrass, K.R., 80
Soards, M.L., 64, 65, 67, 69, 171, 174, 179, 180, 181
Sparling, R.A., 14
Spencer, F.S., 78
Steck, O.H., 69, 70, 71, 72, 73, 74, 75, 76, 77, 78, 79
Stein, R.H., 263
Stewart, A.C., 53
Stewart, R., 27
Stibbs, A.M., 215
Strack, H.L., 23
Stuhlmacher, P., 82, 86, 145, 146, 150, 216
Talbert, C.H., 223
Tannehill, R.C., 174, 184, 185
Taylor, V., 110, 143
Telford, W.R., 88, 89
Theissen, G., 27
Thiede, C.P., 9, 84, 209, 212
Thomas, R., 94
Thornton, C.-J., 103, 112, 116

Troftgruben, T., 188, 189
Turner, N., 115
Unnik, W.C., van, 99
Uytanlet, S., 98
Vielhauer, P., 66, 124
Voorst, R.E., van, 17
Wallace, D., 141
Wansborough, H., 27, 94
Wassell, B.E., 125
Watts, R.E., 144
Wehnert, J., 148
Wenham, D., 113, 144
Wenham, G.J., 129
Wenham, J.W., 38, 39, 47, 83, 108, 117, 118
Westcott, B.F., 83, 86, 92, 94, 96, 117
Wilckens, U., 64, 65, 69, 79, 80, 81, 86, 171
Wilcox, M., 80
Wilkins, M.J., 27, 221
Williams, M.D., 255
Williams, T.B., 116, 258
Wintermute, O.S., 168, 169
Wolterstorff, N., 253
Wrede, W., 152, 153, 154
Wright, C.J.H., 156, 170, 189
Wright, N.T., 149, 177
Wright, R.B., 139
Yarbrough, R., 36, 103, 104, 108
Zager, W., 154
Zahn, T., 32, 33, 34, 35, 117, 120, 121
Zehnle, R.F., 208
Zimmermann, J., 136, 137, 138, 139
Zmijewski, J., 177
Zylla, P.C., 253

Subject and Place Index
Prepared by Alissa Rockney

abomination of desolation, 13
adoption, 143, 241
adversity, 134, 166, 188, 190, 191, 195, 196, 197, 199, 200, 205, 210, 213, 227, 230, 257, 259, 267
aids, mnemonic, 31
alienation, 6, 163, 202, 223, 232, 242
aliens, sojourning, 199, 254, 255, 256
amanuensis, 106, 114, 116, 214
Antioch, 45, 46, 52, 60, 62, 107, 112, 113, 120, 132, 189, 248
    Ignatius of, 48
    Pisidian, 25, 78, 79
    Serapion of, 121
    Syrian, 107, 113
Antiochus IV, 12, 13, 14, 15
apostle, 1, 2, 9, 10, 25, 38, 43, 44, 45, 47, 48, 51, 52, 53, 54, 58, 59, 60, 63, 64, 77, 85, 86, 88, 89, 98, 100, 104, 105, 107, 108, 109, 112, 113, 114, 117, 120, 121, 122, 123, 132, 161, 172, 174, 178, 181, 195, 200, 212, 213, 216, 217, 222, 268, 269, 270, 272
Aramaic, 9, 10, 26, 32, 33, 34, 35, 55, 57, 84, 86, 105, 144, 148
Asia Minor, 4, 19, 60, 107, 115, 116, 134, 197, 198, 203, 254, 255
Atonement
    Jesus's substitutionary, 6, 45, 84, 127, 129, 146, 155, 156, 159, 160, 161, 163, 170, 174, 176, 187, 192, 196, 202, 204, 223, 225, 230, 232, 235, 236, 240, 241, 242, 245, 247, 248, 257, 259, 261, 265, 271, 272
death, 2, 35, 40, 44, 54, 59, 63, 64, 67, 78, 80, 83, 85, 91, 113, 127, 135, 141, 144, 150, 151, 152, 160, 165, 166, 173, 175, 180, 182, 184, 187, 192, 200, 201, 202, 216, 217, 234, 245, 246, 259, 265, 267
sacrifice, 61, 128, 135, 147, 241, 245, 271
attendant, synagogue, 26, 30, 100, 105, 106, 107, 112, 113
Augustus, 17, 19, 20, 21
authority
    apostolic, 48, 54, 59, 60, 70, 114, 129, 130
    canonical, 121
    divine, 38, 56, 57, 61, 82, 84, 147, 155, 178, 241, 266
    ecclesiastical, 56, 132
    ex cathedra, 52
    positional, 20, 22, 42, 90, 113, 148, 163, 199, 205, 208, 244, 249, 251
autonomy, 14, 3, 84, 156, 223, 239
Babylon, fig. use of, 46, 107, 116, 132, 198
barriers
    cultural, 15, 44
    economic, 15
    ethnic, 44, 248
    gender, 248
    language, 45
    philosophical, 15, 45

political, 45
racial, 248
religious, 15, 44
Bethsaida, 9, 10, 11, 35, 125
bind, fig. use of, 52, 55, 61, 62, 63, 129
bios, 83, 87, 88, 89, 90, 91, 92, 93, 103, 118, 122, 269
Bithynia, 46, 197
blasphemy, 149, 178, 239
blindness, fig. use of, 158, 159, 237, 238
born again, 203, 233, 255
bridegroom, messianic, 241
Caligula, 17, 18, 20, 21, 47, 235
canon, 90, 104, 117, 118, 119, 120, 121, 122, 123, 133, 214, 268, 269
canonicity, 119
core, 118, 119, 120, 121
Capernaum, 11, 26, 29, 35
Cappadocia, 46, 197
character, 5, 6, 7, 17, 39, 90, 92, 151, 156, 161, 164, 182, 190, 196, 229, 230, 249, 250, 264, 267, 272
and identity, 15, 5, 160, 165, 166, 187, 193, 196, 220, 268, 271, 273
kingdom, 150, 188, 195
Petrine, 3, 41, 42, 124, 134, 222
character formation, 5, 134, 155, 156, 163, 165, 193, 194, 196, 197, 210, 221, 223, 224, 225, 229, 230, 234
and identity formation, 1, 2, 3, 4, 6, 133, 134, 155, 156, 168, 188, 197, 209, 210, 211, 213, 214, 219, 220, 226, 230, 268, 271, 272
Petrine, 4, 44, 54, 124, 130
character foundation, 5, 155, 156
character traits, 6, 134, 161, 162, 195, 196, 204, 206, 207, 224, 225, 230, 231, 233, 244, 245, 267
and identity traits, 188, 203, 210
characteristic, 224
core, 162, 163, 196, 227, 230, 231
kingdom, 235
of character formation, 204, 206, 207, 224 225, 229
of discipleship, 3, 161, 194, 244
Petrine, 41, 194, 199, 254
Petrine theology, 1, 2, 171, 172, 209, 216, 225, 227, 244
characteristics, 6, 196, 206, 225, 230, 245
core, 161, 162, 196, 205, 206, 208, 209, 210, 225, 227, 229, 245, 272
core discipleship, 3
kingdom, 245
of character formation, 205, 220, 225
of discipleship, 188
of leadership, 4
Petrine, 3, 41, 125, 220, 272
chief shepherd, 62, 129, 130, 146, 202, 204, 223, 249, 271
chreia, 89, 90, 92, 93, 105, 106
Christlikeness, 61, 134, 161, 204, 235, 239, 249, 271
Christology, 1, 3, 4, 65, 77, 124, 133, 134, 159, 163, 166, 167, 168, 177, 178, 182, 183, 200, 209, 211, 213, 214, 215, 216, 217, 219, 220, 226, 268, 271, 272
functional, 181
narrative, 181
titular, 172, 180, 181, 218
circumcision, 13, 45, 46, 223
city, God's, 124, 145, 264, 267, 270, 273

commission, Peter's apostolic, 36,
    42, 47, 50, 51, 53, 54, 59,
    62, 69, 122, 125, 126,
    128, 129, 130, 131, 132,
    134, 269, 270, 271
community, 14, 15, 4, 5, 26, 38,
    40, 55, 56, 61, 83, 129,
    147, 182, 223, 225, 248,
    250, 251, 253, 270, 272
    sojourning, 222, 230, 249,
        255, 256, 265, 272
condemnation, commuted, 57, 243,
    258
confession, 72, 73, 235
    adoptionist, 177
    Christian, 53, 153, 177,
        178
    holistic, 58, 236
    of faith, 26, 167
    of Peter, 38, 42, 50, 51,
        54, 55, 56, 58, 62, 124,
        131, 175, 187, 201
    of rebellion, 72
Corinth, 18, 25, 46, 60, 64
cornerstone, 50, 51, 54, 56, 57, 58,
    62, 63, 122, 124, 262,
    263, 268, 270
covenant, 56, 77, 123, 126, 128,
    146, 167, 169, 170, 172,
    186, 196, 200, 204, 222,
    230, 232, 241, 242, 255,
    256, 258, 260, 261
creation, 125, 135, 169, 186, 214,
    237, 262
creation design, 229, 233, 272
crucible, 230, 256, 260, 261
crucifixion, 18, 84, 91, 135, 150,
    166, 172, 178, 217, 232
deafness, 157
    fig. use of, 158, 254
Decapolis, 16, 152
defilement
    of the heart, 157, 159,
        237, 239, 240, 272
    religious, 136, 204
denial, 23, 56, 66

of Christ, 184, 234, 236,
    253
of Jesus, 161, 184
of Peter's call, 207
of self, 129, 162
Peter's, 38, 41, 60, 111,
    129, 130, 132, 226, 234,
    236, 248, 249, 271
dependence
    on Christ, 3, 6, 54, 68,
        125, 129, 130, 193, 194,
        202, 204, 207, 221, 223,
        229, 235, 244, 248, 253,
        266, 272
    on God, 14, 3, 5, 45, 155,
        156, 164, 166, 182, 188,
        193, 194, 197, 222, 223,
        225, 229, 233, 236, 246,
        247, 249, 250, 251, 266,
        267, 272
    on self, 251
dependencies, God-opposing, 255,
    266
Diaspora
    Christian, 26, 254
    Jewish, 33, 34, 35, 71, 78,
        79, 116, 165, 254
Dionysius of Corinth, 46, 48
discipleship, 14, 15, 3, 4, 5, 6, 53,
    141, 142, 155, 156, 160,
    161, 188, 221, 225, 226,
    244, 247, 266, 272
discourse, 87, 92, 144, 166, 197
    eschatological, 68
Domitian, 21, 116, 198
double crisis of God-perception
    and self-perception, 55,
        155, 156, 161, 163, 164,
        188, 222, 223
doubt, 231, 232, 238
dwelling, God's, 262, 263
Eastern Orthodoxy, 58
Ebed YHWH, 140, 145, 146, 172,
    175, 178, 200, 201, 216,
    218, 245, 260, 271
election, 75

emperor worship/apotheosis, 17, 20, 21
enthronement, Jesus's, 146, 177, 186
eschatology in Acts
    far-expectation, 66, 182, 183
    near-expectation, 66, 67, 68, 183, 217
Essenes, 23, 25
ethics, 3, 4, 5, 23, 24, 202
    social, 273
exaltation, 140, 146, 147, 149, 150, 160, 175, 177, 178, 180, 184, 201, 217, 221, 265
exile, Babylonian, 25, 73, 126, 127, 185, 255
exodus
    from Egypt, 72, 168, 169, 170, 204, 250
    second, 127, 152
expectation, 66, 183, 217, 253
    future, 66, 67, 68, 182, 183, 185, 186, 187, 263
    messianic, 10, 12, 56, 136, 137, 138, 139, 140, 151, 153, 154, 155, 179, 219, 263
    political, 14, 16, 140, 151, 152, 154
    political, Davidic-messianic, 36, 136, 137, 138, 144, 176
expulsion, Claudian, 47, 198
eyewitness, 40, 51, 59, 69, 82, 96, 97, 99, 100, 101, 102, 106, 107, 108, 109, 110, 111, 112, 119, 172, 232
faith, 6, 11, 14, 15, 18, 26, 39, 45, 48, 52, 58, 60, 79, 118, 122, 153, 154, 162, 163, 171, 182, 188, 192, 193, 194, 195, 196, 205, 206, 209, 222, 223, 224, 231, 232, 233, 243, 250, 256, 264, 265, 266, 268, 269, 272
fate
    in a worldview, 20, 24
    of John the Baptist, 144
    prophets' violent, 71, 72, 74, 77, 78, 79, 80
Father
    God as, 4, 5, 135, 142, 143, 149, 150, 161, 166, 167, 172, 173, 176, 177, 178, 184, 185, 187, 188, 195, 200, 215, 233, 234, 235, 243, 245, 254, 258, 259, 260, 266, 267, 270
Felix, 93, 113
Festus, 113
fire, purifying, 128, 197, 230, 237, 247, 256, 258, 260, 261, 264
fishers of men, 41, 42, 125, 126, 127, 128, 132, 261, 266, 271
fishing industry/trade, 35, 110, 125, 127, 128, 129
following Jesus, 3, 5, 7, 10, 19, 35, 41, 51, 53, 60, 62, 81, 84, 87, 92, 112, 122, 125, 128, 130, 131, 132, 133, 155, 156, 157, 161, 162, 163, 164, 182, 187, 188, 191, 192, 193, 197, 201, 203, 204, 208, 209, 210, 217, 220, 221, 222, 223, 225, 226, 227, 229, 230, 231, 232, 233, 234, 235, 236, 238, 241, 244, 245, 247, 249, 251, 252, 253, 257, 258, 260, 261, 262, 264, 266, 267, 268, 271, 272
footwashing, 41, 246, 247, 248
foreknowledge, God's, 200, 216
foreordination, 181, 216
forgiveness, 6, 7, 41, 60, 61, 62, 163, 174, 186, 222, 224,

232, 233, 234, 240, 241, 242
of sins, 76, 141, 147, 155, 171, 174, 175, 179, 184, 187, 194, 217, 218, 241, 242
foundation, apostolic, 4, 47, 50, 51, 53, 54, 57, 59, 60, 62, 63, 118, 119, 122, 123, 124, 131, 132, 249, 268, 269, 270
framework
  interpretive, 39, 65, 66, 71, 72, 84
  narrative (of the Gospels), 83, 85, 86, 122
  redemptive-historical, 67, 214
fruit, fig. use of, 60, 161, 194, 198, 199, 208, 229, 233, 239, 242, 249, 250, 264
fulfillment, 49, 62, 67, 75, 126
  of promises, 186
  of prophecy, 45, 66, 70, 135, 142, 149, 170, 172, 187, 212, 215
  of Scripture, 173, 180
  of the law, 142, 162, 170, 232
Galatia, 46, 115, 189, 197, 254
genre of canonical Gospels, 39, 80, 83, 84, 85, 86, 88, 89, 90, 96, 101, 103, 117, 118, 119, 120, 122, 143, 197, 206, 212, 213, 225
glory, divine, 142, 147, 148, 149, 178, 201, 203, 205, 208, 217, 230, 234, 243, 250, 260, 262
God-fearer, 26, 34, 171
godliness, 5, 130, 163, 170, 198, 199, 204, 205, 208, 209, 233, 243, 249, 257, 258, 264

gospel transmission, oral, 27, 28, 37, 38, 40, 83, 84, 95, 96, 117
Greek language, 9, 10, 31, 32, 33, 34, 35, 57, 58, 66, 69, 84, 86, 92, 93, 95, 98, 104, 105, 107, 113, 115, 116, 269
guarantor, Peter as, 43, 51, 82, 97, 119, 122, 123
hades, gates of, 55, 57
Hanukkah, 12, 14, 20
Hasmonean, 10, 13, 14, 19, 22, 23, 34, 137
healing, 14, 159, 160, 184, 223
  act of, 11, 141, 157, 180, 182, 183, 184, 187, 191, 245, 246
heart, 6, 7, 36, 37, 38, 54, 61, 63, 84, 156, 157, 158, 160, 163, 170, 188, 192, 194, 196, 205, 206, 221, 222, 230, 232, 236, 237, 238, 239, 240, 242, 243, 244, 246, 247, 249, 250, 251, 257, 258, 265
  attitudes of, 6, 157, 206, 238, 239
  hardness of, 70, 75, 78, 79, 154, 158, 159, 162, 237, 238, 239
  shaping of, 5, 6, 39, 54, 84, 111, 158, 192, 208, 236, 241, 265
  watching over the, 41, 146, 161, 162, 163, 168, 170, 194, 195, 196, 197, 204, 205, 206, 208, 224, 227, 237, 238, 239, 240, 253, 267, 272
heart-transaction, 4
heart-transformation, 83, 84
Hebrew language, 26, 31, 32, 33, 34, 35, 84, 86, 92, 103, 105, 269

Hellenistic influence, 14, 18, 19, 33, 34, 78, 79, 80, 93, 97, 107, 126
hellenization, 12, 33
hermeneutēs, 105, 106
Herod 'the Great', 16, 19, 20
Herod Agrippa, 17, 235
Herod Antipas, 11, 17, 19, 22, 34, 35, 159
high priest, non-Zadokite, 12, 13, 14, 22
high priest, Zadokite, 12
Hillel, 29, 31
history, redemptive, 66, 67, 68, 70, 71, 72, 75, 78, 157, 167, 170, 182, 183, 184, 185, 199, 214, 217
Holy Spirit, 4, 5, 37, 39, 54, 61, 69, 78, 84, 130, 131, 160, 163, 166, 167, 170, 173, 178, 181, 182, 184, 187, 188, 191, 192, 193, 194, 195, 196, 200, 204, 208, 215, 221, 222, 234, 237, 241, 242, 248, 254, 259, 260, 266, 270
   outpouring of the, 45, 66, 80, 130, 131, 165, 168, 170, 174, 177, 180, 181, 182, 183, 192
humble, 4, 53, 115, 144, 145, 161, 163, 164, 198, 242, 245, 250, 251, 259, 264, 272
   being humbled, 10, 164, 176, 248, 249, 250
   leader, 251
   surrender, 257
humble service, 114, 205, 245
humility, 41, 42, 53, 62, 147, 155, 163, 195, 196, 197, 205, 206, 224, 227, 242, 243, 244, 245, 246, 247, 248, 249, 250, 251, 252, 253, 259, 260, 261, 264, 267, 272
idolatry, 72, 126, 127, 234, 237, 239

ignorance, Israel's, 76, 184
indicative
   future, 182, 199, 253
   past, 199
injunctions to silence, 140, 152, 153, 154
innocence, Jesus's, 90, 201, 216, 260, 263
integrity, 3, 45, 153, 165, 248, 267, 272
James, 2, 11, 36, 42, 44, 48, 59, 119, 142, 165, 172, 245, 246, 250, 269
   the half-brother of Jesus, 37, 43, 47, 112, 114, 118
   James the Just, 44, 45, 46, 53, 124
Jerusalem, 13, 14, 17, 18, 26, 34, 35, 43, 44, 45, 52, 53, 60, 62, 64, 74, 77, 81, 107, 112, 113, 118, 119, 124, 132, 138, 139, 159, 165, 172, 175, 186, 189, 190, 217, 248, 263, 264
   temple of, 12, 17, 19, 20, 34, 237, 263
Jerusalem Council, 45, 46, 248
Jesus as
   beloved Son of God, 142, 143, 150, 167
   teacher, 28, 36, 37, 38, 83, 254
Jewish Revolt, 13, 18
John Mark, 34, 86, 87, 92, 93, 100, 101, 103, 104, 105, 106, 107, 108, 109, 111, 112, 113, 116, 118, 120, 134, 214
John the Baptist, 11, 19, 36, 80, 81, 113, 144, 180, 232, 241, 242, 256
Joppa, 44, 60, 247
Judaism, Pharisaic, 5, 19, 20, 23, 24, 25, 26, 29, 36, 41, 46, 136, 139, 140, 154, 157, 194
Judaizers, 45, 46, 248

Subject and Place Index

judge, Jesus as, 42, 147, 179, 181, 182, 200, 201, 209, 218, 219, 235, 257
judgment, 70, 71, 72, 73, 74, 75, 126, 127, 128, 150, 158, 173, 180, 192, 207, 209, 217, 227, 246, 256, 257, 258, 259, 260
   cup of, 209, 227, 246, 260
   final, 70, 73, 74, 127, 183, 253, 257, 258, 260
   future, 79, 85
   imminent, 126, 127, 159
   temporary, 127, 260
keys to the kingdom, 52, 55, 57, 60, 61, 62, 182
kingdom of God, 4, 56, 58, 62, 63, 80, 133, 135, 137, 141, 148, 150, 155, 156, 162, 193, 195, 196, 200, 204, 207, 235, 245, 246, 255, 260, 261, 265
kingdom-ministry, 132, 271
kingdom-mission, 89, 127, 268
Last Judgment, 66, 125, 186, 208, 257
law of Moses, 22, 25, 27, 73, 137, 168, 169, 170, 192, 194, 232, 233, 247
leadership, 14, 15, 4, 10, 26, 42, 52, 53, 60, 64, 76, 115, 118, 131, 165, 247, 249, 252
literary
   dependence, 94, 95
   independence, 94, 95, 212
longsuffering (of God with his people), 70
loosen, fig. use of, 52, 55, 61, 62, 129
Lord, Jesus as, 37, 44, 46, 52, 63, 68, 92, 104, 105, 130, 138, 139, 140, 141, 147, 149, 150, 155, 171, 173, 175, 176, 177, 178, 180, 183, 207, 218, 221, 222, 232, 237, 256, 261, 262, 265
love, 6, 42, 44, 129, 131, 155, 156, 160, 164, 203, 205, 206, 207, 208, 209, 223, 224, 240, 243, 250, 251, 257, 266, 272
loyalty, 13, 266
   to Christ, 41, 129, 226
   to self, 226, 266
Maccabeus, Simon, 10, 13
martyrdom, 13, 15, 18, 46, 47, 48, 89, 108, 115, 119, 132, 252, 259
Mattathias, 13
maturity (discipleship), 15, 3, 4, 5, 6, 39, 54, 89, 131, 165, 188, 190, 192, 193, 196, 199, 213, 223, 225, 229, 234, 241, 257, 258, 262, 267
memorization, stereotyped, 38, 83, 91, 117
mentoring, 14, 15, 1, 3, 4, 38, 45, 54, 83, 125, 131, 198, 248
Messiah, 10, 36, 44, 46, 50, 54, 55, 58, 63, 68, 74, 77, 79, 80, 81, 111, 136, 137, 139, 140, 141, 142, 143, 144, 145, 146, 147, 149, 150, 151, 152, 154, 155, 156, 159, 160, 164, 167, 170, 173, 175, 176, 178, 185, 186, 218, 247
Messiah, suffering of the, 42, 55, 140, 141, 144, 146, 152, 154, 175, 176, 185, 201
missio dei, 166, 173, 193, 236, 254
mission, divine, 15, 3, 36, 67, 68, 84, 87, 111, 123, 127, 128, 130, 136, 147, 150, 151, 152, 157, 159, 160, 166, 187, 188, 190, 191, 192, 193, 194, 195, 200, 214, 215, 221, 230, 232, 233, 235, 236, 239, 241,

243, 254, 266, 268, 270, 273
monotheism, complex, 34
names of Peter
   Cephas, 10, 41
   Peter, 10, 41, 48, 57
   Simon, 9, 10, 55
nationalism, Jewish, 11
nature, Jesus's divine, 141, 142, 143, 160, 166, 208, 246, 264
Nero, 17, 18, 20, 21, 46, 47, 198, 252
nomism, covenantal, 24
obedience, 6, 13, 41, 69, 130, 131, 162, 193, 194, 195, 196, 197, 200, 205, 206, 209, 222, 223, 224, 227, 231, 233, 242, 244, 252, 253, 259, 265, 266, 267, 272
opposition, 29, 88, 144, 188, 190, 192, 194, 195, 196, 198, 213, 222, 232, 235, 236, 243, 250, 251, 253, 254, 257, 258, 265
oppression, 13, 14, 15, 12, 14, 15, 16, 17, 20, 49, 57, 139, 152, 179, 199, 218, 236, 245, 247, 251, 252, 254, 260
overseer, 130, 202
Palestine, 14, 4, 10, 14, 16, 17, 18, 26, 27, 28, 30, 32, 33, 34
papal See, 60
Papias, 46, 87, 92, 93, 101, 103, 104, 105, 106, 108, 109, 115
Parousia, 66, 67, 68, 130, 141, 142, 180, 181, 182, 183, 187, 201, 203, 205, 207, 208, 210, 217, 221, 224, 226, 253
   delay of, 67, 182
   imminence of, 66, 182
passio iusti, 80
passion account, 85, 90, 135

Passover, 111, 168, 169, 170, 204, 247
pattern-imitation, 92, 156, 161, 204, 220, 259, 271
Pentecost, 32, 45, 47, 67, 131, 141, 165, 166, 168, 169, 170, 176, 192, 196, 218, 221, 261
   meaning of, 168
   Peter's speech at, 65, 67, 170, 172, 174, 183, 185
people, chosen, 77, 172, 203, 206, 222
persecution, 6, 18, 34, 48, 80, 104, 115, 116, 145, 161, 163, 176, 190, 194, 195, 198, 224, 232, 235, 236, 239, 249, 252, 253, 254, 257, 258, 259, 261, 272
perseverance in trials, 6, 7, 41, 194, 204, 206, 235, 243, 265
Personalkontinuität, 83
Peter, 14, 15, 1, 2, 3, 4, 6, 9, 10, 11, 12, 14, 15, 16, 17, 18, 19, 20, 21, 22, 23, 24, 25, 26, 27, 29, 30, 31, 32, 34, 35, 36, 37, 38, 39, 40, 41, 42, 43, 44, 45, 46, 47, 48, 49, 50, 51, 52, 53, 54, 55, 56, 57, 58, 59, 60, 61, 62, 63, 64, 65, 66, 67, 68, 69, 70, 71, 74, 75, 76, 77, 78, 79, 80, 81, 82, 83, 85, 86, 87, 88, 92, 93, 96, 101, 102, 103, 104, 105, 106, 107, 108, 109, 110, 111, 112, 113, 114, 115, 116, 117, 118, 119, 120, 121, 122, 123, 124, 125, 126, 128, 129, 130, 131, 132, 133, 134, 135, 136, 141, 142, 160, 163, 165, 166, 167, 170, 171, 172, 173, 174, 175, 176, 177, 178, 179, 180, 181, 182, 184, 186, 187, 188, 190, 191,

Subject and Place Index

192, 193, 194, 195, 196,
197, 198, 199, 200, 201,
202, 208, 209, 210, 212,
213, 214, 215, 216, 217,
218, 219, 220, 221, 222,
223, 224, 225, 226, 229,
230, 231, 232, 234, 235,
236, 238, 239, 243, 244,
245, 246, 247, 248, 249,
250, 252, 254, 255, 256,
257, 258, 259, 262, 265,
266, 268, 269, 270, 271,
272, 273
Pharisees, 22, 23, 24, 25, 29, 137, 151, 157, 159, 237
pneumatology, Acts and, 65, 68
Pompey, 14, 16
pondus peccati, 6, 84, 232
Pontus, 46, 197
Pope Stephen, 52
pope, the, 51
portrait, Peter's historical, 3, 43, 111, 213
possessions, 192, 225, 227, 240, 246
prayer, 6, 7, 25, 26, 42, 74, 110,
131, 161, 162, 163, 174,
178, 190, 191, 192, 194,
195, 204, 206, 210, 224,
226, 231, 233, 234, 237,
238, 239, 241, 242, 254,
264, 267
preexistence, Jesus's, 139, 215
priesthood, holy, 204, 206, 222, 239
primus inter pares, 42, 118
procurator, 19, 93, 113
promised land, 127, 221
Prophet like Moses, 142, 145, 167, 173, 179, 218
propitiation, Jesus's, 174, 201
proselyte, 26, 34, 78, 165
pseudonym, 114
purification, 45, 126, 127, 128,
162, 170, 192, 227, 230,

237, 247, 256, 258, 259,
260, 261, 262, 265
of the temple, 13, 262, 264
purity, 15, 208, 251, 261, 272
ceremonial, 23, 247, 262, 264
moral, 198
Qumran community, 56, 137, 139, 202, 263
rabbinic Judaism, 25, 26, 28, 38,
56, 61, 71, 78, 91, 126,
159, 168, 185, 186, 261
ransom, 144, 150, 204, 206, 216, 222, 239, 258
rebirth, 200, 222
reconciliation, 14, 5, 61, 91, 135,
155, 161, 186, 223, 225,
230, 232, 239, 247, 251,
261, 271
rededication, temple, 14, 264
refreshment, times of, 67, 167,
171, 174, 180, 185, 187
regeneration, 61, 62
reinstatement, Peter's, 129, 132, 193, 271
rejection
  by God's people, 78
  divine, 75
  of God's people, 81, 186, 209, 257, 262
  of God's prophets, 70, 76, 78
  of Jesus, 75, 76, 79, 140,
  144, 145, 180, 201, 209,
  215, 217, 226, 243,
  262, 263
religio licita, 18, 21
renewal, covenant, 75, 168, 169, 170
repentance, 25, 61, 62, 67, 70, 71,
72, 73, 74, 75, 76, 77, 78,
79, 80, 146, 159, 170,
171, 172, 173, 174, 181,
183, 184, 185, 187, 192,
204, 208, 222, 224, 230,

232, 238, 239, 241, 242, 245, 269
repentance preacher, Peter as prophetic, 4, 63, 68, 69, 70, 80, 122, 123, 128, 165, 166, 172, 268, 269
repentance speeches, 63, 68, 70, 71, 72, 73, 74, 75, 77, 78, 79, 80, 81, 165, 170, 171, 185, 194, 234, 269
repetition and variation, Jesus's teaching by means of, 38, 39, 40, 158
representative, Jesus as, 77, 146, 147, 178, 258, 260
resettlement of Jews, 15, 16
restitution, 67, 70, 73, 138
restoration, 41, 70, 72, 75, 126, 127, 128, 129, 138, 155, 156, 161, 171, 174, 180, 183, 185, 186, 187, 223, 232, 235, 248, 251, 272
    messianic, 136, 176
    of the kingdom, 14
resurrection
    Christ's, 2, 35, 40, 44, 45, 54, 57, 59, 64, 69, 80, 83, 84, 85, 102, 110, 113, 128, 140, 141, 150, 152, 154, 165, 166, 172, 175, 178, 180, 182, 184, 187, 192, 193, 194, 200, 201, 203, 217, 221, 234, 245, 246, 254, 259, 265
    of the dead, 23, 25, 66, 183, 186

reversal of the fall, 156, 236, 239, 240, 255
rock, Peter as, 2, 4, 10, 41, 42, 47, 50, 51, 52, 53, 55, 56, 57, 58, 59, 60, 62, 69, 103, 110, 117, 119, 122, 123, 129, 131, 213, 268, 269, 270, 272, 273
Roman Empire, 16, 18, 19, 52, 134, 140, 244

Roman pontiff, 58
Rome, 12, 14, 17, 18, 19, 21, 22, 23, 24, 25, 32, 35, 44, 46, 47, 48, 51, 52, 53, 54, 60, 62, 63, 101, 105, 106, 107, 112, 113, 114, 115, 116, 120, 132, 151, 189, 190, 197, 198, 248, 252, 254, 255
rooster, 35
ruler, messianic-political, 136, 139, 151, 176, 186
sacrifice
    living, 261
    of Isaac, 257
    spiritual, 178, 204, 261
    temple, 13, 21, 25, 34, 261
Sadducees, 22, 23, 24, 25
salvation, 46, 70, 75, 76, 79, 97, 102, 128, 170, 171, 172, 174, 177, 179, 180, 182, 199, 203, 205, 208, 217, 218, 222, 235, 236, 241, 248, 264
salvation-historical, 182, 183, 184, 187
Sanhedrin, 22, 29, 44, 61
savior, Jesus as, 179, 181, 207, 208, 218
Scandinavian School, 95
school education, elementary (in Palestinian Judaism), 27, 28, 30, 31, 37, 93
Sea of Galilee, 11, 16, 152
secret, messianic, 140, 151, 152, 153, 154
self-awareness (self-perception), 6, 69, 111, 157, 159, 160, 161, 163, 164, 165, 193, 203, 204
self-control, 19, 195, 209
Sepphoris, 19, 31, 33
servant, 100, 163, 244, 245, 246, 252, 259

Subject and Place Index

Servant, Suffering, 42, 56, 123, 139, 145, 146, 147, 160, 216
servant-leadership, 42, 53, 205, 247, 249, 260
service
    acts of, 105, 195, 245, 247, 254, 261, 266, 272
    public Christian, 121, 122
    synagogue, 26, 30, 32, 140
    temple, 138
Shammai, 29
shepherd, 14, 3, 42, 51, 53, 54, 114, 125, 128, 129, 130, 131, 132, 133, 134, 202, 207, 249, 271
signs and wonders, 117, 180
Silas/Silvanus, 34, 112, 113, 114, 116, 118, 134, 165, 214
sojourners, 198
sojourners, scattered, 6, 204, 206, 217, 222, 225, 227, 254, 255, 262
Son of God, Jesus as, 45, 55, 82, 135, 140, 141, 143, 151, 154, 155, 160, 173, 186, 188, 193, 229, 234, 239

Son of Man, Jesus as, 42, 56, 85, 137, 138, 139, 140, 141, 143, 144, 145, 147, 148, 149, 150, 155, 160, 175, 176, 179, 216, 218, 219, 235, 260, 263
sonship, divine, 207
sonship, ontological, 55
soteriology, 3, 24, 226
sovereignty of God, 24, 65, 180, 190
speech, Peter's temple, 65, 67, 170, 174, 181, 182, 183
speeches in Acts, Peter's, 43, 65, 67, 68, 70, 73, 75, 76, 78, 79, 112, 130, 171, 173, 177, 214, 220, 269

spokesperson, Peter as, 2, 41, 42, 43, 50, 51, 54, 58, 59, 63, 64, 65, 66, 67, 68, 74, 80, 85, 93, 111, 123, 128, 165, 166, 270
spread of the gospel, unhindered, 188, 189
Stoicism, 5, 19, 157, 194, 244
stone
    Jesus as living, 201, 209, 217, 226
    Jesus as messianic, 58
    Jesus as rejected, 262
stone metaphor
    messianic, 200, 202
    rejected, 212
stones, living, 59, 124, 204, 209, 222, 226, 256, 262, 263, 264, 270
submission, 201, 205, 209, 244, 249
succession, apostolic, 50, 51, 52, 53, 54, 58, 59, 60, 62, 124, 131, 270
suffering
    Abraham's, 257
    Christians', 4, 15, 81, 116, 130, 134, 163, 192, 198, 199, 201, 204, 205, 206, 209, 213, 223, 224, 226, 227, 230, 232, 234, 243, 246, 247, 249, 250, 255, 256, 257, 259, 261, 262, 265, 267, 272
    Christ's, 144, 145, 160, 197, 201, 206, 207, 209, 213, 215, 216, 217, 220, 226, 243, 246, 247, 254, 257, 258, 259, 265, 271, 272
    disciplinary, 262
    inflicted by Satan, 236, 265
    Jews', 15, 16, 41, 259
    of God's people, 73, 145, 146, 222, 225

Paul's, 243
Peter's, 81, 116, 188, 192, 193, 196, 197, 198, 222, 243, 252, 259
psalms of, 146
psalms of kingly, 146
sufferings, Christ's, 114
surrender, 6, 41, 53, 161, 162, 163, 191, 194, 195, 196, 197, 205, 224, 225, 226, 227, 231, 232, 233, 238, 242, 243, 244, 247, 250, 251, 252, 253, 257, 261, 264, 265, 266, 267, 272
synagogue, 25, 26, 28, 29, 31, 32, 33, 34, 36, 37, 41
synagogue school, 20, 23, 26, 27, 29, 36, 37, 38, 140, 215
tabernacle, 142, 230, 249, 262, 263
table-fellowship, 45, 46, 248
temple
    communal, 270
    God's people as, 59, 60, 63, 111, 122, 124, 130, 157, 195, 199, 204, 222, 230, 263, 264, 267, 268, 272, 273
    Jesus as, 59, 252, 262, 271
    messianic, 139, 256, 262, 263
temptation, 39, 140, 161, 163, 209, 224, 232, 233, 238, 239, 240, 253, 254
tensions, internal, 188, 190, 191, 192, 265
testimony
    patristic, 96, 103, 107, 108, 109, 110, 111, 114, 121, 133, 134, 213, 214, 219
    Peter's canonical, 1, 3, 53, 54, 59, 133, 134, 202, 210, 213, 214, 215, 219, 220, 221, 222, 224, 225, 229, 230
testing, 192, 193, 256, 265

theocracy, 15, 16, 26
throne of David, Jesus on the, 140, 141, 150, 151, 175, 176, 177, 178, 180, 186, 217
Tiberias, 18, 19, 29, 31, 33
time-frames, eschatological, 132
Titus, 71
tradition hypothesis, modified, 93, 94, 95, 96, 102, 117
Trajan, 46, 115, 116, 198
transfiguration, Jesus's, 141, 142, 143, 207
transformation, corporate, 13, 14, 15, 4, 5, 161
trials, 41, 195, 205, 206, 208, 224, 225, 227, 236, 249, 253, 254, 261, 272
tribulations, 192, 193, 260, 261, 265
Trinity, 124, 167
trust, 3, 41, 51, 160, 161, 162, 163, 164, 166, 184, 191, 192, 193, 194, 197, 205, 222, 224, 227, 231, 232, 233, 238, 242, 243, 244, 248, 251, 255, 258, 259, 264, 265, 267, 268, 269, 272
uprising, Maccabean (revolt), 10, 12, 13, 14, 15, 16, 20, 33, 34, 36, 41, 87, 136, 140, 151, 259, 264
virtue, 5, 6, 194, 208, 244, 245, 272
witness
    holistic, 53, 58, 59, 130, 195, 196, 197, 205, 267, 272
    bold and courageous, 6, 41, 166, 168, 170, 194, 195, 196, 197, 222, 234, 243, 253, 272
    Peter's apostolic, 15, 1, 2, 3, 4, 6, 43, 44, 45, 47, 49, 50, 51, 52, 53, 54, 58, 60, 61, 62, 63, 64, 65, 68, 69, 74, 82, 93, 96, 97, 100, 101, 112, 119, 122, 123,

124, 131, 132, 133, 167,
171, 172, 175, 178, 182,
190, 192, 193, 196, 197,
210, 249, 252, 268
worldview, 14, 6, 20, 84, 243
worship
    of Jesus, 126, 127, 163,
176, 177, 178, 200, 205,
230, 231, 232, 233, 242,
264, 267, 270

    of Son of Man, 147, 148,
149
    temple, 12, 26
Y$_{HWH}$, Servant/Ebed of, 139, 140,
145, 146, 147, 167, 178,
185, 218, 235
Zadokite, 22
Zealots, 25

Index of Biblical and Extrabiblical Writings
Prepared by Alissa Rockney

OT

Genesis
3:1-19	41
3:8	262
12:1-3	199
12:3	222
12:7	199
17:7	186
22:18	174, 222
26:4	174
28:12	263
49:10	136

Exodus
3:5-6	36
3:6	174
3:15	174
4:21	237
19:1	169
24:15-18	142
34:22	168
34:29-30	142
34:33	142
34:35	142
40:34-35	262

Leviticus
11:44-45	199
23:1-21	169
23:29	174
23:42-43	169
26:11-17	263
26:12	262
26:32-42	73

Numbers
12:7	59
17:13	262

Deuteronomy
1:8	186
1:32-33	221
1:36	221
4:1	168
4:25-31	72, 73, 74
4:25-32	73
4:31	73
6:4	149, 167, 215
6:7	25
8:2	237
8:3	258
16:1-8	169
16:1-12	169
16:9	169
18	179, 218
18:15	142, 179, 218
18:15-16	174
18:18	142, 179, 218
18:19	174
18:20	117
21:22-23	172
28:25	254
28:45-68	72, 73, 74
30:1-3	73
30:1-10	72, 73, 74
32:25	61

Ruth
4:11	59

Index of Biblical and Extra-Biblical Writings

2 Samuel
5:2	202
7	136
7:7	202
7:11-14	136
7:12-13	146
7:12-14	140, 151
7:13	140
7:13-14	136, 139
7:16	136, 139, 140, 151
12:13	241
23:3	179, 219

1 Kings
8:27	262
8:46-50	73
8:46-53	72, 73
17:7-20	72
18:4	72
18:13	72
19:10	72
19:14	72

2 Kings
17:7-20	74
17:13	72, 73
22:17	72, 74

1 Chronicles
28:9	237

2 Chronicles
6:18	262
7:1	264
7:3	264
7:9-11	262
15:1-7	72
29:5-11	72, 74
29:16	264

30:6-9	72, 74
30:6b-9	72
36:14-16	72, 74
36:14-21	72
36:17-21	72, 74

Ezra
6:16	263
7:19	148
7:24	148
9	73
9:11	72, 74

Nehemiah
1:9	72, 73
1:11	72
9	74
9:5-38	72
9:30	78

Job
6:6	261

Psalms
2:1	222
2:2	46, 177
2:6	146
2:7	142
2:8-10	146
7:9	237
12:2	237
16:8-11	172, 174, 216
16.10	174, 216
17:3	237
19:14	237
22	146
34	239
34:12-16	200, 216
42:6	237
42:12	237

43:5	237	14:30	237
57:7	237		
69	146		
72:1-2	147	**Isaiah**	
73:26	237	5:1-7	233
78:60-61	262	6:1-6	262
78:70-72	146	6:9-10	158, 159
79:6	73	7:3	56
79:9	73	8:14	58, 200, 217, 226, 262
79:10	73		
79:11	73	9:7	147
79:12	73	10:21	56
89:39	146	11:1	146
89:44	146	11:4-5	147
106:47	73	11:10	146
110:1	140, 149, 150, 172, 173, 174, 176, 177, 178, 216, 218, 235	22:15-23	61
		22:22	60, 61
		24:16	147
		26:13	21
		28:16	58, 200, 201, 202, 217, 226, 262
110:1-2	146		
110:1-5	149, 150		
110:5	140, 149, 150, 173, 176, 178, 235	32:1	147, 179, 219
		37:25-28	262
		40:6	199
110:5-6	146	40:8	199, 200, 217
117:22	200	40:11	146
118	146	42–53	145, 146, 147
118:22	173, 200, 215, 217, 226, 262	42:1–52:12	145
		42:6	145
118:22-23	58	42:8	149
119:7	237	42:18-19	159
132:11	174	43:3	145
132:11-12	146	43:8	159
		43:14	145
Proverbs		44:6	145
1–9	31	44:21	145
4:23	237	44:22	145
4:24-27	237	44:24	145
4:25	237	44:28	146
11:31	200, 216		

45:4	145	53:8	140, 144, 145, 146, 241, 260
45:17	145		
45:22	145	53:8-10	150
45:22-23	149	53:9	200, 216
47:4	145	53:9-10	260
48:10-11	230	53:10	146
48:11	149	53:10-12	147, 216, 260
48:17	145	53:11	147, 216
48:20	145	53:11b	216
49:3	145	53:11-12	216
49:6	145, 254	53:12	144, 146, 150, 200, 216
49:6-7	185		
49:8	145	59:2	239
49:26	145	59:21	170
50:2	145	60:5	237
51	257	61:11	264
51:5-6	145	63:7-10	72, 74
51:17	246, 260	63:10	78
51:22	227, 246, 260	63:11-17	72
52:3	145	63:17	73
52:7	145	64:1-2	73
52:10	145	64:1-4	72, 73
52:13	146, 178, 216	66:1	262
52:13–53:12	145, 146, 147, 178, 201, 216, 218, 235, 260, 271	66:2	242
		66:18-22	185
		Jeremiah	
52:15	146	1:1–16:13	126
53	42, 139, 144, 145, 200, 202, 216, 217, 257	2:30	72, 74
		3:12-14	72
		3:12–4:14	72
53:1-12	140	3:15-16	72
53:2	146	5:21	159
53:3	216	5:21-22	158
53:4-6	145, 150, 216, 260	6:14	237
		7:3-32	72
53:5	200	8:11	237
53:5c	155	14:7-9	72
53:6	146, 200, 202	15:7	254
		16:13-16	247

16:14	126	9:6	257
16:14-15	126	12:2	159
16:14-21	126, 127	14:3-4	237
16:15	126	14:6-7	72
16:16	126, 127, 261	14:6-11	72
16:17	127	14:7	237
16:18	126	18:30-31	72
16:19	127, 170	29:4-5	126
17:12	262	34	146
23:1-5	130	34:1-10	202
23:20	237	34:2-24	130
25:3-14	72	34:4	249
25:15	246, 260	34:11-23	202
25:15-17	227	36:26-27	237
25:17	246	37:21-28	185
25:17-18	260	37:26	170
25:28	246	38:4	126
25:29	257, 260	39:29	170
26:1-24	72		
26:2-4	72	**Daniel**	
29:17-19	72	2:34-35	58
31:31-34	170, 192	2:44-45	58
35:13-17	72	3:12	148
44:1-14	72, 74	3:14	148
49:12	246, 260	3:17-18	148
		3:28	148
Lamentations		3:33	148
1-2	73	4:31	148
1:22	73	6:17	148
3:22-23	73	6:21	148
3:40-41	72	6:27	148
3:64-66	72, 73	7:13	149
4:21	73	7:13-14	42, 140, 147, 149, 150, 176, 177, 218, 235, 260
4:21-22b	72		
4:22	73		
4:22b	73		
5:20-21	232	7:13-27	147, 186
5:21	73	7:14	147, 148, 260
		7:15-27	147, 156
Ezekiel		7:18	148

Index of Biblical and Extra-Biblical Writings

7:18-27	260	3:1	264
7:22	148, 150	3:1-3	258
7:27	147, 148, 150	3:1-15	256
9	73, 215	3:2b-4	256
9:6	72, 74	3:5	256
		3:6-7	72

Joel

2:12-20	72
2:28-32	170, 174
2:32	177, 215

NT

Amos

4:2	126
9:9	6
9:11	59, 136
9:11-12	223

Matthew

4:11	227
4:18-19	125
5:18	83
6:21	238

Jonah

4:2	186

7:24-25	56
10:2-4	42
12:6	264
14:28-33	60

Micah

5:2-4	202
5:3	56
7:7-20	72

16	131
16:5-12	54
16:16	54, 55, 56
16:16-17	55
16:17	160
16:17-18	42
16:17-19	55

Habakkuk

1:14-17	126

Zechariah

1:2-8	72
7:4-14	72
7:12	78
8:1-23	72
9:9	263
11:3-17	130
11:16-17	202
13:7	202
13:9	256, 258

16:18	55, 57, 58, 110
16:18-19	50, 52, 53, 54, 55, 62, 69, 103, 122, 131, 193, 213, 268, 269
16:19	60, 61, 62
16:21-23	55
17:1-8	43
17:24-27	110
18:15a	61
18:15b	61
18:15-20	61, 129

Malachi

18:17b	61	1:17	41, 130, 162, 266
18:18	61, 62		
18:19	61	1:20	35
18:21-35	242	1:21	11, 35
21:35	74	1:24	219
23:26	237	1:29	11, 35, 110
26:17	111	1:30	11
26:33-35	41	1:31	244, 245
26:37	43	1:35	234
26:75	111	1:36	35, 110
28:9-10	43	1:38	235
28:18-20	56, 128	1:38-39	235
28:19-20	132	1:41	141
		2	241
Mark		2:1	35
1–12	144	2:1-10	254
1:1	86, 87, 143	2:2	235
1:2-11	86	2:5	61, 162, 231, 241
1:4	232, 241, 242		
1:7-8	242	2:5-10	241
1:8	87, 215, 241, 242	2:7	241
1:9	219, 241	2:10	141, 144, 147, 155, 241
1:10-11	215		
1:11	143, 150, 161, 215, 226	2:14	162, 266
		2:17a	163
1:12-13	254	2:19-20	241
1:12–9:50	86	2:20	140
1:13	227, 265	2:28	147
1:14	125	3:5	141, 239
1:14-15	68, 150, 226, 230, 231, 235, 245	3:6	254
		3:11	143
		3:13-19	42
1:15	80, 162	3:14	125, 177, 213, 235, 266
1:16	11, 36, 125, 126, 127, 261		
		3:14-15	163
1:16-17	42, 125, 127, 132, 155, 257, 270, 271	3:16	177, 213
		3:16-17	106
		3:28-30	211
1:16-20	110	3:29	162, 239, 241, 242

Index of Biblical and Extra-Biblical Writings 299

3:33-35	222	7	157
3:35	162, 239, 266	7–8	156, 157, 239
4	156, 157	7:1-22	222
4–8	222	7:1-23	232
4:1	235	7:10	239
4:1-20	157, 162, 217, 222, 233	7:14-21	162
		7:14-23	157, 238
4:10-12	158, 159, 222	7:18-19	232
4:13-20	239	7:20-22	157, 158, 239, 240
4:15	236, 254, 265		
4:17	253	7:20-23	238
4:23	162	7:21-22	238
4:25	162	7:22-23	5, 162, 222
4:33-34	159	7:24	151, 154
4:38	141	7:27	217
4:40	162, 232	7:28-29	162
5:7	143	7:31-35	157
5:20	234, 235	7:34	141
5:21	110	8	157
5:34	162, 231	8:2	141
5:36	232	8:4-7	163
5:37	43, 110, 266	8:12	141
6–8	223	8:15	159
6:2	235	8:17-18	158
6:4	219	8:17-21	154, 158, 159, 162, 222, 238, 239
6:6	141, 162		
6:7	125		
6:7-12	226	8:18	37
6:7-13	125	8:22-26	157, 158
6:12	80	8:23	11
6:14-29	74	8:26	11
6:15	219	8:27	129, 266
6:30	125, 213	8:27-28	153
6:34	141, 222, 235	8:27–10:45	266
6:45-52	110	8:27–16:8	159
6:46	234	8:29	54, 110, 129, 153, 159
6:49	231		
6:50	232	8:29-31	218
6:50-52	239	8:30	151, 153
6:52	162, 238		

8:31	40, 80, 141, 144, 145, 160, 176, 215, 217, 235, 266	9:19	162, 231
		9:24	162, 231, 232
		9:26–11:18	266
		9:29	163, 233, 234
8:31-33	154, 160, 217	9:30	151, 154
8:32	213, 216	9:31	80, 180, 215, 217, 246, 263, 266
8:32b	14		
8:32-33	140, 247		
8:32-34	160	9:31-32	154
8:33	110, 141, 238, 240	9:31-50	245, 246
		9:33-37	213, 226, 244, 249, 266
8:34	41, 129, 162, 226, 266		
		9:34	246
8:34-35	162	9:35	163, 244, 245, 246
8:34-37	222, 226, 232, 239, 266		
		9:36-37	246
8:34-38	125	9:37	244, 245
8:35-37	246	9:41	245
8:36	143	9:42	231, 238
8:38	42, 87, 127, 140, 141, 147, 160, 163, 176, 177, 201, 217, 218, 219, 226, 232, 234, 235, 266	9:42-47	162
		9:42-49	239
		9:42-50	127, 128
		9:43	57
		9:43-47	238
		9:43-50	246
9–10	252	9:45	57
9:1	141, 226	9:47	57
9:2	110	9:49	162, 230, 238, 257, 260, 261
9:2-8	141, 155, 160, 215, 217, 226		
		9:50	261
9:2-10	43, 110	10:1–15:20	86
9:2-30	246	10:4-44	245
9:3	142	10:5	239
9:5	110	10:11	162
9:7	142, 143, 150, 161, 215, 226	10:13	226
		10:13-16	163, 245
9:9	86, 140, 151, 152	10:14	141, 245
		10:15	245
9:9-13	154	10:21	162
9:12	216	10:23-27	162

10:27	162, 231		219, 222, 226, 227, 230, 235, 241, 245, 247, 257, 259, 260, 261, 265
10:28	41, 162		
10:28-30	266		
10:29-30	162, 225, 246, 265		
10:29-31	222, 230	10:47	219
10:30	163, 236, 253, 254	10:47-48	219
		10:52	231
10:32	144	11	262
10:32-34	80, 215, 217, 245, 246, 266	11:1-11	263
		11:1-25	222, 226
10:34-44	154	11:10	219, 263
10:35-37	246	11:12	141
10:35-38	227	11:12-14	233, 264
10:35-44	81, 127, 128, 162, 213, 222, 226, 238, 239, 244, 245, 246, 249, 257, 265, 266	11:12-25	264
		11:15-19	264
		11:17	127, 138, 163, 217, 230, 233, 264
		11:21	37, 110
10:35-45	226, 260	11:22	162
10:37	163, 246	11:22-24	232
10:38	209, 246, 260	11:22-25	233, 234, 242, 264
10:38-39	226, 230, 258, 260		
		11:23	238
10:39	209, 227, 260, 262	11:23-24	162
		11:24	231
10:40	247	11:24-25	163
10:42	205, 211, 245, 247, 249	11:25	163, 171, 217, 234, 241
10:42-44	163	12:1-10	74, 77, 81
10:43	232	12:1-12	55, 78, 80, 143, 201, 230, 233
10:43-44	244, 246		
10:43b-44	246, 247	12:6-8	143
10:45	42, 80, 87, 91, 125, 127, 128, 140, 144, 145, 146, 150, 155, 176, 202, 212, 215, 216, 217,	12:9-12	263
		12:10-11	173, 215, 264
		12:10-12	58, 217, 226, 262, 268
		12:13-17	212
		12:14	235

12:17	244	13:33-37	253
12:30-31	266	13:35	191
12:35-37	140, 141, 149, 176, 186, 217, 218, 219	13:35-37	226
		13:37	191, 212, 254
		14:1–16:8	127, 213, 215, 216
12:36-37	177, 178, 218	14:8	254
12:38-40	163, 245	14:13	111, 266
12:44	162	14:21	144
13	68, 182, 217, 235	14:22-24	128, 216, 241, 257, 259, 261
13:3	110, 232	14:22-25	222
13:7-13	226	14:23-24	241, 262
13:9	191, 222, 232, 253	14:24	216
13:9-13	163, 235, 236, 253, 254	14:25	68, 150, 155, 235
13:9-14	232	14:26-31	41
13:10	123, 127, 128, 132, 163, 191, 217, 222, 230, 234, 235	14:27	202, 223
		14:29-31	41, 129
		14:30-31	110
		14:32-36	233, 234
13:10-13	253	14:32-41	254
13:11	162, 212, 222, 227, 232	14:33	43, 110
		14:33-34	141
13:13	222, 226, 232	14:33-42	110
13:14-23	226	14:34	253
13:16-17	232	14:36	127, 128, 143, 144, 227, 235, 240, 241, 245, 260, 267
13:18	191		
13:19	222		
13:20	222		
13:21	231	14:37	110, 213
13:22	222	14:37-38	212, 253
13:23	191	14:37-42	41
13:26	147, 217	14:38	162, 163, 239
13:27	222	14:43-50	202
13:29	226	14:51-52	107
13:31	83, 217	14:54	110
13:32	143, 215	14:54-72	110
13:32-37	208	14:58	263, 264
13:33	163, 191, 254	14:61	201

Index of Biblical and Extra-Biblical Writings

14:61-62	143, 175	3:16	247
14:61-63	177	3:16b	170, 260
14:62	42, 140, 147, 149, 150, 177, 201, 217, 219	3:16-17	128
		3:21-22	174
		4:18-21	177
14:62-63	176, 218	4:33-35	174
14:66-72	42, 129	5:1-11	129
14:67	219	5:4-11	36
14:72	37, 110, 111, 188	5:7	11
		5:8	36
15:21	107	5:10	11
15:21-47	86	6:12-16	42
15:25	241	6:13	213
15:27	216	6:45	237
15:29	264	7:18-23	138
15:32	231	8:1-3	227
15:37	241	9:10	213
15:38	264	9:18-20	63
15:39	143	9:35	177
16:1-8	86, 217, 231	10:18	265
16:6	162, 219, 232	11:49-51	74, 213
16:7	69, 110	12:1	159
16:11	232	12:35	238
16:13	232	12:50	260
16:14	239	13:16	265
16:16	162, 211, 231	13:34-35	74
		14:33	227
Luke		17:5	213
1:1	96, 98, 99, 101	17:20-21	67
1:1-3	101	19:31	177
1:1-4	96, 98, 99, 111	19:34	177
1:2	98, 99, 100	20:17-18	58
1:2-3	172	21:34-36	239
1:3	99, 100, 101	22:8-13	111
1:4	98, 99, 101, 102	22:14	213
1:43	177	22:29-30	63
1:76	177	22:31	129, 265
2:19	37	22:31-34	42
2:35	237	22:31-32	54, 110, 128, 131, 193
2:51	37		

22:32	63	13:1-20	213, 246, 247, 249
22:33	48		
22:33-34	41	13:2-11	41
22:37	216	13:8-9	247
22:61	42	13:14-16	247
22:62	111	13:20	247
24:10	213	13:37-38	41
24:21	140	14–16	167
24:25-27	40	14:15-28	40, 221
24:26	176	14:16-17	188
24:34	43	14:26, 37	120
24:36-43	86	15:26-27	120
24:46	176	16:4	37
24:47-48	102	16:7	221
24:48	213	16:7-15	221
		16:13	120
John		17:5	161
1:14	263	17:20	51, 122, 268
1:40	36	17:24	161
1:40-42	11	19:13	32
1:41	36	19:17	32
1:42	10, 36, 41, 58	20:1-9	43
1:44	11	20:7	128
1:45	58	20:11-29	128
1:51	263	20:14-17	43
2:19	264	20:22	130-31
2:19-21	263	20:23	60, 61, 62, 129
2:22	37	21	131
4:24	230	21:1-6	129
5:2	32	21:1-14	128
5:27	235	21:3-8	36
6:15	140, 151, 152	21:12	129
7:35	254	21:14	128
8:19	40	21:14-19	44
8:23-24	40	21:15	129
10	129	21:15c	129
10:22	12	21:15-17	42, 130, 204, 213
12:16	37		
13	252	21:15-18	48

Index of Biblical and Extra-Biblical Writings

21:15-19	41, 42, 54, 128, 131, 132, 193, 270, 271	1:16	215, 219
		1:16-22	166
		1:20	215
21:15-22	131	1:21-22	54, 59, 86
21:16	129	1:22	69, 114, 180, 194, 213, 217, 222, 234
21:16c	129		
21:17	129, 134		
21:17d	129	1:23-26	166
21:18-19	81	1:24	191, 192, 194, 233, 238
21:19	41, 130, 134		
21:21	134	1:25-26	213
21:22	130	2	66, 67, 70, 76, 78, 79, 165, 170, 173, 217, 243
Acts			
1–5	265	2–5	74, 75, 76, 78, 79, 173, 197, 213
1–9	63, 111, 118		
1–10	44		
1–12	112, 130, 268	2:1-4	80, 192
1:1	221	2:1–8:4	189
1:1-26	189	2:2-4	131, 192
1:1–6:7	165, 166	2:4	222
1:1–9:32	64, 68, 172	2:10	47
1:2	213, 222	2:11	216
1:3	186	2:12	234
1:5	222	2:13	190, 195, 236, 254
1:6	14, 136, 140, 142, 176, 185, 186	2:14	42, 69
		2:14-36	43, 65, 76, 166, 194, 217, 234
1:7-8	170		
1:8	69, 114, 165, 185, 186, 189, 192, 194, 213, 222, 231, 234	2:15	190, 193, 195, 234, 236, 254
		2:16-21	67
		2:16-36	193
1:10	212	2:17	218
1:10-12	216	2:17-21	174
1:11	217	2:18	216
1:13-14	42, 118	2:21	69, 170, 174, 176, 177, 215, 218, 222
1:13-15	166		
1:14	172, 191, 192, 194, 233		
		2:21-24	216

2:22	117, 177, 179, 181, 215, 219	2:38-39	65, 74, 75
2:22-23	212	2:38-40	166
2:22-24	67	2:39	75, 170, 181, 215
2:22-32	215	2:40	76, 174, 213, 217, 222, 223
2:22-36	180		
2:23	180	2:40b	65, 74
2:23-32	217	2:42	99, 192, 194
2:24-31	215	2:42a	54
2:24-36	173	2:42-43	213
2:25	219	2:42-47	189, 236, 253
2:25-28	174, 215-16	2:43	117
2:25-36	186	2:44	194
2:27	57, 181	2:44-45	195
2:29	215	2:44-46	192
2:29-31	179, 219	2:46	192
2:30	140, 141, 150, 151, 174, 176, 186, 217	3	66, 67, 70, 76, 78, 79, 173, 181, 182, 217, 243
2:30-31	176, 215, 217	3:1	192
2:31	57, 173, 174, 180, 181, 216	3:1-5	166
		3:4	166
2:32	69, 114, 180, 213	3:4-7	232
		3:5	212
2:33	167, 174, 180, 181, 182, 215, 221, 241	3:6	166, 179, 180, 193, 219
		3:6-7	63
2:33-34	201	3:7-11	166
2:33-36	217	3:12	181, 232
2:34	173, 177, 219	3:12-26	76, 166, 167, 194, 234
2:34-35	174, 216		
2:36	68, 69, 151, 173, 175, 176, 177, 180, 186, 187, 194, 212, 218	3:12b-26	65, 183
		3:12-33	173
		3:13	75, 150, 161, 167, 173, 174, 178, 180, 181, 184, 215, 216, 217
2:37	166, 188, 213		
2:38	63, 76, 171, 174, 181, 192, 217, 218, 222, 223, 230, 239		
		3:13-14	129, 215

3:13-15	145, 176, 180, 202	3:22-33	173
		3:23	76
3:13-21	85	3:23a	174
3:13a	181	3:23b	174
3:13b-18	181	3:24-26	76
3:14	173, 179, 212, 219	3:25	75, 167, 174, 217
3:14-15	181	3:25-26	181, 222
3:15	69, 114, 161, 167, 173, 179, 180, 181, 184, 213, 215, 217, 218, 234	3:26	63, 150, 167, 174, 178, 180, 215, 216, 239
		4	79, 243
3:15b	184	4:1-3	190, 195, 236, 254
3:15-16	177	4:1-7	166
3:15-26	215	4:1-14	253
3:16	174, 180, 181, 182, 184, 194, 212, 215, 221, 232	4:2	186
		4:3	190, 194
		4:4	189
		4:5-7	190, 195, 236, 254
3:17-21	183, 187		
3:17-26	184	4:7-22	44
3:18	167, 176, 180, 181, 212, 215, 216	4:8-12	166, 191, 194, 234
		4:9	174
3:18-26	66	4:9-12	76, 174
3:19	63, 75, 174, 217, 222, 223, 239	4:10	69, 179, 180, 212, 217, 219
3:19b	74	4:11	58, 122, 173, 177, 201, 209, 215, 217, 226, 262
3:19-20	208		
3:19-21	174, 181, 215, 226		
3:20	167, 176, 180, 185, 215, 218	4:11-12	268
		4:11-13	212
3:20-21	180, 215	4:12	174, 177, 180, 212, 215, 217, 218, 222
3:20-22	181		
3:21	167, 180, 185, 187		
		4:13	115, 222
3:22	167, 174	4:13-18	166
3:22-23	179, 218		

4:18	190, 195, 236, 254	5:8-9	166, 194
		5:9	192, 193
4:19	69, 194, 222, 242, 244, 266	5:11	192
		5:12	117, 192, 213
4:19-20	166, 191, 193	5:12-16	189
4:20	194, 222, 234	5:14-16	191
4:21	190, 195, 236, 254	5:15	166
		5:17-18	190, 195, 236, 254
4:21-23	166		
4:23	186, 218	5:18	190, 194, 213
4:24	180, 192, 215	5:18-20	227
4:24-30	190, 192, 233	5:18-42	44
4:25	215, 219	5:19	235
4:25-30	192	5:20-21	191
4:26	176, 222	5:21b-28	190, 195, 236, 254
4:26-30	236, 253		
4:27	178, 216	5:22	235
4:27-28	180, 215	5:23	101
4:27-30	226	5:25	235
4:28	212	5:26	194
4:29	190, 195, 236, 254	5:29	69, 190, 194, 213, 220, 222, 242, 244, 266
4:30	117, 178, 216		
4:31	131, 194, 217	5:29-32	76, 166, 191, 194, 234
4:32	192		
4:32-37	189, 195	5:30	75, 180, 217
4:33	194, 213, 222, 234	5:31	63, 75, 171, 174, 179, 180, 181, 215, 217, 218, 222, 223, 239
4:34-37	192		
4:35-37	213		
4:36-37	107	5:31b	74
5	78, 79, 243	5:32	69, 114, 194, 212, 213, 220, 222, 266
5:1-4	192		
5:2	213		
5:3	222, 254, 265	5:33	190, 194, 195, 236, 254
5:3-4	166, 194, 238, 239		
		5:40	190, 195, 213, 236, 254
5:4	69, 227		
5:7-9	239	5:41	190, 194, 212, 222, 226, 227
5:7-11	194, 238		

Index of Biblical and Extra-Biblical Writings

5:42	189, 194, 234	8:15	194
6:1	191, 192	8:17-24	194, 238
6:1-6	112, 192	8:18	213
6:2	100, 172, 217	8:18-24	190, 195, 236, 254
6:3-6	191		
6:4	100, 191, 192, 194, 217, 233, 234	8:20	181
		8:20-23	166, 239
		8:21	192
6:5	172	8:21-22	238
6:6	191, 194, 213, 233	8:21-23	194
		8:22	74, 171, 192, 217, 239
6:7	189		
6:7b	194, 266	8:24-25	166
6:8	117	8:25	189
6:8–8:4	112	8:32	223
6:9	190, 195, 236, 254	8:40	189
		9	47
6:11-15	190, 195, 236, 254	9:15	86
		9:22	218
6:14	179, 219	9:26	107
7	75, 77, 79, 173	9:26–11:18	165, 166, 194
7:1-53	76, 78	9:31	59, 189
7:2-53	74	9:32	64
7:48-50	262	9:32-35	191, 233
7:51-53	79	9:32-43	166
7:52	78	9:32–12:24	189
7:58	172	9:32–12:25	189
8:1	165, 189, 194, 213, 223, 254	9:34	166, 232
		9:35	63
8:1-25	166	9:36-41	191
8:4	189, 190, 223	9:36-42	191
8:5–9:31	189	9:40	166, 194, 232
8:7	190, 195, 236, 254	10	45, 76, 93, 123, 194, 197, 213, 232, 236, 252
8:9-13	190, 195, 236, 254		
		10–15	172
8:13	194, 232	10:1-11	85
8:14	213	10:1-33	166
8:14-19	166	10:1-48	247
8:14-25	43, 165	10:9	194

10:9-48	191	10:43	87, 171, 174, 194, 212, 215, 217, 222, 232
10:14	166, 194, 239		
10:15	165, 247		
10:17	231	10:44	248
10:18	85	10:44-46	166
10:21	166	10:45	86, 181, 217, 222
10:21-48	195, 244		
10:21–11:3	244	10:47	166
10:25-26	195, 244	10:48	166
10:26	166	11	123, 194, 232, 236
10:28	171, 195, 244, 266		
		11:1	213
10:28-29	166	11:1-4	166
10:34	69, 212	11:1-18	189, 192
10:34-35	171, 217	11:2-3	191
10:34-36	86	11:3	195, 244
10:34-43	43, 65, 85, 86, 87, 166	11:5	231
		11:5-17	166
10:36	171, 174	11:8	239
10:37-38a	86	11:9	180, 215, 247
10:38	179, 180, 181, 215, 219	11:14	174, 217
		11:16	37, 180, 213
10:38b	86	11:17	181, 222, 232
10:38-41	180, 217	11:18	166, 217, 222, 230, 239
10:39	114, 174, 194, 213, 217		
		11:19	189, 223
10:39a	86	11:19-21	189
10:39b	86	11:19-30	112
10:39-41	69	11:22-24	189
10:40	86, 180, 181, 215	11:23	237
		11:24	189
10:41	86, 194, 213, 222	11:26	212
		12	111, 118
10:41-42	212	12:1-5	194
10:42	79, 87, 179, 180, 186, 201, 212, 215, 218, 219	12:1-6	190, 195, 236, 254
		12:1-10	166
10:42-43	74	12:1-19	165, 166
		12:3	35
		12:5	192, 232

12:5-6	235	15:5	191
12:9	231	15:6	213
12:11	166, 222, 232, 236, 254	15:7	86, 191, 212
		15:7-11	165, 213, 222
12:12	103, 107, 192, 212, 227	15:7b-11	166
		15:7-21	172
12:12-19	166	15:8	74, 181, 222, 238
12:17	35, 53, 64, 119, 122		
		15:8-9	192, 194, 222, 238, 239
12:17b	45, 166		
12:19	64, 190, 195, 236, 254	15:9	222, 223
		15:9-11	232
12:24	189	15:10-11	160, 194, 232, 248
12:25	103, 107		
13	75, 77, 79, 173	15:11	64, 174, 222, 223, 231
13:1–15:35	189		
13:2-13	103	15:12-14	86
13:5	105, 107, 113	15:12-29	166
13:13	107	15:13-21	119
13:16-41	65, 74, 76, 78, 79	15:14	222
		15:16-17	136
13:23	179, 218	15:19	63
13:31	2, 59, 114, 123, 269	15:21	235
		15:22	112
13:47	86	15:22-23	213
13:49	189	15:27	112
14:3	117	15:32	112
14:22b	193, 260, 265	15:35	189
14:23	192	15:36-40	107
15	2, 45, 46, 47, 48, 53, 111, 112, 118, 130, 268	15:36–19:20	189
		15:36–19:21	189
		15:37-40	112
15:1	248	15:40	112, 113
15:1-2	191	16:3	112
15:1-7a	166	16:5	189
15:1-21	119, 192	16:6	189
15:1-29	165, 166	16:17-19	112
15:2	117, 213	16:25	112
15:3-29	191	16:29	112
15:4	213	16:37-38	112

16:40	112	1:15	47
17	173	1:17–3:26	202
17:3	176	3:20-26	241
17:4	112	3:25	260
17:10	112	4:13	186
17:14-15	112	5:1-21	41
17:24	262	8:4	5
17:30-31	79	8:27	237
17:31	179, 219	9:4-5	241
17:32	186	9:5	242
18:2	47	10:4	5
18:5	112, 176	10:14-15	236
18:9-10	234, 235	11:13	86
18:28	176	12:1	261
19:10	189	13:1	199
19:20	190	13:10	5
19:22–28:31	190	15:19	117
20:35	117	16:1-23	47
21:18-26	119		
21:20b	190	**1 Corinthians**	
21:40	32	1:12	46
22	47	3:16-17	264
22:2	32	3:22	46
22:8	179, 219	5:6-8	159
22:21	85	6:19	264
23:31	33	7:10	117
24:15	186	9:5	11, 35, 46, 53
24:27	113	10:4	57
26	47	11:23-25	117
26:3	186	13:1-7	6
26:9	179, 219	15:1-4	102
26:11	218	15:4	44
26:18	265	15:5	43, 46, 217
26:22-23	176	15:25	151
28:14	190		
28:16	101, 112, 172	**2 Corinthians**	
28:30	112	1:19	112, 116
28:31	190	3:3	236
		6:4-10	243
Romans		6:16	264

6:16-18	263
11:16-29	243
12:12	117

Galatians

1:18	2, 45, 47, 172
1:19	47, 59
2	45, 112, 252
2:2	45
2:6	204, 248
2:9	35, 45
2:11	248
2:11-12	160
2:11-14	45, 107
2:11-16	35
2:11-21	45
2:12	45
3:14	170
3:18	167
4:6	167
4:26	198
5:9	159
5:22	250

Ephesians

2:19-22	122
2:20	122, 217, 268
2:20-22	58, 226
2:21	264
2:21-22	124, 222

Philippians

2:1-12	271
2:1-14	188
2:5-11	243
2:6-11	178
2:9-11	149
3:10	259
4:9	237

Colossians

1:12-21	188
1:15-17	265
1:21-22	241
2:23	239
4:10	103, 107
4:10-14	107

1 Thessalonians

1:1	112, 116
2:6-8	53
4:13	68
5:3	68, 101

2 Thessalonians

1:1	112, 116
2:3	68

1 Timothy

2:7	86
4:7b	237
4:15-16	237

2 Timothy

4:11	103, 106, 107, 112
4:11-12	107

Philemon

23-24	107
24	103, 107

Hebrews

1:1-2	78
2:4	117
2:10	179, 218
7:5	240
8:8-12	170
9:5	260

9:11	263	1:6-7	206, 222, 232, 256
9:23-24	262		
10:16-17	170	1:7	201, 205, 217, 218, 249, 253, 255, 261
10:21	58-59		
10:36	233		
11:1-2	231	1:7-8	203
11:2	233	1:8	199, 205, 206, 257, 266
11:8-10	255		
11:13-14	255	1:8-9	231, 233
11:13-16	199	1:9	203, 206, 222
11:14-15	255	1:10	114
11:15	255	1:10-12	200, 212, 215
11:16a	255	1:10-13	218
11:39	233	1:11	200, 201, 202, 215, 217, 218, 219
12:2	179, 198, 218		
13:14	199		
		1:11-12	204, 215, 216
1 Peter		1:12	205, 209, 226, 235
1:1	46, 113, 114, 197, 199, 200, 204, 206, 212, 213, 222, 254, 257, 266		
		1:13	42, 130, 201, 203, 205, 217, 218, 226
		1:13-15	206, 266
1:1-2	200, 255	1:14	203, 205, 222, 239, 266
1:1-3	218		
1:1-11	247	1:14-16	206, 239
1:2	204, 205, 206, 212, 215, 222, 266	1:15	238
		1:15-16	199
		1:17	199, 200, 204, 206, 212, 219, 254, 255, 266
1:2-3	200		
1:3	44, 199, 200, 201, 203, 205, 215, 217, 218, 222, 223		
		1:18	201, 212
		1:18-19	201, 204, 216, 222
1:4	203, 205, 222	1:19	218, 219
1:4-5	255	1:19-20	221
1:5	200, 201, 203, 222	1:20	212, 215
		1:20-21	200
1:6	199, 205, 206, 253	1:21	44, 201, 203, 205, 217, 232

1:21-22	200		239, 254, 255, 257
1:22	204, 206, 222, 239, 240, 257, 266	2:11-12	199
		2:12	200, 203, 205, 218, 235, 255, 257
1:22-23	243, 257		
1:23	200, 203, 222		
1:23-25	217, 233	2:13	205, 244
1:24	199, 203	2:13-14	199, 244
1:25	200, 205, 235	2:13-17	205, 212, 249
2:1	204, 222	2:15	204, 205, 235, 257
2:1-2	206, 239		
2:3	200	2:16	206, 244, 266
2:4	122, 201, 209, 212, 217, 226, 262	2:17	203, 244
		2:18	199, 244, 259
		2:18-25	226
2:4-5	213, 264	2:19	205, 249
2:4-8	58	2:19-20	205, 232
2:4-10	124, 268, 270	2:19-21	201
2:5	131, 200, 204, 206, 209, 218, 222, 262, 263, 264	2:19-24	199
		2:20b	258
		2:20-21	206, 253
		2:21	200, 204, 205, 206, 209, 215, 218, 220, 221, 226, 257, 259
2:6	173, 200		
2:6-7	201, 209, 215, 217, 226		
2:6-8	122, 217, 226, 262	2:21-23	204, 232
		2:21-24	146
2:7	173, 174, 200, 205, 209, 212, 217, 226	2:21-25	145, 216, 223
		2:22	200, 201, 202
		2:22-23	240
2:8	200	2:22-24	201, 216, 219, 260
2:8-10	200		
2:9	151, 199, 204, 205, 206, 212, 222, 233, 235	2:22-25	218
		2:23	200, 201, 205, 206, 209, 226, 231, 242, 243, 249, 253
2:9-10	200, 203, 204, 222		
2:10	174, 217, 223	2:23-24	209
2:11	199, 203, 204, 205, 206, 222,		

2:24	61, 201, 206, 216, 239, 241, 257, 259	3:18	130, 161, 163, 177, 181, 201, 202, 203, 212, 215, 216, 217, 218, 223, 229, 232, 235, 240-41, 247, 262
2:24d	200		
2:24-25	239, 259		
2:25	62, 114, 130, 199, 202, 203, 204, 206, 213, 223, 266		
		3:18-22	200, 265
		3:20	222
2:25a	200	3:21	44, 174, 201, 203, 211, 217
3:1	205, 206, 222, 235, 239, 249	3:22	201, 212, 217
3:2	206, 266	4:1	204, 209, 218, 226, 232, 259
3:4	200, 205, 206, 239	4:2	204, 239
3:5	199, 205	4:3	239
3:6	232	4:3-4	204, 222
3:7	206, 218	4:4	203, 204
3:7-8	205, 249	4:5	179, 201, 217, 218, 219, 235
3:8	204, 205, 206, 244, 249	4:5-6	200, 212
3:8-9	199	4:7	42, 201, 210, 217, 226, 255
3:9-14	232		
3:10-11	206, 239	4:8	114, 204, 257
3:10-12	200, 216	4:8-19	205
3:12	206	4:9	249
3:13	206, 253	4:10	206, 244, 266
3:13-17	199	4:10-11	205, 249
3:13-18	199	4:11	201, 203, 204, 205, 217
3:14	205		
3:14-16	235	4:12	200, 204, 206, 232, 253, 257, 261
3:14-18	259		
3:15	199, 205, 218, 230, 231, 236, 249		
		4:12-13	205
		4:12-16	199
3:15-16	205, 206, 239	4:12-19	198, 232, 249
3:16	203, 206, 232, 242, 257	4:13	199, 201, 204, 206, 216, 217, 218, 259
3:16-17	232, 241, 253		
3:17	204, 206		

Index of Biblical and Extra-Biblical Writings 317

4:13-14	203, 209, 212, 226		204, 205, 217, 218, 223, 233
4:14	199, 204, 205, 211, 212, 226, 235, 236, 253, 257, 258	5:5	114, 243
		5:5a	249
		5:5-6	114, 205, 244, 249
4:15	204, 222	5:5b-11	249
4:16	205, 206, 209, 212, 232, 236, 253, 258	5:6	201, 204, 217, 218, 231, 232, 242, 244, 250
4:16-17b	258	5:6-7	250
4:17	199, 200, 201, 220, 222, 246, 257, 260	5:6-8	41
		5:7	205, 240, 250
		5:8	42, 212, 213, 250
4:17-18	209, 227	5:8-9	239, 254, 265
4:18	200, 216	5:8-11	205
4:19	200, 204, 205, 206, 231, 232, 233, 242, 243, 249, 253, 259	5:9	205, 206, 259
		5:9-10	232, 253
		5:10	199, 201, 203, 204, 205, 206, 217, 218, 250, 265
5	252		
5:1	62, 114, 197, 201, 203, 212, 213, 217, 218, 257, 271	5:10-11	200, 210, 227, 236, 254
		5:11	250
5:1-3	62	5:12	112, 114, 116, 206, 253
5:1-4	129, 131, 132, 213, 249	5:12-13	112
5:1-7	271	5:13	103, 106, 107, 108, 198, 199, 206
5:1-8	253		
5:1-10	53, 198		
5:1-11	249	5:13-14	212
5:2	114, 130, 203, 205	5:14	204
5:2-3	204, 205, 249	**2 Peter**	
5:2-4	202	1:1	113, 207, 208, 213
5:3	205, 211		
5:4	114, 129, 130, 200, 201, 203,	1:2	218
		1:3	208, 218

1:3-11	207	3:12	201, 208, 210
1:4	208	3:13	207
1:5	6	3:14	208
1:5-7	208	3:15-16	48
1:6-7	208	3:16	54
1:8	208, 209, 218	3:18	207, 217, 218
1:9	208, 209		
1:11	151, 207, 217, 218	**Revelation**	
1:13-14	209	1:18	60
1:14	218	3:3	37
1:16	142, 201, 217, 218, 230, 232, 271	3:7	129
		6:8	57
		11:8	198
1:16-18	141, 217, 271	17:18	198
1:17	142, 147	20:13-14	57
1:17-18	207, 208	21:3	263
1:19	208, 218	21:22	263, 264
1:20	208		
1:21	215, 269		
2:1	207, 208, 209		
2:2-3	208	**OT Apocrypha**	
2:4	57	Bar, 72, 73, 74	
2:7-8	208	Jdt, 254	
2:9	208, 210	1 Macc, 12, 13, 14, 15, 23, 28, 56, 69, 71, 87, 91, 93	
2:10	207, 244		
2:10-19	208	2 Macc, 12, 13, 14, 15, 28, 71, 87, 88, 91, 93, 104, 254, 259	
2:11	257		
2:20	218	Sir, 74	
3:1	115	Tob, 72, 73, 74, 75, 90	
3:1-2	209	Wis, 71	
3:1-15	218		
3:2	37, 213, 218	**OT Pseudepigrapha**	
3:3-7	208	*As. Mos.*, 72, 73	
3:4	201	*2 Bar.*, 72, 73, 74, 198	
3:8	217	*1 En.*, 28, 56, 72, 73, 74, 137, 138, 139, 140, 147, 179, 219	
3:9	187, 208		
3:10	217	*4 Ezra*, 72, 73, 74, 198	
3:10-11	208		
3:11	208		

Jub., 28, 69, 72, 73, 74, 168, 169, 261
L.A.B., Ps.-Philo, 72, 73, 74
4 Macc., 15, 28, 71
Pss. Sol., 24, 72, 74, 137, 138, 139, 140, 177, 179, 202
Sib. Or., 198
T. 12 Patr., 72, 73, 74, 137
    T. Ash., 72
    T. Benj., 66
    T. Dan, 72
    T. Iss., 72
    T. Jud., 72
    T. Levi, 62, 66, 72
    T. Naph., 72
    T. Zeb., 72
T. Sol., 63

Qumran/Dead Sea Scrolls
1QapGen, 168
1QH, 57, 61, 126
1QIsa^a, 146
1QM, 61
1QpHab, 263
1QS, 66, 137, 179, 182, 202, 219, 263
1QSa, 28, 56, 136, 137, 138, 150
4Q491, 147
4QCommGen A, 136, 137
4QDibHam^a, 72, 73
4QFlor, 136, 137, 151, 168
4QMessAp, 138, 139
4QTest, 137, 179, 218
11QMel, 147
11QPs^a, 28
11QtgJob, 213

CD, 61, 72, 74, 129, 136, 137, 168, 263

Papyri
P 72, 120
P 125, 120
POxy, 113

Josephus
    Ag. Ap., 31, 97, 98, 101, 105, 106
    Ant., 12, 16, 17, 18, 19, 20, 22, 23, 24, 25, 32, 34, 37, 44, 80, 101, 106, 113, 168, 185, 198, 202
    J.W., 16, 17, 18, 19, 20, 22, 23, 24, 25, 26, 33, 34, 62, 101, 105
    Life, 23, 30

Philo
    Her., 185
    Legat., 21
    Opif., 25

NT Apocrypha and Pseudepigrapha
Acts Pet., 46, 48, 252
Acts Pet. 12 Apos., 48
Acts Pet. Andr., 48
Acts Pet. Paul, 48
Ap. John, 198
Apoc. Pet., 48, 120
Ep. Pet. Phil., 48
Gos. Pet., 48, 120, 121
Gos. Heb., 120

Judgment of Pet., 48
Pre. Pet., 48

Church Fathers
Athanasius, *H.Ar.*, 117
Augustine
    Cons., 109
    Ep., 47
    Serm., 56
Clement of Alexandria, 44, 48, 51, 54, 103, 132
Clement of Rome
    1 Clem., 18, 46, 48, 52, 53, 104, 114, 118, 252
Cyprian
    Unit. eccl., 52
Did., 90, 114, 118, 120
Eusebius
    Chron., 46
    Hist. eccl., 44, 46, 48, 49, 51, 92, 101, 104, 105, 108, 115, 119, 121, 132
Ignatius
    Rom., 46, 48
    Smyrn., 48
Irenaeus, *Haer.*, 46, 47, 48, 51, 52, 87, 103, 105, 106, 115, 121
Jerome
    Vir. ill., 46, 47, 63
Justin (Martyr)
    Apol., 121
    Dial., 48, 89, 106, 114
Origen
    Cels., 52
    Comm. Matt., 52

Polycarp, Pol. *Phil.*, 114
Shepherd of Hermas, 120
Tertullian
    Marc., 48, 106
    Praescr., 48
    Pud., 44, 52
    Scorp., 48

Targumic Texts
Tg. Isa., 145, 146

Rabbinic Writings
Babylonian Talmud
    B. Bat., 25
    Ber., 25, 159
    Ḥag., 29, 31, 61
    Menaḥ, 25
    Šabb., 61
    Sanh., 61, 136, 151
    Sukkah, 25
Mishnah
    'Abot, 30
    Mak., 26
    Meg., 26
    Sanh., 26
'Abot R. Nat., 25
Gen. Rab., 30, 185, 186

Classical Writers
Demosthenes, *Cor.*, 100
Cicero, *Resp.*, 18
Herodotus, *Hist.*, 113
Homer, *Il.*, 28
Pliny, the Younger, *Ep.*, 46, 115
Seneca, *Ep.*, 258

Sophocles, *Oed. Col.*, 57
Strabo, *Geogr.*, 16
Suetonius
    Aug., 17
    Claud., 17, 18
    Nero, 17
    Vesp., 21
Tacitus
    Ann., 17, 18, 93, 198
    Hist., 17, 18, 93
Theon of Alexandria,
    Progymnasmata, 92

Bibliography

Achtemeier, P.J. *1 Peter: A Commentary on First Peter*. Hermeneia. Minneapolis, MN: Fortress, 1996.

Adams, S.L. *Social and Economic Life in Second Temple Judea*. Louisville, KY: Westminster John Knox, 2014.

Ådna, J. 'Jesus and the Temple'. Pages 2635–76 in vol. III of *Handbook for the Study of the Historical Jesus*. 4 vols. Edited by T. Holmén and S. Porter. Leiden: Brill, 2011.

Ådna, J. *Jesu Stellung zum Tempel: Die Tempelaktion und das Tempelwort als Ausdruck seiner messianischen Sendung*. WUNT 2/19. Tübingen: Mohr Siebeck, 2000.

Agan, C.D.J. *The Imitation of Christ in the Gospel of Luke: Growing in Christlike Love for God and Neighbor*. Phillipsburg, NJ: P&R, 2014.

Alexander, L. *The Preface of Luke's Gospel: Literary Convention and Social Context in Luke 1:1-4 and Acts 1:1*. SNTSMS 78. Cambridge: Cambridge University Press, 1993.

Allison, D.C. *The End of the Ages Has Come: An Early Interpretation of the Passion and Resurrection of Jesus*. Philadelphia, PA: Fortress, 1985.

Armerding, H.T. *The Heart of Godly Leadership*. Wheaton, IL: Crossway, 1992.

Aune, D.E. 'The Significance of the Delay of the Parousia for Early Christianity'. Pages 87–109 in *Current Issues in Biblical and Patristic Interpretation*. Edited by G.F. Hawthorne. Grand Rapids, MI: Eerdmans, 1975.

Aune, D.E. *The New Testament in Its Literary Environment*. Library of Early Christianity. Philadelphia, PA: Westminster John Knox Press, 1987.

Backhaus, K. 'Lösepreis für viele (Mk 10,45): Zur Heilsbedeutung des Todes Jesu bei Markus'. Pages 91–118 in *Der Evangelist als Theologe. Studien zum Markusevangelium*. Edited by T. Söding. Stuttgart: Katholisches Bibelwerk, 1995.

Bailey, K.E. 'Informal Controlled Oral Tradition and the Synoptic Gospels'. *Asia Journal of Theology* 5 (1991), 34–54.

Bailey, K.E. 'Middle Eastern Oral Tradition and the Synoptic Gospels'. *ExpT* 106 (1994/95), 363–67.

Bailey, K.E. *The Good Shepherd: A Thousand-Year Journey from Psalm 23 to the New Testament*. Downers Grove, IL: IVP Academic, 2014.

Bainton, R.H., and W.L. Jenkins, eds. *Martin Luther's Christmas Book*. Philadelphia, PA: Westminster Press, 1948.

Baker, C.A. *Identity, Memory, and Narrative in Early Christianity: Peter, Paul, and Recategorization in the Book of Acts*. Eugene, OR: Wipf & Stock, 2011.

Balch, D.L. 'The Canon: Adaptable and Stable, Oral and Written. Critical Questions for Kelber and Riesner.' *Forum* 7.3-4 (1991), 183–205.

Balleine, G.R. *Simon Whom He Surnamed Peter*. London: Skeffington, 1958.

Baltes, G. *Hebräisches Evangelium und synoptische Überlieferung: Untersuchungen zum hebräischen Hintergrund der Evangelien.* WUNT 2/312. Tübingen: Mohr Siebeck, 2011.
Barber, M.P. 'Jesus as the Davidic Temple Builder and Peter's Priestly Role in Matthew 16:16-19'. *JBL* 132.4 (2013), 935–53.
Bar-Ilan, M. 'Illiteracy in the Land of Israel in the First Centuries CE'. Pages 46–61 in *Essays in the Social Scientific Study of Judaism and Jewish Society*. Edited by S. Fishbane and S. Schoenfeld. Hoboken, NJ: Ktav, 1992.
Barnett, P.W. *Jesus and the Logic of History.* Grand Rapids, MI: Eerdmans, 1997.
Barnett, P.W. *Jesus and the Rise of Early Christianity: A History of New Testament Times.* Downers Grove, IL: IVP, 1999.
Barrett, C.K. 'Cephas and Corinth'. Pages 1–12 in *Abraham unser Vater: Juden und Christen im Gespräch über die Bibel.* Edited by O. Betz. FS O. Michel. Leiden: Brill, 1963.
Barrett, C.K. 'Faith and Eschatology in Acts 3'. Pages 1–17 in *Glaube und Eschatologie: Festschrift für Werner Georg Kümmel zum 80. Geburtstag.* Edited by E. Grässer and O. Merk. Tübingen: Mohr Siebeck, 1985.
Barrett, C.K. 'Submerged Christology in Acts'. Pages 237–44 in *Anfänge der Christologie.* Edited by C. Breytenbach and H. Paulsen. Göttingen: Vandenhoeck & Ruprecht, 1991.
Barrett, C.K. 'The Background of Mk 10.45'. Pages 1–18 in *New Testament Essays: Studies in the Memory of T.W. Manson, 1893-1958.* Edited by A.J.B. Higgins. Manchester: Manchester University Press, 1959.
Barrett, C.K. 'The Historicity of Acts'. *JTS* 50 (1999), 515–34.
Bartholomew, C. and M. Goheen. 'Story and Biblical Theology'. Pages 144–71 in *Out of Egypt: Biblical Theology and Biblical Interpretation.* Edited by C. Bartholomew. Grand Rapids, MI: Zondervan, 2004.
Bash, A. *Ambassadors for Christ: An Exploration of Ambassadorial Language in the New Testament.* WUNT 2/92. Tübingen: Mohr Siebeck, 1997.
Bass, J.W. *The Battle for the Keys: Revelation 1:18 and Christ's Descent into the Underworld.* Paternoster Biblical Monographs. Milton Keynes: Paternoster, 2014.
Bateman, H., D. Bock and G. Johnston. *Jesus the Messiah: Tracing the Promises, expectations and Coming of Israel's King.* Grand Rapids, MI: Kregel Academic, 2011.
Bates, M.W. *The Hermeneutics of the Apostolic Proclamation: The Center of Paul's Method of Scriptural Interpretation.* Waco, TX: Baylor University Press, 2012.
Bauckham, R.J. 'The Martyrdom of Peter in Early Christian Literature'. *ANRW* 26.1:549–95. Part 2, *Principat,* 26.1. Edited by H. Temporini and W. Haase. Berlin: de Gruyter, 1992.
Bauckham, R.J. *James: The Wisdom of James, Disciple of Jesus the Sage.* London: Routledge, 1999.

Bauckham, R.J. *Jesus and the Eyewitnesses: The Gospels as Eyewitness Testimony.* Grand Rapids, MI: Eerdmans, 2006.

Bauckham, R.J. *Jude, 2 Peter.* WBC 50. Waco, TX: Word, 1983.

Bauckham, R.J. *Jude, 2 Peter.* Word Biblical Themes. Dallas, TX: Word, 1990.

Bauckham, R.J., ed. *The Gospels for All Christians: Rethinking the Gospel Audiences.* Grand Rapids, MI: Eerdmans, 1997.

Bauernfeind, O. 'Tradition und Komposition in dem Apokatastasisspruch Apg 3, 20f'. Pages 13–23 in *Abraham unser Vater: Juden und Christen im Gespräch über die Bibel.* Edited by O. Betz. FS O. Michel. Leiden: Brill, 1963.

Baum, A.D. 'Anonymity in the NT History Books: A Stylistic Device in the Context of Greco-Roman and Ancient Near Eastern Literature'. *NovT* 50 (2008), 120–42.

Baum, A.D. 'Der Presbyter des Papias'. *TZ* 56 (2000), 21–35.

Baum, A.D. 'Der semitische Sprachhintergrund der Evangelien und die Urevangeliumshypothese: Überlegungen im Anschluss an Guido Baltes'. *TBei* 44 (2013), 306–23.

Baum, A.D. 'Experimentalpsychologische Erwägungen zur synoptischen Frage'. *BZ* 44.1 (2000), 37–55.

Baum, A.D. 'Lk 1,1-4 zwischen antiker Historiografie und Fachprosa: Zum literaturgeschichtlichen Kontext des lukanischen Prologs'. *ZNW* 101.1 (2010), 33–54.

Baum, A.D. 'Papias als Kommentator evangelischer Aussprüche Jesu'. *NovT* 28.3 (1996), 257–75.

Baum, A.D. 'Papias, der Vorzug der *Viva Vox* und die Evangelienschriften'. *NTS* 44.1 (1998), 144–51.

Baum, A.D. 'Paulinismen in den Missionsreden des lukanischen Paulus: Zur inhaltlichen Authentizität der *oratio recta* in der Apostelgeschichte'. *Ephemerides Theologicae Lovanienses* 82.4 (2006), 405–36.

Baum, A.D. *Der mündliche Faktor und seine Bedeutung für die synoptische Frage. Analogien aus der antiken Literatur, der Experimentalpsychologie, der Oral Poetry-Forschung und dem rabbinischen Traditionswesen.* TANZ 49. Tübingen: Francke, 2008.

Baum, A.D. *Lukas als Historiker der letzten Jesusreise.* Monographien und Studienbücher. Wuppertal: Brockhaus, 1993.

Bayer, H.F. 'Christ-Centered Eschatology in Acts 3:17-26'. Pages 236–50 in *Jesus of Nazareth: Lord and Christ. Essays on the Historical Jesus and New Testament Christology.* Edited by J.B. Green and M. Turner. FS I.H. Marshall. Grand Rapids, MI/Carlisle: Eerdmans/Paternoster, 1994.

Bayer, H.F. 'Das Hauptmotiv der südphönizischen und ostjordanischen Reisen Jesu bei Markus'. Pages 205–15 in *Sprache lieben – Gottes Wort verstehen: Beiträge zur biblischen Exegese.* Edited by W. Hilbrands. Giessen: Brunnen, 2011.

Bayer, H.F. 'The Eschatological Prospect in the Context of Mark'. Pages 74–84 in *Looking into the Future: Evangelical Studies in Eschatology*. Edited by D.W. Baker. Grand Rapids, MI: Baker, 2001.

Bayer, H.F. 'The Preaching of Peter in Acts'. Pages 257–74 in *Witness to the Gospel: The Theology of Acts*. Edited by I.H. Marshall and D. Peterson. Grand Rapids, MI: Eerdmans, 1998.

Bayer, H.F. *A Theology of Mark: The Dynamic between Christology and Authentic Discipleship*. Phillipsburg, NJ: P&R, 2012.

Bayer, H.F. and R. Yarbrough. 'O. Cullmanns progressiv-heilsgeschichtliche Konzeption'. Pages 319–47 in *Glaube und Geschichte: Heilsgeschichte als Thema der Theologie*. Edited by H. Stadelmann. 2nd ed. Giessen/Wuppertal: Brunnen/Brockhaus, 1998.

Bayer, H.F. *Das Evangelium des Markus*. 2nd ed. Wuppertal: Brokhaus, 2013.

Bayer, H.F. *Jesus' Predictions of Vindication and Resurrection*. Tübingen: Mohr Siebeck, 1986.

Bayer, O. 'The Theology of Lament'. *Jahrbuch für Biblische Theologie* 16 (2001), 298–301.

Beale, G.K. *A New Testament Biblical Theology: The Unfolding of the Old Testament in the New*. Grand Rapids, MI: Baker Academic, 2011.

Beale, G.K. and D.A. Carson, eds. *Commentary on the New Testament Use of the Old Testament*. Grand Rapids, MI: Baker Academic, 2007.

Beale, G.K. *The Temple and the Church's Mission: A Biblical Theology of the Dwelling Place of God*. New Studies in Biblical Theology. Downers Grove, IL: IVP Academic, 2004.

Becker, J. *Mündliche und schriftliche Autorität im frühen Christentum*. Tübingen: Mohr Siebeck, 2012.

Becker, J. *Paulus, der Apostel der Völker*. Tübingen: Mohr Siebeck, 1989.

Becker, J. *Simon Petrus im Urchristentum*. Biblisch-theologische Studien 105. Neukirchen-Vluyn: Neukirchener Verlag, 2009.

Bell, A.A. *Exploring the New Testament World: An Illustrated Guide To The World Of Jesus And The First Christians*. Nashville, TN: Nelson, 1998.

Bellinger, W.H. and W.R. Farmer, eds. *Jesus and the Suffering Servant: Isaiah 53 and Christian Origins*. Harrisburg, PA: Trinity Press, 1998.

Bengel, J.A. *Gnomon Novi Testamenti: Auslegung des Neuen Testamentes in fortlaufenden Anmerkungen*. Vol. I. Evangelien und Apostelgeschichte. 4th ed. Leipzig: M. Heinsius Successor, 1932 [1877].

Benner, D.G. *The Gift of Loving Yourself: The Sacred Call to Self-Discovery*. Downers Grove, IL: IVP, 2004.

Berger, K. 'Die königlichen Messiastraditionen des Neuen Testaments'. *NTS* 20.1 (1973), 1–44.

Berger, K. *Die Auferstehung des Propheten und die Erhöhung des Menschensohnes: Traditionsgeschichtliche Untersuchungen zur Deutung des Geschickes Jesu in frühchristlichen Texten*. SUNT. Göttingen: Vandenhoeck & Ruprecht, 1976.

Berger, K. *Formen und Gattungen im Neuen Testament.* UTB 2532. Tübingen: Francke, 2005.
Bernett, M. *Der Kaiserkult in Judäa unter den Herodiern und Römern: Untersuchungen zur politischen und religiösen Geschichte Judäas von 30 v. bis 66 n. Chr.* WUNT 1/203. Tübingen: Mohr Siebeck, 2007.
Best, E. '1 Peter and the Gospel Tradition'. *NTS* 16 (1969-70), 95–113.
Best, E. *Disciples and Discipleship: Studies in the Gospel According to Mark.* Edinburgh: T&T Clark, 1985.
Best, E. *Following Jesus: Discipleship in the Gospel of Mark.* JSNT Supplement. Sheffield: Continuum, 1981.
Betz, H.D. *Nachfolge und Nachahmung Jesu Christi im Neuen Testament.* Tübingen: Mohr Siebeck, 1967.
Betz, O. 'Donnersöhne, Menschenfischer und der davidische Messias'. *RQ* 3 (1961-62): 41–70.
Betz, O. 'Felsenmann und Felsengemeinde: Parallelen zu Mt. 16:17-19 in den Qumranpsalmen'. *ZNW* 48 (1957), 49–77.
Beyschlag, K. *Simon Magus und die christliche Gnosis.* WUNT 1/16. Tübingen: Mohr Siebeck, 1974.
Bird, M.F. and J. Willitts, eds. *Paul and the Gospels: Christologies, Conflicts, and Convergences.* London: T&T Clark, 2011.
Bird, M.F. *Are You the One Who Is to Come?: The Historical Jesus and the Messianic Question.* Grand Rapids, MI: Baker Academic, 2009.
Bird, M.F. *Jesus and the Origins of the Gentile Mission.* New York, NY: Bloomsbury, 2007.
Bird, M.F. *Jesus Is the Christ: The Messianic Testimony of the Gospels.* Downers Grove, IL: IVP Academic, 2013.
Bird, M.F. *The Gospel of the Lord: How the Early Church Wrote the Story of Jesus.* Grand Rapids, MI: Eerdmans, 2014.
Black, C.C. *Mark: Images of an Apostolic Interpreter.* Columbia, SC: University of SC, 1994.
Black, C.C. *The Disciples according to Mark: Markan Redaction in Current Debate.* 2nd ed. Grand Rapids, MI: Eerdmans, 2012.
Black, D.A. *Why Four Gospels?: The Historical Origins of the Gospels.* Grand Rapids, MI: Kregel, 2001.
Black, M. *An Aramaic Approach to the Gospels and Acts.* 3rd ed. Peabody, MA: Hendrickson Publishers, 1998.
Blackburn, B. *Theios Aner.* Tübingen: Mohr Siebeck, 1991.
Blomberg, C. *Neither Poverty nor Riches: A Biblical Theology of Possessions.* Downers Grove, IL: IVP, 2001.
Blomberg, C., W. Klein and R. Hubbard. *Introduction to Biblical Interpretation.* Waco, TX: Word Books, 1993.
Bock, D.L. 'The Use of the Old Testament in Luke–Acts: Christology and Mission'. Pages 494–511 in *Society of Biblical Literature 1990 Seminar Papers.* SBLSPS 126.29. Atlanta, GA: Scholars Press, 1990.

Bock, D.L. *A Theology of Luke and Acts: God's Promised Program, Realized for All.* Grand Rapids, MI: Zondervan, 2012.

Bock, D.L. and M. Glaser, eds. *The Gospel According to Isaiah 53: Encountering the Suffering Servant in Jewish and Christian Theology.* Grand Rapids, MI: Kregel Academic, 2012.

Bock, D.L. *Blasphemy and Exaltation in Judaism and the Final Examination of Jesus: A Philological-Historical Study of the Key Jewish Themes Impacting Mark 14:61-64.* Tübingen: Mohr Siebeck, 1998.

Bock, D.L. *Luke.* The NIV Application Commentary. Grand Rapids, MI: Zondervan, 1996.

Bock, D.L. *Proclamation from Prophecy and Pattern: Lucan Old Testament Christology.* JSNTS 12. Sheffield: JSOT Press, 1987.

Bockmuehl, M. 'Whose Memory? Whose Orality?: A Conversation with James Dunn on Jesus and the Gospels'. Pages 31–44 in *Memories of Jesus: A Critical Appriasal of James D.G. Dunn's Jesus Remembered.* Edited by R.B. Stewart and G.R. Habermas. Nashville, TN: B&H Academic, 2010.

Bockmuehl, M. *Simon Peter in Scripture and Memory: The New Testament Apostle in the Early Church.* Grand Rapids, MI: Baker Academic, 2012.

Bockmuehl, M. *The Remembered Peter in Ancient Reception and Modern Debate.* WUNT 262. Tübingen: Mohr Siebeck, 2010.

Böe, S. *Cross-Bearing in Luke.* WUNT 2/278. Tübingen: Mohr Siebeck, 2010.

Bonhoeffer D. *Discipleship.* Dietrich Bonhoeffer Works, vol. IV. Translated by B. Green and R. Krauss. Minneapolis, MN: Fortress Press, 2003.

Borg, M. *Conflict, Holiness, and Politics in the Teachings of Jesus.* Philadelphia, PA: Trinity Press International, 1998.

Boring, E. 'Markan Christology: God-Language for Jesus?'. *NTS* 45 (1999), 451–71.

Botha, P.J.J. *Orality and Literacy in Early Christianity.* Biblical Performance Criticism, Vol. V. Eugene, OR: Wipf & Stock, 2012.

Bottino, A. 'La figura di Pietro quale esponente della fede cristiana negli Atti degli Apostoli'. *StudMiss* 37 (1988), 1–25.

Bovon, F. 'Israel, die Kirche und die Völker im lukanischen Doppelwerk'. Pages 243–63 in *L'oeuvre de Luc. Études d'exégèse et de théologie.* Edited by F. Bovon. Paris: Cerf, 1987.

Bovon, F. *De vocatione gentium. Histoire de l'interprétation d'Act. 10, 1 - 11, 18 dans les six premiers siècles.* BGE 8. Tübingen: Mohr Siebeck, 1967.

Bradley, A., ed. *Aliens in the Promised Land: Why Minority Leadership Is Overlooked in White Christian Churches and Institutions.* Phillipsburg, NJ: P&R, 2013.

Brandenburg, A. and H.J. Urban, ed. *Petrus und Papst: Evangelium, Einheit der Kirche, Papstdienst.* Münster: Aschendorff, 1977.

Bray, G.L. and T.C. Oden. *James, 1-2 Peter, 1-3 John, Jude.* Ancient Christian Commentary on Scripture: New Testament, vol. XI. Downers Grove, IL: IVP Academic, 2000.

Breuning, W. 'Apokatastasis: "Restoring all things"'. *TDig* 31 (1984), 47–50.
Breytenbach, C. 'The Gospel of Mark as Episodical Narrative: Reflections on the "Composition" of the Second Gospel'. *Scripture* (1989), 1–26.
Brooks, D. *The Social Animal: The Hidden Source of Love, Character, and Achievement*. New York, NY: Random House, 2011.
Brown, R.E. 'The Gospel of Peter and Canonical Gospel Priority'. *NTS* 33.3 (1987), 321–43.
Brown, R.E. *An Introduction to the New Testament*. AYBRL. New York, NY: Doubleday, 1997.
Brown, R.E. *The Gospel According to John I–XII*. Anchor Bible Series, Vol. XXIX). New York, NY: Doubleday, 1966.
Brown, R.E. *The Gospel According to John XIII–XXI*. Anchor Bible Series, Vol. XXIX, A). New York, NY: Doubleday, 1970.
Brown, R.E., K.P. Donfried and J.H.P. Reumann, eds. *Peter in the New Testament: A Collaborative Assessment by Protestant and Roman Catholic Scholars*. Eugene, OR: Wipf & Stock, 2002.
Bruce, F.F. 'Eschatology in Acts'. Pages 51–63 in *Eschatology and the New Testament*. Edited by W.H. Gloer. FS G.R. Beasley-Murray. Peabody: Hendrickson, 1988.
Bruce, F.F. 'The Significance of the Speeches for Interpreting Acts'. *SWJournTheol* 33.1 (1990), 20–28.
Bruce, F.F. *New Testament History*. Reprint. New York, NY: Galilee/Doubleday, 1983.
Bruce, F.F. *Peter, Stephen, James and John: Studies in Non-Pauline Christianity*. Grand Rapids, MI: Eerdmans, 1979.
Bruce, F.F. *The Acts of the Apostles: The Greek Text with Introduction and Commentary*. 3rd ed. Grand Rapids, MI: Eerdmans, 1990 [1951].
Bruce, F.F. *The Book of Acts*. NICNT. Grand Rapids, MI: Eerdmans/Exeter: Paternoster, 1988.
Bruce, F.F. *The New Testament Documents, Are They Reliable?*. 5th ed. Grand Rapids, MI: Eerdmans, 1987.
Bruggen, J. van. *Christ on Earth: The Gospels Narratives as History*. Grand Rapids, MI: Baker, 1987.
Bruggen, J. van. *Jesus the Son of God: The Gospel Narratives as Message*. Grand Rapids, MI: Baker, 1999.
Bultmann, R. 'Zur Frage nach den Quellen der Apostelgeschichte'. Pages 412–23 in *Exegetica: Aufsätze zur Erforschung des Neuen Testaments*. Edited by E. Dinkler. Tübingen: Mohr Siebeck, 1967.
Bultmann, R. *History of the Synoptic Tradition*. New York, NY: Harper, 1968.
Burge, G.M. *Jesus and the Land: The New Testament Challenge to 'Holy Land' Theology*. Grand Rapids, MI: Baker Academic, 2010.
Burns, B., D. Guthrie and T. Chapman. *Resilient Ministry*. Downers Grove, IL: IVP, 2013.
Burridge, R.A. 'About People, by People, for People: Gospel Genre and Audiences'. Pages 113–45 in *The Gospels for All Christians: Rethinking*

the Gospel Audiences. Edited by R.J. Bauckham. Grand Rapids, MI: Eerdmans, 1997.

Burridge, R.A. *Imitating Jesus: An Inclusive Approach to New Testament Ethics.* Grand Rapids, MI: Eerdmans, 2007.

Burridge, R.A. *What are the Gospels?: A Comparison with Graeco-Roman Biography.* 2nd ed. Grand Rapids, MI: Eerdmans, 2004.

Byrskog, S. 'The Transmission of the Jesus Tradition'. Pages 1465–94 in vol. II of *Handbook for the Study of the Historical Jesus.* 4 vols. Edited by T. Holmén and S. Porter. Leiden: Brill, 2011.

Byrskog, S. *Jesus the Only Teacher: Didactic Authority and Transmission in Ancient Israel, Ancient Judaism and the Matthean Community.* Stockholm: Almqvist and Wiksell, 1994.

Byrskog, S. *Story as History–History as Story: The Gospel Tradition in the Context of Ancient Oral History.* WUNT 123. Tübingen: Mohr Siebeck, 2000.

Cadbury, H.J. 'Acts and Eschatology'. Pages 300–21 in *The Background of the New Testament and its Eschatology.* Edited by W.D. Davies and D. Daube in Honour of C.H. Dodd. Cambridge: Cambridge University Press, 1964.

Callan, T. 'The Preface of Luke–Acts and Historiography'. *NTS* 31.4 (1985), 576–81.

Calvin, J. *Institutes of the Christian Religion.* 2 vols. Reprint, London: SCM Press, 1961 [1536].

Campenhausen, H. Frhr. von. *Kirchliches Amt und geistliche Vollmacht in den ersten drei Jahrhunderten.* BZNW 58. 2nd ed. Tübingen: Mohr Siebeck, 1963.

Capes, D.B. 'Imitatio Christi and the Gospel Genre'. *BBR* 13.1 (2003), 1–19.

Caragounis, C.C. *Peter and the Rock.* Berlin: de Gruyter, 1990.

Carlston, C.E. and C.A. Evans. *From Synagogue to Ecclesia: Matthew's Community at the Crossroads.* Tübingen: Mohr Siebeck, 2014.

Carroll, J.T. *Response to the End of History: Eschatology and Situation in Luke–Acts.* Atlanta, GA: Scholars Press, 1988.

Carroll, K.L. 'Thou art Peter'. *NT* 6 (1963), 268–76.

Carson, D.A. 'Pseudonymity and Pseudepigraphy'. Pages 857–63 in *DNTB*. Edited by C. Evans and S. Porter. Downers Grove, IL: IVP, 2000.

Carson, D.A. and D.J. Moo. *An Introduction to the New Testament.* 2nd ed. Grand Rapids, MI: Zondervan, 2005.

Carson, D.A. *Jesus the Son of God: A Christological Title Often Overlooked, Sometimes Misunderstood, and Currently Disputed.* Wheaton, IL: Crossway, 2012.

Carson, D.A. *Matthew.* EBC, 2 vols. Grand Rapids, MI: Zondervan, 1995.

Carson, D.A. *The Gospel According to John.* The Pillar New Testament Commentary. Grand Rapids, MI: Eerdmans, 1991.

Carson, D.A., ed. *The Scriptures Testify about Me: Jesus and the Gospel in the Old Testament.* Wheaton, IL: Crossway, 2013.

Carson, D.A., P.T. O'Brien and M.A. Seifrid, eds. *Justification and Variegated Nomism.* Vol. I: *The Complexities of Second Temple Judaism.* Vol. II: *The Paradoxes of Paul.* Tübingen: Mohr Siebeck, 2001 and 2004.

Cassidy, J. *Four Times Peter: Portrayals of Peter in the Four Gospels and at Philippi.* Collegeville, MN: Liturgical Press, 2007.

Catrice, P. 'Réflexions missionaires sur la vision de Saint Pierre à Joppé: Du judéo-christianisme à l'Église de tous les peuples'. *BibVie* 79 (1968), 30–39.

Cavin, R.L. *New Existence and Righteous Living: Colossians and 1 Peter in Conversation with 4QInstruction and the Hodayot.* BZNW 197. Berlin: de Gruyter, 2013.

Chambers, A. *Exemplary Life: A Theology of Church Life in Acts.* Nashville, TN: B&H Academic, 2012.

Chang, P. *Repetitions and Variations in the Gospel of John.* University of Strassburg, Ph.D. diss., 1975.

Chapman, D.W. *Ancient Jewish and Christian Perceptions of Crucifixion.* Grand Rapids, MI: Baker, 2010.

Chapman, D.W. and E.J. Schnabel. *The Trial and Crucifixion of Jesus: Texts and Commentary.* Tübingen: Mohr Siebeck, 2015.

Charlesworth, J.H., ed. *The Old Testament Pseudepigrapha: Apocalyptic Literature and Testaments.* Vol. I. New York, NY: Doubleday, 1983.

Charlesworth, J.H., ed. *The Old Testament Pseudepigrapha: Expansions of the Old Testament and Legends, Wisdom and Philosophical Literature, Prayers, Psalms, and Odes, Fragments of Lost Judeo-Hellenistic Works.* Vol. II. New Haven, CT: Yale University Press, 1985.

Charlesworth, J.H., H. Lichtenberger and G.S. Oegema, eds. *Qumran-Messianism: Studies on the Messianic Expectations in the Dead Sea Scrolls.* Tübingen: Mohr Siebeck, 1998.

Chilton, B. and J. Neusner, eds. *The Brother of Jesus.* Louisville, KY: Westminster John Knox, 2001.

Chilton, B.D. and D.L. Bock, eds. *A Comparative Handbook to the Gospel of Mark: Comparisons with Pseudepigrapha, the Qumran Scrolls, and Rabbinic Literature.* Vol. I of *The New Testament Gospels in Their Judaic Contexts.* Leiden: Brill, 2010.

Ciampa, R.E. 'Decapolis'. *DNTB.* Pages 266–68. Edited by C.A. Evans and S.E. Porter. Downers Grove, IL: IVP, 2000.

Cochrane, A.C. *The Church's Confession Under Hitler.* Philadelphia, PA: Westminster, 1962.

Collins, A.Y. and J.J. Collins. *King and Messiah as Son of God: Divine, Human, and Angelic Messianic Figures in Biblical and Related Literature.* Grand Rapids, MI: Eerdmans, 2008.

Collins, J.J. 'The Son of Man in Ancient Judaism'. Pages 1545–68 in vol. II of *Handbook for the Study of the Historical Jesus.* 4 vols. Edited by T. Holmén and S. Porter. Leiden: Brill, 2011.

Collins, J.J. *The Scepter and the Star: The Messiahs of the Dead Sea Scrolls and Other Ancient Literature.* New York, NY: Doubleday, 1995.
Conn, H.M., ed. *Inerrancy and Hermeneutic.* Grand Rapids, MI: Baker, 1988.
Conzelmann, H. *Die Mitte der Zeit: Studien zur Theologie des Lukas.* 4th ed. Tübingen: Mohr Siebeck, 1962.
Conzelmann, H. *The Acts of the Apostles.* Translated by J. Limburg. Philadelphia, PA: Fortress, 1987.
Coody, J. 'The Motif of Hearing and Seeing in Mark 4-8: Contributions to a Missional Reading of the Second Gospel'. Unpublished Th.M. Thesis, CTS, 2011.
Cook, J.G. *Roman Attitudes Toward the Christians: From Claudius to Hadrian.* WUNT 261. Tübingen: Mohr Siebeck, 2011.
Coune, M. 'Sauves au nom de Jesus (Ac 4, 8-12)'. *AssS* 12 (1964), 14–27.
Cranfield, C.E.B. *The Gospel According to Saint Mark.* 4th ed. Cambridge: Cambridge University Press, 1972.
Cullmann, O. 'Petrus, Werkzeug des Teufels und Werkzeug Gottes: Die Stellung von Mt 16, 17-19 in der ältesten Überlieferung'. Pages 202–13, in *Vorträge und Aufsätze 1925-1962.* Edited by K. Fröhlich. Tübingen: Mohr Siebeck, 1966.
Cullmann, O. *Peter: Disciple, Apostle, Martyr.* Translated by F.V. Filson. Reprint. Waco, TX: Baylor University Press, 2011.
Cullmann, O. *Salvation in History.* Norwich: SCM Press, 1967.
Cullmann, O. *The Christology of the New Testament.* Translated by S.C. Guthrie and C.A.M. Hall. Philadelphia, PA: Westminster, 1959.
Cummins, S.A. *Paul and the Crucified Christ in Antioch: Maccabean Martyrdom and Galatians 1 and 2.* SNTSMS 114. Cambridge: Cambridge University Press, 2001.
D' Souza, A. 'The Sermon of Peter in the Acts of the Apostles'. *Bhash* 4.2 (1987), 117–30.
Dahl, N.A. 'Anamnesis: Memory and Commemoration in Early Christianity'. Pages 11–29 in N.A. Dahl, *Jesus in the Memory of the Early Church* (Minneapolis, MN: Augsburg, 1976).
Dalman, G.H. *Sacred Sites and Ways: Studies in the Topography of the Gospels.* Translated by P.P. Levertoff. London: SPCK, 1935.
Dautzenberg, G. *Sein Leben bewahren: Ψυχή in den Herrenworten der Evangelien.* Munich: Kösel, 1966.
Davids, P.H. *A Theology of James, Peter, and Jude: Living in the Light of the Coming King.* Edited by A.J. Köstenberger. Grand Rapids, MI: Zondervan, 2014.
Davids, P.H. *The First Epistle of Peter.* Grand Rapids, MI: Eerdmans, 1990.
Davies, W.D. and D.C. Allison. *A Critical and Exegetical Commentary on the Gospel According to Saint Matthew.* 3 vols. ICC. Edinburgh: T& T Clark, 1988–97.
Dawsey, J. *Peter's Last Sermon: Identity and Discipleship in the Gospel of Mark.* Macon, GA: Mercer Univ. Press, 2010.

Deines, R. *Die Pharisäer: Ihr Verständnis im Spiegel der christlichen und jüdischen Forschung seit Wellhausen und Graetz*. Tübingen: Mohr Siebeck, 1997.
Deissmann, A. *Light from the Ancient East: The New Testament Illustrated by Recently Discovered Texts of the Greco-Roman World*. Translated by L. Strachan. 4th ed. Grand Rapids, MI: Baker, 1978.
Delling, G. 'Die Jesusgeschichte in der Verkündigung nach Acta'. *NTS* 19.4 (1972–73), 373–89.
Demacopoulos, G.E. *The Invention of Peter: Apostolic Discourse and Papal Authority in Late Antiquity*. Philadelphia, PA: University of Pennsylvania Press, 2013.
Dewey, J. 'The Historical Jesus in the Gospel of Mark'. Pages 1821–53 in vol. III of *Handbook for the Study of the Historical Jesus*. 4 vols. Edited by T. Holmén and S. Porter. Leiden: Brill, 2011.
Dickson, J. *Humilitas: A Lost Key to Life, Love, and Leadership*. Grand Rapids, MI: Zondervan, 2011.
Dietrich, W. 'Das Petrusbild der Judas-Tradition in Acta 1.15-26'. *NTS* 19.4 (1973), 438–52.
Dietrich, W. *Das Petrusbild der lukanischen Schriften*. BWANT 94. Stuttgart: Kohlhammer, 1972.
Dillon, R.J. 'The Prophecy of Christ and his Witnesses according to the Discourses of Acts'. *NTS* 32.4 (1986), 544–56.
Dinkler, E. 'Die Petrus-Rom-Frage: Ein Forschungsbericht'. *ThRNF* 25 (1959), 189–230. 289–335; *ThRNF* 27 (1961), 33–64.
Dinkler, E. 'Petrus, Apostel'. 3rd ed. of vol. V, *RGG*, col. 247–49.
Dockx, S. 'Essai de chronologie pétrinienne'. *RSR* 62.2 (1974), 221–41.
Dodd, C.H. *The Apostolic Preaching and Its Developments*. 2nd ed. London: Hodder & Stoughton, 1956.
Dodd, C.H. *The Founder of Christianity*. New York, NY: Macmillan, 1970.
Donahue, J.R. *The Theology and Setting of Discipleship in the Gospel of Mark*. Milwaukee, WI: Marquette University Press, 1983.
Donelson, L.R. *I and II Peter and Jude: A Commentary*. NT Library. Louisville, KY: Westminster John Knox, 2010.
Dormeyer, D. *Die Passion Jesu als Verhaltensmodell: Literarische und theologische Analyse der Traditions- und Redaktionsgeschichte der Markuspassion*. Münster: Aschendorff, 1974.
Dostoyevsky, F. *The Brothers Karamazov*. New York, NY: Penguin, 2003.
Dryden, J. *Theology and Ethics in 1 Peter: Paraenetic Strategies for Christian Character Formation*. Tübingen: Mohr Siebeck, 2006.
Dschulnigg, P., ed. *Petrus in Neuen Testament*. Stuttgart: Katholisches Bibelwerk, 1996.
Dubis, M. 'First Peter and the "Sufferings of the Messiah"'. Pages 85–96 in *Looking into the Future: Evangelical Studies in Eschatology*. Edited by D. Baker. Grand Rapids, MI: Baker, 2001.

Dubis, M. *1 Peter: A Handbook on the Greek Text*. Baylor Handbook on the Greek New Testament 5. Waco, TX: Baylor University Press, 2010.
Dubis, M. *Messianic Woes in First Peter: Suffering and Eschatology in 1 Peter 4:12-19*. New York, NY: Peter Lang, 2002.
Dungan, D. 'Dispensing with the Priority of Mark'. Pages 1313–42 in vol. II of *Handbook for the Study of the Historical Jesus*. 4 vols. Edited by T. Holmén and S. Porter. Leiden: Brill, 2011.
Dunn, J.D.G. 'Altering the Default Setting: Re-envisaging the Early Transmission of the Jesus Tradition'. *NTS* 49 (2003), 139–75.
Dunn, J.D.G. 'The Messianic Secret in Mark'. *TynBul* 21 (1970), 92–117.
Dunn, J.D.G. *A New Perspective on Jesus: What the Quest for the Historical Jesus Missed*. Grand Rapids, MI: Baker Academic, 2004.
Dunn, J.D.G. *Baptism in the Holy Spirit: A Re-examination of the New Testament on the Gift of the Spirit*. Louisville, KY: Westminster John Knox Press, 1977.
Dunn, J.D.G. *Jesus Remembered: Christianity in the Making*. Grand Rapids, MI: Eerdmans, 2003.
Dunn, J.D.G. *The Oral Gospel Tradition*. Grand Rapids, MI: Eerdmans, 2013.
Dunn, J.D.G. *The Parting of the Ways: Between Christianity and Judaism and their Significance for the Character of Christianity*. London: SCM Press, 1991.
Edwards, J. *Religious Affections*. New Haven, CT: Yale University Press, 1959.
Edwards, J.C. *The Ransom Logion in Mark and Matthew: Its Reception and Its Significance for the Study of the Gospels*. WUNT 2/327. Tübingen: Mohr Siebeck, 2012.
Edwards, J.R. 'Markan Sandwiches: The Significance of Interpolations in Markan Narratives'. *NT* 31.3 (1989), 193–216.
Edwards, J.R. *The Gospel According to Mark*. Grand Rapids, MI: Eerdmans, 2002.
Ehrman, B.D. 'A Leper in the Hands of an Angry Jesus'. Pages 77–98 in *New Testament Greek and Exegesis: Essays in Honor of Gerald F. Hawthorne*. Grand Rapids, MI: Eerdmans, 2003.
Ehrman, B.D. 'Cephas and Peter'. *JBL* 109.3 (1990), 463–74.
Elliott, J.H. *1 Peter*. AB 37B. New York, NY: Doubleday, 2000.
Ellis, E.E. 'Midrashic Features in the Speeches in Acts'. Pages 303–12 in *Mélanges Bibliques*. Edited by A. Descamps and A. de Halleux. FS R.P.B. Rigaux. Gembloux: Duculot, 1970.
Ellis, E.E. 'Preformed Traditions and Their Implications for Pauline Christology'. Pages 303–20 in *Christology, Controversy and Community*. Edited by D. Horrell and C.M. Tuckett. Leiden: Brill, 2000.
Ellis, E.E. 'Preformed Traditions and Their Implications for the Origins of Pauline Christology'. Pages 133–50 in *History and Interpretation in New Testament Perspective*. Edited by E.E. Ellis. Leiden: Brill, 2001.

Evans, C.A. *From Jesus to the Church: The First Christian Generation.* Louisville, KY: Westminster John Knox, 2014.
Evans, C.A. *Mark 8:27–16:20.* WBC 34b. Nashville, TN: Nelson, 2001.
Eyal, R. *Hasmoneans: Ideology, Archaeology, Identity.* Göttingen: Vandenhoeck & Ruprecht, 2013.
Farelly, N. *The Disciples in the Fourth Gospel: A Narrative Analysis of Their Faith and Understanding.* Tübingen: Mohr Siebeck, 2010.
Feldmeier, R. 'The Portrayal of Peter in the Synoptic Gospels'. Pages 59–63 in *Studies in the Gospel of Mark.* Edited by M. Hengel. Translated by J. Bowden. London: SCM, 1985.
Feldmeier, R. *Macht – Dienst – Demut: Ein neutestamentlicher Beitrag zur Ethik.* Tübingen: Mohr Siebeck, 2012.
Feldmeier, R. *The First Letter of Peter.* Waco, TX: Baylor University Press, 2005.
Fiensy, D.A. and J.R. Strange, eds. *Galilee in the Late Second Temple and Mishnaic Periods.* Volume I: *Life, Culture, and Society.* Minneapolis, MN: Fortress, 2014.
Fiensy, D.A. and R.K. Hawkins, eds. *The Galilean Economy in the Time of Jesus.* Williston, VT: Society of Biblical Literature, 2013.
Fitzmyer, J. 'The Languages of Palestine in the First Century AD'. *CBQ* 32 (1970), 501–31.
Foakes-Jackson, F.J. *Peter: Prince of Apostles: A Study in the History and Tradition of Christianity.* London: Hodder & Stoughton, 1927.
Forbes, G.W. *1 Peter.* EGNT. Edited by A.J. Köstenberger and R.W. Yarbrough. Nashville, TN: B&H Academic, 2014.
France, R.T. *The Gospel of Mark: A Commentary on the Greek Text.* Grand Rapids, MI: Eerdmans, 2002.
Frey J. and J. Schröter. *Deutungen des Todes Jesu im Neuen Testament.* WUNT 1/181. 2nd ed. Tübingen: Mohr Siebeck, 2012.
Gäckle, V. *Allgemeines Priestertum: Zur Metaphorisierung des Priestertitels im Frühjudentum und Neuen Testament.* Tübingen: Mohr Siebeck, 2014.
Gambrell, C. 'The Portrayal of Discipleship in Mark 8:34'. Unpublished MAET thesis, CTS, 2013.
Gasque, W.W. 'Did Luke Have Access to Traditions about the Apostles and the Early Churches?'. *JETS* 17.1 (1974), 45–48.
Gasque, W.W. 'The Historical Value of Acts'. *TynBul* 40 (1989), 136–57.
Gasque, W.W. and R.P. Martin, eds. *Apostolic History and the Gospel.* Exeter: Paternoster, 1970.
Gathercole, S.J. *Where is Boasting?: Early Jewish Soteriology and Paul's Response in Romans 1–5.* Grand Rapids, MI: Eerdmans, 2002.
Gaventa, B.R. 'The Eschatology of Luke–Acts Revisited'. *Enc* 43.1 (1982), 27–42.
Gerhardsson, B. *Memory and Manuscript: Oral Tradition and Written Transmission in Rabbinic Judaism and Early Christianity.* Reprint. Grand Rapids, MI/Livonia, MI: Eerdmans/Dove, 1998 [1961].

Gerhardsson, B. *The Gospel Tradition*. Lund: CWK Gleerup, 1989.
Gerhardsson, B. *The Origins of the Gospel Tradition*. Philadelphia, PA: Fortress, 1979.
Gerhardsson, B. *Tradition and Transmission in Early Christianity*. Lund: CWK Gleerup, 1964.
Gibson, J.J. *Peter Between Jerusalem and Antioch: Peter, James, and the Gentiles*. WUNT 2/345. Tübingen: Mohr Siebeck, 2013.
Giles, K. 'Present-Future Eschatology in the Book of Acts (I) / (II)'. *RTR* 40.3 (1981), 65–71 and *RTR* 41.1 (1982), 11–18.
Glombitza, O. 'Der Schluß der Petrusrede Acta 2, 36-40: Ein Beitrag zum Problem der Predigten in Acta'. *ZNW* 52.1-2 (1961), 115–18.
Gnilka, J. 'Die Petrusverheißung in Geschichte und Gegenwart'. Pages 71–80 in *Das Matthäusevangelium*. Vol. II (Excursus 5). Freiburg: Herder, 1988.
Gnilka, J. *Petrus und Rom: Das Petrusbild in den ersten zwei Jahrhunderten*. Freiburg: Herder, 2002.
Godet, F. *Commentary on St. Luke*. New York, NY: Funk & Wagnalls, 1887.
Goppelt, L. *A Commentary on 1 Peter*. Edited by F. Hahn. Translated by J.E. Alsup. Grand Rapids, MI: Eerdmans, 1993.
Goppelt, L. *Die apostolische und nachapostolische Zeit*. 2nd ed. Göttingen: Vandenhoeck & Ruprecht, 1966.
Gourgues, M. 'Exalté à la droite de Dieu (Ac 2, 33; 5, 31)'. *ScEs* 27 (1975), 303–27.
Graf, E. *Durch Leiden geprägt: die gegenwärtigen Leidenserfahrungen der indischen Nathanja-Kirche mit einem Blick auf die paulinischen Gemeinden*. Ph.D. diss., Technische Universität Dortmund, 2012.
Grant, M. *Saint Peter: A Biography*. New York, NY: Scribner, 1995.
Grappe, C. *D'un Temple à l'autre: Pierre et l'Eglise primitive de Jérusalem*. Paris: Presses Universitaires de France, 1992.
Grässer, E. 'Die Parusieerwartung in der Apostelgeschichte'. Pages 99–127 in *Les Actes des Apôtres: tradition, rédaction, théologie*. Edited by J. Kremer. Leuven: University Press, 1979.
Gray, T.C. *The Temple in the Gospel of Mark: A Study in its Narrative Role*. WUNT 2/242. Tübingen: Mohr Siebeck, 2008.
Green, G. *Jude and 2 Peter*. BECNT. Grand Rapids, MI: Baker Academic, 2008.
Green, J.B. 'The Gospel of Peter: Source for a Pre-Canonical Passion Narrative?'. *ZNW* 78 (1987), 293–301.
Grundmann, W. 'Die Apostel zwischen Jerusalem und Antiochia'. *ZNW* (1940), 110–37.
Guarducci, M. *The Tomb of St Peter: The New Discoveries in the Sacred Grottoes of the Vatican*. Translated by J. McLellan. London: G.G. Harrap, 1960.
Guelich, R.A. *Mark 1–8:26*. Dallas, TX: Word Books, 1989.
Gundry, R. 'Further Verba on Verba Christi in First Peter'. *Bib* 55 (1974), 211–32.

Gundry, R., 'Verba Christi in 1 Peter: Their Implication Concerning the Authorship of 1 Peter and the Authenticity of the Gospel Tradition'. *NTS* 13.4 (1967), 336–350.
Guthrie, D. *New Testament Introduction.* 3rd ed. Leicester: IVP, 1978.
Guthrie, D. *New Testament Theology.* Downers Grove, IL: IVP, 1981.
Haacker, K. 'Verwendung und Vermeidung des Apostelbegriffs im lukanischen Werk'. *NovT* 30.1 (1988), 9–38.
Haenchen, E. 'Die Apostelgeschichte als Quelle für die christliche Frühgeschichte'. Pages 312–37 in E. Haenchen, *Die Bibel und wir: Gesammelte Aufsätze 2*. Tübingen: Mohr Siebeck, 1968.
Haenchen, E. *The Acts of the Apostles.* Translated by B. Noble and G. Shinn. Philadelphia: Westminster, 1971.
Hägerland, T. *Jesus and the Forgiveness of Sins: An Aspect of his Prophetic Mission.* Cambridge: Cambridge University Press, 2012.
Hagner, D.A. *The Use of the Old and New Testaments in Clement of Rome.* Novum Testamentum Supplements, 34. Leiden: Brill, 1973.
Hagner, D.A. *Matthew 14–28*. WBC 33B. Dallas: Word, 1995.
Hahn, F. 'Das Problem alter christologischer Überlieferungen in der Apostelgeschichte unter besonderer Berücksichtigung von Act 3,19-21'. Pages 145–54 in *Les Actes des Apôtres: Tradition, rédaction, théologie*. Edited by J. Kremer. Gembloux/Leuven: Université, 1979.
Hahn, F. *Das Verständnis der Mission im Neuen Testament*. WMANT 13. Neukirchen-Vluyn: Neukirchener Verlag, 1963.
Hallesby, O. *Prayer.* Minneapolis, MN: Augsburg, 1937.
Hamm, D. 'Acts 3:12-26: Peter's Speech and the Healing of the Man Born Lame'. *PRS* 11.3 (1984), 199–217.
Hanson, K.C. 'The Galilean Fishing Economy and the Jesus Tradition'. *BTB* 27 (1997), 99–111.
Harrington, D.J. *Jude and 2 Peter.* Sacra Pagina 15. Edited by D.J. Harrington. Collegeville, MN: The Liturgical Press, 2003.
Harris, M.J. *Jesus as God: The New Testament Use of* Theos *in Reference to Jesus.* Reprinted. Eugene, OR: Wipf & Stock, 2008.
Harvey, J.D. 'Orality and Its Implications for Biblical Studies: Recapturing an Ancient Paradigm'. *JETS* 45.1 (2002), 99–109.
Haubeck, W. *Loskauf durch Christus.* Giessen: Brunnen, 1985.
Havelock, E.A. *The Muse Learns to Write: Reflections on Orality and Literacy from Antiquity to the Present.* New Haven, CT: Yale University, 1986.
Head, P. 'The Role of Eyewitnesses in the Formation of the Gospel Tradition'. *TynBul* 52.2 (2001), 275–94.
Heid, S. and R. von Haehling, eds. *Petrus und Paulus in Rom: Eine interdisziplinäre Debatte.* Freiburg: Herder, 2011.
Helyer, L.R. *The Life and Witness of Peter.* Downers Grove, IL: IVP Academic, 2012.
Hemer, C.J. 'Luke the Historian'. *BJRL* 60.1 (1977), 28–51.

Hemer, C.J. *The Book of Acts in the Setting of Hellenistic History.* WUNT 49. Edited by C.H. Gempf. Tübingen: Mohr Siebeck, 1989.
Hengel, M. 'Christology and New Testament Chronology'. Pages 33–47 in M. Hengel, *Between Jesus and Paul.*
Hengel, M. 'Das Gleichnis von den Weingärtnern Mc 12,1-12 im Lichte der Zenonpapyri und der rabbinischen Gleichnisse'. *ZNW* 59 (1968), 9–31.
Hengel, M. 'Der Lukasprolog und seine Augenzeugen: die Apostel, Petrus und die Frauen'. Pages 195–242 in *Memory in the Bible and Antiquity: The Fifth Durham-Tübingen Research Symposium (Durham, September 2004).* Edited by S.C. Barton, L.T. Struckenbruck and B.G. Wold. Tübingen: Mohr Siebeck, 2007.
Hengel, M. 'Der stellvertretende Sühnetod Jesu: Ein Beitrag zur Entstehung des urchristlichen Kerygmas'. *IKZ* 9 (1980), 1–25 and 135–47.
Hengel, M. 'Kerygma oder Geschichte?: Zur Problematik einer falschen Alternative in der Synoptikerforschung'. *TQ* 151 (1971), 323–36.
Hengel, M. 'Petrus und die Heidenmission'. Pages 163–70 in *Das Petrusbild in der neueren Forschung.* TVG. Edited by C.P. Thiede. Wuppertal: Brockhaus, 1987.
Hengel, M. 'The Titles of the Gospels and the Gospel of Mark'. Pages 64–84 in *Studies in the Gospel of Mark.* Edited by M. Hengel. Philadelphia, PA: Fortress, 1985.
Hengel, M. and R. Deines. 'E.P. Sanders' "Common Judaism", Jesus and the Pharisees'. *JTS* 46 (1995), 17–41.
Hengel, M. *Between Jesus and Paul: Studies in the Earliest History of Christianity.* London: SCM Press, 1983.
Hengel, M. *Crucifixion in the Ancient World and the Folly of the Message of the Cross.* Translated by J. Bowden. Philadelphia, PA: Fortress Press, 1977.
Hengel, M. *Judaism and Hellenism: Studies in Their Encounter in Palestine During the Early Hellenistic Period.* Translated by J. Bowden. London: SCM Press, 2012.
Hengel, M. *Saint Peter: The Underestimated Apostle.* Translated by T.H. Trapp. Grand Rapids, MI: Eerdmans, 2010.
Hengel, M. *Studies in Early Christology.* Edinburgh: T&T Clark, 1998.
Hengel, M. *Studies in the Gospel of Mark.* Translated by J. Bowden. London: SCM, 1985.
Hengel, M. *The Four Gospels and the One Gospel of Jesus Christ: An Investigation of the Collection and Origin of the Canonical Gospels.* Translated by J. Bowden. Harrisburg, PA: Trinity Press, 2000.
Hengel, M. *The Hellenisation of Judaea in the First Century after Christ.* London: SCM, 1989.
Hennecke, E. *Neutestamentliche Apokryphen.* Vol. I. Tübingen: Mohr Siebeck, 1968.

Henten, J.W. van and A. Friedrich. *Martyrdom and Noble Death: Selected Texts from Graeco-Roman, Jewish and Christian Antiquity*. London: Routledge, 2002.
Henten, J.W. van. *The Maccabean Martyrs as Saviours of the Jewish People: A Study of 2 and 4 Maccabees*. SJSJ 57. Leiden: Brill, 1997.
Herrenbrück, J. *Jesus und die Zöllner: Historische und neutestamentlich-exegetische Untersuchungen*. WUNT 2/41. Tübingen: Mohr Siebeck, 1990.
Hezser, C. *Jewish Literacy in Roman Palestine*. Tübingen: Mohr Siebeck, 2001.
Hill, C.E. *Who Chose the Gospels?: Probing the Great Gospel Conspiracy*. Oxford: Oxford University Press, 2010.
Hillerdal, G. *Simon Petrus*. Stockholm: EFS-förlaget, 1983.
Hoehner, H.W. *Ephesians: An Exegetical Commentary*. Grand Rapids, MI: Baker Academic, 2002.
Holtz, T. 'Zum Selbstverständnis des Apostels Paulus'. *TLZ* 91 (1966), 321–30.
Hooker, M.D. *Jesus and the Servant*. London: SPCK, 1959.
Hooker, M.D. *The Gospel According to Saint Mark*. London: A&C Black, 1991.
Horbury, W. 'The Messianic Associations of the "Son of Man"'. *JTS* 36 (1985), 34–55.
House, P.R. 'Suffering and the Purpose of Acts'. *JETS* 33.3 (1990), 317–30.
Hübenthal, S. *Das Markusevangelium als kollektives Gedächtnis*. Göttingen: Vandenhoeck & Ruprecht, 2014.
Hunter, J.D. *To Change the World: The Irony, Tragedy, and Possibility of Christianity in the Late Modern World*. Oxford: Oxford Univ. Press, 2010.
Janowski, B. and P. Stuhlmacher, eds. *Der leidende Gottesknecht: Jesaja 53 und seine Wirkungsgeschichte mit einer Bibliographie zu Jesaja 53*. Tübingen: Mohr Siebeck, 1996.
Jay, J. *The Tragic in Mark: A Literary-Historical Interpretation*. Tübingen: Mohr Siebeck, 2014.
Jefford, C. *The Apostolic Fathers and the New Testament*. Peabody, MA: Hendrickson, 2006.
Jeremias, J. *Neutestamentliche Theologie*. Vol. I. Berlin: Evangelische Verlagsanstalt, 1973.
Jeremias, J. *The Unknown Sayings of Jesus*. 2nd ed. London: SPCK, 1964.
Jervell, J. 'The Acts of the Apostles and the History of Early Christianity'. *ST* 37.1 (1983), 17–32.
Jobes, K.H. *1 Peter*. BECNT. Grand Rapids, MI: Baker Academic, 2005.
Johnson, D.E. 'Fire in God's House: Imagery from Malachi 3 in Peter's Theology of Suffering (1 Pet 4:12-19)'. *JETS* 29 (1986), 285–95.
Kähler, M. 'Die Reden des Petrus in der Apostelgeschichte, sprachlich untersucht'. *Theologische Studien und Kritiken* 3 (1873), 492–536.

Kähler, M. *Der sogenannte historische Jesus und der geschichtliche, biblische Christus.* Leipzig: Deichert'sche Verlagsbuchhandlung Nachfolger (Georg Böhme), 1892.
Kant, I. *Critique of Pure Reason.* London: Penguin Classics, 2008 [1781].
Karrer, M. 'Petrus im paulinischen Gemeindekreis'. *ZNW* 80 (1989), 210–31.
Keck, L.E. 'The Introduction to Mark's Gospel'. *NTS* 12 (1965-1966), 352–70.
Kee, H.C. 'Aretalogy and Gospel'. *JBL* 92.3 (1973), 402–22.
Kee, H.C. 'Synoptic Studies'. Pages 245–69 in *The New Testament and Its Modern Interpreters.* Edited by E.J. Epp and G.W. McRae. Atlanta, GA: Scholars, 1989.
Keener, C.S. *Acts: An Exegetical Commentary.* 3 of 4 vols. Grand Rapids, MI: Baker Academic, 2012/2013/2014.
Keener, C.S. *The IVP Bible Background Commentary.* 2nd ed. Downers Grove, IL: IVP, 2014.
Kehlhoffer, J.A. *Conceptions of 'Gospel' and Legitimacy in Early Christianity.* Tübingen: Mohr Siebeck, 2014.
Kehlhoffer, J.A. *Persecution, Persuasion and Power: Readiness to Withstand Hardship as a Corroboration of Legitimacy in the New Testament.* WUNT 2/270. Tübingen: Mohr Siebeck, 2010.
Keil, C.F. and F. Delitzsch, eds. *Commentary on the Old Testament in Ten Volumes.* Grand Rapids, MI: Eerdmans, 1983.
Kelber, W.H. *The Oral and the Written Gospel: The Hermeneutics of Speaking and Writing in the Synoptic Tradition.* Bloomington, IN: Indiana Univ. Press, 1996.
Keller, T. *Center Church: Doing Balanced, Gospel-Centered Ministry in Your City.* Grand Rapids, MI: Zondervan, 2012.
Kendall, R.T. *Why Jesus Died: A Meditation on Isaiah 53.* Grand Rapids, MI: Kregel Academic, 2012.
Kiel, Y. *Sefer Daniel.* Jerusalem: Mossad Harav Kook, 1994.
Kierkegaard, S. *Purity of the Heart is to Will One Thing.* Translated by D.V. Steere. New York, NY: Harper, 1948.
Kim, J. 'Targum Isaiah 53 and the New Testament Concept of Atonement'. *JGRChJ* 5 (2008), 81–98.
Kim, S. *The Origin of Paul's Gospel.* Eugene, OR: Wipf & Stock, 2007.
Kim-Rauchholz, M. *Umkehr bei Lukas: Zu Wesen und Bedeutung der Metanoia in der Theologie des dritten Evangelisten.* Neukirchen-Vluyn: Neukirchener Verlag, 2008.
Kingsbury, J.D. 'The Figure of Peter in Matthew's Gospel as a Theological Problem'. *JBL* 98 (1979), 67–83.
Kingsbury, J.D. 'The Gospel of Mark'. *Int* 47 (1993), 341–409.
Kingsbury, J.D. *The Christology of Mark's Gospel.* Minneapolis, MN: Fortress Press, 1983.

Kirk, A. 'Memory Theory and Jesus Research'. Pages 809–42 in vol. I of *Handbook for the Study of the Historical Jesus*. 4 vols. Edited by T. Holmén and S. Porter. Leiden: Brill, 2011.

Kline, M.G. *By Oath Consigned: A Reinterpretation of the Covenant Signs of Circumcision and Baptism*. Grand Rapids, MI: Eerdmans, 1968.

Körtner, U.H.J. *Papias von Hierapolis: Ein Beitrag zur Geschichte des frühen Christentums*. FRLANT 133. Göttingen: Vandenhoeck & Ruprecht, 1983.

Köstenberger, A.J. *John*. BECNT. Grand Rapids, MI: Baker Academic, 2004.

Kraabel, A.T. 'The Diaspora Synagogue'. *ANRW* 19.1:500–10. Part 2, *Principat*, 19.1. Edited by H. Temporini and W. Haase. Berlin: de Gruyter, 1980.

Kränkl, E. *Jesus der Knecht Gottes: Die heilsgeschichtliche Stellung Jesu in den Reden der Apostelgeschichte*. Regensburg: Pustet, 1972.

Kruger, M. *Canon Revisited: Establishing the Origins and Authority of the New Testament Books*. Wheaton, IL: Crossway, 2012.

Kuhn, H.-W. *Betsaida/Bethsaida - Julias (et-Tell): Die ersten 25 Jahre der Ausgrabung (1987–2011) –The First Twenty-Five Years of Excavation (1987–2011)*. Göttingen: Vandenhoeck & Ruprecht, 2014.

Kümmel, W.G. 'Futurische und präsentische Eschatologie im ältesten Urchristentum'. *NTS* 5 (1958/59), 113–26.

Kümmel, W.G. *Introduction to the New Testament*. Translated by H.C. Kee. Nashville, TN: Abingdon, 1975.

Kurz, W. 'Acts 3:19-26 as a Test of the Role of Eschatology in Lukan Christology'. Pages 309–23 in *Society of Biblical Literature 1977 Seminar Papers*. SBLSPS. Edited by P.J. Achtemeier. Missoula, MT: Scholars Press, 1977.

Kürzinger, J. 'Papias von Hierapolis: Zu Titel und Art seines Werkes'. Pages 69–87 in *Papias von Hierapolis und die Evangelien des Neuen Testaments*. Regensburg: Pustet, 1983.

Kürzinger, J. *Papias von Hierapolis und die Evangelien des Neuen Testaments*. Regensburg: Pustet, 1983.

Laato, A. *Who Is the Servant of the Lord? Jewish and Christian Interpretations on Isaiah 53 from Antiquity to the Middle Ages*. Studies in Rewritten Bible 4. Winona Lake, IN: Eisenbrauns, 2013.

Lane, W.L. *The Gospel According to Mark*. 2nd ed. Grand Rapids, MI: Eerdmans, 1978.

Lapham, F. *Peter: The Myth, the Man and the Writings*. Sheffield: Sheffield Academic Press, 2003.

Lea, T.D. 'How Peter Learned the Old Testament'. *SWJT* 22 (1980), 96–102.

Lessing, G.E. *Über den Beweis des Geistes und der Kraft*. Pages 10–16 in vol. VIII of *G.E. Lessing, Gesammelte Werke*. Edited by P. Rilla. 2nd ed. Berlin: Aufbau Verlag, 1968 [1777].

Lewis, C.S. *A Grief Observed*. Reprint. San Francisco: HarperOne, 2009.

Lewis, C.S. *The Problem of Pain*. Reprint. San Francisco: HarperOne, 2001.

Liebengood, K.D. *The Eschatology of 1 Peter: Considering the Influence of Zechariah 9–14*. SNTSMS 157. Cambridge: Cambridge Univ. Press, 2014.

Lindars, B. *Jesus Son of Man: A Fresh Examination of the Son of Man Sayings in the Gospels*. London: SPCK, 1983.

Linnemann, E. *Is There a Synoptic Problem?: Rethinking the Literary Dependence of the First Three Gospels*. Translated by R. Yarbrough. Grand Rapids, MI: Baker, 1992.

Lohfink, G. 'Christologie und Geschichtsbild in Apg 3, 19-21'. Pages 223–43 in G. Lohfink, *Studien zum Neuen Testament*. Stuttgart: Katholisches Bibelwerk, 1989.

Lohse, E. 'Paränese und Kerygma im 1. Petrusbrief'. *ZNW* 45.1 (1954), 68–89.

Lohse, E. *Die Texte aus Qumran: Hebräisch und Deutsch*. Munich: Kösel, 1986.

Longenecker, R.N. 'Some Distinctive Early Christian Motifs'. *NTS* 14.4 (1968), 526–45.

Longenecker, R.N., ed. *Patterns of Discipleship in the New Testament*. Grand Rapids, MI: Eerdmans, 1996.

Lövestam, E. *Son and Saviour: A Study of Acts 13, 32-37*. Translated by J. Petry. Lund: Gleerup, 1961.

Lüdemann, G. *Early Christianity according to the Traditions in Acts: A Commentary*. Translated by J. Bowden. Minneapolis, MN: Fortress, 1989.

Luz, U. *Matthew 8–20*. Translated by J.E. Crouch. Hermeneia. Minneapolis, MN: Augsburg Fortress, 2001.

Luz, U. *Matthew in History: Interpretation, Influence, and Effects*. Minneapolis MN: Fortress, 1994.

Maier, G. 'Jesustradition im 1. Petrusbrief?'. Pages 85–128 in vol. V of *Gospel Perspectives: The Jesus Tradition Outside the Gospels*. 5 vols. Edited by D. Wenham. Sheffield: JSOT Press, 1984.

Maier, G., ed. *Der Kanon der Bibel*. Wuppertal/Giessen: Brockhaus/Brunnen, 1990.

Manning, B. *The Signature of Jesus*. Sisters, OR: Multnomah Publishing, 1996.

Marshall, C.D. *Faith as a Theme in Mark's Narrative*. Cambridge: Cambridge Univ. Press, 1989.

Marshall, I.H. 'The Synoptic Son of Man Sayings in Recent Discussion'. *NTS* 12 (1965–1966), 327–51.

Marshall, I.H. *1 Peter*. The IVP NT Commentary Series. Downers Grove, IL: IVP, 1991.

Marshall, I.H. and D. Peterson, eds. *Witness to the Gospel: The Theology of Acts*. Grand Rapids, MI: Eerdmans, 1989.

Marshall, I.H. *New Testament Theology: Many Witnesses, One Gospel*. Downers Grove, IL: IVP, 2004.

Marshall, I.H. *The Acts of the Apostles*. TNTC. Leicester: IVP, 1980.

Marshall, I.H. *The Gospel of Luke: A Commentary on the Greek Text.* NIGTC 3. 3rd ed. Grand Rapids, MI: Eerdmans, 1983.
Martin, O.R. *Bound for the Promised Land: The Land Promise in God's Redemptive Plan.* New Studies in Biblical Theology. Downers Grove, IL: IVP Academic, 2015.
Martin, R.A. 'Syntactical Evidence of Aramaic Sources in Acts i-xv'. *NTS* 11.1 (1964–65), 38–59.
Martin, R.P. *Mark: Evangelist and Theologian.* Carlyle: Paternoster, 1972.
Martin, R.P. *New Testament Foundations.* 2 vols. Grand Rapids, MI: Eerdmans, 1987.
Marx, K. 'Zur Kritik der Hegel'schen Rechts-Philosophie: Einleitung'. *Deutsch-Französische Jahrbücher*, 7 and 10 February, 1844, n.p.
Mason, S. *Flavius Josephus on the Pharisees.* Leiden: Brill, 1991.
Mattill, A.J. 'Naherwartung, Fernerwartung, and the Purpose of Luke–Acts: Weymouth Reconsidered'. *CBQ* 34.3 (1972), 276–93.
Maurer, C. 'Knecht Gottes im Passionsbericht des Marcus-Evangeliums'. *ZTK* 50 (1953), 1–38.
McCartney, D.G. 'Suffering in the Teachings of the Apostles'. Pages 108–14 in *Suffering and the Goodness of God.* Edited by C.W. Morgan and R.A. Peterson. Wheaton, IL: Crossway, 2008.
McGowan, A.B. *Ancient Christian Worship: Early Church Practices in Social, Historical, and Theological Perspective.* Grand Rapids, MI: Baker Academic, 2014.
McIver, R.K. 'Eyewitnesses as Guarantors of the Accuracy of the Gospel Traditions in the Light of Psychological Research'. *JBL* 131.3 (2012), 529–46.
Ménard, J.-E. 'PAIS THEOU as Messianic Title in the Book of Acts'. *CBQ* 19 (1957), 83–92.
Metzger, B.M. *A Textual Commentary on the Greek New Testament.* 2nd ed. Stuttgart: Deutsche Bibelgesellschaft, 1994.
Metzger, B.M. *The Canon of the New Testament: Its Origin, Development and Significance.* Oxford: Clarendon, 1987.
Metzner, R. *Die Rezeption des Matthäusevangeliums im 1. Petrusbrief: Studien zum traditionsgeschichtlichen und theologischen Einfluss des 1. Evangeliums auf den 1. Petrusbrief.* WUNT 2/74. Tübingen: Mohr Siebeck, 1995.
Meyers, E.M. and M.A. Chancey. *Alexander to Constantine. Archaeology of the Land of the Bible.* Vol. III. New Haven, CT: Yale University Press, 2014.
Michaels, J.R. *1 Peter.* WBC 49. Nashville, TN: Nelson, 1988.
Milik, J.T. *Books of Enoch: Aramaic Fragments of Qumran Cave 4.* Oxford: Oxford University Press, 1976.
Millard, A. *Reading and Writing in the Time of Jesus.* Sheffield: Sheffield Academic, 2000.

Miller, C.J. *The Heart of a Servant Leader: Letters from Jack Miller*. Edited by B. Miller Juliani. Phillipsburg, NJ: P&R Publishing, 2004.
Minde, H.-J. van der. 'Geschichtliches Denken und theologische Implikationen'. Pages 343–60 in *Der Treue Gottes trauen*. Edited by C. Bussmann and W. Radl. FS G. Schneider. Freiburg: Herder, 1991.
Moessner, D.P. '"The Christ Must Suffer": New Light on the Jesus-Peter, Stephen, Paul Parallels in Luke–Acts'. *NT* 28.3 (1986), 220–56.
Moessner, D.P. 'Paul in Acts: Preacher of Eschatological Repentance to Israel'. *NTS* 1.34 (1988), 96–104.
Moessner, D.P. *Lord of the Banquet: The Literary and Theological Significance of the Lukan Travel Narrative*. Minneapolis, MN: Fortress, 1989.
Montefiore, C.G. and H.M.J. Loewe, eds. *A Rabbinic Anthology: Selected and Arranged with Comments and Introductions*. New York, NY: Schocken, 1974 [1938].
Moo, D.J. *Galatians*. BECNT. Grand Rapids, MI: Baker Academic, 2013.
Moore, A.L. *The Parousia in the New Testament*. 2nd ed. Leiden: Brill, 1970.
Morgenthaler, R. *Statistische Synopse*. Zürich: Gotthelf Verlag, 1971.
Mournet, T.C. *Oral Tradition and Literary Dependency: Variability and Stability in the Synoptic Tradition and Q*. WUNT 2/195. Tübingen: Mohr Siebeck, 2005.
Müller, P.-G. 'Die '"Bekehrung" des Petrus: Zur Interpretation von Apg 10,1–11,18'. *HK* 28.7 (1974), 372–75.
Murphy-O'Connor, J. 'Fishers of Fish, Fishers of Men: What We Know of the First Disciples from Their Profession'. *BR* 25.3 (1999), 22–27, 48–49.
Murray, A. *Humility*. Charleston: CreateSpace Independent Publishing Platform, 2012.
Murray, A. *Lord, Teach us to Pray*. Charleston: CreateSpace Independent Publishing Platform, 2013.
Mussner, F. 'Die Idee der Apokatastasis in der Apostelgeschichte'. Pages 293–306 in *Lex Tua Veritas*. Edited by H. Gross and F. Mussner. FS H. Junker. Trier: Paulinus, 1961.
Mussner, F. *Petrus und Paulus - Pole der Einheit. Eine Hilfe für die Kirchen*. Freiburg: Herder, 1976.
Neudorfer, H.-W. *Der Stephanuskreis in der Forschungsgeschichte seit F.C. Baur*. Giessen: Brunnen, 1983.
Novenson, M.V. *Christ among the Messiahs: Christ Language in Paul and Messiah Language in Ancient Judaism*. Oxford: Oxford University Press, 2012.
O'Brien, P.T. *Colossians, Philemon*. Waco, TX: Word, 1982.
O'Callaghan, R.T. 'Vatican Excavations and the Tomb of Peter'. *BA* 16 (1953), 70–87.
Oden, T.C. and C.A. Hall, eds. *Mark*. ACCS II. Downers Grove, IL: IVP, 1998.

Oegema, G.S. *The Anointed and His People: Messianic Expectations from the Maccabees to Bar Kochba.* Sheffield: Sheffield Academic Press, 1998.

Osborne, R.E. 'Where Did Peter Go?'. *CanJT* 14.4 (1968), 274–77.

Packer, J.I. *Weakness Is the Way: Life with Christ Our Strength.* Wheaton, IL: Crossway, 2013.

Page, S.H.T. 'The Authenticity of the Ransom Logion (Mk 10:45b)'. Pages 137–61 in vol. I of *Gospel Perspectives.* 5 vols. Edited by R.T. France and D. Wenham. Sheffield: JSOT Press, 1980.

Painter, J. *Just James: The Brother of Jesus in History and Tradition.* 2nd ed. Columbia, SC: University of South Carolina Press, 2004.

Palmer, D.W. 'Acts and the Historical Monograph'. *TynBul* 43.2 (1992), 373–88.

Perkins, P. *Peter: Apostle for the Whole Church.* Minneapolis, MN: Fortress Press, 2000.

Perrin, N. *Jesus the Temple.* Grand Rapids, MI: Baker Academic, 2010.

Pesch, R. *Das Markusevangelium.* 2 vols. Vol. I, 3rd ed.; vol. II, 2nd ed. Freiburg: Herder, 1980.

Pesch, R. *Die Apostelgeschichte.* 2 vols. Zürich: Neukirchen-Vluyn, 1986.

Pesch, R. *Die biblische Grundlage des Primats.* QD 187. Freiburg: Herder, 2001.

Pesch, R. *Simon-Petrus: Geschichte und geschichtliche Bedeutung des ersten Jüngers Jesu Christi.* Päpste und Papsttum 15. Stuttgart: Hiersemann, 1980.

Peterson, E.H. *The Pastor: A Memoir.* Reprint. New York, NY: HarperOne, 2012.

Phillips, T.R. 'Hades'. Pages 322–23 in *Baker's Evangelical Dictionary of Biblical Theology.* Edited by W.A. Elwell. Grand Rapids, MI: Baker, 1996.

Plantinga, C. *Not the Way It's Supposed to Be: A Breviary of Sin.* Grand Rapids, MI: Eerdmans, 1995.

Platt, D. *Follow Me: A Call to Die. A Call to Live.* Carol Stream, IL: Tyndale House, 2013.

Plümacher, E. 'Die Apostelgeschichte als historische Monographie'. Pages 457–66 in *Les Actes des Apôtres. Traditions, rédactions, théologie.* Edited by J. Kremer. Leuven: Université, 1979.

Quarles, C.L. 'The Soteriology of R. Aqiba and E.P. Sanders' *Paul and Palestinian Judaism*'. *NTS* 42.2 (1996), 185–95.

Rasco, E. 'Pierre proclame le Salut, Act 10, 34a, 37-43' *AssS* 2.21 (1969), 78–83.

Reicke, B. 'Die Verfassung der Urgemeinde im Lichte jüdischer Dokumente'. *TZ* 10 (1954), 95–112.

Reicke, B. *The Roots of the Synoptic Gospels.* Philadelphia, PA: Fortress Press, 1986.

Rengstorf, K.H., ed. *Das Petrusbild in der neueren deutschen Forschung.* Darmstadt: Wiss. Buchgesellschaft, 1964.

Rese, M. 'Die Aussagen über Jesu Tod und Auferstehung in der Apostelgeschichte – ältestes Kerygma oder lukanische Theologumena?'. *NTS* 30.3 (1984), 335–53.
Rese, M. 'Die Funktion der alttestamentlichen Zitate und Anspielungen in den Reden der Apostelgeschichte'. Pages 61–79 in *Les Actes des Apôtres: traditions, rédaction, théologie*. Edited by J. Kremer. Leuven: Université, 1979.
Rese, M. *Alttestamentliche Motive in der Christologie des Lukas*. Gütersloh: Gütersloher Verlag, 1969.
Rhee, H. *Loving the Poor, Saving the Rich: Wealth, Poverty, and Early Christian Formation*. Grand Rapids, MI: Baker Academic, 2012.
Ricoeur, P. *Memory, History, Forgetting*. Translated by K. Blamey and D. Pellauer. Chicago, IL: University of Chicago Press, 2004.
Ridderbos, H.N. *Redemptive History and the New Testament Canon of Scriptures*. 2nd ed. Phillipsburg, NJ: P&R, 1988.
Ridderbos, H.N. *The Speeches of Peter in the Acts of the Apostles*. London: Tyndale, 1962.
Riesenfeld, H. *The Gospel Tradition and Its Beginnings: A Study in the Limits of 'Formgeschichte'*. London: Mowbray, 1957.
Riesner, R. 'Das Lokalkolorit des Lukas-Sonderguts: Italisch oder Palästinisch-Juden-Christlich?'. *LASBF* 49 (1999), 51–64.
Riesner, R. 'Die Rückkehr der Augenzeugen: Eine neue Entwicklung in der Evangelienforschung'. *TBei* 38 (2007), 337–52.
Riesner, R. 'From the Messianic Teacher to the Gospel of Jesus Christ'. Pages 405–46 in vol. 1 of *Handbook for the Study of the Historical Jesus*. 4 vols. Edited by. T. Holmén and S. Porter. Leiden: Brill, 2011.
Riesner, R. 'Jesus as Teacher and Preacher'. Pages 185–210 in *Jesus and the Oral Gospel Tradition*. Edited by H. Wansborough. Edinburgh: T&T Clark, 2004.
Riesner, R. *Jesus als Lehrer*. 3rd ed. Tübingen: Mohr Siebeck, 1988.
Riesner, R. *Paul's Early Period: Chronology, Mission Strategy, Theology*. Grand Rapids, MI: Eerdmans, 1998.
Roberts, A. and J. Donaldson, eds. *The Ante-Nicene Fathers*. Vol. I. New York, NY: Christian Literature, 1906.
Robinson, J.A.T. *The Priority of John*. Edited by J.F. Coakley. London: SCM Press, 1985.
Roetzel, C.J. *The World that Shaped the New Testament*. London/Atlanta: SCM/John Knox, 1987.
Rollmann, H.-J. and W. Zager. 'Unveröffentlichte Briefe William Wredes zur Problematisierung des messianischen Selbstverständnisses Jesu'. *Zeitschrift für neuere Theologiegeschichte* 8 (2001), 274–322.
Rose, W.H. 'Zechariah and the Ambiguity of Kingship in Postexilic Israel'. Pages 219–32 in *Let us Go up to Zion: Essays in Honour of H. G. M. Williamson on the Occasion of his Sixty-Fifth Birthday*. Edited by I. Provan and M. Boda. Leiden: Brill, 2012.

Rosner, B. 'Acts and Biblical History'. Pages 65-82 in *The Book of Acts in its Ancient Literary Setting.* Edited by B.W. Winter and A.D. Clarke. Vol. I of *The Book of Acts in its First Century Setting.* Edited by B.W. Winter. Grand Rapids, MI/ Carlisle: Eerdmans/ Paternoster, 1993.

Rowe, R.D. *God's Kingdom and God's Son: The Background to Mark's Christology from Concepts of Kingship in the Psalms.* Leiden: Brill, 2002.

Sanders, E.P. *Jesus and Judaism.* Philadelphia, PA: Fortress Press, 1985.

Sanders, E.P. *Paul and Palestinian Judaism: A Comparison of Patterns of Religion.* London: SCM Press, 1981.

Sanders, J.N. 'Peter and Paul in the Acts'. *NTS* 2 (1955-56), 133-43.

Sandnes, K.O. *Paul – One of the Prophets?: A Contribution to the Apostle's Self-Understanding.* Tübingen: Mohr Siebeck, 1991.

Santos, N.F. *Slave of All: The Paradox of Authority and Servanthood in the Gospel of Mark.* JSNTS. London: Continuum, 2003.

Satterthwaite, P.E., R.S. Hess and G.J. Wenham, eds. *The Lord's Anointed: Interpretation of OT Messianic Texts.* Carlisle: Paternoster, 1995.

Saucy, R. *Minding the Heart: The Way of Spiritual Transformation.* Grand Rapids, MI: Kregel, 2013.

Schelkle, K.H. 'Petrus in den Briefen des Neuen Testaments'. *BiKi* 2.23 (1968), 46-50.

Schenk, W. 'Naherwartung und Parusieverzögerung: die urchristliche Eschatologie als Problem der Forschung'. *Theologische Versuche* 4 (1972), 47-69.

Schille, G. *Die urchristliche Kollegialmission.* Zürich: Zwingli, 1967.

Schlatter, A. *Der Evangelist Matthäus: Seine Sprache, sein Ziel, seine Selbständigkeit.* 7th ed. Stuttgart: Calwer Verlag, 1982 [1929].

Schlatter, A. *Der Glaube im Neuen Testament.* 6th ed. Stuttgart: Verlag der Vereinsbuchhandlung, 1982 [1896].

Schlatter, A. *Die Geschichte der ersten Christenheit.* 4th ed. Gütersloh: Bertelsmann, 1927.

Schlatter, A. *Die philosophische Arbeit seit Cartesius.* 3rd ed. Giessen: Brunnen, 1981.

Schlatter, A. *Einleitung in die Bibel.* 4th ed. Stuttgart: Calwer, 1923.

Schlatter, A. *Markus, der Evangelist für die Griechen.* 2nd ed. Stuttgart: Calwer, 1984 [1935].

Schlatter, A. *The Theology of the Apostles: The Development of New Testament Theology.* Translated by A.J. Köstenberger. Grand Rapids, MI: Baker, 1998.

Schmith, T.V. *Petrine Controversies in Early Christianity: Attitudes Towards Peter in Christian Writers of the First Two Centuries.* WUNT 2/15. Tübingen: Mohr Siebeck, 1985.

Schmitt, J.W. and J.C. Laney. *Messiah's Coming Temple: Ezekiel's Prophetic Vision of the Future Temple.* 2nd ed. Grand Rapids, MI: Kregel, 2013.

Schnabel, E.J. *Early Christian Mission.* 2 vols. Downers Grove, IL: IVP, 2004.

Schnabel, E.J. 'Paul, Timothy, and Titus: the Assumption of a Pseudonymous Author and of Pseudonymous Recipients in the Light of Literary, Theological, and Historical Evidence'. Pages 383–403 in *Do Historical Matters Matter to Faith?: A Critical Appraisal of Modern and Postmodern Approaches to Scripture*. Edited by J.K. Hoffmeier and D.R. Magary. Wheaton, IL: Crossway, 2012.

Schnabel, E.J. *Acts*. ZECNT 5. Grand Rapids, MI: Zondervan, 2012.

Schnabel, E.J. *Inspiration und Offenbarung: Die Lehre vom Ursprung und Wesen der Bibel*. 2nd ed. Wuppertal: Brockhaus, 1997.

Schnabel, E.J. *Law and Wisdom from Ben Sira to Paul: A Tradition Historical Enquiry into the Relation of Law, Wisdom, and Ethics*. WUNT 2/16. Tübingen: Mohr Siebeck, 1985.

Schnackenburg, R. 'Die lukanische Eschatologie im Lichte von Aussagen der Apostelgeschichte'. Pages 249–65 in *Glaube und Eschatologie: Festschrift für W.G. Kümmel zum 80. Geburtstag*. Edited by E. Grässer and O. Merk. Tübingen: Mohr Siebeck, 1985.

Schnackenburg, R. 'Zur Frage: Heilsgeschichte und Eschatologie im Neuen Testament'. *BZ* 4 (1960), 116–25.

Schnackenburg, R. *The Gospel According to St. John*. 3 vols. New York, NY: Crossroad, 1987.

Schneemelcher, W., ed. *New Testament Apocrypha*. Translated by R.M. Wilson. Revised edition. 2 vols. Louisville, KY: Westminster John Knox, 1991–92.

Schneider, G. 'Die Davidssohnfrage (Mk 12, 35-37)'. *Bib* 53 (1972), 65–90.

Schneider, G. 'Die Petrusrede vor Kornelius: das Verhältnis von Tradition und Komposition in Apg 10,34-43'. Pages 253–79 in G. Schneider, *Lukas, Theologe der Heilsgeschichte: Aufsätze zum lukanischen Doppelwerk*. BoBB 59. Bonn: P. Hanstein, 1985.

Schneider, G. 'Die zwölf Apostel als "Zeugen": Wesen, Ursprung und Funktion einer lukanischen Konzeption'. Pages 61–85 in G. Schneider, *Lukas, Theologe der Heilsgeschichte: Aufsätze zum lukanischen Doppelwerk*. BoBB 59. Bonn: P. Hanstein, 1985.

Schneider, G. *Die Apostelgeschichte*. 2 vols. Freiburg: Herder, 1980/82.

Schreiner, T.R. 'Sacrifices and Offerings in the NT'. Pages 273–77 in vol. IV of *International Standard Bible Encyclopedia*. Edited by G.W. Bromiley. 4 vols. Grand Rapids, MI: Eerdmans, 1988.

Schreiner, T.R. *New Testament Theology: Magnifying God in Christ*. Grand Rapids, MI: Baker, 2008.

Schreiner, T.R. *Paul, Apostle of God's Glory in Christ: A Pauline Theology*. Downers Grove, IL: IVP, 2001.

Schröter, J. 'Der erinnerte Jesus als Begründer des Christentums'. *ZNW* 20 (2007), 46–61.

Schröter, J. *From Jesus to the New Testament: Early Christian Theology and the Origin of the New Testament Canon*. Baylor-Mohr Siebeck Studies in Early Christianity. Waco, TX: Baylor University Press, 2013.

Schultheiß, T. *Das Petrusbild im Johannesevangelium*. Tübingen: Mohr Siebeck, 2012.

Schulz, H.-J. *Die apostolische Herkunft der Evangelien: Zum Ursprung der Evangelienform in der urgemeindlichen Paschafeier*. 3rd ed. Freiburg: Herder, 1997.

Schürer, E. *The History of the Jewish People in the Age of Jesus Christ – 175 B.C.–A.D. 135*. Edited by G. Vermes, F. Millar and F. Black. Vols I–III.2. Edinburgh: T&T Clark, 1973–1987.

Scobie, C.H.H. 'The Use of Source Material in the Speeches of Acts III and VII'. *NTS* 25.4 (1978-79), 399–421.

Sellew, P. 'Composition of Didactic Scenes in Mark's Gospel'. *JBL* 108 (1989), 613–34.

Selwyn, E.G. *The First Epistle of St. Peter*. 2nd ed. London: Macmillan, 1969 [1946].

Sen, A. *Inequality Reexamined*. Cambridge, MA: Harvard University Press, 1992.

Shanks, H. and B. Witherington. *The Brother of Jesus*. New York, NY: Harper San Francisco, 2003.

Shanks, M.A. *Papias and the New Testament*. Eugene, OR: Pickwick Publishing, 2013.

Smith, G.S. *The Testing of God's Sons: The Refining of Faith as a Biblical Theme*. Nashville, TN: BH Academic, 2014.

Smith, T.V. *Petrine Controversies in Early Christianity: Attitudes Towards Peter in Christian Writers of the First Two Centuries*. WUNT 2/15. Tübingen: Mohr Siebeck, 1985.

Snodgrass, K.R. *The Parable of the Wicked Tenants: An Inquiry into Parable Interpretation*. WUNT 27. Tübingen: Mohr Siebeck, 1983.

Soards, M.L. *The Speeches in Acts: Their Content, Context, and Concerns*. Louisville, KY: Westminster/John Knox, 1994.

Söding, T. *Glaube bei Markus*. Stuttgart: Katholisches Bibelwerk, 1985.

Sparling, R.A. *Johann Georg Hamann and the Enlightenment Project*. Toronto: University of Toronto Press, 2011.

Spencer, F.S. *The Portrait of Philip in Acts: A Study of Roles and Relations*. Sheffield: JSOT Press, 1992.

Stauffer, E. 'Zur Vor- und Frühgeschichte des Primatus Petri'. *Zeitschrift für Kirchengeschichte* 62 (1943/44), 3–34.

Steck, O.H. *Israel und das gewaltsame Geschick der Propheten: Untersuchungen zur Überlieferung des deuteronomistischen Geschichtsbildes im Alten Testament, Spätjudentum und Urchristentum*. Neukirchen-Vluyn: Neukirchener, 1967.

Stein, R.H. 'An Early Recension of the Gospel Tradition'. *JETS* 30 (1987), 167–83.

Stein, R.H. *Jesus, the Temple and the Coming Son of Man: A Commentary on Mark 13*. Downers Grove, IL: IVP Academic, 2014.

Stenschke, C.W. 'The Presentation of Jesus in the Missionary Speeches of Acts and the Mission of the Church'. *Verbum et Ecclesia* 35.1 (2014), 1–18.

Stewart, A.C. *The Original Bishops: Office and Order in the First Christian Communities.* Grand Rapids, MI: Baker Academic, 2014.

Stewart, R. and G. Habermas. *Memories of Jesus: A Critical Appriasal of James D.G. Dunn's Jesus Remembered.* Nashville, TN: B&H Academic, 2010.

Stibbs, A.M. *The First Epistle General of Peter: An Introduction and Commentary.* TNTC. Grand Rapids, MI: Eerdmans, 1988.

Strack, H.L. and P. Billerbeck. *Kommentar zum Neuen Testament aus Talmud und Midrasch.* 6 vols. 5th ed. Munich: C.H. Beck,1969.

Strathmann, H. 'Die Stellung des Petrus in der Urkirche: Zur Frühgeschichte des Wortes an Petrus Matthäus 16, 17-19'. *ZSyTh* 20 (1943), 223–82.

Stuhlhofer, F. *Der Gebrauch der Bibel von Jesus bis Euseb: eine statistische Untersuchung zur Kanonsgeschichte.* Wuppertal: Brockhaus, 1988.

Stuhlmacher, P. 'Existenzstellvertretung für die Vielen: Mk 10,45 (Mt 20,28)'. Pages 27–42 in P. Stuhlmacher, *Versöhnung, Gesetz und Gerechtigkeit: Aufsätze zur biblischen Theologie.* Göttingen: Vandenhoeck & Ruprecht, 1981.

Stuhlmacher, P. *Biblische Theologie des Neuen Testaments.* 2 vols. 2nd ed. Göttingen: Vandenhoeck & Ruprecht, 1999.

Talbert, C.H. 'II Peter and the Delay of the Parousia'. *VC* 20 (1966), 137–45.

Talbert, C.H., *Learning Through Suffering: The Educational Value of Suffering in the New Testament and in Its Milieu.* Collegeville, MN: Liturgical Press, 1991.

Tannehill, R.C. 'The Functions of Peter's Mission Speeches in the Narrative of Acts'. *NTS* 37.3 (1991), 400–14.

Tannehill, R.C. *The Narrative Unity of Luke–Acts: A Literary Interpretation.* 2 vols. Minneapolis, MN: Fortress Press, 1986/1990.

Taylor, V. *The Gospel According to St. Mark.* 2nd ed. Reprint. Grand Rapids, MI: Baker, 1981.

Telford, W.R. *Mark.* Sheffield: Sheffield Academic Press, 1997.

Thatcher, T., ed. *Memory and Identity in Ancient Judaism and Early Christianity: A Conversation with Barry Schwartz.* Semeia Studies 78. Williston, VT: SBL Press, 2014.

Theissen, G. and A. Merz. *Der historische Jesus: Ein Lehrbuch.* 4th ed. Göttingen: Vandenhoeck & Ruprecht, 2008.

Thiede, C.P. and M. D'Ancona. *Eyewitness to Jesus: Amazing New Manuscript Evidence about the Origin of the Gospels.* New York, NY: Doubleday, 1996.

Thiede, C.P. *Simon Peter: From Galilee to Rome.* Exeter: Paternoster, 1986.

Thiede, C.P., ed. *Das Petrusbild in der neueren Forschung.* TVG. Wuppertal: Brockhaus, 1987.

Thielman, F. *Theology of the New Testament: A Canonical and Synthetic Approach.* Grand Rapids, MI: Zondervan, 2005.
Thomas, R., ed. *Three Views on the Origins of the Synoptic Gospels.* Grand Rapids, MI: Kregel, 2002.
Thornton, C.-J. 'Justin und das Markusevangelium'. *ZNW* 84 (1993), 93–110.
Thornton, C.-J. *Der Zeuge des Zeugen: Lukas als Historiker der Paulusreisen.* WUNT 56. Tübingen: Mohr Siebeck, 1991.
Trobisch, D. *Die Endredaktion des Neuen Testaments: Eine Untersuchung zur Entstehung der christlichen Bibel.* NTOA 31. Göttingen: Vandenhoeck & Ruprecht, 1996.
Troftgruben, T. *A Conclusion Unhindered: A Study of the Ending of Acts within its Literary Environment.* WUNT 2/280. Tübingen: Mohr Siebeck, 2010.
Turiot, C. 'Pierre dans le Nouveau Testament'. *SémiotBib* 36 (1984), 1–14.
Turner, N. *A Grammar of New Testament Greek.* Edinburgh: T&T Clark, 1976.
Tyson, J.B. 'The Emerging Church and the Problem of Authority in Acts'. *Int* 42.2 (1988), 132–45.
Unnik, W.C., van. 'The "Book of Acts"– the Confirmation of the Gospel'. *NovT* 4.1 (1960), 26–59.
Uytanlet, S. *Luke–Acts and Jewish Historiography: A Study on the Theology, Literature, and Ideology of Luke–Acts.* Tübingen: Mohr Siebeck, 2014.
Vansina, J. *Oral Tradition as History.* Madison, WI: University of Wisconsin, 1985.
Vielhauer, P. 'Zum "Paulinismus" der Apostelgeschichte'. Pages 9–27 in P. Vielhauer. *Aufsätze zum Neuen Testament.* Munich: Chr. Kaiser, 1965.
Vielhauer, P. *Oikodome, das Bild vom Bau in der christlichen Literatur vom N.T. bis Clemens Alexandrinus.* Munich: Chr. Kaiser, 1986.
Voorst, R.E., van. *Jesus Outside the New Testament: An Introduction to the Ancient Evidence.* Grand Rapids, MI: Eerdmans, 2000.
Wall, R.W. 'Peter, "Son" of Jonah: The Conversion of Cornelius in the Context of Canon'. *JSNT* 29 (1987), 79–90.
Wallace, D. *Revisiting the Corruption of the New Testament: Manuscript, Patristic, and Apocryphal Evidence.* Text and Canon of the New Testament. Grand Rapids, MI: Kregel Academic, 2011.
Wansborough, H., ed. *Jesus and the Oral Gospel Tradition.* Edinburgh: T&T Clark, 2004.
Wassell, B.E. and S.R. Llewelyn. '"Fishers of Humans", the Contemporary Theory of Metaphor, and Conceptual Blending Theory'. *JBL* 133.3 (2014), 627–46.
Watson, D.F. and T. Callan, *First and Second Peter.* Grand Rapids, MI: Baker Academic, 2012.
Watson, F. *Gospel Writing: A Canonical Perspective.* Grand Rapids, MI: Eerdmans, 2013.

Watts, R. 'Jesus' Death, Isaiah 53 and Mark 10.45'. Pages 125–51 in *Jesus and the Suffering Servant: Isaiah 53 and Christian Origins*. Edited by W.H. Bellinger and W.R. Farmer. Harrisburg, PA: Trinity Press, 1998.

Wehnert, J. 'Die Teilhabe der Christen an der Herrschaft mit Christus'. *ZNW* 88.1 (1997), 81–96.

Wenham, D. 'Jesus Tradition in the Letters of the New Testament'. Pages 2041–58 in vol. III of *Handbook for the Study of the Historical Jesus*. 4 vols. Edited by T. Holmén and S. Porter. Leiden: Brill, 2011.

Wenham, G.J. *The Book of Leviticus*. NICOT. Grand Rapids, MI: Eerdmans, 1979.

Wenham, J.W. 'Did Peter Go to Rome in A.D. 42?'. *TynBul* 23 (1972), 94–102.

Wenham, J.W. 'Synoptic Independence and the Origin of Luke's Travel Narrative'. *NTS* 27 (1981), 507–15.

Wenham, J.W. *Christ and the Bible*. 3rd ed. Grand Rapids, MI: Baker, 1994.

Wenham, J.W. *Redating Matthew, Mark and Luke*. Downers Grove, IL: IVP, 1992.

Westcott, B.F. *A General Survey of the History of the Canon of the New Testament*. Grand Rapids, MI: Baker, 1980 [1881].

Westcott, B.F. *An Introduction to the Study of the Gospels*. 6th ed. Cambridge: Macmillan, 1881 [1851]).

Wiarda, T.J. 'Peter as Peter in the Gospel of Mark'. *NTS* 45 (1999), 19–37.

Wiarda, T.J. *Peter in the Gospels: Pattern, Personality and Relationship*. WUNT 2/127. Tübingen: Mohr Siebeck, 2000.

Wilckens, U. *Die Missionsreden der Apostelgeschichte*. 3rd ed. Neukirchen-Vluyn: Neukirchener Verlag, 1974.

Wilckens, U. *Theologie des Neuen Testaments: Studienausgabe in 6 Teilbänden*. 6 vols. Neukirchen-Vluyn: Neukirchener Verlag, 2014.

Wilcox, M. 'A Foreword to the Study of the Speeches in Acts'. *SJLA* 12.1 (1975), 206–25.

Wilkins, M.J. *Following the Master: A Biblical Theology of Discipleship*. Grand Rapids, MI: Zondervan, 1992.

Williams, M. *The Doctrine of Salvation in the First Letter of Peter*. Cambridge: Cambridge University Press, 2011.

Williams, M.D. *Far as the Curse Is Found: The Covenant Story of Redemption*. Phillipsburg: P&R, 2005.

Williams, T.B. *Good Works in 1 Peter: Negotiating Social Conflict and Christian Identity in the Greco-Roman World*. Tübingen: Mohr Siebeck, 2014.

Williams, T.B. *Persecution in 1 Peter: Differentiating and Contextualizing Early Christian Suffering*. Leiden: Brill, 2012.

Willimon, W.H. '"Eyewitnesses and Ministers of the Word": Preaching in Acts'. *Int* 42.2 (1988), 158–70.

Wintermute, O.S. 'Jubilees'. Pages 35–142 in vol. 2 of J.H. Charlesworth, ed. *The Old Testament Pseudepigrapha*. 2 vols. New York, NY: Doubleday, 1983/1985.
Wolterstorff, N. *Lament for a Son*. Grand Rapids, MI: Eerdmans, 1987.
Wrede, W. *The Messianic Secret*. Translated by J.C.G. Greig. Cambridge, MA/Greenwood, SC: James Clarke/Attic Press, 1971.
Wright, C.J.H. *The Mission of God: Unlocking the Bible's Grand Narrative*. Downers Grove, IL: IVP, 2006.
Wright, N.T. *Jesus and the Victory of God*. Minneapolis, MN: Fortress, 1996.
Wright, R.B. 'Psalms of Solomon'. Pages 639–70 in *The Old Testament Pseudepigrapha. Vol. 2: Expansions of the Old Testament and Legends, Wisdom and Philosophical Literature, Prayers, Psalms, and Odes, Fragments of Lost Judeo-Hellenistic Works*. Edited by J.H. Charlesworth. New York, NY: Doubleday, 1985.
Yarbrough, R. 'The Date of Papias: A Reassessment'. *JETS* 26.2 (1983), 181–91.
Zahn, T. *Geschichte des neutestamentlichen Kanons*. 2 vols. Reprint. Zürich: Olms Verlag, 2013 [1888–92].
Zahn, T. *Grundriss der Geschichte des neutestamentlichen Kanons*. Leipzig: Deichert'sche Verlagsbuchhandlung, 1901.
Zahn, T. *Introduction to the New Testament*. Translated by J.M. Trout, W.A. Mather, et al. Edited by M.W. Jacobus. 3 vols. Reprinted 3rd ed. Grand Rapids, MI: Kregel, 1953 [1909].
Zehnle, R.F. *Peter's Pentecost Discourse: Tradition and Lukan Reinterpretation in Peter's Speeches of Acts 2 and 3*. SBLMS 15. Nashville, TN: Abingdon, 1971.
Zimmermann, J. *Messianische Texte aus Qumran: Königliche, priesterliche und prophetische Messiasvorstellungen in den Schriftfunden von Qumran*. Tübingen: Mohr Siebeck, 1998.
Zmijewski, J. *Die Apostelgeschichte*. Regensburg: Pustet, 1994.
Zwierlein, O. *Petrus in Rom: Die literarischen Zeugnisse, mit einer kritischen Edition der Martyrien des Petrus und Paulus auf neuer handschriftlicher Grundlage*. Berlin: de Gruyter, 2009.
Zylla, P.C. *The Roots of Sorrow: A Pastoral Theology of Suffering*. Waco, TX: Baylor University Press, 2012.

www.ingramcontent.com/pod-product-compliance
Lightning Source LLC
Chambersburg PA
CBHW070010010526
44117CB00011B/1488